THE ROUTLEDGE COMPANION TO EXPERIMENTAL LITERATURE

What is experimental literature? How has experimentation affected the course of literary history, and how is it shaping literary expression today? Literary experiment has always been diverse and challenging, but never more so than in our age of digital media and social networking, when the very category of the literary is coming under intense pressure. How will literature reconfigure itself in the future?

The Routledge Companion to Experimental Literature maps this expansive and multi-faceted field, with essays on:

- the history of literary experiment from the beginning of the twentieth century to the present
- the impact of new media on literature, including multimodal literature, digital fiction and code poetry
- the development of experimental genres from graphic narratives and found poetry through to gaming and interactive fiction
- experimental movements from Futurism and Surrealism to Postmodernism, Avant-Pop and Flarf.

Shedding new light on often critically neglected terrain, the contributors introduce this vibrant area, define its current state, and offer exciting new perspectives on its future.

This volume is the ideal introduction for those approaching the study of experimental literature for the first time or looking to further their knowledge.

Contributors: Jan Alber, Jan Baetens, Charles Bernstein, R. M. Berry, Joe Bray, Hillary Chute, David Ciccoricco, Liam Connell, Amy J. Elias, Astrid Ensslin, Andrew Epstein, Ellen G. Friedman, Joanna Gavins, Alison Gibbons, Elana Gomel, Priyamvada Gopal, N. Katherine Hayles, Irene Kacandes, Benjamin Lee, Danielle Marx-Scouras, Brian McHale, Robert L. McLaughlin, Philip Mead, Tyrus Miller, Nick Montfort, Richard Murphy, Aldon Lynn Nielsen, Henrik Skov Nielsen, Lance Olsen, Jessica Prinz, Brian Richardson, Marie-Laure Ryan, Peter Stockwell, Steve Tomasula, Gregory L. Ulmer, John White, and Laura Winkiel.

Joe Bray is Senior Lecturer in Language and Literature at the University of Sheffield, UK.

Alison Gibbons is Senior Lecturer in Stylistics, English Language and Literature at De Montfort University, Leicester, UK.

Brian McHale is Distinguished Arts and Humanities Professor of English at the Ohio State University, Columbus, OH, USA.

"The editors of *The Routledge Companion to Experimental Literature* have produced a marvellously wide-ranging, informative, lucid – and often highly original – discussion of experimental writing in the 20th and 21st centuries. From the historical avant-gardes to avant-pop, digital fiction and code poetry, this *Companion* will be an indispensable guide to new movements and to the intermedia post-generic verbal works that now people our literary landscape."

Marjorie Perloff, *Stanford University, USA*

"Experimental, avant-garde, innovative . . . the recent history of such terms has been confusing because they seem to blur into synonyms, to share family resemblances rather than strict definitions, and to indicate distinctly different things for different disciplines and genres. With a series of short accessible entries by the go-to authorities in a number of fields, this collection sketches the range of critical work performed by labels that have proven as necessary as they are elusive."

Craig Dworkin, *The University of Utah, USA*

THE ROUTLEDGE COMPANION TO EXPERIMENTAL LITERATURE

Edited by
Joe Bray, Alison Gibbons and Brian McHale

Routledge
Taylor & Francis Group

LONDON AND NEW YORK

First published 2012
by Routledge
2 Park Square, Milton Park, Abingdon, Oxon OX14 4RN

Simultaneously published in the USA and Canada
by Routledge
711 Third Avenue, New York, NY 10017

Routledge is an imprint of the Taylor & Francis Group, an informa business

British Library Cataloguing in Publication Data
A catalogue record for this book is available from the British Library

Library of Congress Cataloging in Publication Data
The Routledge companion to experimental literature / edited by
Joe Bray, Alison Gibbons and Brian McHale.
   p. cm.
   Includes bibliographical references.
   1. Literature, Experimental—History and criticism.
   2. Modernism (Literature) 3. Avant-garde (Aesthetics)
   4. Mass media and literature. 5. Discourse analysis, Literary.
   I. Bray, Joe. II. Gibbons, Alison. III. McHale, Brian.
   PN56.M54R68 2012
   809'.9112—dc23
   2011048404

ISBN: 978–0–415–57000–8 (hbk)
ISBN: 978–0–203–11696–8 (ebk)

Typeset in Goudy
by Swales & Willis Ltd, Exeter, Devon

Printed and bound by CPI Group (UK) Ltd, Croydon, CR0 4YY

CONTENTS

PART II
Experiment now: printed matter

FIGURES

CONTRIBUTORS

Jan Alber is Assistant Professor in the English Department at the University of Freiburg (Germany). He has published articles in *Dickens Studies Annual, Journal of Narrative Theory, The Journal of Popular Culture, Narrative, Storyworlds*, and *Style*, and is currently working on a book on the unnatural in fiction and drama.

Jan Baetens is Professor of Cultural Studies at the University of Leuven (Belgium). He has published widely in the field of word and image studies and has co-guest-edited in 2009–2010 a double special issue of *Poetics Today* on constrained writing (30:4 and 31:1).

Charles Bernstein is author of *All the Whiskey in Heaven: Selected Poems* (Farrar, Straus, and Giroux, 2010) and *Attack of the Difficult Poems: Essays & Inventions* (Chicago, 2011). He is Regan Professor of English and Comparative Literature at the University of Pennsylvania (Philadelphia).

R. M. Berry is author, most recently, of the novel *Frank* (Chiasmus, 2005) and the story collection *Dictionary of Modern Anguish* (FC2, 2000). His literary criticism has appeared in *Soundings, Symploke, Philosophy and Literature, Narrative, Rain Taxi, American Book Review*, and numerous anthologies. He is editor with Jeffrey Di Leo of *Fiction's Present: Situating Contemporary Narrative Innovation* (SUNY, 2007) and of the experimental fiction anthology, *Forms at War* (University of Alabama, 2009). From 1999 to 2007 Berry was publisher of FC2. He is currently a Professor and Chair of the Department of English at Florida State University (Tallahassee).

Joe Bray is Senior Lecturer in English Language and Literature at the University of Sheffield (UK). He is the author of *The Epistolary Novel: Representations of Consciousness* (Routledge, 2003) and *The Female Reader in the English Novel: From Burney to Austen* (Routledge, 2009), and co-editor of *Ma(r)king The Text: The Presentation of Meaning on the Literary Page* (Ashgate, 2000) and *Mark Z. Danielewski* (Manchester University Press, 2011).

Hillary Chute is Neubauer Family Assistant Professor of English at the University of Chicago. In 2006, she co-edited the *Mfs: Modern Fiction Studies* special issue on Graphic Narrative, and in 2008 she wrote "Comics as Literature? Reading Graphic Narrative" for *PMLA*. She is the author of *Graphic Women: Life Narrative and Contemporary Comics* (Columbia UP, 2010), and Associate Editor of Art Spiegelman's *Meta Maus* (Pantheon, 2011). Her new book project is *"Disaster is My Muse": Visual Witnessing, Comics, and Documentary Form.*

David Ciccoricco is a member of the English Department faculty at the University of Otago in Dunedin (New Zealand). His research is focused on contemporary narrative fiction, with a particular emphasis on emergent forms of digital literature. He is the author of *Reading Network Fiction*, a book on narrative theory and digital fiction.

Liam Connell teaches English at The University of Winchester (UK). He co-edited *Literature and Globalization: a Reader* (2010). His work on globalization appears in *Critical Survey*, *Journal of Postcolonial Writing*, and *Social Text* and collections including *Globalisation and its Discontents* (2006) and the *Oxford History of the Novel in English* (2012).

Amy J. Elias teaches in the English Department at the University of Tennessee (Knoxville). Her book *Sublime Desire: History and Post-1960s Fiction* won the Perkins Award from the International Society for the Study of Narrative, and she has published widely in the areas of contemporary literatures and culture studies. She is the founder of A.S.A.P.: The Association for the Study of the Arts of the Present and hosted the association's launch conference in Knoxville in 2009. Her second monograph concerns dialogics in the post-1960s arts.

Astrid Ensslin is Senior Lecturer in Digital Humanities at Bangor University (UK). Her main publications include *The Language of Gaming* (2011), *Creating Second Lives* (2011), *Canonizing Hypertext* (2007), and *Language in the Media* (2007). She is Principal Editor of the *Journal of Gaming and Virtual Worlds* and Co-Investigator of the Leverhulme-funded Digital Fiction International Network.

Andrew Epstein is an Associate Professor of English at Florida State University (Tallahassee). He is the author of *Beautiful Enemies: Friendship and Postwar American Poetry* (Oxford) and his essays have appeared in various journals, including *Contemporary Literature*, the *Wallace Stevens Journal*, *Jacket*, and *Raritan*.

Ellen G. Friedman is Professor of English at the College of New Jersey (Ewing, NJ). She is the author and editor of seven books, including *Morality USA* and *Breaking the Sequence: Women's Experimental Fiction*, as well as having published widely in academic and popular journals. She is currently working on a family memoir called *The Seven*.

Joanna Gavins is Senior Lecturer in English Language and Literature at the University of Sheffield (UK), author of *Text World Theory* (Edinburgh University Press, 2007), and co-editor of *Cognitive Poetics in Practice* (Routledge, 2002). She has published widely on stylistics, cognitive poetics, absurd prose fiction and contemporary poetry and is currently completing a monograph, *Reading the Absurd*.

Alison Gibbons is Senior Lecturer in English at De Montfort University (Leicester, UK). Alison has published internationally in a number of journals and collections, including *New Perspectives on Narrative and Multimodality* (Routledge, 2009). She is co-editor of *Mark Z. Danielewski* (Manchester University Press, 2011) and the author of *Multimodality, Cognition, and Experimental Literature* (Routledge, 2012).

Elana Gomel is Associate Professor at the Department of English and American Studies of Tel-Aviv University, Israel. She has been a Visiting Scholar at Princeton (NJ), Stanford (CA), University of Hong Kong and other institutions. Her interests include narrative theory, science fiction and posthumanism. Her latest book is *Postmodern Science Fiction and Temporal Imagination* (Continuum, 2009).

Priyamvada Gopal is the author of *Literary Radicalism in India* (Routledge, 2004) and *The Indian Novel in English* (Oxford University Press, 2009). She teaches in the Faculty of English, University of Cambridge (UK).

N. Katherine Hayles is Professor of Literature and Director of Graduate Studies at Duke University (Durham, NC). Her books include *How We Became Posthuman: Virtual Bodies in Cybernetics, Literature and Informatics*, winner of the Rene Wellek Prize for the Best Book in Literary Theory for 1998–1999. Her new book, *How We Think: Digital Media and Contemporary Technogenesis*, will be out in May 2012 from the University of Chicago Press.

Irene Kacandes is The Dartmouth Professor of German Studies and Comparative Literature at Dartmouth College (Hanover, NH). Author most recently of *Daddy's War: Greek American Stories* (2009), Kacandes has published on German and Italian cultural studies, narrative theory, feminist linguistic theory, Holocaust studies, memory and trauma studies, and life writing.

Benjamin Lee is Assistant Professor of English at the University of Tennessee (Knoxville).

Danielle Marx-Scouras is Professor of French at the Ohio State University (Columbus). She has authored two books: *The Cultural Politics of Tel Quel: Literature and the Left in the Wake of Engagement* (University Park: Penn State University Press, 1996) and *La France de Zebda, 1981–2004: Faire de la musique un acte politique* (Paris: Editions Autrement, 2005). She has also published numerous articles and book chapters on contemporary French, francophone and Italian literature, theory, film, and popular music.

Brian McHale is Distinguished Arts and Humanities Professor of English at the Ohio State University (Columbus). He is the author of three books on postmodernist fiction and poetry – *Postmodernist Fiction* (1987), *Constructing Postmodernism* (1992), and *The Obligation toward the Difficult Whole: Postmodernist Long Poems* (2004) – and co-editor, most recently, of the *Cambridge Companion to Thomas Pynchon* (2012).

Robert L. McLaughlin is Professor of English at Illinois State University (Normal), editor of *Innovations: An Anthology of Modern and Contemporary Fiction*, longtime editor of the *Review of Contemporary Fiction* (1993–2005), and co-author with

Sally E. Parry of *We'll Always Have the Movies: American Cinema during World War II*.

Philip Mead is Chair of Australian Literature at the University of Western Australia (Perth) and author of *Networked Language: Culture & History in Australian Poetry* (2009).

Tyrus Miller is Vice Provost and Dean of Graduate Studies and Professor of Literature at the University of California at Santa Cruz. He is author of *Late Modernism: Politics, Fiction, and the Arts Between the World Wars; Singular Examples: Artistic Politics and the Neo-Avant-Garde;* and *Time Images: Alternative Temporalities in 20th-Century Theory, History, and Art*.

Nick Montfort is Associate Professor of Digital Media at MIT (Cambridge, MA) and President of the Electronic Literature Organization. He co-edited *The New Media Reader*, wrote *Twisty Little Passages*, and is co-author of *Racing the Beam* and the forthcoming *10 PRINT CHR$(205.5 +RND(1)); : GOTO 10*.

Richard Murphy is Professor of German, Comparative Literature and Film. Prior to the University of Sussex (UK), he taught at Columbia (NY) and UC Santa Cruz (CA). He writes on modernism, Weimar cinema, and the contemporary avant-garde, and is the author of *Theorizing the Avant-Garde: Modernism, Expressionism and the Problem of Postmodernity* (Cambridge University Press).

Aldon Lynn Nielsen is the Kelly Professor of American Literature at Pennsylvania State University (Philadelphia). His most recent critical volume is *Integral Music: Languages of African American Innovation*. His most recent collection of poetry is *Mantic Semantic*. He is co-editor with Lauri Ramey of *Every Goodbye Ain't Gone: An Anthology Of Innovative Poetry by African Americans*.

Henrik Skov Nielsen is Professor in the Department of Aesthetics and Communication at the University of Aarhus, Denmark. He has recently contributed to edited collections such as *Postclassical Narratology: Approaches and Analyses* (Alber and Fludernik [eds.], Ohio State University Press, 2010), *Bret Easton Ellis* (Naomi Mandel [ed.]), *Theory, Analysis, Interpretation of Narratives* (Sylvie Patron [ed.]), and others.

Lance Olsen has authored more than twenty books of and about innovative fiction, including the novels *Calendar of Regrets, Head in Flames,* and *Nietzsche's Kisses*. With Mark Amerika, he co-edited *In Memoriam To Postmodernism: Essays on the Avant-Pop*. He teaches experimental narrative theory and practice at the University of Utah (Salt Lake City).

Jessica Prinz is Associate Professor of English at the Ohio State University (Columbus). She is author of *Art Discourse/Discourse in Art* (Rutgers, 1991), a full-length study of language in the contemporary visual arts and articles on Samuel Beckett and the visual arts, among other studies concerning twentieth-century writers and authors.

Brian Richardson is a Professor in the English Department of the University of Maryland (College Park). He has authored or co-authored three books on twentieth-century literature, including *Unnatural Voices: Extreme Narration in Modern and Contemporary Fiction* (2006), and edited several volumes, including *Narrative Dynamics: Essays on Time, Plot, Closure, and Frames* (2002) and *Narrative Beginnings* (2009).

Marie-Laure Ryan is an independent scholar based in Colorado. She is the author of *Possible Worlds, Artificial Intelligence and Narrative Theory* (1991), *Narrative as Virtual Reality* (2001), and *Avatars of Story* (2006), as well as co-editor (with David Herman and Manfred Jahn) of the *Routledge Encyclopedia of Narrative* (2005). She is currently editing the *Johns Hopkins Guide to New Media and Digital Textuality*.

Peter Stockwell holds the Chair in Literary Linguistics at the University of Nottingham (UK), where he teaches stylistics and cognitive poetics. He is the author and editor of over fifteen books, translated into many languages, and fifty research articles. His most recent and well-known books are *Texture: A Cognitive Aesthetics of Reading* (Edinburgh University Press, 2009), *The Language and Literature Reader* (with Ron Carter, Routledge, 2008), *Contemporary Stylistics* (with Marina Lambrou, Continuum, 2007), and *Cognitive Poetics* (Routledge, 2002).

Steve Tomasula is the author of the experimental novels *The Book of Portraiture*; *VAS: An Opera in Flatland*; *IN&OZ*; and *TOC: A New-Media Novel*, which received the Mary Shelley Award for Excellence in Fiction. He teaches fiction writing and twentieth- and twenty-first-century literature at the University of Notre Dame (IN).

Gregory L. Ulmer is Professor of English and Media Studies at the University of Florida (Gainesville), and Joseph Beuys Chair at the European Graduate School (Switzerland). His recent work includes *Miami Virtue* (Community-University Research Alliance, Small Cities Imprint), and *Avatar Emergency* (Parlor Press).

John White, Emeritus Professor of German and Comparative Literature at King's College London, is the author of *Mythology in the Modern Novel*, *Literary Futurism: Aspects of the First Avant-Garde*, *Bertolt Brecht's Dramatic Theory* and *Bertolt Brecht's "Furcht und Elend des Dritten Reiches"*. He has published extensively on fiction, drama, semiotics and Futurism.

Laura Winkiel is Associate Professor in the English Department at the University of Colorado at Boulder. She is author of *Modernism, Race and Manifestos* (2008) and co-editor of *Geomodernisms: Race, Modernism, Modernity* (2005). She is currently working on a book on the modern epic.

ACKNOWLEDGEMENTS

The editors would like to thank all at Routledge for their assistance in the preparation and production of this book. We are especially grateful to Polly Dodson, our first commissioning editor, who originally came up with the idea and did so much to help us get it off the ground.

'The Cage', by David Gascoyne, from *Selected Poems* (Enitharmon Press, 1994). Reprinted by permission of the publisher, Enitharmon Press.

Every effort has been made to trace copyright holders and obtain permission but this may not have been possible in all cases. Any omissions brought to the attention of the publisher will be remedied at the earliest opportunity.

1
INTRODUCTION
Joe Bray, Alison Gibbons and Brian McHale

I. What is experimental literature?

Experimental literature, as the contents of this *Routledge Companion* amply testify, is irreducibly diverse. Unfettered improvisation and the rigorous application of rules, accidental composition and hyper-rational design, free invention and obsessively faithful duplication, extreme conceptualism and extreme materiality, multimediality and media-specificity, being "born digital" and being hand-made – all of these, and many others, are ways of being experimental in literature. Despite this diversity, however, a number of common threads (some of which will be explored below) traverse experimental literary practice across the twentieth century and right up to the present. The one feature that *all* literary experiments share is their commitment to raising fundamental questions about the very nature and being of verbal art itself. What *is* literature, and what could it be? What are its functions, it limitations, its possibilities? These are the sorts of questions that "mainstream" literature, at all periods – commercial bestseller literature, but also the "classics" once they have been canonized, domesticated and rendered fit for unreflective consumption – is dedicated to *repressing*. Experimental literature *unrepresses* these fundamental questions, and in doing so it lays everything open to challenge, reconceptualization and reconfiguration. Experimentation makes alternatives visible and conceivable, and some of these alternatives become the foundations for future developments, whole new ways of writing, some of which eventually filter into the mainstream itself. Experiment is one of the engines of literary change and renewal; it is literature's way of reinventing itself.

In the chapters that follow, the modifier *experimental* is used more or less interchangeably with *avant-garde*, and sometimes *innovative*. Though the terms function roughly synonymously, there are important nuances of difference in connotation, especially between *experimental* and *avant-garde*. *Avant-garde* begins its career in the military context, but then migrates to the political sphere, where the avant-garde is the faction that takes the lead ahead of the rest of a political movement (Calinescu 1987: 95–148). Consequently, aesthetic avant-gardism continues to be allied with political radicalism in a number of twentieth- and twenty-first-century artistic and literary movements. Experimentalism's connotations, by contrast, are scientific. Experiment promises to extend the boundaries of knowledge, or in this case, of artistic practice. Strongly associated with modernity, it implies rejection of hide-bound traditions, values and forms. To call literature *experimental* is in some sense to aspire to compete with science – challenging science's privileged status in modernity and reclaiming some of the prestige ceded by literature to science since the nineteenth century.

The language of *experiment* is a relative novelty in literary discourse, though if one were seeking deep historical roots one might venture as far back as the sixteenth century and Michel de Montaigne, who applied the term *essais* – in the sense of "try-outs" or "attempts" – to his unprecedented thought-experiments in prose. Subsequent centuries saw the emergence of literary forms that in hindsight we would surely be disposed to call "experimental" – the eighteenth-century novel, climaxing in Laurence Sterne's *The Life and Opinions of Tristram Shandy, Gentleman* (1759–1767), is one example – but the model of scientific experiment would not become fully available for describing literary innovation until Émile Zola applied it to the naturalist novel at the end of the nineteenth century. The early twentieth-century avant-gardes – especially the Italian and Russian Futurists, and later the Surrealists – embraced the term enthusiastically, and it is largely thanks to them that we continue to regard unconventional, cutting-edge literature as "experimental," and to associate the term with qualities of shock and affront, iconoclasm and difficulty.

In the last third of the twentieth century, avant-garde writers began to express certain reservations about the category "experimental," which they viewed as dismissive, a way of segregating or ghettoizing innovative literature and preventing it from reaching an audience or infiltrating the mainstream. The British novelist B.S. Johnson, a restless innovator and intransigent avant-gardist, wrote that

> "Experimental" to most reviewers is almost always a synonym for "unsuccessful." I object to the word *experimental* being applied to my own work. Certainly I make experiments, but the unsuccessful ones are quietly hidden away and what I choose to publish is in my terms successful: that is, it has been the best way I could find of solving particular writing problems.
>
> (Johnson 1973: 19)

His American counterparts, the surfictionists Raymond Federman and Ronald Sukenick, shared Johnson's suspicion of the category. Contending that "experimental" is a term that literary "middle-men" use to "brush aside" challenging literature, Federman writes that he does not

> believe that a fiction writer with the least amount of self-respect, and belief in what he is doing, ever says to himself: "I am now going to experiment with fiction; I am now writing an experimental piece of fiction." Others say that about his fiction. The middle-man of literature is the one who gives the label

> EXPERIMENT to what is difficult, strange, provocative, and even original
> . . . . Fiction is called experimental out of despair.
>
> (Federman 1975: 7)

Sukenick's view is that the term "experimental" belongs to the "ephemeral meta-language" of the publishing industry, where it is "used to resolve contradictions between publishing as business enterprise and publishing as cultural institution." In this metalanguage, he writes acerbically, "'experimental novel' . . . means something like 'no sales of subsidiary rights'" (1985: 55).

These are cogent objections from writers with impeccable experimentalist credentials, whose reservations need to be taken seriously. Nevertheless, our hope is that the present *Companion* might go some way toward salvaging the term *experimental*, rescuing it from the contexts where it is a term of dismissal and condescension, and reinvigorating its connotations of edginess, renovation and aesthetic adventure.

II. The structure of this *Companion*

The volume is divided into eight sections arranged into three parts, the first of which is entitled *The Historical Avant-Gardes*. The opening section on modernist-era experimentalism introduces the key early and mid-twentieth-century movements that transformed the meaning of the avant-garde: Futurism, Expressionism, Dada and Surrealism, and Existentialism and Absurdism. The next section turns to experimental innovations across Europe and the US in the period following World War II, whether in poetry (the New York School, the Beats), or prose (the *nouveau roman*, meta- and surfiction). The radical politics and techniques of Lettrism and Situationism are discussed here, along with the creative inventiveness of OuLiPo and proceduralism (or writing under constraints) generally. Many of the developments of this period can be brought together under the heading of postmodernism, a phenomenon that has proved notoriously difficult to define or locate chronologically. The third section of Part One discusses forms of experimental writing in which the notion of identity has been especially contested throughout the twentieth century – the female, African-American and postcolonial avant-gardes – before the final section of Part One examines attempts to put a stamp on the experimental contemporary, whether in the form of theoretical reflections and manifestoes, engagements with popular culture (Avant-Pop, post-postmodernism), wider cultural movements (globalization, altermodernism), or new forms of critical practice (post-criticism).

Part Two of the volume eschews a strictly chronological approach, focusing instead on innovation within and across genres. The first section concentrates mainly on poetic forms of experimentation and their influence on current practice, such as L=A=N=G=U=A=G=E poetry, concrete poetry, hoax poetry, found poetry and other forms of "uncreative writing," and the poetry and other types of language used in visual art. The next section focuses on experiments with narrative and with fictionality more generally, with chapters on unnatural narration, impossible worlds, experimental life writing, and genre fiction and the avant-garde. The final section of this part considers ways in which the novel in particular has experimented in recent years with form and design, with attention to graphic novels, multimodal fiction, the incorporation of information design in the novel and printed interactive fiction. The third and final part of the volume comprises one section and turns to the impact that the digital age has had on experimental literature across media. Chapters on digital fiction, code poetry and new media, computer gaming, and virtual forms of autobiographical writing show the wide range and versatility of contemporary experimentation, and point to the ways in which the first years of the twenty-first century, like those of the twentieth, have been concerned with the radical possibilities opened up by new technologies.

III. The persistence of the historical avant-gardes

The idea of a "tradition of the new" ought to be paradoxical – surely anything truly new in culture should define itself *in opposition to* the traditional? – but that has not prevented people from talking about such a tradition since at least Harold Rosenberg's (1959) book of that title. Indeed, it would be hard to deny that such a tradition exists, even if we leave out of account the kind of retrospective tracing of forebears that Jorge Luis Borges once described in his essay, "Kafka and His Precursors." With the benefit of hindsight it is always possible, as Borges saw, to discover historical precursors of recent avant-garde practices in, say, Romantic irony, eighteenth-century metafiction, Renaissance formal inventiveness, and so on, back into the mists of time. It is a somewhat different matter, however, to recognize the direct genealogical connection between the historical avant-gardes of a hundred or so years ago and late twentieth-century and twenty-first-century experimentalism. The first of these ways of constructing a "tradition of the new" is retrospective, while the second acknowledges the persistence of a particular past in the present.

Many of the general features, and even some of the specific practices, of experimental literature of the second half of the century were anticipated by the avant-garde groups of the period from just before the Great War until the immediate aftermath of World War II, the epoch of the great *isms* of the early twentieth century, including Italian and Russian Futurism, Dadaism, Surrealism, and Expressionism, down to Existentialism and Absurdism (see chapters by White, Murphy, Stockwell and Gavins). Multi- and inter-media experiments, experiments with language, identity, visuality and the creative process, the embrace of transformative new technologies, the testing and transgression of the limits of artistic and social acceptability – all of these, and many other features of recent literary experimentalism, are prefigured by the historical avant-gardes. More than that, the very *model* of an avant-garde group, of what it is and does – group formation and internal politics, identity and "branding," manifestoes, self-promotion and propaganda – derives from the early twentieth-century *isms*.

These models of experimental practice and group behavior are in some cases embraced by later literary experimentalists and adapted to their own uses, in other cases resisted, but they can rarely if ever be ignored. Thus, for example, it is easy to trace the influence of the early twentieth-century French and Russian avant-gardes on the New York poets of the 1950s and 1960s (see Lee, this volume), and that of Dada and Surrealist practice on the "uncreative writing" and Flarf poetics of the 1990s and the new millennium (see Epstein, this volume). Conversely, it is just as easy to see how groups as diverse as the French New Novelists and the Tel Quel circle, the Lettrists and Situationists, and the OuLiPo group all defined themselves *in opposition to* their Surrealist and Existentialist predecessors (see Marx-Scouras, Miller, and Baetens, this volume). Both tendencies – both the reclamation of certain aspects of the modernist-era avant-gardes and wariness toward other avant-garde tendencies of the same era – can be detected in the poetics and politics of the L=A=N=G=U=A=G=E poets (see Bernstein, this volume). For better or worse, the life and work of the historical avant-gardes seem to have been incorporated into the very DNA of the experimental literature that has come after them.

The persistence of the historical avant-garde into the present guarantees a sort of family resemblance among the contemporary varieties of experimentalism. As with real families, resemblance here is not a matter of everyone possessing some essential feature common to all types of experimentalism; rather, it involves a series of overlapping similarities – common threads, which connect subsets of experimental practices. Some of the common threads that we have detected among the experimental practices surveyed in this volume are outlined below; no doubt the reader will find others.

IV. Some common threads

After the historical avant-gardes: postmodernism

Postmodernism, whatever it may be – a period, style, literary movement, or cultural condition – is, by its very name, seen as a successor to the historical avant-gardes and, more specifically, to modernism. And yet, as Brian McHale points out, "nothing about the subject is certain, resolved, or uncontentious." Questions of the when, how, and why of postmodernism loom unanswered. Furthermore, postmodernism's ambiguous politics and debatable relationship to popular culture pose an even greater question: Is the literature of the postmodern experimental at all? It is precisely this controversial topic that McHale raises in his essay for the volume, first recalling the unsettled dispute on the matter between philosopher J.F. Lyotard and architecture critic Charles Jencks, who advocated a postmodern experimentalism rooted in modernism and a postmodern eclecticism associated with the popular, respectively. For McHale, there are two key tropes of postmodern literature that complicate each side of the argument: the process of world-modelling and the presentation of an unpresentable textual sublime.

True to the spirit of postmodernism, McHale ultimately refuses to pit the experimental and the eclectic against each other in a straight dichotomy. Similarly, Elana Gomel in her discussion of popular genre fiction (itself a progeny of the postmodern) interrogates the absolute segregation between genre fiction as low art and the avant-garde as high art. As she says in the opening words to her essay, rather "Two trains collide." Concentrating on the popular genres of fantasy, science fiction and horror, Gomel shows that, like postmodern literature, avant-garde genre fiction is concerned with the creation of new worlds and exploration of ontological arenas, particularly through devices of allegory, displacement, and incoherence. However, while postmodern works often rely heavily on parody and pastiche, avant-garde genre works "create new fictional spaces that attempt to resurrect/reconstruct history, and in doing so, question their own role as commodities."

Focusing on writing of the present, both Liam Connell in his discussion of the literature of globalization and Alison Gibbons in her account of altermodenist fiction suggest that contemporary experimental novels exhibit a heightened awareness of the value of commodities in the international market place. The literature of globalization explores themes of "complex connectivity," the numerous and sometimes intertwined modes of social interaction available today, and the ways in which these interactions produce a perceived sense of "proximity." In exploring these themes, such literary experiments also trouble them, highlighting "the interplay between local and global as mutually interpenetrating forms." In doing so, time and space become intertwined. The concatenation of time and space is one of the commonalities shared by the literature of globalization and altermodernist fiction. Gibbons's account of altermodernism, which stems from the writings of art critic Nicolas Bourriaud, identifies three central tenets of fiction of this period: the representation of time as a spatialized landscape, the conceptualization of identity as nomadic, and the integration of genres and modes. Both altermodernist fiction and the literature of globalisation are interested in "networks" – temporal-spatial, formal, intersubjective and ontological. Moreover, both have subversive intent, challenging forms of contemporary internationalism and offering, in Gibbons's words, "an implicitly politicized aesthetic resistance to globalization."

The politics and manifestoes of experimentalism

The political connotations of experimental literature have been prominent ever since Surrealism, described by Stockwell as "the prototype of the modern *avant-garde*." Noting that "even if it was not a political movement in itself, most of the first Surrealists were marxist communists," Stockwell traces Surrealism's roots to Dada, a somewhat chaotic grouping of writers, artists and performers which emerged in Zurich in 1916. The targets of the group's creative energy were many and various; as Stockwell says of the movement, "it is the anti-X, where X is whatever you can think it is." He shows how, as Dada evolved into Surrealism, the art produced became "more constructively framed, more shaped by principle," and also more infused with "the language of revolutionary socialism." While Dada's ethos had often been anti-establishment in the abstract, Surrealism "excelled in the production of manifestoes, pamphlets, essays and debates."

In her wide-ranging chapter Laura Winkiel also highlights the importance of the manifesto in the construction of the "avant-garde," pointing out that the term was first used by radical groups of Jacobins during the French Revolution. For her the implied metaphor in the term of elite troops sent ahead in battle suggests that "revolutionary battles increasingly became a war of words and ideas," and that it thus encodes "the entwining of aesthetics and politics that structures the manifesto form and determines its functioning for the next two centuries." This "duality" is particularly heightened, Winkiel claims, in the first four decades of the twentieth century, when "manifestos' staunch refusal to accommodate 'tradition' in any form captures the militancy of the artistic avant-gardes." She gives as examples Marinetti's futurist manifestoes, yet her comments could apply equally to Breton's *Manifesto of Surrealism*. Both aimed at, in Stockwell's words, "a radical re-evaluation of society through the medium of an artistic movement."

This aim is also crucial to Lettrism and Situationism, which Tyrus Miller describes as "post-World War II outgrowths of Surrealism." Though early Lettrist enthusiasts such as Isidore Isou and Guy-Ernest Debord often scornfully dismissed current Surrealism as tired and mainstream, they openly acknowledged their debt to the radical ideas that it had advanced in the late 1920s and early 1930s. In journals such as *Internationale lettriste* (1952–1954), *Potlatch* (1954–1957), and *Internationale Situationniste* (1958–1969) Debord and Gil Wolman formulated their proposals for overthrowing the commodified, consumerist "spectacle" of capitalist society, developing key concepts such as *dérive* (the exploration of urban space) and *détournement* (the recontextualizing of appropriated cultural materials). Miller argues that such strategies "possess an 'artistic' status at least equal, if not more important, than those works that relate to recognizable artistic categories such as poetry or film."

Two years after the first appearance of the *Internationale Situationniste*, the literary journal *Tel Quel* was founded by a group of relatively unknown French writers. Though the two journals differed in format and approach, they both played a crucial role in shaping French culture and politics in the tumultuous years leading to the uprisings of May 1968. *Tel Quel* was more literary-focused, and closely aligned with the emergence of the *nouveau roman*, yet as Danielle Marx-Scouras observes, "the cultural politics of the journal were shaped as much by the historical events of the era as they were by theoretical advances in literary studies, semiotics, philosophy, and psychoanalysis." The writers published in the journal, who included Alain Robbe-Grillet, Natalie Sarraute and Jean Ricardou, turned away from Sartrean *engagement*, and its belief that literature passively reflects social practice, promoting instead, under the influence of semiotics and psychoanalysis, a critique of language itself, and a greater understanding of its role in shaping, and sometimes frustrating, meaning. As Marx-Scouras notes, however, this preoccupation with language was not an act of political disengagement; indeed quite the contrary.

A focus on language and its ways of making meaning was also key in the 1970s and 1980s for another, disparate group of writers, based mainly in the U.S. and Canada. The term *L=A=N=G=U=A=G=E* describes less a movement or a school than a "site of conversation," as Charles Bernstein, a leading practitioner himself, notes in his chapter. As with the groups centered around the *Internationale Situationniste* and *Tel Quel*, a serial publication was crucial in shaping a collective rationale, namely *L=A=N=G=U=A=G=E* magazine, which Bernstein edited with Bruce Andrews from

1978 to 1982. Although, in marked contrast to earlier experimental movements, the writers associated with $L=A=N=G=U=A=G=E$ tended to steer clear of manifestoes and explicit statements of intent, the turn to language and an examination of its potential for ideological bias, led, as with the *Tel Quel* group, not to a disassociation from politics and contemporary events, but rather to a deeper, more sustained engagement with them. Bernstein notes that "there was a strong desire to connect oppositional political and cultural views with linguistically inventive writing."

One particular kind of oppositional politics, which according to Bernstein had a significant influence on $L=A=N=G=U=A=G=E$, is addressed by Ellen Friedman in her chapter on women's avant-garde writing in the twentieth century. Highlighting the importance of the poststructuralist turn to language and psychoanalysis in the 1970s and early 1980s, Friedman discusses how Hélène Cixous and other French women theorists advocated *l'écriture féminine* in order to emphasize their difference from canonical male authors. Having traced this non-hierarchical, open-ended style to the modernist experiments of Dorothy Richardson, Virginia Woolf and Gertrude Stein, amongst others, Friedman claims that the female avant-garde becomes harder to identify in the late twentieth century, as experimental tropes and techniques are incorporated into the mainstream. She suggests that contemporary feminist experimentalists, such as Kathy Acker, Bharati Mukherjee and The Guerilla Girls, have been driven to "find new forms of subversion, adapting, for instance, the trickster figure."

Political subversion has indeed been a feature of recent experimental writing across the world. In her chapter on Anglophone postcolonial poetry, Priyamvada Gopal discusses how postcolonial literature has been deemed "always already radical by virtue of speaking from the periphery to the metropole." She is concerned to complicate this picture by distinguishing between both the political motivations and the techniques used in different national traditions. She critiques one especially widely-used term in postcolonial theory in particular: "hybridity." Thus the poetry of Sujata Bhatt in India, Mutabaruka in the Caribbean and Mothobi Mutloatse in South Africa, to take three of her examples, differs not only in form and content, but also as a result of the "political and historical imperatives which variously shape the reception, perception and use of English in the wake of colonial rule" in each region. In each case, however, Gopal emphasizes the potential of experimental poetry as a force for change, through its "refiguring multilingualism as a space of creatively politicized intersection."

Technological influence and innovation

The experimental writing practices of Italian Futurism and Russian Cubo-Futurism were hardly isolated from the politics of the early twentieth century. Italian Futurism, as John White advises, was both "a deliberate riposte to the *passéism* of late 19th century poetry" and "a mode of discourse appropriate to the modern dynamic world of speed, technological efficiency and, ultimately, the mechanized slaughter of the First World War." Indeed, in the turbulent climate of the First World War, Futurist experimentation was "invariably deployed with a political purpose in mind."

Nevertheless, while the political was clearly one motivation for the Futurists, the technological was a central inspiration. The rapid advancement of science and technology at the turn of the century was heralded by founder F.T. Marinetti as an impetus for literary experimentation. As White details, the typographical vision associated with Futurism known as "words-in-freedom" or "the telegraphic device" enabled Futurist poets to express the speed and rapidity of trains and automobiles while "aeropoetry" sought to convey the physical and psychological dimensions of flying. Words-in-freedom generated poems in which onomatopoeias abound, punctuation is replaced by mathematic symbols, and words themselves are dismantled. The Russian Cubo-Futurists take such linguistic deconstruction even further, creating neologisms from the existing lexicon, breaking words down into morphemes, or perhaps allowing only vowels to remain, all of which amount to what White calls "a process of linguistic de-familiarisation."

Contemporary electronic code poetry similarly explores the fabric of language. As Steve Tomasula phrases it, code poetry "foregrounds that code is a language, and also that language is a code." In his chapter on the electronic literature of code poetry and new media, Tomasula discusses a form of experimentalism that is rooted in the technology of its own creation. Code poetry, Tomasula explains, is highly self-conscious, and its aesthetics are concerned with revealing the mechanisms by which it is generated. It is a "practice that sees itself as poetry and programming in equal measure," and thus "code poets have pushed to the foreground the scaffolding of code and its structures that normally reside hidden behind the scene/screen." In contrast, new media fiction and poetry, while reliant upon their technological underpinnings and programming foundations, hide such infrastructure. Instead, such works exist as theatrical and engrossing hybrids of video, sound and music; they are often interactive; and they recast experimental literary art as multimedia experience.

Visual experimentation

Code poetry, new media literature, and the Futurist impulse to experiment with typography all point towards the potentialities of the visual dimension of language, literature and narrative. Concrete poetry explores not only the visuality of language but also of the page, which becomes a canvas, with white space as much a part of the literary work as words themselves. In his essay, Joe Bray outlines the history of concrete prose and poetry. While the origins of concrete prose can be found in early novelists such as Laurence Sterne and Henry Fielding, Bray argues that the fascination with visual form has not abated in twentieth- and twenty-first-century novels, pointing to modernist, postmodernist, and contemporary writers for whom the page is still very much an experimental surface. Similarly, having established the canon of concrete poetry, at its height in the 1950s and 1960s, through recourse to seminal poets such as Stéphane Mallarmé, Guillaume Apollinaire, and of course Eugen Gomringer, Bray considers the way in which contemporary poetry might still be influenced by this heritage.

Alison Gibbons cites concrete poetry alongside modernist poetics, Futurist experimentation, and postmodern fictions, to name a few precursors, in contextualising contemporary multimodal literature, that is, "literary texts that feature a multitude of semiotic modes in the communication and progression of their narratives." She claims that the advent of digital technologies in the late twentieth and early twenty-first centuries has produced an upsurge of literary works which emphasize their own form through visual and material experimentation. In her essay, Gibbons suggests a formal taxonomy for contemporary multimodal literature: illustrated works, multimodal (re)visions, tactile fictions, altered books and collage fictions, concrete/typographical fictions, and ontological hoax.

Although graphic novels are certainly multimodal, Gibbons chooses not to discuss them, preferring instead to view such works as a genre in their own right. In her chapter on graphic narrative, Hilary Chute considers the relationship of comics to literary experimentation. Chute rebuffs the charge that comics are merely popular and low culture artefacts, proposing that they are experimental by way of having "vigorously expanded the rubric of 'literature' over the past thirty years." More pertinently, comics are experimental in the sense that they self-consciously draw attention to their own construction and obstruct normal reading practices. In support of her argument, Chute invites readers on a tour of experimental comic practice starting in the early twentieth century, continuing into the late twentieth century and concluding with the comics of today. Ultimately for Chute, comics, like multimodal literature and concrete poetics, explore "the spaces in between word and image" and "offer a rich and relevant visual-verbal syntax."

While literature has incorporated the visual in experimental practices, art has assimilated the verbal. Reflecting on the presence of words in recent visual art, Jessica Prinz claims that in the twentieth century we witnessed "an eruption of language into the field of the visual arts," an eruption prefigured and stimulated by avant-garde experiments such as Dada and Futurism. A key figure in the historical lineage of words in visual art, Prinz claims, was the avant-gardist Marcel Duchamp, "who influenced an entire generation of artists" in the latter twentieth century "for whom art was not only visual but also linguistic." Moreover, the twenty-first century exhibits a further enhancement of the integration of word and image, with works of language art that are inspired by, offer tribute to, or appropriate literary texts. Consequently, Prinz intimates, the boundaries between art and literature are blurring and dissipating. The literary and the artistic are no longer necessarily distinct types of aesthetic artefact.

Experiments across media

From the beginning of the twentieth century right down to the present, experimental literature has had to find ways to coexist with other, competing media – visual art, music in a range of genres, performance, photography, film, television, digital media – competitors that have expanded in number, power, appeal and market-share over the course of the century. A common thread uniting several of the chapters in this volume is experimentation with these other, adjacent media. In some cases this experimentation has taken the form of collaboration across media, or even co-optation of one medium by another; in other cases, it has been more akin to baiting a threatening competitor, poking at this dangerous beast through the bars of its cage to stir it up and see how it reacts.

Richard Murphy views the Expressionism of the immediate post-Great War and the Weimar years as an avant-garde style that straddles the media of literature and film, which share a common "poetics of animism." In both media, on the screen and on the printed page alike, an unstable, uneasy balance is struck between realism and the fantastic. In Expressionist literary works such as Kafka's *Metamorphosis*, just as in films such as *The Cabinet of Dr. Caligari* or *Metropolis*, subjectivity is dramatized, the protagonist's interior state being projected onto the outside world so that, for the viewer or reader as much as for the protagonist, "exterior" reality becomes a hybrid of inside and outside.

If Expressionism straddles media, the experimental poetics of *The New American Poetry*, Donald Allen's seminal anthology of 1960, modelled itself on adjacent art-forms, especially the bebop jazz and Abstract Expressionist painting of the postwar era, but also dance and performance. According to Ben Lee, in his chapter on post-war avant-garde poetry in the U.S., poets adopted the new music and painting as their models as a strategy for distancing themselves from a modernist literary tradition that they regarded as over-civilized and exhausted. Crucial to the aesthetic formation of this generation of poets was their encounter with experimental, collaborative cross-media practices, which some experienced in the New York artworld while others encountered it at Black Mountain College in rural North Carolina, an incubator of mid-twentieth-century avant-gardism.

A similar cross-fertilization among the arts is explored by Aldon Nielsen in his chapter on the experimental strain in African-American poetry, which he seeks to recover through case studies of two pivotal but undervalued figures: Melvin Tolson and Lorenzo Thomas. Tolson wrote his way out of a conservatively modernist aesthetics into a complexity akin to the "New World neo-baroque" of African Diasporic art throughout the hemisphere. Thomas, whose artistic circles overlapped with the groups represented in *The New American Poetry* – the Beats, the Black Mountain poets, the New York School – experimented like them in mingling poetry with jazz, performance and visual art, as reflected, for instance, in the collage imagery of his own book-covers (often the work of his artist-brother Cecilio "Cess" Thomas).

Cross-media experimentation and the poaching of models from adjacent media, features of both the New American Poetry and the African-American avant-garde, become defining characteristics of the Avant-Pop tendency in contemporary literature. By Lance Olsen's account, Avant-Pop exploits the resources of popular film, television, comics, rock music, advertising and franchising in much the same way that high-modernist writing drew on classical mythology, Christian iconology and the literary canon. Avant-Pop writing appropriates, recycles and repurposes the materials of popular mass-media culture, practicing a form "pla(y)giarism," to use Raymond Feder-man's neologism. It has much in common with jazz, readymade art, collage and montage practices, and sound sampling and mashup in popular music, and its aesthetics are perfectly suited to the newer digital media.

Robert McLaughlin discerns quite a different relation to contemporary popular culture, a much more adversarial one, in the tendency that he calls (not without reservations) post-postmodernism. The post-postmodernist fiction of novelists such as Jonathan Franzen, Richard Powers, Jonathan Lethem, and especially David Foster Wallace responds both to the perceived exhaustion of literary postmodernism and to the growing dominance of television in popular culture. Post-postmodernism arises in a generation fully acclimated to television and deeply suspicious of its corrosive irony and its power to reduce our experience of the world to mere "viewership." The post-postmodernists share with their postmodernist predecessors an acute awareness of the constructedness of reality, but they also aspire, more than their precursors ever did, to engage with a reality beyond mass-media representations.

Artifice

Jan Alber, Henrik Skov Nielsen and Brian Richardson describe unnatural narratives as a "distinctive and important subset of experimental literature." They undertake a wide-ranging survey of different forms of unnatural narration, focusing on recent experiments with the narratorial voice in particular, such as the collective, intermental "we" narration of Ayi Kwei Armah's *Two Thousand Seasons* (1973), and the disconnection between the narrator and the narrated in Bret Easton Ellis's *Glamorama* (1998). For Alber, Nielsen and Richardson, such experiments do not only show the extremes possible in narrative construction, but also "provide an interrogation of the basic elements of realistic narrative practices and a critique of overused narrative conventions." Their examples thus highlight the fact that in all literary fiction there is "a process of dialectical mediation between 'natural' components that reproduce the world as we know it and unnatural components that move beyond our real-world knowledge."

Ralph Berry similarly argues that the various practices that can be grouped under the heading "metafiction" should not be regarded as isolated experimental techniques, but rather as integral to the understanding of all fiction. He claims that the most frequently-cited metafictional writers of the 1960s and 1970s, such as Jorge Luis Borges, John Barth and Flann O'Brien, beyond simply asserting the artificiality of their work, were actually aiming to establish "a properly philosophical relation of fiction to itself, one in which writer and reader engage in something like a critical analysis of the formative conditions of their own activity." For Berry, then, writers of metafiction are not self-consciously playing with ideas of constructedness for their own sake, but rather seriously attempting "to engage reality, not primarily by representing it but by acknowledging its immanence in their medium and practice."

According to Philip Mead similar questions are also raised by various forms of literary hoax. Focusing on one particular example, the matrix of critical discourse surrounding the texts supposedly written by Hiroshima survivor Araki Yasusada, Mead suggests that in challenging notions of authenticity, authorship, political responsibility and cultural guilt, the hoax (apparently perpetrated by the poet and translator Kent Johnson) constitutes "a genuine experiment in poetics." Like other hoaxes, it raises for Mead "important questions about what exactly authenticity and genuineness in writing are, how they are produced, and why readers value them." A history of literary (in)authenticity, from Sidney's *Apologie for Poetrie*, through Chatterton and Ossian to Armand Schwerner's playful take on ethnopoetics in *The Tablets* (1999), reveals for him that "authenticity in literature has always been a form of illusion." Literary fakery is thus, according to Mead, more than dissidence against various forms of institutional authority. Instead it can lead, at its most sophisticated, "to the development of useful diagnostic tools for literary and cultural analysis."

The creative process

"Process" is a key aesthetic category and value in many varieties of experimental writing practice across the twentieth and into the twenty-first centuries, and as a recurrent theme it threads its way through several of the contributions to the present *Companion*. Process-oriented art values the experience of *making* over the *thing made*, and that experience is often a shared one, involving the reader's or viewer's collaboration in the artwork's production. Process-oriented writing invites us into the workshop to witness the experiment as it unfolds, and increasingly, especially with the emergence of interactive digital media, to participate in it directly.

One of the avant-garde groups surveyed here literally describes itself as a workshop: *l'Ouvroir de Littérature Potentielle*, the Workshop of Potential Literature, or OuLiPo for short. As Jan Baetens explains, the OuLiPo group researches and practices procedural or constrained writing; it rediscovers and revives, or invents from scratch, *extra* or *supplementary* rules and conventions of literary production, and then applies them. It literally conducts experiments in writing, and it often does so in plain view. The processes by which OuLiPian works come to be produced are sometimes accessible to the reader's inspection, though not always; yet even when the actual procedure that yielded a specific text is irrecoverable, the reader will generally be aware that *some* constraint has been observed or procedure followed, and this knowledge subtly alters his or her relationship to the text from that of passive consumer to co-conspirator.

OuLiPian practice also has implications for our understanding of artistic or authorial *control*. Insofar as the writer relies on a constraint or procedure to help *generate* a text, doesn't he or she surrender some degree of control over the product? This issue of control becomes even more vexed in the case of what Andrew Epstein (following the poet Kenneth Goldsmith) calls "uncreative writing," including its web-based, search-engine-driven variety, known as Flarf. Uncreative writing is *all* process, as it were. Originating nothing, it appropriates and recycles readymade verbal material, whether read, spoken or culled from the internet. Duplicating texts that already exist, its products are strictly speaking *redundant*, and in that sense valueless. What more profound challenge could be posed to dominant aesthetic ideologies of self-expression, originality and the personal voice?

Recycling and appropriation also figure in the concept – or more properly, the *post*-concept – of the *take* that Greg Ulmer develops in his chapter on "post-criticism."

Criticism and theory have been partners of experimental literature throughout the twentieth century, appearing in aesthetic manifestoes and elsewhere in the writings inspired by avant-garde movements; but now that we find ourselves in the *aftermath* of criticism, Ulmer argues, we need, not new concepts, but something else: call them "post-concepts." The *take* is one such post-concept, peculiarly adapted to the literacy (or what Ulmer calls the *electracy*) of an era of digital technology and internet culture. One model of the *take* is Marcel Duchamp's practice of the readymade – for instance the occasion when he defaced a postcard representation of Leonardo's *Mona Lisa* and added a punning, obscene caption. This act of vandalism implies a strategy: *take a picture*. In the same spirit, Ulmer *takes* a passage from Kafka's notebooks, substituting post-conceptual pastiche for definition (the form appropriate to a critical concept). This process may be applied to passages from any writer whose style, like Kafka's, serves as a vehicle for thought. Just as Duchamp *takes a picture*, so post-criticism *takes thought*.

In their chapters, Baetens and Epstein report on avant-garde groups that usher us into the workshops where writing experiments are conducted, but Ulmer goes a step further. His chapter is *itself* such a workshop, and in visiting it we are privileged to witness how post-criticism is made – the very process of its emergence.

Pathways

Decisions concerning the composition of a novel are part and parcel of the process of creating experimental forms. In writing a novel, authors have to choose how to arrange their text, be it in terms of narrative progression, graphological layout, or conventional structure (such as chapter divisions). In his chapter on information design in the novel, Steve Tomasula makes exactly this point, that "one history of writing is a history of information design: a means of organizing information for effect." Through an exploration of design structures as well as the social-literary context of their structures, from renderings of the Tree of Life and PowerPoint appropriations of Lincoln's "Gettysburg Address" to novels and hypertexts of the twentieth and twenty-first centuries, Tomasula shows that different forms of representation, different information designs, have different effects. Ultimately, information design creates the pathways for reading.

Pathways of reading are fundamental in the arena of digital fiction. David Ciccoricco covers extensive ground in his survey of "networked narratives" which present what he calls "a poetics of the link and node," offering "new insights into the composition and reception of literary art in light of participatory digital media." Ciccoricco offers a diachronic account of the development of digital fiction from the disk-based (floppy or compact) hypertext of first generation manifestations to the predominantly (though not exclusively) multimedia web-based works of the second generation. He also mentions digital interactive fiction (IF) which requires textual input from reader-user-players for narrative advancement. Each type shows that information design, and specifically the form of link and node particular to digital fiction, impacts upon reading pathways, for instance, in the case of re-reading text, recycling nodes and reordering narrative. In Ciccoricco's words, "Repetition and variation comes to characterize both the elements of textual design and the interpretive models we design as we read."

N. Katherine Hayles and Nick Montfort share Ciccoricco's interest in interactive fiction, but discuss print interactive fictions as well as digital IFs. In doing so, they suggest the subdivision of printed interactive works into three categories: random shuffle of cards or loose pages, multiple pathways through bounded codex forms, and multiple paths by way of annotation such as the literary footnote. What is common to both printed and digital forms, according to Hayles and Montfort, is that "the text requires the user to make choices, and that these choices affect how the narrative proceeds in a literal (not merely interpretive) sense." The multiple pathways of information, narrativity and reading for interactive fictions offer various perspectives on the narrative and the world(s) it presents. In their approach, Hayles and Montfort employ a worlds model, specifically David Herman's (2002) model of "storyworlds," which understands narrative worlds as mental representations that readers must cognitively map out. This enables them to offer an analysis which tracks the complex ways in which readers construct, develop and revise storyworlds from their interactions with such texts.

Marie-Laure Ryan also employs a model of worlds as mental representations – that of possible worlds as developed from philosophy and logic. In looking at the impossible worlds of experimental literature, Ryan is interested in texts which transgress logical laws and therefore challenge the imagination. Through the course of her essay, she offers a catalog of the forms of impossibility in experimental literature: contradiction, in which opposing facts, sentences, or versions of narrative events are given; ontological impossibility, in which, through metalepsis, fictional entities transgress the boundary between fiction and reality; impossible space, in which spaces do not cohere to their given properties; impossible time, in which narrative time does not function according to its known rules; and impossible texts, in which literary works feature an invented paradoxical text. The pathways presented by impossible worlds are both ontological in their inconsistency and unfeasibility, and cognitive in the sense that readers must negotiate unresolved paradoxes. Impossible worlds present unnatural reading experiences by challenging readers "to devise new strategies for making sense of texts, even if meaning does not arise from the vision of fully imaginable solutions."

The readerly and the experiential

The importance of the reader's experience is also emphasised in Joanna Gavins' chapter on the absurd in literary prose fiction. Having outlined the imprecision of most literary treatments of the topic, Gavins proposes a "spectrum of absurd experimentalism," ranging from texts which overtly display experimental stylistic techniques to those that explore the concept through a more conventional narrative structure. At one end she places Rudolph Wurlitzer's *Nog* (1968), which creates a sense of narratorial unreliability through an abundance of epistemic modality, while at the other she gives the example of J.D. Salinger's *The Catcher in the Rye* (1951), which contains some of the same uncertainty, but exhibits more realism of detail. Gavins argues that the kind of stylistic analysis she practices in the chapter, when complemented by a greater focus on readers' everyday responses, confirms the absurd "not as a genre, not as a movement, but as a readerly experience."

The reader's navigation of a cline of experimental possibilities is also a theme of Astrid Ensslin's chapter. Ensslin proposes a spectrum between ludic digital literature and literary computer games, arguing that "recent experimental forms of art games and digital experimental literature have merged visual, ludic and literary design techniques and materials," and that as a result computer games can be seen as "*literary* art." Nearer the ludic end of the spectrum is an example such as *The Path*, which is based on *Little Red Riding Hood*, and foregrounds certain aspects of computer game mechanics for the purposes of critical *détournement*, while nearer the other end is *The Princess Murderer*, a take on *Bluebeard*, which contains more prominent metafictional elements, and which acts as a subtle criticism of forms of digital narrative and their accompanying critical theories. In each case, according to Ensslin, unreflective, fully immersive gamer behaviour is challenged and a more attentive and critical kind of engagement promoted.

Irene Kacandes is also concerned with the ways in which experimental literature can be experienced. She points in particular to the importance of the reader's attention to paratext in the interpretation of life writing, arguing that neither Philippe Lejeune's oft-cited "autobiographical pact," nor the concomitant "referential pact," can be analyzed on the basis of the text alone. Kacandes shows how experimental life narratives play with each category in Lejeune's definition. Thus for example, Alexander Masters' *Stuart: A Life Backward* (2006) challenges Lejeune's notion of a retrospective vantage point, while J.M. Coetzee's supposedly autobiographical trilogy undermines the unity of author, narrator and protagonist. Kacandes concludes her chapter with a discussion of her own experiment in life writing, her "paramemoir" *Daddy's War: Greek American Stories* (2009), the writing and reception of which confirm her main argument that "the paratext counts."

Amy Elias's chapter on virtual forms of life writing also discusses the ways in which Lejeune's foundational propositions have been challenged by recent experimental texts. Focusing on autographics, various forms of interface and avatar autobiography, she argues that digital-based life writing particularly disrupts Lejeune's assertions concerning authorial intention and single authorship. According to Elias, virtual life narratives are often "collaborative, social, and networked," and the "dialogical self" that emerges "becomes a kind of collaborative interchange between myself as writer and the interpreting, interactive reader." Thus examples such as Shelley Jackson's online graphic memoir "My Body: A Wunderkammer" (1997) and role playing games such as Second Life® illustrate for her the important role of the reader (or participant) in constructing a virtual self. Elias claims that "the options for self-representation" in these new genres diverge radically from those which shape "traditional print autobiography and memoir," and thus that "online autography, interfaces, and avatar autobiography now seem to be, in fact, the new frontier of experimental life writing."

V. Conclusion: the futures of experimental literature

This introduction began with a qualification of what it meant to experiment, intimating that the history of experimentation in literature might be considered as old as the history of literature itself. But what might the future hold? Already at the beginning of the twentieth century, the Futurists claimed that their experiments enabled them to produce a literature of tomorrow. Well, when *is* tomorrow?

In light of the evidence of this *Companion* – its retrospective view of the historical avant-gardes and of postmodernism and its descendants, its survey of explorations in language, narrative, form, and media, and its account of the aesthetics of the present – it remains to ask: What might we expect from the new frontier of experimental literature?

Futurological predictions inevitably fall short: the millennium bug did not take down the world's computer systems on New Year's Day 2000; we are not (yet) post-human; the book is not (yet) dead. As cultural commentator and author Warren Ellis (2005) puts it, "Welcome to the future. It's the world you're living in":

> People are disappointed with the future they're living in. Since 2001, the refrain has gone up, louder year by year: "This is the future. Where's my flying car? Where's my fucking jet pack?" Pre-millenium, we were living in an unprecedented density of imagined futures, and we assumed it was all waiting for us around the corner. And here we are, around the corner, and none of it is standing here.
>
> (Ellis 2005: n.p.)

Any act of future-thinking is, in itself, a work of fiction, and the imagined possibilities are thought-experiments. Thus, to consider any brave new literary landscape, we can but look at where we've been and where we are now, or as Ellis says, "The best we can do is track the future as it happens."

Political intervention has often been a motivating factor in experimental literature, as demonstrated by literary movements such as Surrealism, Futurism, Situationism, and L=A=N=G=U=A=G=E poetry, or by formerly marginalized groups such as feminist or postcolonial writers. The present experimental literature, of globalization and/or altermodernism, seeks to challenge the forces of cultural and economic globalization, internationalism and capital markets. In keeping with such subversion, recent events such as the "Occupy Wall Street" campaign might fuel experimental literary reactions. Beginning on 17 September 2011 in Manhattan's Financial District, and spreading to other major cities in the Western world, Occupy Wall Street is not unconnected to other recent unrest, including the violent civil uprisings in Egypt, Tunisia and elsewhere in the Arab world in 2010/2011, stemming from political corruption, democratic deficiency, and fiscal problems, and in Greece and Italy in relation to the Eurozone debt crisis. We may, therefore, envisage an experimental literature that addresses what may be seen as the contaminated rule of capitalism. Alternatively, the increasing concern over the environment, global warming and the end of the world, seemingly supported by a surge of natural disasters (earthquakes, tsunamis, floods, catastrophic storms), might spur the development of a politicized, experimental eco-literature.

The proliferation of technology in the late twentieth and early twenty-first centuries certainly suggests further potentialities for literary innovation. What does the e-reader, Kindle, or iPad have to offer the literary work? What more might the World Wide Web have to offer? Media scholars cite the development of Web 2.0 (the interactive sites of the internet such as social networking, blogging, and virtual worlds) as liberating for users. Isn't it logical to assume, therefore, that an experimental literature of tomorrow (be it in the printed book, on the tablet computer, online, or across media in multiplatform environments) might offer greater participatory pleasures for its reader-users? Similarly, another factor to consider in the development of tomorrow's literary experiments is the impact of today's media saturated environment. Will works become progressively more hybridized in form, in terms of genre, modes, and media? And will the incessant flow of data and information (rolling news, Twitter feeds) affect the form and process of texts, leading to still more appropriation or recycling in composition?

However grounded in the past and the present, these previsions of the future, predictions of the forthcoming, are no more than fancy. Inventions. Fabrications. In Ellis's (2005: n.p.) words, "By the time you read this, everything in it will be history. The future's a moving target." Yet as we linger in the interminable pause of the present, waiting for a literary future that will never arrive, there is one thing of which we may be certain: Experiment, we must.

References

Calinescu, M. (1987) "The Idea of the Avant-Garde." In *Five Faces of Modernity*, Durham, NC: Duke University Press, pp. 95–148.

Ellis, W. (2005) "Future Underground," *Brainjuice*, 16 February 2005 (no pagination). [Online.] Retrieved October 2011, from http://www.warrenellis.com/?p=336

Federman, R. (1975) "Surfiction: Four Propositions in Form of an Introduction." In R. Federman (ed.) *Surfiction: Fiction Now . . . and Tomorrow*, Chicago, IL: Swallow Press, pp. 5–15.

Herman, D. (2002) *Story Logic: Problems and Possibilities of Narrative*, Lincoln, NE: University of Nebraska Press.

Johnson, B.S. (1973) "Introduction." In *Aren't You Rather Young to Be Writing Your Memoirs?* London: Hutchinson, pp. 11–31.

Sukenick, R. (1985) *In Form: Digressions on the Act of Fiction*, Carbondale and Edwardsville, IL: Southern Illinois University Press.

Part I
THE HISTORICAL AVANT-GARDES

2

ITALIAN FUTURISM AND RUSSIAN CUBO-FUTURISM

John White

"Although Futurism as such developed only in Italy and Russia, its impact was felt all over Europe" (Lawton 1988: 4). This verdict reflects the general consensus that Italian Futurism and Russian Cubo-Futurism were technically more radical and better attuned to the Futurist sensibility than the numerous coteries anxious to associate themselves with Futurism's meteoric success. Italian Futurism's pre-eminence owed much to the movement's disciplined theoretical coherence, its challenging manifestoes (see Winkiel, this volume for more on *Ars Poetica* and manifestoes), dynamic post-Cubist paintings, replacement of conventional music by mechanical noise-intoners (*intonarumori*), repertoire of avant-garde mini-dramas (*sintesi*), and above all its visually and acoustically experimental "words-in-freedom" (*parole in libertà*). Some of the Italian Futurist and Russian Cubo-Futurist movements' signal achievements prefigure later forms of experimental literature, yet their manifestoes seldom mention the process of experimentation. With the exception of Constructivism's "experiments for the future" (Rodchenko 2005: 108), and Aleksei Kruchenykh's early reference to Cubo-Futurism's "first experiments [in creating] the language of the future" (Lawton 1988: 70), the concept was rare among the proto-Futurist avant-gardes of pre-war Europe.

I. Italian Futurism and science

When "The Foundation and Manifesto of Futurism" (Marinetti 2006: 11–16) was published in 1909, "experimental literature" was primarily associated with *Le roman expérimental* (Zola 1880). Although Émile Zola was acknowledged as one of the "great precursors of Futurism" (Marinetti 2006: 45), the accolade was in recognition of the French novelist's urban themes, not the *Rougon-Macquart* cycle's status as a new, scientifically conceived form of fiction based on an amalgam of Hippolyte Taine's positivism and an influential introduction to experimental medicine (Bernard 1865). Three decades later, Italian Futurism was establishing broader-based connections between scientific experiment and literary experimentation. That is to say, its experimental paradigms were frequently indebted to a broad range of recent discoveries made in many countries outside Italy, rather than being focused on a small number of specialist disciplines, as Zola's *Rougon-Macquart* novels were. Moreover, they were generally conceived with the aim of reconstructing Futurist literature in order to make it an effective vehicle for the improvement of modern life in general during the early decades of the twentieth century. For the Italian Futurists such a program was inevitably a matter of socially applied, not merely theoretical, science.

The Italian Futurists were both ingeniously eclectic and up-to-date in their responses to state-of-the-art science. Despite some fanciful references to technological advances in his "Futurist Visionary Hypothesis" of what Italy would be like in the twenty-first century (Marinetti 2006: 221–5) and his prophecy of the emergence of "Extended Man and the Kingdom of the Machine" (85–8), Marinetti usually cited hard science's experimental paradigms in support of his claim that he and his fellow Futurists were "the Futurists of *tomorrow*, not of *the day after tomorrow*," with their "intense focusing on the present [. . .] preparing the way for a Tomorrow which will emanate directly from us" (146; Marinetti's emphasis). Apart from emulating technological advances, preparing for tomorrow's future was a task predicated on a "vision of the mind and body transformed, giving human beings new mental and physical powers" (Humphreys 1999: 6–10). The program was predicated on a rejection of Italy's *passéist* (antiquated) cultural heritage and an aggressive iconoclasm seldom equalled in subsequent experimental literature.

Recent evidence in *Futurism and the Technological Imagination* (Berghaus 2009) supports the movement's boast to be "based on the complete renewal of human sensibility brought about by the great discoveries made by science" (Marinetti 2006: 120). According to one contributor, "unlike scholars, poets and artists from other periods of history who occasionally borrow thematic material [. . .] from the world of science, the Futurists looked to science for direction of mind [. . .] to articulate their aesthetic perception of reality" (Pietropaolo 2009: 43). The interface between the avant-garde and the sciences – a characteristic of both Italian Futurism and Russian Cubo-Futurism – is of great importance for an appreciation of the two movements' literary experiments.

Marinetti, who once considered "Elettricismo" and "Dinamismo" appropriate titles for Futurism, cites an impressive array of scientific disciplines and topics in his manifestoes: astronomy, biology (Lamarck's pre-Darwinian theory of evolution), chemistry, engineering, mathematics, medicine, metallurgy, physics, technology, sensory perception, chronophotography and, not least, current Futurist experiments with "photodynamism," a field relevant to the depiction of moving objects in Futurist painting, collage and experimental poetry.

Despite the absence of the term "experiment" in Futurist manifestoes, modern scholars (Janacek 1984; Drucker 1994; Berghaus 1998, 2009) have been less reluctant to apply the term. However, when it comes to the movement's boisterous self-presentation, caution is required for Futurism's scientific preoccupations are often expressed in terms that smack of manifesto hyperbole. Take, for instance, the claim to work with "the cool detachment of an engineer" (Marinetti 2006: 196), the Lamarckian belief in "an incalculable number of human transformations" (86) or the recommendation of an electric power station with its distribution columns "bristling with meters, control panels, and shining levers" as "models for [Futurist] poetry" (136). For all the rhetoric, Marinetti expresses an urgent need to discover the scientific "laws" or "formulas" that will help explain certain phenomena. In other fields, including chronophotography (Apollonio 1973: 38–45) or the exploration of sensory perception via "tactile panels" (Marinetti 2006: 370–82), specific experiments were devised and carried out, though these remained divorced from the literary sphere. Of course, one needs to bear in mind the fact that Italian Futurism subscribed to an interdisciplinary ethos, one that encouraged cross-fertilization between media: e.g. text/image collage, the fusion of Machine Art with Mechanical Ballet, innovative stage sets and "robotic acting" (Berghaus 1998: 396–441), as well as such new genres as aeropoetry and Total Theater (Marinetti 2006: 400–7). In such a stimulating environment, ingenious joint ventures were undertaken that were experimental in ways that would have been inconceivable, had Italian Futurism remained an exclusively literary project.

II. "Words-in-freedom" as experimental poetry

In reaction to the over-sentimental, visually static poetry that was still deemed to hold sway in contemporary Europe, Marinetti proposed "a telegraphic lyricism that bears not the slightest hint of books but, as much as possible, the taste of life" (2006: 127). With poetry accused of bookishness and Marinetti, at war with "Mallarmé's static ideal" (128), heralding a "Typographical Revolution" designed to "impose on words (already free, dynamic and torpedo-like) every kind of speed" (128), the stage was set for Italian Futurism's boldest literary experiment.

The ensuing "Technical Manifesto of Futurist Literature," "Destruction of Syntax – Untrammeled Imagination – Words-in-Freedom" and "Geometrical and Mechanical Splendor and Sensitivity Toward Numbers" (Marinetti 2006: 107–19, 120–31 and 135–42, respectively) issued sweeping proposals for the reform of poetry as part of the most radical agenda any European avant-garde had yet contemplated. Not only was conventional syntax to be banished from poetry, further drastic measures were also demanded: verbs were to be used in the infinitive, adjectives, adverbs and conjunctions abolished, punctuation replaced by mathematical symbols and the personal pronoun avoided. In the interests of brevity, the deployment of onomatopoeia in lieu of verbose descriptions, anarchic spelling and other "telegraphic" forms of minimalist communication were prescribed. (Sample results appear as postscripts to the "Technical Manifesto" and "Destruction of Syntax.") A potentially more creative proposal came with the invitation to "dismantle and remake words, cutting them in half, extending and reinforcing their centers or their extremities, increasing or reducing the number of their vowels and consonants" (Marinetti 2006: 131). But as we shall see, it was the Russian Cubo-Futurists who turned to language-generation strategies of this kind. Yet failed experiments are also experiments. Even Italian Futurism's puerile "motsfondus en liberté" (fusedwords-in-freedom) (Marinetti 2002: 126–31), comprising compound neologisms formed from existing words, demonstrated that Romance languages (unlike Russian and German) resist all such exercises in deconstruction and compounding. (On the advantages and limitations of Italian Futurism's telegraphic experiments, see White 1990: 143–214.) Words-in-freedom had a greater impact when they involved reductive processes similar to those used in a telegram.

Marinetti's proposals were formulated with a dual function in mind: (i) as a deliberate riposte to the *passéism* of late 19th-century poetry (Symbolism was as much Marinetti's target as it was that of the Russian Cubo-Futurists and Formalists); and (ii) as a mode of discourse appropriate to the modern dynamic world of speed, technological efficiency and, ultimately, the mechanized slaughter of the First World War prefigured in the movement's founding manifesto. According to the inventor of words-in-freedom,

> the speed of trains and automobiles [. . .] familiarizes us with foreshortened perspectives and visual syntheses [thus creating] a horror of slowness, of minutiae, of analyses and detailed explanations. Love of speed, abridgment, and synopsis: "Tell me everything, quickly, *in a couple of words!*"
>
> (Marinetti 2006: 122)

As a corollary, the true Futurist poet would

> convey [life] telegraphically, [. . .] with the same economical rapidity that the telegraph imposes on reporters and war correspondents in their summary reports. [. . .] the poet's imagination has to be able to make connections between things that have no apparent connection, *without using conductor wires*, but rather condensed *Words-in-Freedom*.
>
> (Marinetti 2006: 123)

It could be argued that words-in-freedom constituted a fruitful form of literary experiment in much the same way as Cubo-Futurist and OuLiPo lipograms did (see Baetens, this volume), in that both are based on a principle of systematic omission, in the one case the omission of one letter of the alphabet, in the other, that of entire grammatical categories. But whereas lipogram-production resembles a literary parlor game, the Italian Futurists' "telegraphic" device was invariably deployed with a political purpose in mind. Although still obliged to communicate his Aesthetic of the Machine Age in conventional Italian, Marinetti expressed his trust in the new Telegraphic Lyricism: "Words freed from punctuation will radiate out toward one another, their diverse magnetisms will intersect, in proportion to the continuing dynamism of thought" (Marinetti 2006: 116). However, Futurism's subsequent free-word experiments demonstrated that syntactical reform was not enough. New typographical layouts, new text/image configurations and unique one-off effects were still called for.

Despite Marinetti's campaign to enshrine words-in-freedom as Futurism's signature style, the movement's poets experimented with a number of literary sub-genres and artistic forms: "synchronic charts" (multi-sensory patterns of words structured to resemble in layout either maps or campaign plans), "designed analogies" and "auto-illustrations" (typographical effects arranged in the shape of designated objects), predominantly verbal collages, aeropoems inspired by the new military vantage-point afforded by flying, tactilist tables (Marinetti 2006: 370–82) and concrete poems consisting exclusively of onomatopoeic sequences and acoustic neologisms. Futurism's most ingenious free-word poet, Francesco Cangiullo, devised a poetry of handwritten stanzas arranged on musical staves to create an anti-bookish template, as well as creating a whole variety performance from a cast of "humanized" letters of the alphabet. Carlo Carrà's war collages in *Guerrapittura* (1915) worked with a combination of verbal effects and images, as did much of the experimental work of the so-called Second Futurists. In the midst of such a flurry of inventive activity, one of the most significant forms of interaction was between the founding Futurist painters' concern with dynamism and the influence this would have on words-in-freedom and Futurist verbal collage.

III. Codifying literature's depiction of speed

"We believe that this wonderful world has been further enriched by a new beauty, the beauty of speed," the founding manifesto declared (Marinetti 2006: 13). "Destruction of Syntax" (1913) counted the joys of living on an "Earth grown smaller through speed":

> a constant desire to know what [our] contemporaries, in every part of the world, are up to. [. . .] a need to communicate with all the peoples of the world. [. . .] An immense expansion of our sense of humanity and an urgent need to determine, at every moment, our relations with the whole of mankind. [. . .] Love of [. . .] the speed of trains and automobiles.
>
> (Marinetti 2006: 122)

Futurist literary manifestoes sang the praises of globalization, urban dynamism and the rapid pace of modernity, while presenting words-in-freedom as the idiom par excellence for the age of "the telegraph, the telephone, and the gramophone, the train, the bicycle, the motorcycle, the automobile, the ocean liner, the airship, the airplane, the film theater, the great daily newspaper," regarded as a symbol of a new world of global communication (Marinetti 2006: 120). Marinetti's poetic program served as a pretext not just to abolish syntax, but to clear the way for a range of diverse literary experiments, many of them at odds with the movement's pro-modernity, pro-war and anti-*passéist* agenda. (On Italian Futurism and modernity, war and the country's allegedly defunct cultural heritage, see Berghaus 2009: 1–34 and Marinetti 2006: 221–48 and 81–150.) Although the results of some still gave the impression of being visually static, Futurism's cult of speed in general and the dynamism of urban life in particular tended to remain a matter of thematic emphasis and hence to require further stylistic reconsideration. The Futurist painters were already showing their literary counterparts the way in this respect. "The Exhibitors to the Public" of 1912 (Apollonio 1973: 45–50) was the first to draw attention to the virtues of force-lines (*linee-forza*). Soon the Futurist painters' deployment of force-lines to communicate dynamism started to influence Futurist free-word poets to work with the "essential force-lines of speed" (Apollonio 1973: 197). Despite the Futurists' claim to have invented force-lines, they have recently been shown to have their equivalents in physics (Pietropaolo 2009: 50–9).

Italian Futurists interpreted force-lines in two ways. In "Futurist Painting: Technical Manifesto" (Apollonio 1973: 27–31), they present them as reflecting a "universal dynamism," while elsewhere interpreting them as reflecting "the particular motion of an individual object" in such works as Giacomo Balla's *Abstract Speed*, Russolo's *Dynamism of an Automobile* and Umberto Boccioni's *Dynamism of a Cyclist*. The distinction is reiterated in "Absolute Motion + Relative Motion = Dynamism" (Apollonio 1973: 150–4). Boccioni's 1914 book *Pittura scultura futuriste*, with its emphasis on creating impressions "in our dynamic consciousness," identifies some geometrical techniques employed to this end:

> a train, a car, a bicycle generates an emotional milieu which takes the form of horizontal penetration at an acute angle. A slowly moving crowd awakens in us the inert milieu of perpendicular directions, whereas the same crowd starting off at a run appears in our dynamic consciousness as a maze of acute angles, obliques and aggressive zig-zags.
>
> (Boccioni 1971: 199, my translation)

The deployment of force-lines in words-in-freedom was a major break with early Futurist poetry's timid horizontal layouts. The Futurist painters' force-line code played an important role in the Futurist poets' and collage-designers' ingenious attempts to give words-in-freedom the same sense of exhilarating dynamism the Futurist painters' work displayed. Although initially associated with the depiction of the dynamism of the modern world, words-in-freedom were soon re-fashioned to play their part in Futurism's depiction of battle-scenes as part of the movement's propaganda campaign to persuade the Italian government to abandon its neutrality and join the war against its natural enemies.

Marinetti's verbal collage *Bombardement d'Adrianople* (reproduced in White 1990: 184) led the way in 1914 with its bold use of force-lines consisting of shaped sequences. Yet as the work demonstrates, force-lines are different in free-word typography – not just for economic reasons, but because they serve a new function when constructed out of printed words. In propaganda contexts shaped poetry must be intelligible, the overall configuration therefore needs to contain lines of words that can be read from left to right, thereby at the same time enhancing the impression of movement in the opposite direction, as was the case with Marinetti's earlier war collage *Irredentism (free-word poem)* (1914) and the verbal explosion of words on the cover of his war epic *Zang tumb tumb* (1914).

Force-lines in Futurist paintings depicting the motion of an individual object usually require images pointing to the left side of the canvas. Motion resulting from dynamic force-lines thus becomes motion in one consistently linear direction. In *Bombardement d'Adrianople*, on the other hand, the shapeless dynamism of battle simultaneously involves a whole confusion of clashing forms, both centrifugal and centripetal, involving collective and individual motion. Shaped lines of handwritten text are, for example, used to suggest the trajectories of mortar shells, while centrifugal patterns created by exploding words take typographical dynamism literally in a number of other directions. By comparison with Marinetti's earlier, largely horizontally structured free-word typography, collages involving exploding shapes and fragmenting pieces of deformed text to convey the nature of modern warfare were a radical advance. Such layouts move words-in-freedom away from the tradition of Apollinaire's shaped poetry in the direction of verbal collage or what the Italian Futurists called "free-word pictures" (*tavole parolibere*). Due to the blatant pro-war propaganda used in these works (Poggi 1992: 25), the amalgam of radical political content and violent imagery has been acknowledged as Futurism's most important technical achievement in the field of literary text/image experimentation.

Marinetti's famous verbal war collages (*Le soir, couchée dans son lit, elle relisait la lettre de son artilleur au front, Après la Marne, Joffre visita le front en auto* and *Bataille à 9 étages du Mont Altissimo*) were published in Paris in 1919. French originals and English translations are reproduced in Marinetti 2002: 116–21; detailed interpretations can be found in Bohn 1986, White 1990 and Drucker 1994. Drafts of each stage of the work-in-progress, combining a series of cut-out fragments, hand-drawn silhouette shapes and written components (reproduced in Hanson 1983: 2–5 and Poggi 1992: 231–5), are preserved in the Marinetti Archive (Beinecke Library, Yale University). Valuable genetic material of this kind affords a rare glimpse into the experimental process of hypothesis-trial-and-assessment as well as the works' sources and their systematic adaptation. This is one of the few instances of the documented vital stages of Futurist experimentation being open to scholarly scrutiny. While Italian Futurism's free-word experimenters were shifting visual poetry in the direction of collage, the Cubo-Futurists in Russia were concentrating on the language-generating value of the autonomous word's individual components. This was a paradigm-shift of greater literary significance than anything words-in-freedom could offer.

IV. Russian Cubo-Futurism's experiments with language

The label "Cubo-Futurism" helped emphasize the program of collaboration between the newly baptized movement's prestigious artists (Kazimir Malevich, Natalya Goncharova, Mikhail Larionov, Olga Rozanova and the Burliuk brothers) and its showcase poets (Velimir Khlebnikov, Aleksei Kruchenykh, Vasily Kamensky and Vladimir

Mayakovsky). Its key task was to register Russian Futurism's major debt to the systematic methodology of Cubism rather than the Italian focus on a Futurist sensibility, modernity and the political issues of the day. (Competing explanations of "Cubo" can be found in Markov 1968: 118–19, Pomorska 1968: 78, and Barooshian 1974: 71.)

The first Russian Futurist manifesto, "Slap in the Face of Public Taste" (1912), displayed sufficient anti-*passéist* contempt and provocation to have met with Marinetti's approval: "Throw Pushkin, Dostoevsky, Tolstoy, etc., etc. overboard from the Ship of Modernity," "*We* alone are the *face* of *our* Time," "From the heights of skyscrapers we gaze at [the Symbolists'] insignificance!" (Lawton 1988: 51). The mission statement from the Hylaea group, soon to become Cubo-Futurism, left no doubt that its main concern was with the predicament of the language of Russian poetry. "We *order* that the poets' *rights* be revered," the manifesto declared, specifically identifying the right to "enlarge the *scope* of the poet's vocabulary with arbitrary and derivative words" and "to feel an insurmountable hatred for the language existing before our time" (Lawton 1988: 51–2). While these two demands account for Cubo-Futurism's linguistic program, those that follow merely strengthen the sense of anger contained in the manifesto's title.

Unlike the Italian Futurists' "free-word" experiments, Cubo-Futurist poetry was to have a substantial impact (chronicled in Pomorska 1968, Steiner 1984, and Eagle 1988) on such adjacent disciplines as contemporary linguistics, Russian Formalism and Structuralism. However, during the turbulent post-revolutionary period, a less cosmopolitan Cubo-Futurism found itself under severe pressure to surrender to the requirements of totalitarian cultural politics. The history of Cubo-Futurism, which was the central part of the Russian Futurist movement as well as a "*direct model* for the OPOYAZ school" (Pomorska 1968: 119), soon demonstrated that renovating the language of poetry had important implications for the subsequent understanding of language *per se*. According to one contemporary, it was impossible "to draw a line between Khlebnikov's poetical work and his philological researches" (Livshits 1977: 56). While there had been no such symbiosis of literary theory and the science of linguistics in Italian Futurism, the discovery of various forms of linguistic de-familiarization and language-generation was among Cubo-Futurism's most innovative literary achievements. Despite the Cubo-Futurists' claim to be the first to say "that in order to depict the new – the future – one needs *totally new words and a new way of combining them*," that their poets engaged in "the first experiments of the language of the future," that they had found new ways of depicting "*movement and a new perception of the world*" and "loosening up grammar and syntax" to create a new "swift language of modernity" (Lawton 1988: 72, 70, 73, 73, 61, respectively), what they called their "linguistic work" (202) was very different from Marinetti's "free-word" program. While the Italian free-word poets belonging to Marinetti's innovative experimental group had little or no knowledge of the semiotic and linguistic experiments of their time, the Russian Cubo-Futurists were in regular contact with various contemporary linguistic circles. As a consequence, the resultant linguistic experiments were in due course to attract the attentions of both Russian Formalists and contemporary linguists. (On the principal differences in this respect between Italian Futurism and Russian Cubo-Futurism, see Barooshian 1974: 145–52, and Eagle 1988: 281–94.)

Russian Cubo-Futurists often saw in poetry a unique experimental science: a "laboratory" or "workshop" for language renewal. As has been pointed out, "the closest *scientific* discipline towards which the [Cubo-] Futurists inclined was contemporary linguistics" (Pomorska 1968: 93), "contemporary linguistics" in this instance being the work of The Society for the Study of Poetic Language (OPOYAZ), among whose membership were such luminaries as Boris Eichenbaum, Osip Brik, Viktor Shklovsky, Jurii Tynianov, Viktor Zirmunsky and Lev Jakubinsky, and the Moscow Linguistic Circle, particularly important because of the influential contributions of Roman Jakobson and Gregory Vinokur. More than either Kruchenykh or Mayakovsky, Khlebnikov took word-dissection and word-generation to more sophisticated levels than had hitherto been attempted. Despite Cubo-Futurism's affinity with what was to become Russian Formalist linguistics, his interests in ornithology, botany, mathematics and history also left their mark on his poetry, theoretical essays and manifestoes.

"There exists no science of word creation," according to "Our Fundamentals" (Khlebnikov 1987: 376), although some, largely subjective, principles can be found in "Teacher and Student," Khlebnikov's most revealing contribution to the theory of non-poetic language (277–87). Word-generation, Khlebnikov's abiding concern, invariably involved a number of procedures: inventing neologisms out of real and pseudo-roots, language reduction (albeit not in Marinetti's telegraphic sense), the application of estrangement tactics to everyday language, the use of "abbreviated and spliced words," "chopped-up words, half-words, and their odd artful combinations," the process of "roughing up the language" and "grammatical irregularity," e.g. "lack of agreement in case, number, tense, and gender" (Lawton 1988: 226, 61, 58, 73, 73, respectively), to which one might retrospectively add the Russian Formalist terms "shift," "de-familiarization," "laying bare" and "deformation" (on the importance of these terms for both Russian Formalism and an understanding of the Cubo-Futurists' experiments, see Steiner 1984).

The dilemma was: where to start with the project of renovation? Evidently not by deconstructing available anachronistic models. In "The Word as Such" (Lawton 1988: 55), Kruchenykh and Khlebnikov suggest that "a poem could consist of *a single word*," hardly a hypothetical position, given that Khlebnikov's "Incantation by Laughter," experimenting with new words from the root of the Russian word for "laughter" (details in Cooke 1987: 70–3), had already appeared in *Studio of the Impressionists* in 1910 and Kruchenykh had even published the first of his poems consisting exclusively of vowels (Lawton 1988: 67). Strictly speaking, neither example of language-generation is confined to a single autotelic word. "Incantation by Laughter" works additively with prefixes, suffixes, infixes and invented morphemes to create a poem largely comprising neologisms: new verbs, nouns, adjectives and adverbs all relating to laughter. The result serves as "a demonstration of the 'self-sufficiency' of the word" as well as "the richness of meaning which can be built from a single root" (Cooke 1987: 70). Using a radically different approach, Kruchenykh's illustration

o e a
i e e i
a e e

(Lawton 1988: 67)

is structured on the sequence of vowels in a Russian prayer. In Khlebnikov's case, word-generation is assumed to shed new light on the concept of "laughter" via a process of linguistic de-familiarization, whereas Kruchenykh's vowel-poem engages with one micro-component isolated from a familiar source, isolation being a key strategy in certain forms of experiment. Both of these poems would subsequently be categorized by their authors as "transrational poetry" (*zaum'*), although, as we shall see in the next section, this was always a hotly disputed concept. Khlebnikov's "Incantation by Laughter" would appear to enrich the available Russian language repertoire by a process of constructing sentences on the basis of neologisms derived from the supposed roots lying dormant in the Russian language, an experiment which results in a memorable poem that lodges itself firmly in the collective memory. There are few Futurism aficionados who cannot recite Cubo-Futurism's most famous language-generating poem. No wonder Shklovsky's *The Resurrection of the Word* spoke admiringly of the Cubo-Futurists' "transrational experiments" (Steiner 1984: 151) and the word "eksperiment" figured so often in OPOYAZ publications. But Khlebnikov's generative mode of experimentation did not stop with "Incantation by Laughter." He adopted a similar strategy with "love," as well as repeatedly theorizing the spiritual significance of roots in the Russian language. While the Cubo-Futurists seemed to echo Marinetti with their manifesto title "The Liberation of the Word" (Lawton 1988: 78–81), the focus in this case is on the primeval roots of the modern Russian language, not on the task of adjusting conventional language to the demands of hyper-modernity.

"Is word-creation possible, and to what degree?" "Poetic Principles" asks (Lawton 1988: 84). As the substantial differences in response to this question embodied in Khlebnikov's "Incantation by Laughter" and Kruchenykh's "HEIGHTS (universal language)" suggest, language reform could mean a variety of things in Cubo-Futurist circles. Although Khlebnikov remained "in the vanguard of experimental work on language" (Cooke 1987: 67), he attached mystical – sometimes religious – importance to the roots of words. At times he would follow the normal laws which govern word formation, while also violating these laws and employing pseudo-derivational procedures (Cooke 1987: 71). His obsession with roots went well beyond standard linguistic procedures. "Within the 'circle' of these roots lay," according to him, "the pivotal point through which the meanings of everyday language could pass and be transformed" (Cooke 1987: 69–70). According to Khlebnikov, words were "of man," their roots were "of God" (Cooke 1987: 69–70). What Cubo-Futurist manifestoes repeatedly refer to as the "self-sufficient word" was, for Khlebnikov, the pure word, the "philosopher's stone" of language, not the discourse of words-in-freedom. Khlebnikov also created an onomatopoeic form of "transrational language" that involved a remarkable degree of acoustic mimesis: e.g. his "sound-paintings" of the Language of the Birds in his play *Zangezi* (details in Cooke 1987: 86–7). Unfortunately, many of his poems, including "Incantation," do not lend themselves to translation, especially into a non-Slavonic language.

Some Cubo-Futurists also saw quasi-mystical significance in other de-familiarization devices. In "New Ways of the Word," for example, Kruchenykh declared that they learned how to look at the word backward: "we enjoy this reverse motion [. . .] *it can be read backward, and then it acquires a more profound meaning!*" (Lawton 1988: 76). *Mirskontsa* (*Worldbackwards*) is the title of a primitivist play by Khlebnikov as well as a mixed-media volume published by Kruchenykh. The latter's poetry contains numerous words written in reverse, a major step towards the Cubo-Futurists' use of the palindrome as a language-estranging device. Given that a word written in reverse will allude to its real counterpart, the device has an affinity with the palindrome strategy of language creation.

Mayakovsky created local palindrome effects through word-splitting, whereas Khlebnikov's palindromic verse included works of prodigious length operating with both pure and impure, visual and acoustically reciprocal types of palindrome (examples in White 1990: 281–3). His verse epics *Stenka Razin* and *Pereverten'* (*Turncoat*) entail the subversion of the Baroque conceit of the palindrome for the dual purpose of estrangement and language renewal. The result has nothing to do with Italian Futurism's Telegraphic Lyricism; instead the cumulative deployment of a specific device encourages a new constructive form of reading against-the-grain. When read in both directions, a line's initial meaning changes to negate the former sense (Pomorska 1968: 100). As has been pointed out, although the palindrome does not necessarily demand neologism, Khlebnikov was not averse to experimenting with a combination of the two devices (Cooke 1987: 93). In a similar spirit, he liked in his poetry to encode names and key words as anagrams. Although opinion is divided on which of these devices is part of the arsenal of *zaum'* (Khlebnikov's more permissive conception of transrational language tended to embrace virtually all Russian Futurism's innovative devices, whereas Kruchenykh's only admitted sounds of no semantic value), they each contributed in their various experimental ways to Cubo-Futurism's project of language enrichment, as did Russian and Ukrainian Futurism's shaped poetry, intensification of onomatopoeia, inventive orthography, deployment of handwritten elements and their juxtapositions of painting and poetry in such works as *Old-time Love*, *A Game in Hell*, *Explodity*, *Le-Dantyu as a Beacon* and *Worldbackwards* (illustrations in Compton 1978). (On shaped poetry, see Bray, this volume.)

V. *Zaum'*: Russian Cubo-Futurism's most radical literary experiment?

During a visit to Russia, Marinetti claimed *zaum'* to be "just the same as [his] 'words at liberty'" (Livshits 1977: 191), a glib judgement far from the truth. But it was a divisive project, not helped by the fact that Khlebnikov and Kruchenykh interpreted the concept in different ways and were inconsistent in their explanations of it. Kruchenykh's "Declaration of the Word as Such" (1913) makes the case for *zaum'*:

the artist is free to express himself not only in the common language (con-cepts), but also in a personal one (the creator as an individual), as well as in a language which does not have any definite meaning [. . .], a transrational language. Common language binds, free language allows for fuller expression. [. . .] The artist has seen the world in a new way and, like Adam, proceeds to give things his own names. The lily is beautiful, but the word "lily" has been soiled and "raped." Therefore, I call the lily, "euy" – the original purity is rees-tablished. Consonants render everyday reality, nationality, weight – vowels, the opposite: A UNIVERSAL LANGUAGE.

(Lawton 1988: 67)

While Kruchenykh is thought to have "considered any 'deformation' of the Russian language [. . .] a form of trans-sense" (Barooshian 1974: 91), he repeatedly illustrated his arguments with radically reduced material. Extreme *zaum'*, as the illustration below from the last part of *Explodity* (Lawton 1988: 65) suggests, is a form which takes the concept to the ultimate limit and is thus more suited to the requirements of manifesto hyperbole:

i
che
de
mali
gr
iu
iukh
ddd
ddd
se
v
m'

Whether encountered in the Cyrillic original or transcribed, such poetry is decidedly neither Russian nor a meaningful attempt at creating a new universal language. The same is true of the illustration offered in "The Word as Such," the most quoted and misquoted example of *zaum'*. As if to discourage attempts at interpretation, the poem is again untitled:

dyr bul shchyl
ubeshchur
skum
vy so by
r l ez

(Lawton 1988: 60)

In this case, provocation was added to incomprehension by the appended claim that "in this five-line poem there is more of the Russian national spirit than in all of Pushkin" (Lawton 1988: 60).

The standard survey of critical responses to *zaum'* (Barooshian 1974: 91–6) is highly instructive, inasmuch as the questions it identifies as having been raised back in the Futurist period have remained in circulation to this day. Was such work poetry or merely an experiment in language-generation? On what criteria were Kruchenykh's examples typical of transrational poetry? Were they Khlebnikov's, Kruchenykh's – or perhaps even Shklovsky's? Given the subjective meanings Kruchenykh attached to certain morphemes, vowels, consonants and sounds, how could his kind of *zaum'* justify the claim that it could become a universal language? If Khlebnikov's examples were not comprehensible, were they language at all? Was *zaum'* of this extreme kind more in the domain of linguistic play than that of poetry? What was the common ground between Khlebnikov's, Kruchenykh's and the Russian Formalists' conceptions of de-familiarization, language-deformation and language's social function? For Russian Futurism's chronicler, *zaum'* was "one of the most original parts of the futurist creed," important not least for having led to the founding of the experimental "41°" group (Markov 1968: 129). While the social and poetic virtues of the various types of *zaum'* are seldom judged comparatively, a strong case could be made for the importance of the Khlebnikov school of *zaum'*, either on linguistic or on poetic grounds.

VI. Cultural politics

Proletkul't was Cubo-Futurism's chief adversary during the early Soviet years. It viewed the literary works as unintelligible to the proletariat, while dismissing its poets as representatives of the intelligentsia, lacking in collective spirit, concerned with formal questions at the expense of social and political themes and too distant from the class Futurism claimed to support and represent. Cubo-Futurism's clashes with Proletkul't and its attempt to establish Kom-Fut have been sympathetically documented (Jangfeldt 1977: 72–117) and Lawton (1988) offers extensive evidence of the group's various attempts to re-ingratiate itself with its ruthless detractors. These attempts all center on the claim that the promised "Language of the Future" was now being designed to be appropriate to the needs of a post-civil war USSR.

After Mayakovsky's and Osip Brik's abortive attempt to shore up Cubo-Futurism's reputation by affiliating it to Kom-Fut, the movement was obliged to continue its "linguistic work" under the aegis of Lef (The Left Front of the Arts). One repercussion was the extent to which creating the "language of the future" was politicized. (There is no comparable politicization of the concept in Futurism after Mussolini came to power.) At this stage in the movement's development, the term "experiment" is repeatedly used to stress that Cubo-Futurism's work is not *"an aesthetic end in itself, but a workshop for the best expression of the facts of the contemporary era,"* i.e. "The work of Futurism is parallel with and identical to the work of communism" (Lawton 1988: 203, 216, respectively). The word "experiment" occurs six times in Mayakovsky's and Brik's "Our Linguistic Work" (Lawton 1988: 202–3), doubtless to align Cubo-Futurism with the great "social experiment" of Soviet communism. "We are not priest-creators," the Cubo-Futurists stress, "but master-executors of the social demand" (Lawton 1988: 203). The consequence of this new role is a change in the concept of "literary experiment," a shift in the kind of linguistics invoked and a more cautiously presented preoccupation with the language of Futurist poetry both on the part of the Russian Formalists and the Cubo-Futurists themselves. As a result, Russian Futurism, as understood by Russian Formalism and its followers, had been forced to abandon its cultural program or leave the arena. In post-Second World War Italy, there were still poets who regarded themselves as Futurists. There were no Cubo-Futurist equivalents in the USSR; the secret police had seen to that.

References

Apollonio, U. (1973) *Futurist Manifestos*, London: Thames and Hudson.

Barooshian, V.D. (1974) *Russian Cubo-Futurism, 1910–1930*, The Hague, The Netherlands: Mouton.

Berghaus, G. (1998) *Italian Futurist Theatre, 1909–1944*, Oxford, UK: Clarendon.

—— (ed.) (2009) *Futurism and the Technological Imagination*, Amsterdam: Rodopi.

Bernard, C. (1865) *Introduction à l'étude de la médecine expérimentale*, Paris: Laillière.

Boccioni, U. (1971). *Gli scritti editi e inediti*. Milan: Feltrinelli.

Bohn, W. (1986) *The Aesthetics of Visual Poetry, 1914–1928*, Cambridge, UK: Cambridge University Press.

Compton, S. (1978) *The World Backwards: Russian Futurist Books, 1912–16*, London: The British Library.

Cooke, R. (1987) *Velimir Khlebnikov: A Critical Study*, Cambridge, UK: Cambridge University Press.

Drucker, J. (1994) *The Visible Word: Experimental Typography and Modern Art, 1909–1923*, Chicago, IL: Chicago University Press.

Eagle, H. (1988) "Cubo-Futurism and Russian Formalism." In A. Lawton (ed.) *Russian Futurism through its Manifestoes, 1912–1928*, Ithaca, NY: Cornell University Press, pp. 281–304.

Hanson, A. (ed.) (1983) *The Futurist Imagination: Word + Image in Italian Futurist Painting, Drawing, Collage and Free-Word Poetry*, New Haven, CT: Yale University Art Gallery.

Humphreys, R. (1999) *Futurism*, Cambridge, UK: Cambridge University Press.

Janacek, G. (1984) *The Look of Russian Literature: Avant-Garde Visual Experiments, 1900–1930*, Princeton, NJ: Princeton University Press.

Jangfeldt, B. (1977) *Majakovskij and Futurism, 1917–1921*, Stockholm: Almqvist & Wiksell.

Khlebnikov, V. (1987) *Collected Works: Vol. 1, Letters and Theoretical Writings*, Cambridge, MA: Harvard University Press.

Lawton, A. (1988) *Russian Futurism through its Manifestoes, 1912–1928*, Ithaca, NY: Cornell University Press.

Livshits, B. (1977) *The One and a Half-Eyed Archer*, Newtonville, MA: Oriental Research Partners.

Marinetti, F. (2002) *Selected Poems and Related Prose*, New Haven, CT: Yale University Press.

—— (2006) *Critical Writings*, ed. G. Berghaus, trans. D. Thompson, New York: Farrar, Straus and Giroux.

Markov, V. (1968) *Russian Futurism: A History*, Berkeley, CA: California University Press.

Pietropaolo, D. (2009) "Science and the Aesthetics of Geometric Splendour in Italian Futurism." In G. Berghaus (ed.) *Futurism and the Technological Imagination*, Amsterdam: Rodopi, pp. 41–61.

Poggi, C. (1992) *In Defiance of Painting: Cubism, Futurism, and the Invention of Collage*, New Haven, CT: Yale University Press.

Pomorska, K. (1968) *Russian Formalist Theory and its Poetic Ambiance*, The Hague, The Netherlands: Mouton.

Rodchenko, A. (2005) *Experiments for the Future*, New York: MOMA.

Steiner, P. (1984) *Russian Formalism: A Metapoetics*, Ithaca, NY: Cornell University Press.

White, J. (1990) *Literary Futurism: Aspects of the First Avant-Garde*, Oxford, UK: Clarendon.

Zola, É. (1880) *Le Roman Expérimental*, Paris: Charpentier.

3

THE POETICS OF ANIMISM

Realism and the fantastic in expressionist
literature and film

Richard Murphy

No-one doubts that the genuine thing cannot be that which appears as external reality. Reality
must be created by us.

(Edschmid 1918: 369; my translation)

I. Introduction

Although the expressionist movement flourished only briefly, during the turbulent
decade of 1910 to 1920, it dominated German modernism and produced the most
radical and wide-ranging impulses in literature, art and film. As an avant-garde and
experimental movement it was concerned with undermining inherited forms of realism. Yet many key works of expressionism nonetheless depend for their effectiveness
upon maintaining a tension between realism on the one hand, and the alternatives
to realism, particularly the mode of the fantastic and its dreamlike situations on the
other (see Murphy 1999: Chapter 5). Certainly expressionism is often characterized
by its unhesitating embrace of certain anti-realistic forms, and by its use for the purposes of abstraction of such strategies as excess, hyperbole, extreme characterization,
and extravagant, theatrical gestures. Yet the most remarkable works of expressionism always hold these elements in tension with realism. They frequently create an
overarching realist framework that provides the context that constrains such hyperbolic expressionist forms, thus making them all the more powerful. To take one brief
example, in "The Metamorphosis," written in 1912 and one of Kafka's key texts of the
expressionist decade, the absurdity of the situation arises not from the fantastic element, namely the transformation itself, but from the tension between Gregor Samsa's
new situation as a bug and his attempt to continue with his "realistic" and quotidian
attitudes, such as his regular, everyday behavior, and all the usual concerns associated
with his workaday world, such as his anxiety about missing the next train to work.
The narrative also proceeds for the most part in a largely sober, restrained and realist
fashion in its descriptions of the bourgeois apartment, the family and its undisturbed

routines, even though the image of the insect at its center stands out as entirely fantastic and at odds with the realist context.

In expressionism, a perfect balance between realism and the fantastic is not always present. This is particularly true of cinema: the visual component tends to push towards the real, emphasizing the object-world, and the horizon of the audience's expectation is often set generically towards approaching film "realistically." Nevertheless, my argument will be that a good number of the most significant scenes and images in expressionist and Weimar films, such as *Metropolis*, are in fact not only attributable to the fantastic – corresponding to their expressionist provenance – but are most readily comprehensible via that mode. Within their overarching narratives such fantastic scenes are often unexpected and so are easily overlooked or written off as simple "hallucination" by a straightforward "mimetic" reading of the narrative. This is particularly true of the kind of reading that is geared primarily towards understanding the text in terms of verisimilar representation and towards finding a workable "realistic" orientation within its object-world. I will argue furthermore that an audience familiar with some of the key characteristics of expressionist literature and theatre is more likely to be able simply to accept at face value and to inhabit the endlessly ambiguous and irresolvably enigmatic world associated with the fantastic – which is typical of many expressionist and Weimar films – and to do so without tying down this enigmatic world to the terms of a realist representation. In other words, such an audience is also more likely to be attuned to the kind of reading that suspends "reality-testing," so to speak, and correspondingly, is more likely to accept such scenes as straightforwardly fantastic even though they are at odds with real world experience.

II. Expressionist projection and abstraction

In expressionist literature and film, the fantastic very often takes the form of a centrifugal projection from the protagonist onto the outside world, so that the "exterior" reality that the subject (and the audience) encounters is a hybrid and subjectivized realm. The common forms of projection here involve a world that does not exist as an observable entity of the kind that might be recorded or represented in an objective fashion, nor an observer who exists discreetly and separately. Instead the world is *co-created* by the subject. Two forms of projection in particular are significant. In the first variety, particularly prominent in much early expressionist poetry, the subject experiences the real world of twentieth-century modernity as overwhelming, alienating or threatening, and the poem registers such effects upon the self in terms of deeply subjectivized images of the world. The war poetry of August Stramm for example deploys fragmented lines and aphasic formulations. In the poem "Patrol" this linguistic dissociation helps to evoke the breathless and horrifying experience of being a soldier exploring dangerous enemy territory, in which he expects an attack any moment:

> The stones hostile
> Window grins betrayal
> Branches strangle
>
> (Stramm 1963: 87; my translation)

Here, the subject projects his anxieties in anthropomorphic fashion upon an environment in which he fears that death lurks around every corner, so that the glint in a window becomes a treacherous smile, the branches of a tree appear to form murderous hands capable of throttling him, and even the very stones around him appear to harbor a threat.

A second, major aspect of this projective mode in expressionism occurs in texts that transform the entire external world into an extension or correlative of the subject. This similarly takes the form of a projection outwards of the inner fears, anxieties and fundamental concerns of the individual. This feature is particularly prominent in expressionist theatre, where the hero's desires and anxieties are immediately "realized" by being dramatized in the outside world. For example, in Paul Kornfeld's *The Seduction* ("Die Verführung" 1918) the protagonist falls in love with a woman from one moment to the next and without further ado murders his new rival, her fiancé. Similarly in Arnolt Bronnen's *Patricide* ("Vatermord" 1915), the son openly desires his own mother, and enacts his extreme oedipal feelings towards the father instantly by murdering him. Walter Hasenclever's *The Son* ("Der Sohn" 1914) also dramatizes the perceived oedipal tyranny of the father in a manner which, from a conventional standpoint, is quite unbelievable and unrealistic but which is entirely typical of the expressionists' strategy of creating hyperbolic and subjectivized images rather than real-life scenarios: the father virtually imprisons his son, and treats him as if he were a young child by placing the 20-year-old under the control of a governess.

This projective structure is typified above all by the so-called expressionist "Ich-drama" ("drama of the self") and "Stationendrama" ("station drama"). These are largely devoid of conventional realist concerns such as setting, characterization, dramatic tension or linear "plot." They commonly consist instead of picaresque and frequently dreamlike encounters, with the central figure wandering amongst reflections of his own persona on the path towards an undefined goal of redemption or enlightenment. The "station drama" follows the lead of August Strindberg's *Dream Play* (1902) in basing the protagonist's dreamlike journey on a path analogous to the Stations of the Cross. Prominent examples here are J.M. Becker's *The Last Judgement* ("Das letzte Gericht" 1919) and Ernst Toller's *The Transformation* ("Die Wandlung" 1919) in which the seemingly independent figures that the protagonist encounters are most readily understood as mere offshoots or correlatives of his own self. The landscape too primarily mirrors psychological impulses or emotional forces emanating from the subject rather than reflecting any substantial aspect of the real world outside. In *The Last Judgment* for example the hero's desire to unite and "merge" with his lover is reflected directly in the environment, which at one point is transformed into a symbolic mise-en-scène whose effect is to efface all signs of difference between the hero and heroine: it takes place in the white-on-white infinity of a "snowy landscape" at dusk.

The dizzying events and rapid changes of personnel and scenery in such expressionist dramatic works do not necessarily make sense in terms of logic, causality, or real-life context. They correspond instead to the shifting of psychological and emotional forces within the mind of the protagonist. Yet where the expressionist play dramatizes the world of the subject by embodying his concerns symbolically in other figures and by producing doubles and split selves of this central individual, it succeeds in playing out in external form those internal conflicts that can be construed as being repressed or concealed from the subject himself.

This creation of an expressionist constellation of selfhood and the manner in which it is projected onto the external world has much in common with dreaming and the functioning of the unconscious. Yet it is important to stress that we are not dealing here with a literary attempt to simulate the dream as such. In "The Metamorphosis" the dreamlike aspects of the transformation are always held in tension with realistic detail, as in the case of Gregor Samsa's understated and thoroughly "bourgeois" attempt to ignore his dilemma and simply catch the next train to work. This tension produces an ambiguity that discourages us from interpreting the narrative merely as a dream. What we are dealing with in such narratives is rather the attempt to draw upon some of the characteristic features and functions of dream as a means of dramatizing the self, and to illuminate the ways in which the self has a particular scope to explore its fears, anxieties and desires within the realms of the dream and the fantastic. In this case, the dreamlike scenario of the insect offers an aesthetic image rather than a logical concept or definition. In other words, it presents a concrete visualization of an abstract psychological issue that would be beyond the grasp of a conventional, rationally-oriented form of representation.

A central tenet of expressionist writers is to abstract what they consider the "essence" of reality, the most typical or vital elements beneath the surface level or sheer appearance of reality. There is a corresponding lack of concern with the superfluous chaff of realism and the real. This process of abstraction is a key element in the programmatic writings by figures associated with the expressionist movement such as Wassily Kandinsky, Wilhelm Worringer, and Kasimir Edschmid. Abstraction is associated with the "visionary" qualities described by Edschmid, and he focuses on the way that the expressionists look beyond the reality in front of them in order to grasp its significance via a more abstract notion beyond. This concentration on the essential often leads firstly to an elliptical and frequently aphasic form of writing – and this applies equally to expressionist prose, dramatic speech and, as we saw with Stramm's "Patrol," poetry too – characterized by syntactical foreshortening, linguistic reduction, the omission of articles and the bunching of single-line images or nouns, as in the so-called "telegram style" of writing. Secondly this tendency is also responsible for the expressionist predilection for visionary proclamations and extravagant gestures, often conveyed via hyperbolic forms such as caricature and melodrama. In emphasizing the visionary, the expressionists correspondingly demonstrate a disregard for lifelike detail or the depiction of the fallen world of facticity. As Edschmid says, the expressionists "did not look. . . .They did not photograph. They had visions." With this anti-realistic focus expressionists attempt not to imitate but to pressurize the real into revealing the world of essence beyond. For in expressionism, Edschmid

maintains, "everything takes on a connection to eternity," so that rather than simply seeing "the sick man who suffers," in the vision of the expressionist the sick man "becomes
sickness itself" (1918: 363; my translation).

III. Expressionist dream poetics and metaphorization

In expressionist literature and, I would argue, in much of expressionist cinema, the
tendency towards abstraction replaces the kind of narrative discourse that is built
upon rationality and intellectual scrutiny and produces instead discourse typified by
dense images and dreamlike metaphors. This creates that expressionist textual characteristic of a sheer accumulation or aggregation of individual impressions, images and
tableaux that always take priority over any linear progression of the narrative. In many
respects the works of Franz Kafka serve as paradigm for all expressionism in this regard,
for it was Kafka who thought of his literature as the representation of his "dreamlike
inner self," and that his fantasies produced "whole orchestras of associations" (Kafka
1983: 387). I would argue that this latter effect is related to the oneiric density of
Kafka's writing, with its indeterminacy, multiple meanings, and endlessly suggestive
yet always understated associative quality – the characteristic of his prose that seems
constantly to highlight its own need for interpretation. But it is above all its "metaphorization," its creation of a narrative based upon the elaboration and extension of a
single, often dreamlike figurative image, which makes Kafka's method essential to the
particular form of abstraction that I want to elaborate upon here.

As we have seen, in the expressionist text the focus on the concerns of the central
subject often operates according to what we might term a "poetics of animism." This
produces in the text an animistic universe, again similar to the dream, in which the
world is centred on the key figure and in which all the other figures as well as the environment function as mere reflections of this subject. This animistic "dramatization
of subjectivity" (Murphy 1999: 148–50) means that even though this environment
appears to operate autonomously the narrative structure is deeply subjective since the
text externalizes the subject's inner concerns. In this regard it is crucial to bear in mind
that with this animistic structure the expressionist text has suppressed the vital distinction between subject and object. For the meaningfulness of the narrative world and its
metaphorical or symbolic density largely derives from its significance for the central
figure. As the case of Kafka's writing illustrates most clearly, any overriding context
that would allow the reader to make sense of the metaphorization "objectively" is
simply not given, and any more determinate material or potentially illuminating clues
as to its significance remain within the limits of the protagonist's private sphere. Consequently all those unlikely events in Kafka's works (such as a man being arrested out
of the blue for unspecified and merely existential crimes, or a captured ape learning
to speak) are presented in a way that treats them as simply objective and taken for
granted. As a consequence of the blurring of the subject/object boundary, such events
are not questioned, not "reality-tested," and so come about in that inexplicable and
dreamlike fashion that is characteristic of the fantastic mode in expressionism.

The method of metaphorization is again deeply intertwined here with the key expressionist notion of "abstraction." The goal for the expressionists is always to abstract the essence of the situation or of the character and push this element into the foreground, disregarding any concerns for realistic representation or real-life context. As Walter Sokel has demonstrated in examining the "extended metaphor" which underlies "The Metamorphosis," it is by these means that Kafka abstracts the essence of the main character Gregor Samsa, and makes him identical with his wish "for irresponsibility and parasitic withdrawal from an active and mature way of life" (Sokel 1959: 46). In the figure of the bug, Gregor Samsa is "transformed into a metaphor that states his essential self, and this metaphor in turn is treated like an actual fact." Clearly the process of abstraction that condenses the character and his fundamental situation into a metaphor for the crisis affecting his identity produces a very different effect from any straightforward attempt at expressing this through a conventionally logical and verbalized form. For the metaphor is deeply ambiguous, and like a dream, it has the dual function of both expressing and simultaneously *disguising* meaning. The dramatic metaphorization of subjectivity is also more than a simple symbolic abstraction of the character's identity, and rather than simply producing any direct and clear-cut explanation for Samsa's existence, this central ambiguous image serves to guide and structure the entire narrative.

The image of the bug then is primarily metaphorical, a conceptual figure which serves as an external correlative for Gregor Samsa's interior world. Yet it is handled as if it were a real-life entity rather than a mere abstraction, as Sokel has demonstrated (1959: 47). Corresponding to the expressionist practice of animism, all those extreme thoughts, unspeakable desires and nightmare anxieties that are normally confined to the interior world are instantly dramatized externally and emerge full-blown within the real world. It is not just that Gregor Samsa's pitiful situation leads him to think of himself as a bug, but that this private self-perception is fantastically transformed into an exterior reality, so that the internal imagining emerges in the outside world as observable fact to which all the other characters must respond. The fantastic provenance of the bug-metaphor continues to be emphasized by the fact that the text furnishes us with certain concrete descriptions pertaining to the reality of the insect body, such as Gregor's "hard, shell-like back," or "curved brown belly" (Kafka 1992: 76–7). Yet besides such occasional indications, the reader is largely left to his or her own devices to produce a mental image of the fantastic creature that fits the otherwise realistic parameters of the story. With no specific details we are forced for example to imagine or calculate the *size* of Gregor Samsa: surely the insect must be large enough to reach and turn the key in his bedroom door? In which case is he a bug or rather some kind of hybrid as big as a human? The impossibility of thinking together or bringing into alignment these two incompatible notions is precisely what characterizes the relation between the fantastic and the realistic within expressionist narratives. For we must constantly reconcile the being of the insect with Gregor's nature as a considerate and still sensitive human who, even in the midst of his unusual predicament, does not want to trouble his parents by falling out of bed with a crash.

Even in those expressionist texts by Kafka and other writers in which there is much more lifelike detail, the realism is once again always held in tension with the fantastic. In Kafka's short story, "In the Penal Colony" (1916), the description of the complex punishment-machine is intricate, with detailed explanations of its function (it inscribes the commandment that has been transgressed upon the body of the offender by means of a set of needles), and its mechanical parts (such as the "harrow" and the "bed"). Yet the more complex the description becomes, the more grotesque is the effect of associating the mechanical rigor and logic of the apparatus with the nightmarish and fully absurd uses to which they are put. A similar paradoxical effect associated with realistic detail can also be seen in Alfred Döblin's "The Murder of a Buttercup" (first published 1910). The text appears at first to be written in a straightforwardly realistic mode, opening with a description of a quotidian setting and an arch-bourgeois protagonist taking a recreational walk in the forest. Yet it soon turns out that the hyper-realistic mode of detailed observation of the protagonist (involving the literary equivalents of cinematic slow-motion and microscopic close-up) as he vents his anger by thrashing at the undergrowth is being used against the grain: the realism is being applied to events which are purely hallucinatory, and as a result the disproportionate detail heightens the absurdity of the character's unfounded belief in the veracity of his delusions. This disjunction between a precise, almost photographic approach to detail, and the fantastic nature of the events concerned is reflected in expressionist and Weimar cinema, and it is to this paradox that I now turn.

IV. Cinema and the expressionist poetics of animism

So far I have explored the way that expressionist literary texts dramatize subjectivity by projecting an animistic vision from an internal sphere onto an external world. I want now to look at three films which have clear links to expressionism and to its poetics of animism: Robert Wiene's *The Cabinet of Dr Caligari* (1920), Fritz Lang's *Metropolis* (1927), and Karl Grune's *The Street* (1923). Of the three, *Caligari* seems at first glance most obviously linked to this animistic structure, with the plot involving an internal frame-narration told by, and centered on the key character, Francis. The hazy and dreamlike world that we encounter in the narrative is not only *centered* on Francis but constructed primarily on the foremost questions concerning his identity: his desires for Jane, the rivalry he feels towards his friend Alan as a competitor for Jane's love, and his oedipal anxieties towards the authoritarian Caligari. It is also mixed with a degree of sexual rivalry towards Caligari and is evident to the viewer not least with the erotic undertones of Caligari's peculiarly exhibitionist approach to Jane in the sideshow tent. Consequently, I would argue that the plot makes sense most obviously if we view it as a dramatization or metaphorical playing out of Francis's own fragile selfhood.

The protagonist Francis is revealed at the end of the film to be an inmate in an asylum, who is relating his nightmarish story to a fellow patient. At the most obvious level of interpretation, he appears simply to have fabricated the entire story of his persecution by the tyrannical and murderous Caligari and by the somnambulist Cesare whom the doctor has brought under his control in order to carry out his crimes as well as to demonstrate the extraordinary reach of his powers: in expressionist terms Caligari is an archetypally omnipotent and manipulative father-figure. From this standpoint Francis appears to have made up his tale – foreshadowing the plot of the American neo-noir film, *The Usual Suspects* (1995) – merely on the basis of the material at hand, drawing upon his surroundings and upon the figures he finds among his fellow inmates in the asylum. Given the other nightmarish dimensions of the scenario, this evokes the regular mechanism of dreaming, which draws for its material strongly upon the contents and characters of the dreamer's waking life during the previous day. Furthermore, the distorted and pointedly dreamlike setting of the film, with its exaggeratedly skewed architecture, its sharp and angular scenery, and its painted and clearly two-dimensional backdrops, emphasizes simultaneously the *constructed* nature of the world inhabited by these figures. To this extent it has a self-reflexive effect, and points not only to the fabricated quality of the narrative, but perhaps also to its origin as a projection and as an extension of subjectivity on the part of the protagonist and storyteller Francis.

Yet there are a number of moments in the film that pointedly short-circuit any clear distinction between the inner, framed narrative and the framing narrative that surrounds it. Perhaps the most prominent short-circuiting effects concern the "mad" markings and streaks of paint on the walls of the asylum, which we might initially assume to be a narratorial signpost indicating the insanity of the nightmare scenario told by Francis as an inmate in an asylum. Yet these markings appear on the walls of the asylum not only when Caligari is put in a straitjacket (in Francis's narrative), but are also prominent when Francis in turn is put into a straitjacket within the supposedly sane world of the outer frame tale. The boundary between the realms of the sane and the insane has been effaced and the subject and object worlds are now clearly interchangeable. Furthermore, if these markings continue to exist in the "normality" of the outer, framing tale, they clearly cannot be taken simply as markers, as indications of the delusions of a madman.

The characteristics linking Fritz Lang's *Metropolis* to the expressionist literary movement have not been explored in great detail by commentators. Yet for anyone familiar with expressionist prose and drama, the protagonist Freder is in many respects a prototypical expressionist son-figure. As in Hasenclever's expressionist play *The Son* (1914), the younger man here has a seemingly traumatized relationship to his controlling father, Joh Fredersen, the industrialist and master of Metropolis. The depiction of the father as an absolute authority owes much to the perennial expressionist inclination towards hyperbolic imagery and father-obsessions. Fredersen is typically pictured in a godlike position at the very top of the tower of Metropolis, controlling and conducting surveillance upon the city from his own high-tech panopticon. This powerful image of the omnipotent and omniscient master is particularly relevant for the father–son relationship, since Fredersen continuously asserts his control over his son and, besides occasionally eavesdropping on him, also deploys a spy, saying, "I wish to be informed of my son's every movement." The oedipal tyranny against which Freder struggles is also embodied in the familiar expressionist constellation of a psychological doubling of father-figures. For there is not only his actual father, Fredersen, to contend with but also his "almost-father," the scientist Rotwang, a former rival of Fredersen for the love of Freder's mother. Freder struggles against the authoritarianism of both father-figures, and the oedipal dimension is demonstrated where he is pictured as troubled by a form of sexual rivalry with them. For example, Freder faints when he finds his beloved Maria apparently embracing his father. The sexual undertones in Rotwang's attentions towards Maria are also emphasized when he kidnaps her and at one point forces her back upon a table, leaning right over her prostate body; or again when he corners her in the dark catacombs and makes a beam of light from his flashlight play along the length of her body, as if it were a vicarious gaze or a caress.

Also typically expressionist is the attempt to overthrow a sterile, mechanical and inhumane form of society – a society that reflects the key characteristics of these two dominant technocrats, the authoritarian and despotic father-figures. The young Freder also clearly espouses the expressionists' value of the liberating spirit ("Geist"), associated with that area of expressionism characterized by "vitalism." He is frequently seen dashing vigorously and purposefully between locations on his higher mission, and this pictorializes the vitalist energy and striving that is central to the narrative. At the same time, Freder embodies a typically expressionist longing for fraternity, notably with his frequent articulation of solidarity towards his brothers and sisters among the exploited lower orders, and particularly, as the recovered footage from the original version of the film now makes clear, with his ploy of exchanging clothes, identities, and lifestyles with one of the anonymous and merely numbered workers.

While the narrative of *Metropolis* does not focus quite so directly upon the characteristic expressionist theme of madness as in *Caligari*, it nonetheless features a large number of passages that are clearly indebted to the related themes of nightmare, fantasy and feverish hallucination. Yet it is significant that many of these passages are presented in the film in such an ambiguous manner that we do not necessarily interpret them in the first instance as hallucinations deriving directly from Freder at all. Early in the film for example Freder witnesses a scene in the machine room when an exhausted worker faints at the controls and allows the pressure in the main machine to build up to a dangerous level. In the explosion that follows, many workers are injured or killed, and Freder appears to be blown against a wall. When the huge machine is then transformed into a carnivorous, sphinx-like monster or "Moloch" devouring the workers, the look on Freder's face and his gesture of trying to wipe clean the space in front of his eyes suggest that he cannot believe what he sees. Indeed, given such outward expressions of his inner turmoil the viewer might be tempted to ascribe the entire occurrence to a hallucination by Freder, were it not for the fact that the rows of workers marching in synchronized step into the mouth of the monster are already familiar from the film's opening scene when they marched into the elevator for the "change of shift." Freder did not witness this, and his particular perspective played no part in its construction or its emergence within the narrative. Yet the "objectivity" of the earlier scene is now merged with the nightmarish and seemingly *subjective* Moloch-scene, thereby blurring the distinction between subject and object in a fashion characteristic of the expressionists' animism.

The subject/object boundary is called into question in similar fashion when Freder, at home in bed recovering from a nervous collapse and, nonetheless, appears to witness the magical scene of the robot Maria's seductive and mesmerizing dance at the distant Yoshiwara nightclub, a spectacle that we know is witnessed "objectively" by both his father and Rotwang (see Murphy 2007).

There are many scenes throughout the film *Metropolis* that, while not presented specifically as hallucinations, nonetheless have an exaggerated, not to say "fantastic" quality about them, and we tend as viewers simply to overlook or to accept these, rather than to question them. For example, at the opening of the film, the syncopated and machine-like movements of the workers, whether they are marching in step to their shift or operating the factory machinery in a shared rhythm and choreographed fashion, are entirely "unrealistic" and, more than anything else, the scene forms a hyperbolic image expressing the reification of the workers. Most of all, the peculiar man-sized clock-machines that the workers operate seem to have little to do with any obviously practical productive purposes or technical processes, and from a realistic perspective one would wonder if at this supposed stage of technological progress and automation it is not completely superfluous for a human worker still to have to struggle and manipulate the huge arms of the clock. Again, from this straightforward, realistic perspective the machines are meaningless, unless of course their purpose is primarily to be found at the level of metaphor: to demonstrate the complete reversal of subject and object, and the subjugation of man to machine. Indeed I would argue that, corresponding to the expressionist poetics of animism, these clock-machines function *primarily* on an abstract level that, as with Kafka's "Metamorphosis" or "Penal Colony," establishes an extended metaphor: in this case a nightmare scenario as an *image* of technology and the way it has become a mode of slavery, capable of torturing reified humanity within its new mechanical organization of human time.

Even in those films of the Weimar period in which the characteristics of expressionism appear much less evident than those features of the realism associated with the "neue Sachlichkeit" ("new sobriety" or "new objectivity"), that artistic movement which began to dominate in the wake of expressionism, I would argue that some of the key moments are nonetheless often still indebted to expressionist imagery, animistic fantasy and the characteristic blurring of the boundary between subject and object. One such pointed moment of the fantastic occurs for example in Karl Grune's city film *The Street* ("Die Straße" 1923). In the opening scene we see a couple's city apartment in which the wife busies herself in the kitchen while the husband lies back upon the sofa looking up at the ceiling and the play of shadows upon it from the streets below. Gradually, however, the random, flickering shadows begin to form into recognizable shapes in which a man approaches a woman, appears to address her briefly, and then saunters off with her. The film narrative leaves it fully ambiguous as to whether the husband actually sees the shadowy reflections of a real encounter below, or simply falls asleep and transforms the shadows in his dreams. But in articulating in external form his own hidden desire this scene becomes a pivotal moment for the narrative by forming a catalyst for a typically expressionist moment of awakening and escape ("Aufbruch") – a fantasy of a radical break with the old routines of a humdrum existence for which Georg Kaiser's story of the errant bank teller in the play "From Mornings to Midnight" (1912) is the prototype. This moment of fantasy motivates the husband's sudden departure, his abandonment of his wife and of his stale marriage, and prompts his attempt to find excitement and amorous distraction in the city.

Another notable moment of the fantastic in the film occurs when the husband later pursues a woman on the street. As he passes underneath a sign in the form of a huge pair of spectacles advertising an optician's office, the giant eyes in the sign suddenly light up unexpectedly and begin to flash, as if the external world were reflecting his inner crisis and the eyes were the outward projection of his own guilty conscience. It is only when the lights go out and the eyes "close" that he feels able to pass underneath, as if he has been given permission by an outside power to pursue his desire.

V. Conclusion

The fundamentally fantastic character of moments like those discussed is easily overlooked in the course of viewing the kind of realist film such as "The Street" that largely calls for a conventional, mimetic reading which tends to exclude the unrealistic and fantastic as simply incompatible. Yet in conclusion it is clear that an awareness of the persistent expressionist elements associated with animist projection motivates us to pay particular attention to the key moments of the narrative that are otherwise easily ignored. It also leads to a corresponding acceptance of certain counterintuitive and uncomfortable interpretative positions, such as the blurring between subject and object, the playing out of enigmatic metaphors (such as human as bug), and the impossible balancing of elements that are incompatible and ontologically opposed to each other. It also allows us to keep in play the important tension between realism and the fantastic that underlies some of the most remarkable achievements not only of modernist literature but of Weimar cinema too.

It is the pointed ambiguity and the effacement of the subject/object boundary that indicates the need to pay particular attention to the significance of the hallucinatory or fantastic elements of such scenes in *Metropolis* and other expressionist films and literary texts. For these are scenes that in the course of viewing or reading we are all too likely to suppress or overlook under the compulsion to make realistic sense of them. As with the vast majority of the key works of expressionist literature, such scenes simply cannot be adequately grasped via a straightforward realist-mimetic approach. Rather, they make sense primarily when understood as the exteriorization of the interior world of the protagonist, such as the typically extreme dichotomization in *Metropolis* in the portrayal of the woman: the "doubled" Maria takes on the extreme forms as either a lustful and treacherous witch inciting discord, or as the maternal and saintly female Messiah preaching harmony to the downtrodden masses. In other words, we begin to get some purchase on these enigmatic images if we can accept and bear in mind that the supposed object world we are encountering is in fact a reality that is deeply colored by the fantastic and by an imagination that treats the metaphorical as fact. Although it has not previously been highlighted in the research on this field, this is a crucial way to approach all expressionist cinema, for an awareness of this animist poetics is necessary in order to comprehend the fundamental structure of such films. For expressionist and Weimar cinema characteristically contains a large number of such ambiguous scenes whose enigmatic and fantastic quality is often simply elided in critical interpretations. Such fantastic elements begin to develop their wider significance only when they are linked more broadly to expressionism and the animistic projection of inner conflicts, and when they are understood as the result of the process of "metaphorization."

References

Döblin, A. (1970 [1910]) "Die Ermordung einer Butterblume." Reprinted in F. Martini (ed.), *Prosa des Expressionismus*, Stuttgart, Germany: Reclam.

Edschmid, K. (1918) "Expressionismus in der Dichtung," *Die neue Rundschau* 29(1): 359–74.

Kafka, F. (1983 [1935]) *Tagebücher*, Frankfurt, Germany: Fischer.

Kafka, F. (1992 [1915]) *The Transformation and Other Stories*, trans. M. Pasley, Harmondsworth, UK: Penguin.

Murphy, R. (1999) *Theorizing the Avant-Garde: Modernism, Expressionism, and the Problem of Postmodernity*, Cambridge, UK: Cambridge University Press.

Murphy, R. (2007) "Modernism and the Cinema: *Metropolis* and the Expressionist Aesthetic," *Comparative Critical Studies* 4(1): 105–20.

Sokel, W. (1959) *The Writer in Extremis: Expressionism in Twentieth-Century German Literature*, Stanford, CA: Stanford University Press.

Stramm, A. (1963 [1915]) "Patrouille." In K. Pinthus (ed.), *Menschheitsdämmerung*, Hamburg, Germany: Rowohlt, p. 87.

4

THE SURREALIST EXPERIMENTS WITH LANGUAGE

Peter Stockwell

I. Surrealism is not

Surrealism was not merely a literary exercise, nor simply a political movement, nor an artistic project alone, nor a cultural shift, but it was all of these things simultaneously and holistically. "Surrealism is *not* a style, it is *not* a school of literature or painting, it is *not* a system of aesthetics," wrote David Gascoyne in his 1935 "Introduction" to *A Short Survey of Surrealism* (Gascoyne 2000: 25). He went on to identify those writers, artists and film-makers of the 1920s and 1930s who "have considerably enriched both literature and painting, as well as the cinema, by their researches." From our standpoint almost a century on, surrealism remains both a very precise expression of the historical inter-war period and also perhaps the most influential artistic movement the world has ever known. It was the first art-form to emerge out of advanced industrialisation and international communications, so it spread rapidly from Zurich, Paris and Berlin, then to Madrid, London and elsewhere in Europe, then to New York and Japan, and finally to everywhere else. Where the eighteenth and nineteenth centuries gave us the image of the individual, tormented Romantic artist or writer, surrealism gave us the prototype of the modern *avant-garde*: collective, politically committed, claiming an egalitarian connection but operating often at an abstruse and abstract level beyond the appreciation of the common populace, challenging, infuriating and difficult.

Surrealism's legacy is its success and its failure: surrealist images, techniques and influence can be discerned today in most contemporary art and writing, in much poetry and song lyrics, and in many film and television works for both children and adults, but also in the images of advertising and corporate branding, in the architecture of multinational headquarters, and framed in the hushed office corridors of investment banks, currency speculators, and in the sleek boardrooms of the operators of the military-industrial complex. Even if it was not a political movement in itself, most of the first surrealists were Marxist communists; though they would not have called themselves a "school" of painting, there was very much a membership and a set of identifiable commitments and principles; and in spite of the multimodal and internationally diverse nature of surrealism, it is indeed possible to sketch out its characteristic aesthetic and styles.

I will explore all these facets in this chapter, but it is also important to understand the self-perception of the surrealists and their historical moment. Gascoyne's final formulation above of surrealist "researches" picks up a phrase commonly used in the statements of the surrealists: they generally regarded their activities as *experimental*. In the sphere of contemporary art and literature, it is largely a legacy of surrealism itself that we regard that word as including associations of controversy, edginess and abnormality; however, for the surrealists it also had something closer to the scientific sense of empiricism. Surrealist writing constituted research into the human condition, rather than any sort of indulgent form of self-expression. The writing, art, sculpture, film, music, and other forms, were all attempts at a method for accessing the true nature of human perception. The word *surrealist*, in contemporary usage, has come to be attached popularly to anything that is fantastical, unreal, or even simply out of the ordinary; however, "surréalisme" is better translated as "hyper-realism" or "heightened realism."

II. Origins in Dada

Surrealism needs to be understood in terms of where, how and when it emerged. It developed out of Dada, a movement that is often treated as a separate precursor to surrealism, but is perhaps more properly regarded simply as surrealism's adolescent and immature self. The founding of Dada can be traced to the opening on February 1st, 1916 of the "Cabaret Voltaire," a regular evening of literary performance in a down-at-heel bar in Zurich, aimed at increasing the sales of beer and sausages. Actor and writer Hugo Ball and his partner, poet Emmy Hennings established the event which quickly attracted a regular and international circle of writers, artists and performers: Hans Arp, Tristan Tzara, Marcel Janco, Richard Huelsenbeck, and others, and the evening became scandalously notorious and popular very quickly.

A typical evening might include the performance of poems and songs, both original compositions and existing works; often several would be recited at high volume simultaneously, and with the asynchronised accompaniment of drums, rattles or other semi-musical noises. Dada activities included performances of "exotic" African and African-American music, both indigenous music regarded as authentically "primitive," and jazz. Children's rhymes and songs, and the work of writers from earlier ages commonly judged as visionaries, mystics and madmen would also feature. In all of these sources, Dada identified a literary culture undistorted by the trappings of western bourgeois rationalism and civilised sensibility.

Ball himself developed "phonetic poetry," or "sound poems," in which the soundscape of the performance itself took priority over any meaningful or signifying content. His original *Phonetic Poem* (1917) runs as follows:

Karawane
jolifanto bambla ô falli bambla
grossiga m'pfa habla horem
égiga goramen
higo bloiko russulla huju
hollaka hollala
anlogo bung
blago bung
blago bung
bosso fataka
ü üü ü
schampa wulla wussa ólobo
hej tatta gôrem
eschige zunbada
wulubu ssubudu uluw ssubudu
tumba ba- umf
kusagauma
ba – umf

(Hugo Ball, reproduced in Richter 1964: 8)

Though there are few recognisable words of any single language here, there is a sense that some of the distinctive sound patterns associated with the phonological systems of different particular languages can be discerned. "Karawane", "bambla", "m'pfa" and "ólobo" sound like African languages; "grossiga" and "eschige" could be Germanic; "jolifanto", "blago" and "bosso" are Romance, perhaps Spanish or Italian; "habla horem" might be Yiddish or even Arabic; "higo" has an Oriental, possibly Japanese tone; "bloiko russulla" is possibly Slavic; though all of these associations are subjective and tenuous. The multiple repetitions of syllables and even full words and phrases suggest a systematic underlying grammar and coherence that is associative and suggestive rather than material. The repetitions of words ("blago bung") and phonemes (what we might in a more conventional text call alliteration) suggest a chanting or musical rhythm. In the printed version of this on a flyer for distribution, each line appears in a different font, further signalling the cultural blending of origins, and diminishing symbolically the dominance of any one source.

Such chaotic activities acquired the name of "Dada," a word that cannot be definitively sourced. It has been attributed to the ironic reiteration of "yes" ("da, da") in Slavic languages; it is the German for both an idiot and the sound a baby makes; it is the French for a rocking horse; it is the English childish form for "daddy"; it is capitalised as "Dada"; it must always appear uncapitalised as "dada"; Dadaism should never be suffixed with "-ist" or "-ism." All of these contrary etymologies can be regarded as equal distractions ridiculing the scientist's or historian's tendency to categorise and classify. Dada resists classification: it is the anti-X, where X is whatever you can think it is. Surrealism is often represented as the reaction to Romanticism, but on a longer timescale it owes perhaps more to Dada's energy as a counter-Enlightenment phenomenon. Rationalism, logic and clarity were illusive and distorting consequences of capitalist industrialisation, the same forces which were at that very moment responsible for slaughtering millions in the trenches a few hundred miles to the north.

> Revolted by the butchery of the 1914 World War, we in Zurich devoted ourselves to the arts. While the guns rumbled in the distance, we sang, painted, made collages and wrote poems with all our might. We were seeking an art based on fundamentals, to cure the madness of the age, and a new order of things that would restore the balance between heaven and hell. We had a dim premonition that power-mad gangsters would one day use art itself as a way of deadening men's minds.
>
> (Hans Arp, translated in Richter 1964: 25)

The tone here is not of art as a distraction nor as escapism but as a fully engaged commitment, a direct reaction and corrective to the corrupt misdirection of capitalism and modernity. When Dada and later surrealist artists depicted human bodies as machines, or faces and the internal workings of heads as mechanical clockworks, the assertion was that they were showing something literal, not a metaphor nor poetic affectation.

Dada was reactive, instinctive and aimed directly at the associations, emotions and visceral senses below the level of consciousness. As it evolved into surrealism, the work became more constructively framed, more shaped by principle, and more explicitly aimed at uncovering the unconscious mind and speaking to and from it. Into the 1920s, those who had been associated with Dada and who now travelled as surrealists explicitly began to express themselves in their public pronouncements in the language of revolutionary socialism and the emerging language of psychoanalysis. When the war ended in 1918, most returned to their own countries. In particular, Dada activities in Paris began to formalise around André Breton, Paul Eluard, Louis Aragon and Philippe Soupault. Though Dada had its manifestoes and statements of purpose, they were largely extensions of the artistic anti-art ethos of Dada itself; by contrast, surrealism excelled in the production of manifestoes, pamphlets, essays and debates.

III. Becoming surrealist

In his 1924 *Manifesto of Surrealism*, Breton defines the word, in his words, "once and for all":

> SURREALISM, *n*. Psychic automatism in its pure state, by which one proposes to express – verbally, by means of the written word, or in any other manner – the actual functioning of thought. Dictated by thought, in the absence of any control exercised by reason, exempt from any aesthetic or moral concern.
>
> ENCYCLOPEDIA. *Philosophy*. Surrealism is based on the belief in the superior reality of certain forms of previously neglected associations, in the

omnipotence of dream, in the disinterested play of thought. It tends to ruin once and for all all other psychic mechanisms and to substitute itself for them in solving all the principal problems of life.

(Breton 1969: 27)

This is unlike anything in Dada, though it can be regarded as sharing something of its mischievous irony: what appears in the form and register of a definitive dictionary definition, and is even introduced as such, occurs not at the beginning of the manifesto but almost exactly in the middle, framed on both sides by a rambling discussion and freewheeling musings that are the exact opposite in tone of the quotation extracted here.

Nevertheless, the emphasis on "belief" and the commitment to objectives and principles are characteristic of surrealism in its mature, post-Dada phase. There is a clear objective: one of rising above any mere aesthetic or moral concern in order to arrive at the truth of things. There is a strong commitment to the actual, to the material reality of the world, but it is a sense of the real that does not set psychic and perceptive aspects of life apart from the tangible objects in the world. Instead, pure psychic experience is the most real and actual raw truth, upon which the material circumstances, cultures and politics of history subsequently begin to work and distort.

The emphatic insistence on this reversal of the Cartesian mind–body distinction is the inevitable consequence of attempting to reconcile Marxist materialism with the primacy of the psychic (we would now say, psychological or cognitive) domain. For Breton, clarifying this message required not so much definitive statements like the one above as multiple different articulations of the notion: his 1924 *Manifesto* was reprinted with a revised preface in 1929, followed by a *Second Manifesto* in 1930, and a new edition of that in 1946, and also an essay towards a prospective but unpublished *Third Manifesto* in 1942 (all collected in Breton 1969).

The project was revolutionary in every sense. The re-evaluation of Enlightenment rationalism, and of the grand narratives of science and civilised culture, set the scene for later, post-modernist theorising of language and history. The belief in a radical re-evaluation of society through the medium of an artistic movement is a precursor to the idealistic phases of the political and social revolutions of the twentieth century, from the 1920s soviets, to the uprisings against them in the 1950s, to the hippy idealism of the 1960s, and the liberating and virtually uncontrollable popular diversity of the multimodal internet. The emphasis on psychological reality is a precursor to the intellectual revolutions in mind that characterise the cognitive turn in philosophy, arts, humanities and linguistics as we enter the twenty-first century.

In the 1920s, however, there was already a tension between the artisanal concerns of the proletariat and what might appear to be the indulgent activities of poets and artists: it was a tension that led to several breakaways, expulsions and arguments between the surrealist group in Paris and the communist party. The evasion of the realm of the purely aesthetic was a key principle for surrealism, aimed at avoiding this dilettante and patronising image:

Surrealism, as an organised movement, was born of a far-reaching operation having to do with language. In this regard it cannot be repeated too often that in the minds of their authors the products of free association or automatic writing that Surrealism brought forth in the beginning had nothing to do with any aesthetic criterion.

(Breton 1969: 297)

Breton goes on here (in his 1953 retrospective *On Surrealism and its Living Works*) to point out the difference between surrealist experimental writing and that of, for example, James Joyce, e.e. cummings and Henri Michaux: their techniques aimed at the imitation of life, and thus remained within the framework of "art," which Breton scornfully derides as the domain of "lettrism." By contrast, the surrealists had freed themselves from such constraints because "we had got our hands on the 'prime matter' (in the alchemical sense) of language" (Breton 1969: 299).

The experimental nature of surrealism for the surrealists can be seen in the establishment in 1924 of the "Bureau of Surrealist Research" in Paris, from where the first of twelve issues of the journal *La Révolution Surréaliste* was published in December of that year. Both the experimental and the revolutionary ethos were captured in the content of the magazine, and also after factional splits in 1929 by the title of Breton's successor journal, *Le Surréalisme au Service de la Révolution*. The first journal, in particular, adopted a pseudo-scientific register similar to that found in Breton's dictionary and the encyclopedia-styled definitions quoted above, with content that was immediately scandalously anti-government and anti-clerical.

What is also significant not only in the definitions of surrealism above, but also in his statements and manifestoes which appeared in the journals, is the primary importance Breton places not so much on the consequential revolution but on the technique of surrealism. To recall his definition, Breton (1969: 27) foregrounds the process "by which one proposes to express – verbally, by means of the written word, or in any other manner – the actual functioning of thought." Here is the primacy in surrealism of writing, even though it is swiftly followed by the recognition that there are other means of realising the surreal moment. In fact, although in principle the "surreal image" was the main theoretical object which could be expressed in sculpture, painting, cinema, performance, music or architecture, in practice it was in writing that the surreal image first and foremost was rendered.

Breton's defining passage is followed by a list of precursors who can be seen as proto-surrealists: Shakespeare "in his finer moments," Swift when he is being malicious, Poe in his adventurousness, Baudelaire in his morality, Rimbaud, Mallarmé, Reverdy and others. For Breton, it is clear that literature and writing are in practice the key mode of surrealism, even though the surrealists in general rejected the identification of surrealism with any single means or mode of expression. Dada began as a literary evening, and surrealism too progressed especially in its early years as an articulation of a revolution in *writing*.

PETER STOCKWELL

IV. Techniques of surrealism

In his 1935 *A Short Survey of Surrealism*, David Gascoyne (2000) denies that there is a "recipe" for surrealist output. Even though Breton (1969: 29–32) appears to set out "Secrets of the Magical Surrealist Art," Gascoyne (2000: 59) points out that both the tone of this sub-heading and the instructions that follow it are somewhat tongue-in-cheek and "should not be taken too seriously." Nevertheless, surrealism is as accessible to stylistic analysis as any sort of literary text; in the rest of this chapter I will outline the main techniques of surrealist writing, even though such an approach would be condemned by the surrealists as "academicism" (Richter 1964: 194).

The first method that Breton (1969: 29) describes is the first method of both Dada and surrealism: *automatism*. In early experiments, the author tries to empty his or her mind of any preconceptions or conscious images or ideas, in order to allow as direct a passage to unconscious intuition as possible. The object was then to write down this stream of images and propositions as fast and unthinkingly as possible. Pure automatism should not involve any editing, redrafting or even semi-conscious shaping of the material as it pours from the pen. The idea is that the writer should be as surprised by the output as anyone else.

This *free association* is what distinguishes psychic automatism from the "stream-of-consciousness" technique in contemporary modernist writers like James Joyce, according to Breton (1969: 298–9). The difference lies in the presence of a sense of wilful imitation (on the part of the artist) as opposed to the absence of any wilful intentionality (on the part of the surrealist experimental researcher). Gascoyne (2000: 94) characterises these early experiments as belonging to the "passive or subjective" phase of research, in which he includes psychic "automatism, spontaneous and 'pure' poetry, and the idea of the synonymity of poetry and dream."

It quickly became obvious, however, that such absolutely free association was almost impossible to sustain. Marcel Duchamp aimed at a similar effacement of intention in his "readymades" – accidentally found objects that were then placed into exhibitions and galleries (his 1917 upturned urinal, entitled *Fountain*, is the most famous of many such recontextualisations that persist as installations in art to the present day). This literal self-effacement aimed at the evasion of aesthetics:

> A point that I want very much to establish is that the choice of these "ready-mades" was never dictated by aesthetic selection. The choice was based on a reaction of *visual* indifference with at the same time a total absence of good or bad taste . . . in fact a complete anaesthesia.
> (Marcel Duchamp quoted in Young 1981: 26)

However, Duchamp abandoned the attempt at automatism when he realised that one part of his mind was surreptitiously shaping what he was writing and making. In 1962 he wrote to Hans Richter, "When I discovered ready-mades I thought to discourage aesthetics. In Neo-Dada [New Realism and Pop Art] they have taken my ready-mades and found aesthetic beauty in them" (Richter 1964: 207–8).

54

Other methods for the effacement of intention were inherited from the Dada tradition: clipping words at random from newspapers, picking words at random from a hat, nominating page numbers from a dictionary, and other means were used to bypass the wilful, artistic shaping of the text in order for it to be a genuine surreal object. Later in surrealism, the practice of *chainpoems* became the principal method of authorial evasion. Here, different lines were written by different writers, often without sight of the previous contributions. Alternatively, lines were written separately and then randomly assembled and published. Or a line was written a word at a time, with the syntactic category (article, adjective, noun, verb, article, adjective, noun) specified, such as "The winged vapour seduces the locked bird," "A corset in July is worth a horde of rats," "Faithful as a boneless cat" (reported by Gascoyne 2000: 66). Issues 9 and 10 of *La Révolution Surréaliste* in October 1927 introduced these techniques with many examples of its product. One of the first such poetic lines ("Le cadavre exquis boira le vin nouveau": *The exquisite corpse will drink the new wine*) gave its name to the activity.

Further "Exquisite corpse" chainpoems involved writers who were disparate geographically as well: the American Charles Henri Ford returned to New York from Paris on the outbreak of the war and established (with Breton's approval) the literary magazine *View*, which was initially surrealist. His "international chainpoems" include the following *Anglo-American Chainpoem*:

> The leaf knows sorrow in this time of thorns,
> Red-gold the country's treasure cropped by sword,
> A gale of bristles blown across the land.
> On days when playing for safety spits out blood and stone,
> And evenings when white revolver, exhalation of the trees,
> Smokes mist across the mouth, men take the signposts down,
> Frozen to the north of the time-cropped town.
>
> Sucking the berry's map, they curse the fired seed
> No noose can amnesty nor eyelid truncheon,
> For they have crossed their rubicons of blood.
> The terrible thunder crushes autumn's insects!
> The twisting eyes on the stalks of rue and reed
> Show Europe's laugh! Europe's pearl rope of death
> Her kings dangle to the masses from imperial fingers.
>
> (assembled by Charles Henri Ford 1945)

The first stanza here is by British poets: Scottish academic James Findlay Hendry, English painter Conroy Maddox, art critic Robert Melville, editor Nicholas Moore, editor John Bayliss, poet Mary Woodman and her husband the novelist Henry Treece, several of whom were members of the Birmingham Surrealist group. The second stanza features American poets: line by line, *View*'s co-editor Parker Tyler, John Hastings, Troy Garrison, H.R. Hays, Robert Friend, Harry Roskolenko and Elgar Houghton.

Where early surrealist chainpoems were assembled "blind" by writers composing a line in isolation or half-blind by only seeing the previous line on a folded-up piece of paper, this example from the war years was passed on in its entirety so that each writer had a cumulatively longer prior text to work with. This can be seen in the relative consistency of the apocalyptic theme in the subject-matter, by lexical choices from coherent semantic fields of autumn, countryside and violent death, and by some of the textual cohesion (such as the echoing of "cropped," the semantic connections between "noose" and "dangle," and the rhymes "down"/"town," "seed"/"reed"). It is perhaps also striking, given the historical context and geography, that the British stanza has a resigned and calm, stoical tone, while the American one is more violent and exclamatory.

Such assembled works represent the later, more actively participatory phase of surrealism. This was to make a virtue out of the necessity recognised by Duchamp (above) and others that intention – even unconscious wilfulness – was impossible to evade. Instead, the surrealists shifted the workings of intention to a sort of transcendental quality of the actual world: phenomena that you perceive as pointedly co-incidental, serendipitous, ironically juxtaposed or poignantly, comically or tragically accidental were in fact evidence of the *objective chance* by which you were seeing the genuine workings of the world untrammelled by your bourgeois rationalist delusions. Just as Freudian "slips of the tongue" afforded access to unconscious desires, so the objective chance of the world of experience presented the viewer with access to the world's heightened realism.

> Automatic writing is no more than the re-introduction of objective chance into language, whereas objective chance is the automatic writing of fate in seemingly raw facts.
>
> (Carrouges 1968: 272)

The early readymades and anti-art objects gradually gave way to these more considered and crafted forms. The technique of *collage* can be seen as a prototypical surrealist method in that it brings together separate elements by objective chance. Chainpoems are examples of the collage technique, and in a related way so are the clippings of newspapers, posters and flyers assembled by artists like Kurt Schwitters, whose objects stand as a blend of literary text and art object. Unusual collocations of words, phrases, registers or textual layout were all examples of the collage technique in the service of objective chance.

The surrealists' commitment to the literal in their conception of objective chance encompassed both their stylistic experiments and their perception of reality. In 1938, the Spanish surrealist Oscar Dominguez threw a glass and blinded fellow artist Victor Brauner. However, seven years earlier, Brauner had painted a self-portrait in which he is shown blinded by an object with a letter "D" on it. Such connections were grasped by the surrealists as empirical evidence of underlying patterns in the mechanics of reality.

In order actively to participate in and record such experiences and events, the *paranoic-critical method* was developed, largely in the hands of Salvador Dali. That which the rational world calls "paranoia" is actually an unconscious linkage of aspects of life that are not rationally connected but which are surreally connected. Dali's method, enthusiastically endorsed by Breton, was to place two or more objects in deliberate dissonance with each other. His most famous surreal object is perhaps the lobster telephone, which demonstrates one outcome of the method. In this surreal object, a standard black working 1930s bakelite telephone has a realistic plaster lobster in place of the handset.

It is clear that the dissonant collocation is an extension of the collage technique. Gascoyne (2000: 59) describes this method as "the fusion of two mutually distinct realities." The lobster telephone is an example of a semantic anomaly in our rational world, which would be expressed linguistically as a xenonym (the opposite of a synonym); in a surreal perception, the synonymy and naturalness of the object would be understood in a sudden, shocking moment, which Breton (1991) termed "convulsive beauty." The final line of his 1928 novel *Nadja* reads: "Beauty will be convulsive or it will not be at all" (Breton 1928). It is clear from this formulation not only that surrealism has an aesthetics and an ethics, but that they are collapsed together. Furthermore, the moment of surreal consciousness is a one-off moment of shock: it cannot be repeated with the same surreal object or image. The lobster telephone, the dissonant xenonymy of accidents in a chainpoem, the urinal in the art gallery and the sound poem at a literary evening are all only singularly convulsive. Just as with Duchamp's realisation (above) that his objects could only convulse the viewer once, Hans Richter (1964: 208) records a talk given by Roger Shattuck in which he points out that a work of art (a Picasso or a Cézanne) can be appreciated repeatedly, indeed it gains in the process of appreciation. Dada and surrealist objects, however, become only ordinary objects once they have been beheld; "the (anti-) artistic value they used to possess has gone back to zero."

I am not entirely sure that this is absolutely true. It may be the case that surrealist objects – such as poems and novels – cease to be ideologically surrealist after their initial moment of convulsive beauty, and thereafter become art objects (contrary to surrealist intentions). However, I do not think their value even as instruments of cognitive dissonance and disturbance returns altogether to zero. Not only do the activities of re-reading and systematic analysis increase the sense of richness of those objects, but in the process new, more subtle and ever more surprising effects are brought above the level of consciousness. I have seen Dali's lobster telephone several times, and it retains its oddity – it does not become less odd on reflection. It increases its humorous effect every time I think of it, and the fact that Dali set the lobster's penis in the mouthpiece position does not become less disturbing the more you think about using the telephone as an actual telephone.

Similarly, the following lines from Hugh Sykes Davies do not become ordinary, easier to resolve or thematically simpler even on a multiple re-reading.

It doesn't look like a finger it looks like a feather of broken glass
It doesn't look like something to eat it looks like something eaten
It doesn't look like an empty chair it looks like an old woman searching in a
    heap of stones [. . .]
It doesn't look like a finger it looks like a feather with broken teeth

                          (Sykes Davies 1938)

Indeed an analysis in which the semantics of plesionymy (near but peculiar synonymy) can be traced through the text (see Stockwell 2000) serves only to increase the appreciation of the poetic mechanics of paranoia and disturbance in the text. This is a good example of a dissonant clash between a syntactic form that looks like someone striving for clarity and a semantic content that resists coherence. Surrealism is the depiction of thought rather than the communication of thoughts, but readers find it almost impossible not to treat the language we encounter as communicative. It is the readerly attempt to resolve this mismatch between appearance and content that generates the convulsive moment, and I think that ever closer attention simply re-iterates and renews that sensation. I have argued elsewhere (Stockwell 2009) that literary emotion is not fake emotion nor fictional emotion, but real emotion that is simply understood to have a literary motivation, and the argument applies to the re-enactments that are real surreal experiences.

Such deliberate category-mixing is a characteristic of surrealist writing. The categories might be from different linguistic levels or features, such as between syntax and semantics in the Sykes Davies example; or the clash might be between different collaged registers, as here where journalistic report is interspersed with idiomatic exclamations:

Nobody said Apples for nearly a minute –
I thought I should die.
Finally, though, the second sardine
From the end, on the left,
Converted a try.
(It brought down the house)
[. . .]
People agreed not to notice.
The band played a little bit louder.
It was all very British.

                          (Smith 1936)

The effect is firstly a sense of confusion, as almost any reader would naturally try to resolve for themselves a coherent image of a speaker of these lines, only to find that absolute consistency is not easily resolvable. My main impression of readers' responses to this text is one of wry amusement as the disparate sources of idioms and phrases are half-recognised just as they are subverted by anomalies.

The ultimate effect, I think, is not primarily confusion but one of a rich sense of the multiplication of meaning. This incremental loading of perceptual activity is apparent most clearly in David Gascoyne's *The Very Image*, which begins:

> An image of my grandmother
> Her head appearing upside-down upon a cloud
> The cloud transfixed on the steeple
> Of a deserted railway-station
> Far away
>
> (Gascoyne 1936a)

Each subsequent stanza adds further images, and then the final stanza rolls "all these images/and many others" together and places them "in model birdcages/about six-inches high." In a brief analysis, Germain (1978) describes the effect:

> Faced with the irrefutable incongruities, the unexpected telescoping and astonishing vividness of the images in the poem, the reader may find his mind filled with a sense of wonder, or perhaps an irritating amusement which suggests the images are somehow significant, even though they are obviously products of mental activities with which normal consciousness is typically unfamiliar.
>
> (Germain 1978: 33–4)

This overloading technique achieves richness by the simultaneous amplification of different levels, features and aspects of language (see an analysis of a Picasso poem that works in a similar way, in Stockwell 2003). The surrealist effect depends very largely, however, on the reader taking the surreal object seriously and literally, however deviant the discourse in which it is articulated. For this reason, surrealist writing tends to feature a high volume of visual, concrete, sensual and tactile evocations. For a quick illustration of several surrealist techniques, here is a complete poem by David Gascoyne, of the London Surrealist Group.

The Cage

> In the waking night
> The forests have stopped growing
> The shells are listening
> The shadows in the pools turn grey
> The pearls dissolve in the shadow
> And I return to you
>
> Your face is marked upon the clockface
> My hands are beneath your hair
> And if the time you mark sets free the birds

And if they fly away towards the forest
The hour will no longer be ours

Ours is the ornate birdcage
The brimming cup of water
The preface to the book
And all the clocks are ticking
All the dark rooms are moving
All the air's nerves are bare

Once flown
The feathered hour will not return
And I shall have gone away

(Gascoyne 1936b)

In spite of its counter-Enlightenment ideology, there is a high occurrence of Romantic and conventional high art motifs generally in surrealism. In *The Cage*, the pearls and birds, the forests and pools, and the brimming cup could have been found in Malory or the Gawain-poet, in Keats or Tennyson, the ornate birdcage and the air's nerves in T.S. Eliot, but "the shells are listening" and "the feathered hour" are surreal objects.

As in much surrealist writing, there is cosmetic coherence: in this poem it is manifest in cohesive repetition, a consistent semantic connection between nature on the one hand and domesticity on the other, and a simple assertive unmodalised clausal syntax. However, like the surrealist examples throughout this chapter, this naturalism and ordinariness is populated by vagueness and disturbing juxtapositions. There is a "brimming" profusion of sound, noise ("all the clocks") and shadows, and a lack of coherence between referents in succeeding sentences.

There is an underlying and highly conventional metaphor through the poem, familiarly expressed as "time flies," but in this as in surrealism generally, metaphor is to be taken seriously and literally: time *is* feathered. Similarly, a clockface and a human face are identical, "ours" and "hours" are the same, if you wake in the night it is the night that wakes, if you listen to the sea in shells, it is they that listen. In our rational world, the two sides of a metaphor are conceptually separate; in the surreal consciousness, they are identical and can be exchanged. Such ambiguities and ambivalences, accidents of sense in the rational world, are merely evidence of the workings of objective chance for the surrealists. "My hands are beneath your hair" would be a gentle and erotic line in a different sort of love poem, but embedded in this anxious and paranoid context it is more literally violent and sinister.

V. The working of objective chance

Though what I have been doing towards the end of this chapter has been treating surrealist writing (not as intended, and illegitimately) as literary art, I think in fact I am not so far from the surrealist spirit as such "academicism" might appear. My sense of an analytical understanding of surrealist writing is a greater awareness of its power rather than a diminution. Its significant experiential effect is real, and surprising, and it retains its capacity, even on re-reading, recontextualising and at a historical distance, to shock and force new evaluations. It may be that objective chance is more real than we might think. For example, it is only now, as I re-read this chapter for typing errors and clarity, that I have noticed for the first time the other possible way of reading my title. I think I intended "The surrealist experiments with language" to be a descriptive noun-phrase, much like the title or caption on a painting. However, of course, I have just this moment realised it can also be read as a present-tense verb-phrase, and taken either as a universalising assertion or as a particularising description of someone – you or me – caught in the act of becoming surrealist. I promise you absolutely I was not aware that I had done it when I first began.

References

Breton, A. (1928) *Nadja*, Paris: Livre de Poche.

—— (1969) *Manifestoes of Surrealism*, trans. R. Seaver and H. Lane, Ann Arbor, MI: University of Michigan Press.

—— (1991) "La beauté convulsive." In *Exhibition Catalogue from Musée National d'Art Moderne*, Paris: Georges Pompidou Centre.

Carrouges, M. (1968) "Le hasard objectif." In F. Alquié (ed.) *Le Surréalisme*, Paris: Mouton, pp. 269–78.

Ford, C.H. (ed.) (1945) "Anglo-American Chainpoem," *View* 5(December).

—— (ed.) (1991) *View: Parade of the Avant-Garde*, New York: Thunder's Mouth Press.

Gascoyne, D. (1936a) "The Very Image," *Contemporary Poetry and Prose* 2(June): 35.

—— (1936b) "The Cage." In *Man's Life Is This Meat*, London: Parton Press (Reprinted in *Selected Poems* [1995], London: Enitharmon Press, p. 43).

—— (2000 [1935]) *A Short Survey of Surrealism*, London: Enitharmon Press.

Germain, E.B. (ed.) (1978) *Surrealist Poetry in English*, Harmondsworth, UK: Penguin.

Richter, H. (1964) *Dada: Art and Anti-Art*, London: Thames and Hudson.

Smith, A.J.M. (1936) "Political Note," *Contemporary Poetry and Prose* 7(November): 130–1.

Stockwell, P. (2000) "(Sur)real stylistics: from text to contextualizing." In T. Bex, M. Burke and P. Stockwell (eds.) *Contextualized Stylistics*, Amsterdam: Rodopi, pp. 15–38.

—— (2003) "Surreal figures." In J. Gavins and G. Steen (eds.) *Cognitive Poetics in Practice*, London: Routledge, pp. 13–25.

—— (2009) *Texture: A Cognitive Aesthetics of Reading*, Edinburgh: Edinburgh University Press.

Sykes Davies, H. (1938) "Poem," *London Bulletin*, 2(May): 7.

Young, A. (1981) *Dada and After: Extremist Modernism and English Literature*, Manchester, UK: Manchester University Press.

5

THE LITERARY ABSURD

Joanna Gavins

I. Experimenting with the absurd

This chapter explores the phenomenon of the absurd in literary prose fiction. Like most preceding attempts to do the same, it begins with a stipulation about the slippery nature of all such endeavours, a sort of critical disclaimer, which will be all too familiar to anyone who has previously sought academic opinion on the absurd from other sources. The concept of the absurd is notoriously nebulous, making it seemingly irresistible to many literary academics, and subject to sustained critical attention for more than half a century. Most importantly, the substantial body of work which has been dedicated to the literary absurd since the middle of the twentieth century has failed to agree on the temporal, generic, or stylistic boundaries which might be set around the concept; the absurd has been identified in texts as diverse as Greek tragedy and multimodal science fiction, and in the works of authors from Amis to Voltaire. Far more frequently, the absurd in literature is defined in terms of what it is not: it is neither a literary movement nor a historical moment; it is neither confined by period, nor by genre. Within the context of the present volume on experimental literature, the absurd presents a particular challenge, since it manifests itself just as frequently in realist prose as it does within more innovative textual forms, occupying both extremes along the spectrum of experimentalism. However, this chapter seeks to resolve some of the critical contradictions of the absurd in fiction and to address the imprecision of preceding accounts. It does so by taking readerly experience as a core consideration, and the theories and methodologies of stylistics as its underlying analytical framework.

II. Philosophical and critical approaches

Having begun by briefly outlining the theoretical and technical imprecision which characterizes most literary criticism on the absurd, it is important now to emphasize that which all critics do agree upon: that all literary absurdity is an artistic expression of human beings' inability to find inherent meaning in their existence. The origins of this viewpoint are multiplex, drawn from nineteenth- and twentieth-century philosophy and theology (see Cornwell 2006: 2–14 for a useful survey), as well as from literary prose and drama. The first origins of the vagueness surrounding the concept of the literary absurd can be traced to the disagreement and discord which permeates many of the movements, disciplines, and sub-disciplines which have influenced its development.

Having said this, Søren Kierkegaard's position as one of the key architects of philosophical absurdism is undisputed. In *Fear and Trembling* (originally published in 1843), Kierkegaard (2006) reflects upon the biblical story of God's command to Abraham to sacrifice his son as demonstration of his faith, presenting the anguished moment when Abraham cannot act, and yet must act, as the epitome of the absurdity of human existence. His interest in such paradoxes also earned Kierkegaard the title of the "Father of Existentialism," yet it is important to understand that the majority of existentialists depart radically from the leap into Christian faith Kierkegaard makes as a result of his deliberations. Existentialism is closely related to absurdist philosophy in its recognition of the intrinsic meaninglessness of human life, but draws as much influence from the writings of Nietzsche and Heidegger as it does from Kierkegaard. Existentialism, in very general terms, holds that the responsibility for the creation of an authentic existence lies with the individual (see Cooper 1999 for a full explication). However, this basic overarching proposition admits a nuanced range of opinion and expression. As Macquarrie (1973: 14) points outs, existentialists do not subscribe to a single doctrine and existentialism is better considered as a "style of philosophizing" than as a unified philosophy in itself.

In literature, existentialism is most often identified with the work of Jean Paul Sartre, and his novel *La Nausée* (1938) in particular. Other authors typically associated with existentialism include Fyodor Dostoyevsky, Franz Kafka, and Albert Camus. Camus' position within the existentialist literary canon is also deeply problematic, due both to his eventual rejection of many of the main tenets of existentialist thinking and to his dramatic public disagreement with Sartre in 1952 over the legitimacy of communist violence (see Aronson 2004, and Sprintzen and van den Hoven 2006, for accounts of Camus' and Sartre's turbulent friendship). However, none of this has prevented the routine inclusion of Camus' work in a range of key critical surveys of existentialism and its literary expression (e.g. Barnes 1959; Friedman 1973; Oaklander 1996). By capturing existential anxiety in his novels, most notably in *L'Étranger* (1942), Camus ensured that his ideas on these matters would endure beyond the philosophical, personal, and political shifts which would occur later in his life.

Camus is, of course, also routinely credited as a founding father of absurdism, but it would seem that another of the root causes of much of the muddied water surrounding the existential and the absurd is the often inextricable relationship between these literary phenomena and the philosophies behind them. For Camus, the absurd is a condition of existence to be explored through fiction, rather than a fictional form in itself. His seminal text, *Le Mythe de Sisyphe* (1942), for instance, is made up of a series of essays in which Camus queries whether life has meaning in order to explore the further question of the legitimacy of suicide. He evokes the Greek myth of Sisyphus as an allegory for the absurd human condition. Sisyphus, having angered the gods, was condemned to rolling ceaselessly a huge stone to the top of a mountain, only to watch it roll back down again under the force of its own weight. Camus explains:

> Sisyphus is the absurd hero. He *is* as much through his passions as through his torture. His scorn of the gods, his hatred of death, and his passion for life won him that unspeakable penalty in which the whole being is exerted towards accomplishing nothing. This is the price that must be paid for the passions of this earth.
>
> (Camus 1975 [1942]: 108)

Much later, the phrase "Theatre of the Absurd" was coined by Martin Esslin, in his 1961 seminal text of the same name (Esslin 1980 [1961]), to describe the dramatic works of, primarily, Samuel Beckett, Arthur Adamov, Eugène Ionesco, Jean Genet, and Harold Pinter. Esslin explains that he sees the term "Theatre of the Absurd" as "a device to make certain fundamental traits which seem to be present in the works of a number of dramatists accessible to discussion by tracing the features they have in common" (Esslin 1980 [1961]: 12). Unfortunately, Esslin fails to specify what these fundamental traits actually are, offering only an impressionistic description of the works of each of his chosen authors without reference to the stylistic features the texts may share.

Esslin does provide more rigorous detail in his differentiation between those writers he considers to be dramatists of the absurd and those, including Sartre and Camus, whom he identifies as belonging to an earlier tradition of "Existentialist theatre" (Esslin 1980 [1961]: 25). He argues that

> these writers differ from the dramatists of the Absurd in an important respect: they present their sense of the irrationality of the human condition in the form of highly lucid and logically constructed reasoning, while the Theatre of the Absurd strives to express its sense of the senselessness of the human condition and the inadequacy of the rational approach by the open abandonment of rational devices and discursive thought.
>
> (Esslin 1980 [1961]: 24)

Esslin is careful to retain a tangible distinction between Camus' philosophical outlook and his prose style. According to Esslin, Sartre, Camus, and their contemporaries can be seen to be expressing the same metaphysical anguish as Beckett, Pinter, and the rest of Esslin's absurdist writers, only in a more conventional, realist form. Indeed, Esslin goes on to describe Camus' writing as displaying 'the elegantly rationalistic and discursive style of an eighteenth century moralist' (Esslin 1980 [1961]: 24), while he claims that Sartre's plays are "based on brilliantly drawn characters who remain wholly consistent and thus reflect the old convention that each human being has a core of immutable, unchanging essence" (Esslin 1980 [1961]: 24).

The Theatre of the Absurd, as Esslin defines it is, by contrast, characterized by its deliberate violation of such literary and dramatic norms, displaying numerous features (such as a lack of plot or limited characterization) which can be seen to defy the conventions which previously defined the qualitative boundaries of the literary canon. However, Esslin is also quick to point out the speed and readiness with which such initially incomprehensible avant-garde work was embraced by its audience and transformed into the "all too easily understood modern classic" (Esslin 1980 [1961]: 11). Indeed, Esslin's own terminology enjoyed a similar rush of popularity following the publication of *The Theatre of the Absurd*, as the phrase swiftly became an umbrella term applied to disparate plays and playwrights of the mid- to late twentieth century.

As a consequence, Esslin made several attempts, both in later editions of his initial monograph and in other subsequent studies of absurd drama (e.g. Esslin 1965), to re-draw and re-emphasize the boundaries of his Theatre of the Absurd, describing the term as having become a "catchphrase, much used and much abused" (Esslin 1965: 7). Esslin seems torn between the need to demarcate and differentiate the Theatre of Absurd from other artistic forms and the desire to broaden his grouping to encompass numerous stylistically and historically diverse texts. More recent developments in literary criticism would appear to suggest that the latter of these forces ultimately prevailed, as the term "absurd" has continued to be employed as a means of describing a vast array of drama and prose fiction (see Brothers (1977) on Green; Galloway (1970) on Updike, Bellow, Salinger, and Styron; Hauck (1971) on Melville, Twain, Faulkner, and Barth; Hilfer (1992) on Heller, Pynchon, Vonnegut, Barth, and Nabokov; Hinchliffe (1969) on, among others, Beckett, Osborne, and Stoppard; Ketterer (1978) on Vonnegut and Dick; Miller (1967) on Faulkner, Whitman, and Dickinson; Penner (1978) on Nabokov; Safer (1983, 1989 and 1990) on Pynchon, Kesey, and Barth; and Weinberg (1970) on, among others, Kafka, Hawkes, and Heller). In the most comprehensive study of the absurd in prose fiction to date, Cornwell (2006) extends the boundaries of the absurd yet further, including Sophocles, Shakespeare, Swift, Sterne, and Dickens in his opening sweeping survey of "antecedents to the absurd" (Cornwell 2006: 33–64). In the process, Cornwell blurs the line so carefully drawn by Esslin between absurd and existential literature. His investigation exemplifies how precision and definition have been sacrificed for the sake of historical breadth in the expansion of literary criticism on the absurd since Esslin's day.

The state of the art in literary-critical approaches to the absurd, then, might appear to be one in which almost anything goes. Delineating the absurd from the existential, the philosophical from the literary, no longer seems to be a central or valued preoccupation in this area. The academic notion of the absurd is now so all-encompassing, so vaguely defined, that its value as a descriptive and analytical term must surely be under question. The remainder of this chapter attempts to determine *why* academic accounts of the absurd in literary prose fiction have persisted in their vagueness and uncertainty well into the twenty-first century. In what follows, I examine the future of the absurd as a critical concept and explore, in particular, the possibility of a more coherent definition of the absurd.

III. Reading the literary absurd

Putting aside the complexities and controversies which pervade literary-critical discussions about the absurd, one thing is certain: "absurd" as a means of describing literary experience has become a highly valued concept far beyond the critical academy. Abundant, easily accessible evidence of this can be found in the proliferation of online reading and discussion groups which have sprung up all over the internet over the last decade or so. One of the most popular of these websites, www.librarything.com, allows users to form networks and to discuss and tag literary texts with labels of their choosing. The tag "absurd" and its aliases (including "absurdist," "absurdism," and so on) had been applied to 1,472 texts by 402 separate users of LibraryThing at the time of writing. These users are, of course, defined to some extent by their passion for literary discussion and include a number of academics with a literary-critical background. Many more users, however, have no such academic training (as can be seen from their public profiles) and are drawn from an array of geographical and social situations.

Most interestingly, the range of texts tagged or described as "absurd" on many websites (including other reading sites such as www.shelfari.com and palimpsest.org.uk, as well as literary weblogs such as *The Elegant Variation* [2010] and *The Literary Saloon* [2010]) is as broad-ranging in period and style as that which has been identified as absurd through the last fifty years of professional literary criticism. Readers participating in literary discussion online clearly share the view that the absurd in literature includes texts from a diversity of historical moments and genres, expressed through varying degrees of stylistic experimentation. The list of the top ten texts most frequently tagged as "absurd" on *LibraryThing* (2010), for example, reads as follows:

1. *Waiting for Godot* by Samuel Beckett
2. *The Stranger* by Albert Camus
3. *Rosencrantz and Guildenstern Are Dead* by Tom Stoppard
4. *Catch-22* by Joseph Heller
5. *The Trial* by Franz Kafka
6. *The Hitchhiker's Guide to the Galaxy* by Douglas Adams
7. *Dirk Gently's Holistic Detective Agency* by Douglas Adams
8. *Alice's Adventures in Wonderland and Through the Looking Glass* by Lewis Carroll
9. *The Myth of Sisyphus and Other Essays* by Albert Camus
10. *The Long Dark Tea-Time of the Soul* by Douglas Adams

Most noteworthy in this list are the appearances of two of Camus' "elegantly rationalistic and discursive" texts, as we have seen them described by Esslin (1980: 24), alongside multiple inclusions of satirical science fiction by Douglas Adams. The diversity of genres represented here exhibits the same sweeping comprehensiveness as the collection of texts categorized as absurd within literary criticism. Challenging though the far-reaching generic and historical boundaries of the absurd may be, then, they are nevertheless reflective of readers' day-to-day interactions with texts in situations outside of the academy. It is, of course, impossible to tell which way the influences have fed here; whether literary criticism has affected how readers categorize fiction, or whether that criticism is deliberately or coincidentally rooted in everyday reading experiences. Either way, these contrasting spheres of reading activity lend convincing weight to each other's highly inclusive conception of the absurd as a cultural and artistic phenomenon.

This is not to say, however, that the state of the art in criticism on the literary absurd, as I have so far characterized it, is satisfactory in its present form. What both academic and non-academic perspectives on absurdity in literature still lack, as far as a stylistician like me is concerned, is an adequate account of the discoursal features which connect these texts over centuries and genres. Despite an apparently common recognition in literary criticism that the absurd may in many cases be linguistically realized, attempts to identify and describe this rigorously are practically non-existent. Cornwell, for example, includes an entire section on what he terms "the socio-linguistic absurd" (2006: 23–7), which in the end progresses no further than a limited summary of early structuralist poetics and a collection of opaque post-structuralist comments on the obvious limits of purely formalist stylistic analysis. It would seem that the majority of literary critics who have focused their attention on the absurd thus far have some sense that they are describing a phenomenon that may involve some kind of innovative language use, yet they lack the linguistic terminology to explain such innovation accurately. The next sections of this chapter propose a different approach to the literary absurd which takes the language of this most nebulous of literary categories as its focal point and shifts discussion of the absurd in literature away from obscure philosophical debate and further towards an in-depth understanding of readers' everyday relationships with absurd prose fiction.

IV. The spectrum of absurd experimentalism

For the first step towards a more coherent understanding of the discourse of the absurd, we can look back temporarily to an early point in the rapid growth of literary criticism on the topic through the latter half of the twentieth century. Weinberg (1970) offers a useful formalization of the academic inconsistencies I have been describing in this chapter so far. Following Esslin closely, she distinguishes between those novels which convey existentialist concerns through a conventional narrative structure and those which strive to achieve a more innovative expression of the absurdity of the human condition. In the former, realist category she includes Camus' *L'Étranger* (1942) and Sartre's *La Nausée* (1938), as well as later works such as J.D. Salinger's *The Catcher in the Rye* (1951) and Bruce Friedman's *Stern* (1963). Weinberg goes on to explain:

> These novels are informed by a vision of absurdity and have at their centre a passive, rationalistic, or hopelessly ineffectual victim-hero, dominated by his situation rather than creating or acting to change it. They have a more or

less realistic surface, with somewhat surrealistic elements. Realism of detail, rather, underscores the madness of the world, its grotesque comedy.

(Weinberg 1970: 10)

Weinberg claims that, by contrast, in novels like Thomas Pynchon's *V* (1963), Joseph Heller's *Catch-22* (1961), and John Barth's *The End of the Road* (1958), the same philosophical themes that form the focus of the realist texts listed above are made manifest through what she terms a "stylized absurd surface" (Weinberg 1970: 11). She goes on to explain:

> The absurd surface exaggerates. Through exaggeration and repetitions; grotesqueries; unique, exotic, bizarre or strange symbols . . . the absurdity found in life is transcribed through surreal descriptions. Special surrealistic situations, too, are created to embody the inexplicable; and somewhat common situations, such as those of war, are exaggerated and distorted to produce a heightened effect of the sort experienced in dreams.
>
> (Weinberg 1970: 11)

Weinberg's separation of absurd prose fiction into two distinct categories, one realist and one non-realist, is a clear extension of Esslin's original classification of existentialist and absurdist drama towards an account of prose fictional forms. The core value of this approach is that it allows us to differentiate between literature of the absurd and numerous other twentieth-century texts which may also make use of a non-realist narrative structure. Although many novels of the last one hundred years or so may, for example, display a disrupted chronology, or contain surrealistic elements and situations, not all of them communicate the existentialist unease which, according to Weinberg, must be present in order for a text to be considered truly absurd.

In order to explore the workability of these ideas in more detail, I turn now to a text which might be considered a perfect example of the kind of the combined expression of existential anxiety through stylistic experimentation which Weinberg describes. Rudolph Wurlitzer's novel *Nog* was first published in 1968 and rapidly became a text with cult status for the counter cultural movement at that time. The text is written in the first person, focalized by a narrator who is, at first, nameless. The opening paragraphs are as follows:

> Yesterday afternoon, a girl walked by the window and stopped for sea shells. I was wrenched out of two months of calm. Nothing more than that, certainly, nothing ecstatic or even interesting, but very silent and even, as those periods have become for me. I had been breathing in and out, out and in, calmly, grateful for once to do just that, staring at the waves plopping in, successful at thinking almost nothing, handling easily the three memories I have manufactured, when that girl stooped for sea shells.
>
> (Wurlitzer 2009 [1968]: 11)

Nog remains a fixed homodiegetic narration throughout (in Genette's [1980] terms), and the reader's only access to the world of the fiction is through the perspective described in the extract above. This perspective is unremarkable to begin with: it describes a realistic beach scene in, for the most part, conventional simple past tense narrative. Save, perhaps, for the puzzling mention in the extract above of three memories which have been "manufactured," the opening of *Nog* is initially unchallenging in its style. As the novel progresses, however, it becomes more and more clear that the narrator of *Nog* may not be entirely reliable. He does not approach the girl on the beach, but instead goes to a local roadhouse, where he relates his desire to move on from the unnamed Californian town in which he lives and begins to describe his memories of a character called Nog. Nog is described as "one of those semi-religious lunatics you see wandering around the Sierras on bread and tea" (Wurlitzer 2009 [1968]: 12), of Finnish extraction, who the narrator says sold him a giant rubber octopus, housed in a water-filled bathysphere, balanced on the back of a truck. Over the course of the first chapter, it becomes apparent that the narrator has been traveling around the countryside for a year, showing the octopus at fairs. Along with the somewhat surreal image of the octopus itself, there are a number of other elements of the narrative which suggest that the narrator's version of events may not be trustworthy. For example, in the middle of an otherwise straightforward account of a conversation between Nog and the narrator about the octopus, the narrator tells us that Nog has "a yellow light that had lately been streaming out of his chest from a spot the size of a half dollar" (Wurlitzer 2009 [1968]: 12). Later on in the same scene, the narrator interrupts his detailed description of the octopus itself, saying "Nog is not quite clear enough. I have to invent more. It always comes down to that. I never get chance to rest" (Wurlitzer 2009 [1968]: 13–14).

Despite recurrent incidents such as these, in which the narrator clearly points to the fabricated nature of his account, the fixed focalization means that the reader must persevere with his version of events in order to form an understanding of the narrative world. Over the course of the rest of the opening chapter, the narrator's behavior becomes increasingly erratic as he goes on to describe a second encounter with the girl on the beach, who takes him to a party where there is a storm and where, yet more bizarrely, he meets an old colonel attempting to build a sea wall from driftwood to keep back the encroaching tide. *Nog*'s narrator is the epitome of Weinberg's "hopelessly ineffectual victim-hero" throughout these pages, as he stumbles without apparent motivation from one disorienting episode to another: he aids the colonel's Sisyphean quest for a while; he stumbles back to the party and misunderstands the hospitality of the female host, Sarah, and undresses completely in front of her; he fills a bath with a selection of drugs from a medicine cabinet and mixes them with water, which he says is "a very reviving thing to do" (Wurlitzer 2009 [1968]: 21); he gets into Sarah's bed and goes to sleep; he is woken by Sarah's boyfriend, with whom he plays table tennis for a while before flinging a basket of table-tennis balls at him and tipping over the table, all without explanation. The first chapter of *Nog* closes with the following paragraph:

What I should have done was get rid of the octopus, what I have been trying to do is get rid of the octopus, what I am beginning just now to remember is that I did get rid of the octopus. I see it now for the first time. I either took it back to the party and put it in the bathtub or danced with it on the beach. No, I did bring it back to the beach but not to dance with. I took off my terry cloth bathrobe and ran down to the truck and got the octopus out of the bathysphere, its tentacles waving all over me. Struggling in the rain and wind, I dragged it back and pulled it up on the sea wall. Such a spectacle gave the colonel enough of a jolt to finish the sea wall. Then together we threw it in the sea, and I went home and went to bed. It was something like that, I can remember something like that, a storm, a party and then the octopus. There was an octopus, although I know deep down that the octopus is still up on blocks. I know too that nothing happened and I haven't traveled with the octopus. But I shall move on anyway, perhaps to New York. I remember great things about New York.

(Wurlitzer 2009 [1968]: 25)

The key stylistic feature through which the narrator's bewilderment and general unreliability is expressed here is the use of modality. The stability of key deictic elements (e.g. the octopus) and story events (e.g. building the sea wall) is undermined through the use of modalization. Specifically, there is an abundance of epistemic modality, the overall discourse function of which is to express degrees of knowledge and belief, ranging from absolute certainty to complete lack of confidence. In *Nog*, the narrator destabilizes unmodalized propositions which have preceded this paragraph as he reveals his uncertainty through the repetition of modal verbs such as "I remember" in these closing lines. Where earlier in the chapter unmodalized forms predominated, such as "I bought the octopus, and for a year I traveled through the country with it" (2009: 13), from here on, with increasing regularity through the rest of the novel, contradictory degrees of belief are expressed: "what I am beginning just now to remember is that I did get rid of the octopus" (2009: 25).

Simpson (1993) has identified an identical narrative style at work in another classic absurd text, Samuel Beckett's *Molloy* (1955). Molloy's unreliability as a narrator is similarly communicated through fluctuating and conflicting modalization, at some points stating definite commitment to the truth of particular propositions, often swiftly followed by expressions of confusion and doubt (see also Gavins 2000, 2003, and 2010 for analyses of the absurd effects of modalization in Flann O'Brien's *The Third Policeman* [1967], Donald Barthelme's *Snow White* [1967], and Emmanuel Carrère's [1998] *The Mustache* respectively). The narrator of *Nog* makes recurrent use of perception modality in particular, a type of epistemic modality referring to the senses (for example, "I see it now for the first time" [Wurlitzer 2009: 25]). He also emphasizes the instability of his narrative through the creation of multiple hypothetical alternatives, such as "I either took it back to the party and put it in the bathtub or danced with it on the beach" (2009: 25). Although he often eventually assigns reality to one of the alternatives he constructs (e.g. "No, I did bring it back to the beach but not to dance with" [2009: 25]), the faltering modality in the rest of the text once again undermines the dependability of this commitment.

The patterns of modalization in *Nog* are by no means the only stylistic feature through which the novel's absurdity is communicated. The narrative structures identified above are offered simply as typical examples of elements of the text's "stylized absurd surface" (Weinberg 1970: 11). The experimentalism of the novel increases as the story progresses, with disrupted chronology, a constantly shifting use of tense, and the construction of impossible spatial deixis all making frequent appearances throughout the rest of the book. It gradually emerges that the narrator *is* Nog (although this only becomes clear through other characters' references to him, rather than through any helpful information he provides), as he continues his hapless journey from one absurd situation to another – through drug abuse, free love, and even murder – never providing a dependable explanation of his actions or their consequences.

Nog, then, can be seen to occupy a position towards one extreme of a cline of absurd experimentalism. At the other end of the spectrum, the absurd begins to blend with existentialism, as the "realistic surface" starts to dominate over more "surrealistic elements" (Weinberg 1970: 10). In these texts, the exploration of common philosophical themes through conventional narrative forms takes precedence over linguistic innovation. Whether or not the gradual nature of this blend and the inevitable fuzzy boundaries it creates between literary categories causes insurmountable critical problems depends on the extent to which one is determined to adhere to Esslin's (and Weinberg's) segregation of the two phenomena. It would certainly seem that the majority of non-professional readers in the twenty-first century have no such difficulties and are often willing to accept and apply the labels "absurd" and "existential" interchangeably. This is likely due, in part at least, to the fact that many of the same stylistic features outlined in experimental literature of the absurd can also be found, albeit in a "weakened" form, in the sorts of realist texts Weinberg discusses. Consider, for example, this extract from J.D. Salinger's *The Catcher in the Rye* (1951), which Weinberg uses as a typical example of a text containing "realism of detail" (1970: 10):

> When I finally got down off the radiator and went out to the hat-check room, I was crying and all. I don't know why, but I was. I guess it was because I was feeling so damn depressed and lonesome. Then, when I went out to the checkroom, I couldn't find my goddam check. The hat-check girl was very nice about it, though. She gave me my coat anyway. And my "Little Shirley Beans" record – I still had it with me and all. I gave her a buck for being so nice, but she wouldn't take it. She kept telling me to go home and go to bed. I sort of tried to make a date with her for when she got through working, but she wouldn't do it . . . I didn't feel too drunk any more when I went outside, but it was getting very cold out again, and my teeth started chattering like hell. I couldn't make them stop. I walked over to Madison Avenue and started to wait around for a bus because I didn't have hardly any money left and I had

to start economizing on cabs and all. But I didn't feel like getting on a damn bus. And besides, I didn't even know where I was supposed to go. So what I did, I started walking over to the park. I figured I'd go by that little lake and see what the hell the ducks were doing, see if they were around or not, I still didn't know if they were around or not. It wasn't far over to the park, and I didn't have any place else special to go to – I didn't even know where I was going to sleep yet – so I went.

(Salinger 1951: 153)

Like *Nog*, Salinger's text has a fixed homodiegetic narration throughout. Although there are countless existential and absurd novels which do not, the narrators of those which do have a greatly increased chance of exhibiting some form of unreliability. Readers of these kinds of text, as I have already stated above, have only one point of access to the world of the novel and are forced to view events through this perspective. Holden Caulfield is one of the most notoriously challenging first-person focalizers in literary history and, while his account may not display temporal, spatial, and conceptual disruption to the extent that has been identified in *Nog*, it nevertheless employs other linguistic techniques similarly to destabilize the dependability of the narrative. Note, for example, in the extract above how the use of modality presents a picture of uncertainty once again. Holden comments, "I was crying and all. I don't know why, but I was. I guess it was because I was feeling so damn depressed and lonesome," expressing a relatively weak epistemic commitment to his own interpretation of events. Particularly towards the end of the extract, Holden talks more and more about what he does not know and is unsure of ("I didn't even know where I was supposed to go . . . I still didn't know if they were around or not . . . I didn't even know where I was going to sleep"). He also has a habit of trying to play down the significance of certain actions and events throughout *The Catcher in the Rye*, e.g. "I sort of tried to make a date with her for when she got through working, but she wouldn't do it." Once again, this serves only to exaggerate the highly subjective nature of Holden's focalization, further undermining his reliability as the filter through which the reader must witness the textual world.

V. Embracing the imprecision of the absurd

The Catcher in the Rye exists on the very border between existentialism and the absurd. The majority of readers discussing the text online favour the former categorization of the text, while elsewhere its narrator has been held up as the personification of the "absurd hero" (see Galloway 1970). These mixed responses to the novel's content are additional evidence of the hazy criteria applied by both professional and non-professional readers in their encounters with texts which in various ways communicate anxiety over the meaninglessness of human existence. Embracing and reflecting such nebulousness, however, does not necessarily condemn academic investigation of the literary absurd to unworkable incoherence. On the contrary, it is essential that critical accounts of all literary expression retain close contact with the reception of, and value attached to, literary artifacts by a far wider community of readers. As this chapter has sought to emphasize, the complex and often contradictory historical and philosophical roots of the absurd further necessitate a flexible understanding of its literary manifestations. Criticism of the absurd only loses currency when it fails to recognize the clear patterns which connect both readers' reactions to absurd texts and the disparate discoursal features through which the absurd is expressed in the texts themselves. Only when a properly rigorous examination of the relationships between the language of the absurd and readers of the absurd is attempted does the absurd reveal itself, not as a genre, not as a movement, but as a readerly experience.

References

Aronson, R. (2004) *Camus and Sartre: The Story of a Friendship and the Quarrel That Ended It*, Chicago, IL: University of Chicago Press.

Barnes, H.E. (1959) *Humanistic Existentialism: The Literature of Possibility*, Lincoln, NE: University of Nebraska Press.

Barth, J. (1958) *The End of the Road*, New York: Doubleday.

Barthelme, D. (1967) *Snow White*, New York: Atheneum.

Beckett, S. (1955) *Molloy*, Paris: Olympia Press.

Brothers, B. (1977) "Henry Green: Time and the Absurd," *Boundary* 2(5): 863–76.

Camus, A. (1942) *L'Étranger*, Paris: Gallimard.

—— (1975 [1942]) *The Myth of Sisyphus*, trans. J. O'Brien, London: Penguin (first published as *Le Mythe de Sisyphe*, Paris: Gallimard).

Carrère, E. (1998) "The Mustache," trans. L. Goodman. In *Two By Carrère: Class Trip and The Mustache*, New York: Henry Holt, pp. 149–318 (first published in 1986 as *La Moustache*, Paris: P.O.L.).

Cooper, D.E. (1999) *Existentialism*, 2nd edn, Oxford, UK: Blackwell.

Cornwell, N. (2006) *The Absurd in Literature*, Manchester, UK: Manchester University Press.

Esslin, M. (1965) (ed.) *Absurd Drama*, London: Penguin.

—— (1980 [1961]) *The Theatre of the Absurd*, 3rd edn, London: Penguin (first published by New York: Anchor).

Friedman, B. (1963) *Stern*, London: André Deutsch.

Friedman, M.S. (1973) *The Worlds of Existentialism: A Critical Reader*, Chicago, IL: University of Chicago Press.

Galloway, D. (1970) *The Absurd Hero in American Fiction: Updike, Styron, Bellow, Salinger*, Austin, TX: University of Texas Press.

Gavins, J. (2000) "Absurd Tricks With Bicycle Frames in the Text World of *The Third Policeman*," *Nottingham Linguistic Circular* 15: 17–33.

—— (2003) "Too Much Blague? An Exploration of the Text Worlds of Donald Barthelme's *Snow White*." In J. Gavins and G. Steen (eds.) *Cognitive Poetics in Practice*, London: Routledge, pp. 129–44.

—— (2010) "'Appeased by the Certitude': The Quiet Disintegration of the Paranoid Mind in *The Mustache*." In B. Büsse and D. McIntyre (eds.) *Language and Style*, Basingstoke, UK: Palgrave MacMillan, pp. 402–18.

Genette, G. (1980) *Narrative Discourse*, New York: Cornell University Press.

Hauck, R. (1971) *A Cheerful Nihilism: Confidence and "The Absurd" in American Humorous Fiction*, Bloomington, IN: Indiana University Press.

Heller, J. (1961) *Catch-22*, London: Jonathan Cape.

Hilfer, T. (1992) *American Fiction Since 1940*, London: Longman.

Hinchliffe, A. (1969) *The Absurd*, London: Methuen.

Ketterer, D. (1978) "Take-off to Cosmic Irony: Science-fiction, Humor and the Absurd." In S. Cohen (ed.) *Comic Relief: Humor in Contemporary American Literature*, Urbana, IL: University of Illinois Press, pp. 70–86.

Kierkegaard, S. (2006) *Fear and Trembling*, trans. S. Walsh, ed. S. Walsh and C. S. Evans, Cambridge, UK: Cambridge University Press.

LibraryThing (2010) Retrieved from http://www.librarything.com/tag/absurd (Accessed November 2010).

Macquarrie, J. (1973) *Existentialism*, Harmondsworth, UK: Penguin.

Miller, J. (1967) *Quests Surd and Absurd: Essays in American Literature*, Chicago, IL: University of Chicago Press.

Oaklander, L.N. (1996) *Existentialist Philosophy: An Introduction*, London: Prentice Hall.

O'Brien, F. (1967) *The Third Policeman*, London: MacGibbon and Kee.

Penner, D. (1978) "Invitation to a Beheading: Nabokov's Absurdist Initiation," *Critique* 20(3): 27–38.

Pynchon, T. (1963) *V*, London: Jonathan Cape.

Safer, E. (1983) "The Absurd Quest and Black Humor in Ken Kesey's *Sometimes a Great Notion*," *Critique* 24(4): 228–40.

—— (1989) *The Contemporary American Comic Epic: The Novels of Barth, Pynchon, Gaddis and Kesey*, Detroit, MI: Wayne State University Press.

—— (1990) "Pynchon's World and Its Legendary Past: Humor and the Absurd in a Twentieth Century *Vineland*," *Critique* 32(2): 107–25.

Salinger, J.D. (1951) *The Catcher in the Rye*, London: Hamish Hamilton.

Sartre, J.P. (1938) *La Nausée*, Paris: Gallimard.

Simpson, P. (1993) *Language, Ideology and Point of View*, London: Routledge.

Sprintzen, D. and van den Hoven, A. (2006) *Sartre and Camus: A Historic Confrontation*, London: Prometheus Books.

The Elegant Variation (2010) Retrieved from http://marksarvas.blogs.com/ (Accessed November 2010).

The Literary Saloon (2010) Retrieved from http://www.complete-review.com/saloon/ (Accessed November 2010).

Weinberg, H. (1970) *The New Novel in America: The Kafkan Mode in Contemporary Fiction*, Ithaca, NY: Cornell University Press.

Wurlitzer, R. (2009 [1968]) *Nog*, Granville, OH: Two Dollar Radio Movement (first published by New York: Random House).

6

SPONTANEITY AND IMPROVISATION IN POSTWAR EXPERIMENTAL POETRY

Benjamin Lee

I. Introduction

Much experimental poetry in the 1950s and 1960s, particularly in the United States, was devoted to some notion of improvisation. This was due in large measure to the energy, dexterity, and cultural cachet of bebop, which in the decades before rock 'n' roll managed to signify both youthful rebellion and high modernist difficulty. Asked to characterize the poetic theory of the era, Charles Olson once remarked: "Boy, there was no poetic. It was Charlie Parker. Literally, it was Charlie Parker" (Olson 1979: 71). Olson's remark, while misleading on one level – his own work demonstrates the intensity and sophistication of postwar experimental poetics – also captures quite accurately the fascination bebop and post-bop exerted on any number of poets included in Donald Allen's famous anthology, *The New American Poetry*. From the long lines and incantatory excess of Allen Ginsberg's "Howl" to the precise syncopations of Robert Creeley's lyric minimalism, jazz investments in improvisation, rhythmic experiment, and the deconstruction of traditional melody were everywhere apparent in Allen's anthology, first published in 1960 and widely regarded as the most influential poetry anthology to appear since World War II. The anthology, in turn, provided a compelling reassessment of modernism while also changing the shape of poetry to come. It expressed and helped publicize what one might characterize, to borrow a phrase from Nathaniel Mackey, as an "unruly pivot" in twentieth-century experimental writing, a moment during which the insights of the historical avant-garde were gathered up, reformulated, and projected forward (Mackey 1993: 191–213).

Bebop's signal influence aside, poets drawn to spontaneous aesthetics in the years following World War II had no shortage of muses. The heightened and idiosyncratic notions of improvisation projected in the music of Parker and his collaborators cross-pollinated with improvisatory approaches in other media, increasing their collective impact. Abstract Expressionists, with their new sense of painting as action, gesture, or event, captured the imagination of New York School poets Frank O'Hara, John Ashbery, Kenneth Koch, James Schuyler, and Barbara Guest. Zen Buddhism drew in Beat poets like Jack Kerouac and Gary Snyder, who began describing their art as part of an ongoing process of unself-conscious being and responsiveness to the environment. The philosopher Alfred North Whitehead's visions of human experience in the flow and flux of the energy field helped shape Olson's important theorization of poetry as "Projective Verse." Olson's theories evolved in dialogue with a group of younger poets – including Creeley, Denise Levertov, and Robert Duncan – associated with Black Mountain College, an experimental school in North Carolina where Creeley taught, Olson served as rector, and collaborative, process-oriented approaches were being explored in dance, music, and visual art as well as in poetry. As Daniel Belgrad has argued, a broad but variegated "culture of spontaneity" emerged in the decades after World War II that propelled much of the most influential art of the era while also "functioning as the basis of a distinct counterculture." Across the arts and in the realms of philosophy, cultural commentary, and everyday life, a movement was afoot that embraced spontaneity as an alternative to American materialism and conformity (Belgrad 1998: 1–2).

This essay focuses on Beat, Black Mountain, and New York School poets, emphasizing their cultural context and shared investment in a poetics of spontaneity. I also want to underscore important differences among these three versions of mid-century avant-gardism. These include differences in tone and technique, disagreements about literary predecessors, tensions over art's attitude towards mass and popular culture, and arguments about poetry's ability to represent a self or intervene in public, political debates. The Beats were the most explicitly countercultural and confessional; the New York School poets favored ironic and painterly effects; the Black Mountain poets inclined towards erudition and were more invested than the other two groups in arguments over poetics. Ginsberg the bohemian elegized O'Hara in a suit and tie, "mouth-smell of martinis," while O'Hara gently mocked Ginsberg's claims to religious and spiritual illumination. "Allen is back talking about god a lot," O'Hara deadpans in "Adieu to Norman, Bon Jour to Joan and Jean-Paul" (Ginsberg 1984: 458; O'Hara 1995 [1971]: 328). Ashbery's famous description of O'Hara as "too hip for the squares and too square for the hips," a poet without "a program" in a "supremely tribal" era, has often been interpreted as an expression of the New York School's shared hesitations about the explicitly anti-establishment stances of Beat and Black Mountain poets, though of course these hesitations hardly kept O'Hara from reading or publishing alongside poets with different temperaments or oppositional investments (Ashbery 2004: 81). In attending to such disagreements, I hope to underscore the variety and shading of aesthetic, affective, and political positions experimental poets adopted in the 1950s and 1960s, and to suggest connections between these positions and the experimental poetics of subsequent decades. As they clash and collaborate, Beat, Black Mountain, and New York School poets begin to anticipate some of the most significant movements in experimental poetry to emerge in the 1970s and 1980s, including L=A=N=G=U=A=G=E poetry (see Bernstein, this volume) and a range of ethnic and multicultural poetries.

II. *The New American Poetry* and poetics

The New American Poetry asserted its novelty and spirit of provocation first and most consistently through its "total rejection of all those qualities typical of academic verse" (Allen 1999 [1960]: xi). It was not a teaching anthology, designed for adoption by college or university professors. On the contrary, it articulated a direct challenge to English faculties, academic journals, and received opinions about poetry in the postwar university, where a New Critical version of the poem as transhistorical artifact – traditionally metrical, symbolically complex, studiously distanced from the author's life and experiences – was then dominant. Schuyler's "Statement on Poetics" in *The New American Poetry* decries the "regression . . . [of] the campus dry-heads who . . . descend tum-ti-tumming from Yeats out of Graves"; Ginsberg hears "ghostly Academics in Limbo screeching about form"; LeRoi Jones/Amiri Baraka asserts that "the diluted formalism of the academy . . . is anaemic & fraught with incompetence & unreality." Perhaps most influentially, Olson theorizes "Projective Verse" in opposition to "The NON-Projective," "or . . . 'closed' verse, that verse which print bred and which is pretty much what we have had . . . and have still got" (Allen 1999 [1960]: 386, 415, 418, 425). *The New American Poetry* presented itself as an "aesthetically revisionist" anthology: it intended to be polemical, to intervene in literary history, and to champion non-canonical poets sharing formally innovative positions (Golding 1995: 30). The fact that so many of the poets included in the anthology are now read as central to the development of contemporary poetry is just one measure of the force and timeliness of its intervention.

Olson's suggestion that there was no experimental poetic in the 1950s beyond a reverence for Charlie Parker points to a couple of important characteristics of Beat, Black Mountain, and New York School poetries. They adopted jazz or painting as primary aesthetic models not just because the new music and painting were beautiful and exciting but also as a strategic and rhetorical position. Celebrating decisive innovations in other media was a way of rejecting the prevailing notions of literature and literary tradition, which these poets perceived as static, unimaginative, and excessively polite. They could challenge the New Criticism, for instance, not just directly but also by shifting the grounds of the debate towards experiments in other media – like Action Painting or musical improvisation – that seemed to privilege feeling and intuition over symbolic unity and metaphysical wit. Nor did all of Olson's friends and fellow travelers embrace poetic theorization as he conceived of it. Jack Kerouac, the best-known of Beat writers, could be as vague in his pronouncements about form and technique as his novels and poems could be dynamic; O'Hara's hilarious statements on poetics convey his impatience with precisely the sort of grandiose, didactic assertions about form and consciousness that typify Olson's. Whereas Olson's "Projective Verse" offers a complex and overarching theory of American free verse after Ezra Pound and William Carlos Williams, O'Hara's "Personism" advises poets not to worry too much about "rhythm, assonance, all that stuff." "You just go on your nerve," he quips (O'Hara 1995 [1971]: 498).

It is not true, however, that there was no experimental poetic in the 1950s. The different versions of spontaneous composition articulated by Olson, Ginsberg, Levertov, Kerouac, Creeley, Baraka, O'Hara and others did constitute something like a shared aesthetic, one that pushed free verse experiment and argued that the poem, "immanent and processual," should take shape as the poet worked through immediate personal and historical material, or explored new modes of everyday perceptual and emotional engagement (Golding 1998: 180–1). "[E]ach speech having its own character," Creeley was fond of quoting from Williams, "the poetry it engenders will be peculiar to that speech also in its own intrinsic form" (Allen 1999 [1960]: 408; Williams 1988: 54). This broadly-articulated "renunciation of the well-made symbolist poem" and search for new forms of poetic energy, particularity, and speech-based immediacy had a lasting impact on English-language poetry (Breslin 1984: xv).

By the late 1970s and early 1980s, critics like James Breslin and Marjorie Perloff could offer influential readings of the transformation of American poetry by mid-century experimentalism. The initial, radically experimental modernisms of the early twentieth century, they argued, had by the early 1950s become a weak orthodoxy in need of renovation. New Critical principles expressed in the work of young formalists like Richard Wilbur or Robert Lowell came to seem stifling even to Lowell, then as firmly established as any poet of his generation, not to mention to vanguard poets still struggling to gain an audience. Poets and readers alike were hungry for the hip rush of personal revelation and longing they found in Beat poems, for Black Mountain's propulsive and theoretical revolt against "closed" verse forms, and for the New York School's clever integration into American poetry of tones and techniques culled from their readings in French and Russian avant-gardism (see White, this volume, and Stockwell, this volume). Previously unacceptable content (sexual, political, comedic, ecstatically spiritual) and a range of newly relevant poetic styles came flooding into the field, radically expanding new poets' sense of how they might approach their work (Perloff 1998 [1977]).

III. Little magazines and countercultural community

The various experimental approaches and local scenes condensed into *The New American Poetry* were not just aesthetically innovative but also insistently countercultural, a set of creative responses to cold war America's overwhelming emphasis on material abundance and conformity. Undoubtedly, experimental poetry communities of the 1950s and 1960s challenged some dominant cultural prescriptions while leaving others in place. They were not always as racially egalitarian as they pretended to be, and male poets of the era often undervalued the aesthetic achievements of women and represented avant-garde creativity and dissent as essentially masculine prerogatives (see Friedman, this volume, and Nielsen, this volume; see also Baraka 1997 [1984]; Davidson 2003; Di Prima 2002; Johnson and Grace 2002; Nelson 2007; and Nielsen 1997). Nevertheless, the collective dissent expressed by Allen's anthology was substantially underwritten by queer, interracial, and bohemian collectivities willing to nurture and sustain anaesthetics of risk and provocation (Damon 1993; Mackey 1993; Moten 2003: 149–69). Thus, for example, Baraka fuses his criticism of academic formalism in poetry with a disparagement of "the formal culture of the U.S.," and the intensity of his engagement with experimental art seems inseparable from his fascination with the social, sexual, and intellectual freedoms he went seeking in downtown New York at the close of the 1950s (Allen 1999 [1960]: 425; Baraka 1997 [1984]). Similarly, poetic innovation in San Francisco during the 1950s and 1960s was fostered by the city's gay subcultures and marked by its long tradition of left political activism (Davidson 1989).

The fundamental "groupishness" or "coterie" poetics of the mid-century avant-garde – with its roots in particular bohemian enclaves – is reflected in Allen's decision to gather the poets in his anthology into different schools. Sections for Beat, Black Mountain, and New York School poets are joined in *The New American Poetry* by a section of San Francisco Renaissance poets and a fifth and final group with "no geographical definition" and yet made up of poets with close connections to at least one of the other coteries. Allen's divisions reflect the energies but may also exaggerate the coherence of a set of porous and overlapping communities (Duberman 1988; Epstein 2006; Gray 2006; Kane 2003; Shaw 2006). Many of the poets in question moved frequently (from Black Mountain to New York; from New York to San Francisco; to Paris, Tangiers, or Mallorca), while the bohemian enclaves with which they are most often associated (in Berkeley, North Beach, or downtown New York) were at once real and imaginary, experienced on site and the products of literary representation and cultural desire.Ginsberg's "Howl," first published in 1956, offers a particularly memorable example of this phenomenon. Its immediate popularity was due in no small measure to the impression it created that it had simultaneously managed to reveal the secret lives of bohemians in New York and San Francisco and to call into being an imagined community with which readers everywhere might affiliate (Ginsberg 1984: 126–33).

Before and after the publication of *The New American Poetry*, the imaginative and cultural strivings of Ginsberg's "angel headed hipsters" were embodied as forcefully as anywhere in the little magazines of the period. Allen's anthology, in reframing so successfully a host of more chaotic publications, has now come to stand in as a synecdoche for a much wider field – of mid-century experimental poetry, but also of experimental approaches to editing, publishing, and distribution. Indeed, Allen's decision to edit an anthology in the first place was inspired by his work editing *Evergreen Review*, and many of the poems he included were taken from other little magazines of the era, including *Black Mountain Review*, *Yügen*, *Measure*, *Chicago Review*, and *Big Table* (Allen 1999 [1960]: 447–9). Cid Corman's *Origin* had been publishing Olson since 1951 and had become closely associated with his poetics of the breath unit and of "composition by field," Olson's term for poems that emerge line by line, or syllable by syllable, over the course of their composition; it helped articulate a vanguard interpretation of modernism that other little magazines varied and expanded (Golding 1998: 132). Suddenly and vociferously, mid-century poets embraced Poundian historical collage, Williams's "variable foot," Zukofksy's Objectivism, Steinian repetition, Lorca and Apollinaire, and a reinvigorated Romanticism. The work of displacing T.S. Eliot's dominance and replacing New Critical interpretations of modernism was ongoing and generative; it infused little magazines with a sense of urgency and common purpose. Technological developments and postwar economic prosperity also played a role. Poets in New York and San Francisco could find cheap apartments and part-time jobs to pay the bills, and they had "[d]irect access to mimeograph machines, letterpress, and inexpensive offset," allowing them to print for themselves and distribute quickly (Clay and Phillips 1998: 14). Suddenly readers hungry for innovative poetry and a sense of cultural transformation could read new work by Beat, Black Mountain, and New York School poets just weeks after it had been written (Di Prima 1973: x).

Thus postwar experimental poets, in response to a literary and intellectual climate they perceived as excessively confining and suspicious, embraced an aesthetic of open form and spontaneity on the level of publication as well as poetry. Their little magazines were mostly short-lived and provisional, expressing a shared aesthetic and sense of interconnectedness rather than a desire for longevity and continued authority. These poets wanted to win their own audiences and poetic reputations, of course, but they hoped to win them through acts of immediate communication and ongoing participation in alternative communities. Poems like Ginsberg's "Malest Cornifici Tuo Catullo" or O'Hara's "Why I Am Not a Painter" resemble letters to other poets or conversations among friends rather than great poems responding to other great poems in the solemn, heavily symbolic language of universal judgment. Reflecting their admiration for new jazz or Abstract Expressionism, such poems – and the mimeographed magazines in which they appeared – tend to present themselves as records of creative activity rather than perfectly crafted art objects. From this perspective, art could be ragged and off-kilter, or even appear as something other than art, for it gained in beauty the more it risked. "[I]n 1950 there was no sure proof of the existence of the avant-garde," Ashbery later observed; "to experiment was to have the feeling that one was poised on some outermost brink" (Ashbery 1989). If, by the end of the 1960s, an aesthetics of spontaneity was beginning to seem too familiar, thus diluting its countercultural charge, then subsequent movements would need to rise to the challenge of reevaluating its underlying assumptions and effects.

IV. Creeley and O'Hara

Robert Creeley and Frank O'Hara are as representative as anyone of the avant-garde poetry and poetics of the 1950s and 1960s. Neither poet favored the sweeping, theoretical statements of Olson, and neither enjoyed the widespread notoriety and literary celebrity of Beat standard-bearers like Ginsberg and Kerouac. Neither has quite achieved the acclaim now enjoyed by Ashbery, whom readers and critics since the 1970s – in Britain as well as the U.S. – have transformed into one of the most celebrated poets of the second half of the twentieth century. Nevertheless, both O'Hara and Creeley are beloved, deeply influential figures whose distinctive styles continue to mark English-language poetry. Both possessed personal and editorial energies that made them galvanizing figures among fellow poets and allowed them to bridge the gaps between various postwar coteries. And both produced countless important meditations on the new rhythms, modes of sociability, and fluid relations between content to form that characterized postwar experimental poetry.

The differences between the experimental vernacular favored by Creeley and O'Hara and the more heavily weighted, formalist approach they opposed are at the heart of a well-known anecdote about a poetry reading from the 1960s. The reading, which featured O'Hara and Robert Lowell, took place at Staten Island's Wagner College in February 1962. After two student poets read, O'Hara opened his reading with "Poem (Lana Turner has collapsed)," a brilliantly campy statement of solidarity with the exhausted, media-hounded Hollywood star. "LANA TURNER HAS COLLAPSED!" the poem exclaims, quoting a headline its speaker has just spotted in the *New York Post*. This sudden burst of information, introduced in the poem's opening line and repeated suddenly in line 11, leads O'Hara's speaker to a set of quick comparisons between New York's dreary weather and the absence of "snow" and "rain" in California, before he concludes in a rush of unembarrassed self-revelation:

> I have been to lots of parties
> and acted perfectly disgraceful
> but I never actually collapsed
> oh Lana Turner we love you get up

> (O'Hara 1971: 449)

O'Hara announced as he introduced the poem that he had written it on the Staten Island Ferry on the way to the reading, and the poem still feels like the product of spontaneous composition by someone who had long practiced writing poems this way. As this poem suggests, O'Hara could improvise on tabloid headlines just as easily as he could write poems about love, death, or friendship; indeed, he often fused pop cultural materials with traditional lyric themes. The audience at the reading was reportedly delighted, Lowell less so. He announced after O'Hara had finished and as he began that he would certainly not be reading a poem he had just composed (Perloff 1998 [1977]: 13–14; LeSueur 2003: 264–6; Gooch 1993: 386–7).

Though perhaps too much has been made of this single encounter, there is little doubt that O'Hara's poetry was categorically different from Lowell's, and that Lowell's style – even after his famous embrace of confessionalism and free verse – represented for O'Hara a set of assumptions and effects he hoped to avoid. Even as Lowell departed in the late 1950s from the New Critical approach that characterized his first books and adopted a more conversational, less densely metrical style, he refused to alter his commitment to the notion of a poem revised to perfection. Further, the explosively confessional content of Lowell's *Life Studies* (1959), though shocking to many and unquestionably influential, struck O'Hara as self-aggrandizing. Lowell's poetry everywhere implied aristocratic authority; it proceeded on the overlapping assumptions that he was the right man to comment on major historical events and that his own personal crises (mental illness, alcoholism, difficulties in marriage) echoed and expressed national crises, from the Vietnam War to the struggle for Civil Rights. This led to famous poems, like "Skunk Hour" or "For the Union Dead," which, while they attested to Lowell's transformation of his own style, still seemed to O'Hara – immersed as he was in Mayakovsky, Reverdy, or new poems by Schuyler or Koch – like an extension of New Critical procedures for writing serious, symbolic, academic poems (Perloff 1998 [1977]: 13–14; Damon 1993: 77–8).

O'Hara's spontaneous aesthetic dodges and dissolves solemnity; instead of speaking with solitary cultural authority, his poems create a sense of intimacy, making readers feel they are overhearing conversations with friends or being addressed directly. This is certainly the case in O'Hara's wintry, improvised lyric for Lana Turner, as in so many of his occasional poems, love poems, poems addressed to friends, and poems about everyday life in New York City. "There's nothing worse / than feeling bad and not / being able to tell you," read the opening lines of "Nocturne" (O'Hara 1971: 224). O'Hara's best-known and widely imitated poems, what he called his "I do this, I do that" poems, draw readers into their accounts of daily movements through, and emotional engagements with, the city. In place of metaphor, they offer readers the concreteness, contiguity, and part-for-whole energies of metonymy: "everything . . . honks," "skirts are flipping above heels," "[a] blonde chorus girl clicks," and newspaper headlines catch the poet's eye, suddenly transforming his experience of time and of the emotional meaning of the day (O'Hara 1971: 257).

Even O'Hara's most familiar and frequently anthologized poems – "Why I Am Not a Painter," "The Day Lady Died," "Personal Poem," or "A Step away from Them," for example – continue to project a remarkable sense of hipness, immediacy, and rhythmic spontaneity. Instead of adopting the public, almost official voice Lowell's speakers sometimes adopt, O'Hara tends to invoke smaller, less official communities: downtown artists, gay friends dancing together "At the Old Place," those holding their breath in a basement club while Billie Holiday "whispered a song along the keyboard to Mal Waldron" (O'Hara 1995 [1971]: 325). The camp accents and broader conversational touches of his poems parallel a range of other postwar vernacular effects, including those found in Jack Spicer's poems of queer, esoteric community, or poems by Baraka, Creeley, or Diane di Prima that adopt the diction and phrasing of hipsterism. Such poems helped introduce new tones into contemporary poetry, tones that emerged from historically specific subcultures to circulate textually and become available to everyone (Lee 2010).

Just as O'Hara, in spite of the broad range of poems he produced in a relatively short career, is best known for his "I do this, I do that" poems, Creeley – whose influence as a poet, teacher, and editor lasted from the 1950s until his death in 2005 – is most often associated with the short, innovative, and unsettling lyrics of early books like *For Love: Poems 1950–1960* (1962). These famously minimalist poems echo various literary sources, from Thomas Campion to Williams, Pound, and fellow Black Mountain poets like Olson, Duncan, and Levertov. They were shaped as well, and pulled closer to the Beat poets with whom Creeley was also friendly, by his constant listening to jazz records, particularly to those of Charlie Parker. "Listening to him play," he once remarked,

> I found [Parker] lengthened the experience of time, or shortened it, gained a very subtle experience of "weight," all some decision made within the context of what was called "improvisation" – but what I should rather call the experience of possibility within the limits of his materials (sounds and durations) and their environment.

> (quoted in Mackey 1993: 9)

As is clear from this quote, the angularity and abrupt changes in pace of Parker's saxophone runs helped Creeley rethink lyric approaches to time. They suggested rhythmic techniques that might be applied poetically, means of creating pauses, hesitations, and ambiguities and setting them against the forward movement of a poem's argument and imagery. The improvisation invoked here is different from the more literal spontaneity implied in O'Hara's "dashing . . . poems off at odd moments," whether at home, in his office, or on the Staten Island Ferry on the way to a reading (Ashbery 1971: vii). More important for Creeley than any pure or literal performance of spontaneity was the sense of a poem's form emerging immanently, in response to its own materials and environment. Creeley arranged the words of his poems with remarkable rhythmic and visual precision, inviting them to respond as dynamically as possible to his mood, surroundings, personal circumstances, or philosophical preoccupations. As Charles Altieri has perceptively suggested, Creeley's poetry is personal enough – in its representations of love, marriage, infidelity, sexual desire, loneliness, and psychological distress – to be compared to the confessional poetry of Lowell or Sylvia Plath. Creeley, however, does not "pursue the imaginary as a set of images for the self," fully formed though psychically divided, as it might appear in Plath, so much as he strives "to express the sensory level at which the imaginary takes hold" in the first place (Altieri 2006: 181–2).

One experiences the rhythmic and imaginative effects Creeley derived from Parker and manifested poetically in one of his most famous poems, "I Know a Man." "As I sd to my / friend," the poem begins, before interrupting itself so that the speaker can comment on his own penchant for continuous chatter. This interruption signals the poem's status as both a conversational digression and a set of rhythmic responses – starts and stops, accents and pauses – to the anxious impression that, as the speaker puts it, "the darkness sur- / rounds us." At the center of the poem, the speaker expresses a vague but overwhelming pessimism about the forces that enclose and constrain him and wonders what might be done in response. Creeley's radical line-breaks splinter and energize this pessimism, giving new weight and strangeness to the poem's familiar diction and often colloquial phrasing. "[W]hat," the speaker asks his friend about the "darkness,"

> can we do against
> it, or else, shall we &
> why not, buy a goddamn big car

(Creeley 1982: 132)

In a gesture of futility or perhaps just for the liberating fun of it, Creeley's speaker contemplates giving in to the exaggerated materialism one can only assume is part of the "darkness": why shouldn't he, he wonders, just "buy a . . . big car" and enjoy himself? Before his rambling can continue, however, his friend interrupts to insist that he pay closer attention to the other decisions he should be making – to the car he may be driving at that moment, for instance, and driving quite poorly.

"I Know a Man" plays games with the countercultural positions of postwar experimental writing: the exuberant vagueness of some of its critiques of dominant culture, its embrace – as in the Beat romance with hopping trains or into a car – of some of that culture's most powerful symbols and commodities, its turn to intimacy and spontaneous conversation in response to the pressures of cold war social life, which seemed to demand conformity and punish dissent. The poem raises doubts about the effects of spontaneity, worrying that an aesthetics of what Ginsberg called "first-thought-best-thought" improvisation can become mindless, isolating, or counterproductive. As Michael Davidson has suggested in an illuminating reading of the poem as an expression of the "Beat 'ethos'" of the 1950s and 1960s, "I Know a Man" captures an aspect of Beat literature that is often overlooked: "the recognition of solitude and vulnerability" that haunts the Beats' commitment to "communalism" and to ongoing, organic "participation" in the world (Davidson 1989: 63–4; see also Saul 2003: 56–7).

None of these ironies and complications, however, mean that the poem has given up on the aesthetic of improvisation Creeley learned from long hours spent listening to jazz. On the contrary, these ironies add a level of precision and self-awareness to an approach frequently criticized for its willingness to court sloppiness or incoherence. How well does the speaker really know his friend, whom he calls "John" though this "was not his / name"? And how does "drive" function in the poem, as a theme or even as an individual word and element of syntax? As careful readers of the poem will tell you, "drive" can be read as extending and punctuating the speaker's desire to buy a car, or, on the contrary, as the beginning of his friend's interjection and demand that the speaker watch out where he's going. The syntactical and structural ambiguities of "I Know a Man" thus make it difficult to read as a confident endorsement of hip conversation or countercultural community, as if Creeley's poem were admitting that the culture of spontaneity doesn't have all the answers. Rather, it is *through* such self-reflexive hesitations that the poem demonstrates most forcefully its embrace of immanent, improvisational, process-based art.

Improvisational procedures, to return to Creeley's reflections on listening to Charlie Parker, forced him to confront "the experience of possibility within the limits of his [own artistic] materials." With enormous intensity and impact, Creeley's early poems explore the possibilities of compression, elision, lineation; his short stanzas and abrupt line breaks separate thoughts into discrete parts and create jagged, angular, oddly rhythmical compositions, reimagining the poetic tradition in the image of Parker or Thelonious Monk. This is just as true of poems that make no apparent reference to jazz, including well-known poems like "For Love" or "The Whip," as it is of poems, like "Stomping with Catullus," "Jack's Blues" or "Chasing the Bird," that invoke jazz improvisation directly (Friedlander 2008: 11–16). In such poems, as in "I Know a Man," one watches in awe as Creeley's improvisational procedures zoom in and then expand outwards, trying to imagine how poetry might help us pay closer attention to our own social and perceptual lives, our own "contradictory states of feeling" (Davidson 1989: 64).

V. After The New American Poetry

My discussions thus far have hardly exhausted the topic of spontaneous aesthetics or touched upon all the poets producing notable and mesmerizing experimental work during the 1950s and 1960s. A longer essay might free itself from American contexts to trace the global movements of these poets, or cross generic boundaries to consider ideas of spontaneity and improvisation as they inflect avant-garde theatre or the experimental prose of Kerouac, William Burroughs, or Thomas Pynchon. There is more to say about the various and sometimes contradictory opinions New American poets held about language and politics, or about the pleasures and dissatisfactions of affiliating oneself with a particular group of poets. Levertov, di Prima, and Guest all embraced experimental forms while criticizing the gender politics that seemed endemic to the avant-garde communities of the era. Olson carried a Poundian critique of mass and popular culture into the postwar moment, while Baraka quoted radio programs and the New York School poets never tired of going to the movies. Duncan's visionary erudition and embrace of tradition cut against the vernacular hipness that characterized so many of the poets he encountered in San Francisco. Though these tensions and disagreements all deserve fuller exploration, I want to close here by funneling them into a brief discussion of two potential continuations of the open forms and improvisational aesthetics of the 1950s and 1960s: that of L=A=N=G=U=A=G=E poetry (see Bernstein, this volume) and the movement toward ethnic or identity-based poetries (feminist, Black Arts, Native American, Chicano, gay and lesbian) in the 1970s (see Friedman, this volume, and Nielsen, this volume).

These two movements have often been set in opposition to one another or taken to represent two different elements of postmodernism (see McHale, this volume) – its unstable textuality and embrace of cultural particularity, as it were. Ethnic poetries, the argument goes, offered immediate meditations on the experience of social exclusion and celebrated emergent, identity-based communities. They most often operated in a free-verse, confessional mode, which made personal speech poetic in an attempt to move or confront the reader. L=A=N=G=U=A=G=E poets, even when sharing the explicit political goals of such poems, opposed the increasing uniformity of this speakerly, expressivist mode. Resisting hierarchy on the level of form, L=A=N=G=U=A=G=E poets worked to undermine the overlapping fictions of coherent subjectivity, authentic speech, and writing as a vehicle for transmitting a set of experiences that self-evidently precede it. Refusing "closure," or the narrowing of meaning that occurs when all poetic elements (narrative, grammatical, symbolic) point "towards a single reading," they instead imagined each line, sentence, stanza, or paragraph as a "meaning generating event," as "maximally open" as possible (Bernstein 2001: 35–6; Hejinian 2000: 42–3).

In spite of these differences, L=A=N=G=U=A=G=E poetry and ethnic poetries share a great deal, not least their resistance to hierarchy, investments in underground publishing, cultivation of local writing communities, and extension of a poetics of improvisation. Nor is it difficult, as this brief catalogue suggests, to see how both movements drew upon and expanded *The New American Poetry*. One movement continued to make the personal political, inhabiting vernacular, powerfully subjective, explicitly countercultural voices as a means of creating immediate poetic effects while opposing the social insults and inequalities of patriarchy, white supremacy, homophobia. Another explored the gaps, disruptions in syntax, and discrete linguistic particularities we find in Creeley; or the tendency in long poems by O'Hara to dissolve personality into the free flow of sound and imagery and the play of multiple voices, contexts, affective registers. As many L=A=N=G=U=A=G=E poets have argued, their experiments were always political as well as textual; like the ethnic and multicultural poetries of the 1970s, they saw themselves extending the cultural politics of the 1960s (Watten 2002). Responding differently to the crises of the Vietnam era, ethnic and language-centered poetries thus spent the 1970s and 1980s exploring two different, though not unrelated, countercultural aesthetics. Poets like Ashbery, Ginsberg, Baraka, Levertov, and Creeley lived on, joining in these explorations while continuing to chart their own courses. Reckless, contradictory, and full of improvisational force, Beat, Black Mountain, and New York School poetries continued to exert their influence.

References

Allen, D. (1999 [1960]) *The New American Poetry: 1945–1960*, Berkeley, CA: University of California Press.

Altieri, C. (2006) *The Art of Twentieth-Century American Poetry: Modernism and After*, Malden, MA: Blackwell Publishing.

Ashbery, J. (1971) "Introduction," *The Collected Poems of Frank O'Hara*, ed. D. Allen, Berkeley, CA: University of California Press.

—— (1989) "The Invisible Avant-Garde," in *Reported Sightings: Art Chronicles, 1957–87*, New York: Knopf, pp. 389–95.

—— (2004) "Writers and Issues: Frank O'Hara's Question," in *Selected Prose*, ed. E. Richie, Ann Arbor, MI: University of Michigan Press, pp. 80–3.

Baraka, A. (1997 [1984]) *The Autobiography of LeRoi Jones*, Chicago, IL: Lawrence Hill Books.

Belgrad, D. (1998) *The Culture of Spontaneity: Improvisation and the Arts in Postwar America*, Chicago, IL: University of Chicago Press.

Bernstein, C. (2001) *Content's Dream: Essays 1975–1984*, Evanston, IL: Northwestern University Press.

Breslin, J. (1984) *From Modern to Contemporary: American Poetry, 1945–1965*, Chicago, IL: University of Chicago Press.

Clay, S. and P. Phillips (1998) *A Secret Location on the Lower East Side: Adventures in Writing, 1960–1980*, New York: The New York Public Library and Granary Books.

Creeley, R. (1982) *The Collected Poems of Robert Creeley 1945–1975*, Berkeley, CA: University of California Press.

Damon, M. (1993) *The Dark End of the Street: Margins in American Vanguard Poetry*, Minneapolis, MN: University of Minnesota Press.

Davidson, M. (1989) *The San Francisco Renaissance: Poetics and Community at Mid-century*, New York: Cambridge University Press.

—— (2003) *Guys Like Us: Citing Masculinity in Cold War Poetics*, Chicago, IL: University of Chicago Press.

Di Prima, D. (1973) "Introduction," *The Floating Bear: A Newsletter*, La Jolla, CA: Laurence McGilvery.

—— (2002) *Recollections of My Life as a Woman: The New York Years*, New York: Penguin.

Duberman, M. (1988) *Black Mountain: An Exploration in Community*, Gloucester, MA: Peter Smith.

Epstein, A. (2006) *Beautiful Enemies: Friendship and Postwar American Poetry*, New York: Oxford University Press.

Friedlander, B. (2008) "Introduction" to Robert Creeley's *Selected Poems, 1945–2005*, Berkeley, CA: University of California Press.

Ginsberg, A. (1984) *Collected Poems, 1947–1980*, New York: Harper and Row.

Golding, A. (1995) *From Outlaw to Classic: Canons in American Poetry*, Madison, WI: University of Wisconsin Press.

—— (1998) "The New American Poetry Revisited, Again," *Contemporary Literature*, 39(2): 180–211.

Gooch, B. (1993) *City Poet: The Life and Times of Frank O'Hara*, New York: Knopf.

Gray, T. (2006) *Gary Snyder and the Pacific Rim: Creating Counter-Cultural Community*, Iowa City, IA: University of Iowa Press.

Hejinian, L. (2000) *The Language of Inquiry*, Berkeley, CA: University of California Press.

Johnson, R. and N. Grace (2002) *Girls Who Wore Black: Women Writing the Beat Generation*, New Brunswick, NJ: Rutgers University Press.

Kane, D. (2003) *All Poets Welcome: The Lower East Side Poetry Scene in the 1960s*, Berkeley, CA: University of California Press.

Lee, B. (2010) "Avant-Garde Poetry as Subcultural Practice: Mailer's and di Prima's Hipsters," *New Literary History*, 41: 775–94.

LeSueur, J. (2003) *Digressions on Some Poems by Frank O'Hara*, New York: Farrar, Straus and Giroux.

Mackey, N. (1993) *Discrepant Engagement: Dissonance, Cross-Culturality, and Experimental Writing*, New York: Cambridge University Press.

Moten, F. (2003) *In the Break: The Aesthetics of the Black Radical Tradition*, Minneapolis, MN: University of Minnesota Press.

Nelson, M. (2007) *Women, The New York School, and Other True Abstractions*, Iowa City, IA: University of Iowa Press.

Nielsen, A. (1997) *Black Chant: Languages of African-American Postmodernism*, New York: Cambridge University Press.

O'Hara, F. (1995 [1971]) *The Collected Poems of Frank O'Hara*, ed. D. Allen, Berkeley, CA: University of California Press.

Olson, C. (1979) *Muthologos: The Collected Lectures and Interviews*, Vol. II, ed. G. Butterick, Bolinas, CA: Four Seasons Foundation.

Perloff, M. (1998 [1977]) *Frank O'Hara: Poet Among Painters*, Chicago, IL: University of Chicago Press.

Saul, S. (2003) *Freedom Is, Freedom Ain't: Jazz and the Making of the Sixties*, Cambridge, MA: Harvard University Press.

Shaw, L. (2006) *Frank O'Hara: The Poetics of Coterie*, Iowa City, IA: University of Iowa Press.

Watten, B. (2002) "The Turn to Language and the 1960s," *Critical Inquiry* 29: 139–83.

Williams, W.C. (1988) *The Collected Poems of William Carlos Williams*, Vol. II, ed. A. W. Litz and C. MacGowan, New York: New Directions.

7

THE *NOUVEAU ROMAN* AND *TEL QUEL*

Danielle Marx-Scouras

I. Introduction

The literary journal *Tel Quel* was founded in the spring of 1960 by a group of relatively unknown writers in their mid-twenties, only one of whom, Philippe Sollers, would remain on board until its dissolution in 1982. The following year, Sollers took his journal from the Seuil publishing house to Gallimard, where *Tel Quel* became *L'Infini*.

In just a few years, *Tel Quel* managed to become one of the most influential literary journals, shaping French intellectual thought and writing for two decades. It published the most innovative, prominent writers and intellectuals of its time, such as Roland Barthes, Georges Bataille, Michel Foucault, Jean-Pierre Faye, Gérard Genette, Jacques Derrida, Tzvetan Todorov, Julia Kristeva, and Marcelin Pleynet. The cultural politics of the journal were shaped as much by the historical events of the era as they were by theoretical advances in literary studies, semiotics, philosophy, and psychoanalysis.

Although *Tel Quel* officially parted ways with the *nouveau roman* (new novel) at the Cerisy colloquium of September 1963, moderated, in part, by Foucault, the influence of this literary current on the journal was significant. *Tel Quel* would probably have never been a journal of both theory and creative writing – refusing, in fact, often to differentiate between the two – had it not been for the ground-breaking work of new novelists such as Alain Robbe-Grillet, Natalie Sarraute, Michel Butor, Claude Simon, Claude Ollier, and Jean Ricardou, who would be interviewed by and published in *Tel Quel* from 1960 to 1964. Of these, Ricardou would remain with *Tel Quel* until 1971.

If *Tel Quel* was "a radical advance on and a critique of the nouveau roman" (Heath 1972: 216), this was because of historical circumstances. The new novel had to establish itself in a very adverse ideological climate, characterized by a theoretical void (Ricardou 1973: 64). *Tel Quel*, on the other hand, benefited from the weakening hold of existentialism and Sartrean *engagement* on French culture (Ricardou 1973: 64; see

Gavins, this volume). By attacking the notion that literature passively reflects social practice, the theory and practice of the *nouveau roman* contributed to the demise of engagement. The critique of the "ideology of the text as reflection" (*Tel Quel*) inevitably led to an awareness of language per se, at a time when semiotics and Lacanian psychoanalysis were emerging as disciplines. As a result, language was no longer considered a mere instrument or decoration, but rather a sign and a truth (Barthes 1987 [1966]: 66). Everything affected by language was thus called into question: philosophy, literature, and the social sciences (Barthes 1987 [1966]: 66).

II. The cultural politics of Minuit

The *nouveau roman* and *Tel Quel* were a literary response to the Manichaean oppositions of the post- and Cold-War years, in which philosophy and literature were subject to a political stranglehold. In the 1960 preface to *Signs*, Maurice Merleau-Ponty argued that there had been a political mania among philosophers, which had produced neither effective politics nor good philosophy (Merleau-Ponty 1964 [1960]: 6). The same holds true for literature: if it was not politically engaged, it was immediately viewed as reactionary by French existentialists and Marxists. For Jean-Paul Sartre, "pure" literature – or what we commonly refer to as "art for art's sake" – was a delusion that reinforced the most conservative social forces. "If literature is not *everything*, it is worth nothing. This is what I mean by 'commitment'": in stating this, Sartre was practically suggesting that literature had to be everything *but itself* (Sartre 1974: 13–14). The alternative was to be either "revolutionary" without "literature," or – since "literature" is "bourgeois" – conservative (Sollers 1968: 398). It was as though literature were, in and of itself, reactionary.

In an interview granted to *Tel Quel* in 1963, the new novelist Alain Robbe-Grillet maintained that Sartrean engagement and Aragonian socialist realism were contrary to the practice of literature (Robbe-Grillet 1963: 39–40). Socialist realism, synonymous with Zhdanovism, presupposed the absolute subordination of art and literature to political ends. Since content necessarily preceded form, for Stalin, formal innovation was considered suspect. Robbe-Grillet's conception of literature was shared not only by apolitical aesthetes such as the founding members of *Tel Quel*, but also by a new generation of Communist militants who felt that it was impossible to be "modern" in literature *and* "militant" in politics. In 1986, the former Communist militant, Jacques Henric, who joined *Tel Quel* in 1971, argued that, unlike the avant-garde writers who had preceded them, the Telquelians never sacrificed their literary and artistic convictions to the political slaughterhouse in the name of false gods like Stalin and Zhdanov (Henric 1986). Like Louis Aragon, who had abandoned the surrealists for the Communist party and Stalinism, Sartre too, in the postwar years, sacrificed literature in the name of politics. Instead of elaborating the doubt regarding the redemptive role he had accorded to the writer, Sartre merely shifted it to the terrain of the intellectual (Lyotard 1986: xi). This type of intellectual, whom Roland Barthes preferred to call an *écrivant* (writer), was a direct descendant of the eighteenth-century revolutionary figure who appropriated language for political means. Such a writer "posits a goal (to give evidence, to explain, to instruct), of which language is merely a means; for him language supports a *praxis*, it does not constitute one" (Barthes 1972: 144, 147). Barthes opposes this type of writer to the *écrivain* (author), for whom writing is an intransitive activity, fusing the creative and critical functions of language.

Barthes maintains that Sartre answered the question "What is literature?" "from the outside, which gives him an ambiguous literary position" (Barthes 1972: 98). Although Sartrean engagement accounted for the social context of literature, it nevertheless failed to free language from an idealist framework where it is considered a mere instrument or ornament. For the engaged writer, language is essentially instrumental: words are "useful conventions, tools which gradually wear out and which one throws away when they are no longer serviceable" (Sartre 1949: 13). Style must pass unnoticed: "Since words are transparent and since the gaze looks through them, it would be absurd to slip in among them some panes of rough glass" (Sartre 1949: 25). In reducing language to an instrument and discarding style as excess, the committed writer fails to take language seriously. Unlike Sartre, the new novelists and Telquelians would remain as close as possible to the literary object by raising "the fundamental problems of language, without which [literature] would not exist" (Barthes 1986: 21).

Literature would continue to have a secondary status so long as it remained subordinate to politics or aesthetics – that is, insofar as language was reduced to being "the convenient instrument or sumptuous décor of a social, emotional or poetic 'reality' which pre-exists it and which it is responsible, in a subsidiary way, for expressing, provided it abides by a few rules of style" (Barthes 1986: 4). If, for Sartrean engagement, man is *Homo significans*, "it is not because he speaks, but because he exists. Meaning is the characteristic medium of his life, not the effect of his speech" (Hollier 1986: 59). Contrasting postwar literary concerns with those of the early 1960s, Foucault contended that the "humanist" literature of the 1940s and 1950s was essentially a literature of signification (What is the meaning of man? of the world?). Then came "something very different, almost resistant to meaning, which is the sign, or language itself" (*Tel Quel* 1964: 38).

The preoccupation with language during the late 1950s and early 1960s was not necessarily an act of political disengagement. According to Barthes, "The origin of semiology was political for me. Weary of the immobile, oratorical character of ideological denunciations, I glimpsed with bedazzlement, in reading Saussure (it was in 1956), that there could be an elegant method (as one says of a solution to a mathematical problem) for analyzing social symbols, class distinctions, and ideological cunning" (Barthes 1974: 28). For Kristeva, the formalist reaction of the late 1950s and early 1960s, exemplified both by structuralist theory and the practice of the *nouveau roman*, served to purge "that subjective or rhetorical edema that our parents had set up to protect themselves against the devastating suffering of wars, or that they had used to construct their martyrdom." It was, she argues, a reaction against the romantic, grandiloquent, and pathetic rhetoric of the postwar years (Kristeva 1984: 263).

Language had supplanted History, which had been a revolutionary concept in the nineteenth century and a watchword for an entire generation of writers and intellectuals who came of age in the 1930s and into prominence in the postwar years (Foucault cited in *Tel Quel* 1964: 77). The disciplines of semiotics, psychoanalysis, and ethnology were repeatedly accused of undermining philosophical and historical thought – the hegemonic disciplines of the postwar years. Highly critical of Foucault's *The Order of Things* (1966/1973), Sartre proclaimed that

> Foucault gives the people what they needed: an eclectic synthesis in which Robbe-Grillet, structuralist linguistics, Lacan and Tel Quel are systematically utilized to demonstrate the impossibility of historical reflection. Behind history, of course, it is Marxism which is attacked. The task is to come up with a new ideology: the latest barrier that the bourgeoisie once again can erect against Marx.
>
> (Sartre 1971: 110)

The theoretical advances in the various intellectual disciplines were actually facilitated by a concrete, historical reality – the "Stalinist truth" – which could no longer be ignored after the events of 1956. After Khrushchev's indictment of Stalin at the Twentieth Soviet Party Congress, the invasion of Hungary by Soviet troops, and the Polish October, French intellectuals could no longer contain the doubts that had plagued them since the early 1950s. Although Sartre proclaimed, in 1960, that Marxism remained "the unsurpassable horizon of our time," he was forced to concede that as an official state doctrine, "Marxism was at a standstill" (Sartre 1960: 29, 25, respectively). Many French left-wing intellectuals turned to the Algerian revolution (1954–1962) and to Third Worldism (*tiersmondisme*) as a means of salvaging Marxist thought through praxis. Others used the paradigm shift of this period to cast new light on Marxist thought, by deconstructing it from within.

For example, Edgar Morin's journal *Arguments* (1956–1962), which was housed at the Editions de Minuit publishing house in Paris, deconstructed the monolithic dogmatism of Stalinism that had clouded French intellectual thought in the early 1950s (and would continue to do so until the mid-1970s when Soviet dissidence was finally taken seriously in France), undertaking a pluri-dimensional revision of all aspects of political and cultural life in France. The Editions de Minuit itself, which began as a clandestine venture in 1941, during the German Occupation of France, managed to house two key journals, not only *Arguments* but also *Critique* (and theirrespective book series), as well as the apolitical *nouveau roman*, while publishing a number of the most controversial texts pertaining to the Algerian war, most of which were censored by the French government. In fact, Marguerite Duras's new novel *Moderato Cantabile* was published at the same time as Henri Alleg's celebrated denunciation of French torture in Algeria, *The Question* (1958). According to Anne Simonin, Minuit had "a subversive publishing strategy: one in the literary domain, the other in the political sphere, thus assuring the temporal coincidence of an aesthetic and political avant-gardism within the same publishing house. The genres co-exist but do not mix" (Simonin 1991: 236).

Minuit could never be accused of being a right-wing publisher. Beginning with Jean Bruller's *The Silence of the Sea*, published under the pseudonym of Vercors, which circulated in a clandestine manner in October 1942, Minuit subsequently published twenty works, under pseudonyms, by established authors such as Paul Eluard, André Gide, Jacques Maritain, Jean Paulhan, François Mauriac, and Aragon. They also published a translation of John Steinbeck's *The Moon Is Down* [*Nuits noires*]. In the wake of this initial Resistance sprit, they went on to publish *Premier combat* (1947) by the noted Resistance fighter Jean Moulin (1947); *La Rose blanche* (1955), by Inge Scholl, the sister of Sophie and Hans Scholl, who were executed in 1943 Nazi Germany for their participation in the non-violent resistance group, the White Rose (this publication would not appear in English until 1970); *Un camp très ordinaire* (1957), by Resistance fighter Micheline Maurel, who spent almost two years at Ravensbrück concentration camp; *Night* by Elie Wiesel (1958); the re-edition of *L'Univers concentrationnaire* by David Rousset (1965); and the series *Auschwitz et après*, by Charlotte Delbo (1970).

During the Algerian war (1954–1962), Minuit once again assumed the subversive role they had played during the Occupation. They published a number of key texts in opposition to the war, in addition to Alleg's *The Question*. These include: Jacques Vergès and Georges Arnaud's *Pour Djamila Bouhired*, prefaced by Simone de Beauvoir (1957), the testimony of an Algerian bomb carrier, raped and tortured by the French, and *L'Affaire Audin* (1958), the story of a French mathematician tortured to death in Algeria. These works clearly demonstrate the complicity of French political forces with respect to military actions in Algeria. In 1972, Pierre Vidal-Naquet's *La Torture dans la République* appeared. The publishing houses of Minuit, Maspero and Seuil (which housed *Tel Quel*) became synonymous with intellectual resistance during the Algerian war.

With the Sartrean notion of engaged writing under suspicion in the mid- and late 1950s, a new form of writing that might have been viewed as right-wing during the Occupation or in the immediate postwar years was legitimated as experimental under the Minuit seal. Jerôme Lindon (who took over Minuit's direction in 1948) was very committed to literature per se; he would repeatedly state that without Samuel Beckett (whose works, previously rejected by numerous publishers, began appearing at Minuit in 1950), Minuit would never have existed. Lindon believed that style translated a moral position and that form could not be disassociated from ethics. Political directions never dictated literary, philosophical, or social science directions at Minuit (*Le Monde* 2001). Robbe-Grillet could thus state in 1957 that commitment for the new novelist now implied "full awareness of the present problems of his own language, the conviction of their extreme importance, the desire to solve them from within" (Robbe-Grillet 1965: 41).

Robbe-Grillet's early novels and screenplays were deliberately devoid of any political content. He did not allude to the Algerian war in his screenplay, *L'année dernière à Marienbad* [*Last Year in Marienbad*] (1961). This was not necessarily an apolitical stance on his part. His association with the politicized Alain Resnais and with Minuit was already indicative of liberal political leanings. Furthermore, in September 1960, he signed, along with other intellectuals such as Simone de Beauvoir, Francois Châtelet, Henri Lefebvre, Sartre, and Duras, the "Manifesto of the 121," a manifesto in opposition to the Algerian war, which was a declaration of the right of insubordination and an act of civil disobedience. Although endorsed by Sartre's journal *Les Temps Modernes*, the manifesto was condemned by the Communist and Socialist parties.

By refusing to refer to the Algerian war in *Marienbad*, Robbe-Grillet was not simply being apolitical; he was defending the responsibility of forms that would become the leitmotiv of writers and theoreticians during the 1960s. Had he alluded to Algeria in his screenplay, he would have conceded that the only way to be revolutionary in literature was to write about class struggle or anti-colonialist war. Unwilling to accept the engaged notion that literature had to focus on a certain content, Robbe-Grillet repeatedly subverted this content with a narrative technique that prevented a story from being told and that attempted to suspend meaning: a technique characterized by endless repetitions, lacunae, and interior duplications (*mises en abyme*; see McHale, this volume). He contended that the subordination of form to content led to a socialist realism that was merely a revolutionary parody of nineteenth-century (Balzacian) bourgeois realism.

III. New novel, new criticism

The *nouveau roman* was less a literary school or movement than a sociological phenomenon (Barthes 1972: 161) of the 1950s associated with the Editions de Minuit. In fact, Robbe-Grillet became the literary consultant at Minuit (from 1955–1985) and played a large role in bringing the other writers to this publisher. The term *nouveau roman* gained currency in 1957 thanks to the Academician Emile Henriot, who used the expression in his review of Robbe-Grillet's *La Jalousie* [*Jealousy*] (1957) and Sarraute's *Tropismes* [*Tropisms*] (1939/1957) in *Le Monde* (22 May 1957). Minuit would adopt the term in 1958. The *nouveau roman* was also commonly referred to as *l'école du regard* (the school of the gaze) because of its so-called objective description, devoid of traditional psychology. In addition to *La Jalousie* and a re-edition of *Tropismes*, Butor's *La Modification* [*A Change of Heart*] and Simon's *Le Vent* [*The Wind*] appeared in 1957. The following year, Ollier's *La Mise en scène* [*The Mise-en-Scene*], Simon's *L'Herbe* [*The Grass*], and Duras's *Moderato cantabile* were published. These novels were characterized by the disappearance of the traditional character, the deconstruction of plot, formal experimentation with space and time, the critique of realism and psychology, the re-examination of author/reader relationships, and a new use of description.

Roland Barthes, who would subsequently be associated with *Tel Quel*, was one of the earliest advocates of Robbe-Grillet and journals such as *Esprit* (1958) and *Yale French Studies* (1959) were among the first to devote special issues to this new literary phenomenon. Barthes wrote four pioneering essays on Robbe-Grillet, three of which appeared in the Minuit journals *Arguments* and *Critique*, beginning in July 1954. *Critique*, founded by Bataille in 1946, began appearing at Minuit in 1950. Its objective was to publish critical reviews of books and articles published in France and abroad, covering all disciplines, including literary studies, politics, philosophy, the sciences, and accessible to a broad public. *Critique* sought to move beyond both journalistic and highly specialized journals. Both a journal and a book series, it published such authors as Gilles Deleuze and Félix Guattari, Luce Irigaray, Emmanuel Levinas, Jean-François Lyotard, Michel Serres, Derrida, and Bataille.

If we consider the objectives of *Critique* both in light of the *nouveau roman* and Barthes's leading role as a representative of the "new criticism," we easily discern a strategy at Minuit aimed at subverting not only knowledge but also the very sites that produce it. With respect to literary criticism, these would be the university and the press, which were both opposed to the new novel and new criticism. Robbe-Grillet, in fact, would take advantage of the notoriety the new novel acquired in the media by assuming an adversarial position in the French weekly *L'Express*, where he responded with a series of nine manifesto essays under the rubric "Literature Today," which appeared from October 1955 to February 1956. A few years later, *Tel Quel* adopted a rubric of the very same name to interview writers and critics such as Barthes, Robbe-Grillet, Sarraute, Butor, and Cayrol. *Tel Quel* also published a "Survey on Criticism" which foresaw the day when criticism would no longer have literature as its object, for literature would have criticism as its object (Genette 1963: 71). In challenging the traditional opposition between the writer and the critic, *Tel Quel* was attempting to define a new notion of writing necessarily uniting the creative and critical functions of language. Like the new novel, *Tel Quel* came into its own at a time when writers were not yet expected to account critically for what they did, and critics were not supposed to "write." The "worn-out myth of the '*superb creator and the humble servant, both necessary, each in his place*'" (Barthes 1987: 64) was still quite visible in the Barthes–Picard polemic of 1965–1966.

If Robbe-Grillet's essays in *L'Express* were a strategic response to journalistic literary critics unable to accept fiction as self-referential and critical of its own procedures, including those of plot, character, and more importantly literary realism, Barthes's *On Racine* (1963) and *Criticism and Truth* (1966) symbolized the avant-garde's attack on the university bastion, guarded by Raymond Picard, the author of *Nouvelle critique ou nouvelle imposture* (1965). Picard's scholarly work on Racine had earned him a chair in French literature at the Sorbonne. With no institutional territory of his own, Barthes nonetheless dared to confront the university; furthermore, by employing semiotics and psychoanalysis in his critical discourse, Barthes challenged the way academic criticism safeguarded a classical author like Racine.

The polemic over the "new criticism," which, like the "new novel" also took place in the press, revealed how literature is linked to institutional power and the monopoly of knowledge. The vocabulary of execution pervading the attacks on Barthes clearly revealed the importance attributed to literature in ideological struggles: "It's an execution," wrote a journalist for the Catholic national daily, *La Croix*; for the *Revue de Paris*, it was the "Pearl Harbor of New Criticism." Summing up the critics and journalists, Barthes wrote, "People have dreamed of *wounding* new criticism, *pricking* its pretensions, *assaulting* it, *murdering* it, dragging it before the *criminal courts*, setting it in the *pillory* or putting it on the *scaffold*" (Barthes 1987: 30–1).

Two of Barthes's three essays, which initially fueled the polemic, appeared in English translation in *The Times Literary Supplement* and *Modern Language Notes* in 1963. In his response to these essays, which was published in *Le Monde* (14 March 1964, p. 12) Picard contended that the "University never responds" but the attacks against academic criticism have become so "dangerous" that a response is warranted. Picard assumes that the University, which he deliberately capitalizes, is untouchable and should not have to participate in mundane, temporal disputes. Nonetheless, he deems it necessary to speak out in France's leading daily. Picard essentially disputes Barthes's claim that the university, as a bastion of the literary institution and a seat of uncontested knowledge, has not evolved. Note that this polemic took place just a few years before May 1968, which led to the de-centralization of the French university and consequently of knowledge. However, Paris IV (or the Sorbonne) would remain the most conservative faculty in literary studies even after May 1968.

Despite Picard's claims that academic criticism was objective and neutral, Barthes insisted that a critical method was always a function of a philosophy, ideology, or worldview. Even Lansonism, which derived from nineteenth-century positivism, was ideology "smuggled into the baggage of scientism like contraband merchandise" (Barthes 1972: 257). In criticizing the determinist nature of Lansonism, which continued to permeate academic criticism in the 1960s, Barthes, first of all, objected to a method of inquiry that focused too heavily on the "circumstances " of the literary work and consequently espoused a partial notion of literature, for it did not really question the "being of literature," thus suggesting that the latter was eternal or "natural." According to Barthes, if "the *resemblances* of the work thus derive from the most rigorous positivism, [. . .] by a singular abdication, its *differences* derive from magic" (Barthes 1972: 251–2). In this respect, Barthes concurs with Sartre, who urged that writers cease being taken for charlatans who make people believe there is something magical about writing (Sartre 1974: 14). *Tel Quel*, too, sought to eliminate "the neoromantic eloquence that deifies the writer, making him into a creator" (Henric 1968: 67). This was clearly the objective of the new novelists and Telquelians who made no effort to conceal the very process of writing in their novels, thereby forcing the reader to be fully attentive to the workings of language, without which there would be no plot or characters, nor any sense of time or place.

Even though traditional critics – whether from *Le Monde* or the Sorbonne – objected to this sort of activity on the part of the writer – who was, in a sense, divesting the critic of his prerogative – writers like Mallarmé, Proust, and Blanchot had long recognized that "language is the very stuff of literature" (Barthes 1987: 55). Since the eve of modernity, a unification of the poetic and critical functions of language had already taken place. The distinction between poets and critics had become obsolete: "there is no longer anything but writing" (63–4). The writer could no longer "be defined in terms of his role or his value but only by a certain *awareness of discourse*" (64).

The same holds true for criticism. Employing Lansonian positivism for his methodology, the academic critic failed to account for the being of literature, dismissing it as creative genius. He also failed to apply this methodology to himself as a critic. Barthes asks:

By what miracle would the profound communication which most critics pos-tulate between the work and its author cease in relation to their own enter-prise and their own epoch? Are there laws of creation valid for the writer but not for the critic? All criticism must include in its discourse [. . .] an implicit reflection on itself; every criticism is a criticism of the work *and* a criticism of itself.

(Barthes 1972: 257)

If Barthes threatened the university, as a critic, it was because he dared to talk about language, rather than merely use it: "Discourse reflecting upon discourse is the object of a special vigilance on the part of institutions, which normally contain it within the limits of a strict code [. . .] To be subversive, the critic does not have to judge, it is enough that he talks of language instead of using it" (Barthes 1987: 33).

Sarraute contended, in 1950, that the French novel had entered "the age of suspi-cion" (Sarraute 1963 [1956]). This was not merely because the contemporary reader distrusted the fictional character, the pivot of Balzacian realism (there are between three and four thousand characters in Balzac's *oeuvre*), and the outdated literary appa-ratus that had assured its power under the guise of nineteenth-century realism. At stake in the demise of the fictional character, which a Marxist critic like Lucien Gold-mann associated with the crisis of the individual in advanced capitalist society, was also the notion of the unary subject as the last bastion of Western idealism. If "it was now so necessary to think through fiction – while in the past it was a matter of think-ing the truth," it was because the "I speak" of contemporary literature ran counter to the Cartesian "I think, therefore I am" of philosophical discourse. Foucault argues that "'I think' led to the indubitable certainty of the 'I' and its existence; 'I speak,' on the other hand, distances, disperses, effaces that existence and lets only its empty emplace-ment appear" (Foucault 1987: 12–13). "No doubt," concludes Foucault, "that is why Western thought took so long to think the being of language as if it had a premoni-tion of the danger that the naked experience of language poses for the self-evidence of 'I think.'" (Foucault 1987: 13) This explains why the Nietzschean "Who speaks?" is reiterated with urgency in the novels of Blanchot, Beckett, Sarraute, Robbe-Grillet, Duras, and Sollers. These novels are characterized by "a being devoid of outline, inde-finable, intangible and invisible, an anonymous 'I', who is at once all and nothing, and who as often as not is but the reflection of the author himself, has usurped the role of the hero, occupying the place of honour" (Sarraute 1963: 84). These works confirmed, in fictional practice, the Freudian discovery that "the position of the subject is not defined by *what* he says, nor by what he talks *about*, but by the place – unknown to him – *from which* he speaks" (Felman 1985: 50).

IV. Tel Quel and beyond

This age of suspicion of the *nouveau roman* of the 1950s and 1960s gave rise to a new theoretical discourse on language as subjective experience with *Tel Quel*. Drawing both on the formalist experimentation of the new novel and on advances in semiotic theory, *Tel Quel's* discourse on language in the mid- and late 1960s was also rooted in psychoanalytical theory. With Foucault and Lacan, *Tel Quel* no longer had to bang its head against the walls of Sartre (Kristeva 1984: 265).

In a 1977 interview, Foucault nevertheless claimed that "the whole relentless theorization of writing which we saw in the 1960s was doubtless only a swansong. Through it, the writer was fighting for the preservation of his political privilege" (Foucault 1980: 127). The search for scientific credentials in the disciplines of linguistics, semiology, and psychoanalysis and the production of mediocre literary products only proved that "the activity of the writer was no longer at the focus of things" (Foucault 1980: 127). One could say that the theorization of writing represented by the *nouveau roman* and even more so by *Tel Quel* was a way to reclaim literature in the wake of Sartrean engagement. Nonetheless, for both the *nouveau roman* and *Tel Quel*, the practice of writing always came first. Not only did the new novelists and Telquelians come to theory from their own practice of writing, they made this very practice of writing the basis for a comprehensive theory. Foucault saw the eclipse of the "great writer" in conjunction with the evolving configuration of the French intellectual. The "universal" intellectual, inaugurated by Zola and perhaps buried by Sartre, was being replaced by the organic, specific, and dissident intellectual. Foucault's notion of the specific intellectual nevertheless made it possible to reunite categories that had been previously kept separate. As "each individual's specific activity began to serve as the basis for politicization, the threshold of *writing*, as the sacralising mark of the intellectual, disappear[ed]" (Foucault 1980: 127). However, Barthes's notion of the "écrivain," for whom writing was an intransitive activity reconciling the creative and critical functions of language, is perhaps not at odds with Foucault's "specific" intellectual.

The "desacralization" of writing was not necessarily problematic, insofar as it allowed literature to be taken seriously, along with other disciplines such as linguistics, philosophy, history, ethnography, and psychoanalysis. While it is true that many Anglophone academics turned to theory in the 1970s to give themselves a privileged status over those purely interested in literature, these academics actually misread French theory, forgetting that thinkers like Foucault, Derrida, and Lacan (who even devoted an essay to Duras) were profoundly marked by literature. As for mediocre literary products, it is perhaps true that the novels of Butor, Robbe-Grillet, Ollier, and Sollers have not stood the test of time like those of Gide, Proust, and Camus. If Duras has become an icon of contemporary French literature and Simon the recipient of the 1985 Nobel Prize for literature, it is to the degree that their later works deviate from the characteristics of the new novel. Simon has been compared stylistically more to Proust and Faulkner than to the other new novelists, and his obsession with war and family histories are emphasized by critics. Duras is less remembered today for her Minuit novel, *Moderato cantabile*, than for the autobiographical writing of *L'Amant* [*The Lover*] (1984), for which she won the Goncourt prize, and *La Douleur* [*War*] (1985). In fact, many new novelists turned to autobiographical writing in the 1980s, including Sarraute (*Enfance* [*Childhood*], 1983), Robbe-Grillet (*Le Miroir qui Revient*

[*Ghosts in the Mirror*], 1984), and Simon (*L'Acacia* [*The Acacia*], 1989). In *Le Miroir qui Revient*, Robbe-Grillet claimed that critics like Barthes, who promoted his "literal" and "objective" literature, perhaps lost sight of the unconscious demons against which he and other postwar writers were struggling (Robbe-Grillet 1984: 38, 69).

By challenging traditional notions of representation and literary realism, the new novelists and Tel Quelians perhaps also helped to pave the way for autobiographical studies, which are now an integral part of the literary institution (on experimental life-writing, see Kacandes, this volume, and Elias, this volume). How ironic too that the nouveau roman was inaugurated by a detective novel, Robbe-Grillet's *Les Gommes* [*The Erasers*] (1953), and that today, in France, one out of four books published is a *polar* or detective novel. Clearly, literature is being desacralized and artificial boundaries between what constitutes autobiography and fiction, good (literature) and bad (popular) writing have been dissolved. Georges Simenon, the Belgian detective novelist is now part of the French canonical Pléiade library. Furthermore, although francophone literature may salvage the international prestige of the French language, it also forces us to redefine "Frenchness" and thus literature per se, insofar as it has joined forces with transnational modernity in the recent guise of world literature.

As for French literature, it may never quite regain the enormous prestige that it enjoyed with the creation of *La Nouvelle Revue Française* (NRF) in 1908, which led, shortly after, to the founding of the most powerful French publishing house, Gallimard. The *NRF* placed literature and the writer at the pinnacle of French culture. The supremacy of literature was bound up with the hegemony of the publishing world, which supplanted, in fact, the power of the university in French intellectual life (Debray 1981: 65–6). Despite the fall of the *NRF* in 1940 (when it came under Nazi control) and the cultural supremacy for which it stood, journals such as *Les Temps Modernes*, *Esprit*, *Critique*, *Arguments*, and *Tel Quel* would continue to be viable cultural forces in the struggle for the conquest and preservation of symbolic power in the wake of World War II. And though they lacked the prestige of Gallimard, the publishing houses of Seuil and Minuit nevertheless represented powerful sites of cultural renewal and intellectual foment from the 1950s to the 1980s. With respect to "experimental writing" per se, the *nouveau roman* and *Tel Quel* afford us the opportunity to see both in theory and practice, what Barthes (quoting Sollers 1970) referred to as a "journey across writing" that would leave its mark on the whole of French intellectual discourse during these years (Barthes 1987 [1966]: 65).

References

Barthes, R. (1972 [1964]) *Critical Essays*, trans. R. Howard, Evanston, IL: Northwestern University Press.
—— (1974) "L'aventure sémiologique," *Le Monde*, 7 June, 28.
—— (1986 [1984]) *The Rustle of Language*, trans. R. Howard, New York: Hill and Wang.
—— (1987 [1966]) *Criticism and Truth*, trans. K. Pilcher Keuneman, Minneapolis, MN: University of Minnesota Press.

Debray, R. (1981 [1979]) *Teachers, Writers, Celebrities: The Intellectuals of Modern France*, trans. D. Macey, London: NLB and Verso.

Felman, S. (1985) *Writing and Madness*, Ithaca, NY: Cornell University Press.

Foucault, M. (1980) *Power/Knowledge: Selected Interviews and Other Writings (1972–1977)*, ed. C. Gordon, New York: Pantheon.

—— (1987 [1966]) *The Thought From Outside*, trans. B. Massumi, New York: Zone Books.

Genette, G. (1963) "Enquête sur la critique," *Tel Quel* 14, 68–91.

Heath, S. (1972) *The Nouveau Roman: A Study in the Practice of Writing*, Philadelphia, PA: Temple University Press.

Henric, J. (1986) "Quand une avant-garde (littéraire) rencontre une autre avant-garde (politique) . . .," unpublished paper, 15pp.

Hollier, D. (1986 [1982]) *The Politics of Prose*, trans. J. Mehlman, Minneapolis, MN: University of Minnesota Press.

Kristeva, J. (1984) "My Memory's Hyperbole." In D. Stanton and J. Parisier Plottel (eds.), *The Female Autograph*, New York: New York Literary Forum, pp. 219–36.

Le Monde (2001) "Jérôme Lindon, cinquante ans de résistance sous l'étoile de Minuit," 13 April.

Lyotard, J.-F. (1986) "Foreword: A Success of Sartre's." In D. Hollier, *The Politics of Prose*, Minneapolis, MN: University of Minnesota Press.

Merleau-Ponty, M. (1964 [1960]) *Signs*, trans. R. McCleary, Evanston, IL: Northwestern University Press.

Picard, R. (1964) "M. Barthes et la 'Critique Universitaire'," *Le Monde*, 14 March, 12.

Ricardou, J. (1973) "Nouveau Roman: Un entretien de Jean Thibaudeau avec Jean Ricardou," *La Nouvelle Critique* 60: 62–70.

Robbe-Grillet, A. (1963) "La littérature aujourd' hui – VI," *Tel Quel* 14: 39–45.

—— (1965 [1963]) *For a New Novel*, trans. R. Howard, New York: Grove.

—— (1984) *Le Miroir Qui Revient*, Paris: Minuit.

Sarraute, N. (1963) *Tropisms and The Age of Suspicion*, trans. M. Jolas, London: John Calder.

Sartre, J.-P. (1949 [1947]) *What is Literature?* trans. B. Frechtman, New York: George Braziller.

—— (1960) *"Questions de method."* In *Critique de la raison dialectique*, Vol. 1, Paris: Gallimard.

—— (1971) "Replies to Structuralism: An Interview with Jean-Paul Sartre," *Telos* 9: 110–15.

—— (1974) *Between Existentialism and Marxism*, trans. J. Mathews, New York: Pantheon.

Simonin, A. (1991) "Les Editions de Minuit et les Editions du Seuil." In J.-P. Rioux and J.-F. Sirinelli (eds.), *La Guerre d'Algérie et les intellectuels français*, Paris: Editions Complexe.

Sollers, P. (1968) *Logiques*, Paris: Seuil.

—— (1970) "La lutte idéologique dans l'écriture de l'avant-garde," [special issue] *La Nouvelle Critique* 39a: 74–8.

Tel Quel (1964) "Une littérature nouvelle?" Décade de Cerisy, September 1963, *Tel Quel* 17.

8

LETTRISM AND SITUATIONISM

Tyrus Miller

The evolving cluster of artistic and cultural-political movements identified with the names Lettrism and Situationism created few artistic works of enduring value, either aesthetically or as collectibles in the commodified world of galleries, museums, and patrons. Their marginal status, extreme oppositional posture, anti-monumental practices, and, in their later phases, programmatically anti-art and anti-aesthetic orientation precluded a major contribution to "art" as institutionally understood. Long after their moment of contemporaneity, however, the movements' theories and overall radical stance continued to have a transformative impact on subsequent artistic and political currents. Arguably, in fact, the groups' fluctuating forms, their ensemble of playful and exploratory activities, and their experience in passing time together constituted their artistic "praxis" (as much in Aristotle's sense of an activity with its end in itself as in the Marxist sense of the term). Collective experience was the complex, distributed object of their artistry and hence their most signal artistic "work." However, one would have to immediately add the proviso that this entails a work that is not a "work" at all, but rather a playful process, a species of intransitive artistry no longer readily identifiable as "art," and thus only discernible in the limited traces of "iterated modes of group self-organization," as Astrid Vicas has described the Situationists' favored medium of activity (Vicas 1998: 381). Accordingly, the most important legacy of Lettrism and Situationism does not appear solely through the poems, visual art works, performances, and films created under these names – although these do offer significant indices of lettrist-situationist theory and practice at particular moments of the movements' development. Rather, we must also consider theoretical writings and exemplifications of technical procedures such as the refunctioning of existing texts and images (*détournement*) as possessing an "artistic" status at least equaling, if not exceeding those works that relate to recognizable artistic categories such as poetry or film, in however unconventional a fashion.

I. Lettrist beginnings

The Lettrist movement was launched by a young Romanian poet, Isidore Isou, whose combination of creative panache, autodidactic ambition, romantic good looks, and almost boundless narcissism made him an ideal figure to lead a noisy, publicity-grabbing artistic movement in the unsettled atmosphere of post-war Paris. Like Filippo Tommaso Marinetti at the outset of the Futurist movement – whose artistic and interventive practices early Lettrism rather unoriginally, if also unwittingly, reprised – Isou instinctively understood how to use calculated provocations and polemics to gain notoriety. His equally developed *parvenu* skills allowed him to capitalize on connections with establishment prestige figures such as André Gide, Jean Paulhan, and Jean Cocteau to gain a publication opening with the prestigious Gallimard house and venues for the screening of Lettrist film experiments. Soon Isou had gained a small circle of adherents, including Gabriel Pomerand, who established a "Lettrist headquarters" at the Bookstore at the Latin Gate in 1947; Maurice Lemaître, who considerably extended the range of Lettrist artistic principles in sound poetry, music, theater, and film; and Guy-Ernest Debord, who along with Gil Wolman would soon break from Isou's circle to found the more radical, more theoretically acute, and more rigorous Internationale Lettriste (1952–1957) and eventually the Internationale Situationniste (1957–1972).

A parallel movement, COBRA (an acronym signaling the home cities of the founders Asgar Jorn, Karel Appel, Corneille, and Constant: Copenhagen, Brussels, and Amsterdam), developed analogous ideas in the visual arts during the years 1949 to 1952. After receiving a copy of Debord's Lettrist International publication *Potlatch* from the painter Enrico Baj, Asgar Jorn corresponded with Debord and initiated a life-long friendship; Jorn, along with other COBRA participants such as Constant, affiliated with the early Situationist International and remained an important financial supporter and ally even after his separation from the formal movement. Isou, meanwhile, having been expelled by the Debordian radical minority from the ludicrously miniscule "Lettrist International," continued his own Lettrist activity in parallel, attempting to codify and expand his artistic, philosophical, and social speculations and to recruit new adherents to his cause. To some extent carried along by broader neo-avant-garde currents and a resurgent interest in sound poetry and performance throughout the 1960s and 1970s, Isou, despite the basic mediocrity of his turgid writing and monomaniacal speculations, was able to retain some degree of relevance as a founding influence on post-war avant-garde practices in poetry, performance, film, and visual arts. Key journals dedicated to Lettrist and Situationist artistic and political ideas included *Ion* (1952), *Internationale lettriste* (1952–1954), *Potlatch* (1954–1957), the Belgian Surrealist group's journal *Les Lèvres nues* (1954–1958), *Internationale Situationniste* (1958–1969), *Spur* (1960–1962), *Mutant* (1962), *The Situationist Times* (1962–1969), *Der deutsche Gedanke* (1963), and *Situationisk Revolution* (1970).

II. Post-Surrealist legacies

In a genealogical sense, Lettrism and Situationism were post-World War II outgrowths of Surrealism (see Stockwell, this volume), which by that time had become somewhat middle-aged and routinized, at least in the eyes of young radicals such as Isou or his still younger protégé Debord. If, however, they reacted with scorn or polemical fury against a late, senescent Surrealism that had fallen (in their view) into dogma, occultism, and mainstream canonization, they nonetheless took serious, even openly acknowledged inspiration from Surrealism's earlier ascendance in the late 1920s and early 1930s. Given the occasional violence of his polemics against the Surrealists in individual instances, for example, Debord offered a remarkably balanced and judicious view of their importance and limitations in an important programmatic essay from June 1957, "Report on the Construction of Situations and on the Terms of Organization and Action of the International Situationist Tendency," which was a document connected to the foundation of the Situationist International. In the course of a survey of avant-garde movements from Futurism to Dadaism to Surrealism, Debord suggested that the height of the movement came with its political radicalization in the 1930s, but that during its first decade Surrealism had made key advances towards a more radical conception of freedom than had previously existed:

> The surrealist program, asserting the sovereignty of desire and surprise, offering a new practice of life, is much richer in constructive possibilities than is generally thought. Certainly, the lack of material means of realization seriously limited the scope of surrealism. But the spiritualistic outcome of its first agitators, and above all the mediocrity of its epigones, oblige us to search for the negation of the development of surrealist theory in its very origin.
>
> (Debord in McDonough 2002: 33)

Surrealism's greatest weakness, Debord argues, was its faith in the fecundity of the unconscious, its belief that dreams and automatic writing and other unconscious manifestations offered an infinite source of cultural renewal, rather than a monotonous, repetitive stream of images. Resting on this romanticized idea of the unconscious, Surrealism's failure is ideological, its having abdicated engaging the spectrum of socially effective ideas and experiences in favor of a mystique of pursuing unconscious novelties and surprises. Not only does this blunt the oppositional force of Surrealism, despite the revolutionary intentions of its founders; it even makes the products of Surrealism vulnerable to appropriation by commerce, entertainment, and collection – available, in short, for "the spectacle," as Debord would later say.

Complex relations with their Surrealist precursors accompanied Lettrism from its very moment of emergence. Isou held Tristan Tzara as at once an ideal to imitate and a mimetic rival, and it was thus no accident that he chose a performance of Tzara's *La Fuite* on 8 January 1946 to create a career-launching provocation that would get the incipient Lettrist program into the papers. Following a plan scripted by Isou, his acolytes interrupted Michel Leiris's introductory remarks to call for a reading of Lettrist poetry and an exposition of the principles of this truly up-to-date avant-garde. Though the performance was eventually allowed to take place, it concluded with Isou taking the stage to declaim his writings. Maurice Nadeau, well-known as a critical advocate of Surrealism, wrote a front-page article in *Combat* entitled "The Lettrists Put Tristan Tzara to Flight" (Curtay 1974: 14–15). For their part, the breakaway "International Lettrists" Debord and Wolman published some of their most important texts of this period in the Belgian Surrealist journal *Les Lèvres nues*, with which the International Lettrists had both a tactical alliance and significant points of political and artistic convergence. In 1954, they even managed to team up briefly with veteran Surrealists André Breton and Benjamin Péret to publish a broadside attack on a bungled Rimbaud centennial tribute. This rapprochement, however, was very short lived and, as their follow-up broadside drily put it, "ended badly." Gil Wolman took responsibility for including in the broadside the following personal invective addressed to Breton:

> Breton, you are bankrupt today. Your business has for too long been
> in deficit. . . .
> > The surrealist movement is composed of imbeciles or
> > **FORGERS**
> > (Wolman, cited in Debord 2006: 165)

III. Generalized poetry

The connection of the Lettrist and Situationist movements with Surrealism runs deeper, however, than either direct influence or such polemical skirmishes would suggest. There is a more fundamental consonance and continuity between them in the extended historical trajectory of radical, politicized avant-gardes of the twentieth century. Astrid Vicas has, for instance, suggested that Tristan Tzara's 1931 "Essay on the Situation of Poetry" published in *Le surrealisme au service de la revolution*, represents a key anticipation of the radical conception of culture that the Lettrists and Situationists would elaborate. Here Tzara introduces a distinction between poetry as a means of expression, which gives rise to poems as literary products, and poetry as an activity of the mind, for which the poem is no longer an autonomous, monumental entity but rather a subordinate trace or index of a creative process, including collective factors impinging upon or entering into this "activity of the mind." Poems become models of the organization of creative collective and individual activity, and by indicating alternative ways that meaning and order may be organized, poetry may gesture beyond the aesthetic towards the political and social domains of experience. In this way, poetry need no longer be seen to be essentially limited to *language*; rather it can be viewed as an all-embracing practice of organizing creative activity, irrespective of medium. "Poetry," in other words, need not take place solely in a specific medium, but may embrace a potentially infinite range of sounds, graphisms, gestures, images, and objects, as well as its more conventional verbal means. As Vicas comments on Tzara's essay: "The form these works are to take is entirely a matter of the circumstances in which they happen to be produced. Moreover, any residue they would leave behind, whether photograph, recording, poster, or film, would serve merely as a pointer to the activity that was the occasion of their production" (Vicas 1998: 402).

This Surrealist-influenced idea of generalized poetry, which also implied the iconoclastic destruction of fixed representation whether in words or images, was foundational for Lettrism and was reiterated, in various registers and contexts, in countless Lettrist and Situationist texts. Already in the early proclamations of Lettrism, Isou framed this problem of division of experience in connection with the semantic resources of poetry, opposing the structured differences of words to the pre-differentiated matrix of letters and their corresponding sounds:

> Begin the destruction of the word in favor of letters.
> Seek to capture between letters every stimulus.
> Endeavor no longer to use apriori measures, words.
>
> (Isou, cited in Curtay 1974: 299)

Isou's pretentious pseudo-philosophical terminology ("a priori") can hardly be taken seriously; his addiction to system building and neologistic terminology would reach grotesque proportions in his later work. Yet despite their conceptual unsoundness, the precepts of Lettrism were artistically generative. Isou thus went on to expand further the generative possibilities of the letter-sound matrix by employing invented notations and rubrics, graphisms and typographical devices to restore the dynamic "non-specialized" universality of poetry that had, in his view, been constrained by the dominance of the word. Isou offered as a demonstrative example a "Poème Clos" entitled "A Girl's Tears," which incorporated Greek alphabetic characters to reference a repertoire of non-semantic sound-gestures, which complement the non-lexical combination of letter-sounds that compose the major body of the poem. I quote four lines from the text and the corresponding sound-legend in the footnotes:

> $Λ^3$o là îhî cnn vîi
> snoubidi î pnn mîi
> A^4gohà îhîhî gnn gî
> klnbidi $Δ^5$blîglîhlî

3. Λ, λ = gargarisme.
4. A, a = aspiration.
5. Δ, λ = râle.

(Isou, cited in Curtay 1974: 195)

Notable here is the error in the lower-case delta (note 5), which is erroneously printed as lambda λ instead of δ – a forgivable mistake for a young autodidact such as Isou. Yet it would also be incorrect to see the note-referenced sound-system as merely an incidental supplement to the poem, since it offers an embodied, affective parallel to the sound-poem. Both are formally structured by rhyme- and chime-structures, most notably the sound couplets in the body of the poem. Similarly, throughout the notes, the suffix "-ment" is regularly repeated, and the note 9 redundantly restates the "translation" provided in note 1 (Θ, t = soupir), thus framing the footnotes with an emotionally appropriate sigh (=soupir). The notes are not so much paratextual, then, as integral to the text itself, literally inserted between the other constitutive letter-sounds and entering into free combination with them.

Isou's practice adumbrated an ever-expanding range of new combinations of sensory elements – sonorous, performative, graphic, notational – in an increasingly non-differentiated poetic activity, which pointed beyond the limited realm of "poetry" to an aesthetically transformed practice of daily life. In many respects, however, despite the noisiness of his proclamations, Isou's artistic conceptions were quite tame, progressing little beyond a reprise of Futurist and Dadaist sound poetry of the earlier twentieth century and, even at that, lacking in the neologistic inventiveness of Vladimir Mayakovsky or Velimir Khebnikov or the sacralizing intensity of Hugo Ball or Antonin Artaud (see White, this volume, and Stockwell, this volume). As sound poet Henri Chopin notes, Lettrism in no way broke with the structural sureties of phoneticism, as both the "metapneumic" soundings of International Lettrist Gil Wolman and nascent experiments with electronically modified poetry would, in contrast, soon do (Chopin 1979: 85). From the perspective of Debord and his followers, however, the problem was not simply one of insufficient artistic radicalism – they saw this as a symptom rather than a cause – but rather predominantly an ideological and political one. Isou's conception of "unitary" or non-specialized activity remained within the specialized boundaries of art. Failing to reach into the larger social ensemble, which for the International Lettrists and Situationists was especially to be grasped in urbanism and architecture, Isou's Lettrist avant-gardism remained pre-political and lacking in theoretical grasp of the social preconditions and implications of the aesthetic revolution he sought to lead.

IV. Potlatch and post-capitalist culture

That further analytic reflection fell to the International Lettrists, with Debord as the most consistent voice and leading intellect among them. As Georges Bataille and other renegade Surrealists had done in the 1930s, Debord referred to the anthropological writings of Marcel Mauss on the "potlatch" as a way of concretizing how a post-capitalist economy might look, when the capitalist division of labor and fragmentation of experience had been overcome. "Potlatch" designates a specific practice of non-reciprocal exchange and sumptuary gift-giving among the Native Americans of the Pacific Northwest, which is nevertheless exemplary of a wide range of economic-social exchange-forms – tributes, glorious expenditures, sacrifices, destructive consumption of riches, and so on – predating capitalist exchange and contradicting its laws of equivalence. Debord would lend this name to the International Lettrist journal that appeared in thirty (brief) issues between 1954 and 1957. In the fourteenth issue, published 30 November 1954, under the title "What is Potlatch" Debord included the following playful questionnaire as a "little homage to the American way of life":

1. A Soviet spy, the main accomplice of Rosenberg, discovered in 1952 by the F.B.I.?
2. A practice of sumptuous gift-giving, calling for other gifts in return, that was the foundation of a pre-Columbian economy of America?
3. An utterance void of meaning, invented by the Lettrists for naming one of their publications?

(Debord 1996: 87)

In the next issue, they summarized the answers, taking a swipe at their critics, who "mistakenly" thought that the answer was 1 or 3:

The most widespread opinions are expressed by the third choice: *utterance void of meaning* (*Franc-Tireur*, Camus, etc.) and the first case: *Soviet spy* (*Aspects de la France*, Breton, G. Mollet, etc.). Meanwhile some of our correspondents ardently subscribe to the second choice: *sumptuary giving*.

It is thus useless to linger over this problem, as muddled as any problem that our society puts up a pretence of posing itself. And also over a solution as blinding as all the others.

(Debord 1996: 94)

Precisely this paradoxical status of the journal's title indicated its most imperative critical task: to disturb polemically the ideological status quo represented by the first and third choices and to assert the radical alternative implied by the second (and represented by those "among our correspondents" capable of choosing correctly). Not only, thus, did the name indicate a theoretical commitment to a collective experience not subjected to the laws of capitalist economy, it also represented an alternative sense of how the journal should relate to its public, through both its ideological and political-economic orientations. As Debord explained in a preface to a reissue of the journal in 1985, "*Potlatch* was delivered freely to certain addresses chosen by the editors, and some people who asked to receive it. It was never sold . . . *Potlatch*, obedient to its title, during the whole time in which it appeared, was exclusively given away" (Debord 1996: 8).

Debord and his associates did not, of course, intend a return to archaic ritual and religious forms of life, but rather used the anthropological metaphor critically to indicate the variety and mutability of human experience and the historical contingency of those forms imposed by capitalist exchange and division of labor. Seemingly obvious and immutable motivational aspects of wealth, competition, reciprocity, accumulation of goods, and so forth might be made to appear strange and groundless in light of the anthropological diversity of manners. In this regard, the concept of potlatch converged with another critical metaphor derived from anthropology, the notion of commodity fetishism in Marx's *Capital* and its full theoretical development by Georg Lukács and other Hegelian Marxists in the 1920s and 1930s. Whereas Lukács' critique of capitalist fetishism lead him to invest messianic hopes in the illusion-shattering activity of an ethically galvanized proletariat, the Lettrists' dialectical counterposing of potlatch to commodity fetishism allowed them to embrace more openly heterodox anarchist and utopian alternatives to existing society. Moreover, whereas Lukács had focused his concerns about reification on *labor* – in the forms of production and in the systemically distorting effects of commodities as objectified labor on social consciousness and the- ory – the Lettrists simply rejected work altogether and focus on problems of leisure and creative play. In this refocusing of Marxist theory from labor to leisure, they believed they were rendering conscious and radicalizing a developmental tendency within capitalism itself, which was already abolishing the classic forms of labor and opening controlled, commodified, "spectacular" forms of leisure. The primary site of struggle in capitalism accordingly had also shifted from spaces of labor – improvement in work- conditions, reduction of work-time, collective representation, and union governance of the workplace – to the terrain of leisure, which under capitalism was anything but "free time." It was for the realization of the incipient chance of a utopian freedom in leisure that the Situationists would wage artistic, theoretical, and political battle.

They formulated this point programmatically in an important collective article lead- ing off issue seven of *Potlatch* in August 1954, carrying as title a quote from the radical Jacobin-terrorist Saint-Just: ". . . A New Idea in Europe." The elided word, signifi- cantly, is "Happiness"; in his 3 March 1794 Report on the Enemies of the Revolution, Saint-Just asserted that "Happiness is a new idea in Europe." Signed by Debord along with his wife Michèle Bernstein, André-Frank Conord, Mohamed Dahou, Jacques Fil- lon, Véra, and Gil Wolman, the editorial focused on the problem of leisure as the "true revolutionary problem," and as a demand both within capitalist society and in any future communist society as well. The Lettrists argued that only one thing was worthy of serious consideration: how to realize an "integral amusement" (*un divertissement integral*). Having begun with the revolutionary Jacobin Saint-Just – whose lineage may be thought to have extended through Marx and Engels to Lenin – they concluded by evoking another French radical thinker whose influence had been largely supplanted by the Jacobin mainstream of revolutionary socialist politics: the utopian socialist Charles Fourier, who conceived of an architectural reorganization of class society along "passional" lines, with freely associated affective groupings replacing the compulsory class groupings imposed and reproduced through the laws of political economy. The Lettrists argued that the solution to the revolutionary problem of leisure rests as much with Fourier as with Saint-Just, Marx, or Lenin: "It would be necessary to permanently reinvent that sovereign attraction that Charles Fourier designated in the free play of the passions" (Debord 1996: 51). In another piece from 30 November 1954, Debord and Jacques Fillon again alluded to Fourier's architectural utopia, in which working and dwelling space has been transformed by its reorganization around the collective system of the passions. "Architecture," they write, "must become passionate" (Debord 1996: 91). Likewise for "Constant" (Nieuwenhuys), one of the founders of the COBRA group and an affiliate of the Situationists in the late 1950s, the social and physical dispensation of the city was the primary site for a post-Surrealist "non-specialized" artistic research, a multimedial and interdisciplinary practice oriented not towards producing new objects of art, but rather new subjects of experience in a transfigured everyday life: "We ought therefore to invent new techniques in all domains, visual, oral, and psychological, so as later to combine them in the complex activity that will produce unitary urbanism" (Constant in McDonough 2002: 76).

In another key respect, too, Debord's Internationale Lettriste lived up to the concept of potlatch: in its ostentatious expenditure of former comrades and collaborators, through expulsion and excommunication. Thus, for example, in the second issue of *Potlatch*, from June 1954, Gil Wolman noted the "elimination of the old guard" of the Lettrists from the new Lettrist Internationale (which had taken place already in 1952) (see Table 8.1). The list of names, along with hilariously excoriating glosses, resembled the registers of excommunicants that populated Breton's Surrealist manifestoes in the later 1920 and 1930s.

Among this list of early Lettrist outcasts the most interesting is Ivan Chtchegloff, who through his psychogeographical speculations made an essential contribution to Debord's group concerning the existential and affective dimensions of urbanism. Chtchegloff's mental condition, however, was fragile ("interpretative delirium"), to the point that he would have to be institutionalized at the clinic of La Chesnie in 1959. Unlike the other excommunicants of the Lettrist and Situationist movements, who became complete non-entities to Debord following their expulsion, Chtchegloff continued to receive correspondence from Debord; Debord included his haunting photograph in the valedictory second volume of *Panegyric* in 1991.

Table 8.1 Wolman's list of lettrists eliminated from the lettrist internationale.

A few exclusions:	*A few reasons:*
ISIDORE GOLDSTEIN, alias JEAN-ISIDORE ISOU	Individual morally retrograde, limited ambitions
MOÏSE BISMUTH, alias MAURICE LEMAÎTRE	Prolonged infantalism, precocious senility, good apostle
POMERANS, alias GABRIEL POMERAND	Counterfeiter, a zero
SERGE BERNA	Lack of intellectual rigor
MENSION	Simply decorative
JEAN-LOUIS BRAU	Militarist deviation
LANGLAIS	Foolishness
IVAN CHTCHEGLOFF, alias GILLES IVAIN	Mythomania, interpretative delirium – lack of revolutionary consciousness

Adapted from Debord (1996: 21).

V. Dérive, détournement, spectacle

If, as I have suggested, the object of the radical Lettrists and Situationists should be understood primarily as the self-formation and working-through of their own group experience, it accordingly becomes somewhat artificial to present their keywords and major concepts as stable entities readily transferable out of their situated contexts. Admitting this, however, I will single out three important notions developed by the movements, both because they were treated to extended application by the participants at the time and because taken together they have, in their subsequent reception, become something of the movement's theoretical signature. These three major concepts are: *dérive* (drift or intentional wandering through urban space), *détournement* (recontextualizing/refunctioning of appropriated cultural materials), and *spectacle* (the systematic distantiation of reality through a socially structured domain of images). I will consider them briefly in turn.

The procedure of *dérive* was central to Lettrist and early Situationist concern with urbanism and urban experience. Its programmatic status was signaled by Debord's dedication of a text to its "theory" ("Théorie de la dérive"). The *dérive* was linked, as Debord wrote, "indissolubly to the recognition of effects of a psychogeographical nature and the affirmation of a ludic-constructive comportment opposed in all respects to the classical notions of the journey or the stroll" (Debord in *Les Lèvres nues* November 1956: 6). Already anticipated in key respects by the Surrealists' collective wandering through the nighttime landscape of the Parc des Buttes Chaumont in Louis Aragon's *Paris Peasant*, the *dérive* involved a kind of free exploration of certain areas of, or itineraries through, urban space, with both intentional planning to facilitate the emergence of new observations and experiences and recounting to record and detail the experiences undergone during the *dérive*. It was intended not only to elicit new physical and social details of urban sites, but also to "map" their psychological and affective dimensions, which Debord took to be an "objective" aspect of the interactions of urban dwellers with the specific atmospheres, shadows, spaces, pathways, and buildings that constitute the physical city. He thus wrote of an objective terrain of the passions ("terrain passionnel objectif") and "a psychogeographical relief of the city" that have their own determinism according to the social and physical morphology of urban space (Debord in *Les Lèvres nues* November 1956: 6). A second crucial aspect of the *dérive*, as a quasi-artistic practice spanning writing and performance, was its exemplary ephemerality, anti-monumentality, and intransitivity – in short, its "situational" character. An unattributed article in the December 1959 issue of *Internationale Situationniste*, "Unitary Urbanism at the End of the 1950s," formulated this facet of the *dérive* explicitly:

> In fact, beyond its essential lessons, the *dérive* furnishes only knowledge that is very precisely dated. In a few years, the construction or demolition of houses, the relocation of micro-societies and of fashions, will suffice to change a city's network of superficial attractions – a very encouraging phenomenon for the

moment when we will come to establish an active link between the *dérive* and Situationist urban construction. Until then, the urban milieu will certainly change on its own, anarchically, ultimately rendering obsolete the *dérives* whose conclusions could not be translated into conscious transformations of this milieu. But the first lesson of the *dérive* is its own status in play.

(*Internationale Situationniste* 1997: 83)

In connecting the ephemeral, game-like activity of the *dérive* to Situationist construction, this text signals the attempt to link up two domains of Situationist urban activity, each with a leading figure temporarily aligned: Debord, in the activity of the *dérive* and the exploration of the passional landscape of the city; and Constant, a founder of the COBRA group and already by the late 1950s at work on the utopian city of situations that came to be know as "New Babylon." Yet as the "Unitary Urbanism" text goes on to suggest, there is a third aspect to the *dérive* that is autobiographical and existential, as much an *ethical* question of "a life" and its destinies as an issue directly pertaining to architecture or urban design. "All the stories that we live," the text reads, "the *dérive* of our life, are characterized by the search for – or the lack of – an overarching construction. The transformation of the environment calls forth new emotional states that are first experienced passively and then, with heightened consciousness, give way to constructive reactions" (*Internationale Situationniste* 1997: 83). In an essay entitled "Architecture and Play," published in the 30 May 1955 issue of *Potlatch*, Debord had similarly argued that "games" such as the *dérive* were important explorations of experiences that could, systematically pursued and instituted, open up new modes of individual and collective comportment, indeed, a new morality: "It is a matter now of making the transition from arbitrary rules of play to a moral foundation" (Debord 1996: 158).

The notion of *détournement* was already implicit in early Lettrist practice, but became a defining procedure for the radical International Lettrists by the mid-1950s and persisted in Debord's writings and films long beyond the dissolution of the Situationist International. The term itself refers to their method of appropriating – "detouring" – existing texts, images, or film sequences, modified through recaptioning or other means and placed in new contexts, which alters their meaning and function while continuing to refer back to their original sources (see Epstein, this volume). *Détournement* became an important tool in the repertoire of the Situationists, not only for negative purposes, for critical parody and exposure of hidden ideological aspects of cultural and commercial goods, but also for positive constructions of new meanings and experiences. Rooted in the Lettrists' admiration for Lautréamont's *Poésies*, with its advocacy of plagiarism against literary property and its exemplification of its own precepts through the modified reuse of passages from Pascal and other classical writers, it received theoretical formulation in an essay co-written by Debord and Wolman and published in the May 1956 issue of *Les Lèvres nues*. Significantly, the front page of the journal announced the authors to be none other than Aragon and Andre Breton; Debord and Wolman thus presented their own theoretical tract as a *détournement* of a Surrealism that had latterly entered into the realm of "classics" available for Situationist plagiarism and redirection. As recent editions of Debord's work have revealed, his application of the technique of *détournement* was pervasive and enduring, including both "artistic" works such as his collaborations with Asgar Jorn *Fin de Copenhagen* (1957) and *Mémoires* (1959; an autobiography including only appropriated sentences) as well as "theoretical" works and films such as *Society of the Spectacle* (1967) and *In Girum Imus Nocte Et Consumimur Igni* (1976).

The concept of "spectacle," the best-known concept associated with Situationism, was theoretically articulated at length by Debord in his 1967 book of short thesis-like numbered paragraphs, substantially constructed out of détourned quotations, entitled *The Society of the Spectacle*. Subsequently, in 1973 he would release a film version of the book, with voice-overs of passages from the book juxtaposed with various photographs and film sequences, as well as two follow-up texts, *Refutation of All Judgments, Both Celebratory and Hostile, That Have Been Passed Up Till Now on the Film "The Society of the Spectacle"* (1975) and *Commentaries on the Society of the Spectacle* (1988). Over the course of the various paragraphs of *Society of the Spectacle* in which the concept was elaborated, "spectacle" took on various connotations, but the fundamental definition was given in the opening and closing paragraphs of the first chapter, entitled "Accomplished Separation." Debord first announced an all-encompassing new manifestation of capital, which had extended itself, as representation, into the basic experience of time and space in contemporary Western society: "All social life in which modern conditions of production hold sway may be characterized as an immense accumulation of *spectacles*. All that was directly lived now separates itself in a representation" (Debord 2006: 766). That representation, "spectacle," he goes on to argue, forms a system of images that increasingly shape experience to their stereotypical measure. Lived experience is transformed through images and into further images by the economic and administrative apparatus of advanced capitalism, which has multiple branches in the state bureaucracy, mass media, consumer goods and leisure services, and culture industry. Under the guise of purveying enjoyment and meaning to an increasingly affluent populace, the spectacle actually produces an impoverishment of experience, an "immiseration" not measurable, as Marx had once argued in the *Communist Manifesto* and *Capital*, in economic terms, but in the diminished quality and intensity of life itself. Misleadingly organized into spuriously individuated parcels of image-merchandise, into branded units of pseudo-communication, the spectacle actually offers only monotonous variations on its own structural reproduction and expansion. This apparent diversification of images together with the real totalizing unity of spectacle reproduces the same in ever-new guises; in this expanding spectacular structure resides the essential dynamic of capital in the contemporary period: "Spectacle is *capital* at that degree of accumulation at which it becomes image" (Debord 2006: 745).

VI. Conclusion

Debord drew far-reaching conclusions from his analysis of contemporary society as a "society of the spectacle," a critique which encompassed within one systematic framework his criticisms of the artistic avant-garde (as feeding the spectacular apparatus rather than destroying it), of the traditional forms of working-class and revolutionary organization (as incapable of grasping the present-day dynamics of capital), of the academy (a domain of careerist managers and suppliers of the spectacle), and of the "life" marketed as a society of leisure and consumable goods (immiseration masquerading as affluence). Two sole possibilities, Debord came to believe, existed to break the hold of the spectacle on consciousness and daily life, and taken together they can be seen as dialectically interrelated aims of the whole of Situationist thought and practice.

The first anti-spectacular possibility was collective, activist, even violent: the largely spontaneous May–June 1968 student revolt and general strike in Paris, in which Situationist ideas and to a certain extent Situationist personalities played a significant role. The Situationist group was tiny, and the revolt extended well beyond any direct influence they might have exercised; yet the May–June 1968 rebellion seemed to embody their goal of provoking a creative outburst of radical criticism that would demand a utopian change in everyday life in the present moment. The other possible way of opposing the spectacle, more or less compulsory for Debord following the ebb of the militancy of 1968, involved strategic withdrawal, patient biding of time while preparing subversive forays against the ever-more encompassing spectacular society. Such radical "patiency" complementing Situationist activism – an infrequently considered but important aspect of Debord's thinking – compelled him to live furtively at the margins and at least metaphorically to go "underground." For a number of years, thus, he lived abroad in a condition of public near-anonymity, in the company of a small circle of friends. It must also be recalled, however, that his strategy of anti-spectacular disappearance was punctuated by two major experiments in anti-spectacular "visibility": his extended cinematic *détournements* entitled *Society of the Spectacle* (1973) and *In Girum Imus Nocte et Consumimur Igni* (1978).

Nonetheless, Debord's plunge into subversive anonymity, accompanied by the encroaching illness caused by heavy drinking, nearly proved all too successful. Although intellectuals influenced by Debord, ranging from the sociologists Henri Lefebvre and Jean Baudrillard to the art historian T.J. Clark maintained the subterranean presence of Situationism in cultural and scholarly life, Situationism itself was largely forgotten in the later 1970s and early 1980s; many of Debord's writings and books were unavailable for years. Not until his late "return" to public life with the publication of *Commentaries on the Society of the Spectacle* and *Panegyric* in the late 1980s and 1990s, followed by his suicide in 1994, did the writings and films of Debord and his Situationist comrades again become available to a broader reading and viewing public, to renew their influence on contemporary radical culture and politics. Arguably, with the ongoing development of far left anti-globalization politics and the burgeoning interest in neo-Situationist "relational aesthetics" in the contemporary art world, Debord's thought and work is likely to continue to experience an active, unanticipatedly rich posthumous life.

References

Chopin, H. (1979) *Poesie Sonore Internationale*, Paris: Jean-Michel Place Éditeur.
Curtay, J.-P. (1974) *La Poesie Lettriste*, Paris: Seghers.
Debord, G. (1996) *Potlatch (1954–1957)*, Paris: Gallimard.
—— (2006) *Oeuvres*, ed. J.-L. Rançon, Paris: Gallimard.
Internationale Situationniste (1997), ed. P. Mosconi, Paris: Librarie Arthème Fayard.
Les Lévres Nues (1954–1958), Brussels, Belgium.
McDonough, T. (ed.) (2002) *Guy Debord and the Situationist Internationale: Texts and Documents*, Cambridge, MA: MIT Press.
Vicas, A. (1998) "Reusing Culture: The Importance of Détournement," *Yale Journal of Criticism* 11(2): 381–406.

Further reading

Berreby, G. (1985) *Document Relatifs à la Fondation de l'Internationale Situationniste*, Paris: Allia.
Jappe, A. (1999) *Guy Debord*, trans. D. Nicholson-Smith, Berkeley, CA: University of California Press.
Kaufmann, V. (2006) *Guy Debord: Revolution in the Service of Poetry*, trans. R. Bononno, Minneapolis, MN: University of Minnesota Press.
Marcus, G. (1989) *Lipstick Traces: A Secret History of the Twentieth Century*, Cambridge, MA: Harvard University Press.
McDonough, T. (2007) *"The Beautiful Language of My Century": Reinventing the Language of Contestation in Postwar France, 1945–1968*, Cambridge, MA: MIT Press.
Situationist International [Online]. http://www.cddc.vt.edu/sionline/index.html (Accessed 6 December 2010).
Wigley, M. (1998) *Constant's New Babylon: The Hyper-Architecture of Desire*, Rotterdam: 010 Publishers.

9

OULIPO AND PROCEDURALISM

Jan Baetens

I. What is procedural writing?

Procedural or constrained writing is not simply a synonym for formalism or rule-based writing. The latter, in a certain sense, is common to any kind of literature and most scholars accept that it is not possible to produce a literary text without following certain rules, be they linguistic (to write in this or that language means to follow its rules – even if one decides to break them) or literary (to write a text as a literary product means to be aware of the ways in which a certain cultural and interpretive community defines the notion of literature – even if one rejects this definition and tries to do something else). Procedural literature should therefore be defined as an "expanded," more radical version of formal or rule-based writing, both at the level of what it is, technically speaking, and at the level of what it means, culturally speaking.

In order to distinguish a constraint from all the other literary techniques, forms, figures, conventions, mechanisms, and so on, that inevitably play a role in the composition of a text, two major aspects come immediately to the fore. As we will see, however, a strictly technical definition of constrained writing is very difficult, if not impossible, given the weight of contextual aspects and interpretive communities in our consideration of what a constraint is or may be.

First of all, a constraint constitutes a *supplementary* rule, i.e. a rule that, far from being already used in a large set of literary texts, appears as something added to certain texts as a special feature. Rhyme as such, for instance, is not a constraint in itself, for it is part of the usual techniques that shape our ideas of poetry. However, it may become a constraint in a literary community that does not use rhyme as a "normal" feature of poetry. To put it another way: a constraint is in principle *self-chosen* (and thus self-imposed), and it is always *more than a convention*; it is either something new or something that is "made anew," rediscovered, refreshed, or metamorphosed (on the distinction between convention and constraint, see Andrews 2003).

Second, a constraint is necessarily a rule that is used *systematically*, i.e. throughout the whole text (exceptions are only accepted if they break the rules in highly sophisticated ways; the OuLiPo has reappropriated the antique term of *clinamen* to label such "failures"). Rules that are only applied loosely or occasionally, rather than being used each time that it is possible to do so, are not constraints. In that case, they are just literary *figures* or techniques. A good example of such a shift is given by the anagram, i.e. the reshuffling of the letters of a given word or (short) sentence. Often used to include a play on the name of a person (Salvador Dali = *Avida Dollars*), it is turned into a constraint when all the graphic units of a larger text are determined by the rule of the anagram, as in several books of the OuLiPian author Michelle Grangaud (1987; for more radical, even "abstract," yet always very poetic forms of the conversion of a literary technique into a constraint, see Lebensztejn 1972: 29–85).

This very broad definition of constraint as a *supplementary and systematic expansion of literary rules and conventions* seems correctly to suggest that, like the notion of form itself, constrained writing is a universal phenomenon. There seems to be no literary tradition that is totally deprived of proceduralism, even if the impact and status of constraints may widely diverge, from the viewpoint of production as well as from that of reception. Certain periods, places, and groups prefer constrained writing more than others. The medieval tradition of the *troubadour* lyricism is an example of a constraint-oriented literature, whereas many avant-gardes seem to proclaim a distaste for all things constrained; in contemporary experimental circles, constrained writing is often actively sought out, whereas other groups and other eras may tend to ignore constrained writing or discard it as futile, excessively formalist or even non-modern or non-experimental.

Yet the very universality of proceduralism should not prevent us from seeing that, beyond the mechanism of constrained writing, quite different poetics can be at work. In this regard it can be argued that the OuLiPo group has introduced a totally new vision of proceduralism, breaking with the traditional interpretation of constrained writing as old-fashioned and empty hyperformalism that has dominated discussions of form and formalism in experimental literature for more than a century.

In Western literature, the experimental styles that we associate with the various avant-gardes (from the Cubist and Futurist movements through the neo-avant-gardes of the 1960s) are often characterized by their refusal of any form of traditional rule or convention, such as rhyme and meter in poetry, to take a material example, or semantic coherence and conventional psychology, to take a content-related example. In certain cases, the avant-garde not only opposed all these regularities, it also made a strong case for its diametric opposite, namely the use of *anti-form* (as in the revolutionary work of many Dada artists, for example) or the use of *chance* as a compositional tool (as in the work of a Fluxus artist like John Cage, for instance). Nevertheless, not only is the opposition between constraint and anti-form or chance procedures less absolute than one may think at first sight but constrained writing itself has become more and more crucial to contemporary forms of experimental writing. This point, which hints at the difficulty of maintaining the stereotyped opposition of *avant-garde* and *arrière-garde* (see Marx 2004 and Compagnon 2005), can best be illustrated by studying the watershed transformations introduced by the OuLiPo group, today's epitome of proceduralism in avant-garde writing.

II. OuLiPo: a short history

OuLiPo (the *Ouvroir de Littérature Potentielle*, or the Workshop of Potential Literature) is the name of a literary group whose works have defined and elaborated the
practice of writing under constraint. Founded in 1960 by two friends, both trained as
mathematicians, François Le Lionnais and Raymond Queneau, and now consisting of
thirty-six writers and mathematicians, this Paris-based yet very international collective has played an essential role in the rediscovery of constrained writing as well as in
the dramatic redefinition of its stakes.

All traditional poetics make room for what is called the "constraints of meter and
rhyme," just as all traditional forms of writing know the practice of "fixed forms,"
i.e. poetic genres obeying strictly defined and often very sophisticated rules such as,
for instance, the sestina. Nevertheless, without having invented the word itself, it is
indeed the OuLiPo that has defined the modern expanded use of constraint as self-
chosen supplementary and systematic rule. This reinvention has taken from the beginning two different forms. First, the OuLiPo has tried to invent new constraints, for
instance the "S + 7" constraint, where each noun (or substantive) in a chosen text is
replaced with the seventh noun following it in a chosen dictionary (on this constraint
– in English "N + 7," for "noun" – see Mathews and Brotchie 2005: 202–3). Second,
the collective has completed their idiosyncratic inventions (which were called *Ouli-
pianisms*) with the rereading, unearthing, or reappraisal of constraints that had fallen
into oblivion but that were appropriated by the group as involuntarily pre-Oulipian (a
phenomenon they ironically called *plagiarism by anticipation*). The best known example
of such a rediscovery is of course the lipogram or letter omission, a very ancient figure
which previous generations saw as, at best, a kind of rhetorical gadget. The OuLiPians
explored the lipogram with great enthusiasm and it is now a major tool in all types of
creative writing in France. The results of both exercises were gathered in the working
papers of the "Bibliothèque de l'OuLiPo," with a very modest print-run of 150 copies.
It was only afterwards, once the group had achieved some notoriety (mainly since the
1980s), that these documents were circulated more widely.

The history of the group can roughly be divided in three periods. In the first years
of its existence, the OuLiPo was mainly a group of friends united in their shared distaste for mainstream literature (characterized or rather plagued, in their eyes, by formlessness) as well as by a shared love of experiment for experiment's sake. The aim
of OuLiPo in these years was to invent new forms of writing, i.e. in the first place
new forms of constraint, and to provide one or more illustrations of these constraints.
Almost immediately, however, it became clear that invention could also mean reinvention, and the OuLiPians started working with forgotten or minor constraints. In
this first period, the essential mark of the group's work is their strictly experimental,
almost conceptual approach to literature (one should not forget that one of the historical members of the OuLiPo was Marcel Duchamp). The constraint was compared
to a kind of mathematical *theorem*, and the textual production that could accompany
it was seen as one of its possible *demonstrations*. During this period, various OuLiPians

continued to pursue a *double practice*: although deeply involved in the activities of the group, their work in print was not necessarily OuLiPo-oriented, and since the presence of the group in the literary public sphere was still insignificant, few presented themselves as members of the OuLiPo or as being under its influence. The diffidence of Raymond Queneau, who already "did" procedural writing in the 1930s but often remained silent about that part of his writing that he put to one side as instrumental or preparatory, was typical of these first years. His most popular books were either non-OuLiPian (*Zazie in the Metro*, Queneau 2001) or pre-Oulipian (*Exercises in Style* dates from as early as 1947 [Queneau 1979]), so that it was perfectly possible for him as well as for the public to discard OuLiPian proceduralism as play, a form of entertainment, if not simply an intellectual joke, that did not affect the heart of these authors' "real work." In the same years, various French New Novelists such as Alain Robbe-Grillet and later Nobel Prize winner Claude Simon had however already been experimenting with constrained-based storytelling, using punning as a device to replace linear narrative by new forms of narrative that could shift from one layer to another to mere word-play (see Marx-Scouras, this volume). A good synthesis of New Novel techniques can be found in a novel by Jean Ricardou, *La prise/prose de Constantinople* (1965), in which the author has tried to invent the story with the help of mere word-play and manipulation, the starting point of the whole book being moreover the word "rien" ("nothing"; for a detailed self-analysis of the genesis of this work, see Ricardou 1978).

The second period of the group coincides with the arrival of Georges Perec in 1967. Perec and others with him proclaimed their membership publicly, pledging allegiance to the experimental spirit of the group and progressively eliminating their non-OuLiPian production. Perec had not started his career in the OuLiPian manner, but after his reception by the collective, he rapidly moved into proceduralism. This increased self-awareness and confidence appear also in the publication of manifestoes and other theoretical and historical texts by various members of the group. The success of some of Perec's books – above all *La Disparition* (1969; English translation *A Void* [1994]), a 300-page lipogrammatic novel written without the letter *e*, the most frequent letter in French – helped make OuLiPo visible for the very first time to the broader public. Yet the basic transformation of OuLiPo in this period had to do with something more profound: the redefinition of the relationship between the constraint as theorem and the constrained text as demonstration of this theorem. By contrast with the first period, with its clear emphasis on the invention of new theorems, OuLiPo in its second period started insisting on the *importance of the resulting text*. This new factor seems to have encouraged the production of OuLiPian texts and, even more importantly, their public presentation as OuLiPian works. Besides Perec, the major new names in that period are Jacques Roubaud (first in poetry, later also in prose) and the non-French writers Italo Calvino, Harry Mathews, and Oskar Pastior. Rooted though it was in French culture, the group had managed to be highly international from the very start.

The third period, probably launched by the colossal success of Georges Perec's *Life A User's Manual* (2009 [1978]), can be described as that of its canonization. OuLiPian works and authors, the leading figure now being Jacques Roubaud, who was seen after

Perec's early death in 1992 as the spokesman of the collective, became more and more productive and also more and more recognized by the literary establishment. Today the group is accepted as one of the chief literary movements of the second half of the twentieth century. The international breakthrough of the movement, partly due to the sustained attention given to OuLiPo by academics outside France (see the pioneering study by Warren Motte 1986) and to important popularizations such as Mathews's *Oulipo Compendium* (2005), has of course not gone unnoticed in France, where the success of the OuLiPo offers a consolation for the collapse of other forms of French experimental writing and, more generally, the disappearance of mainstream French literature from the international scene. Last but not least, the dynamism of OuLiPo is demonstrated by its active cross-fertilization. The notion of constrained writing has not remained a strictly literary phenomenon, but has been successfully exported to other fields such as painting (with the *OuPeinPo* or Ouvroir de Peinture Potentielle) or comics (with the *OuBaPo* or Ouvroir de Bande Dessinée Potentielle). Here as well, the dialectics of old and new has proven extremely rewarding: artistic domains outside literature benefit from the importation of literary constraints, even as they come to the realization that they were already OuLiPians without knowing it (the case of the British film director Peter Greenaway, whose first movies were strongly marked by mathematical constraints, is a clear example of such retrospective proceduralism).

The most exciting effects of canonization are however indirect. The success of the OuLiPo has given renewed visibility to other, non-French examples of procedural writing, such as for instance Walter Abish's *Alphabetical Africa* (1974), an astonishing novel that transforms the figure of alliteration into a real (and lipogrammatic) constraint. The book has 52 chapters, each them containing only words that start with particular letters: the first chapter contains only words starting with *a*, the second chapter only words starting with *a* or *b*, the third only words starting with *a*, *b* or *c*, etc. until in chapter 26 the whole alphabet is available; the second part of the novel repeats the structure but in reverse order, dropping one initial letter per chapter, until it reaches once again a chapter having only words starting with *a*. Another example, written by a Paris-based British novelist strongly influenced by French experimental writing and poststructuralist theory, is Christine Brooke-Rose's novel *Between* (1968), which applies a similar lipogrammatic rule, although no longer restricted to the domain of letters but transferred to the domain of lexical items. The protagonist of this novel is a professional translator belonging to a team that travels throughout the world attending various international conferences on translation. *Between* presents two intersecting narratives, one in the present tense in several different languages and describing the breakdown of the protagonist's marriage, and one containing a series of love letters written in medieval French. In neither of these two narratives does the author use the verb "to be," which for Christine Brooke-Rose is a way of expressing the narrator's disoriented sense of personal identity. A later novel by the same author, *Amalgamemnon* (1984), offers a variation on this constraint. In this novel, Brooke-Rose avoids all use of present-tense verbs in order to stress the temporally and culturally multi-layered stream of consciousness of the female narrator who sits in bed reading Herodotus while her lover is snoring beside her. The narrator's thoughts and sense of word-play explore the tensions between fact and imagination against the background of reflection on the changing status of women in relation to traditional hierarchies.

In addition, OuLiPo has generated new literary vocations all over the world. The most promising case is undoubtedly that of Christian Bök (2003, 2009), to whom we will return later on.

III. OuLiPo and the idea of constrained writing

The importance of the OuLiPo group cannot be reduced to its having put back on the agenda a way of writing that existed before but whose significance had been obliterated by its use and reuse in long-established forms of literature. Nor does it make sense to emphasize the creation of previously unknown types and examples of constrained writing. What really matters in the work of OuLiPo is the totally new approach toward proceduralism, now brought into play in new contexts. In short: what made OuLiPo so different, at least in the beginning, is not its *practice* of constrained writing but its *theory*.

The major achievements of the OuLiPo are threefold. First, the group has successfully challenged the restrictive view of experimental writing as antiformalist as well as criticizing its ideal of formlessness. Second, it has countered the interpretation of constrained literature as a form of extreme formalism, replacing it with a new approach toward invention and freedom in proceduralism. Third, it has also, by trial and error, put forward some of the often overlooked complexities of writing under constraint.

The first accomplishment of the group, the critique of avant-gardism as a law-breaking practice, can only be understood in the wider context of modern French literature. When the OuLiPo group started its activities in the 1960s, its program was not only "positive" (the invention and reinvention of constraints) but also "negative," its principal target being the then hegemonic forms of Surrealist and post-Surrealist writing in poetry (see Stockwell, this volume) and, more generally, the unchallenged reign of free verse and free expression, as exemplarily demonstrated in Surrealist automatism. For the OuLiPo, which was not alone in its critique of Surrealism (see also Caillois 2003), the refusal of any rule whatsoever because of the latter's association with "inauthentic" bourgeois culture, on the one hand, and the priority given to content at the expense of form, on the other hand, can only produce false innovation, if it does not prevent innovation from taking place at all. For the OuLiPians, the highly stereotypical character of Surrealist and post-Surrealist poetry proves that without the help of some rule or constraint, the author is pathetically doomed to repeat what he or she already knows. In this regard, it is crucial to stress that the stakes of this discussion exceed the local polemic between Surrealism and OuLiPo. Behind this debate one finds the basic opposition that structures French literature – and perhaps modern Western literature in general – since the revolution embodied by Rimbaud, namely the opposition between "terrorists" and "rhetoricians." The former, to follow Jean Paulhan's terminology in his essay *Les fleurs de Tarbes* (1941; English translation, *The Flowers of Tarbes*, 2006), contest any form of conventional and even of "literary" language as fake, counterfeit, unauthentic. What counts for them is the "ideas" to be expressed, ideas that can only be betrayed by the literary words one uses to utter them. Since there are no words that escape literary use, "terrorists" have therefore only the choice between two ways of using language: either a negative use, namely the attempt to *reject* all known rules and usages (this is, in a sense, what Surrealist automatism was trying to do, or what the Dada movement sought through destruction), or a "supernegative" use, which is that of *silence* – and indeed French avant-garde writing has been haunted since Rimbaud by the myth of silence as "pure expression." To be an avant-garde writer in France means, to quote Laurent Nunez (2006), to be "against writing" and to consider the refusal of words as the most sublime, if not the only possible form of real writing. The latter group, that of the "rhetoricians," generally agrees with the terrorists' critiques, yet observes that even silence must be uttered to become meaningful. Words are inescapable, and therefore what writers and readers need is a conscious, i.e. not naïve use of literature, a use of language and literature that accepts their essential artificiality and that attempts to turn that artificiality into an advantage, at least into a challenge. The OuLiPo is clearly a representative of this "anti-anti-conventionalist" movement, which has for some time been excluded as reactionary. Thanks to the OuLiPo, it is now once again possible to be *experimental as well as procedural*. The collective has proved time and again that the effects of constrained writing can be as corrosive, as playful, as creative, as revolutionary as the techniques that are identified as the core business of classic avant-garde: chance, montage, and subversion.

The second major transformation that the OuLiPo introduced to our ideas about constrained writing bears on the restrictive interpretation of proceduralism as supreme or excessive formalism. Although the formalist aspects of constrained writing are of course key to any understanding of proceduralism, the use of formal rules, as for instance in the already mentioned lipogram or the palindrome (a variation of the anagram, the rearranging of the letters of a word or phrase to produce a new word or phrase, using all the original letters in a different order), is never a matter of simple formalism. One of the axioms of the OuLiPians is indeed that constrained writing is not a way of adding supplementary layers of formal procedures to a text under construction, but the very possibility of inventing such a text. In the case of the lipogram, for instance, the rule does not say, "write a text without using this or that letter," but: "invent a text by relying on the deletion of this or that letter," which is something else altogether. The *productive* approach toward constrained writing suggests – and all these points are crucial to OuLiPo literature – that rules stimulate inventiveness and innovation, instead of being external "obstacles" that hinder or complicate free expression. This new approach turns the conventional interpretation of the notions of constraint and freedom upside down. A constraint is no longer something that opposes freedom, but on the contrary what makes real freedom (i.e. invention, innovation, creativity) possible, whereas the kind of freedom that rejects rule-based practice or behaviour is condemned to remain at the threshold of invention. What the OuLiPo emphasizes is the impossibility of surrendering the notion of freedom to those writers who associate freedom with the rejection of all rules (for a survey, see James 2009). Constrained writers often believe that the repudiation of rule-bound writing is counterproductive (for it produces works that are bound to other, perhaps unacknowledged conventions), while trying to demonstrate that the practice of constraints is a "superior" form of freedom (the same writers often believe as well that the willing acceptance of rules is a guarantee of surprises and innovations that are unthinkable without the use of constraints). This awareness, which at first sight seems totally counterintuitive in a culture that defines freedom as the absence of all constraints, rules, and limitations, is a watershed moment in the history of avant-garde literature, since it also suggests how traditional and perhaps how unconsciously bourgeois the avant-garde can be in its rejection of all rules. It also opens the way to constrained writing as a tool for inspiration. A constraint is not an *obstacle* (although it can be one of course, as we shall see) but a (possible) *springboard*.

Third and finally, the OuLiPo and the OuLiPian procedural movement have also, throughout their rather long history, thematized and theorized a certain number of questions that a more monolithic approach to constrained writing had never raised. Thanks to the OuLiPo, proceduralism has not remained a literary practice or school or tendency, but has also become the object of much critical and theoretical reflection. Constrained writing as such, apart from its concrete realizations, has been extensively discussed, and these debates have proven extremely fruitful, as we will see in the last section of this chapter.

IV. Procedural writing: a user's manual

OuLiPo has undoubtedly unleashed the complexity of writing under constraint, both as a technique and from an institutional point of view. For clarity's sake, it is possible to structure the numerous debates along three lines. First, are all constraints equal? Is there any possibility to distinguish between "good" and "bad" constraints? Or does this question not really matter, does it simply depend on local circumstances? Second, should the reader be informed about the constraint that is being used or not and, more generally, what role does the reader play in the procedural writing? Third, who owns a constraint, and does constrained writing offer the possibility of inventing new forms of literary community?

The first question may seem a little strange, given our current reluctance to contaminate literary research with value judgments, but it definitely is a question that has fascinated all practitioners, readers as well as writers, of constrained writing. The traditional answer of the OuLiPo to this question has been relatively simple, even if it has always proven easier to define a "bad" constraint than a "good" constraint. Undeniably bad, at least in the beginning, were constraints that were already known or catalogued as too easy. A literary bonus was given to constraints that were simultaneously *new* (and here the criterion of invention plays a crucial role), sufficiently *stimulating* (for technical or psychological reasons, certain constraints apparently did not seduce those who had to make the "demonstration" of the "theorem"; in this case, the productivity criterion was a problem) and *difficult to put into action* (and here the notion of creativity was of course key). Among these three elements, many combinations were possible, but in practice the focus shifted rapidly to the aspect of the constraint's "difficulty." It proved tricky to invent new constraints capable of being accepted by the writing community, while the reuse of existing constraints such as the lipogram or the anagram were more than sufficient to raise fundamental questions on how to write under constraint. Therefore the OuLiPo has often preferred "difficult" constraints to easy ones, certainly in its second period, when the most virtuoso of all OuLiPians, Georges Perec, was leading the dance. A book like *Alphabets* (Perec 1976), for instance, is a dizzying experience in an agrammatic writing, which goes into unknown degrees of rhetorical sophistication, its implicit model being to produce a multiply complexified version of the so-called *magical square*:

SATOR
AREPO
TENET
OPERA
ROTAS

It would be a mistake however to reduce Perec's acrobatics to mere recreation. In most of Perec's writings and in the best OuLiPian works (poignant) humour and (often sublime and tragic) depth are always very present, as is demonstrated as well in the work of Christian Bök, a "para-Oulipian" Canadian poet whose use of constraints clearly competes with Perec's labours of Hercules. These are the opening paragraphs of his final comments on *Eunoia*:

"Eunoia" is the shortest word in English to contain all five vowels, and the word quite literally means "beautiful thinking". *Eunoia* is a univocal lipogram, in which each chapter restricts itself to the use of a single vowel. *Eunoia* is directly inspired by the exploits of Oulipo (*l'Ouvroir de Littérature Potentielle*) – the avant-garde coterie renowned for its literary experimentation with extreme formalistic constraints. The text makes a Sisyphean spectacle of its labour, wilfully crippling its language in order to show that, even under such improbable conditions of duress, language can still express an uncanny, if not sublime, thought.

Eunoia abides by many subsidiary rules. All chapters must allude to the art of writing. All chapters must describe a culinary banquet, a prurient debauch, a pastoral tableau and a nautical voyage. All sentences must accent internal rhyme through the use of syntactical parallelism. The text must exhaust the lexicon for each vowel, citing at least 98% of the available repertoire (although a few words do go unused, despite efforts to include them: *parallax*, *belvedere*, *gingivitis*, *monochord* and *tumulus*). The text must minimize repetition of substantive vocabulary (so that, ideally, no word appears more than once). The letter Y is suppressed.

(Bök 2009: 111–12)

Yet behind the discussions on the difficulty of certain constraints and the possible lack of interest of too easy constraints, more fundamental questions arise. The work of Jacques Jouet, for instance, an unconventional OuLiPian who does not always adhere to the party-line of the movement, illustrates a paradoxical form of "proceduralism without constraint." Jouet – and as we have seen earlier, his position is not so different from what was being practiced by some of the first OuLiPians – sometimes writes under constraint, and sometimes doesn't, claiming that it's the right of the (procedural) writer to do whatever he likes (Motte 2006). This alternative may seem simple – do I stick to proceduralism or not, and for what reasons? – but this internal polemic within OuLiPian circles lays bare very intricate discussions on the status of the rule in proce-duralism or, more precisely, on the relationship between input and output, between constraint and constrained text. Does one have to keep the initial constraint in the final text or can it be "superseded" in the creative process? Is the initial constraint a final goal or an intermediary instrument? How can one use a constraint that produces "ugly" texts (for instance texts that may inspire awe and admiration, but that are bor-ing or pointless)? What happens when a constraint encounters non-constrained ele-ments of the text (for except for works like the magical square or Perec's *Alphabets*, most constrained texts are filled with undetermined elements)? What happens when a constraint A meets a constraint B within the same text? Do they complete each other? Do they ignore each other? Do they struggle with each other? Questions like these are everywhere today, even if not always fully theoretically articulated. They reveal the dramatic shift that has taken place since the first meetings of the OuLiPo: what is stressed now is clearly the "demonstration," no longer the "theorem."

A second group of questions – perhaps the most conspicuous one in the broader discussions on the OuLiPo – refers to the visibility or invisibility of the constraint in the final text. As in the previous set of questions, a technical issue – "Must the writer allow the reader to see which constraint has been used, or not?" – has been wrapped up with value judgments, for certain writers and critics consider it a political impera-tive to inform the reader about the production mechanisms of the text. For them, this knowledge is the only possible way to produce a literary and ethically correct reading, for the absence of such knowledge often induces a double failure. First, it may gener-ate irritating and senseless forms of misreading: for instance when one misses com-pletely the constrained dimension of a text, but also when one invents constraints that are not there (Andrews 2009). Second, it creates an unfair power balance between the knowing author and the unknowing reader, the latter being thus prevented from evaluating – and even criticizing – the "theorem demonstration" advanced by the former. Other voices, however, claim that the difference between input (the initial constraint) and output (the final text) is so dramatic that the writer would actually do a disservice to the reader by revealing too much of the work's genesis. Once the house of the novel has been built, Queneau used to claim, the writer has to take away the scaffold; and others have compared the traces of the constraint to the price label on a suit. Perec as well, whose *Life A User's Manual* is (in)famous for its many "hidden" constraints (Magné *et al.* 1993), was sincerely convinced that too strong an emphasis on the disclosure of the constraint might spoil the reader's pleasure, or divert his or her attention to strictly technical issues. Nevertheless, despite the clarity of these theoretical positions, the practice of the constrained text is often much more ambiguous. For what does it mean to "reveal" a constraint? Does it imply that the author adds a comment (blurb, preface, post face) or delivers a key outside the book (inside information, interview, critical essay)? Or is it sufficient to use constraints that are so obvious that nobody will miss them? But we all know that some of the first readers of *A Void* did not notice at all what the novel is made of, and what it is all about: the absence of the letter *e*! The question of the constraint's visibility should therefore be related as well to the questions discussed above, on the difference between "good" and "bad" constraints.

Finally, the importance of value judgments – and of ethical criticism at the heart of what is often considered the most ultimate form of narrow formalist materialism in literature – is also present in debates on ownership. Contrary to a literary convention or a rhetorical figure, which by definition belong to a whole community, constraints – or at least the new ones especially invented as literary theorems – can be attributed to the "hand" of one specific author: Jean Lescure is the inventor of the S + 7 constraint, Michelle Grangaud elaborated the "melted poem" constraint that produces a shorter poem by sampling from a longer one, various OuLiPians have proposed variations on the traditional sestina structure, etc. Yet this "paternity" does not necessarily imply ownership and copyright; on the contrary. Take the example of one of the forerunners of the OuLiPo, Raymond Roussel, who had prepared the posthumous publications of a book that has had a tremendous influence on twentieth-century procedural writing, *How I Wrote Certain of My Books*, which contains crucial information on extremely productive, yet "hidden" constraints (Roussel 2005). Roussel is a challenge for all those eager to think about the limits and possibilities of self-disclosure in constrained writing, since the more he explains his procedures, the more riddles he provokes. The interesting point however is his declared motivation: instructing the reader, he argues, is a way of sharing knowledge and techniques that may help the audience to reappropriate them in unexpected and surprising ways. This generous statement, theoretically backed by the OuLiPo and practically endorsed by the construction of an inspiring website that represents a marvellous online workspace (http://www.oulipo.net/; accessed August 2, 2010), is a revolutionary procedure as well. It defines ownership in the same terms as Wittgenstein did in the case of meaning: *ownership, as meaning, is use*, and all those willing to test the productivity of a constraint are invited to do so, in the same "creative commons" spirit that characterizes the OuLiPo as a whole. (It is instructive to consider the difference with constraints in visual arts, where special inventions and technical innovations are often patented and trademarked.) The collaborative spirit does not exclude the individuality of the makers (OuLiPo texts are not anonymous, even when they are the result of collective writing), nor is it absolute (even if the OuLiPo is a collective from which no member can be excluded – which distinguishes it from Surrealism (see Stockwell, this volume) – membership is not open to all those who work in the OuLiPian spirit; it is severely restricted and by invitation only). But collaboration and exchange typify the whole procedural movement, inside and outside the OuLiPo; moreover, they do so in a way that goes far beyond the mere issue of constraint ownership. Given the separation of constraint and constrained text, on the one hand, and the possibility of providing always new demonstrations of existing theorems, on the other hand, the OuLiPo has made room for a literary practice that has a less fetishistic relationship to a basic division in the field: between those who *have* access to publication (in book form, that is) and those who *do not* (for good or bad reasons). Thanks to the OuLiPo, writing exceeds the field of the book, and is opened to other, more informal, in a word more experimental forms of production, interaction, and exchange than many avant-garde authors, who above all remained "authors," could dream of.

As the examples and issues raised in this chapter have demonstrated, OuLiPo, and procedural writing in general, represents much more than just a period, a tendency, or a style in the global history of avant-garde writing. First, it clearly exceeds all temporal, geographical, and stylistic boundaries: the type of constraints that OuLiPo has helped us to define and describe more neatly can be found everywhere. Second, and perhaps more surprisingly, its use cannot be reduced to the mere domain of avant-garde or "innovative" writing, which only emphasizes the universal role and status of this kind of literature. Third, constrained writing is not a technique or a device whose stakes are merely technical or stylistic: constraints urge us to reconsider the most basic questions of literature, such as, "what is a writer?", "what does it mean to finish a text?", or "what is the role of the reader?" In this sense constraints can be considered a window into what literature actually means in society.

References

Abish, W. (1974) *Alphabetical Africa*, New York: New Directions.
Andrews, C. (2003) "Constraint and Convention: The Formalism of the Oulipo," *Neophilologus* 87: 223–32.
—— (2009) "Paranoid Interpretations and Formal Encoding," *Poetics Today* 30(4): 669–92.
Bök, C. (2003) *Crystallography*, Toronto: The Coach House Press.
—— (2009) *Eunoia*, Toronto: The Coach House Press.
Brooke-Rose, C. (1968) *Between*, London: Michael Joseph.
—— (1984) *Amalgamemnon*, London: Carcanet.
Caillois, R. (2003) *The Edge of Surrealism: A Roger Caillois Reader*, ed. and trans. C. Frank and C. Naish, Durham, NC: Duke University Press.
Compagnon, A. (2005) *Les antimodernes*, Paris: Gallimard.
Grangaud, M. (1987) *Stations*, Paris: P.O.L.
James, A. (2009) *Constraining Chance: Georges Perec and the Oulipo*, Evanston, IL: Northwestern University Press.
Lebensztejn, J.-C. (1972) *La Fourche*, Paris: Gallimard.
Magné, B., C. Hartje and J. Neefs (1993) *Cahier des charges de la Vie mode d'emploi*, Paris: Zulma/CNRS.
Marx, W. (ed.) (2004) *Les arrière-gardes au XXe siècle*, Paris: PUF.
Mathews, H. and A. Brotchie (2005 [1998]) *Oulipo Compendium*, London: Atlas.
Motte, W. (2003 [1986]) *Oulipo: A Primer of Potential Literature*, Normal, IL: Dalkey Archive Press.

—— (ed.) (2006) "Jacques Jouet" [special issue], *Substance* 30(3).

Nunez, L. (2006) *Les écrivains contre l'écriture*, Paris: Corti.

Paulhan, J. (2006 [1936]) *The Flowers of Tarbes, or Terror in Literature*, trans. M. Syrotinski, Urbana-Champaign, IL: University of Illinois Press.

Perec, G. (1976) *Alphabets*, Paris: Galilée.

—— (1995 [1969]) *A Void*, trans. G. Adair, Harvill: First Edition.

—— (2009 [1978]) *Life A User's Manual*, trans. D. Bellos, Boston, MA: David R. Godine.

Queneau, R. (1979 [1947]) *Exercices in Style*, trans. B. Wright, London: Calder.

—— (2001 [1959]) *Zazie in the Metro*, trans. B. Wright, Harmondsworth, UK: Penguin.

Ricardou, J. (1965) *La prise/prose de Constantinople*, Paris: Minuit.

—— (1978) *Nouveaux problèmes du roman*, Paris: Seuil.

Roussel, R. (2005 [1935]) *How I Wrote Certain of My Books*, trans. J. Ashbery, H. Mathews, K. Koch, and T. Winkfield, Boston, MA: Exact Change.

10

METAFICTION

R. M. Berry

I. Against mimesis

Like other aesthetic concepts, "metafiction" makes unavoidable the problem of all concepts, that they do not precede, either logically or historically, their application. The word first appears in 1970 in William Gass's essay, "Philosophy and the Form of Fiction," originally written for a volume edited by Robert Scholes and then included later that same year in William Gass's first collection of critical essays, *Fiction and the Figures of Life*. Gass uses the word only once, in a characterization of the work of Jorge Luis Borges, John Barth, and Flann O'Brien, "in which the forms of fiction serve as the material upon which further forms can be imposed" (Gass 1970: 25), deriving his neologism by analogy from terms fashionable in philosophy at the time, e.g., "metatheory," "metalanguage," "metaphilosophy." Citing several of his other essays for elaboration, Gass seems to have in mind the already textual constitution of these three authors' texts, their construction from previous constructions or from the constituents (genres, tropes, plots, types) of previous constructions. In the cited essays, he quotes Borges saying that "Perhaps universal history is the history of a few metaphors" (Gass 1970: 130–1), remarks that we all live inside the library of Babel (133), and says of Donald Barthelme that the pop songs, television shows, movies, newspapers, books, and magazines his fiction quotes "supply us with our experience" (100). However, it is far from clear how this inclusion of parts of other fictions in a fiction could be analogous to Wittgenstein's metaphilosophical aphorisms in *Philosophical Investigations* (2001: §109–§133) or Roman Jakobson's metalingual function of speech, "I don't follow you – what do you mean?" (Jakobson 2001: 1263). Gass's term occurs at the conclusion of a polemic in which the metafictional works he mentions instance his claim that "the art of the novel is now a mature art" (Gass 1970: 26), its maturation consisting in the novelist's "ceasing to pretend that his business is to render the world; he knows, more often now, that his business is to *make* one" (24). That is, the metafictional impulse seems continuous for Gass with a particular cultural development, one in which earlier pretenses to representational fidelity have been repudiated. When in the twenty-ninth section of Part Two of *Lolita* Humbert narrates, "Then I pulled out my automatic – I mean, this is the kind of fool thing a reader might suppose I did," Nabokov's 1955 novel exemplifies a familiar version of this repudiation, breaking its own mimetic illusion in the fashion of Bertolt Brecht's alienation effect or René Magritte's "Ceci n'est pas une pipe." Gass's flat assertion, "There are no descriptions in fiction, there are only constructions" (17), would seem, at least on first reading, to align his new concept with disillusionments of just this kind.

Metafiction's subsequent applications have often presumed some such anti-mimetic, counter-realist, or skeptical motivation. Writing in 1976, Larry McCaffery identified metafiction's defining characteristic as its attention to its own constructedness, noting that this attention "force[s] us to consider the book we are reading *as an artefact*, undercutting the realistic impulses of the work" (Curry 1995: 183), and in 1984 Patricia Waugh proposed a similar formulation: "Metafiction is a term given to fictional writing which self-consciously and systematically draws attention to its status as an artefact in order to pose questions about the relationship between fiction and reality" (Waugh 1988: 2). Although Linda Hutcheon's work on narcissistic narrative, originally published in 1980, argued for metafiction's "mimesis of process" to replace realism's "mimesis of product" (Hutcheon 1985: 38–9), her 1988 work on postmodernism and history makes explicit that the suspicion of "empiricist and positivist epistemologies" remains fundamental even to metafiction's historiographic versions (Hutcheon 1988: 106). In the thirteenth chapter of John Fowles's *The French Lieutenant's Woman* (1969), a passage cited ubiquitously by scholarly interpreters of metafiction, either Fowles or his persona abruptly announces, "The story I am telling is all imagination. These characters I create never existed outside my own mind" (Fowles 1970: 80). Waugh argues that Fowles's dispelling of mimetic illusion with this and similar intrusions reminds us "that our 'real' world can *never* be the 'real' world of the novel" (Waugh 1988: 33), and Hutcheon goes further, claiming that even the one breaking the illusion is exposed as part of it: "The voice of the narrator is not an exterior authenticating authorial one; it is the voice of a character" (Hutcheon 1985: 63). The idea is that the undisguised textual constitution of Fowles's representation advances the same anti-representational point as Gass's polemic. That is, Fowles's novel does not describe its world; it constructs it. Or in Raymond Federman's formulation: "[F]iction can no longer be reality, or a representation of reality, or an imitation, or even a recreation of reality; it can only be A REALITY – an autonomous reality whose only relation with the real world is to improve that world" (Federman 1975: 8).

Given such sweeping characterizations of metafiction, one wonders to what, if any, subdivision of literature the concept could still apply. The problem is not just that the difference between a text and its context, which all theories of metafiction emphasize, seems itself undermined by these anti-representational claims, but that literature, the value and relevance of which metafiction questions, emerges from the questioning unaltered, as though the so-called "problematizing" of representation merely involves an attitude. In Hutcheon's realist accommodation, metafictional disillusionments of the kind instanced by Fowles and Nabokov are contained within their own diegesis or frame, making these pseudo-authorial acknowledgments of artifice no different from any dramatized narrator's confession. Only the reader's absorption in fiction, not fiction as such, undergoes a change: "[T]he parody and self-reflection of narcissistic narrative work to prevent the reader's identification with any character and to force a new, more active, thinking relationship upon him" (Hutcheon 1985: 49).

Because *The French Lieutenant's Woman*, which Hutcheon takes as her "model" of metafiction (57), keeps its diegetic levels discrete and its language conventional, it seems much better suited to this kind of normalizing account than such works as Ronald Sukenick's "The Death of the Novel" (1969), Gass's *Willie Master's Lonesome Wife* (1968), John Barth's *Lost in the Funhouse* (1968), or Donald Barthelme's *Come Back, Dr. Caligari* (1964), in all of which the action of narrating and the narrating of action are harder to distinguish. In Sukenick's novella, the authorial I's fictional status seems more a given than a theme. There is little or no dispelling of illusion when the text shifts abruptly from narrated past to narrating present,

> Since it was eleven forty-five, we went outside and I hailed her a cab, for which her father had given her money. I suspect there's a bear around here.
> (Sukenick 2003: 52)

partly because "dislocation" in life and art is its announced subject, and partly because no formal or grammatical markers reinforce these narratological distinctions. More significantly, however, the sweepingly anti-mimetic pronouncements of metafiction's proponents, which lend significance to intrusions like Fowles's, are themselves deprived of authority by Sukenick's work. It is not only that their internal contradictions become obtrusive ("God was the omniscient author, but he died" the author announces with godlike omniscience [41]) or even that all such sublimations are shown to be motivated (they are being spoken while the author's thigh is stroked under the seminar table), but that their contextually justified expression occurs only in the voice of a pathetic, proleptically doomed anti-war protester, Neal. "Nothing is real, said Neal. Maybe jail will be real. / Jesus, if jail is the only thing that's real . . . / I might as well kill myself, right?" (88). If it remains true that Sukenick's fiction questions its relationship to reality, that fact no longer means it simply asserts its artificiality. It means that it asks, if experience and observation no longer connect life with art, how is what the reader and writer are doing still possible? In short, what is fiction – *really*?

II. The real conditions of fiction

It does not require a very sophisticated reading of "Philosophy and the Form of Fiction" to feel that Gass's anti-realist polemic is secondary, if not wholly extraneous, to his interest in metafiction. That interest develops out of Gass's titular subject, the relationship of philosophy to fiction, and it remains integral to his aim throughout Part One of *Fiction and the Figures of Life* to base their relationship on fiction's form, not its content. A properly philosophical approach to novels, in Gass's view, would focus on their conditions of existence, their rules, laws, principles of inference (Gass

1970: 21), all that a logical positivist or Kantian (Gass 1970: 71) would call their representational form, revealing different novelists to be "empiricists, idealists, skeptics, or stoics," not in what they have to say, but in the way their works are composed (Gass 1970: 25). Although Gass complains that "the philosophical analysis of fiction has scarcely taken its first steps" (Gass 1970: 25), he believes that such an analysis could lead to a "comprehensive esthetic" of the novel, providing a systematic basis for critical understanding and aesthetic judgment (Gass 1970: 26). In other words, the interest of Borges, Barth, and O'Brien for Gass is that their works establish a properly philosophical relation of fiction to itself, one in which writer and reader engage in something like a critical analysis of the formative conditions of their own activity. Such an application of the concept of "metafiction" would seem especially fitting for a work such as Barth's *Lost in the Funhouse*, where reflection on its constructive rules, laws, and principles often appears explicit: "The function of the *beginning* of a story is to introduce the principal characters, establish their initial relationships, set the scene for the main action . . ." (Barth 1969: 73). Although Borges's fiction seems less obtrusively self-conscious than Barth's, such fictions as "The Library of Babel" and "Pierre Menard, Author of the *Quixote*" are comprised of little more than commentaries on – almost phenomenologies of – reading and writing, and in O'Brien's *At Swim-Two-Birds* the discussion of stories, genres, writing, and books comprises much of its characters' dialogue. In classifying metafiction as a border discourse between literature and criticism, Mark Currie focuses on this developed capacity for self-commentary, arguing like Gass that it establishes a fiction's internal relation to "metacriticism," Currie's term for postmodern philosophy (Curry 1995: 2). The idea is that, because "the forms of fiction serve as the material upon which further forms can be imposed," these works seem to undertake a philosophical investigation of themselves.

Although focusing on the explicitly self-reflective, metacritical, or theoretical passages of such fictions will not account for all that sets them apart, much less all that Gass and others who have cared about them care about, the frequency of such passages is striking. In the fictions of the sixties and seventies most often prefixed meta, sur, or super – e.g., Nabokov's *Pale Fire* (1962), B.S. Johnson's *Albert Angelo* (1964), Christine Brooke-Rose's *Out* (1964), Harry Mathews's *Tlooth* (1966), Julio Cortázar's *Blow Up* (1967), Steve Katz's *The Exaggerations of Peter Prince* (1968), Robert Coover's *Pricksongs and Descants* (1969), John Hawkes's *The Blood Oranges* (1972), Thomas Pynchon's *Gravity's Rainbow* (1973), Clarence Majors's *Reflex and Bone Structure* (1975), Carlos Fuentes's *Terra nostra* (1975), Sukenick's 98.6 (1975), Federman's *Take It or Leave It* (1976), Susan Sontag's *I, etcetera* (1977), Italo Calvino's *If on a Winter's Night a Traveler* (1979), Gilbert Sorrentino's *Mulligan Stew* (1979), or works by Gass, Barthelme, Barth, Beckett, Borges, and Fowles – one regularly encounters descriptions of the work as though from a position above, beyond, or outside it. These may take the form of statements about literature as such, e.g., the narrator's notorious comment in *At Swim-Two-Birds* that "a satisfactory novel should be a self-evident sham" (O'Brien 1976: 33); or of representations of the writing as it is occurring, e.g., Federman's descriptions of his on-going compositional process throughout *Take It or Leave It*; or of comments on the text we hold in our hands, e.g., the publishers' letters rejecting *Mulligan Stew* at the start of *Mulligan Stew*. In other words, an implication of fiction's transcendental prefixes seems to have been that, even if no longer pretending to represent the world, fiction was still pretending to represent itself. In *Willie Masters' Lonesome Wife*, which McCaffery calls "a remarkably pure example of metafiction" (Curry 1995: 191), the work continuously comments on its own constructive principles. As Sam, "the only English critic," explains, "the figures S, U, N, are purely arbitrary modes of recalling their objects, . . . being nothing *per se*" in contrast to the sun itself, which "is large and orange and boiling" (Gass 1973: unpaginated). This disjuncture of words and objects describes both the work's form and its narrative predicament. "The usual view," the personified text recounts, "is that you see through me, through what I am really – significant sound." However, imaginative discourse differs from scientific and logical in seeking to join "sound and sense," such that "symbols seem to contain their objects." The work's aim is to maintain contact with its reader, not through represented action or character, but through its meaning's materialization: "the words which speak, they are the body of the speaker. It's just the same with me. These words are all I am."

How could saying so matter? It seems clear in retrospect that the early metafictionists were impressed by the kind of disjuncture of form and content, matter and meaning, that Gass's fiction describes. It was as though recent history, both political and cultural, had exposed fiction's received versions as fraudulent, as mere pseudo-sociology, amateur psychology, pop metaphysics, or undisciplined journalism, and whether they considered these versions obsolete, naïve, arbitrary, or just boring, the metafictionists were determined to establish the real conditions for their practice (Federman 1975: 59–74; Barthelme 1997: 15–18; Sorrentino 1981: 14–15, 32; Sorrentino 1990: 107–8). For Barth, such conditions could still be found in fiction's earlier versions, the forms of which were viable if employed ironically. Although novelistic conventions for the imitation of action might be anachronistic, he famously argued in "The Literature of Exhaustion," they could be replaced by novelistic imitations of those same conventions, "which attempt to represent not life directly but a representation of life" (Federman 1975: 29). By contrast, Sukenick advocated a more anarchic approach, insisting both with and against Barth that "it takes form to destroy form" (Federman 1975: 40). He recommended an improvisatory and abstract fiction, one that would assure contact with reality by responding to "the flow of experience" while preserving sufficient distance to avoid imitating "some version of reality other than its own" (44). For Federman, as for Gass, Sorrentino, and Barthelme, the real conditions of fiction were to be found in its verbal medium, making writing "a mere process of letting language do its tricks" (Federman 1975: 8). Both writer and reader needed, in Barthelme's formulation, to follow language as Gertrude Stein did, "wherever it leads (and if it leads nowhere, to make capital of that)" (Barthelme 1997: 5). Although these various versions of metafictional or surfictional practice were affirmed to greater or less extent by virtually all of its practitioners, they would seem less coherent in retrospect than at the time, something Barthelme later acknowledged (Barthelme 1997: 23). As Italo Calvino explained, fiction's self-critique appeared to combine two antagonistic impulses. On the one hand, it expressed a conviction in the linguistic structuration of literature, in fiction's being "merely the permutation of a finite set of elements and functions," while on the other, it involved a desire to transcend this structure, to "escape from the confines of language" and express "that which no dictionary contains" (Federman 1975: 76–7). In other words, what the metafictionists were seeking, the formative principles of their lives and art, might turn out to be, once found, nothing they could just say.

III. The sexual politics of metafiction

Consistent with Gass's strictures on philosophical statements, *Willie Masters' Lonesome Wife* does not content itself with merely saying how it is constructed. On the contrary, Gass uses a variety of techniques to achieve, in reality, the unity of matter and meaning that, according to his fiction, imaginative discourse seeks: fragmentation, disruptive juxtaposition, lyricism, *mise-en-abyme*, typographical variation, color, parody, iconic symbolism, photography, figuration, surface texture, etc. In other words, the stated aim of *Willie Masters' Lonesome Wife*, to transcend the disjuncture of form and content, is not identical with its explicit self-description. It must do something, or become it, over and above what it can say. For McCaffery, what it must do is "never [allow] the reader to forget that literature is made of words and nothing else," something ostensibly accomplished by emphasizing the words' "sensuous qualities" (Curry 1995: 184). But its success seems to depend, for McCaffery as for others, on Gass's organizing metaphor: that reading his fiction is having sex with a woman. In other words, unforgetting language does not occur merely through the accretion of sense data. It occurs through the *eroticizing* of that data, the transforming of words' sensory qualities into "sensuous" ones. What gives the early metafictionists' pronouncements their peculiar mixture of zeal and emptiness is their confidence that what is most desired, immediate contact with reality, is in some sense right before everyone's eyes, combined with their offsetting awareness that, if readers fail to experience it, no amount of direct statement will help. An under-discussed feature of metafictional and surfictional works is how often they are wholly *lacking* in any explicit commentary on themselves. In Coover's "The Baby Sitter" (1969), Pynchon's *The Crying of Lot 49* (1966), or Barthelme's "Marie, Marie, Hold on Tight" (1964), no pseudo-author intervenes to break the illusion and no narrator comments self-consciously on the formative conditions of his or her own narrating. Although the author or pseudo-author of Ishmael Reed's *Mumbo Jumbo* (1972) editorializes continuously, the object of his critical commentary is western culture and the art of high modernism, only indirectly or by implication his own work, and in Sorrentino's *Mulligan Stew*, a fiction replete with discussions of fiction, not only is there no self-conscious narrator, there is no narrator. With the possible exception of Sorrentino's letter to Barney Rosset in the front matter, the entirety of the text is comprised of documents written by characters.

Trying to adjudicate conflicts over the position of women in metafiction of the sixties and seventies, specifically, over whether the male-centered perspective of a work like Gass's is a necessary condition of its desire for transcendence, seems particularly uninviting, but a continuing value of such conflicts is that they locate the problem of metafiction at the right depth (see Friedman, this volume). Brian McHale's productive insight that, despite their anti-representational pronouncements, these early metafictions were confronting ontological rather than epistemological questions, suggests that a verdict on metafiction's sexual politics will prove inseparable from an assessment of what individual metafictions achieve over and above their representations (McHale 1987: 3–25). In other words, if metafiction's aim is to overcome fiction's structural dividedness, its estrangement from its own reality, then the sexual necessities of its construction are part of what its writing and reading must themselves discover. Although it is difficult to imagine how, even allowing for critical distance, the phallocentrism of *Willie Masters' Lonesome Wife* could prove inessential to it, other metafictions arouse a desire for words through less explicitly sexual means. In Barthelme's "Marie, Marie, Hold on Tight" (Barthelme 1964: 115–22), the metaphor for reading the work is attending a demonstration, one in which our relation to the signs of protest, presented on Barthelme's page, is as direct as that of the fictional spectators. What the signs say ("MAN DIES!" "THE SOUL IS NOT!" [119]) is that human being is limited, that our ontology is a finite construction, but their occurrence in the contexts of the story *demonstrates* something quite different. What it demonstrates is partly indicated in the fictional contexts by the spectators' responses, two of which receive detailed treatment. The first is that of a church official who praises the "Kierkegaardian spirit" of the protest but replies, not unreasonably, that "the human condition is the *given*," that "you have to deal with what is" (116, 117, respectively). The second is that of a youth gang who beat the demonstrators severely. Henry Mackie, spokesperson for the demonstrators, dismisses the church official's response as exemplifying the complacency they are demonstrating against, while he takes the gang's violence to mean "they understand everything better than anybody" (121). If protesting against human finitude strikes us, too, as meaningless, a mere refusal "to deal with what is," what about the signs on the page has the youth gang experienced that we are missing?

IV. Poetics

To conceive of metafiction as an attempt to discover fiction's own reality – i.e. its constructive laws, rules, and principles; its linguistic materiality; its inherited or improvised forms; its erotic figuration; etc. – is to distance the term from its application in recent narratology (Fludernik 2003; Nunning 2005), and to align it more closely with what L=A=N=G=U=A=G=E writers have called "poetics." As Lyn Hejinian has explained, the practice of poetics need not be understood as the issuing of theoretical statements about poetry for which poems function merely as illustrations. It can also be a poem's capacity "for speaking about itself" (Hejinian 2000: 1), initiating a philosophical inquiry through its on-going practice and avoiding logical regress through the coincidence of action and object: "Poetry . . . takes as its premise that language is a medium for experiencing experience" (3). In other words, instead of fore-grounding fiction's artificiality and constructedness, the concept of metafiction would subsume narratology's contrasting term "metanarrative," applying broadly to formally experimental works or parts of works in which the action of narrating becomes its own object. Hejinian has described this kind of immanent theoretical practice: "One wants to ask how one gets going, how one keeps going, and how one knows what is going on. . . . But none of these questions is more or less basic than any of the others" (165). Such an application of the concept has the double virtue of acknowledging what those works first called "metafictions" cared about and also of disclosing a genealogy for them in earlier fiction. Such moments as Lambert Strether's entering his imagina-tion's frame in the Lambernet scene of James's *The Ambassadors* (Book Eleventh, III), where the represented action becomes the process of aesthetic construction, or Stein's thematizing of Melanctha Herbert's inability to "tell a story wholly" in *Three Lives*, or Jake Barnes's linking of literariness to fakery in Hemingway's *The Sun Also Rises*, or Matthew O'Connor's wish for the end of writing in Djuna Barnes's *Nightwood*, or Addie Bundren's critique of words in Faulkner's *As I Lay Dying* would all be proto-metafictions, places where epistemology shades into ontology, raising questions about the structure *within which* the epistemological issue achieves language and conscious-ness. At such points the problem *in* the work becomes the problem *of* the work, initiat-ing for both writer and reader a quest for self-knowledge that cannot achieve closure in self-representation. But, as Hejinian remarks, "this is not knowledge in the strictest sense; it is, rather, acknowledgment . . . a preservation of otherness" (2).

Focusing on novelists' attempts in the sixties and subsequent decades to engage reality, not primarily by representing it but by acknowledging its immanence in their medium and practice, distances metafiction from the kind of self-consciousness that was already considered by Gass in 1970 a dead-end, "those drearily predictable pieces about writers who are writing about what they are writing" (Gass 1970: 25). The con-cept would apply to fictions disclosing the significance of their own activity, what "Marie, Marie, Hold on Tight" characterizes as sign-making, which our normal prac-tices of reading and writing tend to repress. In other words, Barthelme's fiction would remain as much a commentary on itself as, e.g., Gilbert Sorrentino's comment in *Imaginative Qualities of Actual Things* (1971) that "everything [fiction] teaches is use-less insofar as structuring your life" (Sorrentino 1991: 215), the significance of which would no longer be its generalization about fiction's uselessness. Although the ironic self-consciousness of sixties and seventies metafictions was probably a necessary regis-ter of their ontological problem, what has made them valuable, both at the time and since, is the relation of that self-consciousness – expressed in pseudo-autobiography, exposed illusion, authorial commentary, or metacriticism – to their innovative uses of form, language, and book art. For example, the caustic irony of Sorrentino's *Mul-ligan Stew* seems far-removed from the politically engaged, often impassioned writ-ing of Theresa Hak Kyung Cha's *DICTEE* (Cha 1982), which, by contrast, seems to exemplify the conflation of literature and life that Sorrentino's earlier quote, and any number of citable others, dogmatically rejects. However, the formal construction of these two works, published only three years apart, appears remarkably similar. Both are composed of documents written by others, and both treat these documents as visual objects whose differences of appearance are preserved on the page. In both works, the autonomy of the linguistic medium, along with being thematic, is acknowledged through passages that, while seeming naturally connected to the narrative, do not advance it: i.e. French dictation and translation exercises in Cha's work and the interminable lists in Sorrentino's. And in addition to the numerous thematic parallels – the recurrent topics of mimicry, voice, embodiment, etc. – Cha's writing can be as acerbic in her lines of dictation ("Oh my God, I am heartily sorry for having offended Thee" [Cha 2001: 14]) as Sorrentino's can be earnest in his appreciation for characters who "never yet have walked from off the page" (Sorrentino 1979: 445).

When metafictions of the sixties and seventies are placed alongside formally innovative fictions published in the U.S. during more recent decades – Paul Auster's *New York Trilogy* (1985), Ronald Sukenick's *Blown Away* (1985), Kathy Acker's *Don Quixote* (1986), David Markson's *Wittgenstein's Mistress* (1988), Carole Maso's *AVA* (1993), Ben Marcus's *The Age of Wire and String* (1995), David Foster Wallace's *Infinite Jest* (1996), Brian Evenson's *Contagion* (2000), Mark Z. Danielewski's *House of Leaves* (2000), Michael Martone's *The Blue Guide to Indiana* (2001), Steve Tomasula's *VAS* (2002), Lidia Yuknavitch's *Real to Reel* (2003), or Leslie Scalapino's *Dahlia's Iris: Secret Autobiography and Fiction* (2003) – it becomes clearer that what fictional self-consciousness and formal experimentation share is a common acknowledgment of their medium's autonomy. For the early metafictionists, what seems to have been most striking about the work of Beckett, Borges, and O'Brien was the way literature acquired an objectivity comparable to, not only its represented world, but even its writer and reader. Writing in 1964 Barthelme assigned the origin of this change to Joyce and Stein, characterizing it as a "mysterious shift" that occurs when "art is not about something but *is* something" (Barthelme 1997: 3) and praising Beckett's creation of fully realized objects that, by contrast, exposed the artificiality and mutilation of their social surroundings. Even in novels that preserve the surface appearance of self-conscious narration, i.e. fictions in which one narrating consciousness takes another as its object or adversary, the aim never appears to be critical distance per se, but rather the work's achievement. In Paul Auster's *City of Glass* (1982), Clarence Major's *My Amputations* (1986), and Lydia Davis's *The End of the Story* (1995), all three of which literalize an author's or reader's critical relation to his or her own activity, the potential for consciousness turning endlessly upon itself is merely part of the narrative predicament, a threat of never-ending self-doubt or of an action's interminable repeating. Instead of progressing toward the identification of represented and representing selves, the direction of the narrative is toward displacement of both self and representation by the object in hand. Auster's novel becomes the material realization of Quinn's red notebook, neither of which is the other's original, while Mason's pursuit of his likeness in Major's novel brings the would-be author to an end, escaping imprisonment in the West's two Atticas (the classical tradition and the New York State Correctional Facility) by submitting to "some unknown . . . event," and the unnamed narrator of Davis's work, having satisfactorily performed *literary* closure, concludes her affair's interminable repetition. In all three, the irresolvable problem of dividedness and self-approximation is resolved, not by identification, but by the problem's disappearance. An object that can only be *narrated* as metaphysically incomplete, in the action of narrating becomes wholly material.

V. Historiographic metafiction

Although works classified as "historiographic metafiction" have been seen by numerous critics as the continuation into the eighties of the work of Pynchon, Coover, Barth, and Gass, this application of the concept turns on metafiction's identification with its anti-mimetic, counter-realist self-descriptions. For Hutcheon who introduced the classification, but also for Waugh, Raymond Mazurek (Curry 1995: 194–205), Susana Onega (Curry 1995: 92–103), and Bran Nicol (2009), metafiction's rapprochement with the historical novel restores the conventions of narrative realism while retaining such anti-mimetic elements as exposed illusions, conflicting accounts, authorial disclaimers, and counter-factual references. In Nicol's summary, although the "primary aims" of Barth and Coover "were to 'explode realist narrative conventions' (Hutcheon 1988: xii), by contrast a work of 'historiographic metafiction' . . . is still committed to telling a long and involving story, full of believable characters, which can be enjoyed by the reader in the manner of nineteenth-century realism" (Nicol 2009: 99). Although historiographic metafiction is taken by most critics to include such challenging works as *Gravity's Rainbow* and *The Public Burning*, Hutcheon's coinage marginalizes explorations of fiction's form, language, and materiality, promoting instead straightforwardly narrative works such as E.L. Doctorow's *Ragtime* (1975), Umberto Eco's *The Name of the Rose* (1980), D.M. Thomas's *The White Hotel* (1981), Graham Swift's *Waterland* (1983), Salman Rushdie's *Shame* (1983), Julian Barnes's *Flaubert's Parrot* (1984), J.M. Coetzee's *Foe* (1986), and Don DeLillo's *Libra* (1988). McHale has shown, however, that even the mild epistemological skepticism favored by Hutcheon remains continuous with the more radical investigations of O'Brien, Borges, Beckett, Barthelme, and Barth. McHale identifies three devices in historiographic metafiction – apocryphal history, creative anachronism, and historical fantasy (McHale 1987: 90–6) – which, because they contest, not merely history's received versions, but the order of the possible, tend to disrupt the long and involving stories Nicol enjoys, producing ontological dislocation and groundlessness.

What seems right about Hutcheon's pitting fictive historiography against metafictional experimentation is that, despite metafiction's drawing its significance from narrative representation, there is something irreducibly anti-narrative and non-representational about it. As Robert Scholes remarked in 1970, "Metafiction . . . tends toward brevity because it attempts, among other things, to assault or transcend the laws of fiction" (Scholes 1979: 114), a remark that, even if too tendentious in referencing "laws of fiction," correctly notes an internal limit on metafictional development. If there is a connection between metafiction's awareness of its constructed condition and its quest for reality, then that connection is simply this inherent potential for radical failure. Unlike historical novels, some metafictions raise the question, not just of whether they are good novels, but of whether they qualify as novels at all. Metafiction's putative challenge to historiography is, in this sense, not an epistemological challenge to the accuracy of historical representation, but a challenge to narrative representation per se, a challenge less like Hayden White's than like Nietzsche's "Use and Abuse of History," where questions about how to live presently get displaced by representations of the past, even when accurate. In works such as Carole Maso's *AVA* (1993), Brian Evenson's "Contagion" and "Watson's Boy" (2000), Steve Tomasula's *VAS* (2002), David Markson's *Vanishing Point* (2004), or Michael Martone's *Michael Martone* (2005), narrative representation continues, often in attenuated or fragmentary form, but the reality with which we seek contact no longer resembles that narratively represented. The chronology of Ava Klein's last day seems as extraneous to Ava's struggle as the fragmentary narrative pieced together from her recollections, and the search among Martone's fifty-two autobiographies for the history of the other fifty-one merely defers the problem of authority raised by the whole. Although Evenson's fictions seem classically narrative, their patterns of abstraction call for an allegory they never provide, and Tomasula's brief tale of domestic tension seems almost incidental to the obtrusive, gorgeous body of his book. Our disappointment with the represented action in all of these works merely expresses our sense that the *real* action is taking place much closer to us.

VI. *Vanishing Point*

From the sixties to the present, the achievement of metafiction, and the source of its continuing attraction, is this eclipse of mimesis by acknowledgment of the work. In David Markson's *Vanishing Point*, as in so many metafictions, it is the obstacle to acknowledgment, not the action of overcoming it, that comprises the representation. This obstacle appears in the second of Markson's roughly two thousand "notes," where we learn that a seascape by Matisse was hung upside down in MOMA for over a month (Markson 2004: 1), while a hundred and sixteen thousand viewers passed without complaint (3). As the ensuing assemblage of anecdotes, gossip, facts, names, and quotes makes clear, this inversion of aesthetic values does not result merely from popular incomprehension. Artists and critics are equally undiscerning. Aaron Copland compared Ralph Vaughan Williams' music to "staring at a cow for forty-five minutes" (3); "Victor Hugo found *Le Rouge et le Noir*" unreadable (13); Heraclitus thought Homer should have been beaten (69); "Schoolboy drivel" was Edith Wharton's judgment of *Ulysses* (156), and Auden thought Brecht deserved capital punishment (174). The history of literature and art in Author's notes encompasses all the stupidity, dogmatism, and blindness of humans generally. Given such disorder, how can we take seriously the statement, "Author is pretty sure that most of [the notes] are basically in the sequence he wants" (8)? If there is any basis for their order, that is not apparent from the history represented in the notes. And yet, where but in history could literature and art's basis be? Although saying that metafiction attempts to transcend the "laws of fiction" merely projects a critic's own presumption onto novelists, Markson's work certainly attempts to transcend the randomness he inherits. If Gass is right that metafiction establishes a philosophical relation to its own laws, rules, and principles, then it should be added with Sukenick, Calvino, and even Henry James, that prior to the work before us fiction's laws remain in doubt.

A familiar effect of reflexivity, acknowledged in some metafictions by direct authorial address, is the establishment of reading and writing as collaboration. In Markson's fiction this dependence on his reader is literalized in Author's acknowledgments of all that he does not himself know: where the book is headed (Markson 2004: 11), what he thinks (22), why he writes on a typewriter (27), where he found his information (59), what makes him suspicious of some quotes (68), why he introduces something he knows in the form of a question (70), what the purpose of his experiment is (96), etc. Although Author's gradual demise in *Vanishing Point* is a fictional representation, it accurately reflects a limit on what Markson's own action can achieve. From Beckett to the present, the metafictional recognition that experience and observation no longer connect art with life has coincided with calls to unrepress fiction's medium – variously its language, inherited forms, principles of construction, materiality, erotic figuration, etc. In praising Beckett's fully realized objects, Barthelme sought to conceptualize fiction as other than either a naturally occurring object or a merely idiosyncratic one. Fiction was as lawful as justice or language, but its formative principles, immanent in past examples, became real only in present applications. In other words, if the reader discovers in Author's notes only what Markson himself put there, *Vanishing Point* does not qualify as a novel at all. For it to *be* something, not merely *about* something, the reader must see what Author sees: the significance of *this* arrangement. Needless to say, this demand for acknowledgement may feel intolerably self-conscious. To anyone asking Henry Mackie's question, "Why does it have to be that way?" (Barthelme 1964: 117), the reply of Barthelme's church official – "You have to deal with what is. With reality." – will sound patently false. Every day humans refuse to deal with what is, with reality. In the context of Barthelme's protest, what the signs demonstrate is that humans are free, that no reader can be forced to acknowledge them. And to those living under material constraint, such a demonstration can seem like an outrage. Most learn to repress it, but the occasional gang of youth understands.

References

Barth, J. (1969) *Lost in the Funhouse*, New York: Bantam.
Barthelme, D. (1964) *Come Back, Dr. Caligari*, Boston, MA: Little, Brown.
—— (1997) *Not-Knowing: The Essays and Interviews*, ed. K. Herzinger, New York: Vintage.
Cha, T. (2001) *DICTEE*, Berkeley, CA: University of California Press.
Curry, M. (ed.) (1995) *Metafiction*, New York: Longman.
Federman, R. (ed.) (1975) *Surfiction: Fiction Now and Tomorrow*, Chicago, IL: Swallow Press.
Fludernik, M. (2003) "Metanarrative and Metafictional Commentary: From Metadiscursivity to Metanarration and Metafiction," *Poetica* 35(1/2): 1–39.

Fowles, J. (1970) *The French Lieutenant's Woman*, New York: New American Library.

Gass, W. (1970) *Fiction and the Figures of Life*, Boston, MA: David Godine.

—— (1973) *Willie Masters' Lonesome Wife*, New York: Knopf.

Hejinian, L. (2000) *The Language of Inquiry*, Berkeley, CA: University of California Press.

Hutcheon, L. (1985) *Narcissistic Narrative: The Metafictional Paradox*, New York: Methuen.

—— (1988) *A Poetics of Postmodernism: History, Theory, Fiction*, New York: Routledge.

Jakobson, R. (2001) "Linguistics and Poetics," in *The Norton Anthology of Theory and Criticism*, ed. V. Leitch, New York: W.W. Norton, 1258–65.

Markson, D. (2004) *Vanishing Point*, Washington, DC: Shoemaker and Hoard.

McHale, B. (1987) *Postmodernist Fiction*, New York: Routledge.

Nicol, B. (2009) *The Cambridge Introduction to Postmodern Fiction*, New York: Cambridge University Press.

Nunning, A. (2005) "On Metanarrative: Towards a Definition, a Typology and an Outline of the Functions of Metanarrative Commentary." In J. Pier (ed.), *The Dynamics of Narrative Form: Studies in Anglo-American Narratology*, Berlin: Walter de Gruyter, pp. 11–58.

O'Brien, F. (1976) *At Swim-Two-Birds*, New York: Plume.

Scholes, R. (ed.) (1970) *The Philosopher-Critic*, Tulsa, OK: University of Tulsa Press.

—— (1979) *Fabulation and Metafiction*, Urbana, IL: University of Illinois Press.

Sorrentino, G. (1979) *Mulligan Stew*, New York: Grove Press.

—— (1981) "An Interview with Gilbert Sorrentino, 'The Act of Creation and Its Artifact'," *The Review of Contemporary Fiction*, 1(1), 5–27, 28–34.

—— (1990) "Working at Grove: An Interview with Gilbert Sorrentino," *The Review of Contemporary Fiction*, 10(3), 97–110.

—— (1991) *Imaginative Qualities of Actual Things*, Normal, IL: Dalkey Archive Press.

Sukenick, R. (2003) *The Death of the Novel and Other Stories*, Tallahassee, FL: FC2.

Waugh, P. (1988) *Metafiction: The Theory and Practice of Self-Conscious Fiction*, New York: Routledge.

Wittgenstein, L. (2001) *Philosophical Investigations*, 3rd edn., trans. G.E.M. Anscombe, Malden MA: Blackwell.

11
POSTMODERNISM AND EXPERIMENT

Brian McHale

I. Is postmodernism experimental?

One of the conventions of writing about postmodernism is to acknowledge (or boast?) that nothing about the subject is certain, resolved or uncontentious – not its provenance, nor its scope, nor what category of "thing" it is (a period? a style? a movement? a "condition" of culture?), nor its relation to modernism, the date of its presumed onset (late-thirties? 1945? mid-sixties? 1973?), its significance and value, its politics, its degree of complicity with late capitalism, whether or not it has ended yet, whether or not it ever really happened. I don't propose to flout that convention here, but to add one more bone of contention to the list: it is a matter of dispute whether or not postmodernism can be experimental – whether or not it is avant-garde. (The two terms, *experimental* and *avant-garde*, will be used interchangeably here.)

The person-on-the-street who consumes the products of postmodern culture seems to be of two minds about it. On the one hand, postmodernism is widely reputed to be "difficult"; on the other hand, nearly everything has been identified at one time or another as "postmodern" – "the décor of a room, the design of a building, the diagesis of a film, the construction of a record . . ., a television commercial, or an arts documentary, . . . the layout of a page in a fashion magazine or a critical journal" (Hebdige 1988: 182); "Disneyland, Las Vegas, suburban strips, shopping malls, mirror-glass building façades . . . the Kronos Quartet, Frederick Barthelme, MTV, 'Miami Vice,' David Letterman, Laurie Anderson, Anselm Kiefer, Paul Auster, the Pompidou Center, the Hyatt Regency" (Gitlin 1988: 35). If *everything* is postmodern, how experimental could postmodernism be?

Nor is a clear resolution of the question to be found among the theorists of postmodernism, who on this issue (as on many others) appear sometimes to be speaking at cross-purposes. J.-F. Lyotard, the philosopher who, more than anyone else, was responsible for introducing the idea of the postmodern to European intellectuals, associated postmodernism unequivocally with avant-gardism. Indeed, for Lyotard "postmodernism" is the name for the avant-garde impulse *within* modernism. He identified it with that part of modernist art that resists being domesticated and reduced to a familiar period style – the intransigent or intractable part of modernism. It is his identification of postmodernism with the avant-garde that enables Lyotard to assert, notoriously, that "A work can become modern only if it is first postmodern," and that "postmodernism is not modernism at its end, but in a nascent state, and this state is recurrent" (Lyotard 1993: 13). It also explains his denunciation of the kind of eclectic postmodernism reflected in the everything-but-the-kitchen-sink catalogues I cited in the preceding paragraph:

> Eclecticism is the degree zero of contemporary general culture: you listen to reggae; you watch a western; you eat McDonald's at midday and local cuisine at night; you wear Paris perfume in Tokyo and dress retro in Hong Kong; knowledge is the stuff of TV game shows.
>
> (Lyotard 1993: 8)

Lyotard associates this postmodern eclecticism – maliciously, but not incorrectly – with the name of Charles Jencks, the architecture theorist who from the mid-seventies onwards campaigned to popularize the idea of the postmodern, first among architecture practitioners, then across a range of cultural domains, including literature and the visual arts. Lyotard derides Jencks, and Jencks returns the favor, labeling Lyotard's calculated paradox of postmodernism being a nascent state of modernism "a crazy idea" (Jencks 1986: 42). Lyotard, in Jencks's view, has simply confused his categories: insofar as the avant-garde impulse has persisted into the post-1945 period it should be identified not with postmodernism but with *late-modernism*. Postmodernism is precisely *not* avant-garde – or rather, while it may preserve an experimental impulse, it dispenses with the avant-garde spirit of aesthetic intransigence and intractability, instead coupling experimentalism with values of accessibility, legibility, popularity and pleasure.

Jencks embraces the eclecticism that Lyotard denounces, but he associates it with postmodernism's practice of *double-coding*. According to Jencks, postmodern artworks – such as the buildings he championed by Robert Venturi, Michael Graves, Robert A.M. Stern, Frank Gehry, and others – appeal simultaneously to two different constituencies: on one level, through their sophisticated reflection on modernist design, structural techniques and materials, to a minority constituency of architects and connoisseurs; on another level, through their playful and pleasurable allusions to familiar historical styles of architecture, to a broader public of consumers. Jencks elevated this architectural practice of double-coding to a general principle of postmodernism in all the arts – something like a period style. He recognized it, for instance, in the novelist John Barth's account of what he called the "literature of replenishment," which "keeps one foot always in the narrative past . . . and one foot in, one might say, the Parisian structuralist present" (Barth 1984: 204). Barth identifies the literature of replenishment with Gabriel García Márquez's *One Hundred Years of Solitude* (1967) and the fictions of Italo Calvino, and he distinguishes it from the "literature of exhaustion" practiced by Jorge Luis Borges, Samuel Beckett and Vladimir Nabokov. Barth's formula for replenishment, viewed from Jencks's perspective, looks just like postmodern double-coding, while his literature of exhaustion would presumably map onto Lyotard's perpetually intransigent avant-garde.

Jencks also cites Umberto Eco, whose international best seller *The Name of the Rose* (1980) combines specialist knowledge and ironic self-reflection with the populist pleasures of historical fiction and the detective story. *The Name of the Rose* exemplifies the kind of double-coded postmodern historical fiction for which Linda Hutcheon (1988) coined the name *historiographic metafiction* (see Berry, this volume). Other high-profile examples include John Fowles's *French Lieutenant's Woman* (1969), E.L. Doctorow's *Ragtime* (1975), D.M. Thomas's *The White Hotel* (1981), Salman Rushdie's *Midnight's Children* (1981), and Patrick Süskind's *Perfume* (1985), all of which deliver the narrative pleasures of historical fiction while at the same time reflecting critically on the limits of historical knowledge and the historical imagination. Another double-coded genre is the kind of fiction that Larry McCaffery calls *Avant-Pop*, which he associates with such writers as Kathy Acker, Mark Leyner, Ronald Sukenick, William T. Vollmann and David Foster Wallace (see Olsen, this volume). Avant-Pop, according to McCaffery, "combines pop art's focus on consumer goods and mass media with the avant-garde's spirit of subversion and emphasis on radical innovation" (McCaffery 1995: xvii–xviii) – double-coding in a nutshell.

So for Lyotard, what Jencks calls postmodern is actually a *faux*-postmodernism, because postmodernism is by definition experimental, while for Jencks, what Lyotard calls postmodernism is really late-modernism, because postmodernism is not avant-garde or experimental in Lyotard's sense, but double-coded. Andreas Huyssen tries to find a way out of this impasse by reframing the respective positions of Lyotard and Jencks in historical and contextual terms. The first wave of postmodernism in the sixties, he argues, was primarily an American phenomenon, affiliated with the Pop Art of Warhol and others, and genuinely transgressive, pitting the energies of popular culture against the aesthetics of an "official," institutionalized modernism. Seen against the backdrop of its own cultural moment, this first-wave postmodernism constituted a true avant-garde (Huyssen 1986: 188–95). Seen from the perspective of Europe, however, where the modernist avant-garde had never ceased to play an oppositional role in culture, the alliance of high art with popular culture in the American scene could only look like a capitulation to consumerism. Thus, in a sense, Jencks and Lyotard are both right, but since they respond to different cultural circumstances, they end up speaking at cross-purposes.

However, Jencks is also wrong, from Huyssen's perspective, because by the time of which Jencks is writing, the seventies and eighties, the alliance of high and low art had lost the aesthetic and even political radicalism it once possessed and, no longer provocative, had faded into the kind of consumerist eclecticism of which Lyotard complains (Huyssen 1986: 195–9). By the mid-eighties, according to Huyssen, the experimental potential of double-coding had subsided into art world business-as-usual, and no-one could any longer be startled or edified by the mingling of high and low art.

As for Lyotard, if he was perhaps too quick to dismiss the avant-garde potential of popular culture (given the right circumstances), nevertheless his caricature of postmodern eclecticism comes uncomfortably close to hitting the mark. Eclecticism is indeed a *topos* not only of everyday consumer habits in the postmodern era ("the degree zero of contemporary general culture"), but of many forms of postmodern expression – including postmodern theory itself. If one convention of writing about postmodernism is making a show of uncertainty, another convention is the deliberately eclectic catalogue of postmodern symptoms – such as the two catalogues I sampled above in my second paragraph, one from Tod Gitlin, the other from Dick Hebdige, each of them already quoted elsewhere at least once by somebody else (Gitlin by John Frow [1997: 27–8], Hebdige in the Wikipedia entry for *postmodernism*). The same aesthetic of eclecticism is discernible everywhere in postmodernist fiction, for instance in the *topos* of the miscellaneous assemblage, such as the barricade of consumer goods and tshotshkes erected against the Indians in Donald Barthelme's "The Indian Uprising" (1965), or the sedimentary strata of detritus covering Slothrop's desk in Thomas Pynchon's *Gravity's Rainbow* (1973).

At another level, eclecticism is reflected in the postmodern aesthetics of the *mashup*, in the sense that this term has acquired in digital music remixing, where two or more preexisting tracks are mixed together to produce a new, hybrid track (as in Danger Mouse's celebrated mashup [2004] of the Beatles' *White Album* with the rapper Jay-Z's *Black Album*). The digital mashup aesthetic is anticipated by genre mashups in the print medium, such as Calvino's *If on a Winter's Night a Traveller* (1979), David Mitchell's *Cloud Atlas* (2004), or Robert Coover's "Phantom of the Movie Palace" (1987), where a bored projectionist finds a way of layering films of different genres to produce "thick collages of crashing vehicles or mating lovers or gun-toting soldiers, cowboys, and gangsters all banging away in unison" (Coover 2007: 22). In less ambitious manifestations, the mashup aesthetic yields amusing literary gags such as *Pride and Prejudice and Zombies* (2009).

Scaled up to the proportions of an entire storyworld, eclecticism becomes the organizing principle of postmodern representations of the city, for instance in Ridley Scott's seminal science-fiction film, *Blade Runner* (1982), or in William Gibson's cyberpunk novels from the eighties and nineties. At this scale, the postmodern *topos* of eclecticism converges with what Michel Foucault called *heterotopia*. Inspired by Borges's account of the impossible organizing system of an apocryphal Chinese encyclopedia, Foucault speculated about a kind of spatial disorder

> where fragments of a large number of possible orders glitter separately in the dimension . . . of the *heteroclite*; . . . in such a state, things are "laid," "placed," "arranged" in sites so very different from one another that it is impossible to find a place of residence for them, to define a *common locus* beneath them all.
> (Foucault 1970: xviii)

This is the kind of spatial (dis)order – eclecticism realized at the level of the world itself – that characterizes a number of postmodernist texts, conspicuous among them Calvino's *Invisible Cities* (1972) – not coincidentally, one of John Barth's prime examples of double-coded "literature of replenishment." It is here, if anywhere, that Lyotard's postmodernism of the perpetual avant-garde converges with Jencks's postmodernism of double-coding, pleasure and popular appeal.

II. Experiments with worlds

Leaving aside for a moment Lyotard's kind of postmodernism – which is experimental by definition – is there any respect in which the other kind – Jencks's kind, i.e., eclectic postmodernism – can itself be thought of as experimental? Perhaps there is, if we reflect for a moment on those eclectic assemblages from "The Indian Uprising" and *Gravity's Rainbow*: the barricade, the impossibly cluttered desk. From a mimetic perspective, these are impossible objects; they could not physically cohere *as* objects, let alone perform the functions for which they were intended (repulse Indians, facilitate bureaucratic labor). Impossible as objects, they reveal themselves to be assemblages of *signs* – of discursive fragments, each fragment deriving from its own discursive "homeworld" and connoting that world of origin: "two ashtrays, ceramic . . .; a tin frying pan; two-liter bottles of red wine; three-quarter-liter bottles of Black & White, aquavit, cognac, vodka, gin, Fad #6 sherry . . .; a hollow-core door" (Barthelme 1982: 109); "an empty Kreml hair tonic bottle, lost pieces to different jigsaw puzzles . . ., a busted cork screwing ukulele string, boxes of gummed paper stars in many colors, pieces of a flashlight, top to a Nugget shoe polish can" (Pynchon 1973: 18). These impossible composite objects collapse the space between disparate discursive universes, forcing them into proximity and foregrounding their incompatibilities. Like the projectionist in Coover's "Phantom of the Movie Palace" who produces genre mashups to while away the long hours in the projection booth, these eclectic assemblages constitute experiments with worlds.

All fictions experiment with worlds, of course, in the sense that they conduct *thought-experiments*. They ask *"What if?"*: What if there were such a person as Elizabeth Bennett, an intelligent, unmarried gentlewoman living in the English countryside? What if a Nantucket whaling captain became so obsessed with a particular whale that he risked his ship and crew to try to destroy it? What if Clarissa Dalloway gave a party on the same day that a young man whom she had never met committed suicide? The philosopher Catherine Z. Elgin writes:

> Like an experiment, a work of fiction selects and isolates, manipulating circumstances so that particular properties, patterns, and connections, as well as disparities and irregularities are brought to the fore . . . . [I]f thought experiments afford epistemic access to cognitively important factors, works of fiction do, too.
>
> (Elgin 2007: 49, 48)

Most fictional experiments observe what Marie-Laure Ryan calls the *principle of minimal departure* (see Ryan, this volume); that is, they depart from reality only to the extent of varying one or more *individuals* – inventing a few characters and their relationships and doings, interleaving a few invented places amid the given places of the real world – but generally leaving *world-models* intact. Some genres of fiction experiment with world-models; science fiction is one such case (see Gomel, this volume). Postmodernist fiction experiments with individuals, and also with models – which explains its affinity for science fiction – but beyond that it experiments as well with the very *process of world-modeling*.

Modernist fiction, by contrast, experimented with *consciousness*. A key constituent of much modernist fiction is embodied consciousness – the mind in its engagement with the world – which underlies and motivates many of modernism's experiments in narration, focalization, the representation of interiority, temporality, and language, as well as its problematizing of knowing and unknowing (Weinstein 2005). Embodied consciousness persists in postmodernist fiction, of course, but it has been relegated to the background. The foreground is occupied not by consciousness but by the category of *world* itself. To put it differently, what has changed is the *dominant* – "the focusing component of the work of art," which "rules, determines, and transforms the remaining components" and "guarantees the integrity of the structure" (Jakobson 2002: 82). Modernist fiction's dominant was *epistemological*, knowledge-oriented; postmodernist fiction's is *ontological*, being-oriented (McHale 1987, 1992).

Postmodernist fiction does not take the world for granted as a mere backdrop against which the adventures of consciousness can be played out, but rather foregrounds the world itself as an object of reflection and contestation through the use of a range of devices and strategies. Postmodernism multiplies and juxtaposes worlds; it troubles and volatilizes them. If, as Eco has written, a text is a machine for producing possible worlds (Eco 1979: 246), then a postmodern text is a machine for producing sites "where fragments of a large number of possible orders glitter separately" – a machine for producing heterotopias.

Horizontal and vertical heterotopias

Heterotopias, these sites where fragments of worlds are arranged experimentally in assemblages, can be produced in various ways. Worlds can, first of all, be arranged *horizontally*, juxtaposed side-by-side or end-to-end on the same plane, as it were; alternatively, they can be arranged *vertically* – stacked or layered.

When multiple worlds are juxtaposed, their internal constitutions and external boundaries are rendered sharply visible. Plural-world narratives can take various forms, such as that of paranoid-conspiracy narratives in which characters discover "secret histories" or suspect that another order of things lies concealed behind the manifest one, as in novels by Pynchon, Don DeLillo and Ishmael Reed, or in Eco's *Foucault's Pendulum* (1988). At some hard-to-determine point, experimental conspiracy fiction shades off into the popular kind that is a staple of paperback thrillers and TV series (e.g., *The X-Files* or *24*). Another strategy involves juxtaposing a recognizably real world with an adjacent fantastic world, or mingling naturalistic and supernatural elements in the same world. Such experiments are typical of so-called *magical realist* fiction, which is often associated with writers from the postcolonial world (see Gopal, this volume), such as García-Márquez, Rushdie, Julio Cortázar, Carlos Fuentes and Junot Díaz, but also with some who lack a postcolonial background, such as Angela Carter, Milan Kundera and Toni Morrison.

The category of world can also be pluralized and foregrounded through *vertical* proliferation by nesting secondary "micro-worlds" within the primary narrative world, for instance by introducing stories-within-the-story, as in John Barth's "Menelaiad" (1968), Calvino's *If on a Winter's Night a Traveller*, Mark Z. Danielewski's *House of Leaves* (2000), or Mitchell's *Cloud Atlas*, or by means of ekphrastic descriptions or remediations of artworks, such as the Remedios Varo painting in Pynchon's *The Crying of Lot 49* (1966), the Eisenstein film in DeLillo's *Underworld* (1997) or the *Navidson Record* in *House of Leaves*. Vertical proliferation creates opportunities for a variety of paradoxes that further foreground the category of world. Among these are *trompe l'oeil*, when the inset world is mistaken for the primary world, as in many *nouveaux romans* by Alain Robbe-Grillet, Jean Ricardou, Claude Simon and others (see Marx-Scouras, this volume); *strange loops*, when an inset world turns out to be continuous with the primary world that frames it, as in Cortázar's famous story "Continuity of Parks" (1956), Christine Brooke-Rose's *Thru* (1975), or Sukenick's *Blown Away* (1986); and *mise-en-abyme*, when the world of an inset story or artwork mirrors the primary world, as in Barth's *Giles Goat-Boy* (1966), Robert Coover's *The Public Burning* (1977) or Gilbert Sorrentino's *Mulligan Stew* (1979). (For more on these paradoxes, see Ryan, this volume.)

Postmodernist fiction also foregrounds the category of world by laying bare the operations by which narrative worlds are constructed. It typically does so by *deconstructing* them right before our eyes. For instance, a narrated event can be *unnarrated*, rescinded or contradicted, or a character or other entity of the narrated world can be erased. Narrative *sous rature*, under erasure, abounds in Beckett's fiction and the novels of the *nouveaux romanciers*, as well as among the American surfictionists (Sukenick, Raymond Federman, Clarence Major and others; see Berry, this volume). A related device involves the proliferation of multiple, mutually contradictory narrative sequences, actualizing a structure that Jorge Luis Borges called "The Garden of Forking Paths" (1941). "Forking-paths" narratives occur in some of Robert Coover's stories, such as "The Elevator" and "The Babysitter" from *Pricksongs and Descants* (1969), as well as in hypertext fictions such as Michael Joyce's *afternoon* (1990) or Stuart Moulthrop's *The Victory Garden* (1992) (see Ciccoricco, this volume).

The ultimate gesture of exposing the nature and limits of a world involves drawing the veil of fiction aside to reveal the material basis of all world-building – or rather its material *bases*, in the plural, for there is more than one way to think about the ultimate ontological *grounding* of a fictional world. There is, to use a term coined by Ronald Sukenick, more than one *truth of the page*. The first truth is the one that Sukenick had in mind, namely that "there's a writer sitting there writing the page" (Sukenick 1985: 25). The author, already a foregrounded presence in modernist *Künstlerromane*, intrudes even more aggressively in works of postmodernist metafiction (Beckett,

Barth, Fowles, Brooke-Rose) and surfiction (Sukenick, Federman, Major), thrusting herself or himself onstage, visibly seizing control of the story and its world. The other truth of the page is that the work *exists* on one, whether a real page or a virtual one, bound in a book or heard on an audio tape or scrolling up a screen. Postmodernist novels foreground the materiality of the book in a multitude of ingenious ways, from Nabokov's *Pale Fire* (1962) and Brooke-Rose's *Thru* to Milorad Pavić's *Dictionary of the Khazars* (1984), Danielewski's *House of Leaves* and hypertext fictions. At this extreme limit, the virtual reality of fiction is eclipsed by the material reality of the book, and the storyworld rejoins the real world in which books exist as objects, in a version of a strange loop.

In the zone

All, or nearly all, of these devices for experimenting with worlds are concentrated in Pynchon's seminal novel *Gravity's Rainbow* (1973), which is one reason why it is so widely regarded as the paradigmatic postmodernist novel.

Like the modernist heroes who preceded him, Pynchon's main protagonist, Tyrone Slothrop, undertakes an epistemological quest, a quest for knowledge – a double one, in fact: to discover the fate of V-2 Rocket 00000, in the closing days of the Second World War in Europe, and to uncover the secret of his own upbringing. Unlike modernist heroes, however, he undertakes these quests in a world so volatile and indeterminate, so plural, that the quests themselves are rendered moot – indeed, the questing hero himself disintegrates.

All narratives produce multiple possible worlds – potential states of affairs, subjective realities, plans, expectations, speculations, dreams, fantasies; but these are normally subordinated to a single actual world, which they orbit like satellites. *Gravity's Rainbow* not only proliferates such potential and subjective alternative realities, but places them in competition with the novel's "real world." Most of its characters, Slothrop included, are exceptionally prone to fantasize and hallucinate, and it is often difficult to determine where their fantasies, hallucinations or dreams leave off and reality begins. Beyond proliferating subjective realities, *Gravity's Rainbow* also multiplies objective (or apparently objective) alternative worlds – sub-cultural enclaves, pocket utopias, "Nationalities . . . on the move" (Pynchon 1973: 549), which together constitute the multi-world heterotopian space of the Zone. Contacts with emissaries from other worlds – angels, apparitions, spirits of the dead – recur throughout the novel. Akin to these visitations from other worlds are cameo appearances by historical figures who have, as it were, strayed from history into fiction – e.g., Walter Rathenau, Mickey Rooney – as well as the migration of characters from one novel to another across the Pynchon canon – Clayton "Bloody" Chiclitz from *The Crying of Lot 49* to *Gravity's Rainbow*, Takeshi Fumimota from *Gravity's Rainbow* to *Vineland* (1990), and so on.

"The chances for any paradox here, really, are less than you think," the novel's narrator assures us at one point (Pynchon 1973: 680), but he is bluffing. In fact, the chances for paradox are very good indeed, not only in the situation to which he is referring – the bumbling comic-book superheroes, the Floundering Four, appear to be performing their adventures onstage and at the same time watching the spectacle from the stands – but throughout *Gravity's Rainbow*. Confusion of narrative levels occurs right at the beginning of the novel, when events that we initially assume to be unfolding in the real world turn out to be the content of a character's dream, and again at the very end, when the entire world of *Gravity's Rainbow* is revealed retrospectively to have been a movie which we ("old fans who've always been at the movies") have been watching (Pynchon 1973: 760) – instances of *trompe l'oeil*, in other words. Throughout the novel, violations of narrative levels occur, or threaten to occur, whenever the narrator (who is heterodiegetic, i.e., he does not exist at the level of the novel's world) appears to address the characters, at a lower level than his own ("Caught *you* with your hand in your pants! Go on, show us all what you were doing or leave the area, we don't need your kind around"), or the reader, at a higher level ("Check out Ishmael Reed. He knows more about it than you'll ever find here") (Pynchon 1973: 695–6, 588).

Of the many episodes placed under erasure throughout *Gravity's Rainbow*, none is more memorable, or more disturbing, than the passage in which the rocket-engineer Franz Pökler commits incest with his putative daughter Ilse, and then flees with her to Denmark, defecting from the V-2 program. Our readerly investment in the narrated event is intense and complicated, no doubt a mix of revulsion (at the incest) and relief (at the defection), so we are pulled up short when it is abruptly rescinded: "No. What Pökler did was" comfort Ilse, not have sex or run away with her (Pynchon 1973: 421). As the narrator puts it elsewhere, in a comparable situation: "Of course it happened. Of course it didn't happen" (Pynchon 1973: 667).

Gravity's Rainbow, then, is certainly exemplary in its postmodernism, but is it also experimental? For all of its complexity and difficulty, *Gravity's Rainbow* is manifestly a popular book – a "cult classic," widely read by fans outside of academic settings – as well as a canonical book, widely taught and studied. Genuine experimentalism, one might suppose, should be incompatible with popular success, as it should be with elevation to the scholarly and pedagogical canon. Where does that leave *Gravity's Rainbow*?

III. The zone of the interior

Is there any respect in which eclectic postmodernism – Jencks's postmodernism, that of *Gravity's Rainbow* and other heterotopian texts – might actually satisfy Lyotard's criterion for genuine – that is, genuinely avant-garde – postmodernism? Lyotard's criterion for avant-garde postmodernism hinges on the artwork's relation to the *sublime*, or what he calls the *unpresentable*. Modernist art, such as that of Picasso or Duchamp, or of Joyce or Proust, "present[s] the existence of something unpresentable," or "allude[s] to something that does not let itself be made present." True postmodernist art goes further; it "invokes the unpresentable in presentation itself" (Lyotard 1993: 11, 13, 15). Does eclectic postmodernism ever do this, and if so, how?

We might begin with Fredric Jameson's controversial analysis (Jameson 1991: 28–30) of the poem "China" (1978) by Bob Perelman, one of the L=A=N=G=U=A=G=E poets (see Bernstein, this volume). Jameson, perhaps the most influential of all the theorists of postmodernism, possesses a more catholic sense of the postmodern than either Lyotard or Jencks. His postmodernism, one might say, includes both Lyotard's and Jencks's, both avant-gardism and populist eclecticism; a "big tent," it extends from Frank Gehry's deconstructed house in Santa Monica to John Portman's crowd-pleasing Westin Bonaventure Hotel, from Doctorow's bestselling *Ragtime* to avant-garde L=A=N=G=U=A=G=E poetry. Jameson exhibits Perelman's "China" as symptomatic of what he regards as postmodernism's "schizophrenic" disjointedness – something akin to the literal incoherence displayed by Barthelme's and Pynchon's impossible, eclectic assemblages, but in a poetic register. However, Jameson also acknowledges that Perelman's poem has a "structural secret" (though he slightly misrepresents it): it is a *procedural* and "*uncreative*" poem (see Baetens, this volume, and Epstein, this volume), based on found material – not a book of photographs (as Jameson mistakenly asserts) but an illustrated primer for Chinese-speaking elementary-school pupils. Unable to read the Chinese captions, Perelman has recaptioned the illustrations, each line of his twenty-seven-line poem corresponding to one of the (absent) pictures.

Where, then, is China in "China"? It withdraws into the distance, mediated not by one but at least two texts, one verbal and present, the other visual but absent, and beyond that by the Chinese language itself, which the second of these two texts (the missing one) is designed to teach. China is out there somewhere, surely, but in Perelman's text it figures only as a rapidly-receding horizon. China's unpresentability reveals the mediacy of language as such, its inevitable second- (and third-, and fourth-) handedness; it reveals, in other words, the unpresentable in presentation itself – Lyotard's criterion for true (i.e., avant-garde) postmodernism. We might put this somewhat differently, and suggest that, beyond the horizontal and vertical heterotopias of postmodernist fiction, we glimpse here a third possibility, *internal* heterotopia: heterotopia folded into the language of the text itself, or language itself as heterotopian.

We could trace this possibility through other postmodern texts – for instance, Lyn Hejinian's *My Life* (1978, 1986), a prose text akin to "China" in its disjointedness, authored by another of the L=A=N=G=U=A=G=E poets. As the title suggests, this is evidently a memoir, and each of its sentences certainly seems to refer to the experiences of a girl and later a young woman growing up in the America of Hejinian's generation. But the sentences do not cohere among themselves, falling into no apparent order, and there is none of the continuous narrative one expects from a conventional memoir. Like "China," this, too, it transpires, is a text with a "structural secret": Hejinian has produced one chapter for each of the 37 years of her age when she composed *My Life*, each chapter being comprised of exactly 37 sentences, though neither the chapters nor the sentences follow the chronological order of her life (Perloff 1991: 162–70). (When Hejinian updated the text at age 45, she added eight completely new chapters, and interpolated eight new sentences in each of the original chapters.) The experience is hers, but mediated, as in "China," by a *procedure*. *My Life* experiments not just with form but with a *world*, which the text both does and does not construct, or constructs and deconstructs, produces and erases; but that world-experiment is folded *into* the very language of the text.

Or consider *Empire of the Senseless* (1988) by Kathy Acker, a novelist who has come to be associated with the Avant-Pop tendency in postmodernism (see Olsen, this volume). The first section of the novel certainly seems to live up to the "pop" part of the Avant-Pop label, evoking as it does the post-apocalyptic, life-among-the-ruins *topos* familiar from so much contemporary science fiction, especially of the cyberpunk school. But *Empire* goes beyond merely evoking cyberpunk's ruined cities to literally *rewriting* sentences from cyberpunk's founding text, William Gibson's *Neuromancer* (1984) (see McHale 1992: 233–6, 239–42). Thus, Gibson writes of his heroine Molly, who is receiving high-tech medical treatment for a broken leg:

> A transparent cast ran from her knee to a few millimeters below her crotch, the skin beneath the rigid micropore mottled with bruises, the black shading into ugly yellow. Eight derms, each a different size and color, ran in a neat line down her left wrist. An Akai transdermal unit lay beside her, its fine red leads connected to input trodes under the cast.
>
> (Gibson 1984: 78)

Acker rewrites Gibson, deleting some (but not all) of Gibson's techno-speak, and adding oddly irrelevant details of her own:

> A transparent cast ran from her knee to a few millimetres below her crotch, the skin mottled *by blue purple and green patches which looked like bruises but weren't. Black spots on her nails, finger and toe, shaded into gold.* Eight derms, each a different colour size *and form,* ran in a neat line down her right wrist *and down the vein of the right upper thigh.* A transdermal unit, *separated from her body,* connected to the input trodes under the cast by means of thin red leads. *A construct.*
>
> (Acker 1988: 33–4; my emphases)

Is this sampling? Plagiarism? Parody? *Détournement* in the Situationists' sense (see Miller, this volume)? Or something more like what Jameson calls *pastiche*, which he defines as postmodern "blank parody," lacking the pointedness, the "ulterior motives," of satirical parody (Jameson 1991: 16–17)? However we choose to characterize Acker's rewriting procedure, as soon as it is recognized, it interrupts the smooth production of a storyworld, introducing an intrusive element of second-handedness, of mediacy. The passage appropriates a fragment of Gibson's storyworld, but also subtly *skews* that world-fragment, producing a sort of double-exposure, one world overlaid on another, or an effect of vacillation between two worlds – an ontological flicker. Once again, as with "China" and *My Life*, the text conducts an experiment in world-making (and -unmaking), but the experiment has been folded *inside* its language, "invoking the unpresentable in presentation itself."

IV. Conclusion

If these three cases – Perelman, Hejinian, Acker – do satisfy Lyotard's criterion, then the gap between avant-garde experiment and "mere" postmodern eclecticism begins to narrow. Perelman's "China" certainly looks like an avant-garde text, but Hejinian's text masquerades as an ordinary memoir, and is often marketed, taught and studied under that rubric, while Acker's *Empire* seems to fit comfortably alongside other texts of Avant-Pop, a quintessentially eclectic, double-coded genre. Three texts, two of them more or less "popular," yet all sharing the same "secret" experimentalism, experiment folded inside – on the strength of these examples, one might begin to wonder whether double-coding and "invoking the unpresentable in presentation" might actually be compatible after all. If in texts such as these – texts with "structural secrets," internally heterotopian – Jencks's double-coding can co-exist with Lyotard's postmodern sublime, then why should this not also be the case with *Gravity's Rainbow* and other eclectic postmodernist texts that wear their heterotopianism on their sleeves, as it were? Despite the polemical derision that each directed at the other, it seems as though Jencks and Lyotard – postmodern eclecticism and postmodern experiment – might be reconcilable after all, even on Lyotard's terms.

References

Acker, K. (1988) *Empire of the Senseless*, New York: Grove Press.

Barth, J. (1984) "The Literature of Exhaustion" (1967) and "The Literature of Replenishment" (1979). In *The Friday Book: Essays and Other Nonfiction*, New York: Putnam, pp. 62–76, 193–206.

Barthelme, B. (1982) "The Indian Uprising" (1965). In *Sixty Stories*, New York: Dutton, pp. 108–14.

Coover, R. (2007) "The Phantom of the Movie Palace" (1987). In *A Night at the Movies*, Normal, IL: Dalkey Archive Press, pp. 13–36.

Eco, U. (1979) "Lector in Fabula: Pragmatic Strategy in a Metanarrative Text." In *The Role of the Reader: Exploration in the Semiotics of Texts*, Bloomington, IN: Indiana University Press, pp. 200–60.

Elgin, C.Z. (2007) "The Laboratory of the Mind." In J. Gibson, W. Huemer and L. Pocci (eds.), *A Sense of the World: Essays on Fiction, Narrative, and Knowledge*, New York: Routledge, pp. 43–54.

Foucault, M. (1970) *The Order of Things: An Archaeology of the Human Sciences*, New York: Pantheon.

Frow, J. (1997) "What Was Postmodernism?" In *Time and Commodity Culture: Essays in Cultural Theory and Postmodernity*, Oxford, UK: Clarendon Press, pp. 13–63.

Gibson, W. (1984) *Neuromancer*, New York: Ace Science Fiction.

Gitlin, T. (1988) "Hip-Deep in Postmodernism," *New York Times Book Review*, 6 November, p. 35.

Hebdige, D. (1988) *Hiding in the Light: On Images and Things*, London: Routledge.

Hutcheon, L. (1988) *A Poetics of Postmodernism: History, Theory, Fiction*, New York: Routledge.

Huyssen A. (1986) "Mapping the Postmodern." In *After the Great Divide: Modernism, Mass Culture, Postmodernism*, Bloomington, IN: Indiana University Press, pp. 178–221.

Jakobson, R. (2002) "The Dominant" (1935). In L. Matejka and K. Pomorska (eds.), *Readings in Russian Poetics: Formalist and Structuralist Views*, Normal, IL: Dalkey Archive Press, pp. 82–7.

Jameson, F. (1991) *Postmodernism, or, The Cultural Logic of Late Capitalism*, Durham NC: Duke University Press.

Jencks, C. (1986) *What is Post-Modernism?* London: Academy Editions/New York: St. Martin's Press.

Lyotard, J.-F. (1993) "Answer to the Question, What Is the Postmodern?" (1982). In *The Postmodern Explained: Correspondence 1982–1985*, Minneapolis, MN: University of Minnesota Press, pp. 1–16.

McCaffery L. (1995) "Avant-Pop: Still Life After Yesterday's Crash." In L. McCaffery (ed.), *After Yesterday's Crash: The Avant-Pop Anthology*, New York: Penguin, pp. xi–xxix.

McHale, B. (1987) *Postmodernist Fiction*, New York: Methuen.

—— (1992) *Constructing Postmodernism*, London: Routledge.

Perloff, M. (1991) "The Return of the (Numerical) Repressed: From Free Verse to Procedural Play." In *Radical Artifice: Writing Poetry in the Age of Media*, Chicago: University of Chicago Press, pp. 134–70.

Pynchon, T. (1973) *Gravity's Rainbow*, New York: Viking.

Sukenick, R. (1985) *In Form: Digressions on the Act of Fiction*, Carbondale, IL: Southern Illinois University Press.

Weinstein, P. (2005) *Unknowing: The Work of Modernist Fiction*, Ithaca, NY: Cornell University Press.

Further reading

Bertens, H. (1995) *The Idea of the Postmodern: A History*, London: Routledge.

Bertens, H. and D. Fokkema (eds.) (1997) *International Postmodernism: Theory and Literary Practice*, Amsterdam: John Benjamins.

Calinescu, M. (1987) *Five Faces of Modernity: Modernism, Avant-Garde, Decadence, Kitsch, Postmodernism*, Durham, NC: Duke University Press.

DeKoven, M. (2004) *Utopia Limited: The Sixties and the Emergence of the Postmodern*, Durham, NC: Duke University Press.

12

SEXING THE TEXT

Women's avant-garde writing in the
twentieth century

Ellen G. Friedman

Part of the task in describing a women's avant-garde is to justify this grouping. Why separate out women? This task seems to have been different in the 1980s and early 1990s than it is today. Currently, the category "woman" does not have the explanatory power it had in the twentieth century. Generalizing statements about identity categories such as gender, most feminists would say, essentialize them, a practice of reduction that erases the multidimensionality and variability of identity. Identities may be better described as intersectional – that is, marked not only by the social construction of gender but also by other social constructions, such as race, class, religion, sexuality, nationality, and ethnicity, which necessarily come into play in the delineation of women and their productions. Moreover, in the postmodern, identities are seen as provisional and unstable linguistic constructs. If we follow this logic, the avant-garde itself must be seen as a linguistic construct with variable and arbitrary features. Earlier in the twentieth century, however, before intersectionality was brought to the table of feminism, the avant-garde was recognized by its formal experiments and the justifications for separating women out had to do with exclusion and difference.

I. Exclusion

For the most part, women experimental writers in the twentieth century were absent from surveys of innovative writing, and they were also absent from studies that focused entirely on women writers. The few studies that did center on the category of, or on individual figures among, the female avant-garde were archaeological and compensatory. Such studies tended to concentrate on biographical revelation and speculation rather than textual practice. Early critics of Gertrude Stein, for instance, described her radical aesthetics as a strategy to cover over the lesbian content in her texts. Even today, more ink is expended on Anaïs Nin's relationships with Henry Miller and her father than on her innovative writing. Association with famous male writers, in fact, has driven a great deal of the critical attention on avant-garde writers such as H.D., Jean Rhys, and Jane Bowles. Although Djuna Barnes has received some brilliant exegeses for her masterpiece *Nightwood*, it is best known as a *roman à clef*. Biographical gossip often trumps literary interpretation and appreciation of these writers' revolutionary texts (see Friedman and Fuchs 1989).

II. Difference

Drawing on poststructuralist theories of language and psychoanalysis, French women theorists during the 1970s and early 1980s advocated new writing that was feminine and emphasized difference from canonical male authors. Hélène Cixous coined the term *l'écriture feminine* in her classic essay "The Laugh of the Medusa" (1975) a feminist manifesto that called for putting the woman in the text:

> I shall speak about women's writing: about *what it will do*. Woman must write herself: must write about women and bring women to writing, from which they have been driven away as violently as from their bodies – for the same reasons, by the same law, with the same fatal goal. Woman must put herself into the text – as into the world and into history – by her own movement.
>
> (Cixous 1981: 246)

The style of writing she advocates is non-hierarchical, nonlinear, polyphonic, open-ended, and has multiple climaxes. Writing *l'écriture feminine* means inscribing the female body in texts. It follows a pattern of female sexual pleasure and is distinct from the linear, single-climax pattern of traditional narratives Cixous associates with male sexuality. She pleads for women to write with the "white ink" of their breast milk (1981: 252). For Cixous, *l'écriture feminine* has no particular gendered signature and may be written by anyone. Although she advocates a future in which women will practice this writing, her examples come mainly from male modernists such as James Joyce. In Cixous' economy, whether male or female, the writer who disrupts the forms of conventional narrative disrupts the dominant social structure these forms iterate and opens a space for the culturally repressed, for the feminine to erupt into consciousness.

In contrast to Cixous, some French feminists demanded a female signature for feminine writing. Claudine Herrmann, for example, called for a literature in which a woman can "conserve some space for herself, a sort of *no man's land*, which constitutes precisely what men fail to understand of her" (169). Decades before Cixous issued her manifesto, narrative reform in the name of the feminine already had advocates and practitioners but ones that like Herrmann demanded a female signature. Early in the twentieth century Dorothy Richardson and Virginia Woolf explained the innovations in their texts as a means of representing female consciousness. Although signature mattered for them, it was not only signature. Certainly women had created literature, but their productions followed masculine models, thus reinforcing dominant social codes. When the character Hypo advises Miriam, the protagonist of Richardson's *Pilgrimage* to write like George Eliot, she barks back, "Writes like a man." In order to create a literary space for women, they called for new writing that dismantled canonical structures. In the Foreword to *Pilgrimage*, her unfinished thirteen-volume novel, Richardson announces a "fresh pathway" that would "produce a feminine equivalent of the current masculine realism" (9). She isolates the qualities from which *Pilgrimage* would distance itself, including the imposition of a linear plot, the manipulation of characters' points of view, the relentless drive to the resolution of the conflict, and the author-imposed moral. The traditional novel was less about representing life, she felt, than about representing the author's ego: "Bang, bang, bang, on they go, these men's books, like an L.C.C. tram, yet unable to make you forget them, the authors, for a moment" (Richardson 1967: 239). Dissatisfaction with the conventions of her predecessors for representing female experience drove Richardson's own innovations. When contemplating Henry James and Joseph Conrad, Richardson's main character Miriam feels "left out," even "torment":

> Even as you read about Waymarsh and his "somber glow" and his "attitude of prolonged impermanence" as he sits on the edge of the bed talking to Strether, and revel in all the ways James uses to reveal the process of civilizing Chad, you are distracted from your utter joy by fury over all he is unaware of. And even Conrad. . . . The torment of *all* novels is what is left out. The moment you are aware of it, there is torment in them.
>
> (Richardson 1967: 239)

Richardson's innovations in the name of a literature written by women about women pertained to subject matter as well as form. She legitimized women's lived reality of daily chores, friends, gossip, and the inhabiting of domestic indoor spaces as topics for literature. Without authorial interference or explanation, she attempted to reproduce the flow of female thought as Miriam moved through her day. Importing the phrase from the philosopher and psychologist William James, May Sinclair identified this technique as "stream of consciousness" in a 1918 review for *The Egoist* of Richardson's fiction. Her use of this technique was a deliberate, radical strategy to distinguish her novel from those of the nineteenth century.

She interpreted all constraints on the presentation of characters' consciousness as evidence of the writer's authoritarianism. As she declares in her Foreword, "feminine prose . . . should properly be unpunctuated, moving from point to point without formal obstructions." She abandoned not only periods, commas, and semi-colons but the entire architecture of fiction, including beginnings, middles, and ends. In leaving *Pilgrimage* unfinished at her death after publishing multiple volumes and over two thousand pages, Richardson rescued her protagonist Miriam from the inevitable fate that awaited any heroine in that era, a fate which could include only three options:

marriage, madness, or death. As I have written elsewhere, "By insisting on the incompleteness of *Pilgrimage*, Richardson created a revolutionary option for her female protagonist. Miriam simply goes on; she grows progressively wiser, more complex, more confident. Her fate is to live, not to die, not to be subsumed in marriage to a superior male as is Emma but to remain at the center of the narrative" (Friedman 1988: 357). This shift was more than aesthetic; it was the very delineation of difference, an attempt to "provide a new ground for narrative that could accommodate the feminine" (357).

In contrast to the friendship among male modernists, women modernists were not kind to one another. Richardson refused to review Woolf's *The Years*, opting instead to review Joyce's *Finnegans Wake*. Woolf disparaged Gertrude Stein, and Stein had nothing to say about either Woolf or Richardson. Her compliment for Djuna Barnes was that she had nice legs. Woolf was more gracious to Richardson, but far from enthusiastic. In a lukewarm *Times Literary Supplement* review dated February 13, 1919 of Richardson's 4th volume *The Tunnel*, Woolf wrote:

> Here we are thinking, word by word, as Miriam thinks. The method, if triumphant, should make us feel ourselves seated at the centre of another mind, and, according to the artistic gift of the writer, we should perceive in the helter-skelter of flying fragments some unity, significance, or design. That Miss Richardson gets so far as to achieve a sense of reality far greater than that produced by the ordinary means is undoubted.
>
> (Woolf 1966)

But, cautions Woolf, Richardson does rise far enough above the quotidian.

As far as we know, Woolf did not acknowledge that her project of disrupting the expected structures of fiction in the name of women was similar to Richardson's. She put her ideas for a feminine fiction forward in Chapter 5 of *A Room of One's Own* (1957 [1929]). In one brief paragraph, through a fictional surrogate named Mary Carmichael, Woolf introduces lesbianism as a fit subject of fiction, as well as formal narrative innovation, such as "breaking" the traditional sentence and the expected sequence of fiction:

> I am almost sure, I said to myself, that Mary Carmichael is playing a trick on us. . . . Mary is tampering with the expected sequence. First she broke the sentence; now she has broken the sequence. Very well, she has every right to do both these things if she does them not for the sake of breaking, but for the sake of creating. . . . Are there no men present? Do you promise me that behind that red curtain over there the figure of Sir Charles Biron is not concealed? We are all women you assure me? Then I may tell you that the very next words I read were these – "Chloe liked Olivia . . ." Do not start. Do not blush. Let us admit in the privacy of our own society that these things sometimes happen. Sometimes women do like women.
>
> (Woolf 1980: 82)

To "break" the proper English sentence and canonical novelistic structure or "sequence" is to disrupt the political and social forces that authorize normativity and also to open up the possibility of relaxing compulsory heterosexuality. A 1931 lecture on the "Professions for Women" describes the hurdles she must overcome in order to meet her own standards in defining a female narrative practice. One hurdle, "killing the Angel in the House," exorcising the good girl who is socialized to please, she slyly muses, "I think I solved." However, as the French feminists articulated decades later, writing that is feminine must inscribe the very physicality of womanhood, something Woolf struggled with: "Telling the truth about my own experiences as a body, I do not think I solved." As a woman writer, "she has still many ghosts to fight, many prejudices to overcome. Indeed it will be a long time still, I think, before a woman can sit down to write a book without finding a phantom to be slain, a rock to be dashed against" (Woolf 1970: 236–8).

Woolf's experiments in fiction are dazzling, made more profound by the context of her feminism. *Jacob's Room* (1922) unwinds as a story in which the central character Jacob is missing, presented only through the memories of others (Woolf 1959). He is a soldier who died in World War I, his room the only physical evidence of his existence. It sits undisturbed as if in anticipation of his imminent arrival. On one level at least, the text offers an allegory of absence calling for presence, such as the feminine that Woolf so desperately wished to evoke. Each of Woolf's novels offers another experimental structure in the effort to break the sequence of traditional narrative. *Orlando* (1978 [1928]) plays with the physics of time and biology, rendering them supple and changeable. Gender, time, and death all yield their inexorability to Woolf's pen as she playfully manipulates and undermines the staid elements of nineteenth-century fiction. Perhaps the most innovative of her texts is *The Waves* (1931). This text is all rhythm, voice, and pulse; letting go of distinct characters and discernible plot. In a Diary entry, she describes her text as voices "running homogeneously in & out, in the rhythm of the waves" (Woolf 1980: 312). Through the disembodied voice of a character named Bernard, *The Waves* describes the buried content Woolf attempts to reach in her narratives: "There is always deep below it, even when we arrive punctually at the appointed time with our white waistcoats and polite formalities, a rushing stream of broken dreams . . ." (Woolf 1959: 354). Each new narrative offered a fresh strategy to bring the inhibited text to the surface and required relinquishing more and more elements of conventional narrative as Woolf sought inscription of her womanhood.

Unlike Richardson and Woolf, Gertrude Stein claimed innovation without at the same time claiming the feminine as its basis. As a lesbian, she claimed for herself a half-masculine identity, comparable to Sappho's, and therefore, she judges, superior (Stimpson 1977: 497). Despite her claiming a third sex identity and thus distinguishing herself from both male and female modernist writers, she is tied to Richardson's and Woolf's feminist aesthetics in several ways. American feminist literary critics of the 1980s tie Stein's radical aesthetics to the same elements Richardson and Woolf used to describe their own quests in innovative female writing – difference and a new language to evoke it. Catharine Stimpson characterized Stein's writing as the "very discovery of difference" (1986: 4) and Sandra Gilbert and Susan Gubar write that she "remakes English itself into a foreign language" (1985: 529). Stein's own description of her path to innovation with *Tender Buttons* (1914) resembles the aspirations for feminine writing described by Woolf and Richardson: "It was my first conscious struggle with the problem of correlating sight, sound and sense, and eliminating rhythm; – now I am trying grammar and eliminating sight and sound" (1928, quoted in Williams 1970: n.p.). Stein rejects the assumption that conventional narrative logic is inherent: "The narrative in itself is not what is in your mind but what is in somebody else's" (Stein 1970: 102). Her most direct gesture of distancing herself from specifically the male tradition is in "Patriarchal Poetry":

> Patriarchal Poetry.
> Their origin and their history.
> Patriarchal Poetry their origin and their history
> their history patriarchal poetry their origin patriarchal poetry
> their history their origin patriarchal poetry their history patriarchal poetry
> their origin patriarchal poetry their history their origin.
>
> (Stein 1980: 115)

Unlike the male modernists Pound and Eliot who were preoccupied with tradition, Stein recoils from its suffocating effect, divorcing her texts from literary history, so that even today they fascinate through their unfamiliarity.

In the generation that followed the early women modernists, women innovators were also often conscious of themselves as *women* writers who sought something unavailable in the entire history of literature that would register that experience. Anaïs Nin repeatedly described the difference of her writing (see e.g. Friedman 1993: 247; Felber 1995: 316). Like many of the female avant-garde, she articulates how her writing aims for what has not yet been expressed: "It is to reach a greater reality (authenticity) that I abandon realism (Nin 1968: 45; see Friedman 1993: 246). Of the female avant-garde who followed on the heels of the pioneers, Anaïs Nin was most direct and public in defining her innovations as singularly feminine. "What was left for me to do? To go where Henry [Miller] cannot go, into the Myth. . . . To write as a woman, and as a woman only" (1966: 128). Like Woolf, she feels a responsibility for provoking the lost feminine into consciousness: "It is the woman who has to speak. And it is not only the Woman Anaïs who has to speak, but I who have to speak for many women. . . The mute ones of the past, the inarticulate, who took refuge behind wordless intuitions . . ." (Nin 1966: 289). Even as Henry Miller, Edmund Wilson, and Lawrence Durrell cautioned her to abandon her beloved Diary, what Durrell called her "womb," Nin wants to write from within it, uncannily foreshadowing the vocabulary of Cixous when she describes in the 1930s what the future of women's writing must be:

Woman's creation far from being like man's must be exactly like her creation of children, that it must come out of her own blood, englobed by her womb, nourished with her own milk.

(Nin 1967: 233)

Wildly popular as a women's consciousness-raising figure during the 1970s and 1980s Women's Liberation Movement, Nin is known as much for her fiction as for her diaries. In her fiction, her female protagonists tend to be nomadic; at their most typical, they are traveling, homeless and shift their identity. A Spy in the House of Love follows a quest narrative pattern and then subverts it. The main character glides from one unsatisfactory identity to another, seeking to coalesce her fragmented self into a whole. Unlike traditional stories of the integration of self, this character at the end becomes reconciled to the volatility of her selfhood, finding it preferable to a unified self disciplined by social constraint. Like Richardson, Nin avoids conventional narrative resolution in the name of the feminine.

The diaries offer other versions of nomadic, shifting subjectivity. In the diaries of the 1930s she describes herself as "tormented" by the "multiplicity of selves." She confesses her difficulty in being "sincere" since "each moment I must choose between five or six souls" (Nin 1966: 47). Just as her protagonists are trickster-like figures in their shape shifting, her diaries not only turn on unstable identities but also destabilize the diary genre. (See Kacandes on experimental life-writing, this volume.) The published diaries that she edited are extreme distillations of the originals. Deirdre Bair who wrote a popular biography of Nin and had access to her actual, original diaries, disputes the "truth" of the published diaries (Bair 1995: 203). They are so literary and shaped, that their distance from the actual lived life is incalculable – yet they are marketed as "diaries," the account of a life. There are now several editions of some of the diary volumes; the versions of Nin proliferate and continue in their liberating variability.

Indeed, she goes further, playing the ultimate trick on the dominant culture, repeatedly having the diary subject, herself, invoke incest, the taboo upon which, according to Freud and Lévi-Strauss, civilization is built. Incest does more than raise the bar of transgression beyond Woolf's Mary Carmichael writing "Chloe liked Olivia." Its excess is inassimilable (see Friedman 2001). To seduce the father, as Nin claims she did in a posthumous volume called Incest, seems a foundational moral break. She is fascinated with its shattering power to put everything into question. In the 1986 Henry and June, posthumously published excerpts culled from the unexpurgated diary, 1931–1932, she writes:

I have remained the woman who loves incest. I still practice the most incestuous crimes with a sacred religious fervor. I am the most corrupt of all women. . . . With a Madonna face, I still swallow God and sperm, and my orgasm resembles a mystical climax.

(Nin 1986: 246)

Incest in Nin's works may speak literally of her affair with her father (as an adult who had not seen him for decades), but more importantly for the development of the female avant-garde, it is also a trope in her work for the woman artist's relationship to traditional narrative (see Nin 1992). In the *House of Incest* (1936), the trope of incest, the desire for the father, who represents culture, suggests creative stagnation and constraint: "Their love like the ink of squids, a banquet of poisons" (Nin 1958: 52). In Nin's inventive narrative practice, it is a militant move to expose the utter difference at stake in women's innovation.

III. Homelessness

Estrangement from fathers, from God the father, from home, and the condition of orphanhood, are recurring elements in the female avant-garde that follows Woolf, Richardson, and Stein. They are strategies for the writers' sense that their creative space is as yet, outside and unavailable. Jane Bowles' brilliantly quirky novel *Two Serious Ladies* (1943) delivers this message over and over with bent logic. In the past, "God watched over everybody, and all men were brothers. Now there is nothing to carry with you from one place to another, and as far as I'm concerned these people might as well be kangaroos; yet somehow there must be someone here who will remind me of something. . ." (Bowles 1978: 40). The absence of both fathers and God represent a kind of liberation. In Bowles, as in Nin, it results in a sense of fragmentation that is freeing: "I *have* gone to pieces, which is a thing I've wanted to do for years . . . . but I have my happiness, which I guard like a wolf, and I have authority now and a certain amount of daring . . ." (Bowles 1978: 197; see Friedman 1993).

The pursuit of a sustaining location beyond the constraints of culture seems an irrepressible current in female innovative writing of this generation. Djuna Barnes' *Nightwood*, an anti-quest narrative, makes the character Robin Vote the object of other characters' longing. No one is able to detain her for long however. She keeps escaping to continue an objectless quest, for what she seeks is beyond representation, beyond language and culture. As she flees from the series of men and women who pursue her, Robin chooses homelessness over domesticity. She prefers the alterity of her "desperate anonymity" to conforming to the image of their desires. Finally at the end of the text, Robin reaches beyond speech, beyond even the human to become the "woman who is beast" (Barnes 1961: 37). In drawing Robin, Barnes attempts to elicit what is not yet present in culture (see Friedman 1993). In key passages, she is described as something "not yet in history" (Barnes 1961: 44, 113), outside language and representation.

Jean Rhys inspired discomfort among some feminist literary critics because her female protagonists are written as passive and dependent (Borinsky 1986: 299). They repeatedly undermine success scripts for women and position themselves as vulnerable others, outsiders – as black when they are not, as mad, and even as ghosts. They invite cruelty and usually succeed in attracting it. This slavish positioning poignantly exposes the malicious underbelly of mainstream culture and its restraining codes. Rhys' publications spanned much of the twentieth century, from the 1920s to the 1970s.

Like Anna in *Voyage in the Dark* who identifies with blacks, and Antoinette in *Wide Sargasso Sea*, who becomes the madwoman in the attic in Rhys' novelistic prequel to Charlotte Brontë's *Jane Eyre*, Rhys was born in the West Indies, colonized by the British. Her Creole beginnings inspired a reformulation of the Creole madwoman in Brontë's text (see Friedman 1989a, "Breaking the Master Narrative"). Rather than the beastly creature delaying Jane Eyre's nineteenth-century happiness, Rhys' madwoman is the exploited victim of English contempt for anyone from the colonies, particularly women, whom they often used and threw away. Rhys' prequel to Brontë's text turns on Rochester being sent to Dominica to marry a wealthy wife because his older brother is slated to inherit the family wealth.

Rhys reverses the codes in Brontë's canonical text. In her narrative, the mad Antoinette, renamed "Bertha" by Rochester, possesses not only the poetry and passion that has little purchase in England, but also the moral weight. Not at home in her native Dominica where the black natives are hostile to the Creole plantation owners and not at home in England, Antoinette locates a place to be in madness, a construction of identity and liberation that points an accusing finger.

Even at the end of the twentieth century when avant-garde techniques were assimilated by mainstream writers such as Toni Morrison, the terms for representing feminine presence remain consistent. Constructed solidly in the tradition of the female avant-garde, Morrison's *Paradise* (1998) complicates the trope of the homeless feminine with the trope of race in a text of magical realism. The novel *Paradise* is based on historical post-civil war self-segregated all-black towns. The self-isolating community of Ruby is tightly controlled by a black male hierarchy that severely disciplines transgressions of its rigid, masculinist order (see Friedman 2002: 702–5). Ruby comes in conflict with the Convent, a nearby sanctuary for female homeless outcasts and runaways of various races and ethnicities. In an outrageous act of vigilantism, the men of Ruby murder the women who inhabit the Convent, naming them as a threat to their order, as witches. In the aftermath of the killing spree, Ruby changes, making its boundaries permeable to the outside world and finally integrating with the rest of the nation. Though ostensibly dead, the women, in magical realist episodes, nevertheless come back, one by one, evoking the return of the repressed feminine. Their return is foreshadowed by one of the women of Ruby, Delia, who understands that the feminine powers the men of Ruby thought they eliminated have only been submerged and will reappear. In prose reminiscent of Cixous, she asks:

> When will they reappear, with blazing eyes, war paint and huge hands to rip up and stomp down this prison calling itself a town? . . . She hoped with all her heart that the women were out there, darkly burnished, biding their time, brass-metaling their nails, filing their incisors – but out there.
>
> (Morrison 1998: 308)

Morrison associates the condition of being a woman – of whatever race, ethnicity, or sexuality – with at best containment, such as the women of Ruby experience or in the extreme, complete suppression. Yet what is left unexpressed in the feminine is ultimately irrepressible; it eventually breaks through to disturb things as they are.

IV. The female trickster

As mainstream writers incorporate the tropes and forms once reserved for the avant-garde, contemporary feminist experimentalists find new forms of subversion, adapting, for instance, the trickster figure. This figure is usually interpreted as a moral agent whose offences are disciplinary measures. "By acting at the boundaries of order," Brian Street explains, the trickster "demonstrates where the boundaries lie" (Doty and Hynes 1993: 19). Traditionally, the trickster is a force patrolling the borders of civilization. When female tricksters appear in the narratives of women experimentalists, however, they do not reinforce the normative.

The Guerrilla Girls, a group established in 1985 of women artists who appeared unexpectedly and anonymously and used the names of famous dead women, such as Kathë Kollwitz, Frida Kahlo, and Gertrude Stein, are icons out of pop culture that illustrate this point. In a rude visual pun that also plays with expectations of women's beauty, they wear gorilla masks. They provide a useful paradigm for the experimental women writers' trickster type. This trickster's chief trick is to shock expectation, transforming the quotidian into the abhorrent, and inassimilable. As the western male trickster helps society to stay in balance, the trickster in the feminist avant-garde impedes or throws off-balance normative social narratives.

Among the Guerrilla Girls' most dramatic tactic is revision of classic male art. In 1989, the Guerrilla Girls revised a classic nude in a poster appearing on buses in New York City. They reproduced, in garish yellow, black, and pink, Ingres' *Odalisque*, a painting of a reclining nude, back view. Rather than the original image of ideal feminine beauty, this re-visioned nude has a defiant gorilla head with mouth open and teeth prominent (Guerrilla Girls 1995: 8, 9). Another image, reproduces Velasquez's *Venus and Cupid*, 1649–1651, with one important variant. This reclining nude, is leaning on her elbow, her gaze directed at a mirror that Cupid is holding up for her. Looking back out of the mirror is not the Velasquez Venus, however, but a gorilla mask.

Explicit tampering with master works is not new in art or literature (for instance, see Epstein on appropriation, this volume). The revisionary fairy tales and the novels and poems that take on paternal myths by offering the perspective of a female or another oppressed minority figure in the myth are common revisionary strategies. However, in savaging male representation, the feminist trickster has assumed a more formidable agenda than the revision of received ideas. She is not adding a feminist perspective to existing readings or expanding a narrow, masculinist culture, but attempting to undo it altogether. She wants to kill the cultural father symbolically by thwarting the constructions of his desire, such as those painted by Velasquez and Ingres.

Among the most flamboyant of the trickster writers is Kathy Acker (on Acker, see also McHale, this volume). All her works "plagiarize" (her term) male masterworks just as the Guerrilla Girls "plagiarize" Rembrandt, Velazquez, and Ingres (see

Friedman 1989b: 37–49). The epigraph to Kathy Acker's *Don Quixote* is an explanatory note on her work, which is largely cut and pasted from male works, such as Cervantes' *Don Quixote*. Set in caps, it reads, "Being born into a part of a male world, she had no speech of her own. All she could do was read male texts which weren't hers" (Acker 1986: 39). Acker attributes this philosophy to the artist Sherrie Levine, who faithfully reproduced masterworks and signed her name to them to demonstrate that, "As a woman, I felt there was no room for me . . . The whole art system was geared to celebrating these objects of male desire. Where, as a woman artist, could I situate myself?" (Levine 1986: 96–7). Acker's and Levine's object is to question the masterwork's "sources in paternal authority and male desire" (Friedman 1989: 43).

At the same time that Acker exposes male authority and desire, her quest narratives explore the borders of that authority and desire. Through lewd and violent episodes that include murder, rape, and incest, her nomadic tricksters, often tattooed, orphaned, and sexually obsessive female outsiders attempt to move beyond the border of culture to constitute themselves, to acquire a subjectivity that is independent of constraining social constructions. Their tricks may miss their object, but it is important to understand that their object falls outside of the law of the father. Unlike male Western tricksters, their excesses do not point to cultural borders but beyond them.

Also published at the end of the twentieth century, Bharati Mukherjee's *Leave It To Me* (1997) follows a similar trickster paradigm. Devi Dee, an orphan, is named after the many-armed Hindu goddess, and uses a variety of transgressive strategies, including the suggestion of incest to accomplish her trick – to move beyond the Freudian triad to another basis for identity (Friedman 2002: 706). In a narrative that makes confetti of the nuclear family, her biological father is murdered by the mother's former lover who has also killed her mother, and whom Devi kills in turn. As the police make their way to the crime scene, an earthquake conveniently covers up the damage – the wrecking of familial relations – allowing Devi to escape. Just as Cixous recasts the Medusa into a powerful force for the feminine, Mukherjee recasts Devi, Hindu goddess of creation and order who protects equilibrium, into a force of disequilibrium and instability. A nomad, Devi disengages from the oedipal narrative through disguises in the tradition of the Guerrilla Girls, and like her feminist literary predecessors Nin and Acker, makes inassimilable moves against the family, the basic unit of the social order. Like other feminist trickster figures constructed by women writers, Devi navigates through her plot alone, looking towards what lies outside of the order of law and paternal authority. Her extreme transgressions summon an earthquake, which she survives in a boat, the primordial watery and perhaps generative location for something new, something to follow the collapsing structures of the familial and known.

Literary conventions in the early twenty-first century are not what they were when pioneers such as Virginia Woolf and Dorothy Richardson theorized experimental narratives for women. Mainstream and best-selling women writers, such as Joyce Carol Oates and Toni Morrison, experiment with unconventional narrative through which they assert their feminism. Although one could arguably identify a set of formal practices that would distinguish the "experimental" writer Acker from the more "mainstream" writer Morrison, these practices could not be generalized to characterize all experimentalists. Such distinctions and categories are as unstable and complicated as those associated with gender. As the twentieth century progressed, the terms for representing the repressed feminine became more expansive, more apocalyptic, and more available. Dorothy Richardson discarded punctuation and point of view as well as the structures of nineteenth-century realism. Woolf gave up more structures of fiction to inscribe the physical experience of being a woman. Nin, Barnes, Acker, Mukherjee, and other, more mainstream writers had a much larger arsenal of tropes available to them. They could imagine beyond the borders of culture and society.

V. Conclusion

Luce Irigaray's justification of the category "woman" describes the kind of understanding the women writers of the twentieth-century avant-garde, with some exceptions, have shared. Irigaray argues that womankind should have her own specificity, not only that created by male desire (Irigaray 1991: 32, 149–50, 172). Producing disruptive or expansionary categories or complicating existing categories for women helps to do this work. Such taxonomical moves are given further weight by Judith Halberstam, who makes the following point: Rather than see "categories as perpetually suspect," she embraces "categorization as a way of creating places for acts, identities and modes of being which otherwise remain unnamable." For Halberstam giving "new names for formerly uninhabitable locations" transfigures traditional categories. The production of "different categories," forces people "to use them and widespread use of these categories does utterly change the landscape of gender politics" (Halberstam 1999: 2). From the beginning of the twentieth century, gender functioned as literary explanation, and in functioning as explanation, it also interfered with normative social expectations. As literary critics reproduced the category "women experimental writers" it acquired explanatory power as well as use as an instrument of intervention. Although the singular category "woman" currently seems to require additional identity markers – such as race, class, ethnicity, and sexuality, to be a sufficient object of inquiry – perhaps the intersecting elements involved in the category "women experimental writers," the practitioners of which, as we see, do invoke numerous social locations, allow the category to remain viable and transformative. For the twentieth century and perhaps beyond, women experimental writers may be a category that in being named has the power to both explain and influence.

References

Acker, K. (1986) *Don Quixote*, New York: Grove.
Bair, D. (1995) *Anais Nin: A Biography*, New York: Putnam.
Barnes, D. (1961 [1936]) *Nightwood*, New York: New Directions.
Borinsky, A. (1986) "Jean Rhys: Poses of a Woman as Guest." In S. Suleiman (ed.) *The Female Body in Western Culture*, Cambridge, MA: Harvard University Press, pp. 288–302.

Bowles, J. (1978 [1943]) *Two Serious Ladies. My Sister's Hand in Mine: The Collected Works of Jane Bowles*, expanded edition, New York: Ecco, pp. 1–201.

Cixous, H. (1981) "The Laugh of the Medusa," trans. K. Cohen and P. Cohen. In E. Marks and I. de Courtifron (eds.) *New French Feminisms*, New York: Schocken, pp. 245–64.

Doty, W.G. and Hynes, W.J. (1993) "Historical Overview of Theoretical Issues: The Problem of the Trickster." In W.J. Hynes and W.G. Doty (eds.) *Mythical Trickster Figures: Contours, Contexts, and Criticisms*, Tuscaloosa, AL: University of Alabama Press.

Felber, L. (1995) "The Three Faces of June: Anaïs Nin's Appropriation of Feminine Writing," *Tulsa Studies in Women's Literature* 14(2): 309–24.

Friedman, E.G. (1988) "'Utterly Other Discourse': The Anticanon of Experimental Women Writers from Dorothy Richardson to Christine Brooke-Rose," *Modern Fiction Studies* 34(3): 353–70.

—— (1989a) "Breaking the Master Narrative: Jean Rhys's *Wide Sargasso Sea*." In E.G. Friedman and M. Fuchs (eds.) *Breaking the Sequence: Women's Experimental Fiction*, Princeton: Princeton University Press, pp. 117–28.

—— (1989b) "Now Eat Your Mind: An Introduction to the Works of Kathy Acker," *Review of Contemporary Fiction* 9(3): 37–49.

—— (1993) "Where Are the Missing Contents? (Post) Modernism, Gender and the Canon," *PMLA*: 240–52.

—— (2001) "Sex With Father: The Incest Metaphor in Anaïs Nin." In A. Salvatore (ed.) *Anaïs Nin's Narratives*, Gainesville: University of Florida Press, pp. 79–89.

—— (2002) "Postpatriachal Endings in Recent U.S. Fiction." *Modern Fiction Studies* 48(3): 694–712.

Friedman, E.G. and Fuchs, M. (eds.) (1989) "Contexts and Continuities: An Introduction to Women's Experimental Fiction in English." In E.G. Friedman and M. Fuchs (eds.) *Breaking the Sequence: Women's Experimental Fiction*, Princeton: Princeton University Press, pp. 3–51.

Gilbert, S.M. and Gubar, S. (1985) "Sexual Linguistics: Gender, Language, Sexuality," *New Literary History* 16: 515–43.

Guerrilla Girls (whoever they really are). (1995) *Confessions of the Guerrilla Girls*, New York: Harper Collins.

Halberstam, J. (1999) "Masculinity Without Men: Annamarie Jagose Interviews Judith Halberstam About Her Latest Book, *Female Masculinity*," *Genders* 29: 2.

Herrmann, C. (1981) "Women in Space and Time," trans. M. R. Schuster. In E. Marks and I. de Courtifron (eds.) *New French Feminisms*, New York: Schocken, pp. 167–8.

Irigaray, L. (1991) *The Irigaray Reader*, ed. M. Whitford, Cambridge, MA: Basil Blackwell.

Levine, S. (1986) "Art in the (Re) Making," *Art News* 85: 96–7.

Morrison, T. (1998) *Paradise*, New York: Knopf.

Mukherjee, B. (1997) *Leave It To Me*, New York: Knopf.

Nin, A. (1958 [1936]) *House of Incest*, Denver: Swallow.

—— (1966 [1954]) *A Spy In the House of Love*, Chicago, IL: Swallow.

—— (1966) *The Diary of Anaïs Nin. Vol. I, 1931–1934*, New York: Harcourt.

—— (1967) *The Diary of Anaïs Nin. Vol. II, 1934–1939*, New York: Harcourt.

—— (1968) *The Novel of the Future*, New York: Macmillan.

—— (1986) *Henry and June: From the Unexpurgated Diary of Anaïs Nin*, New York: Harcourt.

—— (1992) *Incest: From a Journal of Love. The Unexpurgated Diary of Anaïs Nin: 1932–1934*, New York: Harcourt.

Rhys, J. (1982 [1966]) *Wide Sargasso Sea*, New York: Norton.

—— (1985 [1934]) *Voyage in the Dark*. In *Jean Rhys: The Complete Novels*, New York: Norton.

Richardson, D. (1967) *Pilgrimage*, London: Dent.

Sinclair, M. (1918) "The Novels of Dorothy Richardson," *The Egoist* 4: 57–9.

Stein, G. (1970 [1940]) *What Are Masterpieces*, New York: Pitman.

—— (1980) "Patriarchal Poetry." In R. Kostelanetz (ed.) *The Yale Gertrude Stein*, New Haven: Yale University Press, pp. 106–46.

Stimpson, C.R. (1977) "The Mind, the Body, and Gertrude Stein," *Critical Inquiry* 3: 489–506.

—— (1986) "Gertrude Stein and the Transposition of Gender." In N.K. Miller (ed.) *The Poetics of Gender*, New York: Columbia University Press.

Williams, W.C. (1970) "The Work of Gertrude Stein." In *Imaginations*, New York: New Directions.

Woolf, V. (1957 [1929]) *A Room of One's Own*, New York: Harcourt.

—— (1959) *Jacob's Room and The Waves: Two Complete Novels*, New York: Harcourt.

—— (1966 [1919]) Review of *The Tunnel*. In J. Guiguet (ed.) *Contemporary Writers*, New York: Harcourt, pp. 120–2.

—— (1970 [1942]) "Professions for Women." In *The Death of the Moth and Other Essays*, New York: Harcourt, pp. 235–42.

—— (1978 [1928]) *Orlando: A Biography*, New York: Harcourt.

—— (1980) *The Diary of Virginia Woolf: 1925–1930*. Vol. 3, ed. A. O. Bell with A. McNeillie, New York: Harcourt.

13

EXPERIMENTS IN BLACK

African-American avant-garde poetics

Aldon Lynn Nielsen

I. Introduction

The American republic has, throughout its history, been thought of as something of an experiment. Certainly my home institution, the Pennsylvania State University, was venturing some mode of experiment when, in 1894, it hired Fred Pattee as the first professor of American Literature at an American University. Pattee's 1896 essay "Is There an American Literature?" asked a question I was still hearing during my own graduate student days. It was a particularly inhumane experiment in slavery that brought Phillis Wheatley from her home in Africa to New England in childhood, where she promptly took up the study of the classics and became the first African American to publish a volume of poetry. Centuries later, Kenneth Warren has published a critical book whose title, *What Was African American Literature?*, seemingly implies that the experiment that began with Wheatley (though in his view African American literature as *a literature* begins considerably later) ended with the Civil Rights era. The very status of "experimental poetry" has always been a fraught subject; all the more so the very idea of black experimental writing, this despite the palpable existence of experimental modes of African American poetry visible on the library shelves of America. The very idea; among the many benefits of the Civil Rights, Black Power and Black Arts moments of the twentieth century's second half was the bringing into critical view of such works as Jean Toomer's Harlem Renaissance era modernist, multi-genre *Cane* and Langston Hughes's wildly innovative, late modernist *Ask Your Mama*, published in 1961. Yet as quickly as these works were recovered, the idea of experimentalist black poets, a given in any anthology of black American poetry of the late 1960s or early 1970s, was subsumed by a critical literature more given to endless celebration of mainstream creative writing, leavened by a seemingly unending academic fascination with the innovations of Hip Hop and the poetic grandchild of the Black Arts and of 1960s rap sessions, Rap, now codified with the appearance in 2010 of the Yale University Press *Anthology of Rap*.

The fact, evident for any who care to look, is that mid-century black America was rife with poetic experiment. At the height of the Black Power era, you could drop by any African American barber shop and find among the aging magazines in the waiting area copies of *Black World*, the Johnson publication ably edited by Hoyt Fuller, and given to publishing experiments such as putting radical young poets on the cover and featuring writing by William Melvin Kelly that twisted English into new shapes and sounds never before heard or seen. I have written at length elsewhere (Nielsen 1997, 2004) of the varied communities of poets and individual innovators who built a radical, new African American poetry out of the shards of modernism, *Negritude*, jazz, projective verse, black American idioms and the legacies of African art's abstractions. Out of that heady mix emerged the Umbra Society of writers (including Ishmael Reed, Askia Muhammed Toure, Tom Dent and David Henderson), Cleveland's *Free Lance* group (with Russell Atkins as perhaps the most prominent advocate for the experimental), the Howard University/ *Dasein* poets (including Percy Johnston and Walter De Legall), Beat writers such as LeRoi Jones, Ted Joans and Bob Kaufman, projective verse poets such as Stephen Jonas, jazz surrealists on the order of Jayne Cortez, and free ranging experimentalists such as Clarence Major, Elouise Loftin, Lloyd Addison, etc. There remains, however, considerable critical confusion over the evolution, or even existence, of experimental poetries by black American artists during the period stretching from the Harlem Renaissance to the Black Arts Movement of the 1960s and 1970s and beyond. By examining the movement that Melvin B. Tolson made from one mode of modernism to another, and the emergence at the same time as the New York School of a poet such as Lorenzo Thomas, we may begin to see the broad outlines of what was happening among the more radical African American poets as the black modern gave onto its own post.

II. The transfiguration of Melvin B. Tolson

In an oft-cited passage in *John Brown's Body*, Stephen Vincent Benét, though he had populated his 1928 Civil War epic with numerous representations of African American figures, confessed his heart too white to assume a role as singer of the "blackskinned epic" he believed American poetry still needed, predicting, much as Emerson before him had prophesied the coming of the true American poet, that one day a black poet would rise to sing that "epic with the black spears" with "truth and mellowness" (Benét 1954: 337). There is much to remark in this passage. Apparently Benét was unaware of already existing epics by black poets, and readers of Ralph Ellison may have found some amusement in the fact that the edition of *John Brown's Body* republished just two years after *Invisible Man*'s appearance was issued by a press named "Rinehart." Still, there were many who read in Benét's declaration a confirmation of their own aspirations. While I suspect that Melvin B. Tolson knew of the nineteenth-century epic length poems of an Alberry Whitman, a poet born in slavery who had come to be known in some quarters as the "poet laureate to the Afro-American race," Tolson felt that the time had come for a truly modern "blackskinned epic" and that he was just the poet to produce it. Tolson's epic aspirations produced the two late volumes (1953 and 1965) with which contemporary readers have become at least somewhat familiar, *Libretto for the Republic of*

Liberia and *Harlem Gallery, Book I: the Curator*, but the many controversies produced by Tolson's late style, and by the dueling prefaces to those books contributed by Allen Tate and Karl Shapiro, have not only obscured from view the earlier epic penned by Tolson but also have sewn confusion about Tolson's path to that late style.

Tolson early on saw himself as the potential author of what he was to term the first modern Negro epic. Writing of Paul Laurence Dunbar, he had once remarked: "Dunbar himself wanted to write an e[p]ic, but the American public wanted only Negro stereotypes, so he took his unwritten epic to the grave. But not before he had written that terrible indictment of the pandemic psychosis that made him a falsely grinning comedian – the poem called We Wear the Mask" (Tolson Papers. Container 5. "Miscellaneous Notes"). Tolson's first magnificent effort in this direction did not see the light of day till after his death. Titled *A Gallery of Harlem Portraits* and largely written in the 1930s, that volume encompassed more than two hundred pages of free verse portraiture adding up to a panoramic exploration of Black America in the twentieth century. What Tolson wrote about the later *Harlem Gallery* was clearly already part of his plan in composing this earlier epic. He noted that his gallery featured "shifts in the Jamesian sense from one reflector to another – one mirror to another to reveal the complex destinies of black folk in America" (Tolson Papers. Container 5. "Similes, Metaphors etc." 3). We know from the humorous essay Tolson wrote about his efforts to get *A Gallery of Harlem Portraits* published (titled "Odyssey of a Manuscript" and itself published posthumously), that he had written to H.L. Mencken, Carl Sandburg and Mark Van Doren hoping to interest them in his manuscript, though each in turn turned down the opportunity to read the poems. When the elderly Edwin Markham was scheduled to read in the chapel of Tolson's own college, the younger poet thought out loud to his patient wife, "if Edwin Markham could help the man with a hoe he could help the man with an epic!" But while Tolson summoned enough nerve to read to Markham an ode he had composed in honor of his visit (which Markham said he'd have inserted in his biography), Tolson somehow choked and couldn't bring himself to broach the subject of his epic. "I'm a damned fool" he said to his wife at dinner following the occasion. "Amen!" his wife "sanctioned fervently." Tolson was less reticent with Langston Hughes, whom he had met in Harlem in years previous, and so when the Governor of Texas dispatched Tolson to represent his state at the San Diego International Exposition in the mid-1930s, the unpublished bard stood by while his working manuscript was surveyed by Hughes, who sighed and chuckled and at one point said of a poem he'd just read, "That's a perfect picture." "You've got something there," Hughes finally pronounced, but he went on to observe, "It's so hard to get a publisher for poetry." Tolson didn't live to see his first epic work into print, but neither did he entirely put it behind him.

We can see in that early volume that he was already working towards his own solution to the problems of structuring a modern epic, a problem he shared with Ezra Pound, William Carlos Williams, H.D., Charles Olson and so many others. The idea of the gallery stayed with him and was his chosen device for his last great work, which he had planned to comprise five books, of which Book 1 and a few scattered drafts are all that he lived to write. Within that Gallery structure he sought further means of creating an architecture for his vast work, thus the published *Harlem Gallery* is built of cantos organized by the letters of the Greek alphabet, and the gallery itself is organized into four wings corresponding to the four directions of the compass. A similar structuring device is at work in the earlier *Gallery of Harlem Portraits*, in which the individual portraits appear in sections organized much as an actual gallery might be, with wings for chiaroscuro, silhouettes, etchings and pastels. That these sections mirror the four-fold structure of his later gallery is probably not incidental. Tolson was quite self-conscious about the significance of his recasting of his poetic forms and style. Not above writing notes about himself for others (such as his college president) to use when speaking of his work and accomplishments, Tolson frequently wrote of himself in the third person. Among his notes is one asserting that "as Yeats rewrote the prose version of 'Byzantium' Tolson rewrote the free verse version of *Harlem Gallery*" (Tolson Papers. Container 5. "Similes Metaphors etc." 3). In his own notes to his last book, Tolson is quite clear what he thinks he is about:

> The autobiographical Book I, The Curator vivifies in myth and metaphor and symbol ideas and places, persons and things, which have given meaning to his life as a man and a collector of works of art. Here, for the first time in poetry, the Afroamerican artist discovers his identity in the complexities that have made him and his people (variegated heritage) what they are today.
>
> One hundred years after the Emancipation Proclamation, a Balsacian gallery of lowbrows and middlebrows and highbrows emerges from that province of Color in the Great White World: Doctor Nkomo, the Bantu expatriate and Africanist; Hideho Heights, the folk poet of Lenox Avenue; Mr. Guy Delaporte III, the tycoon of Bola Boa Enterprises, Inc.; Snakehips Briskie, a forerunner of the Twist; John Laugart, the half-blind artist from the Harlem Catacombs; Martial Kilroy, president of Afroamerican Freedom; Igor Shears, the West Indian patron of the Harlem Symphony Orchestra; Black Diamond, the kingpin of the policy racket; the Zulu Club Wits, the Bohemian eggheads of the Twilight Zone of Afroamerican culture; Black Orchid, the blues-singing, striptease artist of the Bamboo Kraal.
>
> (Tolson Papers. Container 6. Poetry. Harlem Gallery Notes)

This could just as well be a description of the chromatic cast of characters encountered in *A Gallery of Harlem Portraits*, and many of those earlier portraits clearly serve as drafts for the personalities who appear thirty years later in Tolson's final versioning of his materials.

What happens across the span of those intervening decades is that Tolson continuously revises his poetics in the direction of ever greater complexity of structure, allusion and language, moving from a poetic language akin to that of Sandburg and Hughes towards something like an African American cousin of Hart Crane's diction, all in an attempt to produce an aesthetic equal to the myriad complexities of black American modernity. Like C.L.R. James and W.E.B. DuBois, Tolson argued forcefully that, far from being mere subjects of modernism, New World African peoples were producers of the modern, as were their African progenitors. In his *Libretto for the Republic of Liberia* we read of Benin:

> The lily lyricism of whose
> ivory and gold figurines larked
> space oneness on the shelf ice
> of avant-garde Art . . .

(Tolson 1999: 184)

The common take on Tolson is that he was a poet who revised himself from a fairly conventional versifier into a high modernist. This would only ring true if we chose as a starting point that schoolboy ballad on the sinking of the Titanic that made its way into his home town newspaper and became the subject of a Sunday sermon by a white Baptist minister, perhaps drawn by the poem's closing "climactic apostrophe to the deity" ("Odyssey"). It would be far more accurate to say that Tolson wrote his way from one mode of modernism to another. A *Gallery of Harlem Portraits* is much in the vein of the free verse revolution of Carl Sandburg and Edgar Lee Masters, though structurally it surpasses those models in complexity. In his interview with Herbert Hill, included in the landmark collection *Anger and Beyond*, Tolson spoke of his early admiration for Masters, of his appreciation of Robert Browning's psychological depths of characterization and his internalizing of a Whitmanian exuberance. As his biographer and early critic Robert Farnsworth points out in his afterword to A *Gallery of Harlem Portraits*, of equal weight in Tolson's variegated background was the blues, which, with its own psychological depths and powers of characterization and imagery, had worked powerfully in the modernizing experiments of Langston Hughes and Sterling Brown, poets Tolson had studied as a graduate student and had come to know as friends. The movement from the language and structure of Tolson's first book manuscript to the style that dominates his late works might be seen as a parallel to the evolution from blues and spirituals to jazz. But a parallel is not an equivalence; what Tolson undertakes, as musical as it turns out to be, is another order of similar invention. The ever-increasing complexity of Tolson's verse is of a piece with what many critics have described as a New World neo-baroque.

In her own first book, Vera Kutzinski brought the discussion of the neo-baroque from the world of Latin American literary studies into the realm of African Diasporic cultural studies, a work I see as drawing a strong connection to the concept of neo-African culture popularized earlier by Janheinz Jahn and reread to great effect by such poets as Nathaniel Mackey. Here, too, we see yet again a missed opportunity in the construction of genealogies of poststructuralism. In so much of the critical discussion of Gilles Deleuze's analysis of the fold in Leibniz and the Baroque, the African contributions to the Baroque, so immediately evident to Picasso and Lorca, are elided. So far as I have been able to determine, Tolson never knew of Deleuze, but he certainly knew of Leibniz and of the Baroque, and he certainly knew a great deal of Africa and of the Moorish conquests. Tolson's contemporary Robert Hayden, a poet who studied with W.H. Auden and was later to become the first African American Consultant in Poetry to the Library of Congress, was traveling along a similar path during these years, and even referred to his "baroque period," during which, in the reading of Keith Leonard, "he pursued the complexity of metaphor and the interaction between the presumed objectivity of poetic form and the subjectivity of both the reader and the poetic speaker that made such poetic form a necessary expressive channel for the baffling and potentially alienating dynamics of the mind" (Leonard 2006: 169). While Tolson would have found nothing intrinsically alienating about the dynamics of the mind (in fact, he suggested more than once that the black poet might show the path away from the alienation the white world seemed to trumpet), in significant ways, Tolson's late poetry is an instance of the New World neo-baroque, and his revisions are a fold within which modernism comes to differ from itself, something we can already see at work in the production of one of his earliest anthology pieces.

At his reading in the Library of Congress not long before his death from cancer, M.B. Tolson (having for that period adopted the Eliotic mode of self-identification) invited his audience into what he called the poet's workshop, a virtual visit to the Zulu club of his home's basement refuge. He spends quite a bit of time guiding his listeners through the decisions he made as he arrived at the final form of several lines involving the Bola Boa. Not only is the Bola Boa an African snake, but its appearance in his poem affords Tolson an opening to make several insistent comments on the role of Africa in the development of poetic elements that had come to be seen as characteristically modern. The Bola Boa reappears in his composition of *Harlem Gallery* as the name of a company headed by the black bourgeois Mr. Guy Delaporte III. Readers can construct a similar workshop experience by examining the revisions that produced the poem by Tolson known widely as "African China." The version of that piece that most of us read in anthologies over the years was the one that originally appeared in the journal *Voices* in the winter 1950 issue. What we could not have known then (in my case because I wouldn't be born for several more months, but for most because of the non-publication of *A Gallery of Harlem Portraits*) was that there was an earlier, quite different "African China" and that the 1950 poem had been unfolded from two predecessor poems. In *A Gallery of Harlem Portraits* we encounter two Chinese figures who operate businesses in Harlem: Wu Shang and Lou Sing, both of whom are in the laundry trade. The experiences of the two separate figures are recomposed into a singular Wu Shang in the later poem. The original "African China," featuring Lou Sing, opens with a premonitory quatrain, italicized to indicate that it represents the folk wisdom of the community:

> *East is East an' West is West,*
>   *You heahs de People say,*
> *But when you mixes East an' South*
>   *De devil is to pay.*

(Tolson 1999: 8)

This poem from the depression era marks a rare instance of more traditional dialect in Tolson's poetry, but we should never see this quatrain's disappearance from the final poem as in any sense a rejection of the vernacular. For one thing, that final poem does still feature dialect, in the line that reads: "Good Gawd, / China and Africa gits wed" (Tolson 1999: 128). More to the point, Tolson has followed the practice of James Weldon Johnson, Sterling Brown and others, writing a poetry more interested in conveying the flavor and structures of actual Black American idioms rather than the sort of preconstituted and stereotypical dialect he had remarked in Dunbar (albeit with great respect for Dunbar's technical mastery of the form). The central material of the original "African China," in a pattern that will become familiar to scholars researching the Tolson papers, is reworked for the later poem and reassigned from Lou Sing to Wu Shang. That core material is the love story of Lou Sing and his employee, Mable, a love that endures the skepticism of their Harlem neighbors and eventually produces the child known along Eighth Avenue as "African China" who has the facial features of his Chinese father and the ebony skin of his African American mother. Mable's verse says it all: "Lou Sing is a restful oasis . . . Blessed by Allah . . ." (Tolson 1979: 8). This is precisely the variegation and complexity of black diasporic life that Tolson found so fascinating, seeing in the relation between this family and their neighbors a transnational race study living and breathing before him. In taking over the central role in the later "African China," Wu Shang brings with him a portion of his own story, the tale of a man who hates his work in the laundry as much as he loves "elegant phrases," the beauty of which come to serve as "a balm of Gilead" (Tolson 1979: 210) to his friends and customers. In arriving at the final form of "African China," Tolson moves to a six-part structure composed in shorter, often rhyming lines. Further, the language moves increasingly towards the elegance that Wu Shang appreciates. For one example, in the final version Wu Shang is not simply a lover of elegant phrases. Now he resides among "bric-a-brac / metaphysical" and is described as "a connoisseur of pearl / necklace phrases" (Tolson 1999: 125). The newly introduced sections of the poem correspond to Wu Shang's interactions with his customers as they had been outlined in the earlier poem, but now instead of falling in love with Mabel, an employee, he falls for Dixie Dixon, who fell on Lenox Avenue, breaking her leg, which leads in turn to Wu Shang's helping her home and aiding her recovery, followed by, in Tolson's words, "old kismet" knotting the two "unraveled destinies" (Tolson 1999: 127). In this final rendering their child has a name, Wu Shang Junior, and while the neighbor children still assign the poem's title as Junior's nickname, here the final lines introduce an element not present in the original:

in accents Carolina
on the streets they never made,
the dusky children tease,
"African China!"

(Tolson 1999: 128)

Thus a poem that was already about, among so many other things, the constructedness of race, also underscores both the unconsciousness of that construction and the movements of history that lie behind it. All of this in a language that has become largely that of Tolson's final books of the 1950s and 1960s:

> Later, late, Wu Shang remarks,
> "Siroccos mar the toughest palm."
> The bigger thing, as always, goes unsaid:
> the look behind the door of big John's eyes,
> awareness of the steps of *Is*,
> the freedom of the wise.

(Tolson 1999: 127)

These same modes of revision can be seen throughout Tolson's work. A memory of his visit to Liberia, in the course of which a paramount chief met during a reception at the home of President Tubman makes a bet with Tolson about which country produces the strongest liquor (a story, mind you, in which the actual signifying monkey puts in an appearance), is reworked through multiple versions into a virtuoso performance involving a paramount chief and a Greenwich Village poet, the poem "Dark Laughter" that was found among Tolson's papers. Lines interpolated into the "Ti" section of *Libretto for the Republic of Liberia* between the time of its appearance in *Poetry* magazine (an appearance which caught the eye of William Carlos Williams, who immediately saluted them in *Paterson*) and its final book form begin to meditate on color ("melamin or melanin dies to the world and dies") then proceed through a litany of rivers and civilizations, recalling Langston Hughes's early poem "The Negro Speaks of Rivers," reminding readers of "the dusky peers of Roman, Greek, and Jew" (Tolson 1999: 170). The evolving story of "The Chitterling King" gives readers a glimpse of the rich directions Tolson's planned succession of books of the *Harlem Gallery* were meant to take. In each instance we see the same thing. Starting with a fold within the texture and text of black modernity, Tolson works to elaborate language and structures that fold back upon themselves in ever more generative loops of difference.

III. Lorenzo Thomas's New York School

> through a park, then I cross St. Nicholas,
> Eighth Avenue, Seventh, and I come to the Y,
> the Harlem Branch Y, where I take the elevator
> Up to my room, sit down, and write this page:

(Hughes 1994: 409)

These lines, with their perambulating persona making his way through those same "Negro Streets" traversed at the outset of Allen Ginsberg's "Howl," sound like nothing so much as one of Frank O'Hara's "I do this; I do that" poems, or perhaps the product of one of O'Hara's many progeny among the New Yorkish poets of the post-WWII years. The poem is, of course, neither. It is Langston Hughes's "Theme for English B," one component of his *Montage of a Dream Deferred* and first published in a 1949 issue of *Common Ground*. In our zeal to school our poets we often seem doomed to repeat the *de facto* segregation of those days, hence Langston Hughes is never spoken of as a New York School poet (though he is often deemed a Harlem poet, and was already so deemed when he was living in D.C.). We arrange our poets into coteries as often as we group them by aesthetic leanings, thus a stage full of poet contemporaries in New York in the early 1960s would easily and did accommodate Beat, Black Mountain and New York School poets, all of whom were close friends, indeed belonged to the same coterie (see also Lee, this volume). The Village apartment of LeRoi Jones in the days before he became Imamu Amiri Baraka was a gathering of just those groups, as was Jones/Baraka himself. O'Hara read Hughes, as had Baraka, and they all went to the Five Spot and held their breath.

> You know, I keep coming back to the Crown
> Delicatessen. It reminds me of you
> I see your happy face in every blond table, my
> Red embarrassed smirk in the edges of beer
> Bottles. The irresponsible public hero above
> The stainless steel "take out" counter.
> My picture is in that cheap frame
> And you are that first dollar pasted on the mirror
> I have been so busy of late, translating
> "Two or Three" chants by Leopold Senghor and
> Thinking about the coming revolution.

(Thomas 1981: 17)

These lines are not Hughes, not O'Hara or a New York School ephebe, not Baraka. This is an early poem by New York poet Lorenzo Thomas, dating to 1964, and foregrounding many of the surface features that could, perhaps should, be seen as linking poets of the New American poetry across coterie boundaries. By this time, Don Allen's *New American Poetry* is out and has been read by the younger poets of Thomas's generation. Baraka's *Preface to a Twenty Volume Suicide Note* has become a touchstone among many on the aesthetic left, and the casual, attitudinal, gestural poetics here visible have become a taken-for-granted part of the vocabulary of innovative poets. Gathering with his mostly older colleagues in the Society of Umbra, Thomas was learning as much from the highly distinctive aesthetics of a Lloyd Addison, another New York poet, as he was from O'Hara or Baraka. Like O'Hara, and like Hughes, who translated many of them, Thomas was reading the small presses to see what the poets in Ghana and elsewhere in Africa were doing. But here, too, there was an element of racialized reception that Thomas was reading and dealing with. The poem quoted here, "The Unnatural Life," opens with a telling epigraph from Aimé Césaire: "What I am is a

176

man alone / imprisoned in white." Thomas's poem takes a turn not found anywhere in O'Hara, though pointed to in works like the 1959 "Personal Poem," the poem in which Baraka brings O'Hara news of the beating of Miles Davis by the New York police:

> My copy of Muhammed Speaks covers the table and the wind, and
> The door hanging open, frightened because I am here
> That I might forget these young delusions of love, afraid
> As I emerge from my fashionable jacket my brain turns
> Black and hateful. Like a beast, your color rising in my nose
> And you are raped and murdered in the usual manner.
> The same peach tree in the backyard spreads on the white house
> Behind your house. It is a simplified heart,
> See the blind aorta sketched over the vacant windows.
> I should never have moved into your neighborhood!
>
> (Thomas 1981: 17–18)

The invocation of the "white house behind your house" points back to the Harlem Renaissance and the Claude McKay poem titled variously, with and without his permission, "The White House" and "White Houses," while at the same time reaching back yet farther to Charles Chesnutt's *The House behind the Cedars*. The more violent imaginings of the poem parallel elements of Baraka's "Black Art," "Black Dada Nihilismus," "Poem for Black Hearts" and other contemporaneous works, but with an ironic edge Baraka was rapidly de-emphasizing, along with his family name. That final line of Thomas's poem is a send-up of anti-integrationist logics in an era that still saw redlining, block busting and various government sponsored means of insuring *de facto* segregation. (A cartoon that ran in *Esquire* magazine in those days showed a beer-bellied, unshaven slob of a white man sitting on his porch, watching a properly besuited African American man moving his tastefully attired family into the house across the street. The white man observes to his wife, "there go the property values." It was a *Raisin in the Sun* era, when even poets could get a laugh out of neighborhood race boundaries.) Thomas's line additionally may be read as a satiric commentary on the increasingly integrated bohemian arts scene of New York's Lower East Side in those days, as Umbra's artists moved into formerly ethnic enclaves. "If one wanted to be a poet in the early 60s," Thomas was to write later for *African American Review*, "the Lower East Side was the place to be" (Thomas 1993: 575). And the place to be at two in the morning if you were an Umbra poet was the Polish café "Stanley's" at 13th Street and Avenue B, which quickly became a gathering ground for poets and other artists, and was a bit later the birth place of the Fugs in performance. Then, too, the line may be seen as addressing another sort of mixing that was going on at Stanley's, as Ishmael Reed, Tom Dent, Lorenzo Thomas and the other Umbra alums rubbed elbows with white artists, including Aldo Tambellini, who operated a store front studio and gallery space nearby ($65.00 per month in those days) and who was later to marry Umbra poet N.H. Pritchard's ex-wife. Black poets had entered the aesthetic neighborhoods of the New American Poetry, had, in fact, helped bring them into being, though, as with residential neighborhoods, they were slow to be accepted in the anthology districts of American verse.

Between that Césaire epigraph and its Senghor bookend in Thomas's poem is lodged another satiric barb. As black Americans used to joke that they could gain entry to otherwise restricted dining rooms simply by donning African garb and adopting an accent, Thomas was not the only poet to wonder at the acceptance of African poetry in quarters not noted for their hospitality to African American writers. (In a later reminiscence, introducing a poem, Thomas remarks wryly that his investigations at the time revealed that the only black poets getting published routinely were poets from Africa, badly translated. He then read a poem he claimed was written in an effort to mimic that more acceptable manner.)

Like Jack Kerouac and Amiri Baraka, Thomas was raised on radio, and Fats Waller. A 1964 poem is titled, "One Never Knows, Do One," and out of this mashup of *The Shadow* and Waller emerges scathing dissection of Civil Rights era racial aesthetics:

> You and my mother both, you will be so
> Pleased to hear what I have to tell you. I agree with
> You now, I really like "Cabin in the Sky". You'll
> Be so glad to know that now I also agree with
> Your vision and judgement of my own handsomeness,
> That I did not get that process I wanted.
>
> (Thomas 1981: 19)

At nearly this same moment, Amiri Baraka published his poem "Duncan Spoke of a Process," but he meant something else, didn't he? Donald Reeves titled his 1972 memoir *Notes of a Processed Brother*, walking over that bridge from the whitening process of America's racial cosmology to Whiteheadian process theory left by his predecessors. Lorenzo Thomas kept his natural; never got that process he wanted. He came to value rags and hollers over do rags, as he came to a non-ironic appreciation of the talents of a Rex Ingram, even as he rejected the white man's hellish imaginings of the hereafter Ingram was employed to preside over. Ingram had the distinction of playing Lucifer in *Cabin in the Sky* and De Lawd in *The Green Pastures*, perhaps confirming the wisdom of the folk saying: the white man's heaven is the black man's hell.

Part and parcel of the New York scene in those post-war years was the intimacy among the arts and artists, and the intermedia projects this inevitably brought into being. Thomas writes:

> Because they were all outsiders in an immigrant community, the avant-garde artists became a community. Because those who were African American came there to become artists, not to avoid being black, there was a kind of integrated society that did not exist elsewhere.
>
> (Thomas 1993: 576)

Just as Archie Shepp would follow Jackie McClean in the Living Theater's production of *The Connection*, by Jack Gelber, and Cecil Taylor would not only perform in that play but would also lend a hand in getting out the LeRoi Jones/Diane DiPrima little mag *The Floating Bear*, poets and visual artists, Aldo Tambellini among them, would collaborate on small press projects that grew out of their being in the same aesthetic and geographic neighborhoods. Thomas's 1966 volume *Dracula* bore a ghoulish collage by Britt Wilkie that, with its juxtaposition of the vampire with gas company logos, police and images of the tourist, was of a piece with the emerging underground comics scene (see Chute, this volume). Thomas's most long-lasting and productive collaborative relationship proved to be with his own brother, Cecilio "Cess" Thomas. An early production was the 1971 *Fit Music*, whose annunciatory cover opened onto a world where, as they really did in the 1960s, the Beach Boys shared room in the stanzas with James Brown. Inside the book there was another Cess Thomas collage that combined schoolbook lessons ("Learning about Space") instructing students on the intricacies of elliptical orbits with a crowning elliptical reference to Lorenzo Thomas's military service. Lady Liberty is seen shaking hands with a black Navy man.

> And the orders came down
> As your prophets demanded. Strange FM stations
> And astrological phone calls hastened to soothe you
>
> (Thomas 1981: 69)

These lines of Lorenzo Thomas's *Fit Music* seem as if broadcast from the orbiting imagery of his brother's collage work.

Thomas was a poet given to the hieroglyphic extension of Ezra Pound's imperatives (*Fit Music* opens with an Epigraph from Pound's "Canto XIII"). "The Bathers" incorporates lines of Egyptian writing, enacting the Art Ensemble of Chicago's long-term slogan, "Great Black Music, Ancient to the Future." A 1974 poem, "Hurricane Doris," like some of the avant-garde cinema of its day, literally looks out of the page at the reader (see Figure 13.1). An arrow, tracing the sine wave referenced in the poem, gives

A signal sine wave mayday in a glance

Figure 13.1 Lorenzo Thomas, "A signal sine wave" from "Hurricane Doris" (1974). Courtesy of literary executor.

on a glance leading our view off the page to something sited beyond the margin yet encompassed in text.

Figure 13.2 shows 1992's *Sound Science*, with its punning title, featuring a cover illustration of even then aging technology, a 1960s vintage Webcor reel-to-reel tape recorder. This was technology that promised sound science, truly high fidelity

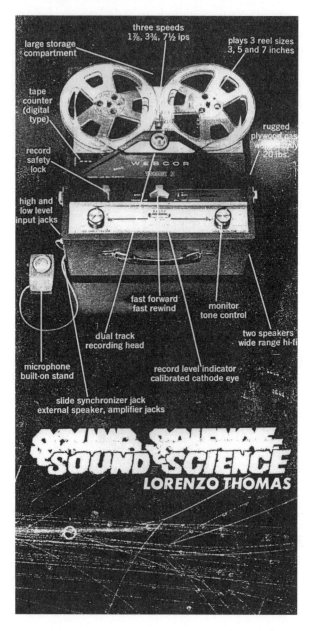

Figure 13.2 Lorenzo Thomas, *Sound Science* (1992) [cover illustration]. Courtesy of literary executor.

reproduction of speech by means of electronic tracings on magnetic tape. The "calibrated cathode eye" of the record level indicator was yet another instance of our technologies looking back at us, as this image looks back at us from our futuristic past.

Thomas's use of such imagery clearly prefigures the later practice of a poet like Claudia Rankine in her recent volume *Don't Let Me Be Lonely* (even as that book's title simultaneously honors the past represented by James Taylor's song, and the more recent past represented by The Isley Brothers' masterful deformation of that musical text). Contemporary poet Harryette Mullen was a dear friend of Thomas's dating back to her Texas years and her poetry makes joyful reference to the "Umbra alums" who meant so much to the evolution of her poetics. Thomas's concerns with sound technology are of a piece with the recording practices of the younger poet/songwriter Gil Scott-Heron, so frequently credited (often against his will) as the godfather of Rap, and those concerns find their digital echoes in the sound poetry of a poet such as performance artist Tracie Morris. The call of the baroque unfoldings of Melvin B. Tolson's verse histories in poems like *Libretto for the Republic of Liberia* find their contemporary response in works like Amiri Baraka's *Wise Why's Y's* or Nathaniel Mackey's *Splay Anthem*. Clearly, if we are to comprehend the innovations of a Claudia Rankine (or of The Isley Brothers, for that matter), we must attend to the experimental ruptures in the standard narrative of black poetics earlier occasioned by a Lorenzo Thomas and a Melvin B. Tolson.

References

Benét, S.V. (1954) *John Brown's Body*, New York: Rinehart.

Hughes, L. (1994) "Theme for English B." In A. Rampersand and D. Russell (eds.) *The Collected Poems of Langston Hughes*, New York: Alfred A. Knopf, pp. 409–10.

Leonard, K. (2006) *Fettered Genius: The African American Bardic Poet from Slavery to Civil Rights*, Charlottesville, VA: University of Virginia Press.

Nielsen, A.L. (1997) *Black Chant: Languages of African American Postmodernism*, Cambridge, UK: Cambridge University Press.

—— (2004) *Integral Music: Languages of African American Innovation*, Tuscaloosa, AL: University of Alabama Press.

Thomas, L. (1981) *The Bathers*, New York: I. Reed Books.

—— (1992) *Sound Science*, Houston: Sun Be/Am Associates.

—— (1993) "Alea's Children: The Avant-Garde on the Lower East Side, 1960–1970," *African American Review* 27(4): 573–8.

Tolson, M.B. (1979) *A Gallery of Harlem Portraits*, ed. R.M. Farnsworth, Columbia, MO: University of Missouri Press.

—— (1999) *Harlem Gallery and Other Poems of Melvin B. Tolson*, ed. R. Nelson, Charlottesville, VA: University of Virginia Press.

—— *The Melvin B. Tolson Papers*, Library of Congress, Washington, DC.

14

THE LIMITS OF HYBRIDITY

Language and innovation in Anglophone
postcolonial poetry

Priyamvada Gopal

I. Introduction

The project of elaborating the "postcolonial" in relation to the experimental or the avant-garde poses two challenges. The first is the sheer unwieldiness of the category of the "postcolonial" itself, covering as it does dozens of national and cultural contexts, multiple languages, and very different, often internally variegated, literary histories. Were it even possible to narrow the terms of engagement down to experimental writing in English alone, the scope of the category remains vast, ranging from modernist novels from the Indian subcontinent and rewritings of Greek tragedy in Nigeria to protest poetry in South Africa, feminist fiction in New Zealand and the short story in Zimbabwe. The catalogue of experimental writers in English would range from Amos Tutuola (Nigeria) and G.V. Desani (India) to more recent talents like Dambubzo Marachera (Zimbabwe), Salman Rushdie (India/Britain) and Mudrooroo (Australia).

The thornier challenge derives from the fact that postcolonial literary studies is a field that, in its most influential incarnations, has presented itself as *constitutively* avant-garde. As the relatively staid field of "Commonwealth Literature" – comprising English-language writing from former British colonies – transformed itself into the distinctly hipper specialism of "postcolonial studies," the close association with deconstruction and post-structuralism in the work of leading critics like Homi Bhabha and Gayatri Spivak meant that postcolonial studies came to be seen, *tout court*, as possessed of a critical-theoretical cutting edge. Simultaneously, its most iconic literary figures, such as Salman Rushdie, Derek Walcott, Wilson Harris, Ben Okri and Wole Soyinka, among others, were received and critically analysed precisely in terms of their own putative avant-gardism. Magical realism became regarded as the most fundamentally innovative dimension of postcolonial literature as a postmodern aesthetic of fragmentation, linguistic play, anti-realism and generic mixing achieved critical primacy. Even when writers pointedly worked with more established literary conventions – such as the "Onegin stanza" in Vikram Seth's *The Golden Gate* and realism in

A Suitable Boy – the dominant framework of *reception*, nevertheless, deemed such texts to be participating *sui generis* in some form of experimentation through appropriation, mimicry and rewriting. Postcolonial literature was, then, deemed always already radical by virtue of speaking from the periphery to the metropole.

Accordingly, "writing back" to and against a metropolitan linguistic and literary norm became the central critical trope in the field. Iconic status was conferred upon the cursing figure of Shakespeare's Caliban who, according to the Cuban critic, Roberto Retamar, resists by using the coloniser's language against him (Retamar 1989). Retamar, it is worth noting, was speaking very specifically of the *mestizo* in the Americas and of people who have been left no choice other than to use the coloniser's language in the face of cultural genocide. Generalised against the grain of Retamar's historically specific argument across all postcolonial contexts, notions of literary subversion that emphasised such "mimicry" interlocked usefully with a term that has become postcolonial theory's most popular aesthetic and theoretical coinage, "hybridity." Theories of "hybridity" overlapped fortuitously with accounts of linguistic processes such as "creolisation" and "metissage," whereby metropolitan languages such as French and English were remade in interaction with native vernaculars and indigenous speech patterns. Articulated famously by Homi Bhabha, the "hybrid" in postcolonial studies is a "Third Space" which allows us "to find those words with which we can speak of Ourselves and Others . . . [and] elude the politics of polarity and emerge as the others of ourselves" [1995: 209]. Hybridity as a weapon of discursive subversion appeared to be exemplified by the multilingual wordplay that became the currency of postcolonial literature's avant-gardism. Salman Rushdie's witty paean to the ethnic and linguistic hybrid, the "bastard" embodies this perspective in its knowing wordplay:

> I was both, and nothing: a jewholic-anonymous, a cathjew nut, a stewpot, a mongrel-cur. I was – what's the word thse days? – *atomised*. Yessir, a real Bombay mix.
>
> [. . .]
>
> *Bastard*: I like the sound of the word. *Baas*, a smell, a stinky-poo. *Turd*, no translation required. Ergo, *Bastard*, a smelly shit; like, for example, me.
> (Rushdie 1995: 104)

While literary engagements with hybridity in postcolonial literatures have tended to focus on prose, in an influential recent work, *The Hybrid Muse*, Jahan Ramazani has made a case for "hybridity" as the primary analytic through which to investigate an otherwise disparate range of poetic texts across Anglophone postcolonial literatures. Arguing that postcolonial poetry is "hybrid not only in language but also in form," Ramazani suggests that it is precisely the dimension of experimentation with non-indigenous languages and genres that justifies, privileging hybridity as analytical lens (2001: 17). In a later work, he argues that beyond the linguistic dimension, the fact of globalisation also speaks to a constitutive hybridity: "Without losing sight of the losses inflicted by a globalizing modernity, we can explore how poets, working in a genre with especially abundant formal and linguistic traces, have also imaginatively transvalued and creolized these global forces to bring into expression their specific experiences of globalized locality and localized globality" (2006: 10).

Contra Ramazani, this essay argues that the "breaking" and "remaking" of English, while an integral part of poetic and linguistic experimentation across Anglophone post-colonial contexts, is too differentiated a process to be subsumed under the rubric of "hybridity." Paradoxically, if "hybridity" is something of a given in Anglophone litera-tures, then the innovative dimensions of a literary text cannot be identified simply by identifying it as a hybrid in language and form. Deployed as a generic term to discuss experimentation in poetic language, "hybridity" is ultimately a blunt instrument, too neglectful of the specificities of different aesthetic projects and their experimental aspi-rations. Below, I show how even self-conscious poetic experimentation with English and multilingualism in three iconic literary contexts – the Caribbean, India and South Africa – not only differ radically in form and content but do so in symptomatically spe-cific ways. These derive from the political and historical imperatives that variously shape the reception, perception and use of English in the wake of colonial rule, factors often elided in discussions of postcolonial wordplay. While theories of literary hybridity have been correct in their apprehension of the general phenomenon of traces and mixture, they often suffer not only from a weak sense of linguistic or cultural specificity but also fail to address the relationship between the aesthetics and politics of the Anglophone, specifically, the ways in which English is perceived and deployed very differently across postcolonial contexts. English in India, a minority language, certainly a minority litera-ture, is freighted with different political resonances from the language of the townships in apartheid South Africa, where English has an "omnipresence" that can be "inconven-ient and suffocating and induce a sense of disempowerment and exclusion" reinforced by formal racial hierarchies (Albie Sachs quoted in De Klerk 1996: 7). Caribbean English – marked by creolisation – in turn has a different demographic. Defined famously by Kamau Brathwaite as "nation-language," English in places like Trinidad and Jamaica "in its contours, its rhythm and timbre, its sound explosions, it is not English, even though the words, as you hear them, might be English to a greater or lesser degree" (1984: 13). By contrast, the English-speaking upper classes in India, according to the poet Agha Shahid Ali, "have not allowed English to come into any 'real' contact with Indianisms . . . not let even a pidgin English develop in India" (2008: 150). These contextual differences, as we shall see, are reflected in and refracted through the prism of poetic experimentation.

II. India: the other's tongue

Deployed from the outset as part of the colonial project of creating between colonial rulers and "the millions whom we govern; a class of persons, Indian in blood and colour, but English in taste, in opinions, in morals, and in intellect," Indian English writing – very much the practice of an elite – has consistently evinced an anxiety of authenticity (Macaulay 2006 [1835]: 375). The problematic was famously adumbrated by the novelist, Raja Rao: "One has to convey in a *language* that is not one's own the *spirit* that is one's own" (1963 [1938]: vii). In Anglophone poetry – which has lagged behind fiction in terms of innovativeness and range – the disjuncture in consciousness identified by Rao would itself become a thematic preoccupation, articulated at times with Miltonian ponderousness as in R. Parthasarathy's "Homecoming":

> My tongue in English chains
> I return, after a generation to you
> I am the end of my Dravidic tether . . .
>
> (Parthasarathy 1977: 30)

Later, it would be more deftly apostrophised by Vikram Seth:

> English! Six armed god,
> Key to a job, to power,
> Snobbery, the good life,
> This separateness, this fear.
>
> (Seth 1999: 66)

The fear of separateness was occasionally displaced on to mockery in works like Nissim Ezekiel's well-known "Goodbye Party for Miss Pushpa, T.S":

> You are all knowing, friends,
> what sweetness is in Miss Pushpa.
> I don't mean only external sweetness
> but internal sweetness.
>
> (Ezekiel 1989a: 190)

While possibly intended to provoke reflections on the unintended ramifications of Macaulay's famous project of Anglicising a race of people, the poem comes off as little more than a classed parody of "babu" English, the language of lower-level administrators for whom it is a workplace patois and definitely not a first language. In "Soap," from the collection "Very Indian Poems in Indian English," where a man with limited English skills unwittingly parodies himself:

> That shopman he's giving me soap
> but I'm finding it defective version.
> So I'm saying very politely –
> though in Hindi I'm saying it,
> and my Hindi is not so good as my English.
>
> (Ezekiel 1989b: 269)

Such parody, however well-intended, is symptomatic of the circumscribed milieu from which Anglophone poetry in India emerges. Reliant on the simultaneous command of English and other Indian languages (as opposed to a more widespread *non*-Anglophone multilingualism), this poetry is confidently cosmopolitan, able to assert ownership of, rather than mere facility in, more than one language. "Hybridity" in this milieu is dependent on a certain economic and international mobility. Deployed in poetry as theme and technique, it ultimately enables very particular reflections on the condition and concerns of the class that commands English. In recent years, the anxiety of being Anglophone – and the separateness this engenders – has been addressed by some poets through a self-conscious engagement with "bhasha" or vernacular languages, i.e. active experimentation with English in proximity to and interaction with other Indian languages.

This turn is typified by the innovative work of Sujata Bhatt whose own biographical trajectory as a Gujarati speaker educated in English and living first in the US and then Germany, shapes many of her poems. Bhatt's preoccupation with language is famously encapsulated in her widely-anthologised poem," Search for my Tongue," a condition generated:

> if you had two tongues in your mouth,
> and lost the first one, the mother tongue,
> and could not really know the other,
> the foreign tongue.
> You could not use them both together
> even if you thought that way.

(Bhatt 1997: 35)

In a literary gesture that has now become something of a trademark, Bhatt attempts to actualise linguistic alienation – for a reader presumed to not be multilingual in the same way – by experimenting with multilingualism, bringing in substantial amounts of Gujarati and other Indian languages into the body of her work. These unfamiliar words and visuals appear in variations of the Devanagari script, usually accompanied by transliteration. Often there are implied or explicit translations while at other times, these lines stand on their own, deliberately indecipherable and/or opaque to the non-native speaker. The following lines

પરં તુ રાત્રે સ્વપ્નામાં મારી ભાષા પાછી આવે છે.

(parantoo rattray svupnama mari bhasha pachi aavay chay)

have already been partially translated into English in the preceding lines as "but overnight while I dream" but the reader who is unschooled in Gujarati has no way of knowing this (Bhatt 1988: 36). The meaning of the poem as an entirety is only available to a specific breed of Anglophone polyglot.

Despite the sophistication of Bhatt's literary technique and fluency with languages, there is at the heart of the poem's self-conscious thematic and formal hybridity, a didacticism which both occasions and constrains it. Routinely included as the "multicultural" component of secondary school English syllabi, the poem is overtly experimental and yet curiously schematic, a teachable poem "about" the condition of "living between two cultures." In a thoughtful essay on the Anglophone Indian poet's relationship to the English literary canon, the poet Agha Shahid Ali describes the position of the contemporary Indian writer in English as a privileged one with "ownership" of multiple languages and traditions: "I can use the Indian landscape, and the subcontinent's myths and traditions, from within, and I can do so for the first time in what might seem like a new idiom, a new language – subcontinental English . . . I have three major world cultures available to me without effort, cultures that I can appropriate, mix and exploit" (Ali 2008: 149–50).

This very command of languages – in a context where English is the language of command, to evoke Bernard Cohn's evocative phrase, rather than a vernacular, accounts for the scholastic quality of the carefully constructed linguistic hybridity in Bhatt's poem. To the extent that Anglophone poets from India belong to a small but powerful cultural elite, literary anxieties about hybridity and loss articulate the concerns of a minor milieu, compelling in their own right but not generalisable to a "postcolonial condition" or even a particularly "Indian" one. This disjuncture between the Anglophone and the vernacular is thematised in Bhatt's thoughtful work, *Devibhen Pathak*, where the interlacing of multiple languages and orthographies opens out into a compelling narrative meditation on semiotic (in)flexibility. Returning to the past of a young girl who will "one day be my mother," the poetic voice invokes Devibhen, the grandmother who takes a precious lump of gold to a jeweller to be worked into an heirloom necklace and to choose a shape for the ruby pendant. It is the year 1938 but "she didn't hesitate":

> For her it was clearly the geometric sun
> a wheel for life and luck,
> a four-petalled flower
> twisting out of a circle, in turned encircled
> by a hexagon
>
> (Bhatt 1991: 48)

Years later, her poet grand-daughter sequesters this matrilineal inheritance in a box, unable to wear

~v

> this yellow gold snake heavy symbol?
> I'm unable to believe the swastika
> is untouched by history.
>
> (Bhatt 1991: 49)

The juxtaposition of Gujarati, Hindi, English and Sanskrit combined with translations and transliteration keeps open the hopeful possibility of commensurability and

mutual understanding. Yet shared etymology is rendered starker by horrifying mutations of meaning

> (swasti, swasti,)   they used to say
> Meaning: Be well, be well!
>
> (Bhatt 1991: 51)

The four-pronged swastika finds family resemblances in still benevolent icons "*Hak-
enkreuz*, fylfot / . . . also St Brigid's plaited fancy cross" (1991: 51). Ironically, this
very plasticity of meaning, the necessary historicity of symbols, itself forecloses the
possibility that the narrator might access a different symbolic register: there can be
no "pure form" in the face of a local history turned global. Once the swastika assumes
its demonic twentieth-century incarnation, the generation of meaning itself appears
to come to a standstill. As European history becomes world history, just as its wars
become world wars, the narrator's cosmopolitanism becomes the barrier between her
self and her inheritance, a seemingly impermeable barrier between histories.

Yet grandmother Devibhen herself remains a question mark within the poem, which
ends, appropriately enough, on a series of questions. Asked by the jeweller,

> (aray bhen, tamnay khabar nathi . . .?)
> . . .
> Oh bhen, don't you know . . .?
>
> (Bhatt 1991: 48)

the grandmother's implicit response is simple if shocking:

> Who was Hitler? Mahatma Gandhi
>   was her daily news,
>   her truth.
>
> (Bhatt 1991: 48)

The historical and interpretative lacunae that separate grandmother and poet-grand-
daughter are also symptomatic of the location of Anglophone modernist poetry of
India. Devibhen's refusal to concede hermeneutic defeat in the face of a globalising
history ("she was right / and she was wrong"), also evokes a fissure between the concerns of the vernacular and the Anglophone (Bhatt 1991: 49). This is not to make
the crude claim that world-historical questions are absent from the former – the jeweller's surprised question in Gujarati makes clear that they are not. However, the poet-
narrator's concerns and her crafting of the multilingual are clearly specific to her
cultural formation – Anglophone, self-consciously cosmopolitan, and geographically
mobile. The poet's anguish about the conflicts generated by her own hybridity is specific to an English-speaking polyglot (the subcontinent has many polyglots who do not
speak English) privileged enough to cross national borders.

The academicism that inflects the poem's experimentation with multilingualism is even more apparent in works such as "Russown" from Bhatt's 1995 collection *The Stinking Rose*, which contains numerous odes to garlic (Bhatt 1995a). Here Hindi sits unobtrusively next to Gujarati, the two scripts similar enough to deceive the inattentive or unfamiliar eye. Elsewhere in the same collection, Bhatt issues a poetic challenge to the appropriation of languages in a charged, belligerent question that opens the poem "*Shantih*":

> Why did you latch on
> to that word
> when you probably never used it
> in common speech or prayer?
>
> (Bhatt 1995b: 78)

The unnamed "you" here is opposed to an assertive "we who use it for everything" (1995b: 78). Bhatt's question – "Are the resonances of *peace, peace, peace* deeper / if you call it *shantih*?" – targets forms of Western modernist exoticism that have appropriated Sanskrit terms like "shantih" (most famously in the closing lines of T.S. Eliot's *The Waste Land*). "Given this multiple heritage, why shouldn't I be envied?" writes Agha Shahid Ali of the "privileged minority" he belongs to (Ali 2008: 148). "After all, I can use *shantih* without being exotic, as Eliot clearly was in The Waste Land, a use that strikes one as full of irony when one remembers his customary fuss over the mind of Europe" (2008: 151).

Bhatt attacks the appropriative modernism of a culture that, on the one hand, declares itself universal and, on the other, uses the weaponry of mass destruction to segregate and destroy. "What is the true sound of *shantih*?" is answered thus:

> the sound of children sleeping
> a sound that is so different
> if one of them has only
> one leg.
>
> (Bhatt 1995b: 79)

To some extent, the poetic assertion of authenticity is strategic; the extensive quotations from Sanskrit scriptures and an insistence on Sanskrit terms as "Every-day words I took / for granted" resurrect linguistic barriers as acts of resistance to appropriation. Nevertheless, there is something odd about the claim that Sanskrit – an elite, upper-caste and far from quotidian language – is the stuff of the everyday for the poetic voice: "The Sanskrit becomes so simple / when I translate it" (Bhatt 1995b: 79). Ironically, at the point of articulating its own hybridity, the poetic voice seemingly reifies the colonial categorisation of languages and cultures into distinct monolithic categories while simultaneously eliding its own caste and class position. The innovative work of Bhatt's Anglophone multilingual poetry illuminates cultural interstices but also inadvertently reveals points of conflict and constraint, generated by the hierarchy of languages in which English cannot quite overcome the legacies of its own historical entanglements with power and violence on the subcontinent.

III. The Caribbean: "dis poem"

If, as Ali argues, the Anglophone classes of India have steadfastly kept quotidian cre-olisation at bay, despite the whimsicality and wordplay of some literary reworkings of English, the former British Caribbean or the West Indies, as this group of nation-islands is usually referred to, is the site of some of the most well-known literary deploy-ments of English as a creole. "English and African at the same time" according to Edward Brathwaite, Caribbean English "is much more closely allied to the African experience in the Caribbean" (1984: 13). Where Ali enjoins Indian writers not to reject the legacies of Milton and Shakespeare, the Guyanese writer, David Dabydeen celebrates the implications of "Not Being Milton" (Dabydeen 1990). The subversive potential of "nation-language" is perhaps best encapsulated by a famous John Agard poem (first published in 1985):

> I ent have no gun
> I ent have no knife
> But mugging de Queen's English
> Is the story of my life

> (Agard 1998: 318)

If "mugging" – a deliberate reclamation of racist stereotypes – is one approach to experimentation in Anglophone Caribbean poetry, it would be a mistake to regard it as a shared poetic project across a vast range of poets. While exploiting the subver-sive possibilities of creole has indeed given joy to poets as different as Una Marson, Kamau Brathwaite, Louise Bennett and The Mighty Sparrow, it is not the case that breaking and remaking English for its own sake accounts for innovation in Caribbean poetry.

Unlike the self-conscious multilingual experimentation seen above in Anglophone Indian poetry, some of the most compelling poetic experiments with language in Car-ibbean poetry takes for granted the hybridised quality of the language it uses, probing instead the relationship between language and the work of poetry. What Dabydeen provocatively calls "nigger talk" is a repudiation of the conventions of traditional metre and diction: "The hurricane does not roar in pentameters," Brathwaite famously pronounced (1984: 10). Poetry is put in the service of insightful reflections on poetics itself, particularly on the relationship between literary aesthetics and the politics of history. Something of the flavour of this project emerges in Dennis Scott's well-known "black apostrophe" to lynching, which evokes congruence between racialised killing and standardised language:

At least that's how
they tell it. It was long ago
and what we can recall of a dead slave or two
except that when we punctuate our island tale
they swing like sighs across the brutal
sentences, and anger pauses
till they pass away.

(Scott 2005: 175)

Scott was among a handful of early poets who struggled with the choice between drawing on the resources of creolised English and using standard forms. Here, standard English is not rejected but works rather as a quiet reminder of the limits of language, its inability to represent the horrors of the collective past of slavery during which language was also deployed as strategy, Brathwaite reminds us, to hide and disguise. Some of the most innovative Caribbean poetry emerging from an already hybrid, yet fluid, linguistic tradition, is engaged less with gaps between cultures or languages than with the lacunae between the discursive and the material.

Mutabaruka's "dis poem," for instance, cannot be easily categorised as "writing back" or even, in another dub poet's words, as "burnin thru slang and syntax" even as it both addresses a canonical poetic tradition and experiments with language and literary form. Dub is an innovative form of performance poetry, prepared not improvised, but often tweaked through stylised chanting or recitation.

dis poem
shall speak of the wretched sea
that washed ships to these shores
of mothers crying for their young
swallowed up by the sea

(Mutabaruka 2005: 278)

Although both the title and opening lines of Mutabaruka's poem promise direct representation, what follows is a deceptively simple series of evasions, definitions and riddles that require the reader to work not just with content, but with the idea of poetry itself. Not only will "dis poem" say "nothing new," it "will not change things." It is "like all the rest" but "it will not be recited by poetry enthusiasts" (2005: 279). Forcing an agile and constantly active interpretation, "dis poem" is all the more challenging for the apparent simplicity of language, short syntactical units, and incantatory rhythm. The mimetic and the anti-mimetic are held in contrapuntal tension alongside the performative and the anti-performative. At times "dis poem" speaks and calls while at others it merely *is* "knives . . . bombs . . . guns . . ." Yet:

dis poem will not change things
dis poem needs to be changed

dis poem is the rebirth of a people . . . awaking . . . overstanding . . . .
. . . dis poem speak
is speakin . . . has spoken

(Mutabaruka 2005: 279)

"dis poem" (which may also be a pun on "diss" or name-calling) declares that it will "call names" but rather than invective, we get a litany of names from lumumba and kenyatta to hannibal and akeneton, deliberately not capitalised, evoking pan-African solidarity. The pleasures of ontology are manifest in the incantatory catalogues of nomenclature, the drumming out of names unfamiliar to readers of standard Anglophone poetry, alternative cultural filiations and genealogies, the unfamiliar nouns allowing for an assertive infiltration of other languages. While the content is pan-African, each term draws on different African languages, places, names or historical events with all of Africa itself moving inexorably towards "uhuru" (freedom).

ashanti
maumau
ibo
yoruba
nyahbingi warriors

(Mutabaruka 2005: 279)

In insisting, with a seeming perversity, on its non-innovativeness ("dis poem is just a part of the story his-story . . . her-story . . . our-story"), Mutabaruka's work calmly shrugs off the distinction between subject of representation and aesthetic object. While this distinction is elided in language itself "dis poem" does not make the facile claim that all reality is reducible to speech acts. Rather than allow for this complacent elision, the poem demands of its listener-reader a constant alertness and interpretative responsibility. Mutabaruka's poem sets up a more demanding relationship between word and world:

dis poem is watchin u
tryin' to make sense from dis poem
dis poem is messin up your brains
makin you want to stop listening to dis poem

To be is "dis poem's" job; to do is the listener's. The poet is not dead – "dis poem has no poet" – he does not exist at all.
    The change to be effected by "dis poem" is not offered in the form of either easy slogans or utopian/dystopian endings. Ultimately

dis poem is to be continue
in your mind . . .

in your mind . . .
in your mind . . .

(Mutabaruka 2005: 280)

The newness generated by change is not, then, contained by the series of actions "dis poem" undertakes – calling, speaking, blazing, revolting, ringing, talking, irritating, watching, messing, disappointing, continuing – but is left open as a possibility for a future for which no template is provided. The instability of "dis poem" as poetic object is not, therefore, merely an ethnographic feature provided by orality (though each printing of it is slightly different from the other as is each spoken performance) but an enabling lacuna that demands the listener's creative labours. If the poet's insistence on handing over authorship, an embracing of his own irrelevance, opens up the possibility of collective contribution to "dis poem," through a range of activities, there is also an insistence on the poetic work's obstreperous immortality, albeit of a different sort:

dis poem shall continue
even when poets have stopped writing
dis poem shall survive . . . u . . . me

(Mutabaruka 2005: 279)

The multiple ontological and existential possibilities that inhere in "dis poem" emerge as a series of slippages, but they are nevertheless constellated around a clear ethical question: how can art, along with other human actions, from which it cannot be separated, be the change it wants to be?

IV. South Africa: proemdra

Questions of change and the role played by language and art were, however, more immediate in contexts such as apartheid South Africa, a uniquely challenging one for poets and poetry. A regime of censorship and repressive legislation meant that all protest writers, and black writers in particular, had to "look for survival away from the explicit if not to the cryptic then to the implicit" (Nadine Gordimer, cited in Patke 2006: 113). Poetry provided that genre more readily than others.

You can go to prison for saying
Some words.
Like . . . sorry I'm not allowed to say that.

(Smallberg 1992: 134)

For black writers, creating literary hybrids was a poetic act that was also political in a very different way from literary hybridity in the work of Bhatt or Rushdie. In the context of forbidden racial mixing, the mixing of languages has clearly subversive political resonances while using opacity and difficulty to evade incrimination. Language and its workings are a preoccupation for many South African protest poets across racial categories but in symptomatically different ways from the Caribbean and the Indian poetry discussed above. In Keith Gottschalk's poem, "Awareness Programme: The Grammar Lesson," prose is figured as the language of power and conformity:

> mood: imperative
> case: possessive
> tense: pluperfect
> voice: passive, negative
> person: singular

(Gottschalk 1992: 472)

Poetry, in contrast, is an active verb that will create a "transformational grammar":

> let's poem.

> mood: indicative
> case: accusative
> tense: the future
> voice: active and positive
> person: collective

(Gottschalk 1992: 472)

In a context where language is policed, experimentation must take place in the service of specific oppositional tasks. For Gottschalk, language is eminently well-suited to undertake the task of undermining power precisely because of its slipperiness and polyvalence; "forbidden couplets cuddle" where interracial coupling is illegal, and pass-free "armed poems slip across patrolling frontiers . . . dig caesuras to trap statutes" (473).

Barolong Seboni's poem "Punctuation" (1978) begins

Why

?

does africa resemble a continent of question marks?

(Seboni 1983: 370)

Optimistically triumphal about the possibility of this situation changing, Seboni pronounces:

the 3rd world
is overturning
emerging from
a comma,
and will in a brief period;
dot your dreary eyes and punch a full stop to all this

> anglo-owen-american double-carter-dealing internal –
> smith-settlement vostered-bantu pluralistic
> bullshit.

(Seboni 1983: 370)

Hyphenating a series of historical events in 1977, including US President Carter's controversial visit to South Africa, to forge a giant compound noun, is turned here into an act of mastery; everything will be contracted into "bullshit" to be ended, "period."

Others are less optimistic about the scope of words though no less attuned to their significance. In Dennis Brutus's "Black Bells," for instance, words are also racialised entities that entrap the poet and, as such, are not easily appropriated or subverted for oppositional purposes.

> AND
> Words,
> Make pain,
> Like poverty can make pain.
> . . .
> I know I'm trapped.
> Helpless
> Hopeless
> Trapped me whitey. Meem wanna ge aot Fuc
> Pschwee e ep booboodubooboodu blllll

(Brutus 1973: 26)

For Brutus, who was imprisoned and many of whose books were banned, language here offers only a mock-transcendence (or transubstantiation), as English, Afrikaans, patois and deliberately broken words and syntax merge into a skewed and nonsensical blessing:

> Flesh blood words shittrr Haai,
> Amen.

Compound nouns and multiple languages are also abundant in a work that seeks deliberately to create a hybrid genre, the "proemdra," an attempt to undo the distinctions between prose, poem and drama. Mothobi Mutloatse's "Ngwana wa Azania: a *proemdra for oral delivery*" is a bilious paean to the "recalcitrant" child of Azania (an oppositional name for South Africa, of uncertain etymological origin). Mutloatse coined the term "proemdra" as a way of rejecting what he decried as an externally imposed aesthetic division of labour between the genres of prose, poetry and drama. In the preface to his 1980 anthology, *Forced Landing*, he describes it as "an exciting experimental art form" through which to, using an Afrikaans word, "*donder* conventional literature . . . We are going to experiment and probe and not give a damn what the critics have to say" (5). The implied target is the oft-repeated charge that protest poetry was just journalism in poetic form, a charge Mutloatse aggressively appropriates as a project: "We'll write our poems in a narrative form; we'll write journalistic pieces in poetry form; we'll drama-tise our poetic experiences; we'll poeticise our historical dramas" (1980: 5).

Despite this call to undo borders and merge genres, Mutloatse's own proemdra is no simple celebration of hybridity. If, on the one hand, the hybrid genre of the proemdra polemically undoes separations in a society and culture that is viciously segregated and reliant on division to perpetuate power, on the other, hybridity itself is the monstrous product of apartheid, necessitating these awkward compounds and clunky nominalisa-tions. The multivocal proemdra, invokes a child who is never only a child, but always yoked to an adjective in multiple languages, almost none with positive connotations. S/he is a "ngkonochild," "mkhuluchild," "umtwana," "child of despair," "this ngwana of redemptive suffering," "child of nowhere," "child of rags to rags," "child of eviction" and "child of the donga." The linguistic admixture in the work – there are no less than four southern African languages here, including Zulu, Sotho and Xhosa in addition to Afrikaans and English – signals neither joyously subversive creolisation nor a Cali-banesque "cursing," but rather a chaotic concatenation of despair, incomprehension and destruction. Only the most wide-ranging of South African polyglots would be able to understand the proemdra in its entirety; as with Sujata Bhatt's work, untranslated opacity is deliberate but deployed in the service of a very different end.

In telling contrast to Rushdie's celebrated "baas-turd," Mutloatse's "child of bas-tardised society" is the "child of raw indecision and experimentation" and the "child of an insane and degenerated society"; he will "shit in the bedroom-cum-lounge-cum-kitchen" which he is condemned to live in (2005: 360–1). If Mutloatse is culpable of a moralistic denunciation of "illegitimate" children (the proemdra is replete with pejorative references to rape, prostitution and children born without fathers), it is also true that the poet is angry on behalf of a child for whom instability, uncertainty and vulnerability to multifarious intersecting vicissitudes have become a physically and mentally "crippling" existential condition:

> This child of dissipation shall loiter in the she been in earnest search for its parents and shall be batterd and abused to hell and gone by its roving parents when reunited in frustration in an alleyway.
> This child of bastardised society and bastard people-in high-office and colour-obsession and paranoid of communism and humanism, shall break through and snap the chain of repression with its bare hands . . .
>
> (Mutloatse 2005: 362)

The spaces of oppression are themselves hybridised like those above and "deadend-streetcamps" in which the children "speak animatedly of love and rage under the influence of glue and resistance" (Mutloatse 2005: 360). The child's destiny is the "labourglobe" in which his "dear living bread winning" is rewarded by a "thanks-for-nothing-thanks-for enriching-the rich-kick in the arse" (361). Hybridity here is an imposed condition born, ironically enough, of segregation and exploitation rather than inherently emancipatory, a term haunted by racism: "He shall photograph how the superior doctor addresses his unkempt mother in untailored talk as if mother-stupid had conceived of a baboon child" (361). Horst Zander somewhat misses the point in arguing that Mutloatse's proemdra does not "break new ground with regard to the distinction between fictional and factual discourse" because it does not mix generic conventions (Zander 1999: 17). Mutloatse seeks less to create a recognisable generic hybrid of traditional Western literary genres than to push passionately at the boundaries of linguistic bricolage, refiguring multilingualism as a space of creatively politicised intersection. Language can both generate meaning through heteroglossia and render itself opaque, but either way, refuses assimilation and reconciliation.

V. Conclusion

This essay has argued that despite its wide purchase, "hybridity" is of limited critical value in thinking about experimentation in postcolonial aesthetics. While it is now commonplace to deploy terms such as "transnational" and "cross-cultural," these are phrases that, along with hybridity, are often blunt instruments that ultimately obscure rather than elucidate the innovative dimensions of postcolonial literary works. To the extent that English poetry from non-Anglophone cultures is necessarily "composite," "mongrel," and "compound," hybridity offers little more than a stating of the obvious. If, as Ramazani convincingly argues, creolisation and hybridisation should be seen as integral to modern poetry and innovation, rather than exoticised, then attention is due to the specificities of context – linguistic, political and cultural – in seeking to understand how these processes play themselves out within the innovative practice of particular poets and traditions. If modern (ist) poetry is constitutively cross-cultural, there can be little purchase in identifying specific works as "cross-cultural" poems.

At their best, studies of postcolonial literatures articulate the paradigmatic (generalisable) and the comparative (specific). Mixing, contact and transculturation, while common to all colonial and postcolonial contexts, are always embedded in particular histories and frequently attest to very different kinds of cultural politics. An awareness of these histories must inflect our understanding of how linguistic innovation and experimentation work in different contexts. As Ramazani argues, "in poetry, more than perhaps in any other literary genre, the specificities of language matter" (2006: 19). While no language is the product of a single national context, all attempts at innovation and reinvention are inflected by specific historical exigencies, political imperatives and cultural formations. To read poetic innovation and language alongside these imperatives, far from reducing poems to political projects or constraining them within national contexts, ultimately enables more finely calibrated and fuller understandings of what they achieve.

References

Agard, J. (1998) "Listen Mr Oxford don." In S. Armitage and R. Crawford (eds.) *The Penguin Book of Poetry from Britain and Ireland since 1945*, London: Penguin Press.

Ali, A.S. (2008) "A Darkly Defense of Dead White Males." In D. Tobin and P. Triplett (eds.) *Poet's Work, Poet's Play: Essays on the Practice and the Art*, Ann Arbor, MI: University of Michigan Press.

Bhabha, H.K. (1995) "The Commitment To Theory." In B. Ashcroft, G. Griffiths and H. Tiffin (eds.) *The Postcolonial Studies Reader*, London: Routledge.

Bhatt, S. (1988) "Search for My Tongue." In *Brunizem*, Manchester, UK: Carcanet.

—— (1991) "Devibhen Pathak." In *Monkey Shadows*, Manchester, UK: Carcanet.

—— (1995a) "Russown." In *The Stinking Rose*, Manchester, UK: Carcanet.

—— (1995b) "Shantih." In *The Stinking Rose*, Manchester, UK: Carcanet.

—— (1997) "Search for My Tongue." In *Point No Point*, Manchester, UK: Carcanet.

Brathwaite, E. (1984) *History of the Voice: The Development of Nation Language in Anglophone Caribbean Poetry*, London: New Beacon Books.

Brutus, D. (1973) "Black Bells." In R. Royston (ed.) *To Whom it May Concern: An Anthology of South African Poetry*, Johannesburg: AD Donker.

Dabydeen, D. (1990) "On Not Being Milton: Nigger Talk in England Today." In C. Ricks and L. Michaels (eds.) *The State of Language*, London: Faber.

De Klerk, V. (1996) "Introduction." In V. de Klerk (ed.) *Focus on South Africa*, Amsterdam/Philadelphia: John Benjamins.

Ezekiel, N. (1989a) "Goodbye Party for Miss Pushpa, T.S." In G. Patel (ed.) *Nissim Ezekiel: Collected Poems 1952–1988*, Delhi: Oxford University Press.

—— (1989b) "Soap." In G. Patel (ed.) *Nissim Ezekiel: Collected Poems 1952–1988*, Delhi: Oxford University Press.

Gottschalk, K. (1992) "Awareness Programme: The Grammar Lesson." In A.W. Oliphant (ed.) *Essential Things: An Anthology of New South African Poetry*, Johannesburg: COSAW.

Macaulay, T.B. (2006 [1835]) "Minute on Indian Education." In B. Ashcroft, G. Griffiths and H. Tiffin (eds.) *The Post-Colonial Studies Reader*, second edn, London: Routledge.

Mutabaruka (2005) "dis poem." In S. Brown and M. McWatt (eds.) *The Oxford Book of Caribbean Verse*, Oxford, UK: Oxford University Press.

Mutloatse, M. (1980) "Introduction." In M. Mutloatse (ed.) *Forced Landing: Africa South: Contemporary Writings*, Johannesburg: Ravan Press.

—— (2005) "Ngwana wa Azania: A Proemdra for Oral Delivery." In M. Chapman (ed.) *A Century of South African Poetry*, Johannesburg: AD. Donker.

Parthasarathy, R. (1977) "From 'Homecoming.'" In S. Ameeruddin (ed.) *Indian Verse in English*, Madras, India: Poet Press, p. 30.

Patke, R. S. (2006) *Postcolonial Poetry in English*, Oxford, UK: Oxford University Press.

Ramazani, J. (2001) *The Hybrid Muse: Postcolonial Poetry in English*, Chicago, IL: University of Chicago Press.

—— (2006) *A Transnational Poetics*, Chicago, IL: University of Chicago Press.

Rao, R. (1963 [1938]) "Foreword" to *Kanthapura*, Bombay, India: New Directions.

Retamar, R. (1989) "Caliban." In *Caliban and Other Essays*. Minneapolis, MN: University of Minnesota Press.

Rushdie, S. (1995) *The Moor's Last Sigh*, New York: Vintage Books

Scott, D. (2005) "Epitaph." In S. Brown and M. McWatt (eds.) *The Oxford Book of Caribbean Verse*, Oxford, UK: Oxford University Press.

Seboni, B. (1983) "Punctuation." In T. Couzens and E. Patel (eds.) *The Return of the Amasi Bird: Black South African Poetry 1891–1981*, Johannesburg: Ravan.

Seth, V. (1999) "Diwali." In *Collected Poems*, Delhi: Penguin India.

Smallberg, M. (1992) "Signals." In A. W. Oliphant (ed.) *Essential Things: An Anthology of New South African Poetry*, Johannesburg: COSAW.

Zander, H. (1999) "Prose-Poem-Drama 'Proemdra': 'Black Aesthetics' versus 'White Aesthetics' in South Africa," *Research in African Literatures* 30(1).

15
AVANT-POP
Lance Olsen

I. *After Yesterday's Crash*: definitions

Unlike the coinage of many literary-historical terms, that of "Avant-Pop" is relatively straightforward. In 1987 critic Larry McCaffery happened across jazz trumpeter Lester Bowie's album from the year before entitled *Avant-Pop* (1986), on which Bowie takes such oldies as "Blueberry Hill" and, in collaboration with the Brass Fantasy nonet, reconfigures them into improvisations that complicate and expand the comparatively simple Pop energies of the originals. Four years later, Surfictionist Ronald Sukenick mentioned to McCaffery in passing that Mark Leyner's work, celebrated for its dense, blitzkrieg style, absurdist humor, and televisual texture, had a certain "'Avant-Pop' feel to it"; Sukenick's use of the term struck McCaffery as "absolutely right" (L. McCaffery, personal communication, 4 June 2010). The comment reminded him of Bowie's album, which McCaffery shared with Sukenick while the two sat listening to jazz and discussing current cultural trends at McCaffery's desert retreat in Borrego Springs several hours east of San Diego near the Salton Sea. It struck both men that a similar sort of transformational gesture typified much of what was going on around them in experimental writing, music, film, television, and criticism (Olsen 1998: 556).

Phenomena comprising popular culture, Bowie's retoolings suggested, were more than mainstream boorishness. They could also serve as rich generative material for artists creating in various disciplines. "While normally seen as being fixed or confined in terms of their 'meaning' and arrangement," McCaffery argues three years later in his introduction to *After Yesterday's Crash*, the second of two anthologies of Avant-Pop fiction that he edited (the first was FC2/Black Ice's *Avant-Pop: Fiction for a Daydream Nation* [1993]), pop-cultural pieces "actually contain an inexhaustible source of hidden resonances and recombinatory arrangements" (McCaffery 1995a: xxi).

Following Fredric Jameson's reasoning in "Postmodernism: or the Cultural Logic of Late Capitalism," McCaffery further contends that pop culture has colonized and commodified, not only the physical space surrounding us, but also the internal space of our memories, dreams, and desires. One cannot position oneself outside it. The challenge facing contemporary innovators is how, not to "halt or deflect" the progress of the juggernaut called hyper-consumer capitalism, along with its relentless infection of our unconscious, but how to learn to "coexist" (xii) with it, "how to survive in these new conditions" (xiv). Although survival may be difficult for all serious art – all art that doesn't structure and thematize itself primarily as entertainment and distraction – it is especially so for serious fiction, which since World War Two has found itself increasingly adrift on the cultural peripheries.

How, then, to "coexist" alongside the beast and learn to "survive in these new conditions"? "Coexist" may be the wrong word, since it denotes a harmonious relationship between the Avant-Pop and the dominant cultures. Rather, the Avant-Pop's heterodox solution for survival, like those songs on Bowie's album, is to destabilize hyperconsumer capitalism's aesthetic merchandise by means of recycling and reinvention. "Avant-Pop," McCaffery writes, "combines Pop Art's focus on consumer goods and mass media with the avant-garde's spirit of subversion and emphasis on radical formal innovation" (1995a: xvii–xviii). To get a sense of what this means in practical terms, consider David Cronenberg's film *Videodrome* (1983). In one emblematic scene, the new flesh morphs into the static of a television screen that literally oozes out of its veined, throbbing, eroticized black box in the form of Nikki Brand's lips to engulf the head of the protagonist, Max Renn, who has lost his ability to discriminate between inside and outside. The uncanny image drives home with astonishing transgressive force how the virtual and actual have become hybridized (Seegert 2010: 63–5), how the human has become identical with the ubiquitous commodified mediascape.

Whether manifested in music (Laurie Anderson: *Big Science* [1982]), film (Satoshi Kon and Iginio Straffi: *Paprika* [2006]), television (*Max Headroom* [1987–1988]), theory (Steven Shaviro: *Doom Patrols* [1996]), or fiction (Manuel Puig: *Betrayed by Rita Hayworth* [1968]), the Avant-Pop expresses an essential optimism – an "intention of creating a sense of delight, amazement, and amusement" (McCaffery 1995a: xix). Moreover, McCaffery claims it situates itself beyond the "stinking, grotesquely bloated corpse" of Postmodernism (Olsen 1998: 562). (See Lee; Marx-Scouras; Miller; Baetens; Berry; and McHale, this volume.) Perhaps paradoxically, McCaffery adds that the Avant-Pop is "less an artistic 'movement' with manifestoes and specifically agreed upon goals than a set of related aesthetic and thematic tendencies" (McCaffery 1995b: 40).

"Paradoxically" because one wonders whether McCaffery's writing on the Avant-Pop is supposed to be descriptive, prescriptive, or both. His insightful, influential introduction to the fictions in *After Yesterday's Crash* is shot through precisely with the unskeptical exuberance associated with manifestoes (see Winkiel, this volume). His stress on the Avant-Pop's optimism occasionally comes close to echoing the strains of the misguided utopianism running through modernist manifestoes by Tristan Tzara, André Breton, and, most disconcertingly, F.T. Marinetti with his proto-Fascistic glorification of youth, speed, and immachination. One also wonders why McCaffery mentions so few non-U.S. creators in his discussion, when so many (Tomas Alfredson, Italo Calvino, David Clark, Umberto Eco, Damien Hirst, Haruki Murakami, to name the first half-dozen that fly to mind) exist.

Nor is it quite clear how J.G. Ballard's or Steve Erickson's work – both included in *After Yesterday's Crash* – could be considered optimistic, "delightful," and/or "amusing," any more than could Guy Debord's theoretical tracts (cited in McCaffery's "Random Sampling of Avant-Pop Works" following his introduction [xxx–xxxi]), or (not cited by McCaffery), say, Dave Soldier, Komar, and Melamid's *The People's Choice Music* project, for which the trio in 1996 conducted a poll about respondents' musical preferences on Dia's website and then used the results to write Pop melodies and lyrics to what presumably should have been the most wanted and unwanted songs in the world (Ubuweb: Sound 2010). Its biting critique of the commodification of the current Pop music industry and its colonization of its audience's ears and needs is hardly delightful. Pop taste, it argues, has become an act of demographic finesse, mainstream art an act of manufacturing by committee, and the McDonaldization of aesthetics a *fait accompli*.

It is also debatable that the Avant-Pop situates itself beyond Postmodernism (see McLaughlin, this volume). One may view aesthetic histories either as a necklace of ruptures or continuities. McCaffery chooses the former. But if one accepts Brian McHale's contention that Postmodernism, like all literary instants, is a construction, a potentially useful language game (1992: 1), then the question becomes, neither whether or not there is such a thing as Postmodernism, nor whether or not the Avant-Pop has somehow found a way to displace it, but rather whose construction of Postmodernism one can productively employ to better place and understand the Avant-Pop. Turn to Andreas Huyssen's *After the Great Divide* (1986 – the same year, serendipitously enough, as the appearance of Lester Bowie's *Avant-Pop* album), and one locates an approach that emphasizes the volatile blurring of high and mass culture as Postmodernism's defining feature. If so, it is difficult to see how the Avant-Pop is less a surpassing/supplanting than it is a valuable shorthand for a constellation of Postmodern attitudes and methods that have gained ascendancy since the 1950s (including a Pop aesthetics, absurdism, appropriation and manipulation, and formal/thematic experimentation) with the advent of increased leisure time; invention of the teenager; explosion of mass media; proliferation of processed/digitized nature; suffusion of the entertainment industry into all aspects of our lives; rise of conurbation, globalization, corporatization, and conglomeration; appearance of the internet, email, social-networking sites, news feeds, and text messages (see Connell; Gibbons, this volume).

By situating the Avant-Pop in the last decade of the twentieth century, McCaffery firmly and problematically periodizes the concept. If we conceptualize the Avant-Pop as said shorthand, McCaffery's identification appears belated. The present continuously shapes and reshapes our perspective on and categories of the past. Avant-Pop activities have arguably brought to our attention what has been evident in works at least as far back as the early Post-War years, if not the beginnings of Modernism – which may be a roundabout way of saying that periodization and categorization are nothing if not profoundly permeable, polymorphous, contingent affairs.

II. Genealogies, continuities, contexts

"The fact is," Borges announces in his essay about Kafka's retro-influence on Browning and others, "that every writer *creates* his own precursors. His work modifies our conception of the past, as it will modify the future" (1964: 201). The same is the case for constructions like the Avant-Pop. Read back through its lens, and one encounters a faintly different *Waste Land* than one encountered previously: a poem nearly as infused with a pop-cultural awareness (Eliot's appropriation of ragtime rhythms and phrasing, cinematic montage, pub hubbub, and general awareness of heightening speed and globalization in the early twentieth century) as it is with Weston's discourse on the Grail legend and Frazer's on fertility cults, or a faintly different *Ulysses*, whose satiric Aeolus chapter, set in the offices of the *Freeman's Journal and National Press* and *Evening Telegraph*, borrows its structure from the vocabulary of headlines, as well as the commotion and data rush of contemporary media, in order to show it all as so much hot air – if not, like the newspaper filled with advertisements Bloom carries with him in the Lotus Eaters chapter (along with the church he visits there, the gambling he discusses with Bantam Lyons, and so on), a kind of pop-cultural narcotic.

Far from representing a break from earlier theoretico-aesthetic forces, the Avant-Pop shares a number of concerns/approaches with many subsumed under the umbrella of Modernism – not only Italian Futurism with its fixation on youth culture, velocity, technology, permanent innovation, and the connection between arts and politics, but also Cubism with its investigation of collage and multiple relativistic perspectives; Dada with its acclamation of anti-art and the aleatory, as well as its virulent rejection of capitalism's logic; and Surrealism with its signature juxtapositions of radically different elements within a single space to achieve jarred viewing, listening, and/or reading experiences on its audience's part (although, as we shall see, the Avant-Pop eschews Surrealism's investigation into the unconscious). (See White, this volume, on Futurism; Stockwell on Surrealism.)

Simultaneously, the Avant-Pop shares concerns/approaches with Cyberpunk. A case could be made that Cyberpunk operates as a subset of the Avant-Pop in its stress on appropriation of pop-cultural genres, its thematics of mediazation and mediation, and its politically and aesthetically subversive attitude. Recall Cyberpunk's defining propensity for hijacking tropes from SF and reprocessing them into disquieting structures (Anthony Burgess' *A Clockwork Orange* [1962], J.G. Ballard's *The Atrocity Exhibition* [1970], and my own novel, *Tonguing the Zeitgeist* [1994]); its inquiries into the subject's colonization and manipulation by information technologies and commerce; its curiosity about the limiting and liberating possibilities of machine–human interfaces; and its hacker/punk accent on casts of dissenters dedicated either to trying to exist outside dominant systems and/or using those systems' apparatuses against themselves.

William S. Burroughs' *Naked Lunch* (1959), generally regarded as an exemplary Beat novel, is also one of the first in which Avant-Pop formal strategies and thematics – tinted with proto-Cyberpunk shadings – evince themselves in full. Burroughs considered experimental writing a plastic art that rhymes more with Jackson Pollock's gestural abstraction, where visual fields consist of spontaneous clashes foregrounding the physical act of painting, than with conventional mimetic narrativity. The resulting disjunctive "plot" involves protagonist William Lee's addiction to opiates and apomorphine treatment. His journey leads him to Mexico, a limbo called

Freeland, the anarchic Interzone, the manipulative behaviorist Dr. Benway, and a far side that hints that Lee's "quest" (which may have been no more than the disjointed memories and hallucinations of his withdrawal) has taken him nowhere. The novel unwrites itself through a number of genres (SF, noir detective novel, Swiftian satire, Borscht belt shtick, etc.) into a series of cut-up passages that over the course of its final pages splinter language, chronology, and Freudian characterization into something very near illegibility. Lee's dependence on opiates intimates – as does Joyce's Lotus Eaters chapter – a culture of narcotics pushers and addictions committed to making the body into a biological site of entrapment. The human organism materializes as a virus feeding compulsively upon a host hyper-consumerism bent on maintaining its own control (technological, psychological, political, semiotic) by means of distraction, chemical and otherwise. Through its linguistic, ontological, and nonsequential, proto-hypertextual deformations, *Naked Lunch* disorganizes the assumptions of that host.

Innovative authors working chiefly in the 1950s, 1960s, and early 1970s (Vladimir Nabokov, John Hawkes, *et al.*) were raised less on pop-cultural phenomena than on diverse strands of Modernism, which they tended to position themselves concurrently within and against. Those beginning to work in the mid-1970s forward (Kathy Acker, William Gibson, *et al.*) represented another species altogether. They embody the first generations of authors raised primarily on TV, commercials, B-films, pop-cultural genres, and, increasingly, digital forms of entertainment from early video games to Wii, Walkman to the iPod, and Macintosh computers to the iPad. If classical and Christian mythology, Shakespeare, Dante, and Joyce were the literary/cultural home chords many writers working before the mid-1970s returned to for inspiration and quotation, then comics, rock'n'roll, and the universe of Pop iconography are the paraliterary and pop-cultural ones many working after the mid-1970s tended to cite and mine. These writers take ideas like hybridity and information density/speed for granted, while affirming, along with Thomas Pynchon in his introduction to *Slow Learner*, "May Road Runner cartoons never vanish from the airwaves, is my attitude" (1984: 19) – a statement that would have been incomprehensible to Robbe-Grillet or Doris Lessing, let alone Thomas Mann or Virginia Woolf.

Many comprising these new generations (David Foster Wallace, Mark Danielewski, Lidia Yuknavitch, *et al.*) studied philosophy and/or theory as undergraduates and/or graduates. Many received advanced degrees in literature and theory as well as creative writing. And many went on to teach at colleges and universities. Their exposure to emerging theoretical discourses, from Deconstruction to Cultural Studies, Post-Coloniality to Gender Theories, revealed itself in their fiction as a sophisticated awareness of themselves as consuming subjects in the late capitalist pluriverse described by Jameson (1984); citizens of Guy Debord's (1995) society of the spectacle, where commodity fetishism is structured to distract us from thinking about our alienation from others, ourselves, and our environment; and strangers in Paul Virilio's (1989) strange land where velocity has in a sense abolished physical movement itself, so that it now seems more efficacious to sit still and accelerate information past/through ourselves by means of various interfaces than to travel relatively unmediated through tangible space. The consequence for these authors is nothing if not a deeply conflicted relationship with popular culture.

III. Pla(y)giarist ecologies: formal strategies

In "Critifiction: Imagination as Plagiarism" (written in 1976), Surfictionist Raymond Federman, himself influenced by appropriative and improvisational constructions of jazz, argues for a conception of text as intertext traversed by multiple discourses not its own, a zone of "pla(y)giarism" (Federman 1993: 51) where "I do not know . . . where my own language [begins] and where it converge[s] with that of others" (52) – an idea itself pla(y)giarized from the poststructuralists, most notably Barthes (1977), who in "The Death of the Author" conceives of the text as "a multi-dimensional space in which a variety of writings, none of them original, blend and clash" (146). Pla(y)giarism is arguably the Avant-Pop's principal formal strategy, displaying itself in a multitude of innovative loci and at a variety of strata: junk/trash aesthetics (Duchamp's found art; Kenneth Goldsmith's uncreative writing (see Epstein, this volume)), where "writers don't need to write anything anymore," but rather "just need to manage the language that already exists" (Jones 2008); visual/linguistic collage/montage/quotation practices (Sergei Eisenstein, Michael Graves); sound sampling and mashup (industrial and electronic music, hip-hop).

By way of literary examples, Robert Coover, Angela Carter, and Aimee Bender, among many others, recycle fairy tales to assorted unruly ends, while Jay Cantor reprocesses George Herriman's famous comic strip in *Krazy Kat: A Novel in Five Panels* (Cantor 1987) to examine the Cold War nuclear threat. Dave Gibbons and Alan Moore undo the conventional superhero comic in their groundbreaking graphic novel *The Watchmen* (Gibbons and Moore 1987) by introducing elements from nineteenth-century realist fiction (fully-rounded characters with pasts, fears, and desires) and innovating the form by inserting cinematic techniques (zoom, extreme close-up, montage, jump-cut) and tropes from detective noir and alternative-universe SF, in addition to *trompe l'oeil* devices that call attention to the materiality of the page: letters that appear to have been produced on a typewriter, pasted-in book entries, police reports, photographs, business cards, and paper clips.

At the nexus of pla(y)giarism, improvisation, structural velocity, linguistic density, and hypertextuality, one locates a key proto-Avant-Pop novel from the 1960s, Donald Barthelme's *Snow White* (1967). Its title refers, not to the Brothers Grimm's folk version, but to the 1937 saccharine animated-film adaptation by Disney. Barthelme's interference resets the tale in an absurd commune in Manhattan peopled by seven dull men and one bored woman. Coming to political awareness, the latter feels herself abused in her role as "horsewife" (Barthelme 1967: 49) by the scripts (Freudian, suburban, pop existentialist) that write her and which under scrutiny start seeming as outmoded as the fairy tale that she and her sidekicks find themselves inhabiting – or at least trying to; the contemporary world, Snow White learns, is no more able to supply her with a prince in shining armor than it is "the correct ending to the story" (138) – let alone any sense of coherent plot that explains and comforts. Barthelme's collage text, made up of non-chronological scenes, quasi-philosophical musings, headlines, high-speed nonsensical passages, a clash of "high" and "low" diction from a multiplicity of cultural sites, and an intermission in the form of quiz asking the reader how she/he has been faring so far, uses a paratactic (and hence radically democratic) aesthetics, where every component is equal to every other, in order to critique the empty, brutalized language out of which those confining scripts are generated. Barthelme incorporates a hyperbolic version of what one character refers to as its "sludge quality" to turn the language of control against itself while revealing how Kierkegaard's worst nineteenth-century fears about what he called The Age of Journalism – in which speed of information delivery and skimmed surfaces pass for wisdom, and brash literal-mindedness swamps complexity and subtlety – are being born out today in sobering abundance (Morace 1992: 170).

It would be tautology to point out that Avant-Pop writing is by nature metafictive – that it is continuously self-conscious about its own methods, (mis)use of semiotics, and fictive processes. Less obvious is that much Avant-Pop writing also participates in what Ihab Hassan terms "paracriticism" (1975), Greg Ulmer "post-criticism" (1983; see also Ulmer, this volume), and Federman "critifiction" (1993): blurring the traditional division between fiction and theoretical discourses in an effort to execute and explore "the apparent collapse of criticism into its object" (Connor 1997: 227). Avant-Pop work regularly disfigures the conventional critical monograph's layout and aims with techniques from avant-garde writing practices (lyrical prose, allegory, inserted poems and letters, non-linear and/or contradictory thought, manifold voices, typographical and other paginal mischief, inventories, even fleshed-out characters, scenes, plots, etc.). Antecedents encompass such generically amphibious work as Nietzsche's oeuvre, Cixous' 1975 "Sorties" (Cixous 1998), and Derrida's *Glas* (1974). Besides Hassan's *Paracriticisms*, which advances that avant-theory must subvert the academy's conservative fixities, must through a strategy of decreation overturn "the theoretical solemnity of modern criticism" that "ignores the self-destructive element of literature" (9), Avant-Pop post-criticism spans such heterogeneous projects as the jocoserious narratological inquiries in John Barth's *Lost in the Funhouse* (1969) and Joe Amato's mixture of juxtaposed aphorisms, personal narrative, polemics, documentary reportage, and the vernacular in *Industrial Poetics: Demo Tracks for a Mobile Culture* (2006).

IV. Pla(y)giarist demythologies: the problematics of representation and the subject

Laundry lists cataloguing principle formal strategies, however, fail to address the more vital question about the Avant-Pop: *What are its objectives in employing such strategies?* Two of the most salient are the problematization of: (1) traditional notions of representation; and (2) traditional notions of the subject position. Once again, both fall comfortably within the scope of several Postmodernisms.

In his appendix to *The Postmodern Condition*, Jean-François Lyotard contends that Postmodern work – for him an extension of the avant-garde (a mode which "denies itself the solace of good forms, the consensus of a taste" [Lyotard 1984: 81]) – struggles continuously if paradoxically to find a way to present the unpresentable. Whether in the shape of one of Ad Reinhardt's all-black canvases or Beckett's *Unnamable* (1953), the Postmodern project attempts to "enable us to see only by making it impossible to see"; to "please only by causing pain" (Beckett 1994: 78). There are some circumstances, Lyotard maintains, which by their very nature cannot be thought about or articulated within the bounds of reason and aesthetic convention. There are some events – he cites Auschwitz; 9/11 or BP's catastrophic Deepwater Horizon oil spill are more recent examples – whose atrocious complexities refuse to be reduced to habitual understanding, predictable storylines, anything other than what they are: manifestations of unimaginable difficulty and radical existential/narrative unease.

The contemporary is unpresentable in another way as well. For Jean Baudrillard, simulation has replaced the natural. Signs no longer connect with the world they represent, but are "exchanged against each other rather than against the real" (1998: 489). Take, by way of illustration, the Most Photographed Barn in America in DeLillo's *White Noise* (1985). Jack Gladney, the novel's protagonist, one day drives twenty two miles into the country to show the barn to his friend and colleague, Murray. They arrive to find a full-fledged tourist site complete with people bearing cameras and a booth selling postcards and slides. "No one sees the barn," Murray realizes. "Once you've seen the signs about the barn, it becomes impossible to see the barn." Instead of taking pictures of the barn, people are "taking pictures of taking pictures" (12–13).

If the contemporary is always-already beyond belief, unimaginable and unimaginably synthetic, then how do experimental practices go about their business, and what, precisely, has that business become? For Avant-Pop creators, one answer is to search out formal strategies that help re-present that existence, rethink narrativity, not simply to innovate structure, but to better capture how it feels to exist now. One answer, then, is to embrace, not some sort of anti-realism, but an array of neo-realisms for a hyper-mediated, late-stage capitalist "reality" that is no longer perceived to be real. Another is to create compositions that focus on the very problematics of representation itself, such as Steve Tomasula's *Book of Portraiture* (2006). Tomasula organizes his multi-genre critifiction less like a conventional novel with a central set of characters than an essay with a central thesis. Chapter one narrates the invention of the phonemic alphabet in the ancient world and the concomitant gap that yawns between signifier and signified. Chapter two relates Velázquez's worrying in the seventeenth century of Catholicism's powerful representational procedures through works like his own metafictive *Las Meninas* (1656). Chapter three recounts a case of Freudian psycho-sexual depth (mis)analysis of female consciousness and the attendant modulation in the early twentieth century from external to internal representation. Various contemporary technological remediations of the disappearing subject position (video surveillance, commercial modeling, digital forgery) comprise chapter four, while a story of bio-representation in the shape of an artist modifying a mouse's DNA to produce a new kind of aesthetic object in a new kind of alphabet comprises chapter five.

Each age may get the literature it deserves, but then each also gets a fresh complex of reading strategies and languages with which to discuss the new kinds of textuality and narrativity it finds itself confronting. N. Katherine Hayles makes the useful distinction in this regard between two cognitive modes, *deep attention* and *hyper attention* (2007; see also Ensslin, this volume). Deep attention, usually associated with serious writing and reading, can concentrate on a single object for an extended period of time; think, for instance, of engaging with a James novel. Hyper attention, on the other hand, can switch focus rapidly and often; think, for instance, of navigating *Grand Theft Auto*. Conventional narratological formations ask the reader to employ deep attention. Avant-Pop works ask the reader to employ an oscillating combination of both. Consider one's experience of reading *Gravity's Rainbow* (Pynchon 1973) or Danielewski's *House of Leaves* (2000), or the opening of Patrik Ourednik's *Europeana* (2001):

> The Americans who fell in Normandy in 1944 were tall men measuring 173 centimeters on average, and if they were laid head to foot they would measure 38 kilometers. The Germans were tall too, while the tallest of all were the Senegalese fusiliers in the First World War who measured 176 centimeters, and so they were sent into battle on the front lines in order to scare the Germans. It was said of the First World War that people in it fell like seeds and the Russian Communists later calculated how much fertilizer a square kilometer of corpses would yield and how much they would save on expensive foreign fertilizers if they used the corpses of traitors and criminals instead of manure.

> (Ourednik 2005: 1)

Ourednik crams several micro-fictions into three paratactic sentences. Each phrase challenges the reader to readjust both his/her focus and the web of references to which the phrase gives rise in order to make meaning. The ironic linguistic collage that results is what David Foster Wallace refers to in Mark Leyner's fiction as "less a novel than a piece of witty erudite extremely high-quality prose television. Velocity and vividness – the wow – replace the literary hmm of actual development." For Wallace, this sort of fiction is at once "hilarious, upsetting, sophisticated, and extremely shallow" (Wallace 1993: 192).

The representation of character (emblematic of a culture's understanding of the subject position) and scene (emblematic of a culture's understanding of space and place) are unsettled, too. If mediation of the natural, the effects of hyper-consumer capitalism, and the rest radiate unremittingly through us and around us, and if traditional distinctions between public and private, objective and subjective, therefore no longer hold, then, literally, the question becomes, in all senses of the phrase: Where am *I?* In the aftermath of poststructuralism's demythologizing philosophies of radical uncertainty, ideas of selfhood – and its corollaries, race and gender – have shivered into unstable quantum fields, reminding us that the pronoun (the heart of character and subjectivity) is no more than a sort of hoax foisted upon us by the culture's language. The rules of grammar don't amount to a metaphysics. In Avant-Pop undertakings, one locates something closer, not to the reverberant Freudian depth-subject, but to the schizoid subject Baudrillard describes in "The Ecstasy of Communication": a network for the data flowing within and without, "bereft of every scene, open to everything in spite of him[/her]self, living in the greatest confusion" (1983: 133).

Utilizing Flash animation techniques, Young-Hae Chang and Heavy Industries' text-film *Traveling to Utopia: With a Brief History of Technology* (2005) takes the form of multiple black and green words in Helvetica font racing simultaneously across the top, middle, and bottom of a bright white screen at a speed the reader/viewer cannot control. She/he often needs five or more sittings before being able to assemble the information presented. Across the top runs a narrative in Korean characters, indecipherable to most English speakers at any speed. Across the bottom runs one in English that recounts the Kafkaesque dream of a nameless (and ambiguously gendered) narrator stopped by three policemen at a subway station that may be in Seoul, but may also be in Paris, questioned briefly, and allowed to go on her/his way. Across the middle runs the story of a (probably) different nameless female narrator's life with technology from her first encounter with a computer in her father's office to her own first laptop and beyond. Walking through a metal detector at an airport one day, she sets off the alarm. A visit to the doctor reveals a chip used to track endangered species implanted in her abdomen. Her story concludes with the narrator reporting that she has taken to living in airports, which for her represent a temporal, non-spatial spaces that make her feel safe. All three narratives are interrupted briefly, once, by a screen-sized smiley face clock, while an upbeat jazz score at odds with the narratives' content plays throughout.

Hayles highlights the importance of Media-Specific Analysis (MSA) when approaching any text (2004). Most contemporary readers, she argues, have been raised on hardcopy print texts that have remained virtually unchanged in appearance for 500 years. As new paginal and surpaginal forms appear, it is essential to employ "a mode of critical attention which recognizes that all texts are instantiated and that the nature of the medium in which they are instantiated matters" (67). Chang's text-film could not have been imagined except as a reaction to and conversation with conventional linear narrativity and hypertextuality, the ubiquity of film, and Flash technologies which enable it, not only to talk about, but to enact the book's disembodiment while placing the reader/viewer in the same position as the narrator(s) with respect to technology: unable to control it even as it broadcasts from outside and inside, dematerializing even as it tracks the subject. Through MSA procedures, Chang's work performs its thematics through a troubled interface with its reader/viewer, suggesting the new flesh (in this case the female abdomen, site of bio-reproduction) has become impregnated with media (the site of semiotic reproduction) that knows more about us than we do about "ourselves" – a realization that returns us to that uncanny image of Max Renn's head disappearing into the TV set in *Videodrome*.

V. Conclusion

The Avant-Pop is far from being a subset of the Postmodernism theorists like Jameson typify as caught in a prison-house of language, unable to engage with institutional contexts and functions (1975) – if such a beast ever existed. Rather, it accords with the Postmodernisms advocated by Marjorie Perloff, who lauds the participatory art of a John Cage or Robert Smithson, late outriders of Futurism's drive to dissolve the distinction between art and non-art, hermetically sealed aesthetic objects and their sociopolitical/philosophical/ecological environments (Perloff 1986), or by Lyotard, who conceives of the Postmodern as a re-distillation of late nineteenth- and early twentieth-century avant-garde intensities, "but in the nascent state, [where] this state is constant" (Lyotard 1984: 79). Impulses which envisage art as a space of possibility that allows one to picture the text of the text and the text of the world other than they are, and thus to contemplate change in both.

Avant-Pop activities run the risk of accepting and perpetuating a vapid popular culture. Yesterday's *détournement* all-too-quickly dissolves into tomorrow's *récupéra- tion*. The "radical" all-too-quickly becomes reincorporated into the culture at large, commodified, made palatable, and sold to readers, listeners, and viewers in ways that make them feel edgy and unique. Disruption quickly devolves into fashion. Within a few seasons of Grunge's appearance in the late 1980s, the Gap was selling the unkempt thrift-store look (produced in Saipan sweatshops), as middle-class teenagers across the country bought faux-rebellious identities off the rack at the local mall in order to impersonate their peers. For the Avant-Pop to remain vital, it must exist in a continu- ous state of (mis)appropriative reinvention.

References

Amato, J. (2006) *Industrial Poetics: Demo Tracks for a Mobile Culture*, Iowa City, IA: University of Iowa Press.

Avant-Pop. (1986) [Album] Featuring Lester Bowie and Brass Fantasy, Munich, Germany: ECM.

Ballard, J.G. (1970) *The Atrocity Exhibition*, London: Jonathan Cape.

Barth, J. (1969) *Lost in the Funhouse*, New York: Bantam.

Barthelme, D. (1967) *Snow White*, New York: Atheneum.

Barthes, R. (1977) "The Death of the Author" trans. S. Heath, in *Image Music Text*, New York: Hill and Wang, pp. 142–48.

Baudrillard, J. (1983) "The Ecstasy of Communication." In H. Foster (ed.) *The Anti-Aesthetic: Essays on Postmodern Culture*, Port Townsend, WA: Bay Press, pp. 126–34.

—— (1998) "Symbolic Exchange and Death." In J. Rivkin and M. Ryan (eds.) *Literary Theory: An Anthology*, Malden, MA: Blackwell, pp. 488–508.

Beckett, S. (1994 [1953]). *Three Novels: Molloy, Malone Dies, The Unnamable*, New York: Grove.

Big Science. (1982) [Album] Featuring Laurie Anderson. New York: Warner Bros.

Borges, J. L. (1964) "Kafka and His Precursors." In D. A. Yates and J. E. Irby (eds.) *Labyrinths: Selected Stories and Other Writings of Jorge Luis Borges*, New York: New Directions, pp. 199–201.

Burgess, A. (1962) *A Clockwork Orange*, London: William Heinemann.

Burroughs, W. S. (1959) *Naked Lunch*, New York: Grove Weidenfeld.

Cantor, J. (1987) *Krazy Kat: A Novel in Five Panels*, New York: Collier.

Chang, Y.-H. (2005) Young-Hae Chang and Heavy Industries Website. *Traveling to Utopia* [Online] Available at: www.yhchang.com/ [accessed 23 June 2010].

Cixous, H. (1998) "Sorties: Out and Out: Attacks/Ways Out/Forays." In J. Rivkin and M. Ryan (eds.) *Literary Theory: An Anthology*, Malden, MA: Blackwell, pp. 578–84.

Connor, S. (1997) *Postmodernist Culture*, Cambridge, MA: Blackwell.

Danielewski, M. (2000) *House of Leaves*, New York: Pantheon.

Debord, G. (1995) *The Society of the Spectacle*, trans. D. Nicholson-Smith, New York: Zone Books.

DeLillo, D. (1985) *White Noise*, New York: Viking Penguin.

Derrida, J. (1974) *Glas*, Paris: Galilée.

Federman, R. (1993) "Critifiction: Imagination as Plagiarism." In *Critifiction: Postmodern Essays*, Albany: SUNY Press, pp. 48–64.

Gibbons, D. and Moore, A. (1987) *The Watchmen*, New York: DC Comics.

Hassan, I. (1975) *Paracriticisms: Seven Speculations of the Times*, Urbana, IL: University of Illinois Press.

Hayles, N.K. (2004) "Print is Flat, Code is Deep: The Importance of Media-Specific Analysis," *Poetics Today* 25(1): 67–90.

—— (2007) "Hyper and Deep Attention: The Generational Divide in Cognitive Modes," *Profession* 13: 187–99.

Huyssen, A. (1986) *After the Great Divide*, Bloomington, IN: Indiana University Press.

Jameson, F. (1975) *The Prison-House of Language*, Princeton, NJ: Princeton University Press.

—— (1984) "Postmodernism: or the Cultural Logic of Late Capitalism," *New Left Review*: 53–92.

Jones, R. (2008) *Bookforum*. (June/July/August 2008) *Uncreative Writing* [Online.] Retrieved from http://www.bookforum.com/inprint/015_02/2462 (accessed 18 June 2010).

Lyotard, J-F. (1984) *The Postmodern Condition: A Report on Knowledge*, trans. G. Bennington and B. Massumi, Minneapolis, MN: University of Minnesota Press.

Max Headroom. (1987–1988) [TV program] USA: Cinemax.

McCaffery, L. (1993) *Avant-Pop: Fiction for a Daydream Nation*, Boulder and Normal: Black Ice Books/FC2.

—— (1995a) *After Yesterday's Crash: The Avant-Pop Anthology*, New York: Penguin.

—— (1995b) "13 Introductory Ways of Looking at a Post-Post-Modernist Aesthetic Phenomenon Called 'Avant-Pop.'" In L. Olsen and M. Amerika (eds.) *In Memoriam to Postmodernism: Essays on the Avant-Pop*, San Diego, CA: SDSU Press, pp. 32–47.

McHale, B. (1992) *Constructing Postmodernism*, London: Routledge.

Morace, R. (1992) "Donald Barthelme's *Snow White*: The Novel, the Critics, and the Culture." In R.F. Patteson (ed.) *Critical Essays on Donald Barthelme*, New York: G.K. Hall and Company, pp. 164–72.

Olsen, L. (1994) *Tonguing the Zeitgeist*, San Francisco: Permeable.

—— (1998) "Avant-Crit and the Advent of Theory in a Musical Idiom: A Polylogue with Larry McCaffery," *Paradoxa: Studies in World Literary Genres* 4(11): 556–602.

Ouredník, P. (2005) *Europeana*, trans. G. Turner, Normal, IL: Dalkey Archive Press.

Paprika. (2006) [Film] Directed by Satoshi Kon and Iginio Straffi. Japan: Sony Pictures Classics.

Perloff, M. (1986) *The Futurist Moment: Avant-Garde, Avant Guerre, and the Language of Rupture*, Chicago, IL: University of Chicago Press.

Puig, M. (2009 [1968]) *Betrayed by Rita Hayworth*, trans. S.J. Levine, Champaign, IL: Dalkey Archive.

Pynchon, T. (1973) *Gravity's Rainbow*, New York: Penguin.

—— (1984) *Slow Learner*, Boston, MA: Little, Brown, and Company.

Seegert, A. (2010) *Cybercultural Ecologies: Interfacing Nature, Virtuality, and Narrative*, Doctoral thesis, University of Utah, Salt Lake City, UT.

Shaviro, S. (1996) *Doom Patrols*, New York: Serpent's Tail.

Tomasula, S. (2006) *The Book of Portraiture*, Tallahassee, FL: FC2.

Ubuweb: Sound. (2010) *The People's Choice Music*. [Online.] Retrieved from http://www.ubu.com/ sound/komar.html (accessed 6 June 2010).

Ulmer, G. (1983) "The Object of Post-Criticism." In H. Foster (ed.) *The Anti-Aesthetic: Essays on Postmodern Culture*, Port Townsend, WA: Bay Press, pp. 83–110.

Videodrome. (1983) [Film] Directed by David Cronenberg. Canada: Canadian Film Development Corporation.

Virilio, P. (1989) "The Last Vehicle." In D. Kamper and C. Wulf (eds.) *Looking Back on the End of the World*, trans. D. Antal, New York: Semiotext(e), pp. 106–19.

Wallace, D. F. (1993) "E Unibus Pluram: Television and U.S. Fiction," *Review of Contemporary Fiction* 3(2): 151–94.

16

POST-POSTMODERNISM

Robert L. McLaughlin

Post-postmodernism is a movement in U.S. fiction that took shape in the late 1980s as a response to both a perceived exhaustion of American postmodernism and the growing dominance of television in American popular culture.

I. Contexts

Cultural conservatism and U.S. postmodern fiction

Concomitant with the pendular swing toward political conservatism in the 1980s United States was a cultural reaction against postmodern fiction as it had been practiced by such American writers as Thomas Pynchon, Robert Coover, Kathy Acker, Ishmael Reed, William Gaddis, and John Barth. The *New York Times* of 1 October 1979 featured an opening volley in this reaction. John Leonard's review of Barth's *LETTERS* began by complaining that this massive and complex novel, intended as a summation of the first half of the author's career, was "written for graduate students and other masochists" and concluded by whining, "'Letters' is full of ideas, while empty of people. In the library it huffs and puffs and leers, a series of tricks to be taught, not a passion to experience or a language redeemed. It is the most boring novel by a serious writer since 'The Black Swan' and 'The Glass Bead Game'" (Leonard 1979: C15). Leonard was not afraid of big postmodern novels – he went to the mat with the Pulitzer committee over *Gravity's Rainbow* – and perhaps *LETTERS* simply didn't speak to him. Nevertheless, this review is representative of a turning away from postmodernism on the part of American public intellectuals. Reviewers began to favor a different kind of fiction, minimalism in the spirit of Raymond Carver, which seems the antithesis of postmodern style. Where in the anything-goes 1960s and 1970s, postmodern fiction's experiments with form, its attacks on the conventions of traditional narrative and readers' expectations, its challenging of the coherence of the individual self, and its problematization of knowledge were celebrated, through the Reagan years and to the present, they have been greeted with an increasingly testy impatience: Why can't these authors put aside their postmodern games, their annoying stylistic tricks, and give us characters we can care about and a plot in which we can lose ourselves?

These kinds of complaints reached something of a climax in the notorious essay "Mr. Difficult," in which Jonathan Franzen abjures the postmodern fiction he once admired and embraces the more conventional and accessible.

Of course, postmodern fiction didn't really disappear at this time any more than realism disappeared with the advent of modernism and, later, postmodernism (Harris 2002). Nevertheless the discontent with postmodern fiction, articulated in different ways and some twenty years apart by Leonard and Franzen, can be discerned in the work of another group of authors, most of whom began publishing in the late 1980s and 1990s. I include in this group such U.S. writers as David Foster Wallace, Richard Powers, Rick Moody, William T. Vollmann, Mary Caponegro, Bradford Morrow, Michael Chabon, Denis Johnson, Colson Whitehead, A. M. Homes, Jonathan Lethem, Cris Mazza, and Susan Daitch, among others. These authors were in many cases inspired to write fiction by the work of the great postmodernists, but where the postmodernists tended to celebrate the deconstruction of language, the breakdown of master narratives, the fragmentation of coherent identity, and the explosion of epistemological systems, this new generation more cautiously recognizes all these things as pervasive and deleterious elements of an increasingly fractious and isolating society. Inheriting the postmodern fascination with representation, the layers of text, discourse, narrative, and image that construct our experience of the world, these authors seek in general to acknowledge but penetrate through the layers, aiming, perhaps quixotically, to reconnect with something beyond representation, something extralinguistic, something real. *Post-postmodernism* is a clumsy term, but it is nevertheless appropriate to these authors who work within a culture and aesthetic constructed by postmodernism from which they seek to break out.

The television generation of U.S. authors

If Barth's "The Literature of Exhaustion" was a postmodernist's *cri de coeur*, the post-postmodern equivalent is David Foster Wallace's "E Unibus Pluram: Television and U.S. Fiction," first published in 1993. Wallace places his generation of authors in the context of the 1960s intersection of television as a ubiquitous appliance and the pervasive influence of postmodern fiction (Wallace 1997). Postmodern fiction continually questioned all epistemological, ideological, and narrative authority through self-referential irony. It cut to the hypocritical heart of post-World War II America's myths – about the American dream, American exceptionalism, the family, justice, equality – that were promulgated through television. As postmodern techniques and attitudes – especially irony – trickled down to popular media, authority-questioning became the dominant mood on television. The values, wisdom, and authority of the father embedded in shows like *Father Knows Best* and *Leave It to Beaver* were shaken by shows like *All in the Family* and shattered completely by *The Simpsons*. The result, Wallace writes, is that "the only authority figures who retain any credibility on post-'80s shows . . . are those upholders of values who can communicate some irony about themselves, make fun of themselves before any merciless Group around them can move in for the kill . . ." (Wallace 1997: 62). In the story "My Appearance" Wallace presents David Letterman as the manifestation of TV's postmodern irony, the mocker of all who still think language can be used sincerely. An actress about to appear on his show is advised, "Act as if you knew from birth that everything is clichéd and hyped and empty and absurd, and that that's *just* where the fun is" (Wallace 1989a: 183). In *Infinite Jest* (1996) Wallace includes a character's seventh-grade essay, which notes the transformation of the modern TV hero, exemplified by *Hawaii Five-O*'s Steve McGarrett, master of events, his environment, and narrative closure, into the postmodern hero, exemplified by *Hill Street Blues*'s Frank Furillo, dominated by events, lost in his environment, and overwhelmed by open-ended narratives and indeterminate knowledge (Wallace 1996: 140–2). Thus, Wallace writes, TV creates "an authority vacuum. And then guess what fills it. The real authority on a world we now view as constructed and not depicted becomes the medium that constructs our world-view" (Wallace 1997: 62). TV-as-authority then reproduces its own irony-laced cynicism in the viewer: "the most frightening prospect, for the well-conditioned viewer, becomes leaving oneself open to others' ridicule by betraying passé expressions of value, emotion, or vulnerability. Other people become judges; the crime is naïveté" (Wallace 1997: 63).

Wallace includes himself among the first generation of writers to grow up with television always there, as necessary a part of the household as the refrigerator. Like most other Americans in the TV era, these writers have become watchers of the TV world rather than engagers with the world outside TV, living in what Franzen calls "atomized privacy" (Franzen 2002b: 70). Heirs to postmodernism's exploding of American myths and absorbers of television's all-purpose irony, contemporary writers find themselves painted into a corner. Self-referential irony, which for the postmodernists was revolutionary, has become reactionary as it makes impossible a sincere assertion about the world: sincerity is always subject to the Letterman-esque smirk and eye-rolling, a "hip cynicism, a hatred that winks and nudges you and pretends it's just kidding" (Wallace, quoted in McCaffery 1993: 147). Wallace sums much of this up in his interview with Larry McCaffery:

> Irony and cynicism were just what the U.S. hypocrisy of the fifties and sixties called for. That's what made the early postmodernists great artists. The great thing about irony is that it splits things apart, gets us up above them so we can see the flaws and hypocrisies and duplicities. . . .The problem is that once the rules for art are debunked, and once the unpleasant realities the irony diagnoses are revealed and diagnosed, *then* what do we do? Irony's useful for debunking illusions, but most of the illusion-debunking in the U.S. has now been done and redone. . . . All we seem to want to do is keep ridiculing the stuff. Postmodern irony and cynicism's become an end in itself, a measure of hip sophistication and literary savvy. Few artists dare to try to talk about ways of working toward redeeming what's wrong, because they'll look sentimental and naive to all the weary ironists. Irony's gone from liberating to enslaving.
> (Wallace, quoted in McCaffery 1993: 147)

In its popular manifestations postmodernism reifies the ideological status quo through a weary inertia: we accept the mendaciousness of our culture because we lack the imagination to envision how it might be better.

In his conclusion to the TV essay, Wallace calls on writers to reject the ironic worldview in favor of sincerity and love:

> The next real literary "rebels" in this country might well emerge as some weird bunch of *anti*-rebels, born oglers who dare somehow to back away from ironic watching, who have the childish gall actually to endorse and instanti- ate single-entendre principles. Who treat of plain old untrendy human trou- bles and emotions in U.S. life with reverence and conviction. Who eschew self-consciousness and hip fatigue. . . .The new rebels might be artists willing to risk the yawn, the rolled eyes, the cool smile, the nudged ribs, the parody of gifted ironists, the "Oh how *banal*."
>
> (Wallace 1997: 81)

Wallace is not calling for an impossible return to innocent, non-self-aware language, a rejection of postmodernism, or a retrenching in realism (see the essays in Brooks and Toth [2007] for considerations of the nuances of realism in post-postmodern fiction). Rather, he is saying that the challenge of the post-postmodern author (a term he uses ironically) is to write within the context of self-aware language, irony, and cynicism, acknowledge them, even use them, but then to write through them, to break through the cycle of self-reference, to represent the world constructively, to connect with oth- ers. Jonathan Lethem appropriates some of Wallace's words and demonstrates the challenge of writing out of a discourse-saturated world: "in reimagining what human life might truly be like over there across the chasms of illusion, mediation, demograph- ics, marketing, imago, and appearance, artists are paradoxically trying to restore what's taken for 'real' to three whole dimensions, to reconstruct a univocally round world out of disparate streams of flat sights" (Lethem 2007: 63). The difficulty of this challenge is revealed in a telling moment in the McCaffery interview, when Wallace says of his goal in writing, "You've got to discipline yourself to talk out of the part of you that loves the thing, loves what you're working on. Maybe that just plain loves. (I think we might need woodwinds for this part . . .)" (Wallace, quoted in McCaffery 1993: 148). Note the need to append the parenthetical wink and nudge, the preemptive acknowledgment that the previous, too sincere assertion opens the speaker to charges of sappiness. Wallace both undercuts his assertion and demonstrates the difficulty of the practice he's espousing for the TV generation of writers. This difficulty is one he would wrestle with in his fiction for the rest of his too short life.

II. Characteristics of post-postmodernism

If we accept, then, that post-postmodernism can be understood as a reaction by this generation of U.S. writers to the legacy of their postmodern forebears and to that legacy's deleterious pervasiveness in popular culture, as an acknowledgment of the self-referential nature of discourse linked to an impulse to break through to a reality outside of language, and as a desire to escape the atomized privacy of contemporary culture so as to connect with others – to be Thou- rather than I-directed – we can address some of the formal, stylistic, and thematic characteristics that draw a fine but distinct line between postmodernism and post-postmodernism.

Killing the postmodern father

The first of these characteristics is the working out of a Harold Bloomian anxiety of influence. We can see this need to distinguish oneself from the previous generation of writers most blatantly in the "Mr. Difficult" essay, in which Franzen dismisses as boring, ludicrous, and self-important most of the fiction of William Gaddis with some whacks at Barth, Pynchon, Coover, and others (Franzen 2003a). Franzen seems deeply attention-needy in his critical writings, often making provocative claims so as to be the center of a commotion. (To be fair, as Burn argues, Franzen's critical writings don't offer a good guide to his own fiction [Burn 2008: 46–51].) His arguments here, however, and in some of his other essays, for example, "I'll Be Doing More of the Same" (Franzen 1996) and "Why Bother?" (Franzen 2003b) – hit on points that concern many of his contemporaries. He argues that postmodern authors frequently abrogated an implied contract with their readers to entertain them; that in creating self-consciously difficult work, they in effect ceded contemporary literature to pointy-headed English professors who use it for their own ideological, theoretical, and multicultural purposes; and that fiction is essentially a conservative art form whose conventions support interesting stories about intriguing characters. These concerns connect to what seems to be a wider post-postmodern de-emphasis of formal experimentation and a reemphasis of a more stylistically translucent representation of the world.

Other authors practice their patricide in their fiction. Wallace declares his independence in "Westward the Course of Empire Takes Its Way," a long and complexly layered story first published in *Girl with Curious Hair*. Its title alludes to Emanuel Gottlieb Leutze's 1861 painting depicting the nineteenth-century master narrative of Manifest Destiny with its clear journey from east to west. This invocation of straightforward narrative and physical direction is in tension with the story's action, a journey whose destination, a reunion of all the people who have ever appeared in McDonald's commercials, is never reached, and its style, a *Tristram Shandy*-like narration in which the digressions gradually overwhelm the main plot. The main characters are students in a creative-writing class at the East Chesapeake Tradeschool taught by Professor Ambrose, the author of and the main character in the postmodern classic *Lost in the Funhouse*. Ambrose, an obvious stand-in for John Barth, the real author of *Funhouse*, and Drew-Lynn Eberhardt, one of the students and a self-proclaimed postmodernist, serve as the targets of the story's critique of postmodernism. Ambrose's fiction, as the Tradeschool setting suggests, is now more craft than art. Further, Ambrose has licensed the *Funhouse* story to public-relations mogul J. D. Steelritter who plans to open Funhouses in every major city; Barth's funhouse as metaphor for self-conscious fiction in the postmodern era will be transformed into literal buildings, half amusement park, half mall, distributed across the map like any other chain. The critique is aimed less at Ambrose for selling out than at the way U.S. culture at large has reoriented itself to his fiction: late twentieth century's commercial capitalism can absorb and make use of anything. Drew-Lynn produces stories that are determinedly self-referential, clever for the sake of being clever, having no goal beyond the clever-ness because, for her, there is nothing real beyond the play of language. This picture of postmodernism is contrasted with Steelritter's advertising enterprises, which have flourished because of his ability to harness them to society's fears and desires. Adver-tising speaks to people's deepest emotions, co-opting the role art used to play, but it does so in a cynical, commercial way.

Set against this presentation of postmodernism is the narrator and his story of another of Ambrose's students, Mark Nechtr. The narrator, a nameless student in Ambrose's class, is struggling within the contradictions of his own writing. On the one hand, he frequently interrupts the narrative flow to digress, comment on his digres-sions, apologize for taking so long to get the characters from here to there, and reflect on the future of fiction, all self-referentially entertaining and all revealing his immer-sion in the tricks of postmodernism (see Berry, this volume). On the other hand, he insists that his story is not metafiction and mocks postmodern conventions "aimed at drawing the poor old reader's emotional attention to the fact that the narrative bought and paid for and now under time-consuming scrutiny is *not* in fact a barely-there win-dow onto a different and truly diverting world, but rather in fact an 'artifact,' an object, a plain old this-worldly thing . . ." (Wallace 1989b: 265). This confusion about his own writing perhaps explains the narrator's interest in Mark. He too is dissatisfied with the legacy of postmodernism. He too is searching for a new way to write, one that can use the conventions of postmodern fiction, now familiar and safe, but use them to betray the reader, to make her feel love and make her feel hurt, to reclaim from advertising the discursivity of fear and desire. In the story he presents to Ambrose's class, Mark creates a character, significantly named Dave, who struggles through the paradoxes of existence – that love and hate are intertwined, that guilt and innocence can be the same thing, that the self is chosen and constructed – and concludes that selflessness, the giving of oneself to others, is the flip side of selfishness, holding on to an ideal – honor, integrity, self-love – when the world demands it be given up. This, Wallace's story suggests, is the direction the next generation of fiction writers needs to take.

Another, more desperate, but nevertheless brilliant example of patricide is Mat-thew Remski's 1998 novel *Silver*. *Silver* begins as a parody of *V.* and *Gravity's Rainbow*, as Remski tries self-consciously to write himself out from under Thomas Pynchon's intimidating shadow. The implied troubled son–father relationship is mirrored in the novel by the character Jesus Christ (who, as it turns out, died and rose but did not ascend into heaven and so wanders the earth) with His invisible and inscrutable Father. Remski captures Pynchon's narrative style, as well as his characters (some historical, some bizarre, some both), surreal events, and encyclopedic knowledge. The sprawling plot begins with investigative reporter Tyrone Pynchon scuffling through pre-war Germany, uncovering the dangers associated with the ascendant Nazis and pursuing a fascination with the Shroud of Turin. Purportedly the result of primitive photography, the Shroud manifests Tyrone's desire to understand the transcendent through its representation, a desire the novel shows is difficult to the point of impossible. As the novel moves to postwar America, we see that the Nazis, though defeated militarily, have managed to spread their fascistic worldview through layers of representation. The desire to objectify others, most evident in the Holocaust, takes shape in the United States in a sexism that has been internalized by men and women through a variety of pop-cultural phenomena. The Barbie doll, with its impossible image of female beauty and its lessons about commodification, is created by escaped war criminal Klaus Barbie. *Playgoy* magazine, which turns the girl next door into a sexual object of desire, is the brainchild of Nazi Hans Hugo Heffner. The climax of the novel is the murder of Playmate Dorothy Stratten, sacrificed to the culture's worship of the image and rejection of the real. The novel leaves Tyrone reaching hopelessly for an unattainable, illusory reality and visited in a dream by Matthew Remski who tries to explain the trap he is caught in: "This is how the mind falls in love with its fictions. This is how the fictions learn to hate the mind that wants to possess them. This is how human attention destroys the subject it desires to shine upon" (Remski 1998: 374). Interestingly, despite his monumental effort, Remski seems to have written himself into a dead end; his author's note on the cover tells us that "since writing this novel," he "has forsworn literature" and indeed to date he has published no new fiction.

Escaping discourse

A second seminal characteristic of post-postmodernism is the recognition that the world as we perceive it is constructed by a complex interweaving of representations and the need to write and live one's way out of representation and into something more real. To a certain extent, post-postmodernism shares this concern with postmodernism. Many postmodern works focus on situations wherein characters find their once-secure sense of the real deconstructed, exposed as an arbitrary or manipulated construction, behind which lies no concealed real but ambiguity and contingency (see McHale, this volume). Post-postmodernism is not so much different in this as it is differently focused, in two ways. First, post-postmodern narrators and characters tend to be much more media savvy than their forebears and thus more prepared to engage a world of images and discourse. Second, post-postmodern fiction tends to be less formally and stylistically self-referential than postmodern fiction (though not always: see Wallace). Where postmodern authors often used self-reference to expose their own fiction's artificiality so as to mirror the exposure of the world as constructed of images their characters undergo (what McHale calls shifting "the site of immediacy from the interior of the fictional world . . . to the interface between the text and its reader" [McHale 2008: 257]), post-postmodern authors tend to offer an idiosyncratic respect for the suspension of disbelief, spending less time reflecting on their narratives as narrative and discourse as discourse and more on exploring the protean and factitious nature of what their characters consider to be reality. This change of focus is the main reason many critics have noted a sea change in fiction, a transition from postmodernism to something that seems to be different. It is also the reason some critics and reviewers define this sea change as a return to some kind of realism. (Richard Powers's *Gain* [1998] and *The Time of Our Singing* [2003] have been hailed or critiqued, depending on one's perspective, for returning to straightforward realism. Maliszewski [2008] and Dewey [2008] have demonstrated the ways each novel in fact productively violates the conventions of realism, but no one had to write an article to prove that *Gravity's Rainbow*, *J R*, or *The Public Burning* were not playing by the rulebook of realism – it was self-evident.) Realism, however, presumes both a style that doesn't draw attention to itself as style, making representation transparent, and an objectively knowable world to represent. Post-postmodern style varies as to levels of translucency, but it never represents an unproblematically knowable world or treats representation unproblematically.

Some examples will help illustrate this double change of focus. Denis Johnson's epic Vietnam War novel *Tree of Smoke* (2007), in minimal style and with a clear organizational formula, follows the experiences of several characters in Southeast Asia from 1963 to 1970, with a 1983 epilogue. Skip Sands, a novice CIA operative working under the tutelage of his legendary rogue-agent uncle, known universally as the colonel, arrives first in the Philippines, then in Vietnam, not so much idealistic as certain of basic truths and distinctions: right/wrong; good guys/bad guys; democracy/communism. His certainty begins to crack when his uncle makes him an unwitting accomplice in the assassination of an American missionary priest on Mindanao. Later, in Vietnam he sees distinctions blur and collapse as American soldiers wound and kill each other, the loyalties of both the South and North Vietnamese are ambiguous, the military and intelligence bureaucracies engage in in-fighting, and the American presence generates a parodic re-creation of American popular culture. The colonel assigns Skip to organize and cross-reference thousands of file cards he has assembled over his career, each with bits of seemingly random information. Skip eventually realizes that the cards can never be cross-referenced in any way that will actually structure them into knowledge; the information they contain is disconnected, lacking context, and unnarrativized. This disheartening conclusion relates to the colonel's unorthodox theories of intelligence. Seeing that policy-makers embrace or ignore intelligence depending on what policy they want to construct, what fiction they want to presume is real, the colonel imagines an intelligence network that, instead of sending hard intelligence up the bureaucratic pipeline, creates fictions for the policy-makers, seizing the responsibility for defining the real. His aide-de-camp enthusiastically sums up, "We're on the cutting edge of reality itself. Right where it turns into a dream" (Johnson 2007: 255). This, the novel suggests, is the Vietnam War: an American dream imposed on a reality that can't support it.

Jonathan Lethem's *Chronic City* (2009) is set in the near future in a recognizable but reimagined Manhattan, where an insidious power elite disseminates fictions through the media, fictions that create a hyperreality masking the real. The narrator, Chase Insteadman, a semi-retired actor famous since adolescence as a regular on a sitcom, is drawn into the circle around broadside artist and rock and film critic Perkus Tooth, rebellious, compulsive, and convinced that the interweaving of real and image results inevitably in the loss of reality. Perkus's circle becomes fascinated by chaldrons, something of a combination of a chalice and a vase, which represent for them a gateway through a world of images to something transcendent. Perkus is shattered when he discovers that chaldrons were invented for a computer game and the only one he's seen in person is a hologram. He suddenly doubts his own reality, wondering if he is only data in someone's computer, and he begins the process of learning to live inside a daydream conjured by others. Chase, naive and not terribly bright, learns Perkus's lesson slowly and only after discovering that he has been an unwitting actor in one of the mayor's made-for-the-media dramas, living in a fiction that he thought was real. He concludes, "The world was ersatz and actual, forged and faked, by ourselves and unseen others. Daring to attempt to absolutely sort *fake* from *real* was a folly. . . .So retreat. Live in a Manhattan of your devising . . ." (Lethem 2009: 449).

Rick Moody's *The Diviners* (2005), set in the aftermath of the contested 2000 U.S. presidential election, is a multilayered novel with multiple narrative voices and a huge cast of characters, most of whom are involved collaboratively or competitively in a hot miniseries project, a thirteen-part epic stretching from ancient Mongolia to the founding of Las Vegas, held together by divining, the semi-supernatural ability to find water in even the driest places. Everyone wants a piece of the miniseries, but it doesn't exist. It's the desperate improvisation of a production company assistant who's lost a film treatment. The characters share media- or image-obsession, many of them think deeply about film and television as contemporary myth-makers, and in the novel's centerpiece they briefly become a community when, across the country, they watch the hit show *The Werewolves of Fairfield County*. However, this is a mock-community, with viewers in their separate living rooms, which masks their atomized privacy and temporarily alleviates their desire for human connection. Paradoxically, the miniseries, a Hollywood product, is offered as a possible alternative to TV-centered aloneness. Its subject, divining, represents the possibility of peace in the face of war, of resisting the official realities created for us by the mass media, of quenching the thirst that almost all the characters feel for something more than their vapid consumer culture can give them. This possibility is lost when *Bush v. Gore*, always in the background, is decided by the Supreme Court. The interregnum during which the action takes place is over. The temporary uncertainty offered a chance to remake reality, a chance the characters missed in their pursuit of the chimerical miniseries.

Living with the limits of knowledge

A third characteristic of post-postmodernism involves attitudes toward knowledge. Postmodernism reacted against the modernist conception of epistemological systems as totalizing structures that sought to account for all phenomena and contain them in one absolute truth and that sought to disseminate that truth through a controlling will to power. Postmodernism tended to deconstruct these systems, undercutting their claims to truth and subverting their desire to be the sole representation of reality. Thus postmodernism explored the limits of knowledge, systems that exist behind systems, and multiple, alternate realities (see Bauman 1991; Hutcheon 1988). Postmodernism is sympathetic with systems theory, which rejects deterministic, linear, totalizing knowledge in favor of dynamic, fluid, interdependent knowledges (see LeClair 1989). Post-postmodernism offers not a move away from this attitude but rather, again, a change of focus. Where postmodernism exposed the uncertainty within totalizing systems' claims to truth, post-postmodernism takes the uncertainty of epistemological systems for granted and explores instead what to do with it, how to live in the world with incomplete systems of knowledge, how various systems of knowledge can be linked together or embedded within one another to create a contingent but useful structure. One example is Richard Powers's *The Echo Maker* (2006) in which a character, as the result of a horrific accident, develops Capgras Syndrome. Although he remembers and recognizes everything, he suspects that his sister is an impostor, a substitute for his real sister, who he imagines is being kept from him. His confusion is used to explore the workings of the mind and the nature of relationships, but the novel never suggests that he may be right and is actually the victim of a conspiracy. Compare this with *Gravity's Rainbow* (1973), where rocket scientist Franz Pökler suspects that the daughter who visits him for one week each summer is never the same girl but rather a series of substitutes. Pynchon never settles the ambiguity, using it instead to undermine Pökler's faith in deterministic science to reveal the truth and in the inviolability of the coherent self.

This post-postmodern attitude toward knowledge can be seen in several novels that look back to World War II, far removed from this generation's lived experience, as an epistemological turning point. In *The Final Solution* (2004) Michael Chabon finds Sherlock Holmes in 1944, eighty-nine years old and long retired, drawn into a mystery involving a murder and the kidnapping of a parrot, which has come to England with a young refugee from Nazi Germany. The murderer thinks that the numbers the parrot recites represent Swiss bank accounts holding assets seized by the Nazis. Holmes, who leads the police to the murderer and recovers the bird, thinks they connect to German codes, a hypothesis military intelligence debunks. The reader, however, understands that they are the numbers on the sides of boxcars shipping Jews east to Auschwitz. This is a mystery Holmes cannot solve: his career has been based in an Enlightenment logic, where clues, signs in the world, can be arranged into knowledge representing the truth and where the pursuit of such truth is the highest aspiration of the human mind. He is incapable of the leap into a different system of knowledge in which the Holocaust denies logic and the essential progress toward perfection of human intelligence. He ends by dismissing the numbers as meaningless, but they are all too meaningful for the burgeoning postwar era; the limits of his epistemological systems create a space where a new, darker epistemology can begin to construct reality.

In a similar manner Bradford Morrow in *Trinity Fields* (1995), Jay Cantor in *Krazy Kat* (1987), and Richard Powers in *Prisoner's Dilemma* (1988) all look to the first use of the Atomic Bomb as the event that shattered previous epistemologies and the moment from which new ones had to be conjured so as to make living possible in the postwar age. In *Prisoner's Dilemma* Eddie Hobson Sr. suffers from a strange physical anemia and spiritual malaise stemming, we eventually find out, from his having witnessed the Trinity A-Bomb test. To cope with his condition, he records an alternate history of his times, in which, instead of the dream of technological progress betrayed to the science of war and democratic ideals betrayed to the pragmatism of waging war, World War II teaches us the value of the individual and the need for human community. This lesson comes too late for Eddie, but the novel suggests that his children, who live inside their minds, behind the defenses of ironic language, will use it to create a productive narrative of their own times. Recognizing that multiple knowledge-containing narratives exist simultaneously and that no one of them contains the absolute truth isn't enough. As we end one century and begin another, the stakes are too high for us to dismiss the differences among knowledges. Which narratives we use to guide us in the world is a vitally important decision.

III. Conclusion

U.S. post-postmodernism arises from a particular cultural moment marked by an increasing political and social conservatism and by the pervasive influence of American television's socially stultifying adoption of postmodern self-referentiality. The American post-postmodernists write out of the complex dilemma bequeathed them by postmodernism: while understanding that truth is contingent, to speak the truth; while acknowledging that representation is self-referential, to represent the real; while conceding that the human subject is constructed via socially charged discourse, to value the individual; while knowing that epistemological systems are contingent, to commit to an ethical and productive knowledge. Some outstanding fiction from other countries functions aesthetically in a manner similar to American post-postmodernism. Fiction by such authors as Roberto Bolaño, Orhan Pamuk, Daniel Kehlman, Kazuo Ishiguro, and Ariel Dorfman, to name only a few, exhibits many of the characteristics associated with American post-postmodernism, but they are reactions to their own cultural circumstances. Some critics, most notably Nobel Prize secretary Horace Engdahl, have complained about the cultural isolation of contemporary American literature, and the U.S.-centrism of most of the American post-postmodernists might seem to support them. One might see instead, however, an opportunity for a cross-cultural understanding of the reactions to the various worldwide constructions of postmodernism as well as the specific cultural manifestations out of which they arise.

References

Bauman, Z. (1991) *Modernity and Ambivalence*, Ithaca, NY: Cornell University Press.
Brooks, N. and J. Toth (eds.) (2007) *The Mourning After: Attending the Wake of Postmodernism*, Amsterdam: Rodopi.
Burn, S.J. (2008) *Jonathan Franzen at the End of Postmodernism*, London: Continuum.
Cantor, J. (1987) *Krazy Kat*, New York: Knopf.

Chabon, M. (2004) *The Final Solution*, New York: Fourth Estate/HarperCollins.

Dewey, J. (2008) "Little Knots, Tied in the Clothing of Time: *The Time of Our Singing* as a Dual-Time Narrative." In S.J. Burn and P. Dempsey (eds.) *Intersections: Essays on Richard Powers*, Champaign, IL: Dalkey Archive Press, pp. 198–214.

Franzen, J. (1996) "I'll Be Doing More of the Same," *Review of Contemporary Fiction* 16(1): 34–8.

——(2003a) "Mr. Difficult." In *How to Be Alone*, New York: Farrar, Straus, and Giroux, pp. 238–69.

——(2003b) "Why Bother?" In *How to Be Alone*, New York: Farrar, Straus, and Giroux, pp. 55–97.

Harris, C.B. (2002) "PoMos's Wake, 1," *American Book Review* 23(2): 1, 3.

Hutcheon, L. (1988) *A Poetics of Postmodernism: History, Theory, Fiction*, New York: Routledge.

Johnson, D. (2007) *Tree of Smoke*, New York: Farrar, Straus, and Giroux.

LeClair, T. (1989) *The Art of Excess: Mastery in Contemporary American Fiction*, Urbana, IL: University of Illinois Press.

Leonard, J. (1979) "Review of *LETTERS*, by John Barth," *New York Times* 1 October, C15.

Lethem, J. (2007) "The Ecstasy of Influence: A Plagiarism," *Harper's* (February), 59–71.

——(2009) *Chronic City*, New York: Doubleday.

Maliszewski, P. (2008) "The Business of *Gain*." In S.J. Burn and P. Dempsey (eds.) *Intersections: Essays on Richard Powers*, Champaign, IL: Dalkey Archive Press, pp. 162–86.

McCaffery, L. (1993) "An Interview with David Foster Wallace," *Review of Contemporary Fiction* 13(2), 127–50.

McHale, B. (2008) "Afterword: Two Presents." In R.M. Berry and Jeffrey Di Leo (eds.) *Fiction's Present: Situating Contemporary Narrative Innovation*, Albany, NY: State University of New York Press, pp. 255–64.

Moody, R. (2005) *The Diviners*, New York: Little, Brown.

Morrow, B. (1995) *Trinity Fields*, New York: Viking.

Powers, R. (1988) *Prisoner's Dilemma*, New York: William Morrow.

——(2006) *The Echo Maker*, New York: Farrar, Straus, and Giroux.

Pynchon, T. (1973), *Gravity's Rainbow*, New York: Viking.

Remski, M. (1998) *Silver*, Toronto: Insomniac.

Wallace, D.F. (1989a) "My Appearance." In *Girl with Curious Hair*, New York: Norton, pp. 173–201.

——(1989b) "Westward the Course of Empire Takes Its Way." In *Girl with Curious Hair*, New York: Norton, pp. 231–373.

——(1996) *Infinite Jest*, Boston, MA: Little, Brown.

——(1997) "E Unibus Pluram: Television and U.S. Fiction." In *A Supposedly Fun Thing I'll Never Do Again*, Boston, MA: Little, Brown, pp. 21–82.

Further reading

Cohen, S. (2009) *After the End of History: American Fiction in the 1990s*, Iowa City, IA: University of Iowa Press.

Hoberek, A. (ed.) (2007) "After Postmodernism" [special issue], *Twentieth Century Literature* 53(3).

Moraru, C. (2001) *Rewriting: Postmodern Narrative and Cultural Critique in the Age of Cloning*, Albany, NY: State University of New York Press.

Prosser, J. (ed.) (2008) *American Fiction of the 1990s: Reflections of History and Culture*, New York: Routledge.

Wallace, D.F. (ed.) (1996) "The Future of Fiction" [special issue], *The Review of Contemporary Fiction* 16, 1.

Wegner, P.E. (2009) *Life between Two Deaths, 1989–2001: U.S. Culture in the Long Nineties*, Durham, NC: Duke University Press.

17

GLOBALIZATION AND TRANSNATIONALISM

Liam Connell

I. Introduction

One of the pithiest definitions of globalization is arguably John Tomlinson's claim that it represents "complex connectivity" (1999). In sketching out this definition Tomlinson sees globalization as producing a "'proximity' that comes from the networking of social relations across large tracts of time-space, causing distant events and powers to penetrate our local experience" (9). A number of important ideas are contained within this statement; it acknowledges the sheer range of cross-cutting and interrelated forms that contemporary social interactions take and it points to the interplay between the local and global as mutually interpenetrating formations. For thinking about how literary texts might engage with globalization it is useful to note two related tendencies at work in Tomlinson's description. In the first instance, globalization involves a high degree of concatenation, as various local actors are strung together by processes or "networks" that transcend their immediate locality. Somewhat contradictorily this leads to a second tendency towards concentration where the local becomes the nodal point for acting out these transnational relations. In terms of Tomlinson's account, it is important to think of these processes as experiential. Roland Robertson makes a similar point when he talks of globalization as a twofold process; referring "both to the compression of the world and the intensification of consciousness of the world as a whole" (Robertson 1992: 8). Robertson's sense that the phenomenological integration of globalization is matched by the *perception* of this process is vital for understanding globalization's force as a descriptive term.

One way to understand globalization is to see it as a particular way of narrating contemporary internationalism. To that end its status as a recent neologism is revealing. It has been hard to date the term precisely and, whereas the 2009 edition of the *Oxford English Dictionary* provides quotations dating back to 1930, the previous edition dated the term only to as far back as the 1960s. This new evidence of an earlier use of globalization is, paradoxically, not proof of a widespread use at an earlier date but, rather, proof of recent interest in the word and its development. The importance of the relative novelty of globalization as a term resides in the way that it speaks of processes which require a new vocabulary precisely because they lack any exact precedent. In this respect, a useful way to understand globalization is to see it as fulfilling our desire to rename our international relations in order to signal a rupture with the past and with earlier forms of transnationalism.

It is not my intention to reduce globalization to a terminological question. It is clear that the word describes a range of socio-economic changes dating from the early 1970s and widely associated with neoliberalism. These changes include the international dispersal of production and consumption; the development of rules-based free-trade regimes which locked national economies into economic deregulation; rapid technological development, especially in communicative technology and a concomitant expansion of speculative capital and the dematerialization of value. A substantial part of the literary response to globalization has been the attempt to thematize it through a discussion of these issues. Given the mass-market appeal of globalization as a term, the kinds of texts that have sought to do this work have been varied in form, ranging from the conventionally realist novel to the formally experimental. Although it is possible to see even realist fiction attempting to grapple with the supposed novelty of globalization, my use of the term experimental is intended to refer to texts that self-consciously explore their own techniques of representation and narration. I want to suggest that the thematic presentation of globalization has tended to reproduce the combination of concatenation and compression that we saw in Tomlinson and Robertson's accounts of globalization. Where experimental writing has differed from other kinds of work is where it has sought to trouble this combination. By disturbing the easy link between connectivity and proximity, these kinds of literary experiments draw attention to their own capacity to represent globalization successfully. In doing so, they arguably also challenge the efficacy of globalization as a description of the forms of contemporary internationalism.

II. Concatenation and concentration in the global novel

As an example of the way that literary texts combine the idea of concatenation with concentration it is possible to point to a large number of works that juxtapose or interleave a range of separate narratives, often focalised through separate characters, which are then gradually drawn together into a single narrative time and space. A notable example of this is the pioneering science fiction writing of William Gibson. In *Count Zero* (1987) for instance, the apparently separate plot lines of Turner, Bobby Newark (the eponymous Count Zero) and Marly Krushkova eventually find the characters fighting alongside each other in a single room. Critics are divided on how experimental Gibson's fiction might be regarded and it seems clear that while, in certain respects, his work is attempting new forms of representation, in other ways it is rather conventional. Where Gibson is experimental is in his attempt to explore the new interactions with technology and, perhaps more interestingly, his invention of slang-vocabularies which might be capable of articulating these interactions. Joseph Tabbi has praised this last aspect of Gibson's fiction for its refusal of a clear translation or complex expla-nation, which he regards as representing the "image" of technology rather than tech-nology itself (Tabbi 1995: 218). Tabbi makes connections between Gibson and more recognizably postmodern authors such as Thomas Pynchon, though it is worth noting a likely debt to earlier dystopian fiction such as Aldous Huxley's *Brave New World* (2007 [1932]) or Anthony Burgess' *A Clockwork Orange* (1996 [1962]). Both these novels rely upon a depiction of linguistic evolution to make their future reality appear plausible and, arguably, Gibson's lexical innovation is less immersive than Burgess'. Indeed, it is possible to suggest that this kind of lexical inventiveness is a characteristic of science-fictional texts throughout the twentieth century (Stockwell 2000: 60).

As an account of globalization Gibson's fiction has been lauded for setting out the early contours of the dematerialized geographies of cyberspace (Adams 1997). Yet, strikingly, given his early envisioning of the virtual relations produced by advanced and speculative communicative technologies, Gibson's narrative method consistently resorts to face-to-face interaction rather than the disembodied simulations of post-modern culture. Correspondingly, critics have pointed to the relative conservatism of Gibson's writing which contains "little sense of anything hypertextual" (Annesley 2006: 95) and which remains committed to "old geographic interpretations of space" that encode ideologies of home and abroad, inside and outside, centre and periphery (McCallum 2000: 350). It could be argued that Gibson's narrative method domesti-cates the potential strangeness of globalizing technologies by using coherent char-acters and narrative space to moor the reader in the face of the disorientations that these technologies produce. Nevertheless, Gibson's work manages to represent some of the key elements of globalization. In the first instance, his reduction of the global to the local seems characteristic of the experiential modalities of globalization, through which the local is persistently the theatre in which the global is performed. Further-more, his interest in emerging technologies seems to align his work with a discursive emphasis upon futurity in discussions of globalization. Although "globalization" refers to a process rather than a state of being, at the discursive level it quickly becomes a teleology in which the process of globalization "promises an almost-but-not-quite-there globality" (Tsing 2000: 332) while seeming simultaneously to cause the very social change which brought it about (Cameron and Palan 2004: 55). In similar ways, and in contrast to the narration of technological innovation in later works such as *All Tomorrow's Parties* (Gibson 2000), the dramatization of speculative technologies in Gibson's early novels bypasses the process of their emergence and actualises their promised arrival.

Gibson's main narrative method of juxtaposed plot-lines that gradually converge in time and space is a methodology that is employed in a number of recent works which thematize globalization in other ways. A good example of this is Robert Newman's *The Fountain at the Centre of the World* (2003) which is organised around the interconnect-ing narratives of three members of the same family who, for reasons of circumstance, are estranged and reside separately in Britain, Mexico and Costa Rica. Through the course of the novel each character makes his way to Seattle to take part in the 1999 meeting of the World Trade Organisation either as a delegate or a protester. In this climactic section of the novel we are presented with several incidents where the same event is narrated and re-narrated from the perspective of the different characters who are unaware, or only dimly aware, of the others' presence. If this resembles Paul Virilio's notion of "simultaneity" (1998), it is still formally realist with little attempt to disrupt the narrative coherence of any of the perspectives that the novel offers. Indeed the novel is closest here to direct reportage and it appears to draw heavily on documentary accounts of the clashes in Seattle such as Cockburn, St. Clair and Sekula (2000), with which it shares both events and descriptive vocabulary. For instance, where Cockburn *et al.* describe the "Seattle police attired in black body armor and Darth Vader-like helmet" (2000: 21), Newman describes "riot police" walking "clubs at the diagonal, long black Darth Vader capes swinging over the top of their high black boots" (2003: 276). There seems little attempt to transform Cockburn *et al.*'s journalistic simile in Newman's account and the Seattle section of his novel offers us little opportunity to think about how globalization might provoke an experimental response to problems of representation.

For other writers however, the techniques of concatenation and concentration may open up more self-conscious representational strategies that do try to experiment with fiction's capacity to represent globalization. One novel that attempts this is Karen Tei Yamashita's *Tropic of Orange* (1997) which uses so-called magic realism and cognitive mapping (Jameson 1991) to offer a modified form of realism as a way of understanding the related themes of international income inequalities, trade and labor migration. How experimental magic realism might now be considered is a moot point (see McHale, this volume) but Yamashita uses it in her novel to attempt to reconfigure or interrogate some of the spatial hierarchies that globalization involves. Arguably, this is a feature of some of the more famous works of magic realist fiction. Gabriel García Márquez's iconic work *One Hundred Years of Solitude*, for instance, explicitly attributes the notion of magic to acts of law and capital which ensure the dominance of northern investors over the rights of local workers in Maconda (1978: 245). In *Tropic of Orange*, Yamashita uses the device of an orange travelling from Mazatlán in Mexico to Los Angeles in the United States as a way of confronting high-income economies with the sublimated presence of low-income labor. Carried by the mythical figure, Arcangel, en route to a wrestling match with a personified NAFTA, the orange pulls with it the latitude of its origins transforming the climate and character of the Californian destination along the way. Through the orange, the novel challenges the notion of the political border by moving the Tropic of Cancer north with illegalized Mexican laborers who travel in search of employment in the USA. As with García Márquez, Yamashita's use of magic realism's playful aesthetics is more purposefully political than simply a form of postmodern disruption. Yamashita uses this technique as a modification of the kinds of juxtaposition that we see in Gibson's or Newman's novels, and *Tropic of Orange* interlaces the discrete but interconnected narratives of seven individuals to suggest the connections between events in different regions of the world. Significantly, this also relies upon the strategy of concentration as the various narrative strands point towards a final convergence in Los Angeles.

The details of Yamashita's plot lines speak of overlapping concerns that transcend location or personal history. For instance, the character Rafaela Cortes flees Mazatlán when she discovers that her neighbour's son Hernando is both a drug smuggler and a trafficker of body parts for transplant. His mother describes his work as "Export. Import" and the realization that the exportable good is a child's heart destined for a patient in the high-income economies of the north dramatically exposes the horror of global inequality and labor commoditization (Yamashita 1997: 118–19). Meanwhile, her estranged husband, Bobby Ngu, encounters a similar scenario which has little if anything to do with their personal connection. A naturalized American who entered the USA by posing as a Vietnamese refugee, Bobby is asked to pay people smugglers for the passage of a Chinese migrant, who may be his cousin, to prevent her sale into prostitution (100). Like Hernando's trade, the possibility of this girl's exploitation by her traffickers renders the bodies of low-income workers as consumables and this is tied to high-income consumerism in explicit ways. For the girl to gain access to the USA from Tijuana she must pose as an American consumer by buying Levi jeans, Nike trainers and a Malibu t-shirt (203). The connections here are obviously thematic but they also point to structural relations between different kinds of economies which the novel's modification of realism seeks to expose. The use of magic realism for the framing device allows the whole text to interrogate these relations by suggesting that the political boundaries that regulate the global division of labor are a purposeful fiction. In doing so it tries to shift the focus of the reader away from the locally particular by showing how a range of disparate localities are, at the very least, linked to observable planetary structures.

Arguably then, Yamashita's use of magic realism points us back to Robertson's notion of globalization as a "consciousness of the world as a whole" by seeking to cognitively map a string of individual points onto the globe as a totality. This is exaggerated by a further device through which Yamashita simultaneously draws attention to and challenges the concatenation of the different narrative strands. This is achieved at the start of the novel by two tables of contents which offer the reader different ways to navigate her text. Both tables contain chapter numbers and titles, as well as an indication of the chapter's setting. The specified locations are varied and, rather than being markers of the physical setting, they frequently indicate a means of interacting with regulated physical spaces. For instance, Chapter 29 occurs on the "World Wide Web" while Chapter 43 takes place "Over the Net" as the journalists Gabriel Balboa and Emi communicate via the internet. By contrast, Chapter 40 takes place on "I-5," the Interstate that navigates the Western coast of the USA from Mexico to Canada, but signifies the first location inside the USA that is visited by Bobby Ngu's "cousin" after he has rescued her from Tijuana. This chapter location is therefore actually a reference to the illegalized migrant's successful navigation of the infrastructures of trade which are designed to extract the value from low-income labor while debarring low-income workers from the benefits of this value. As his "Little cuz" looks at her new Nike trainers, Bobby notes that they are "Made in China. Nikes get in. But not [Chinese people]" (Yamashita 230). The apparent precision of place that the chapter listings offer us is then really an invitation to read space politically rather than geographically.

What is perhaps more interesting about the two tables of contents is the way that they offer different perspectives on the narrative sequence of the novel. The first listing is organised chronologically from Monday to Sunday listing each chapter in the novel sequentially with the relevant page references. It clearly prioritises time and suggests a linear narrative that is entirely in keeping with realist aesthetics. This presentation does not announce the interweaving of the different narrative strands, but it encourages readers to experience it by inviting them to read the novel from start to finish which necessarily involves cutting between the different storylines. The second table of contents, which follows immediately from this, is set out horizontally across two pages and lists the novel's "Hyper Contexts." It provides a graphical map of the novel with the days of the week along the x-axis and character names running down the y-axis. The presentation of this second listing could be seen as an invitation for readers to follow individual characters in isolation; offering us "an atomistic sense of each character's life," in which "each chapter seems to stand on its own with little continuity from" those around it (Lee 2007: 506; see also Heise 2006: 212–14). Yet we might also think about how this presentation offers us a diagrammatic conceptualization of the world as observable in both space and time. This presentation offers us a forward momentum for each character as they move through the week but also as they move across space towards Los Angeles as a nodal location. Though it disaggregates the concatenation of the different narratives it also makes apparent the technique of concentration which is the twin feature of globalization's presentation of internationalism.

III. Mark Lombardi's narrative poems

Yamashita's "Hyper Context" chapter map could be seen as one way of using writing to visualize global geographies as they form social interaction. In this respect it is limited in the range of connections and in the scale of the geographical area that it covers. Nevertheless, as a model of what might be possible it invites comparison with the images in Mark Lombardi's *Global Networks* (Hobbs 2003). Although he saw himself as a visual artist with connections to a long line of visual representation – identified by Robert Hobbs as including history-painting of the eighteenth and nineteenth centuries, and modernist and postmodernist artists such as Duchamp, Beuys and Haacke (Hobbs 2003: 12, 34) – Lombardi consciously described his work as "narrative structures" (13) and compared it to that of "early storytellers" who relied "on drawing" as a way "to communicate their narratives" (14). Moreover, Hobbs also notes Lombardi's debt to the "model offered by French modernist poet Guillaume Apollinaire's visual/verbal *Calligrammes*" (36), an influence which clearly ties him to a tradition of visual poetry (see Bray, this volume). This combination of influences, combining visual poetry and narrative storytelling, suggests a way of reading Lombardi's drawings as narrative-poems which offer us a model for a certain kind of experimental literature of globalization that is focused on the world as a conceivable object determined by lines of connection that are social, economic and political. Lombardi's works seek to map the contours of interconnection between politicians, security agencies, drug cartels and US banks by using a self-devised system of diagrammatic connections that links together remote institutions and personalities. Often focusing on the collapse of financial institutions or political scandals, Lombardi shows prominent actors such as George H.W. Bush, Oliver North and Bill Clinton entangled in an intractable network of relations which possess both a spatial and temporal element. The seven versions of *World Finance Corporation, Miami, ca.1970–84* are perhaps the most interesting illustration of this approach since while the first five track a temporal process in illustrating the involvement of World Finance Corporation's head, Guillermo Hernández-Cartaya, in Colombian drug-trafficking and C.I.A. and Mafia-funded attempts to assassinate Fidel Castro (1966–1971), in the final two versions Lombardi dispenses with the temporal analysis to show instead the spatial interconnections of capital flows from and to World Finance Corporation (see Figure 17.1). Correspondingly, the work shifts from an elongated spine, with curving and overlapping tendrils representing Hernández-Cartaya's financial benefactors and his misappropriation of funds, to roughly spherical patterns, which seek to track the synchronic flow of capital. While the earlier versions of this work are suggestive, if somewhat obliquely, of world maps in their geoidal form,

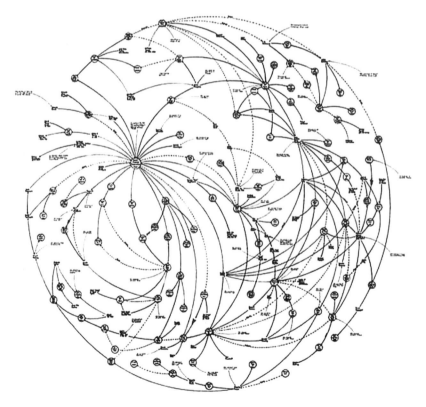

Figure 17.1 Mark Lombardi, World Finance Corporation and Associates c.1970–84, Miami-Ajman-Bogota-Caracas (7th version). Courtesy of Pierogi gallery.

the later versions take on a "quasi three-dimensional quality" (66) which is suggestive of the globe as a discernible, planetary, object. What is striking about this presentation is that it appears to achieve a combination of both aspects of globalization as Robertson defines it. The spherical appearance of these works responds to our "consciousness of the world as a whole," while its structure is composed of the various textual components which are able to suggest a "compression of the world" by connecting remote nodes of capital and governance into a coherent shape.

When reading Lombardi's work, however, his aesthetic approach breaks apart the twin aspects of Robertson's definition by making it impossible to read them simultaneously. The visual coherence of globalization as a physically-observable connectivity can be apprehended only from a distance, taking in the whole work. However, from this perspective, the textual content which describes the various people and organizations that are connected is illegible. It is only by stepping forward that we can read the words and from this vantage point we lose sight of the whole. As a result, the two layers of the work, which describes local events but also how these cohere as globalization, remain separated. Accordingly, by making convergence possible only at the level of the globe, Lombardi's work rejects the tendency of thematic representations of globalization to combine concatenation with concentration at the local. One consequence of this is, arguably, that it draws our attention to the ways that globalization seems to defy apprehension. To that end, we should be cautious about any claims that Lombardi's work makes the global knowable. For instance, Hobbs notes that Lombardi could not "verify the accuracy of all the events, people, and financial numbers cited in his drawings"; nor can we now (51). In this respect it is useful to note Bill Maurer's claim that our "enjoyment" of Lombardi's work derives from our sense that "we have discovered something when we look at his elegant diagrams" when what they really record "is the sustenance of our own ideal(ist) projects, the denial of the asymptotic relation between reasonable care and truth in the clean lines and clear nodes of the network he traces" (2005: 498). The clarity of Lombardi's work represents an act of wish-fulfillment in which we read his lucid rendering of complexity through our own desire to know that which cannot be known. Nevertheless, while never able to certify its vision, Lombardi's work remains able to speak of the enormous scale of globalization by suggesting its geographical diffuseness, and also allows us to retain a sense of the process of its materialization as an observable object.

IV. Hypertextuality and multitextuality

Reading from Yamashita's tentative combination of text and space to Lombardi's more fully realised visual poems, a combination of the literary and the visual begins to seem one of the most productive means of experimenting with ways of representing globalization (see Prinz, this volume). To that end it is worth considering a text such as Douglas Coupland's recent novel *JPod* (2006) which similarly gestures towards the experiments of visual poetry but which also constructs a literary model of hypertextuality which challenges the text's presentation of itself as a closed site of meaning.

Like Lombardi, Coupland trained as a visual artist and this has had a substantial influence on his writing practice. His first novel *Generation X* (1991) radically disrupts the textual flow by breaking the paragraphs with marginalia of slogans and cartoons that evoke the détournement of the Situationist International (Ford 2005; see Miller, this volume). In *JPod*, the disruption of the narrative is more intermittent and, in some respects, more easily integrated into the plot because the interruptions relate more directly to adjacent narrative events. Yet at the same time this integration is somewhat implicit, and the interruptions are most frequently connected with the narrative-content by association rather than being directly deigetic. Moreover, Coupland's use of alternate font sizes, typesetting and Chinese logograms breaks up the formal integrity of the page in ways that more profoundly disrupt the narrative form.

A significant example occurs when the protagonist-narrator flies to China to rescue his erstwhile boss who has been trafficked to work on a Chinese production line. When he arrives in a "city" called simply "Special Economic Zone" or "SEZ" he is confronted by the development of modern Chinese consumerism, where high-end luxury cars have become "the new dream" of modern China (Coupland 2006: 264). Arriving at his hotel the narrator goes to sleep and the novel then provides a seven-page digression showing large Chinese logograms with slogans of modern consumerist activities underneath: Shopping, Boredom, Pornography, Cosmetic Surgery, Tourism, Internet browsing and TV (see Figure 17.2).

The relation of these words to the plot is tangential rather than narrative, and the novel provides no explanation for their appearance or context. As a result it is not clear from the text whether the English words beneath the logograms are actual translations or not. Johanna Drucker's suggestion that late twentieth-century visual/verbal work owes a debt to both "Concretism" and "to mass media commercial design and electronic (video and computer) technology" (1996: 39) offers a way to read Coupland's commingling of the visual and the verbal here. The labelling of the city after its economic function transforms Chinese geography into an entity of markets rather than politics. Similarly, although the presentation of the Chinese characters in large centred type seems to emphasize their aesthetic quality, the choice of vocabulary evokes consumerism and connects their visual appeal to the aesthetics of billboards. The scale of the logograms in comparison to the English type, emphasizes a visual rather than a semiotic appreciation but the fact of their translation speaks to a negotiation between difference and universalism whereby these images might stand as a locally particular expression of the universal (Robertson 1992: 102).

Figure 17.2 Two examples of the Chinese logograms, "Boredom" and "Pornography," in Douglas Coupland's (2006), *Jpod*, pp. 266–7.

In other instances, the textual interruptions in Coupland's novel gesture towards a hypertextual aesthetics. At the narrative level his characters frequently resort to Google in order to answer the kind of speculative questions that Coupland uses as a form of character interaction in all his fiction. In *JPod*, the frequent lack of a purposeful connection between the plot and retrieved information speaks to the randomness of our interactions with the world through the internet and at times appears to consciously mimic the so-called "spoetry" found in spam-emails (Gallix 2008; see Epstein, this volume). Coupland also acknowledges the global scale of these interactions by pointing to the way that they play on our assumptions about the nature of international relations, such as in his choice to reproduce a Nigerian embezzlement money-transfer-scam (Coupland 2006: 27). The reader cannot know whether this email is a genuine fake or an imitation of Coupland's own making. Yet this hardly matters because, as a result of their ubiquity and their endless repeatability with minor variations, the meaning of such emails is constituted in their form just as much their actual content. The fact that meaning here resides in the form more than in the obvious content of these emails complements the previous example, where the logograms seem to signify difference more than their translatability. What is more, moments like this allow Coupland's novel to suggest the ungoverned movement of the hypertext from one point to another. Though his novel involves an obvious narrative sequence, its attempt to represent the internet as a pool of potentially limitless content means that the possibility of digression is constantly present. In different ways both Suman Gupta (2009: 77–85) and Berthold Schoene (2011) have argued that hypertexts represent the literariness of globalization and both are interested in the way that hypertextuality is visible in existing literary practices (see also Tomasula, this volume; Hayles 2004). Coupland's approximation of hypertext's nonsequential juxtapositions may be one way that this is achieved.

A more provocative example of this kind of approach is found in the novel *Looking for Headless* published since 2007 as part of Goldin+Senneby's larger Headless project. The concept for Headless is that the two Swedish artists, Simon Goldin and Jakob Senneby, set out to explore the potential connections between an offshore-fund called Headless and a secret society known as Acéphale founded by Georges Bataille and the Collège de Sociologie in the late 1930s (Goldin+Senneby 2009a). To explore this idea they hired the author John Barlow to ghost write the novel *Looking for Headless*, as the pseudonymous "K.D." a fictionalized version of offshore financier Kate Dent. As part of a series of exhibitions of the project, actors were paid to play "the fictional author" K.D. and each chapter was read publicly before its publication (Cohen 2009: 53). Styled as a murder mystery, the novel is composed of thinly fictionalized real-life events including Barlow's attempt to find the company called Headless, a meeting of academics assembled by Goldin+Senneby to discuss the project, and a series of art exhibitions in which the work is displayed. Most of the "characters" in the novel are also personae of real people who have collaborated with Goldin+Senneby as "outsourced workers" (K.D. 2007–2010: 126). Moreover, along with Barlow, the novel hints that its authors are also drawn from this cast of characters: Chapter Seven, for instance, is narrated by an actor who plays K.D. at the Bienal Internacional de São Paulo and may have been written by actor and writer Noemi Marinho who collaborated in this exhibition (Goldin+Senneby 2009b: 48–9; K.D. 2007–2010: 146–56). In his contribution to Headless, as both an emissary for Goldin+Senneby and as a character in *Looking for Headless*, Angus Cameron describes multiple-authoring as a multitext (K.D. 2007–2010: 163). However, we might also think about the way that the novel itself resembles the hypertext through its blurring of real and fictional words. For instance, early in the novel the persona John Barlow wonders why Goldin+Senneby are so paranoid about Kate Dent:

> Barlow has seen the video footage of Kate, he's Googled her; she exists, and she works for Sovereign, the company who G+S claim was registered by Sovereign as an off-shore company here in the Bahamas in 2002 . . .
> (K.D. 2007–2010: 45)

Combined with the uncertainty produced by the layers of Headless, and the frequent inclusion of real people as novelistic personae, the declarative "he's Googled her" immediately becomes an interrogative "have you Googled her?" and an imperative "'Google her': I have and she does exist." Likewise, Chapter Two, which recounts Barlow's travel to the Bahamas in search of Headless, is interspersed with extracts from a travel blog that Barlow wrote on his actual trip (2008). The URL is supplied at the start of the chapter (K.D. 2007–2010: 32) and in this way the reader is invited to move between the novel and its co-texts. This technique seems to be imitative of hypertextuality in a similar way to *JPod*. However, whereas Coupland's interest is with construction of subjectivity within globally dispersed mediated-networks, *Looking for Headless* and the Headless project "appropriate or mimic strategies of the offshore" by concealing authorship and responsibility for the narrative (Einarsson 2009: 37). Such strategies challenge the very notion of the centre, of the rooted, or of agency in order to construct a commentary on the kinds of secrecy which the offshore represents (Figure 17.3).

V. Conclusion

A useful way to grasp Goldin+Senneby's representation of globalization as decentred integration is through the "Mind Map" that they provide to accompany their installations, which is reproduced in the catalogue to the exhibition in Toronto's Power Plant (Goldin+Senneby 2009b). Nicky Marsh has compared this map to Lombardi's work, suggesting that its "huge entangled networks . . . demonstrate . . . that the offshore confounds easy mapping or visual representation" (Marsh 2011: 93). Read alongside Maurer's reading of Lombardi as providing an illusion of knowledge which is finally impossible, we can read Goldin+Senneby's map as promising explication but signalling only entanglement. The ever-knowing *Looking for Headless* seems to acknowledge this when it portrays the persona of Angus Cameron speculating about the operation of offshore finance and using the map to pull "everything together in my mind" to

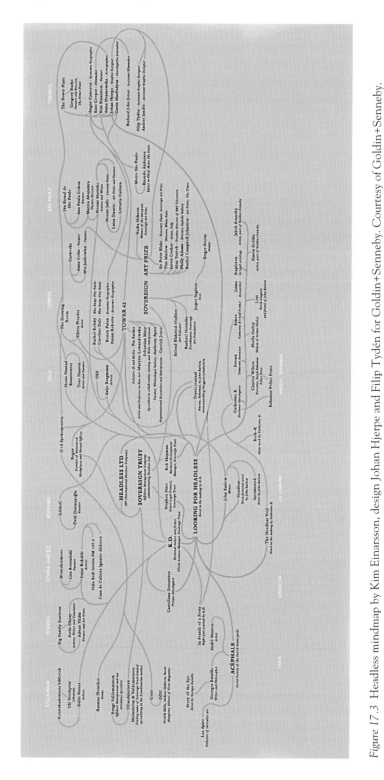

Figure 17.3 Headless mindmap by Kim Einarsson, design Johan Hjerpe and Filip Tydén for Goldin+Senneby. Courtesy of Goldin+Senneby.

help "form a map of my own arguments" (K.D. 2007–2010: 162). Revealingly, the coherence which the map provides is associative rather than hermeneutic. Points on the map are connected but the nature of these connections is obscure and imprecise. As such the map exists as a sign of coherence in general without making fully readable its own diffuse connectivity. Tellingly, and in keeping with the more experimental literature of globalization, it rejects the combination of concatenation with concentration and leaves connectivity as a kind of active problem for the text. This sense of openness might evoke familiar critical judgements about experimental literature, but it is crucially also a feature of globalization's status as a descriptive term. If *Looking for Headless* frustrates our attempts to map the processes of its construction, we might equally say the same for globalization, which purports to describe processes that, by their nature, frustrate description or easy comprehension. The tension for any attempt to represent globalization is the need to alternate between highlighting structures of coherence and integration and highlighting the processes of occlusion and dispersal that these structures produce. Works such as those by Yamashita, Coupland, Lombardi and Goldin+Senneby offer us models for thinking about the productive ways that this tension can be manipulated.

References

Adams, P.C. (1997) "Cyberspace and Virtual Places," *Geographical Review* 87: 155–71.

Annesley, J. (2006) *Fictions of Globalization: Consumption, the Market and the Contemporary American Novel*, London: Continuum.

Barlow, J. (2008) "Going to the Bahamas", Retrieved from http://www.travelblog.org/Central-America-Caribbean/Bahamas/Nassau/blog-259665.html (accessed 25 June 2011).

Burgess, A. (1996 [1962]) *A Clockwork Orange*, London: Penguin.

Cameron, A. and R. Palan (2004) *The Imagined Economies of Globalization*, London: Sage.

Cockburn, A., J. St. Clair and A. Sekula (2000) *Five Days That Shook the World: Seattle and Beyond*, New York: Verso.

Cohen, A. P. (2009) "The Practice of Instituting." In Goldin+Senneby (ed.) *Goldin+Senneby: Headless*, Toronto: The Power Plant.

Coupland, D. (1991) *Generation X*, London: Abacus.

—— (2006) *JPod*, London: Bloomsbury.

Drucker, J. (1996) "Experimental, Visual and Concrete Poetry: A Note on Historical Context and Basic Concepts." In K.D. Jackson, E. Voss and J. Drucker (eds.) *Experimental, Visual Concrete: Avant-Garde Poetry since the 1960s*, Amsterdam: Rodopi.

Einarsson, K. (2009) "Headless. To the Public Record: Interview with Angus Cameron." In Goldin+Senneby (ed.) *Goldin+Senneby: Headless*, Toronto: The Power Plant.

Ford, S. (2005) *The Situationist International: A User's Guide*, London: Black Dog.

Gallix, A. (2008) "Spam Lit: The Silver Lining of Junk Mail?" *The Guardian*. [Online.] Retrieved from http://www.guardian.co.uk/books/booksblog/2008/jul/01/spampoetry?INTCMP=SRCH [accessed 30 June 2011].

García Márquez, G. (1978) *One Hundred Years of Solitude*, Basingstoke, UK: Picador.

Gibson, W. (1987) *Count Zero*, New York: Ace Books.

—— (2000) *All Tomorrow's Parties*, New York: Berkley.

Goldin+Senneby (2009a) "Goldin+Senneby » Blog Archive » Headless." Retrieved from http://www.goldinsenneby.com/gs/?p=116 (accessed 23 June 2011).

—— (ed.) (2009b) *Goldin+Senneby: Headless*, Toronto: The Power Plant.

Gupta, S. (2009) *Globalization and Literature*, Cambridge, UK: Polity.

Hayles, N.K. (2004) "Print Is Flat, Code Is Deep: The Importance of Media-Specific Analysis," *Poetics Today* 25: 67–90.

Heise, U.K. (2006) "1970, Planet Earth: The Imagination of the Global." In B. McHale and R. Stevenson (eds.) *The Edinburgh Companion to Twentieth-Century Literatures in English*, Edinburgh, UK: Edinburgh University Press.

Hobbs, R. (ed.) (2003) *Mark Lombardi: Global Networks*, New York: Independent Curaters International.

Huxley, A. (2007 [1932]) *Brave New World*, London: Vintage.

Jameson, F. (1991) *Postmodernism or, the Cultural Logic of Late Capitalism*, New York: Verso.

K.D. (2007–2010) *Looking for Headless*, Goldin+Senneby.

Lee, S.-I. (2007) "'We Are Not the World': Global Village, Universalism, and Karen Tei Yamashita's Tropic of Orange," *MFS Modern Fiction Studies* 53: 501–27.

Marsh, N. (2011) "Goldin+Senneby's 'Headless': From the Public Record 2009," *Wasafiri* 26: 92–4.

Maurer, B. (2005) "Due Diligence and 'Reasonable Man,' Offshore," *Cultural Anthropology* 20: 474–505.

McCallum, E.L. (2000) "Mapping the Real in Cyberfiction," *Poetics Today* 21: 349–77.

Newman, R. (2003) *The Fountain at the Centre of the World*, London: Verso.

Robertson, R. (1992) *Globalization: Social Theory and Global Culture*, London: Sage Publications.

Schoene, B. (2011) "From *253* to 6775235741: Global Narration, Hypertext and Community in Geoff Ryman's Online Tube Theatre and Print Remix," Unpublished conference paper, Manchester Metropolitan University, Manchester, UK.

Stockwell, P. (2000) *The Poetics of Science Fiction*, Harlow, UK: Longman.

Tabbi, J. (1995) *The Postmodern Sublime: Technology and American Writing from Mailer to Cyberpunk*, Ithaca, NY: Cornell University Press.

Tomlinson, J. (1999) *Globalization and Culture*, Cambridge, UK: Polity.

Tsing, A. (2000) "The Global Situation," *Cultural Anthropology* 15: 327–60.

Virilio, P. (1998) "A Traveling Shot over Eighty Years." In J.D. Derian (ed.) *The Virilio Reader*, Oxford, UK: Blackwell.

Yamashita, K.T. (1997) *Tropic of Orange: A Novel*, Minneapolis, MI: Coffee House Press.

18

ALTERMODERNIST FICTION

Alison Gibbons

I. Introduction: altermodernism

Tate Britain first launched its Triennial exhibitions in 2000, the purpose of which has consistently been to showcase the best in contemporary British art. The 2009 exhibition was the largest and most ambitious Triennial to date. Led by internationally renowned curator and art critic Nicolas Bourriaud, it focused on what he called *Altermodern*; the cultural milieu, Bourriaud argues, in which we now find ourselves. Such a sensibility reflects social and cultural changes affecting the world in this era of globalization and the World Wide Web. Bourriaud's theorization of the altermodern is set out in his introductory essay to the Tate Triennial 2009 (2009a) and ensuing monograph *The Radicant* (2009b), both of which concentrate upon visual art. This chapter introduces altermodernist fiction. First, I define and expound altermodernism before providing a conceptualization of experimental fiction of the epoch in Section II through recourse to W.G. Sebald. In Section III, the boundaries of the genre are extended through the analysis of three case studies of altermodernist fiction: Liam Gillick's *Erasmus is Late* (1995 [2000]), Brian Castro's *Shanghai Dancing* (2003 [2009]), and Charles Avery's *The Islanders* project (2010a). Section IV concludes the chapter by identifying other writers whose works might also be considered as altermodern.

Bourriaud claims that the "term 'altermodern', which serves both as the title of the present exhibition and to delimit the void beyond the postmodern, has its roots in the idea of 'otherness' (Latin *alter* = 'other', with the added English connotation of 'different') and suggests a multitude of possibilities, of alternatives to a single route" (2009a: 12). As Bourriaud's words suggest, altermodernism is conceived as something post-postmodern. While defining the temporal parameters of cultural epochs is always problematic, Bourriaud cites the significance of 1989 as a precursor to altermodernism in opening the way for the second stage of postmodernism in the form of postcolonialism. The year 1989 was the fall of the Berlin Wall, implying a victory for capitalism and the collapse of a utopian alternative (also highlighted by Brooks and Toth [2007] as an important date in Postmodernism's demise). The turn of the millennium, with

238

the anxiety that foreshadowed it, and the events of September 11, 2001, is also vital. 9/11 particularly brought about two significant paradigm shifts: first, it showed up fissures in the liberal capitalist utopia of the 1990s, and second it caused a shift in the conceptualization of time. Indeed, this latter notion is put forth by Don DeLillo in "In the ruins of the future" (2001), where he suggests that in light of the events of September 11, 2001, time can no longer be understood as an ongoing linear process since now the future is haunted by the past and the past haunted by imagined temporal possibilities. Toth and Brooks boldly claim, "if postmodernism became terminally ill sometime in the late-eighties and early-nineties, it was buried once and for all in the rubble of the World Trade Center" (2007: 3). Thus, Altermodernism emerges from the debris, compounded by the global financial crisis of the late 2000s and in particular "the collapse of the globalised financial system in Autumn 2008 appears to mark a definitive turning-point in history" (Bourriaud 2009a: 16).

While McLaughlin (this volume) defines post-postmodernism as a US-centric movement materializing in the late 1980s through a television-culture generation of writers reacting against and wrestling with the paradoxes of its postmodern heritage, for Bourriaud the present period is in many ways marked by a return to or at least a reclamation of modernism: Today is a historical juncture, "ripe to reconstruct the 'modern' for the present moment, to reconfigure it for the specific context in which we are living" (2009b: 15). Bourriaud draws parallels between the rise of modernism in the nineteenth century and the emergence of altermodernism at the turn of the twenty-first century: in particular, the influence of industrialization on the historical avant-gardes, the resulting fervor for new technologies and the progress of the modern urban environment, is paired with the impact of globalization on the world today. Rather than embracing capitalist industry, as early modernism appeared to, altermodernism stands in opposition to the effects of globalization, both culture and capital. Modernism arose from the early capitalist explosion; postmodernism was a mourning of the loss of the grand-narrative and the stable self under the logic of late capitalism (see Jameson 1991); Postcolonialism was driven by an essentialist need to seek origins as global capitalism took hold. Altermodernism, rather than embrace, mourn, or enroot, is defined by an implicitly politicized aesthetic resistance to globalization, refusing standardization, stability, or stasis. Indeed, the influence of global capitalism on the condition of altermodernist fiction means that it shares more commonalities with the experimental literature of globalization (see Connell, this volume) than with post-postmodernism (McLaughlin). (On Modernism, see Part 1 of this volume; Postmodernism, see McHale; Postcolonialism, see Gopal.)

According to Bourriaud, the archipelago provides a suitable metaphor for global culture and altermodern practice, in a shrinking world in which digital technologies (satellite surveillance, Google Earth, the World Wide Web and the hypermobility it entails) transform our experience of territory, locality, and home. An archipelago, an extensive system of islands, is "an example of the relationship between the one and the many" (Bourriaud 2009a: 12). Thus, altermodernism sees a cacophony of matter constructed into meaningful networks. In doing so, altermodernist art and fiction deals in the "aesthetics of heterochrony . . . it brings together heterochronic elements", so that "delay (analogous to the 'pre-recorded') coexists with the *immediate* ('to live') and with the anticipated", all with "the aim of revealing our present, in which temporalities and levels of reality are intertwined" (Bourriaud 2009a: 21). Navigating this heterochronological territory, authors, artists, and characters, take on the role of travelers and their narratives represent a contemporary experience that is pluralized, decentralized, and itinerant.

II. Altermodernist fiction

Works of altermodernist fiction materialize in the twenty-first century, though there are some exceptions of forward-thinking works published in the mid-to-late 1990s. Based upon Bourriaud's writings, I define altermodernist fiction by its treatment of form, time, and identity.

> FORM: Altermodernist writing is formally experimental. It weaves disparate elements together, be it a mixing of genre (literary, autobiographical, historical, artistic) or of mode (words, drawings, sculptures, photographs). So doing, it seeks to reframe reality; often, components of everyday Western culture (corporate logos, media images) are integrated into the literary work, an act which underscores the precarious ontology of altermodernist fiction.

> TIME: In the altermodern, time is heterochronic. Cultural standardization is resisted by understanding history as a series of pluralized accounts, and acknowledging the dialogues between these accounts. Time is explored as a spatialized landscape whereby past, present, and future can be woven together into a complex network (an archipelago) which, in itself, enables a re-examination of our present reality and experience.

> IDENTITY: Altermodernist conceptions of identity are centered upon the notion of "setting roots in motion" through the journey format, while the figure of the traveler, the nomad, provides a character whose movement through time and space traces out intersubjective memories and identities.

While Bourriaud suggests these characteristics in relation to visual art in *The Radicant*, he gives no indication of how they might be manifested within a literary work. I now turn to the work of W.G. Sebald, an author cited by Bourriaud, in order to investigate the stylistic practices of altermodernist writing.

First acknowledging Sebald in the Tate Triennial introduction, Bourriaud advocates, "Sebald's writings – wanderings between 'signs', punctuated by black and white photographs – they appear to me as emblematic of a mutation in our perception of space and time, in which history and geography operate a cross-fertilisation, tracing out paths and weaving networks" (2009a: 12). In *The Radicant*, Bourriaud adds:

> Sebald shows how the memory of the people and the events of the past haunt our lives and shape the space around us. For him, the experience of travelling represents a privileged form of access to memory: thus, he finds history's traces in buildings, museums, and monuments as well as in hotel rooms and conversations with the individuals he meets.
>
> (Bourriaud 2009b: 129)

Throughout Sebald's opus, genre is treated as malleable and capricious, blurring the boundaries between literature, history, travel writing, and autobiography. Fact and fiction intermingle, so that in many ways Sebald's writing appears to consistently delve into aspects of his own personal identities and histories. Born in Bavaria in a war-torn 1944, his father a German prisoner of war, Sebald's childhood took place in a Europe recovering from the horrors of the Third Reich, while after his university years Sebald moved to England as an academic. Sebald's own life haunts his fiction with *The Emigrants* (1993) chronicling the lives of four exiles who left their homes in the wake of the Holocaust, and *Austerlitz* (2001) recounting Jacques Austerlitz' search for his true identity after discovering a childhood in which he was evacuated on a kinder transport from Nazi Germany. Both these works are typical of Sebald's fiction in that they are written from the perspective of an anonymous first-person narrator, presumably a counterpart of the author, while the narratives stem from the narrators' own wandering journeys.

The Rings of Saturn (1995) is perhaps the most itinerant of Sebald's prose fictions, detailing a coastal expedition on foot across East Anglia. The opening displays many of the properties of altermodernist fiction, as does the book generally. It begins:

> In August 1992, when the dog days were drawing to an end, I set off to walk the county of Suffolk, in the hope of dispelling the emptiness that takes hold of me whenever I have completed a long stint of work. And in fact my hope was realized, up to a point; for I have seldom felt so carefree as I did then, walking for hours in the day through the thinly populated countryside, which stretches inland from the coast. I wonder now, however, whether there might be something in the old superstition that certain ailments of the spirit and of the body are particularly likely to beset us under the sign of the Dog Star. At all events, in retrospect I became preoccupied not only with the unaccustomed freedom but also with the paralysing horror that had come over me at various times when confronted with traces of destruction, reaching far back into the past, that were evident even in that remote place. Perhaps it was because of this that, a year to the day after I began my tour, I was taken into hospital in Norwich in a state of almost total immobility. It was then that I began in my thoughts to write these pages. I can remember precisely how, upon being admitted to that room on the eighth floor, I became overwhelmed by the feeling that the Suffolk expanses I had walked the previous summer had now shrunk once and for all to a single blind, insensate spot. Indeed, all

that could be seen of the world from my bed was the colourless patch of sky framed in the window.

(Sebald 2002 [1995]: 3–4)

At this point the narrative is punctuated by a black and white photograph depicting a window, presumably the hospital window just mentioned.

Notable about the opening passage is the way in which it subtly obscures the boundaries between past and present. It begins with a temporal locative, "August 1992", soon complemented by the proper noun "Suffolk", thus instantly grounding the narrative in a specific time and place. While the narrative begins in past tense, with the narrator looking back to the "dog days" of summer that "were drawing to an end", shifts in tense start to occur. The narrator "set off to walk", a past tense construction that combines past and infinitive, but his motivation is relayed to the reader in present tense: "in the hope of *dispelling* the emptiness that *takes* hold of me". This is then followed with the conjunction "whenever" which emphasizes a non-specific but recurring time, before present-perfect tense, "I have completed a long stint of work". The opening sentence thus entwines past and present, an effect which continues throughout, and is particularly remarkable within the second sentence and the penultimate sentence. The second works similarly to the first: "I *have seldom felt* [present-perfect] so carefree as I *did then* [past tense and distal adverb], *walking* [present-continuous] for hours in the day . . .". The penultimate sentence opens in present tense, "I can remember", but with a main verb that semantically looks back to the past. It continues in past ("being admitted", "became overwhelmed") which not only shifts the tense again but its passive mood suggests the fragile state of the narrator in hospital. The tense then remains in the past, but is interrupted by present tense adverb in "had now shrunk".

The opening passage initially evokes the narrator's walks through Suffolk with exactness and immediacy for the reader, particular since it is the act of walking and the narrator's cognitive experiences which tend to be expressed in present tense. The predominance of the past tense, however, nevertheless roots these experiences in the past. As a piece of altermodernist writing then, Sebald's alternating use of past and present tense serves to show up the vivacity of memories, and the ways in which the subjection of personal histories are, as Sebald says in interview, "determined by the inequality or unevenness of time" (Bigsby 2001: 141). Moreover, while such memories are vivid at first, the countryside they occupy transforms from a sprawling land-mass, realized through active present-tense verbs such as "stretches" and spatialized nouns like "expanses", to an "insensate spot". The passage closes by moving the time and space of the narrator's reminiscences into both the past and the distance using the semantic motion of the verb "shrunk" and consigning them beyond the hospital window.

The brief analysis offered above begins to provide a sense of the temporal texture of altermodernist writing. In *The Rings of Saturn* past and present intermingle to create a fuzzy or heterochronic temporality that enables Sebald to explore the interrelated themes of time and memory. And in Sebald's work, memory is both personal and historical: the opening chapter alone moves from Suffolk in August 1992 to the hospital in 1993 to recollections from Kafka; from memories of friends to seventeenth-century history and art. The photograph is also important in showing Sebald's work as altermodern. It is but one of many throughout the book, and while multimodality in literature (see Gibbons, Part II, this volume) is not essential to altermodernist fiction, it is part of its formal experimentation. Moreover, as Bourriaud notes, altermodernism is an era that "valorizes the links that texts and images establish, the paths that artists forge in a multicultural landscape, the passageways they lay out to connect modes of expression and communication" (2009b: 44).

In the next section of this chapter, I extend the understanding of altermodernist fiction through the discussion of three case studies, beginning with the work of Liam Gillick who also includes images within his writings. In altermodernist fiction formal experimentation is used to accentuate themes of time and identity, since as Bourriaud claims of both Sebald's and Gillick's works, "remembering can never be reduced to the act of telling: the past is reconfigured through a patient collection of visual and linguistic detail" (Bourriaud 2009b: 129).

III. Case studies

Liam Gillick: *Erasmus is Late*

In addition to Sebald's writings, Bourriaud does acknowledge one further author, Liam Gillick. Gillick is a British artist, based in London and New York, whose work comprises installation art, sculpture, architectural practice, criticism, and fiction, and it is not unusual for an art exhibition to develop from or with a piece of writing. Speaking of Gillick's practice, Bourriaud comments, "Gillick's entire oeuvre could be described as an echo chamber in which the aesthetic procedures of the avant-gardes and the history of the work would call to each other across a tightly woven network of forms and texts" (Bourriaud 2009b: 129). Thus, the concept of the network is once again evoked, as is the fusion of forms.

Gillick's *Erasmus is Late* (1995) manifests a network design on both a narratological and stylistic level. The novella (it is less than 100 pages) is divided into twelve chapters all set in a different London location with each site illustrated by a single line-drawing, created by the artist's mother Gillian Gillick (see Figure 18.1). In narrative terms, *Erasmus is Late* follows its central character Erasmus Darwin, brother of Charles Darwin, as he wanders through London stopping for pause and reflection at each of the chapter-sites. Erasmus's journey is, however, more complicated than it seems, for as he wanders Erasmus moves between his home-time in the early 1800s and 1997. He is on his way to a dinner party he is hosting, and is late for, a dinner party whose guests include: Harriet Martineau, the nineteenth-century pamphleteer and social commentator; Elsie McLuhan, mother of media theorist Marshall McLuhan; Masaru Ibuka, co-founder of Sony; Robert McNamara, Secretary of Defense

CHAPTER TWO

A SHOP IN TOTTENHAM COURT ROAD

The traffic flows in one direction. There is no real break. The vehicles are indistinct. Darkness on the road is peculiar given the number of shops here. But for Erasmus there are four more glowing retail sites to visit and the first lies across the steady stream. Still caught in the reflections of the non-debate with Harriet, there is no urgency in his movements. The priority stands on the other side. It was the signage that first attracted his attention. The vast number of logos in the form of names. The choice of

such names often came about through the desire to create something understandable across many borders. Ibuka knows all about that. But will the availability of various components, all connected to recording discussion provide any kind of answer for our guests? The appeal of the stuff is clear enough but Erasmus did not remember the places ever having been there. It is clear that something is taking hold of him. There is a feeling that the dinner tonight is taking place at a crucial moment. It is a question of naming. And the signs are all part of that. Erasmus is standing in front of a projection that encompasses future profits and a desire for market share.

In the house. A dark, narrow hallway. A staircase leads straight up from the front door. A passage twists around the plain dominance of the sweeping stairs and takes you through to the back of the building. Upstairs. The second floor is faintly illuminated. Some activity is taking place with sounds of conversation. The interior is too dark to allow full view of the décor. But it's only early evening. A few people have gathered but the central character is absent. They sit around a heavy table. Its surface lightened by a clean white cloth. Harriet has been speaking but now she is silent. A mantelpiece carries photographs, drawings and a small pot. None of the people pictured there are

14

15

Figure 18.1 Example of a line drawing from *Erasmus is Late*, Liam Gillick, Published by Book Works (2000 [1995]), pp. 14–15. Courtesy of Book Works.

under Kennedy and later President of the World Bank; and Murry Wilson, songwriter and father to Brian Wilson of The Beach Boys. While the array of characters may seem bizarre, they stand as figureheads for socialist politics, capitalist enterprise, and popular culture.

Erasmus is Late begins, "Erasmus is late. The table will have to wait. His insomniac wanderings have produced a guide to places that require further thought. A debate about the Other Man. A set of parallel histories" (Gillick 2000 [1995]: 8). This aperture initiates many of the novel's altermodernist themes: the way in which the narrative is built around Erasmus's wanderings through the streets of London, its comingling of temporal coordinates (1810 and 1997). Moreover, the reference to "the Other Man" hints at the way in which Erasmus's walk, thoughts, and conversations across time and space with the dinner guests provide a vehicle for political debate. Indeed, art critic Peio Aguirre writes that Gillick's work suggests a ". . . return to one of the aspirations of Western Marxism: the re-politicization of aesthetics and the political validation of form" (Aguirre 2009: 26).

Gillick's critique of global capitalism is triggered by the locations Erasmus visits. As the first chapter draws to a close, Erasmus walks towards Tottenham Court Road; "A place for shopping. Somewhere to buy all the things he could want. Devices to help with communication. The shop has him mesmerised. The glow from the window lights his face" (Gillick 2000 [1995]: 12). There is an implicit irony in Gillick's articulation of "all the things he could want", and an acknowledgement of consumerist desire. This continues throughout the novella, with electronic shop light being cast as captivating emanation: There are "glowing retail sites" (14) and later "Erasmus remains caught

244

within the attraction of the shop windows. Stuck, unable to complete his crossings" (18). Connected is Gillick's musings on the mass of company logos in the shop windows (commentary that connects to the altermodernist integration into art of everyday Western culture): "The vast number of logos in the form of names. The choice of such names often came about through the desire to create something understandable across many borders. [. . .] the signs are all part of that. Erasmus is standing in front of a projection that encompasses future profits and a desire for market share" (18). This is the strong allure of capitalism, and the glittering promises of wealth it suggests.

It is the parallel temporalities of *Erasmus is Late* that Gillick uses in order to engage in a political critique and to search out future possibilities. For instance, in Chapter Three, Erasmus ruminates:

> I am in the middle and I function as a conduit for what has happened and what might be possible. I am the other man. [. . .] For tonight the mob become the workers and after this point all the procedures with which to abuse power structures will be irrevocably altered. For now, for just one night, everything remains. Laid out, layered, and compressed.
>
> (Gillick 2000 [1995]: 18)

While the reference to "the mob" suggests the fixed social structures of Georgian society, "the workers" are those for whom modernist and postmodernist capitalist production offered the opportunity for social and economic ascendance. Gillick's use of parallel histories is what Aguirre calls his "ellipsis or the elliptical literary form" in which he is intentionally "leaving a gap between two events" (2009: 10). The sociopolitical circumstances of 1810 and 1997 in *Erasmus is Late* are brought together to create dialogues between times, and from such dialogue is an implicit sense of future possibilities. Maire writes that through Erasmus's journey, "time can now be thought of as a knot in which past, present, and future merge, not only by the mere fact of temporal retroactions, but by the emergence of a transhistorical community" (Maire 2009: 178). For Gillick, this enables a "futurology" (Gillick 2000 [1995]: 39) or what Haberer calls "'prevision,' i.e. seeing forward" (2007: 8), but while the altermodernist strategies of *Erasmus is Late* provide both critical reflection and implicit political subversion, the vision for the future is uncertain. There are no grand statements of conviction, no Utopias, but rather a recognizable blend of skepticism and optimism. Thus at the end of the novel, when Erasmus eventually reaches home, his guests have already left: "If you think of the empty room, so recently vacated, then it might be possible to imagine the sound of the key in the door", Gillick (2000 [1995]: 84) writes, "And heavy footsteps approach up the stairs".

Brian Castro: *Shanghai Dancing*

Brian Castro is an Australian author, whose challenging and stylistically innovative writing has garnered critical acclaim, particularly in his home country. His novels consistently interlace fiction and reality, as well as creating dialogues between different cultures, principally those pertinent to his own hybridized cultural identities – Australian, Chinese, Portuguese, and English. Interestingly, Castro has cited Sebald as a literary influence, and there are correspondences between the two authors biographically (both, for instance, became academics) and in terms of their textual aesthetics.

Shanghai Dancing (2003) is Castro's seventh novel and, like Sebald's work, it mixes genres, modes, and registers. *Shanghai Dancing* contains Pillow Books (bedside journals in Japanese tradition), legal documents such as wills, biblical invocations, letters, dictionary definitions, maps, calligraphy, music, and photographs. The novel depicts the journey of protagonist, António Castro, who after his father's death leaves Australia for Shanghai – the city from which his father ran an empire – in order to unravel the histories of his Chinese, Portuguese, and English heritage, and overcome the ghosts of memories which haunt him. Described in the jacket blurb as a "fictional autobiography" (see also Kacandes, this volume), the novel opens with a double-page spread of the Castro family tree; while this family tree pertains to the fictional António Castro, its cultural composition mirrors Brian Castro's own, born in Hong Kong with parents of Portuguese, Chinese, English, and Spanish descent. Although the reader's imaginative journey begins in Shanghai, as António discovers and reminisces about the lives of his ancestors, the novel becomes a complex oscillating web of stories, temporalities, and locations: The narrative drifts from contemporary Hong Kong to China at the start of the twentieth century; from seventeenth-century Brazil to the Philippines in the nineteenth century; on his search, António visits Macau, London, Liverpool.

The narrative proper starts in a chapter titled, "Slow Boat to China", therefore emphasizing the journey motif. It commences:

> Winter had descended on Shanghai.
>
> There was no real hope of finding tomatoes. You went looking anyway. It was a cure of sorts. No, not the tomatoes, but the search.
>
> Sometimes you suffocate when you think of the past; of a life that never was, flashing up in sepia. Memory which is creamy-yellow, cracked; composed of protagallic acid, protosulphate of iron, potassium cyanide. Let's not get too technical. Not right now. It makes for too much exposure. Still in the dark, you remember that in Shanghai they used to wrap tomatoes in tissue paper. Like this story. Like the way everything in history is always wrapped in tissue; of words, of memories, of lies.
>
> Dancing. Now that's another matter. You have to have infinite patience with that. Time and timing. Grace and desire. Swaying back and forth like the tide until something is washed up; something always washed up.
>
> Shanghai-dancing. Nothing there yet. No bluish epiphany; no flaring gas jet above my head.
>
> I wanted to find out what it was but all I had was a sheaf of photos wrapped in cellophane and they had become creased, flaky, sticking to the plastic window in my wallet where the credit cards should go.

> Shanghai-dancing; sounds like the high life or the low life; maybe both.
> My father mentioned it only once, but it wasn't to me.
>
> (Castro 2009 [2003]: 3–4)

While the first sentence locates the narrative in Shanghai in early Winter, the remainder of the extract reads like the thoughts of a drifting consciousness, or what Brennan calls "confusing narrative arabesques" (2008: 149). This impression is aided by the fluctuating point of view and shifts of thematic focus.

The second paragraph appears to initiate a narrative event, making use of the second-person pronoun in "You went looking anyway", though the colloquial tone is suggestive of a narrative voice. The concretized nature of the specified act suggests that the "you" is a particular storyworld character. The theme here is also important for altermodernist fiction, since Castro assigns more import to the act rather than the potential goal, the search for tomatoes rather than the tomatoes in themselves. The third paragraph shifts the anchorage of the second-person pronoun so that it feels less definite and more self-reflexive in nature. A rumination on the nature of memory, it enacts a metaphorical mapping, with photography-specific lexis working to instigate a comparison between memories and photographs: chemicals used to develop photos, "exposure", and the pun on the phrase "still in the dark" which is simultaneously suggestive of both the dark room and a lack of understanding, through the cultural association of light with knowledge. The reference of "you" shifts again as it is reoriented to the deictic location of "Shanghai", and a particular memory relating to "tomatoes". The narrative then appears to turn in on itself through metatextual comment, "Like this story. Like the way everything in history is always wrapped in tissue; of words, of memories, of lies." These last remarks, foregrounded through repetitions, highlight the duplicitous nature of memories and of storytelling (a central theme of the novel), problematizing what has already asserted itself as a changeable and peripatetic opening. This, of course, is all interlinked with Castro's use of photographs, a medium that, while supposedly objective and reliable documentation, is in fact as fragile and subjective as memory itself.

Shanghai Dancing is a novel which does not sit still, in theme, narrative, or style. Castro's prose performs relentless shifts, creating an itinerant instability that relates to notions of identity, time, and form. Indeed, meaning itself is even challenged. In the opening to the novel, quoted above, the term "Shanghai-dancing" is cited, firstly with the appendage "Nothing there yet", and later tagged by "sounds like the high life . . .". In fact, there are numerous repetitions of the phrase within the first chapter:

> Shanghai-dancing. Nothing there yet. No bluish epiphany; no flaring gas jet above my head. (3)
> Shanghai-dancing; sounds like the high life or the low life; maybe both. (3)
> Shanghai-dancing. Stuck in my head. (4)
> Shanghai-dancing. Something in my bones. (5)
> *Shanghai-dancing*. To cast a line from an old spool: it is the attainment of disorientation and instability. (6)

Shanghai-dancing: *sb. unkn. (Naval slang?) syphilis.* (17)
Shanghai-dancing. To come through something. A rite of passage. (22)
shanghai: *v. to drug or otherwise render insensible and ship on board a vessel wanting hands.* (23)
shanghai: *sb. (Austral. & NZ) a catapult.* (26)

(Castro 2009 [2003]: all italics original)

These are nearly always stand-alone sentences, and often they are set apart as isolated paragraphs for further emphasis. Brennan refers to these as Castro's "now familiar etymological games, offering his reader a plethora of possibilities" (2008: 149). More than this, because the phrase is attributed to António's father, it is an important psychic puzzle for the narrator. Of course, it is a puzzle that is not, and perhaps cannot, be solved, thus the meaning of the phrase, the reader's interpretation, and António's sense of self, are drawn into a state of perpetual semantic deferral, or if they are defined it is, as Bourriaud writes of the subject of altermodernist art, "as a construction or montage, in other words, as a work born of endless negotiation" (2009b: 56).

Charles Avery: *The Islanders*

The final case study is Scottish artist Charles Avery's *The Islanders* project. In 2004, Avery, whose work featured in the 2009 Tate Triennial, embarked upon a series of large-scale drawings, sculptures, installations, and writings all united in their goal of creating a new world. Avery's books have been produced on one hand to catalogue his works, while on the other, as fictional travelogues and pieces of altermodernist fiction (see Figure 18.2). Two such books currently exist, *The Islanders: An Introduction* (2010a), soon followed by *Onomatopoeia: The Port* (2010b). The project clearly has an altermodernist aesthetic not only in its use of diverse forms and artistic media, but also in the way in which it creates a topological arena, an island, whose very creation reverberates back on our own epoch. In interview, Avery muses, "There are countries in our own world that for me are merely a blob on a map, or less – just a name. There are huge cities in China that I have never heard of, and yet I have an intimate knowledge of cracks in the tiles that line my bath". He adds, *The Islanders* project is "all underwritten by my sincere declaration as to the reality of this place, completely free of any irony" (Morton 2010: 163). Indeed, in the contemporary world, space seems to be negotiated anew as we may now travel around the world with unprecedented ease and speed, by car, boat, train, plane, and Ethernet; we might talk to people on the other side of the world more often than we speak to our next-door neighbors. Bourriaud goes one step further, arguing that in "our globalised universe, where even the slightest square meter has been charted by satellites and is accessible on websites like Google Earth, the invention of a world has a completely different meaning". He adds, *The Islanders* "is about territorialising an idea in the era of capitalist deterritorialisation. It 'smoothes' the entire planet, erases frontiers and homogenises cultures" (Bourriaud 2010: 150).

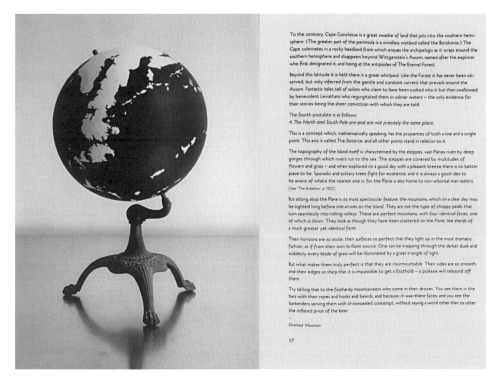

Figure 18.2 Example of illustration and text from Charles Avery, *The Islanders* (2010a), pp. 36–7. Courtesy of the artist and Pilar Corrias Gallery.

The Islander's prologue begins, "I first came to the island at the end of the great kelp rush, although I was not aware of that at the time. On the contrary, I had sought this strange land with a view to being its discoverer" (2010a: 9). From the start, the fiction is established as a discourse of discovery, written in past tense with a first-person narrator. As this narrator, named Only McFew, settles on the Island, he catalogues its creatures and inhabitants, and learns to become a hunter. He also informs the reader of the religious, mystical, and cultural beliefs of the islanders. In a chapter entitled "Creeds", he writes:

> Speaking from the point of view of an Islander, which I now regard myself to be, there are two states: the Island and Triangleland.
>
> The term Triangleland refers to the character of the tourists, their apparent desire to label and classify everything and their complacency in their ability to do so. The first thing they will ask is, "What is the name of the island?" This appears an absurd and irrelevant question, for it is akin to asking, "What is the name of everything?" Or, "What is Tom's name?" Being the continent from which all the other islands in the archipelago are isolated it is the archetype and as such does not require a name.
>
> (Avery 2010a: 103)

Essentially, Avery is distinguishing between the Island and its inhabitants and the reality of the Western world. In Only McFew's comments on the tourists of Triangleland, there is, therefore, a nestled criticism of the cultural standardization brought about by globalization. Indeed, Bourriaud writes:

> The "ground" is giving way; we are told to compromise our rituals, our culture, and our history, now confined to standardized urban contexts that no longer reflect the image of us, except in locations reserved for that purpose: museums, monuments, historic districts. Our environments no longer reflect history; rather, they transform it into a spectacle or reduce it to the limits of a memorial.
>
> (Bourriaud 2009b: 33)

Avery's depiction of the Trianglelanders shows tourists who are less interested in the experience of a place than in its commercial identity. To paraphrase Bourriaud (2009b: 32), it is the portable nature of national and cultural identities, what can be "snapped" by digital camera or souvenir-ized, that is favored over local reality.

Avery also appears critical of the reader's complicity with Western society. In the chapter "The Hunter", Only McFew recounts how he killed an Aleph (a creature of the island). One of the illustrations which accompany the narrative depicts two "Triangleland Bourgeoisie studying the head of an Aleph", as shown in Figure 18.3. Implicitly, then, there is an art gallery context being inscribed here. Is Avery suggesting our own collusion with both *The Islanders* project and the capitalist global market? The Island, however fictional, is something we lay witness to in his exhibitions, and globalization something with which, in the way we live out our twenty-first-century lives, we inevitably collude.

Interestingly, when Tom Morton, curator of the Hayward Gallery in London, interviewed Avery he suggested that the narrator functioned as an "avatar" of the artist himself (2010: 156). Additionally, the narrator can be seen as an avatar or a site of projection for the reader. Indeed, the book's consistent use of first person can be seen to encourage this. It seems as though Avery entices the reader into the world of the Island through a series of identifications: with the narrator, complicity with the Triangleland tourists, collusion with the art voyeurs. Additionally, Avery takes this one step further in his conclusion, closing *The Islanders* with a tantalizing direct address: "I cannot tell you how this world really is – I have no idea – I can state only the facts as I perceive them. You must be satisfied with this or you must travel there yourself sometime, and see these beings in their natural environment, for this place is utterly subjective" (2010a: 141).

IV. Conclusion

While altermodernist art has been discussed at length by Bourriaud, the fiction of the epoch has not. This chapter takes the first steps towards redressing this balance by

Figure 18.3 "Triangleland Bourgeoisie studying the head of an Aleph." From Charles Avery, *The Islanders* (2010a), p. 28. Courtesy of the artist and Pilar Corrias Gallery.

introducing the experimental genre of altermodernist fiction, a literature of our contemporary globalized world. I have sought to offer insight to the themes, styles, and modes of narration of such works through reference to four examples, W.G. Sebald's *The Rings of Saturn*, Liam Gillick's *Erasmus is Late*, Brian Castro's *Shanghai Dancing*, and Charles Avery's *The Islanders*. A number of other works also fall under the remit of altermodernism, not least other novels by the above authors. Beyond this, works such as *The One Facing Us* by Ronit Matalon (1998), *Istanbul: Memories of a City* by Orhan Pamuk (2005), Mark Z. Danielewski's *Only Revolutions* (2006), *Headless* by Goldin+Senneby (2009), Jennifer Egan's *A Visit from the Goon Squad* (2010), *Open City* by Teju Cole (2011), and the work of Rana Dasgupta may also be considered altermodernist.

For Bourriaud, a key feature of altermodernist art is its employment of heterochrony and its spatialization of time. As more attention is paid to altermodernist fiction, critical tools and narrative frameworks will be developed. For now, I'd like to propose the applicability of Herman's term "polychrony": "It includes both the more and less 'radical' types of inexactness of coding, as well as both the multiple and partial ordering of events. Polychrony thus entails self-conscious, self-subverting modes of narration in which alternative or multiple ways of sequencing events are entertained" (Herman 2002: 213). Furthermore, "it can also entail modes of narration that make it possible to reconstruct a global sequence or overall temporal interval, yet militate against interpreters' efforts to establish temporal positions for particular events within that larger span of time" (213–14). As a term, polychrony relates to the three key concerns of altermodernist fiction: form, time, and identity. Form is experimental and hybridized; time is heterochronological, and identities (of both characters and readers) are fluid and shifting. In altermodernist fiction, form, time, and identity, are intertwined in an intricate narrative network, a polysemous archipelago.

References

Aguirre, P. (2009) "Elusive Social Forms." In M. Szewczyk (ed.) *Meaning Liam Gillick*, Cambridge, MA: MIT Press, pp.1–27.

Avery, C. (2010a) *The Islanders: An Introduction*, London: Koenig Books.

—— (2010b) *Onomatopoeia: The Port*, London: Koenig Books.

Bigsby, C. (2001) "In Conversation with W. G. Sebald." In *Writers in Conversation, Vol.2*, Norwich, UK: Arthur Miller Centre for American Studies and EAS Publishing, pp. 139–65.

Bourriaud, N. (2009a) "Altermodern." In N. Bourriaud (ed.) *Altermodern: Tate Triennial*, London: Tate Publishing, pp. 11–23.

—— (2009b) *The Radicant*, New York: Lucas & Sternberg.

—— (2010) "Charles Avery: A Topology," trans. A. Spira. In *The Islanders: An Introduction*, London: Koenig Books, pp. 147–52.

Brennan, B. (2008) *Brian Castro's Fiction: The Seductive Play of Language*, Amherst, MA: Cambria Press.

Brooks, N. and Toth, J. (eds.) (2007) *The Mourning After: Attending the Wake of Postmodernism*, Amsterdam: Rodopi.

Castro, B. (2009 [2003]) *Shanghai Dancing*, New York: Kaya Press.

DeLillo, D. (2001) "In the Ruins of the Future," *The Guardian* 22 December 2001. [Online.] Retrieved 16 March 2004, from http://www.guardian.co.uk/books/2001/dec/22/fiction.dondelillo

Gillick, L. (2000 [1995]) *Erasmus is Late*, London: Book Works.

—— (2009) *All Books*, London: Book Works.

Haberer, L. (2007) "Liam Gillick: Parallel Thinking Between Structure and Fiction." In L. Gillick and L. Haberer (eds.) *Factories in the Snow: Texts by Lilian Haberer; Works by Liam Gillick*, Zurich: JRP/Ringer, pp. 3–46.

Herman, D. (2002) *Story Logic: Problems and Possibilities of Narrative*, Lincoln, NE: University of Nebraska Press.

Jameson, F. (1991) *Postmodernism, or the Cultural Logic of Late Capitalism*, London: Verso.

Maire, B. (2009) "The Aesthetics of the End of Time." In M. Szewczyk (ed.) *Meaning Liam Gillick*, Cambridge, MA: MIT Press, pp. 159–81.

Morton, T. (2010) "An Interview with Charles Avery." In C. Avery, *The Islanders: An Introduction*, London: Koenig Books, pp. 155–63.

Sebald, W. G. (2002 [1995]) *The Rings of Saturn*, London: Vintage.

Toth, J. and Brooks, N. (2007) "Introduction: A Wake and Renewed?" In N. Brooks and J. Toth (eds.) *The Mourning After: Attending the Wake of Postmodernism*, Amsterdam: Rodopi, pp. 1–14.

19

MANIFESTOS AND ARS POETICA

Laura Winkiel

I. Genealogies

No matter at what historical moment one opens the manifesto archive – in the late sixteenth-century France where the manifesto served as "a public writing in which one or more responsible politicians make known their views or explain their conduct" (*Trésor de la langue français*, quoted in Hjartarson 2007: 174), amongst the Diggers and Levellers in seventeenth-century England (Lyon 1999: 16–23), or as part of the theological polemics and the Swabian peasant riots of the Lutheran reformation (Puchner 2006: 13–15) – the critical consensus is that the manifesto began its history as a public, political document capable of heralding *and* producing formidable historical and social change. It is also axiomatic that the late eighteenth century marks a watershed moment in the history of the form. During the tumultuous period of the Enlightenment revolutions, especially the French, the manifesto came to embody the myth of modernity as a form of historical rupture. This embodiment consists of the following basic structure: a declaration of a break from history understood as a repetition of the same; a formation of a collectivity dedicated to leading society in a radically new direction; and an advancement of a program of change. This format reflects the shift in the manifesto from its authoritarian institutional location (the church, the state, the military) to its predominant Enlightenment-era position amongst literate common people in the streets and the coffee shops. Signaling *le peuple* as opposed to the bourgeois *citoyen*, the dissenting political manifesto declared a break from bourgeois history in order to claim a space within the public sphere so as to lead society in radically new directions.

From this seizure of the means of public dissent, the manifesto helped to popularize the term "avant-garde." Rooted in French military language, the "avant-garde" began to be used by radical groups of Jacobins during the French Revolution to describe a revolutionary political stance intended to reach past military circles towards a broader audience of "patriots" (Calinescu 1987: 100–11). Evoking the image of elite shock troupes in battle, sent ahead of the massed body of soldiers to attack the enemy, this metaphor suggests that revolutionary political battles increasingly became a war of words and ideas. The Romantic use of the term "avant-garde" in a literary-artistic context, Calinescu writes, was directly derived from the language of revolutionary politics: "It is not difficult to explain the appeal of the [military] metaphor for various kinds of revolutionary, and therefore future-oriented, philosophies" (1987: 101). In this way, the term "avant-garde" codes the entwining of aesthetics and politics that structures the manifesto form and determines its functioning for the next two centuries.

The manifesto's duality depends on two modes of speech: the first is the political one of action, and the second relies upon poetic and often dramatic language. The manifesto is both a founding act of building a new society and a signal of great formative activities to come. Its break from the past combines future expectations and speech act efficacy (doing things with words) in the present. It marks an imaginative stirring of new ideas and practices and provides a script for action that will unfold in as yet undetermined ways. The manifesto, as a document of action, recursively reflects on the grounds necessary for achieving that action. It dramatizes the possibility of its own authority and anticipates the creation of the world it imagines. In so doing, it combines politics and aesthetics even as it separates them: the manifesto's program will be realized when its readers assent to its demands by acting according to its vision. Political action is deferred in favor of developing a utopian (aesthetic) image of the world to come. Despite this deferral, the manifesto's language is striking. The root sense of *manifest* suggests a mode of communication that differs from the premium on rational communication that subtends theories of bourgeois public political discourse. *Manifest* presents a literalness that seemingly does not require interpretation. It is a piece of evidence that is clearly revealed to the eye, open to view or comprehension. Its deictic nature (do this, now!) arrests attention on the seemingly unmediated present. The manifesto's evidential quality contributes to its penchant to wield words as weapons in which the absolute certainty of its message contains the threat of violence. Its refusal to accommodate differences of opinion and its often aggressive, militant stance is suggested also by an *OED* etymology of "manifesto" in which the word emanates from "*manus*" (hand) and "*festus*" (cf. *infestus*, dangerous, which is the root of *of-fendre* and *de-fendre*). The primary meaning of this derivation would thus be "palpable" or, more literally, "dangerous" or "hostile hand," which carries with it violent overtones. This threatened spillage of mere words into the category of deeds relates to manifesto writers' impatient desire to change history with their words (Winkiel 2008: 11–12).

Despite the manifesto's insistence on changing the world – now! – its status as a recognizable genre and as a language act mediates its urgent insistence and proclaimed self-evident nature (see Honig 1992, and Derrida 1982, 1986). Claude Leroy's characterization of the historical avant-garde and its use of the manifesto form cogently summarizes the mutually constitutive feedback loop of performative discourse. He writes, "the manifesto has certainly become the discursive formation of the avant-gardes *par excellence* because it regards itself as the avant-garde of discourse" (quoted in Hjartarson 2007: 174). This chiasmus, in which the manifesto produces the avant-garde because it *is* avant-garde, suggests that representation (aesthetics) precedes politics (speech act efficacy in which saying something does something). In actuality, however, such causality is undecidable. Puchner has usefully discussed this fundamental aporia of the manifesto genre through reference to speech act theory and notions of drama and performativity. The problem of the manifesto form, he argues, begins with the difficulty of posing a serious threat to authority by means of a mere document. The manifesto struggles with trying to change words into instruments of action, and this transitivity is the subject of speech act theory, the study of situations in which saying something actually *does* something. For instance, a speech act occurs when one achieves the legally binding state of matrimony by means of uttering the words, "I do." This legally binding action only occurs when those words are said before a justice of the peace or a religious figure (and if one is heterosexual in most U.S. states and the U.K., in their right mind, not already married, over the age of consent, etc.). Given that manifestos utter their speech acts in situations devoid of the institutional authority that gives weight to what is said, their speech acts are considerably more complex than that of a marriage ceremony. The manifesto wants to create the context that will authorize their utterances in the future, a temporal state described by the verb tense of the future anterior: "Their authority will have been provided by the changes they themselves want to bring about" (Puchner 2006: 24). This prolepsis, Puchner suggests, indicates that theatricality is, along with performativity, at the heart of manifestos.

Manifestos suggestively enact the future they want to produce. Puchner states:

> Theatricality describes a space between absolute powerlessness and the secure position of the sovereign, a play that the manifesto exploits without yet knowing whether the project of usurping power will work out. Without theatricality, in other words, there would be no pose, no presumption, no projection, no futurity; without theatricality there would be no manifesto.
>
> (Puchner 2006: 26)

Puchner describes a political crisis of language in which the manifesto writers' desire for absolute certainty and instrumentality is undermined by the very nature of linguistic indeterminacy as well as by their institutional locations outside of power structures. This crisis, he writes, is best encapsulated by Marx's eleventh thesis on Feuerbach that "formulates this desire for political action as a command: 'The philosophers have only *interpreted* the world in different ways; the point is to *change* it'" (2006: 27, italics in original). Marx broke from philosophy here both through content and form: philosophical argument takes the form of a polemical aphorism that names a new practice of philosophy as action.

The connection between the manifesto and the philosophical fragment is striking and apposite. Returning to the Enlightenment crisis during the French Revolution, we can trace there the imbrication of poetry, philosophy and self-conscious reflection on poetry and philosophy (theory) in the Romantic fragment as a form of poesis. *Poesis* highlights the active sense of *making* the work of art. Philippe Lacoue-Labarthe and

Jean-Luc Nancy argue that the fragment "involves an essential incompletion" that is identical to the *project* which they define as a "'fragment of the future,' insofar as the constitutive incompletion of the project is its most valuable quality" (1988: 42–3). Deferring its perfection into the future – "it should forever be becoming and never be perfected" – the fragment, like the project, nonetheless contains the totality (the possibility) of its own perfection within itself (1988: 43). The Romantic fragment is not coherent perfection, but, rather, when located within a collection of fragments, it embodies a "'motley heap of sudden ideas,' whose profound, substantial unity rests on the 'free and equal fellowship' of its parts" (1988: 44). These collective, often anonymous, exchanges of ideas stage a dialogue by which the fragment comes to stand in for "the romantic ideal of drama" (1988: 45), the process and activity of arriving at some future "truth."

The fragment, like the manifesto, stands both within and without "literature," as it serves as a form of meta-critical reflection on the form and function of aesthetic imagination in producing a new society. The common aphoristic form of manifestos (for example, Mina Loy's "Aphorisms on Futurism," Italian and Russian Futurist manifestos, Dada manifestos, Pound's "Axiomata": see Caws 2001: 170–363; also White, this volume, and Stockwell, this volume) – a quick series of polemical statements that most certainly comprises a "motley heap of sudden ideas" – also points towards a future in which the utopian vision ("truth") it only gestures to might be realized. Lacoue-Labarthe and Nancy highlight an important development in the genealogy of the "romantico-modern" conception of literature that occurs in Friedrich Schlegel's philosophical fragments produced for the *Athenaeum* between 1798–1800. Calling the group of writers clustered around the journal *Athenaeum*, "the first 'avant-garde' group in history" (1988: 8), these writers (being powerfully influenced by Schlegel who remained somewhat outside the circle) developed a concept of literature that was, Lacoue-Labarthe and Nancy argue, the *production* of something entirely new:

> The romantics never really succeed in naming this something: they speak of poetry, of the work, of the novel, or . . . of romanticism. In the end, they decide to call it – all things considered – *literature*. This term, which was not their own invention, will be adopted by posterity . . . to designate a concept – a concept that may still be undefinable today, but which the romantics took great pains to delimit. They, in any case, will approach it explicitly as a new *genre*, beyond the divisions of classical (or modern) poetics and capable of resolving the inherent ("generic") divisions of the written thing. Beyond divisions and all definition, this *genre* is thus programmed in romanticism as *the* genre of literature: the genericity, so to speak, and the generativity of literature, grasping and producing themselves in an entirely new, infinitely new Work.
>
> (Lacoue-Labarthe and Nancy 1988: 11, italics in original)

Such a capacious definition of literature includes self-critical reflections on the making of literature as well as genre-blurring forms and collective works such as anthologies and little magazines. In effect, the self-reflexive writing of manifestos as the making of the conditions of revolutionary action is anticipated here, though writers at this point in history utilize the manifesto genre solely to make programmatic political statements of revolutionary intent rather than to craft self-reflexive statements on art's utopian aspirations for society as they would, increasingly, after 1870.

The Jena Circle, as this group of writers came to be called, placed literature between philosophy, on the one hand, and theory, as the hybrid of poetry and philosophy, on the other. Schlegel writes in his *Ideas*, "Where philosophy stops, poetry has to begin," and, on the other side of the series, remarking on the relation between literature and theory, he writes in the *Athenaeum* fragments that "poetry should describe itself, and always be simultaneously poetry and the poetry of poetry" (Brown 2005: 13). We have in this formulation something akin to *Ars Poetica*: the metalanguage in which a poem reflects on its own art of poetry. Best known from Archibald Macleish's eponymous poem (1925) with its famous line: "A poem should not mean / but be," *Ars Poetica* has been criticized (by none other than John Cage: see Haislip, 136) as being too didactic and too close to propaganda to be "good" (i.e., autonomous, formal) poetry. This comment reveals the close kinship of *Ars Poetica* to the manifesto in its propagandistic and metacritical language. It both announces its aesthetic project and attempts to imagine the conditions under which such a project will be achievable. John Haislip writes, "'Ars Poetica' does not do what it says should be done in the composition of a poem – largely because it is impossible to write a poem that is and only is an object to behold as a static object without meaning, without message. This is the central paradox of 'Ars Poetica'" (137). Its incompletion and simultaneous anticipation of a future completion further confirms more generally *Ars Poetica*'s affinity to manifestos: they both gesture towards the overcoming of their own impossibility.

II. Emerging avant-gardes

The abbreviated genealogical section above concentrates on the manifesto's European origins. This next section globalizes Europe by tracing "The Founding and Manifesto of Futurism, 1909" as its rhetoric underscores Italy's bid to become a modern, imperial power. By situating the manifesto in a global, rather than in a solely European geography, I prepare the conceptual ground for the following section's discussion of how the manifesto has circulated as part of global modernity, rather than as simply emerging as a European phenomenon. This section's attention to the literary marketplace and the avant-garde's use of the manifesto to both compete within the sphere of commodity culture and differentiate itself from those reified forms suggests that the European avant-garde – despite its differentiation – partook in a linear, progressivist history that universalizes European culture as a form of imperial domination.

The nineteenth-century European avant-gardes deployed the manifesto to distinguish their art and literature from commercial forms. Hjartarson summarizes:

> In the course of the nineteenth century the manifesto and other types of programmatic texts are to an increasing degree used by writers and artists to

explain and justify their modern aesthetics. The emergence of the aesthetic manifesto in the nineteenth century is closely related to transformations of the literary and artistic market which made writers and artists dependent on a new public. The need to produce manifestos is caused by a breach in communication between author or artist and public. The work of art no longer seems capable of mediating its own message or intention, it is in need of a meta-aesthetic discourse to fulfill this intermediary function.

(Hjartarson 2007: 176)

Literary manifestos served as a form of self-marketing and differentiation amongst various aesthetic schools that circulated and competed for cultural capital much as commodities circulate within their markets, though the notion of aesthetic autonomy or "art for art's sake" sought nominally to remove the artist and the work of art from the commodifying pressures of marketplace. This removal, however, sundered the confluence of the writer and his/her public. The manifestos written under such auspices tended to be meandering, prosaic, lengthy documents. Some characteristic texts include Jean Moreas's "Le Symbolisme" (1886), Pierre-Louis's (Maurice Denis) "Definition of Neo-Traditionalism" (1890), and Jules Romaine's "Les sentiments unanimes et la poesie" (1905). These texts, though sometimes aphoristic (e.g., Pierre-Louis, Wilde, Whistler: see Caws 2001: 3–21) were seldom performative (Whistler's "The Ten O'Clock" is the exception). Sometimes iconoclastic – consider Oscar Wilde's concluding statement in the preface to *The Portrait of Dorian Gray* that "all art is useless" (Caws 2001: 18) – they uniformly lacked the kinetic dimension of the avant-garde manifesto that F.T. Marinetti was to invent in 1909.

The important shift in the manifesto's rhetoric and form first occurred in F.T. Marinetti's "The Founding and Manifesto of Futurism, 1909," published on the first page of France's leading newspaper *Le Figaro* (see White, this volume). Rather than disengage from commodity culture and its mainstream bourgeois audience, Marinetti sought entry into this sphere of mass consumption by means of theatrical provocation. His manifesto narrates the mythic transformation of the modern subject from a state of individual decadence (evocative of the nineteenth-century "art for art's sake" autonomous aesthetic) to one of collectivist modern action. The manifesto's call to violence (theatrical and otherwise) aimed to generate cohesion, heroism, and the enhancement, rather than the annihilation, of bodies by modern technologies.

The manifesto constructs its cohesive community by means of the myth of the racial other. In the manifesto, Marinetti mingles with the factory cesspool and emerges abjectly – torn, filthy, stinking – from the haunches of his *car*. His rebirth as man-machine is diametrically opposed to the consumable body of the Sudanese nurse metonymically related to the cesspool. The recollected nurse's body allows for the fantasy of absolute cultural difference which allows for the formation of the futurist collective and their ecstatic manifesto declaration: "We intend to sing the love of danger, the habit of energy and fearlessness" (Apollonio 2001: 21). The violence of the accident, rather than being figured as traumatic shock, is cast as ecstasy that Jeffrey Schnapp reads as "sunder[ing] bonds to the past and in their place, forge[ing] new links between men, machines, and their environment" (1999: 7–8). These "metallicized" subjects – Marinetti and his cohorts – are immune to threats posed by "degeneration, fatigue, mortality and an overburdened historical consciousness" (1999: 8). They enact their superiority over passive, inert others, leading Italy through a "revolution of the mind" (Gentile 1994: 72) that will impose its will on other territories and compete effectively with other imperial nations (Winkiel 2008: 84–91).

Marinetti's manifestos and futurist movement relied, too, on literal theatricalization. He performed his manifestos on stage and developed elaborate multimedia scenarios for their delivery (including dropping manifestos from bell towers and automobiles). This change in strategy signals how Marinetti attempted to compete with commodity culture for the attention of popular audiences rather than distancing himself from the fray. Indeed, early twentieth-century avant-garde manifestos harnessed the energies of modernity (with its culture of abundance) in order to change it from within. So, too, these manifestos' staunch refusal to accommodate "tradition" in any form captures the militancy of the artistic avant-gardes in the first four decades of the twentieth century. However, by heralding a complete overcoming of the past by the futurity of revolution, the avant-garde and its interlocutors maintained, despite themselves, the paradigm of historicism.

Historicism narrates temporal unfolding as a progressive overcoming of regressive forces and it is this narrative that Calinescu connects to the avant-garde: "It was modernity's own alliance with time and long-lasting reliance on the concept of progress that made possible the myth of a self-conscious and heroic avant-garde in the struggle for futurity" (1987: 95). One sees the trap of historicism in avant-gardists' self-conscious acknowledgement of their own redundancy and obsolescence in which they predict all too accurately how the new inevitably becomes old as other innovative artist groups supersede them. F.T. Marinetti's "The Founding and Manifesto of Futurism, 1909," for instance, proclaims, "When we are forty, other younger and stronger men will probably throw us in the waste basket like useless manuscripts – we want it to happen!" (Apollonio 2001: 23). That the Futurists use irony to distance themselves from their vanguardist position serves to highlight the theatricality of their art manifesto, but their irony does nothing to displace the historicist narrative of progression and supersession. Indeed, the references in Marinetti's "The Founding and Manifesto of Futurism, 1909" to imperial competition also makes clear that what was at stake in the first few decades of the century was nothing less than the future of capitalist modernity and global hegemony.

III. Global circulations

When itinerant artists from the European periphery and its colonies deployed the avant-garde manifesto, they put its theatricality to a different use than did the European historical avant-gardes. Puchner claims that the avant-garde, forged as it was within the cosmopolitan centers of Europe and beyond, fostered a sense of geographical and linguistic displacement, intercultural encounter and cross-fertilization. Speaking of the work of Chilean avant-gardist Vincente Huidobro, Puchner writes:

> Paris is not so much a center as one of the nodal points where avant-garde activity is concentrated. Other such points, for Huidobro, are New York, Milan, Madrid, Barcelona, Zurich, Berlin, and Buenos Aires. The crossing paths of figures such as Tzara, Picabia, Huidobro – one could add Huelsenbeck, Duchamp, and Breton – do not respect origins (although they may try to create and project them) . . . Whether Marx in Brussels, Engels in London, Tzara in Zurich, Breton and Picabia in New York, Trotsky in Mexico, Pound in Rome, or Huidobro in Madrid and Paris – the list could go on – writers of manifestos use this genre to establish and fabricate new points of departure.
>
> (Puchner 2006: 173–4)

Puchner highlights how the cosmopolitan nature of the avant-garde worldwide drew writers to the manifesto form as a means of displacing narratives of origin. But he neglects to consider the uneven nature of global development. The postcolonial avant-gardes, it is my contention, went a step further: Only those cosmopolitan writers who sought to carve out an enunciative position for non-Western peoples explicitly confronted the colonized and racialized history of those originary narratives.

The anthropologist Arjun Appadurai suggests that "the circulation of forms produces new and distinct geographies, within which forms co-exist in uneven and uneasy combinations" (2010: 8). This section takes up this idea to consider how the global circulation of the manifesto form interacts with different histories, locations and geographies to produce new understandings of modernity in the world/colonial system. In effect, the global circulation of forms (intensified by colonization which accelerates the process of global circulation) carries the meaning of the modern in itself. I begin with some of the first non-European avant-gardes, those of Latin America. Let me expand a bit on why avant-gardes from the colonies critiqued the Eurocentrism of the European avant-gardes in their manifestos even while they deployed similar iconoclastic gestures: As Enlightenment thinkers produced a Eurocentric account of modernity, they relegated the global south to the premodern, the condition of being outside of or coming late to modernity. One can think of Homi Bhabha's notion of writing out of the colonial time-lag: when so-called "primitive" peoples always come late to modernity, how can they ever catch up? (1994: 252). Their belatedness in relation to modernity is inscribed within the very discourses of modernity themselves. Bhabha's theorization of the colonial time lag, along with Stuart Hall's economic and cultural theories of "societies structured in dominance," (1996: 16–60) allow us to recover the overlooked significance of the postcolonial avant-garde and to talk about these "untimely" modernisms. These include, for instance, C.L.R. James's *The Black Jacobins* (1936) in which the disavowed Haitian Revolution figures prominently among world-historical revolutionary events. In featuring this revolution, James displaces linear narratives of modernity that construct a center-periphery geography in order to articulate a global modernity crucially integrated *from the colonial outset* with the south. This articulation describes the differences and similarities in economic as well as political modernity between Paris and Port-au-Prince. In short, James's work allows for similarities to be tracked across global modernity, but it also insists on crucial differences – gaps in development where societies are "structured in dominance" – that describe Eurocentric narratives of modernity justified by the colonial time lag. If we *begin* with the notion of uneven development in which all parts of the world-system are understood to be contemporaneous, the story of modernity's achievements and failures takes on a different cast. Its movement across the colonial divide brings with it altered experiences and effects of modernity while registering the urgency of understanding the significance of multiple modernisms and avant-gardes (Winkiel 2008: 9–36). The "modern/colonial world system" contains within its name an essential structuring gap between the centers of empire and their colonial peripheries. Walter Mignolo argues that this border is part of a system that

> introduces the subaltern perspective articulated on the basis of memories and legacies of the colonial experience, that is, the colonial experience in their historical diversity. [. . .] Once coloniality of power is introduced into the analysis, the "colonial difference" becomes visible, and the epistemological fractures between the Eurocentric critique of Eurocentrism is distinguished from the critique of Eurocentrism, anchored in the colonial difference – being articulated as postcolonialism.
>
> (Mignolo 2000: 37)

Mignolo's postcolonial critical lens refuses to disavow the dark underside of modernity. The often positive forces of modernity (industrialization, urbanization, literacy, democracy, rights, and individualism) are structured and made possible by coloniality (conquest, exploitation, resource extraction, absolutism, and forced migration). Latin America's postcolonial location ensures that its avant-garde saw both the promises of modernity and their exclusion from full participation in it. This contradictory positioning, Rosenberg argues, produces a heightened geopolitical awareness of Latin America's role in the world-system. The Latin American avant-garde, being cognizant of such a historical position, refuses merely to imitate the European avant-garde (dissolving its own historical particularity within a European universality). So, too, Rosenberg argues, critics must resist the "pervasive inclination to reduce spatial position to stages of temporal progress in discussions of modernity." Instead,

> the term "geopolitics" has been a conceptual key to understanding the global distribution of symbolic power and the possible ways to locate folds or niches of resistance in it and to it: from the inception of the notion of geopolitics as a way for the nineteenth-century imperial sciences to identify location and physical environment as variables in the struggle for global power, to its use as a way of viewing discrete entities – nations – in their mutual interconnectedness; to the

more recent world-system analysis, in which the predominance of the nation as the only privileged agent in the global power game is challenged and new actors and new ways to gain cultural agency emerge.

(Rosenberg 2006: 15)

The point of advancing this geopolitical model is simply that we must approach the postcolonial avant-gardes with a different critical and historical lens than we would with the European avant-gardes. Their positioning within the modern/colonial world system necessitates that their aesthetic form and language work to different aims than those of their European cohorts. It also signals a critical skepticism towards the presumed universality of the European avant-garde as proclaimed in their manifestos.

IV. The Cannibal Manifesto

Surely one of the most remarked-upon Latin American avant-garde events was the publication of Oswald de Andrade's "Cannibal Manifesto" in São Paulo in 1928. This manifesto, which reworks the primitivist discourse of colonial indigeneity into an ironic performative stance, illustrates a spatial aesthetic of simultaneity rather than a linear temporal framework of primitivism/futurity. The "Cannibal Manifesto" provocatively turns the tables on primitive/civilized dichotomy by appropriating cannibalism as a performative trope. Its most iconic line – "Tupi or not Tupi: that is the question" – refuses the colonial role of exporting primitive resources (its indigenous cultures) in order to innovate European art (as well as the exportation of material resources to build European wealth). Rather, it reverses the trajectory of appropriation, "cannibalizing" Shakespeare in order to assert an ironic self-distance from its own indigeneity while simultaneously asserting the positive value of that indigenous culture in forming a distinctive Latin American identity. The fact that the altered line is drama highlights indigeneity here as part of the modern, a self-fashioned identity that is performed in tandem with recognizably European forms of modernity. But more than affirming a positive hybrid identity for Latin America, a recognizably national construction, the "Cannibal Manifesto" situates Latin America as a region within the world system of modernity/coloniality:

> The struggle between what we might call the Uncreated and the Created – illustrated by the permanent contradiction of man and his taboo. Daily love and the capitalist modus vivendi. Cannibalism. Absorption of the sacred enemy. To transform him into a totem. The human adventure. Earthly finality. [. . .] Once carnal, it turns elective and creates friendship. Affectivity, or love. Speculative, science. It deviates and transfers. We arrive at utter vilification. In base cannibalism, our baptized sins agglomerate – envy, usury, calumny, or murder. A plague from the so-called cultured and Christianized, it's what we are acting against. Cannibals.
>
> (Andrade 1928: n.p.)

Andrade outlines the stereotypical "otherness" of Latin America, how it is perceived by Europe to be in an "uncreated" state of nature as opposed to Europe's cultured (developed) state. Rather than repressing the taboo of cannibalism (and thereby internalizing their colonial inferiority), Andrade embraces the taboo tongue-in-cheek, turning it into a mark of identity, a totem. Simultaneously, he undermines the absolute otherness of cannibalism by imbricating it within the "capitalist modus vivendi," the economic, social and political structures of modernity. Anthropophagy, in this narrative, Rosenberg remarks, highlights "an active Brazilian role in its colonial status, back to the first encounter in 1500" (2006: 78). At the first point of contact, the "innocent but savvy savage would swallow and digest for his own benefit whatever is or stands for Western or modern, which would nevertheless come from elsewhere" (2006: 78). In digesting the foreign element, it becomes native. Such incorporation refuses to recognize origins, and foregrounds instead the workings of a global market (colonial trade), accepting interdependency and exchange as well as a lack of autonomy.

Embracing the heterogeneity of both North and South, nature and culture, the manifesto proclaims a freedom from the strictures of European morality "against all the importers of canned conscience" that labels colonial peoples and cultures evil. Instead, it proclaims an ironic and performative avant-gardism: "Screenplays. Screenplays. Screenplays. Screenplays. Screenplays. Screenplays. Screenplays" (Andrade 1928: n.p.). The repetition renounces originality and evacuates European universality in the endlessly proliferating mass cultural forms of cinema. Appropriating the liberatory possibilities within modernity's mass culture forms, the cannibal manifesto seizes upon Hollywood performance to defamiliarize the present and unleash the transformative potential of a disavowed populist history as revolution. This strategy – as subsequent Brazilian history bears out – is a mystification, though, insofar as populism "rests on a conflation of the interests of labor and capital into a single, mythic entity" (Brown 2005: 187). Even while heralding the next revolution, the manifesto rejects the linearity of history as progress:

> Filiation. The contact with the Brazilian Cariba Indians. Ou Villegaignon print terre. Montaigne. Natural man. Rousseau. From the French Revolution to Romanticism, to the Bolshevik Revolution, to the Surrealist Revolution and the technological barbarity of Keyserling. We're moving right along.
>
> (Andrade 1928: n.p.)

The heavy irony of the manifesto halts sweeping transformative change and instead embraces: "The golden age proclaimed by America. The golden age. And all the girls." Happiness, dream worlds, and screenplays: these are the resources Andrade names to envision a world unleashed from a universal historical narrative. The march of progress is halted in favor of anarchic libidinal popular energies. To conclude, Andrade's use of cannibalism to name an aggressively colonizing modern world system is fundamentally different from the European avant-garde's trope of cannibalism. (See "Dada Cannibalistic Manifesto" in Caws 2001: 316–17.) There, it names the irrationality and barbarity of European modernity without reconceptualizing modernity as being a world/colonial system from its outset. It proclaims, "Dada alone does not smell: it is nothing, nothing, nothing. / It is like your hopes: nothing. / like your paradise: nothing. / like your idols: nothing" (Caws 2001: 317). This nihilism sweeps European modernity and colonial otherness into the same basket of nothingness. Such blanket statements do nothing to destabilize the structure of this world system. It erases colonial histories once again. "Your paradise" and "your idols" appropriate colonial territories and indigenous religions in order to attack European imaginaries.

V. Futures

Whither the manifesto? Until very recently, it was a critical commonplace to declare the avant-garde completely commodified by market culture and the manifesto useless (see Puchner 2007). This tide has turned, though in the recent global era the role of the aesthetic has been largely subsumed within capitalism. This fact, however, simply means that manifestos intervene from within the beast. Indeed, there are scores of new political, aesthetic, and technological manifestos, published in print and, increasingly, in digital media. A small sampling includes: Donna Haraway's "Cyborg Manifesto" (1985), Lars Von Trier's filmmaking manifesto "Dogme 95" (1995), Jean Bernabé's, Patrick Chamoiseau's, and Raphaël Confiant's "In Praise of Creoleness" (1988), "The Blogger's Manifesto" (2002), "Avant-Pop Manifesto" (1993) (see Olsen on Avant-pop, this volume), Nick Piombino "Writing and Remembering" (1993), Lyn Hejinian "If Written is Writing" (1978), Susan Bee (Laufer) and Charles Bernstein "Style" (1978), Charles Bernstein "The Conspiracy of 'Us'" (1979), "The Conservative Party Manifestos" (1900–2001), and the Zapatista National Liberation Army's (ELZN) communiqués (1995–1998, see Marcos 2004). The manifesto has also become a commodity itself: it names a furniture store, a wine, a U.K. record label, a book series from Blackwell Publishing, and serves as a slogan for a cosmetic company (see "Manifestos" [n.d.], http://www.manifestos.net/titles/ for an excellent public archive of various recent and historical manifestos). And there are many websites featuring instructions on "how to write a manifesto" (a phenomenon that echoes Tristan Tzara's 1918 Dada Manifesto: see Caws 2001: 297; see also Stockwell, this volume). Though some "manifestos" are mere metaphors (using the term "manifesto" simply to mean "a strongly worded statement"), others are passionate appeals to radically new ways of doing things.

One key difference from the historical avant-garde (modernist) manifestos discussed in the first two sections is that contemporary (postmodern) manifestos tend to be more uniformly explicit about the long history of manifesto writing they invoke (and there's more history *to* invoke). Take, for instance, the stir around David Shields' anti-novel *Reality Hunger: A Manifesto* (2010). It begins with an "Overture":

> Every artistic movement from the beginning of time is an attempt to figure out a way to smuggle more of what the artist thinks is reality into the work of art. Zola: "Every proper artist is more or less a realist according to his own

eyes." Braque's goal: "To get as close as I could to reality." E.g., Chekhov's diaries, E.M. Forster's *Commonplace Book*, Fitzgerald's *The Crack-Up* (much his best book), Cheever's posthumously published journals (same), Edward Hoagland's journals, Alan Bennett's *Writing Home*. So, too, every artistic movement or moment needs a credo: Horace's *Ars Poetica*, Sir Philip Sidney's *Defence of Poesie*, Shelley's *A Defence of Poetry*, André Breton's "Surrealist Manifesto," Lars von Trier's "Dogme 95" statement. My intent is to write the *ars poetica* for a burgeoning group of interrelated (but unconnected) artists in a multitude of forms and media (lyric essay, prose poem, collage novel, visual art, film, television, radio, performance art, rap, stand-up comedy, graffiti) who are breaking larger and larger chunks of "reality" into their work. (*Reality*, as Nabokov never got tired of reminding us, is the one work that is meaningless without quotation marks.)

(Shields 2010: 3–4)

Unlike earlier manifestos that sought Enlightenment universality, postmodern manifestos name their particular locations and cite key manifestos and other iconoclastic texts as precursors. However, the "reality" principle of integrating art with life – whether by reaching a large audience beyond the military (as in early French manifestos), or beyond the institution of art (as in the historical avant-garde), or beyond the institutional confines of various media and genres (in postmodernism) – remains the same. So, too, whether the manifesto writers are European or from the global South, they occupy a marginal location and seek via the manifesto to establish a position tangential to a given order (Yu 2009: 14). In effect, as cultures around the world register conflict and change, the manifesto will be marking *and* producing those struggles.

References

Andrade, O. de. (1928) "Cannibal Manifesto." [Online.] Retrieved 28 July 2010, from http://feastof-hateandfear.com/archives/andrade.html.

Apollonio, U. (2001) *Futurist Manifestoes*, Boston, MA: MFA Press.

Appadurai, A. (2010) "Circulation-Forms." *The Salon*, vol. 2 (2010): 5–10 [Online.] Retrieved 25 October 2010, from http://jwtc.org.za/the_salon/volume_2/arjun_Appadurai_circulation_forms.htm.

Bhabha, H. (2004) *The Location of Culture*, New York: Routledge Press.

Brown, N. (2005) *Utopian Generations: The Political Horizon of Twentieth-Century Literature*, Princeton, NJ: Princeton University Press.

Calinescu, M. (1987) *Five Faces of Modernity: Modernism, Avant-Garde, Decadence, Kitsch, Postmodernism*, Durham, NC: Duke University Press.

Caws, M.A. (ed.) (2001) *Manifesto: A Century of isms*, Lincoln, NE: University of Nebraska Press.

Derrida, J. (1982) "Signature, Event, Context." In *Margins of Philosophy*, Chicago, IL: Chicago University Press, pp. 309–30.

—— (1986) "Declarations of Independence," *New Political Science* 15: 7–15.

Gentile, E. (1994) "The Conquest of Modernity: From Modernist Nationalism to Fascism," *Modernism/Modernity* 1(3): 55–87.

Haislip, J. (1997) "Archibald MacLeish: 'Ars Poetica' and Other Observations." In D.Z. Baker (ed.) *Poetics in the Poem: Critical Essays on American Self-Reflexive Poetry*, New York: Peter Lang, pp. 132–47.

Hall, S. (1996) "Race, Articulation, and Societies Structured in Dominance." In H.A. Baker, M. Diawara and R.H. Lindborg (eds.) *Black British Cultural Studies*, Chicago, IL: Chicago University Press, pp. 16–60.

Hjartarson, B. (2007) "Myths of Rupture: The Manifesto and the Concept of the Avant-Garde." In A. Eysteinsson and V. Liska (eds.) *Modernism*, vol. 1, Philadelphia, PA: Johns Benjamins Publishing, pp. 173–94.

Honig, B. (1992) "Towards an Agonistic Feminism: Hannah Arendt and the Politics of Identity." In J. Butler and J.W. Scott (eds.) *Feminists Theorize the Political*, New York: Routledge, pp. 215–35.

Lacoue-Labarthe, P. and J.-L. Nancy (1988) *The Literary Absolute*, Albany, NY: State University of New York.

Lyon, J. (1999) *Manifestoes: Provocations of the Modern*, Ithaca, NY: Cornell University Press.

"Manifestos" (n.d.) [Online.] Retrieved 30 November 2010, from http://www.manifestos.net/titles/

Marcos, S. (2004) *Ya Basta: Ten Years of the Zapatista Uprising*, Oakland, CA: AK Press.

Mignolo, W.D. (2000) *Local Histories/Global Designs: Coloniality, Subaltern Knowledges, and Border Thinking*, Princeton, NJ: Princeton University Press.

Puchner, M. (2006) *Poetry of the Revolution: Marx, Manifestos, and the Avant-Garde*, Princeton, NJ: Princeton University Press.

—— (2007) "Five Theses on the Future of the Manifesto." In K. Nygärd and E. Prestsæter (eds.) *Dokumenterer Fremtiden*, Norway: Rett Kopi, pp. 182–3.

Rosenberg, F.J. (2006) *The Avant-Garde and Geopolitics in Latin America*, Pittsburgh, PA: Pittsburgh University Press.

Schnapp, J. (1999) "Crash (Speed as Engine of Individuation)," *Modernism/Modernity* 6(1): 1–49.

Shields, D. (2010) *Reality Hunger: A Manifesto*, New York: Knopf.

Winkiel, L. (2008) *Modernism, Race and Manifestos*, New York: Cambridge University Press.

Yu, T. (2009) *Race and the Avant-Garde: Experimental and Asian American Poetry Since 1965*, Stanford, CA: Stanford University Press.

Further reading

Perloff, M. (1986) *The Futurist Moment: Avant-Garde, Avant-Guerre, and the Language of Rupture*, Chicago, IL: Chicago University Press.

Somigli, L. (2003) *Legitimizing the Artist: Manifesto Writing and European Modernism, 1885–1915*, Toronto: University of Toronto Press.

Yanoshevsky, G. (2009) "Three Decades of Writing on Manifesto: The Making of a Genre," *Poetics Today* 30(2): 257–86.

20

POST-CRITICISM

Conceptual takes

Gregory L. Ulmer

To laugh at philosophy (at Hegelianism) – such, in effect, is the form of the awakening – henceforth calls for an entire "discipline," an entire "method of meditation" that acknowledges the philosopher's byways, understands his techniques, makes use of his ruses, manipulates his cards, lets him deploy his strategy, appropriates his texts.

(Jacques Derrida 1978: 252)

I. Theory: concept

This essay introduces a post-critical experiment – the invention of a concept adapted to the conditions of electracy. Electracy is to digital technologies what literacy is to alphabetic writing. Critical thinking is a practice specific to literacy, so to speak of an electrate concept for digital reasoning is like referring to an automobile as a horse-less carriage. We live in a transitional moment, however, with experimental modernist literature serving as a bridge between epochs. Post-criticism adapts philosophy to Internet culture. We still need theoretical thinking in electracy, but the old alphabetic techniques of inference are no longer adequate to the task. A methodology for post-criticism is heuretics (the logic of invention). *Heuretics* (Ulmer 1994) appropriated from the history of discourses on method a generative formula for the creation of new forms and practices. The acronym CATTt identifies the set of resources needed for our invention: Contrast, Analogy, Theory, Target, tale. This generator guides our proposal for a hybrid concept (combining features of word and image). The particular quality of thought that we need our concept to support is judgment, individual decision making. "Action proceeds from an exchange between the body and its double; deliberation and decision express this fundamental dialogue. We have two bodies, the physical body and the virtual body. The virtual body consists of all the internal models that comprise the elements of the body schema and allow the brain to simulate and to emulate reality. This body is the one we perceive when we are dreaming. It, too, has a phenomenal reality" (Berthoz 2003: 128). Consciousness, Berthoz proposes, is the product of a dialogue between these two bodies, between "I" and "me." This essay describes the invention of a post-critical concept, to be called "take," that supports this self-communication of decision.

The Theory for inventing this transitional concept is derived from Deleuze and Guattari, especially from *What Is Philosophy?* They argue that the concept as practiced in philosophy still has a role to play in contemporary civilization. Such concepts function through a kind of cinematic *mise-en-scène*. Their working parts include a persona, a problem in the world, an anecdote that dramatizes the thought, a mode of presentation of the scene, and a name for the idea. Socrates, as presented in Plato's dialogues, is the prototype. Socrates embodied the persona of "gadfly," buttonholing citizens in the streets of Athens in search of someone wiser than himself, in order to refute the Delphic oracle's declaration that no man was wiser than Socrates. He dramatized "dialectic" as a mode of thought. We need to generate similar features for our conceptual "take."

A post-critical concept is not confined to the professional or disciplinary parameters of philosophy, but is a means for theoretical thinking native to a civilization of the Internet, in which digital imaging supersedes alphabetic writing. The historical record shows that each innovation in forms and practices of thought preserves some parts of the previous mode, abandons some parts, and adds some new elements. An electrate concept, in this spirit, does not simply reproduce Deleuze and Guattari's proposal, but revises it with our purpose in mind, looking for those aspects of their poetics that lend themselves to digital imaging, while deemphasizing other aspects relevant only to the literate apparatus. In what follows we will work through each resource of the CATTt, making one pass through the generator, to propose a style of written reasoning valid in electracy. Here is our CATTt: Theory by Deleuze and Guattari; Contrast is Commercial advertising; Analogy is experimental modernist arts; Target is the public sphere, deliberative rhetoric, the practice of good judgment needed for a democratic society; tale (the tail of the CATTt), referring to the actual technique used to compose the concept, is pastiche, specifically a pastiche of an aphorism by Franz Kafka. Our version is an invitation to readers to propose their own pass, revising the recipe to taste.

II. Contrast: commerce

Deleuze and Guattari named our Contrast – Commerce – which they credit with having taken over concept production in our era, along with everything else in the order of public discourse. We need a resource to document this domain. Roland Marchand's (1986) history of the creation of the commodity sign is a useful candidate. He begins in the 1920s, which is not the beginning of advertising, but the first full separation of exchange value from use value in guiding promotional thought. Contrast is not a rejection of its source, but an inventory of materials to discover what sorts of concepts Commerce makes. Philosophy can learn something from Commerce about how to adapt to the conditions of electracy. We accept the formal discoveries of Commerce (use of icons, schemas, scenarios, tableaux and the like) but reject its propaganda stance on behalf of corporate profit. Our goal is thinking, not selling/buying. The real craft of using the CATTt generator comes at this point: How do we create (invent) a synthesis, a hybrid of our Theory and Contrast, to formulate an emergent set of instructions for constructing an electrate concept?

Our inventory of Marchand covers what Commerce got right, understanding that the emergence of electracy in a capitalist society is a contingency of history. Marchand describes advertising as the discourse primarily responsible for converting the citizens of the industrial city to the worldview of the new apparatus, which dates from the beginnings of the industrial revolution. This worldview is based in aesthetics, referring to the sensory faculty of taste described by Immanuel Kant in the eighteenth century. The aesthetic image is to electracy what the analytical word is to literacy. The commodity form, separating exchange value from use value, desire from product, expression from object, allowed the pedagogy of aesthetic judgment to operate autonomously. Advertisers realized they were selling not the steak but the sizzle. Electrate intelligence, not just commerce but civics and ethics (practical reason), functions in the dimension of *sizzle*. Advertising discourse disseminated throughout America (and the emerging global economy) the inventions of Paris, including not only "fashion" but the new logic of taste, and the design styles of modernist arts. The appropriation in ad practices of popular culture forms from tabloid magazines to celebrity gossip and movies contributed to the didactic value, assisting the public in internalizing the new native discourse of the image apparatus.

Within this general frame of Commerce as advice on modernization, the ads specifically demonstrated how to construct concepts in the emerging mass media discourse, and this is what Deleuze and Guattari recognized as a direct challenge to Philosophy. An important point of alignment between Deleuze and Guattari and Marchand is precisely here. The philosophical concept includes a *conceptual persona* to mediate between the "name" of the concept (the idea) and the problem plane or discursive field addressed by the idea (between the general and the particular). Literate concepts foreground *idea*; commercial concepts foreground *persona*. Everything that Marchand describes about the strategies of ad campaigns is relevant to the design of post-critical conceptual personae: social tableaux, parables, visual clichés, fantasies and icons. Betty Crocker and her peers are to Commerce what Socrates is to Philosophy. Plato's parable of the cave in the *Republic* dramatizes the essential gesture of philosophy: *conversion*. One prisoner turns around, away from the shadows cast on the walls of the cave, to behold the true light of the sun outside the cave. *Diversion* (the "vert," turn or trope of Commerce) is a conceptual stand of reassurance, crystallizing majority opinion around a few key figures (scenes). The instruction from Contrast is to foreground a persona to dramatize our idea, to show how to stand and turn in a problem field (understanding "turn" as "trope"). Each resource of the CATTt contributes to the final emergent poetics of our post-critical concept in an unpredictable way. The next resource whose contribution we need to inventory is Analogy.

III. Analogy 1: Montmartre Cabaret

Electracy dates from the late eighteenth century, the epoch of revolutions (industrial, bourgeois, representational, technological). We orient ourselves to our own epoch by

269

analogy with the invention of literacy in classical Greece. The term "apparatus" in this context (derived and expanded from media studies) is used to notice that the invention is a matrix including institution formation and identity behavior (individual and collective). A relevant point of the analogy is that in Athens Plato and his students (including Aristotle) created a new institution (the Academy), which opened a new zone in the city within which they invented the devices of "pure thought." This new kind of thought was different from the oral apparatus (religion, ritual, spirit, tribe). It has been dubbed "natural history" retroactively, and eventually became hegemonic, or at least fully independent, in the seventeenth century, the inception of "science" in the modern sense. "Science" as a stand first became possible within the literate apparatus. The related identity inventions are "selfhood" as experience and behavior, and the democratic political state.

Our present moment is the heir of the two previous apparati (orality and literacy), providing two axes guiding (in unstable syncretism) our collective deliberations: right/wrong (oral); true/false (literate). Electracy does not eliminate or replace these two historical orientations, but supplements them with a third stand. The formal practices of electracy are invented primarily in nineteenth-century Paris. *Paris is the Athens of electracy.* The template from Athens maps the dynamics of apparatus creation. Simultaneous with the emergence of bourgeois hegemony, a counterculture zone opened first in Paris, known as "bohemia." The original bohemia was the neighborhood of Montmartre, on the outskirts of Paris. The taverns and bistros of the area provided cheap wine, prostitution, song and dance (all the vices). The first official Cabaret associated with the avant-garde is Le Chat Noir, founded in 1881, followed by the Lapin Agile and the Moulin Rouge. These Cabarets are to electracy what the Academy and Lyceum were to literacy. A good account of the institution formation related to this scene is Pierre Bourdieu (1996). Aesthetic experience is the relevant human capacity to be augmented in the prosthesis (the electrate apparatus), and *pure art* is the means. Bourdieu identifies Baudelaire and Flaubert as the inventors of this stand and formal operation, with Manet as their equivalent in painting. "Before Baudelaire," Walter Benjamin wrote in his study of Paris as the capital of the nineteenth century, "the apache, who lived out his life within the precincts of society and of the big city, had had no place in literature. The most striking depiction of this subject in *Les fleurs du mal*, 'Le Vin de l'Assassin,' inaugurated a Parisian genre. The café known as Le Chat Noir became its 'artistic headquarters.' 'Passant, sois moderne!' was the inscription it bore during its early, heroic period" (Benjamin, 2006: 108). The vanguard revolution more generally subsequently develops and institutionalizes this stand or attitude. The future of electracy involves unfolding the potential of pure art, just as the history of literacy records the unfolding of the potential of pure reason. The new form is an adaptation to the shock of life in the industrial city.

The philosophical account of this historical gambit is familiar, beginning with Kant's promotion of aesthetic judgment (the faculty of taste) to equal status with pure and practical reason. The third faculty added to the axes orienting thought is that of pleasure/pain (Spinoza's joy/sadness). Embodied experience, in other words, is the ground

270

of electrate intelligence. The responsibility of this dimension (distinct from oral salvation or literate engineering) is well-being (thriving). We noted that the commodity form contributes to the invention of electracy by initiating a reformation in Western identity, the most profound since Rome converted to Christianity. In this case it is the conversion to "pleasure" (sensory satisfaction) albeit in the guise of consumerism: the old values of "character" (self-denial) are displaced by "personality" (self-indulgence), opening a new dimension of identity formation. The implications for politics and ethics are substantial: what happens when pleasure/pain (attraction/repulsion) has equal voice relative to right/wrong and true/false in contemporary policy formation? Our post-concept is intended to think precisely this register of experience, *the capacity to be affected*. Both branches of the Western tradition (Greco-Roman and Judeo-Christian) deprecated visceral experience and even condemned human embodiment as misfortune or sin. The challenge of post-criticism is to design practices of thought for an augmented aesthetic prosthesis that make affect intelligent.

IV. Analogy 2: pure attitude

What is the state of mind to be dramatized in the conceptual persona of our post concept? The "pure art" created in Cabaret achieved international recognition ultimately in Dadaism (see Stockwell, this volume), product of Cabaret Voltaire in Zurich (where the scene moved during the World War). The Readymades in general, and "Fountain" in particular (the urinal submitted as a joke to a supposedly non-juried exhibition) make Marcel Duchamp the Aristotle of electracy. "Mona Lisa with a Pipe" (by the artist known as Sapeck, 1887) is emblematic of the attitude that is the "Spirit of Montmartre"expressed in these works. The attitude is *fumisme*, used to name the mocking humor that characterized the Cabaret scene of bohemian Paris. The anchoring term is the verb *fumer* (to smoke), but with a usage in agriculture, "to manure." A *fumiste* is a chimney sweep, with slang extension to name a joker, crackpot, fraud. An immediate point of interest is the background that Sapeck's Mona Lisa provides for Duchamp's more famous readymade (the mustachioed Mona Lisa), composed much later. The choice of iconic image to profane is motivated in part by the term *fumisme* itself. The hazy smoke referenced in this semantic field resonates with one of the important terms used to identify Leonardo's style: *sfumato*. *Sfumato* is a term coined by Leonardo da Vinci to refer to a painting technique which overlays translucent layers of color to create perceptions of depth, volume and form. In Italian *sfumato* means "blended" or "smoky" and is derived from the Italian word *fumo* meaning "smoke." The best example of a *sfumato* painting is Leonardo's *Mona Lisa*.

A "wit" is different from a *fumiste*, a distinction used to clarify the intent of Sapeck's illustrations:

> Whereas the former made fun of idiots in terms that they were not always able to understand, the *fumiste* accepts the ideas of the idiot and expresses their quintessence . . . The *fumiste* avoids discussions of ideas, he does not set

up a specific target, he adopts a posture of withdrawal that makes all distinctions hazy, and he internalizes Universal Stupidity by postulating the illusory nature of values and of the Beautiful, whence his denial of the established order and of official hierarchies. From this point of view, which is that of the sage, the dandy, the observer, and the skeptic, everything has the same value, everything is one and the same thing.

(Grojnowski 1999: 104)

The image of thought mocked in *fumisme* is Descartes' cogito, since, as Deleuze and Guattari observed, the stand of the subject in Descartes' radical doubt (I think, therefore I am) is that of "idiot" in the classical sense of "private person," one who does not participate in the public sphere. This alienated subject finally goes crazy in modernity, they explain, with reference to Dostoevsky.

The key to our concept is to learn from the CATTt how a vital anecdote associated with a conceptual persona performs the desired thought. The relevant documentation in *What Is Philosophy?* is the references to modernist arts practices (literature, painting, music). The mental landscape of thinking relates to the problem plane by means analogous to those invented by Cézanne (for example) to express the physical landscape. The CATTt directs us to adopt the modernist arts plane of composition (invented in Paris) as a relay (Analogy) for treating the conceptual anecdote, in order to create a vector or a different turning within the problem, to challenge the commodity version of contemporary embodiment. The instruction from our Analogy, then, for how to compose a vital anecdote, is Duchamp's Readymade. An example of a Readymade is a postcard representation of Leonardo's *Mona Lisa*, to which Duchamp added a mustache and goatee, plus a caption, L. H. O. O. Q. (the letters punning on a phrase in French meaning "she has a hot ass"). The formal instruction includes not only the attitude, but the device: *take a picture*. The phrase alludes to the technology of imaging, and suggests a name for our concept: *take* (verb/noun). Post-criticism *takes* thought.

V. Target: judgment

How does one *take* a stand or make a turn away from or towards a position by means of our post-concept? Paolo Virno (2008) provides a source for Target (specifying the need or lack to be supplied by our concept). Conceptual thinking continues to be relevant in electracy to the extent that a democratic public sphere is still possible in an Internet civilization. Our concept must support judgment in decision making. Judgment (practical reason) means drawing upon the lessons of the past to make a decision in the present situation promising the best outcome for the future well-being of the community. Good judgment requires the virtue of *phronesis*, prudence. Prudence is a virtue, meaning that it is a matter of disposition, a quality of character. The practice of deliberative rhetoric in the civic sphere follows the paths of inference, beginning with *abduction* from the particular conditions to the rules (an archive of maxims and proverbs representing the wisdom of experience or tradition and its associated respected authorities). Common-sense rules supplied the premises for *deductions* formulating hypothetical cases, which in turn *inductively* were applied to the situation. The problem with practical reason today, Virno observes, is that there is not now, and never has been, a rule for applying the rule to a case. The application requires a decision, and this decision represents the *aporia* (impasse) of ethics.

The *aporia* is even more implacable than Virno admits, since in the sublime conditions of the industrial city the archive of maxims and proverbs recording the wisdom of collective experience lost all authority. Moreover, the locus of causality disappeared from everyday life, to become accessible only to scientific expertise supported by technology. Commerce filled the void, promoting through advertising the conversion of citizens to an entirely new stand, oriented along the axis of pleasure–pain (attraction/repulsion). Wisdom is reduced to taste. Marchand cites a pronouncement made by one advertising agency in the 1920s to note the role Commerce attempted to play:

> The product of advertising is public opinion; and in a democracy public opinion is the uncrowned king. It is the advertising agency's business to write the speeches from the throne of that king; to help his subjects decide what they should eat and wear; how they should invest their savings; by what courses they can improve their minds; and even what laws they should make, and by what faith they may be saved.
>
> (Marchand 1986: 31)

Virno's proposal assumes that we are now living in conditions of a permanent "state of exception," in which the rules guiding judgment may be open to revision, to innovation, to testing against experience. Here is an opportunity for post-criticism. His suggestion to replace valid reasoning with the deliberate use of fallacies, in order to expose the enthymemes, the assumptions and values determining the ineffective deductions guiding decision-making, acknowledges the unconscious as a site of ethical decision unsuspected in pre-modern philosophy. Ethics we now understand is beyond the reach of both reason and will. Fallacies and joke-work are transitional forms manifesting the fourth mode of inference invented in Cabaret: *conduction*. The primary instruction derived from Virno is based on his proposal to adopt logical fallacies (exploiting the structure of joke-work: condensation, displacement, secondary elaboration) as sources of innovative inference practice in conditions of ethical/political crisis. "Jokes and innovative action displace the 'rotational axis' of a form of life by means of an openly 'fallacious' conjecture, one that nonetheless reveals in a flash a different way of applying the rules of the game: contrary to the way it seemed before, it is entirely possible to embark on a side path or to escape from Pharaoh's Egypt" (Virno 2008: 163). Joke-work surprises thought from an unexpected direction.

Here is a call for the rhetoric of *fumisme* proposed by our Analogy. The pragmatics of laughter and the forms that elicit it are guides to the site of interface, the moebius twist, crossing body and language. The two sides of language (biology and culture) are hinged here, enabling discourse and desire (unconscious satisfaction, that the French call *jouissance*) to coexist in one practice. This is the point of departure for electracy as metaphysics. Literacy ontologized the semantic register of writing; electracy ontologizes the libidinal register (the signifier).

The logic of crisis is most evident in the articulation between instinctual apparatus and propositional structure, between drives and grammar. Each attempt at delineating a different normative "substratum," though it unravels within wholly contingent sociopolitical circumstances, retraces and compounds, on a reduced scale, the passage from life in general to linguistic life. Anomalous inferences are the precision instrument by virtue of which verbal thought, delineating a different normative "substratum," recalls, each time anew, the anthropogenetic passage. Their anomaly lies in the manner in which language preserves within itself, though transfigured to the point of being barely recognizable, the original nonlinguistic drive (Virno 2008: 160).

Instruction: Style gives access to embodied (sensory, aesthetic) thought. The lesson of our Target resource, then, is to create a concept capable of supporting judgment (decision) conducted in an aesthetic style. The goal is to activate and administer in writing the drives that accompany meaning. Style is the element of philosophy that survives in electracy.

VI. Tale: Kafka

Tale functions as vehicle for the CATTt inventories. Users encounter the emergent poetics of the invention through a form that partly demonstrates and partly explains the invention. Plato introduced his concept of "method" in the form of "dialogue." Commentators remind us that Plato invented this form, but we recognize in it the vital anecdote: the scene of Socrates conversing with interlocutors is an interface, embedding the encounter with dialectic in a familiar situation. Dialectic (method) is a core practice of literacy, unfamiliar in the oral culture of Athens, transitioning from orality to literacy. In the terms of our CATTt, "Socrates" is Plato's conceptual persona. Part of the nature and purpose of "method" as concept is communicated by the aura associated with Socrates as an iconic type: the gadfly. The image of thought associated with this icon is complex, including the representation of Socrates as a sophist in Aristophanes's *The Clouds*. Deleuze and Guattari give many examples of this holistic effect of the conceptual persona portraying an image of thought.

> Kierkegaard's "knight of the faith," he who makes the leap, or Pascal's gambler, he who throws the dice, are men of a transcendence or a faith. But they constantly recharge immanence: they are philosophers or, rather, intercessors, conceptual personae who stand in for these two philosophers and who are concerned no longer with the transcendent existence of God but only with the infinite immanent possibilities brought by the one who believes that God exists.
>
> (Deleuze and Guattari 1996: 74)

The tale is usually selected from among the forms available within one of the other resources of the CATTt. Analogy is often used, since it already proposes a version of the desired invention. A prototype for a vital anecdote in which to present the stand of take may be selected from among those writers most expressive of the experience of the modernist city. Perhaps any modernist or experimental writer could fulfill this role and be our Socrates, although the specific choice inflects the thought necessarily (here is an opportunity for further experiment). Most of the themes relevant to *judgment* (our Target) are treated in the work of Franz Kafka, so let Kafka be our conceptual persona. The contextual rationale for this choice is testimony that Kafka laughed when he read his stories to his friends in the cafés. Kafka's laughter is the vital anecdote of take, especially since few readers are in on the joke. Part of the semantics of "take" as operational concept, then, includes the aura of "Kafka" (the Kafkaesque), exemplifying the stand of the subject as modern "idiot" (the cogito gone mad). More specifically, the parable "Before the Law," introduced as a play-within-the-play in *The Trial*, suggests the nature of the threshold position occupied by the post-concept. The heuretic method of our experiment is not to "be Kafka," but to seek what he sought, borrowing his writing strategies, such as the parable and aphorism, the way Plato borrowed Socrates's questioning. The man from the country (the rube, the idiot) comes to the city and encounters the "law" as a gateway guarded by a doorkeeper (a threshold guardian, a daimon). The ambiguous lesson (the man waits his whole life before the doorway, and it finally is closed as he approaches death, since it existed only for him) is kairotic: *kairos*. *The Trial* and *The Castle* both treat this theme of the Moment, and the fear of missing it, the missed encounter, the failed promise of happiness or fulfillment. In both stories the protagonist comes very close to the "bridge," to the moment that would open the link between two realms (whatever they might be – immanence and transcendence) (Calasso 2005: 226).

The importance of Kafka for electracy is that he shows us a world in which the literate *category* has become total and absolute. What recommends Kafka for our persona is not only his existential metaphysics, but that his aesthetic strategy is to literalize or extend a commonplace phrase, idiom, figure or trope as a device for his own use, turning clichés into probes. His writing technique is that of the modified readymade, and in this he fulfills Baudelaire's ambition to invent a new kind of cliché. *The Trial* may be read in this light as imagining a world in which the accusatory mood present in the etymology of the word "category" (originally associated with the vocabulary of the courts and the practice of indictment) spreads from metaphysics into all experience. As Milan Kundera (among many others) observed, Kafka's vision of a society run by "tribunal" became reality for millions of people in the Camps. To live "categorically" is a nightmare. "The trial brought by the tribunal is always *absolute*; meaning that it does not concern an isolated act, a specific crime (theft, fraud, rape), but rather concerns the character of the accused in its entirety: K. searches for his offense in 'the most minute events' of his *whole* life" (Kundera 1993: 227). In a conceptual take, aesthetics replaces jurisprudence as the source for a turn away from "category."

VII. Conclusion: take

We *take* for the tale of our CATTt, for the presentation of our post-concept, the following passage from Kafka as a template for writing a judgment. The goal is for writers themselves to *receive* a feeling accessible exclusively through the style of writing (the musical, libidinal dimension of language). The procedure is *pastiche*, one of the devices of imitation of an existing work in the family that includes parody dear to Parisian *fumistes*. To practice take requires composing an imitation of an existing text, adapting it to evoke a thought of one's own. This passage by Kafka (from the *Blue Octavo Notebooks*) outlines an affective thought (numbers added for subsequent analysis). These notebooks, composed in the final years of Kafka's life, were self-addressed (famously, Kafka asked his friend Max Brod to burn all his writings). You may use the following passage to test the practice, or select some other one.

> 1) Is it possible to think something unconsoling? Or, rather, something unconsoling without the breath of consolation? A way out [Ausweg] would seem to lie in the fact that recognition as such is consolation. 2) And so one might well think: You must put yourself aside, and yet one might maintain oneself, without falsifying this recognition, by the consciousness of having recognized it. 3) That, then, really means having pulled oneself out of the swamp by one's own pigtail. 4) What is ridiculous in the physical world is possible in the spiritual world. *There* there is no law of gravity (the angels do not fly, they have not overcome any force of gravity, it is only we observers in the terrestrial world who cannot imagine it in any better way than that), which is, of course, beyond our power of conception, or at any rate conceivable only on a very high level. 5) How pathetically scanty my self-knowledge is compared with, say, my knowledge of my room. (Evening). Why? There is no such thing as observation of the inner world, as there is of the outer world. At least descriptive psychology is probably, taken as a whole, a form of anthropomorphism, a nibbling at our own limits. The inner world can only be experienced, not described. 6) Psychology is the description of the reflection of the terrestrial world in the heavenly plane, or, more correctly, the description of a reflection such as we, soaked as we are in our terrestrial nature, imagine it, for no reflection actually occurs, only we see earth wherever we turn.
>
> (Kafka 1991 [composed 1917; first published 1953]: 14)

Kafka's aphoristic composition may be generalized into a genre. This passage was analyzed by Richard T. Gray (1987), which is the basis for the following heuretic recipe. (1) Begin with a keyword, contextualized by a thought problem: *Ausweg* – a way out, a dodge or expedient; it also evokes the "no way" (*Ausweglos*) of aporia, the impasse whose primary manifestation structuring our lifeworld is mortality (but any keyword may be substituted). Kafka exploits the multivalence of the term. (2) Take the question literally, or apply it to a concrete circumstance, such as a person contemplating suicide (?). The rhetorical trick: to recognize that there is no consolation is itself a consolation. (3) Find an analogy (or metaphor) in art, in this case in one of the tales attributed to Baron von Munchausen (this source could be the origin of the exercise, to appropriate a commonplace as a parable for your own feeling). (4) Recast the analogy as a proposition (the dichotomy dividing the physical and spiritual world). Explain the principles organizing this imaginative stance (free of the laws of physics). (5) Apply to one's own world-view (draw a personal conclusion). (6) Recast the personal insight as a tag line, or generalize it in aphoristic form. Use this sequence to generate one's own attitude toward the same keyword, or with respect to another such term of one's own repertoire, finding your own proverbial commonplace to use as pivot image.

In practice, take replaces definition with pastiche, which may be applied to a passage from any writer whose style is accessed as a vehicle for thought, to tap into the libidinal side of language. In order to feel the thought, and occupy the stand, you must compose your own version, your own take. Each take is singular. Here is my turn, reflecting on the potential of post-criticism in my own situation:

> Is it possible to receive your own post as if for the first time, as if it were news about yourself originating from abroad? This prospect articulates the aporia, the no/way or im/passe in the circuit of auto-affection. The probe is self-addressed (middle voice), in order to attune and open the channel of take as relation. To subscribe to this channel one must use the good offices of a surrogate, a go-between (a prosopon). That, then, really means recognizing your autobiography in the schtick of a Punch and Judy show. What is commonplace, even stereotyped, in the physical world is obscure, indeterminate in the spiritual one. There are no stock characters, no plot formulas, or rather, it is only we self-observers who continue to miss the point of our love for puppet shows. How pathetically scanty is my self-knowledge compared with, say, my knowledge of my home town. (Past). And so? Any observation of the inner world is accomplished through sketches of the outer world. At least expression is doubtless a form of improvisational theater, an abstract graphing of one's own shape. The inner life may be figured, not narrated, described, or analyzed. Expression is the opening of a passage between the two sides of life (the im/material). Or, more correctly, the invention of an aesthetic effigy that neither resembles nor indexes either dimension of my nature, since, immersed as we are in spectacle, we only see programming wherever we turn.

Pastiche retrieves from its source text a thought specifically evoked by style (Dyer, 2007). A written take is self-addressed. The communication channel in need of augmentation in electracy is between I and Me (for each one of us). Take as Internet concept is a product of our CATTt. It is not merely a synthesis of the CATTt, but an extrapolation emerging unpredictably from the intertext of the CATTt sources. The CATTt resources included: Contrast (advertising discourse); Analogy (Parisian Cabaret vanguard arts); Theory (Deleuze and Guattari, *What Is Philosophy?*); Target (practical reason, judgment); tale (Kafka's *Blue Octavo Notebooks*).

To summarize our *post-concept* itself (following the formula of Deleuze and Guattari): Name (Take); Persona (Kafka); Anecdote (Kafka laughing as he read his works to his friends in a Prague cafe); Presentation (aphoristic pastiche); Stand (the affect experienced through Kafka's style, primarily by the composer, but also by the reader). The vital anecdote of take includes the dramatization of judgment between two trials. The post-critical thought is *an experience of limitation*, achieved by recognizing one's own feeling in an appropriated style. We saw this event of measure with Socrates, at the beginning of Western metaphysics. Socrates consulted his *daimonion* (only a voice) at his doorway, before leaving to attend his trial for corrupting the young, and hears nothing, meaning that his decision to cooperate with the court was just. Aristotle, thereafter, used the term for "indictment" (*Kategory*) to name the new classification system of literacy, thus signaling a changed stand from Plato's "apology" ("apology" meaning originally "defense" in court). The arc nears completion with Kafka's *The Trial* (including the parable of the Law), dramatizing the saturation of modern experience by "indictment" (to be under arrest). The doorkeeper plays daimon for the man from the country in Kafka's parable. Now I take Kafka as my daimon (to take my measure). Assignment (for post-critics): take the measure of the joy/sadness (attraction/repulsion) axis for yourself, since electrate *judgment* happens in your body (in a blink) and may only be undergone (aesthetically), not understood (logically). It is not universal but singular. To get it you have to write.

References

Benjamin, W. (2006) *The Writer of Modern Life: Essays on Charles Baudelaire*, ed. M. W. Jennings, trans. H. Eiland *et al.*, Cambridge, MA: Harvard University Press.

Berthoz, A. (2003) *Emotion and Reason: The Cognitive Neuroscience of Decision Making*, trans. G. Weiss, New York: Oxford University Press.

Bourdieu, P. (1996) *The Rules of Art: Genesis and Structure of the Literary Field*, trans. S. Emanuel, Stanford, CA: Stanford University Press.

Calasso, R. (2005) *K*, trans. G. Brock, New York: Knopf.

Deleuze, G. and F. Guattari (1996) *What Is Philosophy?* trans. J. Tomlinson and G. Burchell III, New York: Columbia University Press.

Derrida, J. (1978) *Writing and Difference*, trans. A. Bass, Chicago, IL: University of Chicago Press.

Dyer, R. (2007) *Pastiche*, New York: Routledge.

Gray, R. T. (1987) *Constructive Destruction: Kafka's Aphorisms*, Tübingen, Germany: M. Niemeyer.

Grojnowski, D. (1999) In P.D. Cate (ed.) *The Spirit of Montmartre: Cabarets, Humor, and the Avant-Garde, 1875–1905*, Piscataway, NJ: Rutgers University Press.

Kafka, F. (1991) *The Blue Octavo Notebooks*, trans. E. Kaiser and E. Wilkins, Cambridge, MA: Exact Change Press.

Kundera, M. (1993) *Testaments Betrayed*, trans. L. Asher, New York: Harper Collins.

Marchand, R. (1986) *Advertising the American Dream: Making Way for Modernity, 1920–1940*, Berkeley, CA: University of California Press.

Ulmer, G.L. (1994) *Heuretics: The Logic of Invention*, Baltimore, MD: Johns Hopkins University Press.

Virno, P. (2008) *Multitude: Between Innovation and Negation*, trans. I. Bertoletti *et al.*, Los Angeles, CA: Semiotexte.

Part II
EXPERIMENT NOW
Printed matter

21

THE EXPANDED FIELD OF *L=A=N=G=U=A=G=E*

Charles Bernstein

L=A=N=G=U=A=G=E magazine, which I edited with Bruce Andrews, published its first issue in 1978 and its last in 1982. In our preface to *The L=A=N=G=U=A=G=E Book* (1984), we provided a summary of our editorial project:

> Throughout, we have emphasized a spectrum of writing that places its attention primarily on language and ways of making meaning, that takes for granted neither vocabulary, grammar, process, shape, syntax, program, or subject matter. All of these remain at issue. Focussing on this range of poetic exploration, and on related aesthetic and political concerns, we have tried to open things up beyond correspondence and conversation: to break down some unnecessary self-encapsulation of writers (person from person, & scene from scene), and to develop more fully the latticework of those involved in aesthetically related activity.
>
> (Andrews and Bernstein 1984: ix)

At its most fundamental level, *L=A=N=G=U=A=G=E* was an editorial action: a frame for selecting and combining a range of disparate poetic practices and critical thinking. We didn't capture an already-existing, fully formed aesthetic as much as participate in its creation. The approaches to poetry explored in *L=A=N=G=U=A=G=E* were emerging in the mid-1970s in several small press magazine and presses and in a number of local reading series. *L=A=N=G=U=A=G=E* poetry, under its many different names – Language Poetry, Language Poetries, Language Writing, Language-Centered Writing – mark different frames of a field of poetic activity that has no unified stylistic consistency. Bruce Andrews's epithet, "so-called," and more precisely, "so-called so-called language writing," suggests an ongoing ambivalence about labeling, for one of the obsessions of (one fraction) of this poetic constellation was a resistance to (or phobia about) naming, characterization, and standardized modes of representation. So the description is part of the "problematic," and it remains an open question whether this constellation of activity was a movement or school, aesthetic tendency or convenient label, and whether the names for the phenomena were insulting labels or a standard for group solidarity.

For some practitioners and advocates, the local scene played a fundamental role, for others it was a set of defining aesthetic principles, while for others still the most important thing was the exchange across geographic borders. All three aspects are vital parts of the story. Overall, there was a commitment to poetry as a social activity – an equal commitment to exchange value as to the value of individual works.

$L=A=N=G=U=A=G=E$ was a site of conversation about a set of marked issues, a place to air differences but not necessarily to settle them. That conversation was radically distinct from the values of the official verse culture of the time, not only in terms of what poetry is, what it does, and how it works, but also in terms of the commitment to group and community formation through conversation. $L=A=N=G=U=A=G=E$ and the poetry and poetics surrounding it was formed in controversy and remained controversial because its unity was not a set of agreed upon aesthetic principles, but rather an aversion to the conservative dogmas of much of the dominant poetry of the time. Yet, despite its unruliness, the ensemble of activities that falls under this rubric does share a family resemblance – to use Wittgenstein's term. Both the poetry and poetics posed a stark alternative to the prized poetry of the era.

$L=A=N=G=U=A=G=E$ made a turn from some aspects of modernist avant-garde formations, staying clear of univocal manifestoes, though not from polemic intervention. This is not to say that social or aesthetic insularity, or the promotion of particular styles, was not present, but that it was neither governing nor defining. Indeed, a pervasive wariness about, combined with a peculiar devotion to, some of the more doctrinaire aspects of the modernist avant-garde formations was one of the constituent interests in the formation of the work in and around $L=A=N=G=U=A=G=E$.

$L=A=N=G=U=A=G=E$ primarily focused on poets from the U.S. and Canada born from the mid-1930s to the mid-1950s. Some of these poets had a greater affiliation with the project while others (call them fellow travelers) were more averse to affiliation; both pulls, one to the idiosyncratic and the other toward group solidarity, are constituent of the field. It is my intention to note the contributions across this spectrum. Many of the key poets were born during the Second World War and much of their work was formative to the development of the expanded field of $L=A=N=G=U=A=G=E$, at the time and after, even if as individuals some were skeptical of some of the theoretical articulations or group framing. In hindsight, among the signature poets of this older half-generation are Clark Coolidge, Lyn Hejinian, Robert Grenier, Ted Greenwald, Susan Howe, Rosmarie Waldrop, Leslie Scalapino, and Michael Palmer. The poets born in 1945 and after had a sometimes different generational consciousness that affected our poetics; in hindsight, among the signature poets of this younger half-generation are Ron Silliman, Steve McCaffery, Bruce Andrews, Johanna Drucker, Rae Armantrout, Harryette Mullen, Bob Perelman, Bernadette Mayer, Barrett Watten, and Mei-mei Berssenbrugge. Jackson Mac Low, Hannah Weiner, and David Bromige, though of the New American Poetry generation (see Lee, this volume), became part and parcel of our work. Dozens of other poets made crucial contributions to the field, so such a list necessarily leaves out many of the most significant contributions, a few of which are detailed in what follows; indeed, as a call for poems for a new, highly ephemeral, magazine rightly insisted in the early 1990s: *you may be a language poet and not know it.*

Key geographic centers for this work were New York, the San Francisco Bay Area, Washington, DC, and Toronto, with perhaps the most intense reformulation and extension of the work occurring in the late 1980s and 1990s in Vancouver, with the Kootenay School of Writing. (For a list of key magazines and anthologies, see *Further Reading,* below.)

Linguistically innovative British poetry has had a close connection to its American cousin, while remaining distinctive and self-generating. Bob Cobbing's Writer's Workshop spawned a generation of mostly London-based VVV poets (*verbal-vocal-visual,* in James Joyce's phrase), whose "messy" mimeo productions combined word and image. In contrast, Cambridge has been the site of intensely compacted "sprung" lyric production. If Tom Raworth's open, speedy, socially charged poems are one pole, then J.H. Prynne's tightly wired renunciations are the other. In between there are Allen Fisher's process-oriented explorations of discrete forms and vocabularies, Maggie O'Sullivan's exuberant recreation of a virtually magical charm-melos, Denise Riley's stunning engendering of the lyric, cris cheek's conceptual performances, Bill Griffith's syntactic invention and accentual insistences. The fine poet Ken Edwards published in the U.K. some of the earliest L=A=N=G=U=A=G=E-related works in the 1970s and 1980s. But perhaps the most striking parallel to many of the ideas explored in L=A=N=G=U=A=G=E is to be found in Veronica Forrest-Thomson's critical work *Poetic Artifice* (1978).

A few of the younger British and Irish poets continuing in these directions include Caroline Bergvall, Drew Milne, Catherine Walsh, Tim Atkins, Miles Champion, and Redell Olsen, who, along with Robert Sheppherd, John Wilkinson, Peter Middleton, and Fisher have made a significant commitment to poetics as well as poetry. In New Zealand, there has been a strong connection with Wystan Curnow, Alan Loney, Michelle Leggott, and the late Leigh Davis. In Australia, John Tranter's *Jacket Magazine,* probably the best web literary magazine of the past decade, did a remarkable job of covering the broader field of English language innovative poetries.

There are many international associations with the expanded field of L=A=N=G=U=A=G=E, which has in the twenty-first century moved toward a transnational use of English as a medium for radical poetic practice by non-native speakers, as advocated by Finnish poet Leevi Lehto. Strong affiliations have been established between the U.S. and Canadian poets and those in other parts of the Americas (Brazil, Argentina, Cuba, Mexico), Europe (including Russia and Scandinavia) and China. But the link with French poetry stands out for its historical continuity and density, with a number of active poet/translators, including Rosmarie and Keith Waldrop, Ron Padgett, Cole Swenson, Norma Cole, Michael Palmer, and Stacy Doris, who have translated Emmanuel Hocquard, Claude Royet-Journoud, Anne-Marie Albiach,

Dominique Fourcade, Danielle Collobert, Christopher Tarkos, and Olivier Cadiot. Many the American poets discussed here have been translated into French, through such groups as Bureau sur l'Atlantique, the Royaumont literary center, and Double Change, as well as in a pair of anthologies edited by Hocquard and Royet-Journoud (1986, 1991).

I. Poetics and literary history

$L=A=N=G=U=A=G=E$ published not poetry but poetics; the importance of an activist poetics – thinking with the poem – is a crucial feature of the expanded field of activity around the magazine. Poetics is different from literary criticism or journalism in its primary engagement with *poesis* and *faktura*, the art of making. In $L=A=N=G=U=A=G=E$, poetics was conceived as reflections, investigations, and speculations by and for poets. In particular we emphasized nonexpository approaches to critical thinking, discursive writing where the compositional imperatives of poem-making were manifest. In the Bay Area in the 1970s, Perelman started a series of "talks," which encouraged informal thinking out loud; this format was picked up by San Francisco's 80 Langton Street and proliferated from there. For American poetry, one of the unique contributions of this emphasis on poetics has been an unprecedented number of books of critical writing published by poets in the larger $L=A=N=G=U=A=G=E$ context, including Silliman, Hejinian, Scalapino, McCaffery, Susan Howe, Palmer, Watten, Nick Piombino, Fanny Howe, Rosmarie Waldrop, Mullen, Andrews, Armantrout, Nathaniel Mackey, Ann Lauterbach, Messerli, Madeline Gins, Hank Lazer, Eileen Myles, Abigail Child, Susan Stewart, Loss Pequeño Glazier, Perelman, Lorenzo Thomas, Rachel Blau DuPlessis, Pierre Joris, Kathleen Fraser, Grenier (in ms.), Stephen Ratcliffe, Anne Waldman, Ron Padgett, Dick Higgins, Erin Moure, Adeena Karasick, Norma Cole, George Quasha, Marlene NourbeSe Philip, and Joan Retallack. The work of literary critics provided an increasingly significant dialog with the poets. Marjorie Perloff's "The Word as Such: Language Poetries in the Eighties" (1984) was instrumental to bringing this work to a wider audience; Perloff's subsequent essays, along with books and essays by Jerome McGann, Jed Rasula, Michael Davidson, Alan Golding, and A.L. Nielsen extended and deepened the poetics of $L=A=N=G=U=A=G=E$.

While few of the $L=A=N=G=U=A=G=E$ poets were connected to universities in the 1970s, by the 1990s, several of the poets had taken teaching jobs (some after completing graduate studies and some not). In 1991, Robert Creeley, Susan Howe, Raymond Federman, Dennis Tedlock and I founded the Poetics Program at SUNY-Buffalo. Following on such nontraditional arts programs as Black Mountain College, this was a Ph.D. program in which innovative poets taught literature rather than creative writing, and graduate students combined work as active poets, editors, and scholars.

$L=A=N=G=U=A=G=E$ is associated not only with poetic practice but also with an active effort to reclaim the legacy of radical modernist poetry from revisionist, anti-modernist accounts. Strenuous efforts to place Gertrude Stein's work at the center of first-wave modernism have largely succeeded; equally important has been the greater attention to the second-wave modernists such as Louis Zukofsky, George Oppen, Lorine Neidecker – the Objectivists – as well as Laura Riding and Mina Loy. There was also a clear, and much acknowledged, connection to Russian Formalism and Futurism (see White, this volume).

Unlike some modernist avant-garde movements, the poets in the expanded field of *L=A=N=G=U=A=G=E* were as much involved with an extension of the aesthetic and political radicalism of their poetic predecessors as breaking with them to create new works. For a few, Blake, in his "Mental Fight," remained a preceding poetic angel, as did Mallarmé and Baudelaire, Poe and Dickinson.

Still, the greatest literary debt for most of these poets was probably the immediately prior generation of the *New American Poetry*, to use the title of Don Allen's 1960 anthology as a convenient label for the poetry and poetics of the New York School (Barbara Guest, John Ashbery, Frank O'Hara, James Schuyler), the Beats (William Burroughs, Allen Ginsberg, Jack Kerouac), the San Francisco Renaissance (Jack Spicer, Robin Blaser, Robert Duncan, Philip Whalen), the Black Arts Movement (Amiri Baraka), Projectivism/Black Mountain (Larry Eigner, Charles Olson, Robert Creeley, John Wieners), Ethnopoetics (Rothenberg), and Talk/Performance poetry (David Antin). (See Lee, this volume.)

II. Frames and contexts

Philosophy and linguistics

Ludwig Wittgenstein is a foundational thinker for the turn to language, taken up, some might say with a vengeance, in *L=A=N=G=U=A=G=E*. Wittgenstein's work cannot directly be translated into a poetic practice and his emphasis on ordinary language puts him at some distance from poetry that emphasizes invented and queer language. And yet, Wittgenstein's recognition of how the language we use shapes how we perceive the things of the world is fundamental to the work in and around *L=A=N=G=U=A=G=E*. Some of the poets specifically cite Wittgenstein – his propositional style is a ghostly presence in the early poetry of Palmer, while the fullest poetic account of this work comes in Rosmarie Waldrop's *Reproduction of Profiles* (1987), where she turns his philosophical dialogues into gendered conversation. Among linguists, Roman Jakobson, who was closely associated with the Russian Futurists, provides the most influential account of the poetic function – verbal language that foregrounds its material (acoustic and syntactic) features, providing an understanding of poetry as less about communicating a message than an engagement with the medium of verbal language itself. Another crucial philosophic source is the work of Walter Benjamin, both his interest in "language as such" in the context of media theory, and his engagement with found or citational language.

A larger context for these philosophical dispositions might be found in Ralph Waldo Emerson's essays, where process is valued over predetermined or fixed goals and where mood and inconsistency is found to be a stronger affective ground than stylistic uniformity and continuity. Emerson's emphasis on "aversion of conformity," stressed by contemporary American philosopher Stanley Cavell, resonates with some of the poetics in and around $L=A=N=G=U=A=G=E$, despite Emerson's attraction to reconciliation, which is at odds with the more polemical agonism and ideological conflict of the later poets. $L=A=N=G=U=A=G=E$ was contemporary with the rise of post-structuralism in the U.S., and while post-structuralist thinking and that of $L=A=N=G=U=A=G=E$ overlap, the latter's project was to relate such thought to a radical poetry of invention. In this context, there is surely a symbiotic relation to the work of Jacques Derrida, Michel Foucault, Emmanuel Levinas, Gilles Deleuze and Felix Guattari, and, more specifically, Roland Barthes's writing about writing, as in *Writing Degree Zero* (1953). More recently, the work of linguist George Lakoff on the importance of metaphors in framing meaning directly connects with the approaches to breaking frames and reframing that is ubiquitous in much of the poetry under consideration here.

Ideology

The poets associated with $L=A=N=G=U=A=G=E$ came of age during the protests against the Vietnam war, with the shadow of the Second World War still hanging over us. Several of the participants were active in the anti-war movement of the 1960s and all were deeply affected by the civil rights movement of the 1950s and 1960s. The mid-century catastrophe of the Holocaust and the atomic bombing of Japan created, for this generation of poets, a skepticism toward received ideas of technological, economic, and cultural progress – well known from accounts of the Sixties and its counter-cultures, from psychedelic counter-realities to sexual counter-genders.

There was a strong desire to connect oppositional political and cultural views with linguistically inventive writing, breaking sharply from leftist art that was representational and conventionally populist. At the most basic level, there was a sense that words did not always mean what they said, that language is never neutral but rather always betrays an ideological interest and unstated messages. This was the focus of the anthology, *The Politics of Poetic Form: Poetry and Public Policy* (1990), which I edited. The idea was not that poetry can be "pure" and beyond such interests – the sort of Romantic ideology (in McGann's phrase) that was rejected by the poets – but that poetry can "lay bare the device" by "making strange" or "defamiliarizing" (*ostranie*) (the terms are from the Russian Formalist Viktor Shklovsky); that is, poems can make the metaphoricity of our perception in and through language more palpable. This approach also related to Bertolt Brecht's "alienation" or "distancing" effect (*Verfremdungseffekt*): the idea that one can look aslant at what one is experiencing, to get glimmers of its means of production. Surely the influence of Marx hovers over all this, and especially that of his latter-day interpreter Louis Althusser in "Ideology and Ideological State Apparatuses" (1970). The Frankfurt School's ideological critique, especially the work of Theodor Adorno, provides another useful frame for understanding these issues. But it should be noted that many of the most brilliant poets of this field did not read, and were not directly influenced by, the political, philosophical, and linguistic thinkers detailed here. Still, the ideas were in the air for all to breathe, as was the desire to formulate an "oppositional poetics," to quote the title of an influential essay by Erica Hunt from *The Politics of Poetic Form*.

Feminism

The feminism of the 1970s had a powerful effect on both poetic practice and social formation, which is not to say that the poets involved were free of the effects of misogyny among ourselves and in our culture. (Davidson [1995] has written about compulsory homosociality in the New American Poetry communities.) Formally, feminism offered a tangible and tantalizing diacritical perspective on the gender narratives of both grammar and the lyric, as exemplified by the work of Quebec poet Nicole Brossard. Hejinian's signal essay, "The Rejection of Closure" (Hejinian 2000: 40–58), is closely related in a critique of the Faustian desire to possess knowledge, which Hejinian contrasts with an epistemology figured in terms of Scheherazade's refusal of closure. Hejinian's critique, informed by feminism, provides a grounding for an alternative, exploratory, research-oriented poetics.

How (ever), edited by Kathleen Fraser starting in 1983, provided a crucial space for the exploration of these issues, which have been specifically addressed in critical writing and poems by Howe, Drucker, DuPlessis, Scalapino, Carla Harryman, Armantrout, Mullen, Hunt, Waldrop, Lauterbach, O'Sullivan, Moure, Myles, Joan Retallack, and Chris Tysh, among others, and pursued – in very different, often unexpected ways – by such younger writers as Juliana Spahr, Bergvall, Lisa Robertson, Nada Gordon, and Tracie Morris.

Transparency, reference, meaning, and the reader

Silliman's 1977 essay "Disappearance of the Word, Appearance of the World" (reprinted in Andrews and Bernstein 1984: 121–32) focused on the transparency effect of much conventional writing, where language is used instrumentally, like a window, to reveal only what is on the other side of the pane. To Silliman, the erasure of the traces of glass – the social materiality of the linguistic – makes language into a commodity, valued for what it produces while its process of production is repressed.

Silliman advocated a poetry that makes the social materiality of language more apparent (or opaque). Around the same time, McCaffery and Andrews were exploring the "politics of the referent" and advocating a poetry that foregrounded sound and syntax. Meaning and reference do not disappear from this new poetry, but other ways of making meaning, and a greater range of possibilities for linguistic reference, are activated. Such "language-centered" writing was not intended to replace all other forms of writing but rather to open up new spaces for poetry and to combat the dogma that the only goal of writing is to produce transparent, conventionally representational works or I-centered lyric utterances – direct expressions of an author's feelings (as if unmediated by language).

In this sense, Silliman, McCaffery, and Andrews were arguing for a poetry that did not use words instrumentally but rather created a non-purpose-driven aesthetic space, which allowed for the pleasure in reflection, projection, and sensory engagement with verbal materials. This writing would create a very different role for the reader, as Mac Low argued: the work was not language centered but perceiver- (or reader-) centered. The imaginations of readers were activated: they were not told what to think or feel or see but encouraged to make intuitive leaps: to *interenact* – as I like to say it – rather than passively consume. Certainly, many of the poets created a "small (or large) machine made of words" (in William Carlos Williams's phrase), semi-autonomous objects or contraptions that don't so much *tell* as *do*. In this way, poetry becomes an act of construction rather than a transfer of pre-existing information.

Expression, self, voice, rhetoric, affect

The move toward opacity and away from transparency reflected a view that poetry was a mode of rhetoric not an expression of unmediated truth. However, the typically pragmatist poetics of $L=A=N=G=U=A=G=E$ rejected a hermeneutics of suspicion – the idea that truth and meaning are fundamentally unknowable – often associated with post-structuralism in theory and postmodernism in the arts. $L=A=N=G=U=A=G=E$ was not about deconstruction as an end in itself but about reconstruction, emplacement, and enactment: it was constructivist. In $L=A=N=G=U=A=G=E$ poetry, syllogistic logic and naturalistic plot gave way to intuitively felt, aesthetically designed, or programmatically arranged connections among elements of a work. The poem was imagined not as the fixed voice of a self-contained ego conveying a predetermined, or paraphrasable, message but a collage or constellation of textual elements: not voice, but voicings. The expression in the poem lies not in the message of the poet's autonomous lyric voice but in the process of an affective and dynamic compositional field. While the conventional lyric of the time stated or named its emotional content, this new poetry enacted its affective state. The move was from emptied-out emotional behavior to a new linguistic sentience. The self was not something assumed in such poems, but found in the act of collaboration with the language of the poem and the reader's response.

Speech

Grenier's assertion, "I HATE SPEECH," from the first issue of *This* magazine (1971) is often mistakenly taken as a manifesto against speech; it should not be missed that the remark is itself a speech act. Grenier's call is against the way utterance is tamed and indeed reified in much conventional voice-centered poetry. Indeed the vernacular, dialect, slang, and speech acts – voicings more than " *voice*"– pervade the poetry under discussion here. Greenwald's work, with its down-to-earth vocabulary, is rooted in the spoken, even if it spins the spoken into artifice or variation and recombination. Marked local accent also plays an important part in the work of Raworth, Lorenzo

Thomas, and Michael Gizzi. Mullen's *Muse & Drudge* (1995) is a masterpiece of the vernacular, taking demotic (everyday) "folk" material such as nursery rhymes and African-American songs, calls, and speech to quilt a wild lyric ballad, rooted in its embodied rhythms.

Minimalism

From the late 1960s to the mid-1970s, Clark Coolidge and Aram Saroyan created poems with very basic linguistic units, from a single word on a page, to juxtapositions of two words, from a work made up of only prepositions to works with permutations of a restricted vocabulary. Greenwald's *Makes Sense* (1975) and Raworth's *Ace* poems (1974) with single word lines might be considered in this context, as well as Kit Robinson's *Dolch Stanzas* (1976), made up of a small set of the most frequently used words in English. Carl Andre's 1970s grid poems are also related. Such minimalism focused attention on small units of language, which were rhythmically charged by the repetition and displacement inherent in their serial or permutational forms. Grenier's *Sentences* (1978) consisted of 500 large-format index cards, each with a short poem or utterance; freed from the constraint of a bound book, the work could be read in any order; this was not a collection of tiny poems but a long-poem with shifting relations among the parts.

Disjunction, fragment, recombination, collage, overlay, and constellation

One of the most typical stylistic features associated with the *L=A=N=G=U=A=G=E* poetries of the 1970s and 1980s is disjunction, or parataxis. Logical connectors between elements have been elided to create a poetic force field that relies on sound, rhythm, motif, intuitively felt connections, or structural programs/constraints. On one end of the spectrum, there is Silliman's *Tjanting* (1978), which uses the Fibonacci series to determine the number of sentences in each paragraph. At the other end are Susan Howe's rhetorically thrilling juxtapositions of historical material as a way to giving voice to the silenced. In her poetry, Scalapino has worked with linguistic displacement/replacement to create four-dimensional sonic holograms, with deep affective resonance. These approaches – and they are just a few of very many – work not toward fragmentation but from fragmentation (often considered the social given). The works use disjunction and overlay to create constellation (to use Benjamin's term) and rhythmic oscillation, making manifest new textual pleasure at each turn.

Procedure, program, constraint

Averting apparently "natural" writing styles as well as traditional forms also gave rise to the extensive use of constraints, procedures, programs, invented structures, and syncretic forms. Though influenced by Mac Low's use of "chance" operations (text-selection procedures) on found language (what he called "diastic," for reading *through* these given texts), and also the use of constraints by the French OuLiPo group, much of the $L=A=N=G=U=A=G=E$ work used such programs either to generate material that was incorporated into a poem or to determine the external form of the poem while freely composing its text within the invented form or constraint. And often constraints were mixed or violated. Retallack, who often works with procedural form, considers the importance of John Cage in *The Poethical Wager* (2003). Since 1990, the use of constraints and algorithms has increased, with the emergence of digital poetics and poetry in programmable media. Glazier, Chris Funkhouser, Matthew Kirchenbaum, John Cayley, Jim Rosenberg, and Brian Kim Stefansare pushing the work discussed here into new frontiers. (See Baetens, this volume.)

Craig Dworkin, in his poetry and essays, has expanded the possibilities of the conceptual poetics of procedure, exploring extreme constraints that approach the unreadable and the unconscious. The most renowned recent work of constraint-based poetry is Christian Bök's *Eunoia* (2001), a work in prose format in which every chapter uses just one vowel. Bök is now pushing constraints beyond the human horizon, working on a biopoem generated via DNA sequencing; irony is useful in considering his projects.

Prose

Many of the works of poetry in and around $L=A=N=G=U=A=G=E$ use prose, rather than verse, format. This use of prose is distinct from the genre of "prose poem" that has developed in the wake of Baudelaire's prose poems. The poets have developed two distinct modalities: imploded syntax and serialized sentences.

$L=A=N=G=U=A=G=E$ also called for a new approach to the essay, averting exposition in favor of wild combinations, shifts of mood and tone, hyperbole, enigma, lyric exuberance, rhythmic propulsion, telegraphic immediacy, digression, aphorism, contradiction, investigation, and dialog. We see this in such works as Nathaniel Mackey's ongoing epistolary novel/essay *From a Broken Bottle Traces of Perfume Still Emanate* (1986, 1993, 2001, 2008), Susan Howe's *My Emily Dickinson* (1985) and later essay collections, Scalapino's *How Phenomena Appear To Unfold* (1994) and later collections, Ben Friedlander *Simulcast* (2004), rewriting Poe's essays with current content, Bruce Boone's *My Walk with Bob* (1978), Joe Brainard's *I Remember* (1970), Alan Davies's *Signage* (1987), as well as in the dialogic (multi-voiced) criticism of McGann. Nick Piombino's *Boundary of Blur* (1993) and *Theoretical Objects* (1999) have most fully explored the relation of self-disclosure, free-association, and psychoanalysis (both in the form and content of these works).

Free writing

Imploded syntax prose is sometimes thought of as "free writing" or improvised prose, even "automatic" or unconscious writing (putting on paper whatever comes into your head, without analytic planning): phrases tumble on phrases, words bouncing off one another in extended sentences, if there are sentences at all. In fact, there is a great deal of artifice in this approach and a variety of concepts determine the form and style. Bernadette Mayer's *Memory* and *Studying Hunger* (both 1976) are exemplary, while Coolidge's "prosoid" works from the 1970s and 1980s suggest jazz-inflected improvisation. At around the same time, Peter Seaton forged perhaps the densest, most magisterial, and awesomely refractory work of this kind (sometimes mixing verse and prose), while Lynne Dreyer create prose works which she likened to the experience of swimming. In contrast, James Sherry engaged and poetically exploded discursive aspects of genre prose. A diaristic/journal feel often pervades some of these works, most explicitly in Hannah Weiner's *Clairvoyant Journal* (1975), composed of three conflicting "voices": one clairvoyantly seen (in CAPS), one commenting (*in italics*), one narrating. For Weiner, visually arranged prose (with juxtaposed type fonts) was an ideal medium to map consciousness, understood not through a single or unified voice but through a melded clashing of voices.

The new sentence

Silliman introduced the term "new sentence" to describe the serial or disjunctive ordering of grammatical sentences, such as one finds in *Tjanting*. There are many works of this type, but the best known is Hejinian's *My Life* (1980), an autobiography written when she was 37, comprising 37 prose sections of 37 sentences each; key sentences recur in different orders throughout the work (she revised and expanded the work to 45 sections of 45 sentences each when she turned 45). Another remarkable work in this mode is Perelman's *A.K.A* (1978), where paradigmatic sentences move from statement to aphorism to philosophical reflection to autobiography to lament. David Bromige's acutely funny "My Poetry" (1980) paratactically wove together reviews of his work. Such approaches to prose poetry have been extended more recently by Spahr in the riveting, woven prose of *The Transformation* (2007), as well as in the pervasively citational, politically acute work of Canadians Jeff Derksen and Kevin Davies.

Sprung lyric

The lyric is a vexed term for the post-1975 poetics of invention; such lyric resistance has paradoxically led to a resurgence of new lyric intensities in startlingly varied forms. Sprung lyric stands between the sentence-driven and discursive drives of the new prose-format poems and the traditional I-centered free verse lyric of personal sincerity or epiphany. In the 1970s, Diane Ward published a series of books that seemed to actualize the space of interpersonal relationship, from attachment to distancing. Lauterbach has developed an open field of crystallized, sometimes elegiac, processual lyrics, using fragments in the service of sonic excess: torn moments of language are left "as is" so as readers we can piece them together as we grapple toward a shared articulation. Palmer has developed a related form of analytic (non-I-centered) lyric, often more propositional in texture.

Armantrout has created a unique form of new-sentence lyric, where each sentence-like unit is broken into phrasal elements, each part cracked open to show its dark matter. The parts come together into a whole the way a puzzle with missing pieces comes together in a dream. Armantrout's often dark poems hover between irony, whimsy, and astringent social critique. As with Elaine Equi, bemused popular cultural references vie with sardonic commentary on everyday life in America. Douglas Messerli's sprung lyrics of the 1970s and 1980s often used riddles and puns to created a linguistic pop and pull in the poems. John Yau has pioneered a surrealist inflected social lyric, exploring cultural identity and interpersonal relationships. Fred Wah's social lyrics have moved toward improvisation.

Norman Fischer, a zen priest, has used lyric and an open-ended form for reflection and meditation. Hank Lazer has written eloquently on his and Fischer's fusion of zen, jazz, and open-ended reflection in the new non-I centered lyrics. Alan Davies's preternaturally precise, uncanny, enigmatic, poignantly beautiful poems are also influenced by zen.

Sprung lyrics party with wild forms – what I've called "Nude Formalism" – from Ted Berrigan's serial love poems, *The Sonnets* (1964), peppered with unattributed literary "steals," to Joseph Ceravolo's syntactically ecstatic *Fits of Dawn* (1965) to, in subsequent decades, Will Alexander's rhapsodic "exobiotic" excursions into the hyper-reality of the cosmos to Maggie O'Sullivan's "colliderings" – her trembling, warbling, stuttering charm-poems. Work by slightly younger poets that inhabits this range of poetic possibilities include Peter Gizzi's "threshold songs," with their abstraction and attenuated rhythms; Nada Gordon's zany "high" syntax and lyric exuberance (in her 2007 *Folly*); Lee Ann Brown's often balladic polyversity; Elizabeth Willis's synthesis of the Pre-Raphaelites, epistemology, and historical counter-narratives; Stacy Doris's conceptual forms; Myung Mi Kim's tense negotiations between Korean and English; and Rod Smith's laconic wit.

Appropriation, citation, quotation, originality, documentary, and the found

The move away from directly self-expressive lyric poetry entailed a questioning of originality: the self was seen as quintessential social rather than autonomously individual; verbal language was viewed as a vast collective record to be mined for poetic use, whether in a documentary mode or in a collage or palimpsest, or through the pervasive use of "sampling" in a work. Such repurposing of found language was partly fueled by an aesthetic interest in the sensation of the citational, the palpable sense of something being quoted, or put on display: nontransparent "language to be looked at" (to use a phrase of Robert Smithson's).

Since the 1990s, both "Flarf" and "Conceptual" poetry have further explored this line of inquiry (see Epstein, this volume). K. Silem Mohammed's Flarf in *Deer Head Nation* (2003) is one of a number of works using digital "data mining" as a poetic tool; in this case, the book title was a Google search term, producing poems – often with grotesque Americana motifs – from the resulting search pages. Jena Osman has pursued a new documentary poetics. Kenneth Goldsmith has created (or assembled, since "Uncreative Writing" is his calling card) a series of epic works in which the found material (transcribed weather or traffic reports, for example) appear to be presented uncut and unedited. Goldsmith is something of a magician or trickster figure, conjuring up loads of creative thought and solid-gold frames of invention from the base materials of found language.

Collaboration

As an extension of the exchange that was at the heart of L=A=N=G=U=A=G=E, collaboration among the poets was frequent and became a stylistic foundry for some of the most inventive works of the milieu. L=A=N=G=U=A=G=E published the supersized *Legend* (1980) by Andrews, McCaffery, Silliman, Ray DiPalma, and me; Mayer collaborated with Coolidge, Hejinian with Harryman and Scalapino, McCaffery with bp Nichol. Collaborations between the poets and artists in other mediums were even more common, with Steve Clay's Granary Books emerging in the 1990s as a key publisher of poet/artist collaborations.

Poetry Plastique

In 2001, Jay Sanders and I co-curated the *Poetry Plastique* show in New York, focusing on poetry that moved off the page, from visual and concrete poetry to poetry sculpture, painting, and installation. Drucker, in her book art and several of her critical studies, has most fully explored the visual materiality of poetry. From 1986 to 1996, Susan Bee and Mira Schor edited M/E/A/N/I/N/G, focusing on artists' writing and partly extending the work of L=A=N=G=U=A=G=E. Vito Acconci's and Bernadette Mayer's magazine 0–9 (1967–1969) is a rich source for the intersection of poetry and conceptual art. Arakawa and Madeline Gins's *The Mechanism of Meaning* (1971) set a crucial precedent for L=A=N=G=U=A=G=E. It is illuminating to consider the work of language and book artists such as Robert Smithson, Lawrence Weiner, Tom Phillips, Richard Tuttle, Xu Bing, Alison Knowles, Dick Higgins, and Ligorano/Reese in this context, which would also include Grenier's hand-drawn poems, DiPalma's rubber stamp books, and McCaffery's typewriter works, Tan Lin's ambient installations, and Ronald Johnson's *Ark*. Site-specificity, beyond the book, is another dimension of Poetry Plastique. The acute relevance for poetry of Smithson's engagement with site specificity has been taken up recently by Lytle Shaw in *Fieldworks* (in press).

Translation, transcreation, ideolect, nomadics

Writing poems in a made-up language is a legacy of Russian Futurism and also of Lewis Carroll, with strong connections to both visual and sound poetry. Frank Kuenstler's *Lens* (1964), David Melnick's *Pcoet* (1975), as well as much of P. Inman's work of the 1970s and 1980s foregrounded the possibilities for *ideolect*, taking nonstandardization down to the level of the word. In 1983, Melnick followed up *Pcoet* with *Men in Aida*, a queerly homophonic Homer, translating the sound of the Greek into an ideolectal American. The poetics of translation inform many aspects of the expanded field of *L=A=N=G=U=A=G=E*, and there is a kinship with the critical explorations on this topic of scholar/translator Lawrence Venuti and Pierre Joris, as well as the Seventies speculations on translation by McCaffery and Nichol (writing at the Toronto Research Group): translation as metaphor, or better to say metaphor as translation – from English to English, dialect to ideolect, thought to text, visual to verbal, and so on. Joris makes the case for a "nomadic poetics" in the space between languages – both for poetry as an othering of language and for poetry as a second language. M. NourbeSe Philip's poetry focuses on the anguish of writing in the other's language. A new horizon may be multilectal poetry, as for example Theresa Hak Kyung Cha's *Dictee* (1982) and Anne Tardos's *The Dik-Dik's Solitude* (2003).

Performance

In *L=A=N=G=U=A=G=E*, all poetry is a performance rather than a statement or disembodied content. At the most fundamental level, the poetry reading provides a site for the work to come into a new life in sound. Many of the poets have developed quite distinct performance modes, from the very understated to the extravagant. *Close Listening: Poetry and the Performed Word* (1998), a collection of essays which I edited, explores this topic. In their 2010 anthology *The Kenning Anthology of Poets Theater: 1945–1985*, Kevin Killian and David Brazil include plays by Harryman, Perelman, Waldman, Robinson, Greenwald, Andrews, Gordon, Scalapino, the Waldrops, Steve Benson, Thomas, Alan Bernheimer, and Fiona Templeton. Charles Borkhuis should also be mentioned in this context. Killian is a central force in the Bay Area poet's theater, infusing it with something of the queer energies of Charles Ludlam's Ridiculous Theater Company. Messerli, both in his publishing and his own work, has also been a strong force for poet's theater. Templeton and Mac Wellman are poet-playwrights whose work, like that of Richard Foreman, has become a key force for poet's theater in New York. Sound poetry and its conceptual extensions is another aspect of performance, pursued in and around *L=A=N=G=U=A=G=E*. In the 1970s and 1980s, McCaffery's and Benson's work were deeply tied to performance, while in 1982 Andrews began an ongoing series of sound performances accompanying dancer Sally Silvers. New modes of what Bergvall calls "performance writing" have been taken up by Bergvall herself, Bök, Rodrigo Toscano, and Morris. Morris combines aspects of performance poetry and sound poetry to create electrifying pieces that verge on song; her work is often inflected by African-American sounds and themes.

Many of these poets have collaborated with musicians, filmmakers, and dancers. Henry Hills's 1985 film *Money* documents the New York scene at the time. Like Hills, filmmaker-poet Abigail Child was a central figure in that New York scene, just as filmmaker Warren Sonbert was a vital to the Bay Area scene.

Ecopoetics

In the 1970s and 1980s, Christopher Dewdney wrote a set of geologically stratified poems in a pulsing, imploded-syntax prose, both visionary and dystopian. The collage lyric of Johnson explores heart, hearth, and earth. *Ecopoetics*, as framed by Jonathan Skinner in his magazine of that title, brings together radical formal forays into writing as ecosystems and environment of/as/against language. Berssenbrugge, in her long lines of attenuated lyrics, uses language as a medium for hyperperception and expanded, non-ego-centered, consciousness.

III. Onward: dissonance, ambiance, and the pataque(e)rical

The more open the legacy of *L=A=N=G=U=A=G=E*, the more successful our approach. Both a historical moment in North American poetry and poetics and a philosophical and political orientation toward poetry and the language arts, the expanded field, both *after* and *next to L=A=N=G=U=A=G=E*, has been characterized by the ingenuity of its appropriations, deformations, and reorientations.

L=A=N=G=U=A=G=E pursued a poetry averse to convention, standardization, and received forms, often prizing eccentricity, oddness, abrupt shifts of tone, peculiarity, error, and the abnormal – poetry that begins in disability (see Davidson 2008). This is what I call the *pataque(e)rical* imperative (a syncretic term combining "queer" and "query" with "'pataphysics," French protomodernist Alfred Jarry's "science" of exceptions, imaginary solutions, and swerves). Dissonance is certainly a signal manifestation of the pataque(e)rical and marks perhaps the starkest break from the harmonious or melodic or tonal lyricism of much free verse poetry. In the 1980s, Andrews perfected a dissonant, often angry poetry, breaking down cultural detritus at the microlevel and remixing it into something strangely exquisite in its consciousness of itself. In contrast, starting in the new millennia, Lin has created an "ambient" poetics: easy listening, low key, sampled at a macro-level from readily identifiable materials.

The future horizon for *L=A=N=G=U=A=G=E* lies between imaginary poles: dissonance and ambiance, opacity and radical legibility, concept and aesthesis, with the full force of the irony of these artifices and the artifice of these ironies.

Beyond the expanded field, it is the task of this poetics to acknowledge errancy, malformation, system failure.

We are all pataque(e)rical now.

References

Andrews, B. and C. Bernstein (eds.) (1984) *The L=A=N=G=U=A=G=E Book*, Carbondale, IL: Southern Illinois University Press.

Bernstein, C. (ed.) (1990) *The Politics of Poetic Form: Poetry and Public Policy*, New York: Roof.

Davidson, M. (1995) "Compulsory Heterosexuality: Charles Olson, Jack Spicer, and the Gender of Politics." In S.-E. Case, P. Brett, and S. L. Foster (eds.), *Cruising the Performative: Interventions*

into the Representation of Ethnicity, Nationality, and Sexuality, Bloomington, IN: Indiana University Press, pp. 197–216.
—— (2008) *Concerto for Left Hand: Disability and the Defamiliar Body*, Ann Arbor, MI: University of Michigan Press.
Forrest-Thomson, V. (1978) *Poetic Artifice: A Theory of Twentieth-Century Poetry*, Manchester, UK: Manchester University Press.
Hejinian, L. (2000) *The Language of Inquiry*, Berkeley, CA: University of California Press.
Hocquard, E. and C. Royet-Journoud (eds.) (1986) *21 + 1: Poètes américains d'aujourd'hui*, Montpellier, France: Delta.
—— (1991) *49 + 1: nouveaux poètes américains*, Royaumont, France: Un Bureau sur l'Atlantique/ Action poétique.
Perloff, M. (1984) "The Word as Such: Language Poetries in the Eighties," *American Poetry Review* 13(3), 15–22.

Further reading

Other collections edited by Charles Bernstein

Bernstein, C. (2009) *American Poetry after 1975* [special issue], *boundary 2* 36(3).
—— (1998) *Close Listening: Poetry and the Performed Word*, New York: Oxford University Press.
—— (1985) *43 Poets (1984)* [special issue] *boundary 2* 14(1/2).
—— (1982) "Language Sampler," *The Paris Review* 86:75–125.

Some influential magazines and presses of the 1970s and 1980s

Beckett, T. (ed.) *The Difficulties.*
Davies, A. (ed.) *100 Posters.*
Eshleman, C. (ed.) *Sulfur.*
Friedlander, B. and A. Schelling (eds.) *Jimmy & Lucy's House of "K".*
Hejinian, L. (ed.) *Tuumba Press.*
Hejinian, L. and B. Watten (eds.) *Poetics Journal.*
Hickman, L. (ed.) *Temblor.*
Messerli, D. (ed.) *La Bas* and Sun & Moon Press.
Perelman, B. (ed.) *Hills.*
Sherry, J. (ed.) *ROOF* magazine and press (a part of Sherry's Segue Foundation).
Silliman, R. (ed.) *Tottel's.*
Watten, B. (ed.) *This* magazine and press.
Young, G. (ed.) The Figures press.

Some key anthologies and collections from the 1970s through the 2000s

Beach, C. (ed.) (1998) *Artifice and Indeterminacy: An Anthology of New Poetics*, Tuscaloosa, AL: University of Alabama Press.
Hoover, P. (ed.) (1994) *Postmodern Poetry: A Norton Anthology*, New York: W.W. Norton.
Messerli, D. (ed.) (1987) *Language Poetries*, New York: New Directions.
—— (1994) *From the Other Side of the Century: A New American Poetry 1960–1990*, Los Angeles, CA: Sun & Moon Press.
Nielsen, A.D. and L. Ramey (eds.) (2006) *Every Goodbye Ain't Gone: An Anthology of Innovative Poetry by African Americans*, Tuscaloosa, AL: University of Alabama Press.

Rothenberg, J. (ed.) (1974) *Revolution of the Word: A New Gathering of American Avant Garde Poetry, 1914–1945*, New York: Seabury Press.

Rothenberg, J. and P. Joris (eds.) (1998) *Poems for the Millennium: The University of California Book of Modern and Postmodern Poetry*, vol. 2, Berkeley, CA: University of California Press.

Silliman, R. (ed.) (1975) "The Dwelling Place," *Alcheringa* New Series 1, 2.

—— (1982) "Realism: An Anthology of 'Language' Writing," *Ironwood* 20:10.

—— (1986) *In the American Tree*, Orono, ME: National Poetry Foundation.

Web resources

Eclipse digital archive (english.utah.edu/eclipse)
Electronic Poetry Center (epc.buffalo.edu)
PennSound (writing.upenn.edu/pennsound)

22

CONCRETE POETRY AND PROSE

Joe Bray

I. Introduction

Concrete poetry emerged simultaneously in Switzerland and Brazil in the early 1950s and soon spread all over the world. As a movement it is diverse and thus difficult to define, though most critics agree that in the strictest sense concrete poems are brief, pared-down pieces of text that are intended to be seen rather than read aloud. This phenomenon, which flourished in the 1950s and 1960s, can nevertheless be placed in the context of a much broader tradition of poetry which draws attention to its visual shape. The patterned or shaped poem can be traced to the ancient world, and was particularly popular (though often derided as trivial) in England in the late sixteenth and early seventeenth centuries. Though this type of poetry went out of fashion in the eighteenth century, the influence of an emphasis on visual layout can be felt in some of the key texts of the early novel, as I will discuss. I will argue further that visual experimentation tends to become heightened and more significant when generic boundaries are elided or brought into question, when the physical formats of prose and verse are combined. The chapter finishes with an examination of a collection by a contemporary writer who, though not obviously a "concrete poet," plays with layout in subtle ways, transforming the conventions of the "prose poem." What connects the authors studied here is their desire to experiment with the possibilities afforded by the page, and in particular to explore the potential of that often-overlooked site of meaning which will be the focus of this chapter: white space.

II. Concrete poetry

The term concrete poetry refers to a worldwide movement that arose in the early 1950s. As Mary Ellen Solt put it in the introduction to a key 1970 anthology: "the term 'concrete poetry' is now being used to refer to a variety of innovations and experiments following World War II which are revolutionizing the art of the poem on a global scale and enlarging its possibilities for expression and communication" (1970:

7). Though these "innovations and experiments" took place around the world, two particular areas are often associated with the start of the movement. As Solt observes, "what has mushroomed into a world-wide movement was founded in Europe by a single poet Eugen Gomringer of Switzerland, who adheres to the strictest concrete practice, and almost simultaneously in Brazil by the Noigandres group – Haroldo de Campos, Decio Pignatari and Augusto de Campos – who derived their new concept of form from closest study of poets who preceded them" (8). This "strictest concrete practice" is, even by 1970, hard to define; Solt notes that "there are now so many kinds of experimental poetry being labeled 'concrete' that it is difficult to say what the word means" (7), while in 1967 Emmett Williams, in the foreword to another key anthology, observed that the "international movement" "is blessed with a disunity that unshackles it from the aims and aesthetic principles of the many manifestoes it has engendered" (1967: vii).

Most critics of concrete poetry have focused on its visual characteristics. In Solt's view, for example, the "new visual poem" is "intended to be seen like a painting" (1970: 7), and is in direct opposition to what she calls "the oral tradition," which "neglected the visual power of words" (61). She claims that "to write a completely silent poem" is "probably the ultimate goal of the visual concrete poet" and that "all true poems are said to aspire to silence, the silence of the spirit at their centre" (60), giving as an illustration Gomringer's "silencio," one of the best-known early concrete poems, in which the role of white space in the poem is clearly crucial. The "silence" of the title is enacted at the center of the text, as the noisy black type is replaced by a silent gap. It is as if the white space trumps the linguistic attempt to represent silence; it achieves what words cannot. Its dominance over language in the poem is also suggested by the way it dwarfs the text on the page, surrounding and diminishing it. The proportional use of white space to convey meaning here is typical of Gomringer's work; according to Solt, he "makes semantic use of space," and "much of the meaning in his poems, particularly spiritual content, comes through as a result of the delicate relationship between the scale and weight of his letters and words and the space they occupy" (62). As in much early concrete poetry, the interaction between the black type and the white space on the page is crucial. In the succinct formulation of Augusto de Campos, quoted by his brother Haroldo to accompany one of Augusto's poems from 1956: "Concrete poetry: tension of things-words in space-time" (originally published in the review, *ad – arquitectura e decoração*, n. 20, november/december 1956, São Paulo, Brazil).

Following the first flourishing of the concrete movement in Switzerland and Brazil, it soon became a world-wide phenomenon, to be found not just in poetry, but also painting, architecture, even music. Amongst those commonly cited as concrete artists are the German typographer Hansjörg Mayer, the Austrian composer Gerhard Rühm, and the Mexican painter and architect Mathias Goeritz. The most notable English-language concrete poets include Emmett Williams, whose book-length poem *Sweethearts* (1968) contains only the letters in "sweethearts" and is designed to be read back to front; Aram Saroyan, whose poem "lighght" (1965), which consists of this single word at the centre of a blank page, caused controversy when it was included in *The American Literary Anthology*; and the Scottish poets Ian Hamilton Finlay and Edwin Morgan. The former uses a variety of natural, often sea-related, materials in his poetry; in "wave rock" (1966), for example, light shining through blue sandblasted glass illuminates forms of the word "wave" gradually moving towards the word "rock," while in the sculpture poem "purse-net boat" (1969) the sea is polished aluminum, on which are five embossed forms of the word "seiner" (the net) and one of the word "silver" (the fish). Morgan's collections *Emergent Poems* (1967) and *The Second Life* (1968) use a wide variety of typographical shapes, as do his *Newspoems* (1965–1971), which consist of cuttings from newspapers pasted on to sheets of paper and photographed. One of his favorite techniques is to select isolated letters from a quotation and add more letters from line to line, always in their correct position, to create new space-filled words and combinations, until the full quotation is formed at the bottom of the page (see for example "Plea" [1967], "Nightmare" [1967] and "Message Clear" [1968]). The wit and ingenuity of Morgan's concrete poems shows the wide range of possibilities that the work of Gomringer and the Noigandres group had inspired and the different directions that their original impulse had taken, even by the late sixties.

III. Pattern poetry

Though the concrete movement was certainly innovative and experimental, the "visual poem" was far from new. As Dick Higgins noted in 1977, "the impression of visual poetry as a peculiarly modern movement [. . .] is misleading" (1977: 4). Concrete poetry is indebted to, and indeed partly emerges from, a rich historical tradition of what is sometimes called pattern or shaped poetry. Broadly defined, pattern poems are simply those, in M.H. Abrams' words, "which experiment with the visual shape in which a text is presented on the page" (1993: 34). Claiming that "the pattern poem has a far richer tradition, ancient and contemporary, than is generally supposed" (3), Higgins asserts that "visual poetry [. . .] has existed in many languages from antiquity to the present, though more so at some times and places, and it should certainly not be considered as some bizarre deviation" (5). He gives examples from both the *Greek Anthology*, a tenth- or eleventh-century compilation of surviving poems assembled in Germany in the Palatine manuscript, and some Latin poets who used strikingly visual forms, including Porphyrius (c. 400 AD), to whom an altar-shaped poem can be attributed, and Venantius Fortunatus (c. 530–600 AD), who wrote a number of grid poems, as well as a cruciform one.

A history of shaped forms in poetry is also given in George Puttenham's widely-read and influential *The Arte of English Poesie* (1589). In chapter 12 of Book 2, Puttenham describes his fifth type of proportion, "proportion in figure," which involves reducing metres "by good symmetry [. . .] into certain geometrical figures" (2007: 179). He gives examples of geometrical poetic forms, including "the Lozenge," "the Triangle or Triquet," the "Roundel or Sphere," the "Square or Quadrangle Equilater" and "the Figure Oval." He claims not to have found any examples in Greek or Latin poets, except for what he calls "Anacreon's egg" (actually a poem more commonly attributed to the Greek poet Simias of Rhodes). Though Puttenham goes into great detail on these various shaped forms, he is nervous about their poetic worth, observing that they are "fittest for the pretty amorets in court to entertain their servants and the time withal" (180). Puttenham sees shaped poems as witty and ingenious, certainly, but also somewhat frivolous and trifling, an impression reinforced by his dubious claim not to have found any Greek or Latin examples. Before listing his shapes, he remarks defensively that "at the beginning they will seem nothing pleasant to an English ear, but time and usage will make them acceptable enough" (180).

Despite the evident stigma surrounding the shaped poem in *The Arte of English Poesie*, Puttenham's work helped to inspire a vogue for pattern poetry in the late sixteenth and early seventeenth centuries. From this surge of interest emerged two of the best-known and most widely-imitated shaped poems: George Herbert's "The Altar" and "Easter-Wings," both first published in *The Temple* (1633). Several critics have shown that these are considerably more than witty conceits. Joseph Summers, for example, claims that in both cases the use of the "visual hieroglyph" enables Herbert to fuse "the spiritual and the material" and "the rational and the sensuous" (1954: 145) (see also Elsky [1983]). After the appearance of *The Temple* pattern poems gained in popularity, with practitioners including Robert Herrick and Thomas Traherne. Yet the quality of most was notoriously low, prompting Addison to write in the *Spectator* in 1711 that "The first species of false wit which I have met with is very venerable for its antiquity, and has produced several pieces which have lived near us as long as the Iliad itself: I mean these short poems, printed among the minor Greek poets, which resemble the figure of an egg, a pair of wings, an axe, a shepherd's pipe and an altar" (no. 58, May 7, 1711).

IV. Twentieth-century visual poetry

After Addison's dismissal, the traditional narrative then has the shaped poem fading from prominence in the eighteenth and nineteenth centuries until a re-emergence in the early twentieth. Stéphane Mallarmé's *Un Coup de dés* (1897) and Guillaume Apollinaire's *Calligrammes* (1918) are often cited as key impetuses behind a resurgence in visual poetry. The latter in particular combines shaped poetry in the tradition of Herbert and others with an interest in the spaces between words which is typical of later concrete poets. The text of "le miroir," for example, creates a mirror-like space which contains the words "Guillaume Apollinaire." This is more than just black type; the text makes clear that the space is to be imagined as filled by the poet's living presence: "Dans ce miroir je suis enclos vivant et vrai."

Inspired by Mallarmé and Apollinaire, many Modernist poets experimented with the appearance of the text on the page. The typography of the second section of *The Waste Land* (1922), "A Game of Chess," conveys T.S. Eliot's subtle merger of the rhythms of pub conversation and Shakespearean verse, while the numerous Chinese ideograms in Ezra Pound's early *Cantos* (1925) create meaning through their placement on the page as much as their translation into English (see Xie 1998). In America these Modernist experiments were taken further by, amongst others, e.e. cummings, whose poems frequently mix syntactic and typographic irregularity, especially in his early collections *Tulips and Chimneys* (1923) and *XLI Poems* (1925), and William Carlos Williams, whose early poems of the 1920s combine the imagist philosophy that Pound and others had developed a decade earlier with an interest in photography. The result, in such poems as "Spring and All" and "The Red Wheelbarrow" from the sequence *Spring and All* (1923), is an attempt at a pictorial style of representation, which depends as much on visual layout as on semantic content. Williams especially was an important influence on Charles Olson's 1950 theory of "Projective Verse," which called for a poetry of improvisation and a rejection of traditional poetic forms, and on the Black Mountain poets who took this as their manifesto (see Lee, this volume).

The emergence of concrete poetry in the early 1950s can thus be linked to innovations in American poetry, especially amongst the Black Mountain poets, who were simultaneously experimenting with visual form (see Fraser 1999). Though there are important differences between the two groups (for example, the Black Mountain poets tended to retain the notion that verse should consist of lines, however disjointed), there are points of connection too. Denise Levertov's "A Silence," for example, from the collection *Here and Now* (1957), uses space in a similar, if less immediately obvious, way to Gomringer's "silencio":

A Silence
Among its petals the rose
still holds
       a few tears of the morning rain that
broke it from its stem
         In each
shines a speck of
        red light, darker even
than the rose. Phoenix-tailed
slateblue martins pursue
      one   another, spaced out
in hopeless hope, circling
      the porous clay vase, dark from
the water in it. Silence
surrounds the facts. A language
still unspoken.

(Levertov 1957: 12)

Here the extra space in the tenth line between "one" and "another" captures the gap between the pursuing, "spaced out," "slateblue martins," and the ever-circling futility of their chase, while the white spaces at the start of the third, fifth, seventh, tenth and twelfth lines suggest the "porous" quality of the verse and the fragility of the images it is designed to capture. As in the earliest concrete poems, the typography of the page, the white space in and around the black type, is crucial. As the poem concludes: "Silence/ surrounds the facts. A language/ still unspoken."

V. The visual shape of prose: the early novel

It is not just in verse that white space can be an important site of meaning. While pattern poems may have gone out of fashion in the eighteenth and nineteenth centuries, the appearance of the text on the page became important in another, emerging genre. Janine Barchas, amongst others, has pointed to the "graphic diversity" of the early novel, and complained that "the insipid uniformity of modern paperback editions of eighteenth-century fiction" is such that "it is difficult to resurrect the genre's lost visual dynamism" (2003: 6). Claiming that "writers of prose fiction during roughly the first half of the eighteenth century experimented broadly (and, broadly speaking, every publication was an experiment) with the material presentation of the novel as well as its narrative content" (13), Barchas emphasizes the "extent to which the early novel depends for its literary effects upon its graphic appearance as a printed book" (7–8). An obvious eighteenth-century example of visual experimentation is of course Laurence Sterne's *Tristram Shandy* (1759–1767), which uses a variety of graphic devices, such as a black page and squiggly graphs to represent the action of each volume, in order to tease and challenge its readers. Yet *Tristram Shandy* is not so much an innovation in visual design as a compendium of techniques and practices which had been widespread in the early novel for almost half a century.

One early novelist who is rarely considered in this context is Henry Fielding. In comparison with his contemporary and rival Samuel Richardson, who as a printer guided his own novels through every stage of their publication, Fielding's innovative use of graphic design in his novels has tended to be overlooked. *Joseph Andrews* (1742), for example, plays cleverly with the use of white space in the breaks between chapters. In the first chapter of Book II, Fielding's narrator humorously describes the practice of "dividing our Works into Books and Chapters" as a considerable "Mystery or Secret" in "Authoring." Dismissing the charge that the sole purpose of "this Art of dividing" is "to swell our Works to a much larger Bulk than they would otherwise be extended to," he maintains that the practice is for "the Advantage of our Reader, not our own; and indeed many notable Uses arise to him from this Method":

> [. . .] for first, those little Spaces between our Chapters may be looked upon as an Inn or Resting-Place, where he may stop and take a Glass, or any other Refreshment, as it pleases him. Nay, our fine Readers will, perhaps, be scarce able to travel further than through one of them in a Day. As to those vacant Pages which are placed between our Books, they are to be regarded as those Stages, where, in long Journeys, the Traveller stays some time to repose himself, and consider of what he hath seen in the Parts he hath already past through; a Consideration which I take the Liberty to recommend a little to

the Reader: for however swift his Capacity may be, I would not advise him to travel through these Pages too fast: for if he doth, he may probably miss the seeing some curious Productions of Nature which will be observed by the slower and more accurate Reader. A Volume without any such Places of Rest resembles the Opening of Wilds or Seas, which tires the Eye and fatigues the Spirit when entered upon.

(Fielding 1999 [1742]: 76)

The comparison of white spaces between chapters to inns at which refreshment can be imbided of course reflects the actual events of the novel, in which Joseph and Parson Adams are continually stopping off at alehouses and getting into various scrapes. Developing the analogy, the narrator describes the "Contents prefixed to every Chapter" as "so many Inscriptions over the Gates of Inns (to continue the same Metaphor,) informing the Reader what Entertainment he is to expect, which if he likes not, he may travel on to the next" (77).

Fielding's careful and extensive use of white space in *Joseph Andrews* is modelled in part on contemporary poetic practice. John Lennard has noted how a characteristic of poetry from the early eighteenth to mid-nineteenth centuries is its "heavy leading," which, he explains, is "the amount of page left white," depending on "whether the lines are single-spaced or double-spaced, and how much space is left between stanzas (if the poem is stanzaic)" (1996: 50), and the Preface to *Joseph Andrews* suggests that the novel quite consciously models itself on poetic conventions. The narrator claims that comic epic poetry "may be likewise in either Verse or Prose," since although metre may be lacking, "when any kind of Writing contains all its other Parts, such as Fable, Action, Characters, Sentiments, and Diction, and is deficient in Metre only; it seems, I think, reasonable to refer it to the Epic" (3). Thus, clearly with his own work in mind, he asserts that "a comic Romance is a comic Epic-Poem in Prose; differing from Comedy, as the serious Epic from Tragedy: its Actions being more extended and comprehensive; containing a much larger Circle of Incidents, and introducing a greater Variety of Characters" (3–4). This description of the genre of *Joseph Andrews* as an "Epic-Poem in Prose" suggests a blend of techniques and styles associated with verse and prose, explaining in part the text's systematic use of graphic design and its concern with visual layout.

VI. Innovation in twentieth-century prose layout

The early novel's experiments with typography have proved influential in the subsequent history of the genre. There is unfortunately not room here to discuss the Victorian novel's concern with its materiality; a useful summary is given in Hack (2005). It is clear though that the potential for visual experimentation in the novel increased dramatically with the advent of Modernism, with *Ulysses* (1922) in particular transforming the way prose could be presented on the page. Especially innovative chapters from a typographical point of view are "Aeolus," which mimics the format of a newspaper, "Circe," which is set out entirely as a play script, and "Penelope," in which spaces are closed up in order to represent Molly Bloom's interior monologue. Later twentieth-century novelists explored and developed the possibilities opened up by Joyce's experimentation. Brian McHale has coined the term "concrete prose" to describe pieces of prose which either "imitate through their shapes the shapes of objects or processes in the real world," or, more commonly, like Mallarmé's *Un coup de dés*, are non-mimetic, but rather, like abstract expressionist painting, "focus attention on the ontological 'cut': on the one side of the cut, the world projected by the words; on the other side, the physical reality of ink shapes on paper" (McHale 1987: 184). He cites Raymond Federman's *Double or Nothing* (1971), Christine Brooke-Rose's *Thru* (1975) and Ronald Sukenick's *Long Talking Bad Conditions Blues* (1979) as novels which are particularly inventive in their use of "shaped typography" (see also McHale, this volume). There are many other late twentieth-century examples; from B.S. Johnson's *Albert Angelo* (1964) with its cut-through pages which enable the reader to skip forward, to Alasdair Gray's *Lanark* (1981), which contains an "Index of Plagiarisms" as running notes in the margins of its "Epilogue," to Jerzy Kosinski's *The Hermit of 69th Street* (1988), whose pages are dominated by abstruse and inconsequential footnotes. (On informational design in experimental fiction, see Tomasula, this volume.)

Many of the innovations in late twentieth-century prose layout are brought together in Mark Z. Danielewski's dazzling *House of Leaves* (2000), which includes, amongst a plethora of graphic devices, extensive footnotes in different voices, nearly blank pages, and a "duct note" running through twenty-five pages of the book, in which the verso text is the mirror-image of that on the recto (see Fordham 2011). The pages also present mimetically the journey of the characters through a mysterious, ever-expanding hallway, with the words on the page at one point arranged in the form of a ladder (Danielewski 2000: 440–1). The "house" of the title is thus both a "real," though frighteningly unknowable, structure in the world of the novel, and an unstable edifice of ever-shifting type (see also Gibbons, this volume, and Hayles and Montfort, this volume). For all its spectacular inventiveness, *House of Leaves* cleverly draws for many of its visual effects on techniques which have been part of the history of the novel since its inception. Just as the "vacant pages" represent "Stages" in both the reader's and the characters' journeys in *Joseph Andrews*, so the reader's experience of the text on the pages of Danielewski's novel mirrors that of the characters through the house's mysterious passages. In both cases, in McHale's terms, the ontological "cut" between the projected world and the physical shape of the text is foregrounded.

VII. The prose, or "story" poem

McHale stresses the commonalities between concrete prose and concrete poetry (1987: 187), and Fielding's innovative blend of the conventions of verse and prose in his "Epic-Poem in Prose" suggests that visual experimentation may reach a peak when generic boundaries are crossed, or at least subjected to more intense pressure. In the final section of this chapter I will concentrate on another mixed, or hybrid, genre which displays a similar kind of emphasis on the layout of the text on the page. Again the use of white space will be seen to be particularly crucial, suggesting the possibility of a continuum between the earliest concrete poetry of Gomringer and others, and more recent experiments with poetic form and layout. I will consider in particular one contemporary poet whose generic playfulness involves an interest in visual design. Just as Fielding borrowed some of the visual techniques of poetry to craft the look of his novel *Joseph Andrews*, so the poet Simon Armitage, I argue, combines prose and verse to create subtle visual effects in his latest collection *Seeing Stars* (2010).

All of the thirty-nine poems in the collection are written in what looks like paragraphs, with right-hand margin unjustified and very few, if any, end rhymes. They thus in part resemble "prose poems," a genre which has tended to elude precise definition. For M.H. Abrams these are "densely compact, pronouncedly rhythmic, and highly sonorous compositions which are written as a continuous sequence of sentences without line breaks," while Martin Gray's description is "a short work of poetic prose, resembling a poem because of its ornate language and imagery, and because it stands on its own, and lacks narrative: like a lyric poem but not subjected to the patterning of metre" (Abrams and Gray both quoted in Delville [1998], p. 2). In his history of the form, Michel Delville is sceptical of such formulations, claiming that "Baudelaire's generic *enfant terrible* now seems to have developed almost as many trends as there are poets practising it, so that any attempt at a single, monolithic definition of the genre would be doomed to failure" (1998: 1). He instead prefers an approach which "attend[s] to the specific generic conventions alternately introduced and negated by the genre," arguing for a consideration of the contemporary prose poem as "representative of how individual works can subvert the very codes and narratives by which they exist and can expose them as the product of specific historical moments" (9).

An approach which emphasises the subversive potential of the prose poem seems especially appropriate for Simon Armitage's use of the form, which eschews some of the "monolithic definitions" given above. Of the thirty-nine poems in *Seeing Stars*, for example, twenty-nine have at least one line break (twenty-three have one and six have two). None of them could be said to be strictly "lyric" poems which "lack narrative," in Gray's terms, and those with one or more line break in particular clearly contain narrative elements, as the break often marks a gap or transition between one event and another. It is perhaps this which has led Armitage to insist that they are not "prose poems" but "story-poems" (for example at a reading at Sheffield's "Off the Shelf" festival, 13 October, 2010). As the critic Alastair Beddow notes in an early review, "perhaps deliberately eschewing the more rarefied term 'prose-poem', Armitage's 'story-poems' combine the narrative instinct of the short story (often employing the twist or inversion ending) and the sensibility and language of poetry" (Beddow 2010).

An example of a poem in the collection that seems especially keen to integrate these narrative and poetic elements is "The Personal Touch," which explicitly concerns a kind of "space," in this case the request of the "cohabitee" for "space [. . .] and plenty of it" in their relationship. This clichéd demand is playfully transformed by the way in which "space" is then treated as a tangible object in the poem, as the narrator sets off to find a space in the hardware shop: "'Got any space?'/ I asked the man in the brown overalls. 'Sure,' he said./ 'What kind of thing were you looking for? Doesn't come/ cheap, mind.'" The narrator is offered various different kinds of space, including "hexagonal space," "deep ocean space," "space/ that glowed in the dark" and "space that/ giggled when you poked it," before settling for the "'pretty neutral, standard spec., no trimmings to/ speak of'" variety recommended by the shopkeeper. He has the package gift-wrapped and writes on the gift tag "'Here's what you asked for, my sweetheart. I only hope/ it's enough'" (Armitage 2010: 55–6).

The story-poem also depends for its meaning on a different kind of space, as can only be fully appreciated by considering its original layout. A line break after the ninth line signals a transition between the initial conversation between the couple, and the hardware shop. It therefore enhances the narrative aspect of the text, marking a gap between the first event and what follows; after the hardware shop, later events in the second section occur in the newsagents, at the doorstep, and "along Quarry Road." It also serves to represent iconically the key theme of the text and hint at the dynamics between the couple; the narrator's acceptance of his partner's demand for space is indicated by a line of actual white space. His feelings about his task and the relationship as a whole are however unstated, as is typical of other poems in the collection; it can perhaps be inferred that he is not happy about her "pretty demanding" request from the way he drops the package of space on the doorstep at the end of the poem, yet this is never made explicit; instead the white space on the page is frustratingly silent and oblique, perhaps suggesting a kind of angry passivity on the narrator's part. As in Gomringer's "silencio" then, the white space represents a silence, a range of unexpressed emotions which cannot be captured in words. This silence is heightened all the more by being preceded by the typographical marker of a raised voice as the cohabitee's insistence is literally spelt out in capital letters: "'Paul, space is what I want/ and space is what I need. Do I have to SPELL IT OUT?'"

The space after the end of the poem is also crucial to its meaning. Having dropped the package of space on the doorstep for his partner, the narrator "zoomed off in the Roadster,/ faster than I'd ever travelled in my whole existence,/ straight along Quarry Road." The "quarry" of "Quarry Road" perhaps surprisingly suggests a kind of pursuit, as though the narrator, in seeking to get away from his cohabitee as quickly as possible, is himself seeking something of his own, though he may not know what this is. The open-endedness and unattainable vastness of his quest is suggested by the visual appearance of the text, as after this last line, the rest of this page (its majority) is white space. The narrator zooms off into the unknown, as again the text is frustratingly silent as to his emotions. After giving his partner her required space he drives off into a typographical space of his own, exiting "faster than I'd ever travelled in my whole existence." The appearance of the poem's second page indicates then both each partner's desire for space, and the vast, "deep ocean" between them that results.

VIII. Conclusion

The white spaces of "The Personal Touch" are thus examples of what John Hollander, himself an acclaimed writer of shaped poetry, has claimed is widespread in "contemporary verse formats": "the odd sorts of interruption and linkage being developed – extensions of the more archaic white spaces between stanza breaks – in order to handle complex sorts of transition that defy ordinary syntactical punctuation" (Hollander 1975: 283). His observation that white space can "become operative and can indeed be *glossed*" (270) applies in one sense to all poetry, and to many kinds of experimental prose too. Yet it seems to become especially pertinent when generic boundaries are crossed. Not only prose and poetry, but also prose poetry, and variations on this hybrid genre, depend for much of their meaning on the gaps between the words on the page, on often-overlooked blanks which can be sites of both humour and gravity, play and reflection. Within all literary genres, and especially across them, these flexible spaces continue to re-define and re-shape the "concrete."

References

Abrams, M.H. (1993) *A Glossary of Literary Terms*, 6th edn., Fort Worth, TX: Harcourt Brace.

Armitage, S. (2010) *Seeing Stars*, London: Faber and Faber.

Barchas, J. (2003) *Graphic Design, Print Culture, and the Eighteenth-Century Novel*, Cambridge, UK: Cambridge University Press.

Beddow, A. (2010) "Review of 'Seeing Stars by Simon Armitage'," [Online], *The Literateur* (1 May 2010). Accessed from: http://literateur.com/seeing-stars-by-simon-armitage/

Danielewski, M. Z. (2000) *House of Leaves by Zampanò with introduction and notes by Johnny Truant*, London: Doubleday.

Delville, M. (1998) *The American Prose Poem: Poetic Form and the Boundaries of Genre*, Gainesville, FL: University Press of Florida.

Elsky, M. (1983) "George Herbert's Pattern Poems and the Materiality of Language: A New Approach to Renaissance Hieroglyphics," *ELH*, 50(2), 245–60.

Fielding, H. (1999 [1742]) *The History of the Adventures of Joseph Andrews*, ed. D. Brooks-Davies, rev. with new intro. by T. Keymer, Oxford, UK: Oxford University Press.

Fordham, F. (2011) "Katabasis in Danielewski's *House of Leaves* and two other recent American novels." In J. Bray and A. Gibbons (eds.) *Mark Z. Danielewski*, Manchester, UK: Manchester University Press, pp. 33–51.

Fraser, K. (1999) "Translating the Unspeakable: Visual Poetics as Projected through Olson's 'Field' into Current Female Writing Practice," in *Translating the Unspeakable: Poetry and the Innovative Necessity*, Tuscaloosa, AL: University of Alabama Press.

Hack, D. (2005) *The Material Interests of the Victorian Novel*, Charlottesville, VA: University of Virginia Press.

Higgins, D. (1977) *George Herbert's Pattern Poems: In Their Tradition*, West Glover, VT: Unpublished Editions.

Hollander, J. (1975) *Vision and Resonance: Two Sense of Poetic Form*, New York: Oxford University Press.

Lennard, J. (1996) *The Poetry Handbook: A Guide to Reading Poetry for Pleasure and Practical Criticism*, Oxford, UK: Oxford University Press.

Levertov, D. (1957) *Here and Now*, San Francisco, CA: City Lights Pocket Bookshop.

McHale, B. (1987) *Postmodernist Fiction*, New York: Methuen.

Puttenham, G. (2007 [1589]) *The Art of English Poesy, A Critical Edition*, ed. F. Whigham and W.A. Rebhorn. Ithaca, NY: Cornell University Press.

Solt, M.E. (ed.) (1970) *Concrete Poetry: A World View*, Bloomington, IN: Indiana University Press.

Summers, J. (1954) *George Herbert: His Religion and Art*, London: Chatto & Windus.

Williams, E. (ed.) (1967) *An Anthology of Concrete Poetry*, New York: Something Else Press.

Xie, M. (1998) *Ezra Pound and the Appropriation of Chinese Poetry: Cathay, Translation and Imagism*, London and New York: Routledge.

23

FOUND POETRY, "UNCREATIVE WRITING," AND THE ART OF APPROPRIATION

Andrew Epstein

I. Culture in the age of the remix

To adapt a famous statement by W.E.B. DuBois, a major problem of the twenty-first century is the problem of *the quote line*: the relation between the older and the newer versions of a text or cultural product, between source and quotation, original and copy, the content we consume and the content we produce. True, Ecclesiastes sounded the warning thousands of years ago that "there is nothing new under the sun," and litera- ture has from its inception been woven together from the shreds and patches of earlier works. Virgil reworked Homer, Shakespeare filched from Ovid, Plutarch, and Holin- shed; the history of literature is a long narrative of borrowings, echoings, and thefts. In the twentieth century, many writers and artists went another step: they forcefully rejected the Romantic concept of "genius" and musty, outdated notions of originality, inspiration, and heroic creativity, and invented radical new ways of appropriating and recycling pre-existing forms of expression.

Recent technological and social transformations have only made the relationship between artistic inspiration and appropriation blurrier than ever, and debates over the meaning of originality, creativity, and authorship have intensified. The consensus seems to be that we are presently living in a period of tumultuous change, in which the reproduction, sampling, and recycling of cultural materials – by writers, artists, and musicians but also by legions of "ordinary" consumers – has become a dominant expressive mode, if not *the* dominant one. Today, the remix and the mash-up rule.

The last two decades have witnessed the emergence of a wide range of interrelated phenomena which have helped to usher in this new paradigm: for example, the ubiq- uity of sampling in popular music and ensuing legal battles over copyright infringement; the emergence of the music file-sharing service Napster and the lawsuits that eventually shut the site down; the arrival of digital photography, video, music, and books, which has made it increasingly easy for individuals to reproduce and alter those forms; and the dramatic rise of "Web 2.0," exemplified by new media phenomena such as blogging, social networking, and Twitter (which have made copying, pasting, and linking to other texts essential acts of expression), and YouTube (in which users can generate content by grabbing and remixing existing images, music, and words).

As a result, fierce, unresolved debates are raging in the broader culture about the fate of copyright and intellectual property – not to mention the work of art – in an age of digital reproduction. This fraught issue has reared its head in far-flung spheres of culture, from law to ethics, politics to literature. Should the fruits of culture be considered "free," a kind of "cultural commons," an "open source" archive accessible to all, or should they be carefully guarded by legal boundaries of ownership and intellectual property? Where does one draw the line between originality and plagiarism in an era that takes the recycling and recombination of existing materials to be key expressive techniques? Among the many books on intellectual property and originality that have appeared in recent years, see Lessig 2005; Boon 2010; and Johns 2010. It seems safe to say that from the vantage point of the early twenty-first century, the idea of originality is in serious crisis.

Confronted with the dynamics of this new era, contemporary experimental writers have begun to grapple with its meaning, promise, and perils. "Our immersive digital environment demands new responses from writers," the poet Kenneth Goldsmith argues. "What does it mean to be a poet in the Internet age?" (2009). Recent innovative poetry has been energized by the question Goldsmith poses. New poetic forms based on plagiarism and plunder, on the manipulating and re-contextualizing of found texts, have become pervasive. The most prominent examples of this tendency are two self-styled avant-garde poetic movements which emerged in the late 1990s and which have generated heated controversy and extensive discussion among poets and scholars of contemporary poetry over the past decade: "Conceptual writing" (associated with Goldsmith and his brand of "uncreative writing") and "Flarf" (a movement which creates poems by collaging together found language gathered from the web).

At the same time, appropriative projects have sprung up in the work of poets unrelated to these two groups, across a wide spectrum of contemporary writing, which suggests just how widespread, and even acceptable, this phenomenon is becoming; once deemed marginal and questionable, such procedures are increasingly viewed as valid, worthy of notice, debate, and study. In 2007, the celebrated novelist Jonathan Lethem published a widely-read piece in *Harper's* called "An Ecstasy of Influence: A Plagiarism Mosaic," a lively tribute to the joys of appropriation and sampling, their rich history, and their vital importance to contemporary culture. Only when readers turned to the end of the essay did they learn that virtually every single word of Lethem's essay had been, appropriately enough, lifted from a wide range of other sources and stitched seamlessly together. In 2010, the fiction writer David Shields published a spirited defense of appropriation entitled *Reality Hunger: A Manifesto*, which seemed to pick up where Lethem's essay left off. Published by an esteemed mainstream press, Alfred A. Knopf, reviewed in major newspapers and magazines, and the subject of much discussion and hand-wringing (the chief *New York Times* book critic called it "deeply nihilistic"), Shields' book is a collection of numbered aphorisms and paragraphs, most of which, it turns out, are borrowed from other sources (Kakutani 2010). (Like Lethem, Shields includes an appendix with citations, explaining that his publisher's lawyers forced him to attach it to prevent legal difficulties.)

Within the world of poetry, the use of found language as a vehicle for poems has drawn a good deal of attention and discussion, some of which has moved far beyond the precincts of experimental poetry. The *Wall Street Journal* (Naik 2010) and *Poets and Writers* (Fischer 2009) magazine have published features on Flarf's brand of found web poetry, and in 2010 the *New York Times* even ran an online contest in honor of National Poetry Month, in which students were invited to submit "found poetry" made from its own newspaper articles (Schulten 2010). In 2009, *Poetry* magazine, regarded by many (fairly or not) as an organ of the American poetry establishment, had a special feature devoted to Conceptual Writing and Flarf poetry, and one of the premier art institutions in the country, the Whitney Museum of American Art in New York, hosted an evening that playfully pitted one movement against the other. Moreover, one of the most influential scholars of avant-garde poetry, Marjorie Perloff, has turned her attention to this phenomenon in her latest, field-defining book, *Unoriginal Genius: Poetry by Other Means in the New Century* (2010). Perloff's study makes a strong case that an aesthetics of recycling and citation is not only what the age demanded, but also what it needs.

II. Pioneers and precursors: appropriation in modernism and postmodernism

Although space will not allow a detailed discussion here of the vibrant earlier tradition of appropriation, collage, and citation, any account of recent experiments in this arena must acknowledge the pioneering contributions of visual artists and avant-garde authors from both the modernist and post-World War II period. In the early twentieth century, many modernists grew suspicious of the idea of "originality" and the notion of the artist as a divinely-inspired creator of unique, sui generis works. "Art is theft," Pablo Picasso announced (quoted in Shields 2010), while T.S. Eliot famously declared that "immature poets imitate; mature poets steal; bad poets deface what they take and good poets make it into something better" (1975: 153). This ethos led to the development of a whole range of ground breaking practices at the heart of modernism: the creation of collages out of juxtaposed fragments, a fascination with allusion, quotation, montage, and pastiche, and a belief in the creative potential of found materials.

Some crucial examples in the modernist visual arts include the cubist collages of Picasso, which featured actual pieces of fabric and newsprint pasted onto the canvas, and the work of Dada and Surrealist artists, like Kurt Schwitters, and later Joseph Cornell, who made collages and constructions out of found objects and cast-off trash, initiating a century's worth of mixed media assemblage art fashioned from found materials (see Stockwell, this volume). One of the most important figures behind today's fascination with appropriation is Marcel Duchamp, who pioneered the idea of recontextualizing found objects, which he called "ready-mades," as art, as in his notorious piece "Fountain," which consisted of a urinal which Duchamp found, turned upside down, and signed. Duchamp also performed a classic work of subversive appropriation when he notoriously reproduced Leonardo Da Vinci's masterwork, the *Mona Lisa*, irreverently painted a moustache and goatee on it, and gave it a mischievous title (*L.H.O.O.Q.*), which was a dirty joke in French (see Ulmer, this volume).

In the realm of modernist literature, indispensable precursors include T.S. Eliot's *The Waste Land*, a polyglot patchwork of quotations and allusions drawn from a wide variety of texts and sources, and other modernist poets, like Ezra Pound, Marianne Moore, William Carlos Williams, who developed complex forms dependent upon citation, sampling, and collage, and the Objectivist poets, like Charles Reznikoff, whose poems turned transcripts from legal cases and war crimes trials into verse (see Gregory 1996).

In the post-World War II period, this cut-and-paste proclivity only intensifies, as these practices become increasingly viewed as one of the distinguishing features of what comes to be known as "postmodernism" across the arts. In his influential essay "The Death of the Author" (1968), Roland Barthes dethroned the writer-as-creator and jettisoned the notion of originality in favor of endless intertextuality, when he famously declared that "a text is a tissue of quotations drawn from the innumerable centres of culture" (2001: 1468). In the visual arts, practices of appropriation, collage, and pastiche became even more central in the postwar period – for example, in Robert Rauschenberg's "combines," hybrid constructions made from found objects and junk materials, in the painted American flags of Jasper Johns, in Andy Warhol's Campbell soup cans and Marilyn Monroe silk-screens and other instances of Pop Art's reliance on the re-framing of images from popular culture, and in the turn to found materials in Conceptual Art. Appropriation art came to dominate in the 1970s and 1980s in the work of the young artists associated with "the Pictures Generation," like Richard Prince, Cindy Sherman, and Barbara Kruger, whose work depended upon the politically driven, ironic subversion of photographic imagery. Perhaps the most extreme example of pure appropriation can be found in the controversial work of Sherrie Levine, who took Duchamp another step: Levine re-photographed the iconic Depression-era photographs of Walker Evans and hung them, unaltered, in a gallery show as works by Sherrie Levine.

In postwar experimental writing, these practices continued to proliferate, as can be seen in the use of sampling and recycling in works by New York School poets (as in John Ashbery's *The Tennis Court Oath* and Ted Berrigan's *The Sonnets*), the experiments in "writing through" various found materials undertaken by Jackson Mac Low and the avant-garde composer and writer John Cage, and the constraint-based procedures deployed on pre-existing texts by writers affiliated with the largely French movement known as OuLiPo (see Lee, this volume, and Baetens, this volume). An interest in found language also became key to the work of poets within the avant-garde movement known as Language poetry, like Bruce Andrews, Charles Bernstein, Susan Howe, and Ron Silliman, whose poems often present phrases drawn from a diverse array of discourses, high and low, arranged into discontinuous collages (see Bernstein, this volume). The most notorious instance of appropriation in postmodernist fiction can be found in the work of Kathy Acker, whose entire oeuvre is founded upon an aesthetics of plagiarism and piracy; Acker felt that plundering and subverting other, usually male-authored, texts was an essential tool in a radical feminist attack on contemporary capitalist, patriarchal culture (see Dettmar 1999; also McHale, this volume).

Citation, copying, and appropriation can be found across a wide range of media and arts in the age of postmodernism, from the French New Wave films of Jean-Luc Godard, to the sound collage pieces by the avant-garde classical composer Steve Reich, to the magpie borrowings of Bob Dylan. The most prominent and widespread example in music, of course, can be found in the development of hip-hop since the 1970s. Exploiting the possibility of new technologies, rap revolutionized the use of samples and remixing, a phenomenon which has spread to other forms of popular music, and has become in some ways the lingua franca of contemporary culture itself.

III. The resurgence of appropriation in contemporary poetry

Clearly, the act of adopting and juxtaposing existing images and texts is hardly new nor the sole property of the twenty-first century – a fact not at all lost on the recent practitioners, who readily acknowledge that they are perpetuating some quite familiar gestures. But what are some of the reasons for this burst of interest in appropriation and recycling in recent poetry? As I have mentioned, it can be seen as a response to the crisis of originality and authorship brought on by the evolution of new media. But there are other factors as well. For one thing, appropriation and sampling have become central poetic tools because they offer a powerful way of paying close attention to the nature of everyday life in modernity. The idea that poetry must grasp and represent daily life and ordinary events and objects has been a prevailing goal of poetry and poetics since modernism, if not before, from the mundane "red wheelbarrow" of William Carlos Williams upon which so much depends to Frank O'Hara's "I do this, I do that" poems that chronicle daily urban life (see Lee, this volume), from Wallace Stevens's "Ordinary Evening in New Haven" to the poems of Billy Collins, which are celebrated for making the familiar and humdrum surprising. Recent poets have turned to found language and the reframing of existing texts in order to document and present the quotidian without elevation or distortion, transformation or elaborate aestheticization. These revitalized strategies enable new possibilities for the difficult task of representing, and in some cases critiquing, daily life in today's echo chamber of hyper-mediation and information overload.

Second, the cultivation of "uncreative writing" practices, the championing of boredom, and the creation of "unreadable" texts made up entirely of words swiped from others, have also allowed experimental poets to challenge what they view as the narrow, retrograde model of writing that still governs "mainstream" contemporary poetry, thanks to the "creative writing industry" associated with the flourishing of graduate programs in creative writing, such as the MFA (Master in Fine Arts) degree programs that have come to dominate the teaching and writing of poetry over the past several decades in the United States. What could be more alien to the creative writing workshop model – where self-expression, originality, and the fostering of a poet's distinctive "voice" still reign supreme – than *uncreativity*, plagiarism, impersonal and neutral transcription, extreme boredom, and unreadability? In this sense, Goldsmith's "uncreative writing," like Flarf and other examples of poetic appropriation, can be viewed as shots fired in the long battle against the expressivist, voice-centered model of lyric poetry – a fight waged most ferociously by Language writers since the 1970s, but now adapted for the Internet age.

More specifically, these tactics have given poets license to incorporate subjective experience and emotional material without fetishizing the lyric ego, the personal "I" – in effect, they permit poets to write about personal experience while sidestepping the problems of sentimentality, narcissism, and autobiographical excess that many poets still find dogging much contemporary lyric poetry (see Ashton 2008/2009). As Robert Fitterman, a poet who relies heavily on appropriation, puts it in his book *Rob the Plagiarist*, "what happens to personal experience in all of this? I am interested in the inclusion of subjectivity and personal experience; I just prefer it isn't my own" (2009: 18).

Third, strategies of appropriation have also proven useful as a vehicle of political critique and dissent for contemporary writers. As I will discuss below, many recent experimental projects have been written in explicit opposition to the extreme political dynamics of the post-9/11 period, the war in Iraq, and the conservative administration of President George W. Bush. In particular, writers have experimented with reproducing, assembling, and hijacking pre-existing language and images, often from the media, the news, or government sources, in order to expose, and perhaps to resist, the manipulation, deceit, and stupidity of contemporary political and media discourse.

IV. Kenneth Goldsmith, uncreative writing, and the everyday

In many ways, Kenneth Goldsmith has become the poster child for "unoriginality" and the recent surge of interest in appropriation as a poetic tool. After beginning his career as a visual artist steeped in the lineage of Pop Art, minimalism, and conceptual art, Goldsmith (who is also a DJ with a deep knowledge of experimental classical and rock music) left the art world and turned his attention to poetry after being exposed to the experiments of Language writing in the 1990s.

Part-prankster, part-visionary, Goldsmith has declared poetry's need both to catch up with the other arts and to confront the realities of the digital mediasphere in which we all float today. With his playful, evasive persona and sometimes faux-naïve pronouncements, he has self-consciously positioned himself in the tradition of Duchamp,

Cage, and especially Warhol. He has aggressively promoted Conceptual Writing – a movement that also includes writers like Christian Bök, Craig Dworkin, Robert Fitterman, Caroline Bergvall, and Vanessa Place – as "a poetics of the moment, fusing the avant-garde impulses of the last century with the technologies of the present, one that proposes an expanded field for 21st century poetry" (Goldsmith 2008: n.p.). In Goldsmith's definition, Conceptual Writing "employs intentionally self and ego effacing tactics using uncreativity, unoriginality, illegibility, appropriation, plagiarism, fraud, theft, and falsification as its precepts; information management, word processing, databasing, and extreme process as its methodologies; and boredom, valuelessness, and nutritionlessness as its ethos" (2010: n.p.).

Goldsmith seems unruffled by claims that his self-proclaimed avant-garde movement is little more than "Duchamp: The Remix," or "Warhol 2.0." "Conceptual writing obstinately makes no claims on originality," Goldsmith writes. "What we are doing has been done decades ago in the art and music worlds. We're just bringing those ideas, for the first time, into the writing world" (2010: n.p.). Goldsmith insists – perhaps hyperbolically, given the range of precursors discussed above – that poetry has suffered a peculiar lag in contrast to the other arts in this department: while the appropriation of existing images and texts has been an accepted, even expected practice, in contemporary art since Duchamp, and sampling has been at the basis of contemporary music for decades, Goldsmith believes that literature, especially poetry, has yet to fully accept or explore the possibilities of such practices. In her study, Perloff concurs, noting that "in the poetry world . . . the demand for original expression dies hard: we expect our poets to produce words, phrases, images, and ironic locutions that we have never heard before" (2010: 23).

In the mid-1990s, Goldsmith embarked on a series of conceptual, constraint-based projects that have become touchstones and flash points for contemporary avant-garde writing. His first major book remains one of his most impressive achievements, a 600-page tome entitled *No. 111: 2.7.93–10.20.96*, that he has referred to as a "useless encyclopedic reference book" (1997). Over the course of three years, Goldsmith collected an enormous number of phrases – many from the web – that ended in an "r" sound, and then arranged them alphabetically, in sections based on syllable count, beginning with a section of single syllable sounds and moving through collections of increasingly lengthy phrases, syllable by syllable. The final section consists of an entire short story by D. H. Lawrence (which ends with the letter "r," of course), lifted verbatim, and pasted into his book. A compendium of contemporary language in all its variety, ordinariness, and strangeness, *No. 111* is a wild archive of late twentieth-century daily life composed out of found shards of our existence.

Goldsmith's other key projects that seek to reinvigorate a poetics of everyday life include *Soliloquy* (2001), an unedited transcript of every word Goldsmith spoke for a week that runs to 600 pages. Like Warhol's *a: a novel* (1968), an important precursor for this work, *Soliloquy* is a remarkable experiment in collecting, transcribing, and archiving that ends up making ordinary language strange and fascinating. A similar effect is achieved in one of Goldsmith's most extravagant and widely discussed works,

Day (2003) – a verbatim, cover-to-cover reproduction of an entire *New York Times* for a single day that runs to over 800 pages. To create the book, Goldsmith has claimed that he spent months "uncreatively" retyping every word, number, and letter for a randomly selected day, September 1, 2000. (At the same time, Goldsmith also mentions that he digitally scanned and pasted much of the text rather than painstakingly retyping it, an unresolved contradiction). More recently, Goldsmith has completed his "American Trilogy": *The Weather* (2005) (a transcription of New York City weather reports over the course of a year), *Traffic* (2007) (a day's worth of traffic reports from the radio), and *Sports* (2008) (a verbatim rendering of the television commentary heard during a Red Sox–Yankees game).

These unusual, playful projects have garnered Goldsmith a great deal of attention from literary scholars and established literary venues like *Poetry*, not to mention prestigious university presses (Columbia University Press and Northwestern University Press will publish his latest books, rather than the small publishers he has published with in the past). Perhaps the apotheosis of "uncreative writing" was reached when Goldsmith received a rather surprising invitation to perform at the White House for "An Evening of Poetry" hosted by President Obama in May 2011.

However, as Perloff notes, "Goldsmith's provocative equation of poetry with 'word processing' or 'information management' has met with strong resistance from the poetry community – not just from the Establishment but, perhaps surprisingly, from such well-known experimentalists as Ron Silliman" (2010: 149). Silliman and other experimental writers have criticized Goldsmith's work for boldly going where many writers have already gone many times before, as well as for its refusal to engage with history and politics: "For in merely recycling the words of others . . . Goldsmith denies the very possibility of the poet's ability to have perspective on the cultural moment, much less to critique it" (149).

Further, as Perloff observes, Goldsmith has been attacked for the "egotism" lurking in his writing, in which the self-proclaimed unreadability of the work leads readers to turn, instead, to "the cult of the artist as his own work of art" (149). This aspect of Goldsmith's work was thrown into relief by another recent experiment with appropriation that provoked uncomfortable questions about where we might locate the limits of such practices, as well as about the ethics of appropriation. The poet Kent Johnson – known for subversive literary antics and hoaxes, such as the Araki Yasusada affair (see Mead, this volume) – decided to take Goldsmith's conceptual project of reframing an unaltered found text one step further: in a Sherrie Levine-like gesture, Johnson placed a sticker with his own name over Goldsmith's name on the front cover of copies of *Day*, declared the new work " *Day*, by Kent Johnson," and put the books up for sale (Johnson 2009). Despite the fact that Johnson's playful act of appropriation is quite similar to the spirit and theory behind Goldsmith's own work, his project did not seem to be well-received by Goldsmith and his fellow Conceptual writers, who greeted it with either silence or hostility. From Johnson's perspective, this chilly reception only serves to highlight the limitations of the contemporary Conceptual poetry project, in that it seems to stop short of truly relinquishing the idea of authorship, ownership, and property. In other words, the Johnson/Goldsmith episode may indicate that it is one thing to appropriate the words of others, another to have one's own work appropriated (see Freind 2010).

If nothing else, Goldsmith's tireless provocations have dramatically re-energized the practice of, and the critical thinking about, using found materials and sampling in contemporary poetry.

V. The rise of Flarf in the age of Bush

Like Conceptual Writing, the controversial movement known as "Flarf" takes seriously the idea of what it means to be a poet in the age of the Internet, even if it does not always take itself too seriously. It too finds creative fuel in found language and explores the possibilities of digital media for poetry. In the case of Flarf, poets have developed a technique they refer to as "Google sculpting," in which the poet trawls the internet for ready-made language, usually by running searches on Google for combinations of intentionally silly or offensive keywords ("pizza" and "kitty," or "Rogaine" and "bunny," "pussy" and "turtleneck") and then making strange, funny, and unsettling collages out of the results. Flarf is clearly an extension of twentieth-century avant-garde collage aesthetics, from Dada to Language poetry precursors like Bruce Andrews. One writer associated with Flarf, Michael Magee, acknowledges its debt to such earlier forms of poetic appropriation and collage, but argues that the extensive use of Google search results represents a "willful democratization of the method" (Magee, Mohammad and Sullivan 2003). In addition to Magee, some of the founders and practitioners of Flarf include Gary Sullivan, K. Silem Mohammad, Nada Gordon, Drew Gardner, Katie Degentesh, Sharon Mesmer, and Jordan Davis (see Snyder 2006).

As Flarf poems and books have appeared over the past decade, the movement has gone from being considered something of an inside joke to constituting an actual aesthetic intervention in contemporary poetics. The name "Flarf" is a neologism which Sullivan defines as "a kind of corrosive, cute, or cloying, awfulness. Wrong. Un-P.C. Out of control. 'Not okay.'" It is also, he explains, a verb, meaning "to bring out the inherent awfulness, etc., of some pre-existing text" (thus, one can "flarf" any unsuspecting piece of writing) (Magee *et al.* 2003).

What do the results of this Google sculpting methodology look like? Books like Mohammad's *Deer Head Nation* (2003), Mesmer's *Annoying Diabetic Bitch* (2008), Magee's *Mainstream* (2006), and Drew Gardner's *Petroleum Hat* (2005) present a polyvocal, disjunctive poetry made from "junk language," the verbal detritus which teems on the web and saturates our culture. Filled with deliberately outrageous and absurd content and offensive language, the poetry is often rebarbative, abrasive, and distasteful, but its humor and strangeness can be powerfully affecting. Despite the movement's own claims about the awfulness of the writing, Flarf poems – like those in Katie Degentesh's *The Anger Scale* (2006) – can be unsettling, emotionally potent, and oddly beautiful.

Some Flarf poets and critics have made political claims on its behalf, explaining that Flarf emerged as an antidote to the repressive political climate of the Bush years. Sullivan argues that Flarf took on a different, more serious and politicized cast after September 11: "instead of inside-jokes about minor annoyances, the target was the New Era" (2009). Magee explains his own participation in the Flarf project as a dissi-dent response to the nightmarish absurdity and deceit of the post-9/11 era: "I feel com-pelled in the face of this to interrogate dumbness, ridiculousness, stupidity; to work undercover in the middle of it, to pretend to be it if necessary, all the while reporting back to the reader. I have in mind, always now, Frederick Douglass's words, 'At a time like this, scorching irony, not convincing argument is needed'" (2006: 95). This brand of "scorching irony" can perhaps be seen in the socially and politically-charged language stew of a poem like Drew Gardner's "Chicks Dig War" (2005), which assem-bles chunks of disturbing found language in order to blast the macho nationalism, militarism, and xenophobia at work in ordinary language and daily life under George W. Bush (2005: 20).

At the same time, some have questioned the efficacy of these political gestures. In a widely read attack, Dan Hoy slammed Flarf for its complicity with the corporate struc-tures it claims to be critiquing (personified by Google), noting its "willful dependency on corporate tools to do the searching, selecting, and contextualizing of poetic mate-rial" (2006). Others have criticized Flarf for exhibiting a patronizing and elitist stance towards the "low" and "common" materials it appropriates, and have raised ethical questions about whether Flarf's reproduction of hateful, offensive language perpetu-ates rather than critiques harmful stereotypes and prejudices.

VI. Recent directions in the poetics of appropriation

Although Conceptual Writing and Flarf have received the lion's share of attention, examples of recycling, sampling, and "unoriginality" in contemporary writing extend well beyond the borders of these two movements. A wide range of poets, including Claudia Rankine, Susan Howe, and Jorie Graham, have in recent books relied on slabs of language mined from various sources. Poets like C.D. Wright, Mark Nowak, and Juliana Spahr have demonstrated a renewed interest in the kind of politically charged documentary poetics pioneered by Williams, Reznikoff, and Muriel Rukeyser. Eliot Weinberger's celebrated piece, "What I Heard About Iraq" (2005), hailed as a "classic anti-war book," is an essay-meets-prose poem that consists of a long list of statements, almost all verbatim quotations taken from Bush Administration officials and media accounts of the war in Iraq, each prefaced with the words "I heard" (Lezard 2005).

Recent years have also seen a mini-trend of "erasure poetics," as critics like Brian McHale (2005) and Travis MacDonald (2009) have shown, in which poems are wrought by erasing parts of an existing text and presenting the remainder as the work of art. There are precursors for these projects, to be sure, including Rauschenberg's *Erased De Kooning Drawing*, in which Rauschenberg took Duchamp's gesture of defac-ing the *Mona Lisa* another step by asking one of his idols, the painter Willem de

Kooning, to let him erase one of De Kooning's own drawings. Perhaps the ur-text for a poetry of erasure is Ronald Johnson's *Radi Os* (1977), which the poet created by erasing enormous portions of Milton's *Paradise Lost*, leaving behind a lapidary, spare poem of his own. The past several years have witnessed a rush of such works: for example, Jen Bervin's *Nets* (2003) erases Shakespeare's sonnets, while Janet Holmes's *MS OF M Y KIN* (2009) erases *The Poems of Emily Dickinson* and Mary Ruefle's *Little White Shadow* (2006) whites out most of an obscure nineteenth-century book. Similarly, the Conceptual poet Robert Fitterman's prose piece "The Sun Also Also Rises" was created when "I erased my way through Hemingway's original text, leaving behind only the phrases that begin with the pronoun I" (2009: 107). The best-selling novelist Jonathan Safran Foer has joined the erasure trend, as well – his most recent book, *Tree of Codes* (2010), is an artist's book in the tradition of Tom Phillips' masterpiece of erasure, *A Humument* (1970) (an erasure of an unheralded nineteenth-century novel), that Foer created by literally carving out words from the text of Bruno Schulz's novel *The Street of Crocodiles* (1934).

VII. Towards a typology of the poetics of appropriation

Given the abundance and diversity of such projects, it is worthwhile to recognize that not all acts of appropriation are the same and to confront the fact that the practice of appropriation raises a whole battery of thorny aesthetic, ethical, and political questions that we have only begun to consider. For example, why have such works proliferated in the last two decades? Has the digital revolution irrevocably altered ideas of ownership and intellectual property? Is the writer who re-uses the words of others simply lazy, unimaginative, or unethical or can re-framing existing language be a deeply creative act? Furthermore, can works of appropriation be subversive, dissident works of resistance, or are they guilty of merely repeating and thereby reinforcing dominant ideologies? Is it unethical or exploitative to borrow and adapt the voices and words of others, particularly the words of those who are marginalized in our society? (For example, see Abe Louise Young [2010], who argues that a recent book by Raymond McDaniel, which borrows words from survivors of Hurricane Katrina, is an instance of unethical appropriation.)

If, as it seems clear, appropriation and sampling are not going to go away, what is needed now is a rather dramatic shift in our critical vocabularies, our means of assessing creative works, and our concepts of originality and creativity. It behooves us to think deeply about why these practices are so much with us, what they mean, where they come from, and where they – and we – are going.

References

Ashton, J. (2008/2009) "Sincerity and the Second Person: Lyric After Language Poetry," *Interval(le)s* 2(2)–3(1), retrieved from http://www.cipa.ulg.ac.be/intervalles4/8_ashton.pdf [accessed 12 November 2010].

Barthes, R. (2001 [1968]) "The Death of the Author". In V. Leitch (ed.), *The Norton Anthology of Theory and Criticism*, New York: W.W. Norton, pp. 1466–70.

Boon, M. (2010) *In Praise of Copying*, Cambridge, MA: Harvard University Press.

Dettmar, K. (1999) "The Illusion of Modernist Allusion and the Politics of Postmodern Plagiarism." In L. Buranen and A. Roy (eds.) *Perspectives on Plagiarism and Intellectual Property in a Postmodern World*, Albany, NY: SUNY Press, pp. 99–110.

Eliot, T.S. (1975) "Philip Massinger" (1920), in *Selected Prose*, New York: Harcourt, pp. 153–60.

Fischer, S. (2009) "Can Flarf Ever Be Taken Seriously?" *Poets and Writers*, retrieved from http://www.pw.org/content/can_flarf_ever_be_taken_seriously [accessed 12 November 2010].

Fitterman, R. (2009) *Rob the Plagiarist*, New York: Roof Books.

Freind, B. (2010) "In the Conceptual Vacuum: On Kent Johnson's *Day*" retrieved from http://jacketmagazine.com/40/freind-johnson-day.shtml [accessed 12 November 2010].

Gardner, D. (2005) *Petroleum Hat*, New York: Roof Books.

Goldsmith, K. (1997) *No. 111: 2.7.93–10.20.96*, Great Barrington, MA: The Figures.

—— (2001) *Soliloquy*, New York: Granary Books.

—— (2003) *Day*, Great Barrington, MA: The Figures.

—— (2008) "Conceptual Poetics," *Poetry Foundation*, retrieved from http://www.poetryfoundation.org/harriet/2008/06/conceptual-poetics-kenneth-goldsmith/ [accessed 12 November 2010].

—— (2009) "Introduction to Flarf vs. Conceptual Writing," *Electronic Poetry Center*, retrieved from http://www.epc.buffalo.edu/authors/goldsmith/whitney-intro.html [accessed 12 November 2010].

—— (2010) "If I were to raise my children the way I write my books, I would have been thrown in jail long ago," *Poetry Foundation*, retrieved from http://www.poetryfoundation.org/harriet/2010/04/if-i-were-to-raise-my-children-the-way-i-write-my-books-i-would-have-been-thrown-in-jail-long-ago/ [accessed 12 November 2010].

Gregory, E. (1996) *Quotation and Modern American Poetry: "Imaginary Gardens with Real Toads,"* Ann Arbor, MI: University of Michigan Press.

Hoy, D. (2006) "The Virtual Dependency of the Post-Avant and the Problematics of Flarf: What Happens When Poets Spend Too Much Time Fucking Around on the Internet," *Jacket* 29, retrieved from http://jacketmagazine.com/29/hoy-flarf.html [accessed 12 November 2010].

Johns, A. (2010) *Piracy: The Intellectual Property Wars from Gutenberg to Gates*, Chicago, IL: University of Chicago Press.

Johnson, K. (2009) *Day*, Buffalo, NY: BlazeVOX.

Kakutani, M. (2010) "Texts Without Context," *The New York Times*, 21 March.

Lessig, L. (2005) *Free Culture: The Nature and Future of Creativity*, New York: Penguin Press.

Lethem, J. (2007) "An Ecstasy of Influence: A Plagiarism Mosaic," *Harper's Magazine*, retrieved from http://harpers.org/archive/2007/02/0081387 [accessed 12 November 2010].

Lezard, N. (2005) "War: The Case Against." *The Guardian*, May 28, retrieved from http://www.guardian.co.uk/books/2005/may/28/iraq.middleeast [accessed 12 November 2010].

MacDonald, T. (2009) "A Brief History of Erasure Poetics," *Jacket* 38, retrieved from http://jacketmagazine.com/38/macdonald-erasure.shtml [accessed 12 November 2010].

Magee, M., K.S. Mohammad and G. Sullivan (2003) "The Flarf Files." *Electronic Poetry Center*, retrieved from http://epc.buffalo.edu/authors/bernstein/syllabi/readings/flarf.htm [accessed 12 November 2010].

Magee, M. (2006) *Mainstream*, Buffalo, NY: BlazeVOX.

McHale, B. (2005) "Poetry Under Erasure." In E. Müller-Zettelman and M. Rubik (eds.) *Theory into Practice: New Approaches to Poetry*, Amsterdam: Peter Lang, pp. 277–301.

Naik, G. (2010) "Search for a New Poetics Yields This: 'Kitty Goes Postal/Wants Pizza,'" *Wall Street Journal*, May 25.

Perloff, M. (2010) *Unoriginal Genius: Poetry by Other Means in the New Century*, Chicago, IL: University of Chicago Press.

Schulten, K. (2010) "Student Challenge: Create a New York Times 'Found Poem.'" The Learning Network blog, *New York Times*, April 5, retrieved from http://learning.blogs.nytimes.com/2010/04/05/student-challenge-new-york-times-found-poem/[accessed 12 November 2010].

Shields, D. (2010) *Reality Hunger: A Manifesto*, New York: Alfred A. Knopf.

Snyder, R., 2006. "The New Pandemonium: A Brief Overview of Flarf," *Jacket* 31, retrieved from http://jacketmagazine.com/31/snyder-flarf.html [accessed 12 November 2010].

Sullivan, G. (2009) "Flarf: From Glory Days to Glory Hole," *Brooklyn Rail*, retrieved from http://www.brooklynrail.org/2009/02/books/flarf-from-glory-days-to-glory-hole [accessed 12 November 2010].

Weinberger, E. (2005) "What I Heard About Iraq," *London Review of Books* 27(3), 3–11.

Young, A.L. (2010) "The Voices of Hurricane Katrina, Part I: What are the Ethics of Poetic Appropriation?" *Poetry Foundation*, retrieved from http://www.poetryfoundation.org/journal/article.html?id=239906 [accessed 12 November 2010].

Further reading

Evans, D. (2009) *Appropriation*, Cambridge, MA: MIT Press.

Miller, P. (2008) *Sound Unbound: Sampling Digital Music and Culture*, Cambridge, MA: MIT Press.

Rubinstein, R. (1999) "Gathered, Not Made: A Brief History of Appropriative Writing," *American Poetry Review*, 28(2), 31–4.

24

WORDS IN VISUAL ART

Jessica Prinz

I. Introduction: the language arts

The use of language within art is hardly new. Early fusions of the verbal and the visual occur in Egyptian hieroglyphs, Chinese ideograms, and Mayan glyph writing. Illuminated manuscripts, seventeenth-century emblem books, pattern poetry (from George Herbert to the present; see Bray, this volume), and William Blake's mixed art are among some of the diverse and "curious" combinations of media that predate our time. It is in the twentieth century, though, that an eruption of language into the field of the visual arts can be witnessed. This eruption began early in the century, exploded onto the conceptual art scene, and is still evident today in performance modes, multimodal artworks, and multimedia installations (see Gibbons, "Multimodal Literature," this volume). Indeed, the pervasiveness and variety of language works produced during the twentieth century are remarkable. Hybrid works including words appear in paintings with words as dominant images (Edward Ruscha), or words painted directly on walls (by conceptualists Lawrence Weiner, Robert Barry, and Mel Bochner as well as painters whose inspiration has sources in graffiti art, like Jean-Michel Basquiat). Some artists produce visual signs contextualized by theoretical essays (Daniel Buren), essays on aesthetics presented as art and wall texts that are stories (Art and Language Group), collage or sculptural objects with fictional texts (Edward Kienholz), performed texts (Joseph Beuys, Laurie Anderson), books (Lawrence Weiner, Dan Graham), card files (Robert Morris), postcards with words (On Kawara), puns conveyed through body art (Bruce Nauman, Chris Burden), thesaurus works (Joseph Kosuth, Vito Acconci), scripted events (George Brecht, John Cage), the exchange of spoken or written secrets (Vito Acconci, Douglas Huebler), multimedia installations with texts (Jonathan Borofsky, Marcel Broodthaers), photographs (Barbara Kruger), neon signs (Jenny Holzer), and more. Numerous art movements generated during the twentieth century are also defined by their use of language: conceptual art and performance art include programs for using language as a primary material. Since the 1960s, language has become as important to many artists as the brushstroke has remained to others.

In the following chapter I discuss how the innovations of the avant-garde, especially Dada and Futurist experiments, paved the way for later variations and creations based on the interplay of verbal and visual components. In the 1960s, two factors conjoined to produce the preoccupation with language as a subject and medium for art: (1) the art of the sixties was a direct response (or "answer") to earlier artists like Duchamp and Marinetti; and (2) the pervasiveness of language in art produced during the sixties also reflected a general concern for language and its meaning within the culture and philosophy of the time. Finally, the conceptual art of the sixties in turn became the touchstone for later artists also concerned with and employing words in their work.

II. The early twentieth century and conceptual art

What is most distinctive in the art of the sixties is the way in which the debate concerning art's possibilities, limits, and boundaries is no longer centered on art's visuality alone, but extended to include the verbal mode, too. Words are used not only in the production of art (Kosuth, Wiener, Barry, and Huebler), but also in the production of theories that become inseparable from it. Traditionally, artists create objects and leave critics free to formulate the conceptual implications of their art. "As such," Kosuth says, "the traditional artist functions like the 'valet's assistant' to his marksman master (the critic)" (Kosuth 1991: 100). The Art and Language Group, Joseph Kosuth, Daniel Buren, Robert Smithson, and Joseph Beuys are just some of the artists who appropriate the critic's role and create critical discourse as an essential part of art; they generate the ideas through which the artistic objects and actions are viewed, or present theoretical discourse as the substance of art. Of course, each artist manipulates the relation of theory and art in a slightly different way. Members of the Art and Language group write essays that are presented as visual art. Smithson intertwines art criticism and art forms, sustaining a shifting balance through a constant interplay of verbal and visual components. Theory becomes performance in Beuys's "How to Explain Pictures to a Dead Hare" (1965) in which the artist tours a gallery talking to a dead hare about art, making the piece a poignant commentary on the necessity and the futility of talking about art. Kosuth places priority on theory: his visual "forms of presentation" are secondary manifestations of his ideas; nevertheless, they constitute procedures essential to his art. (See also Winkiel on manifestos, this volume.)

The most immediate and important context for a discussion of language works (both now and in the 1960s) is modernist-era works of collage and linguistic experimentation by such figures as George Braque, Juan Gris, Stuart Davis, Gino Severini, Carlo Carra, and Filippo Tommaso Marinetti. Braque's "The Portuguese" (1911) was the first Cubist collage to include lettering, and it paved the way for numerous canvases with words used as elements in the composition. As Douglas Cooper (1970) suggests, the fragments of verbal material in a Cubist painting serve a double function: they operate as mimetic elements, heightening the representational aspect of the work, while at the same time foregrounding the two-dimensionality of the canvas. Richard Kostelanetz (1980) proposes that Cubist paintings represent a complementary art, like opera, where a libretto can viably be separated from the music, rather than an intermedium where one element is entwined with the other. A brief comparison of Juan Gris and Marcel Duchamp will bear out this distinction.

Juan Gris's "Still Life with a Poem" (1915) is an example of a complementary art: it contains a poem by Pierre Reverdy painted on one of the many frames within the work. The words do not verbalize the painting, nor does the painting resolve any of the poem's ambiguities. Here the poem and the painting remain distinct and autonomous. In contrast, Duchamp's "The Bride Stripped Bare by Her Bachelors, Even" (1915–1923), intertwines the verbal and the visual aspects of the work. "The Green Box" includes Duchamp's fragmented narratives, drawings, and anecdotes for "The Bride Stripped Bare." When the images are seen "through" this text and the text, as it were, seen "through" the glass, "The Large Glass" as a whole is suddenly animated, lively, intriguing, and even in a strange way, beautiful. Suddenly the mechanical images are comically humanized and implicated in a complex love story, an erotic encounter with an indecisive conclusion. "The Large Glass" is a hybrid work – visual, pictorial, literary, narrative, aleatory, linguistic, poetic and philosophical. Any of the following terms would apply to it: transmedial, intermedial, plurimedial and multimedial (on the complexity and "fuzziness" of these terms, see Ryan 2010: 1–7), but generally all of these suggest some relation between different media. "My research," Duchamp said, "was in the direction of finding some way of expressing myself without being a painter, without being a writer, without taking one of those labels" (quoted in Schwarz 1970: 7). Duchamp's hybrid approach is a perfect example of what Kostelanetz would call an "intermedial" art (1980: 3). (See also Ulmer, this volume.) Ryan, for instance, follows the transformations of fictional and narrative components from one medium to another (book to film, to TV and to the Web), which she calls "transfictionality." The term, intermedial, also (and more appropriately for my discussion here) includes works that are themselves hybrid and complex mixtures of visual and verbal elements. "The Large Glass" is just such a work.

Although clearly influenced by Duchamp, the use of language in sixties art also reflected a general emphasis in Western cultures on language and its possibilities and meanings. Structuralism and semiotics were just two of the many theoretical approaches manifesting the whole orientation of postmodern culture toward language. "The sixties," writes Julia Kristeva, "witnessed a theoretical ebullience that could roughly be summarized as leading to the discovery of the determinative role of *language* in all the human sciences" (Kristeva 1980: vii). In the words of Wendy Steiner, "structuralism in general turned to language as a model for understanding all cultural phenomena" (Steiner 1982: 51). However different these theorists may be, they seem to agree that language itself is somehow central to their work and culture as a whole. Viewed in this context, the prioritization of language in conceptual art, where the texts themselves become the art, was not an aberration of art history so much as the fullest expression of the intellectual thought of its time. It is not a coincidence that one of the most important texts on the postmodern style was titled *The Language of Post-Modern Architecture* and that in it Charles Jencks asked us to attend to architectural "syntax" and "semantics" (Jencks 1981: 39; see also McHale, this volume).

Following Duchamp, then, language and image are now frequently presented without priority, and there is a concern for the interplay of sign systems rather than any hierarchy between them (see also Gibbons, "Multimodal Literature," this volume). Robert Smithson, Laurie Anderson, and other artists like Jonathan Borofsky and Ann Hamilton set image and text in constantly changing relations to one another. These artists would concur with W.J.T. Mitchell's observation that the real task – not only of theory but of artistic production as well – "is not to renounce this dialogue" between word and image (Mitchell 1986: 46). Furthermore, the very notion of multimodality (in linguistics and narrative theory), emphasizes the way some works appeal to the various senses, using different semiotic codes and multiple systems of discourse. Michael O'Toole's *The Language of Displayed Art* (1994) and *Reading Images* by Kress and van Leeuwen (2006 [1996]), along with a host of more recent works in the field analyze the multiple channels and modes of communication by which some fictional (and nonfictional) works communicate to an audience.

III. The later twentieth century: after Duchamp

Duchamp thus influenced an entire generation of artists (including Kosuth, Weiner, Huebler, and Barry) for whom art was not only visual but also linguistic. Kosuth in particular produced an art influenced by language philosophy and poised dramatically between philosophy and art. His dictionary definitions and his book, *Art Investigations and "Problematics" Since 1965* (1973), present art as an exploration of linguistic meanings (and the meaning of "art"). Kosuth writes: "Being an artist now means to question the nature of 'art'" (1973: 54). "Painting is a kind of art. If you make paintings you are already accepting (not questioning) the nature of art" (Kosuth in Rose 1969: 23). His work, "One and Three Chairs" (1965) is perhaps an icon for the movement, especially for the de-materialization of the art object (Lippard 1973) and the rejection of painting and "retinal" art. The work includes a real wooden chair; a black and white photograph of the chair blown up and posted to the left; and a photostat of a dictionary definition of the work, "CHAIR," which hangs to the right. This work may be simple in form and color, but it generates an amazingly complex network of alternative readings and ideas (see Figure 24.1).

First, we are confronted with a simple, domestic, and commonplace object in a work that is about language and naming. On one level, the words and things seem to be equivalent, implying a one-to-one relationship between the object and its name. Wittgenstein acknowledges that this is one way (among many others) that language works. He says, "Nominalists make the mistake of interpreting all words as *names*, so of not really describing their use" (1958: 383). On one level, then, Kosuth practices just such nominalism in which words define or label a thing. At the same time, though, a different theory of language is also expressed in this work, one more consistent with Wittgenstein's later theories. Here the key link is not between word(s) and object(s), but between the word and the linguistic system in which it is used. The elements of the piece, "One and Three Chairs," all remain distinct from each other, and all are separate sign systems that produce their own unique meanings. Kosuth writes, for example,

Figure 24.1 Joseph Kosuth, "One and Three Chairs," Digital Image © The Museum of Modern Art/
Licensed by SCALA / Art Resource, NY.

> With normal usage either the text or the image is subservient to the other.
> Here, both have equal weight. The text does not explain the image, nor does
> the image "illustrate" the text . . .
>
> (Kosuth 1991: 200)

Regardless of whether Kosuth is alluding to the early or to the later Wittgenstein, or
neither, one thing is certain: the art is comprised of language and concerns the relation of words to things. As such it reflects the inherently linguistic nature of art, which
(Kosuth argues) has always has been contextualized by words and texts (titles, essays,
theories, monographs, histories, biographies, artists' statements, lectures, essays, cartoons, teaching and interviews, etc.). He posits that art has always been "framed by
language" (Kosuth 1991: 53).

Fundamental to this idea of art is the understanding of the linguistic nature of all art
propositions, be they past or present, and regardless of the elements used in their construction (Kosuth 1991: 40 and 74). Here, the artist is no longer the maker of "visual
kicks" (Kosuth 1991: 51) and instead is a maker of meanings and ideas (Kosuth 1991:
216), especially those concerning art and its "definition." Kosuth seems more intent
on proliferating and generating various meanings, possibilities and ideas rather than
conveying "one" (essential) thematic arc or through-line.

Briefly during the 1960s, Kosuth was a member of the Art and Language Group, a predominantly British association of artists (including Terry Atkinson, Michael Baldwin, David Bainbridge, Harold Hurrill, Charles Harrison, and others) whose work (like Kosuth's own) has by now spanned five decades of experimentation and creativity. As the name of the group suggests, language is and was central to them. They published essays and journals as art. They rejected all of the "old" genres and concentrated on works with a linguistic or verbal element. Books, for example, were treated as "exhibition sites" (Guttman 1998: 425), and publications, in general, served as the central medium for these "visual" artists. Expressing the de-materialization of art, they took as their subjects substances like gas, air, water, or other material that cannot be seen or which cannot be defined in anything but words. They were very much opposed to traditional venues for art (galleries and museums), as were other artists during this time, such as Robert Smithson, Christo, and Daniel Buren, as well as other more recent artists, like Stelarc and Barbara Kruger.

In the 1990s the Art and Language Group produced a series titled "Hostages" that combined silkscreen, text and paper, glass, oil and canvas. Here the text appears in a rectangle and the canvas is divided into geometrical sections, some with varying kinds of confusing imagery (birds? trees? leaves?). Here is the text from "Hostage LXVI" by Art and Language:

> The convertible exploded. It went roar thump. The body accelerated upwards, away from the heavier mechanical parts. The roof tore open at the front. The rear axle and part of its subframe assembly caught up with and passed through the rearbody, upwards and forwards. The doors and the windshield burst. A few passers-by were injured. Some were deafened by the concussion, others were lacerated by glass.
>
> (Harrison 2001: 120)

Charles Harrison compares the geometric organization of this piece to paintings by Barnett Newman or Mark Rothko. However, it is also clearly influenced by the discursive component of Futurist art. That is, in some ways, it reads like a contemporary version of Marinetti's "First Futurist Manifesto" of 1909, which describes the artist's furious and speedy adventure in a car and the way it lands in a ditch – because it was going so fast (10–15 miles an hour!) (see White, this volume). A short passage from the "First Manifesto" expresses how exhilarating this speedy ride was, and how it ended with the car (and its passenger) swerving into a ditch:

> Oh! Maternal ditch!, almost full of muddy water! Fair factory drain! I gulped down your nourishing sludge; and I remembered the blessed black breast of my Sudanese nurse. When I came up – torn, filthy, and stinking – from under the capsized car, I felt the white-hot iron joy deliciously pass through my heart.
>
> (Marinetti 1972: 40–1)

Both of these – Marinetti's original text and Art and Language's variation on it, include buffoonery, hyperbole, and parody. In both cases, despite a gap of almost a century between them, a text becomes central to the art.

Robert Smithson is another interdisciplinary and intermedial artist whose writings constitute an essential component of his art. "The Spiral Jetty" (1970) cuts across three media: earthwork, essay, and film. In it, Smithson presents linguistic data as solid objects. "Language tended to inform my structures, " he says. "I guess if there was any kind of notation, it was a kind of linguistic notation" (Smithson 1979: 154). Language may, in fact, be one of the many axes around which the verbal and visual materials of "The Spiral Jetty" accumulate. Among the words and linked linguistic meanings underlying the piece, which itself intertwines verbal and visual elements, are the following:

Helix: A spiral in many dimensions, in which the Jetty "could be considered one layer";

Helicopter: "From the Greek, helix, helikos meaning spiral" (Smithson 1979: 113);

Helicline:A curving ramp that ascends gradually. "The Spiral Jetty" curves and "ascends" ("scala . . . a means of ascent") (Smithson 1979: 112);

Heliogram: Signaling by flashing sun's rays from a mirror. The water serves as a "vast thermal mirror" reflecting sunlight;

Heliotypes: printed reproductions. Smithson's work in general is presented as a series of duplications and replicas for lost and absent originals;

Helios: The sun. The film begins with a shot of the sun and fictively ends in "sunstroke." The narration includes a definition of sunstroke from Black's Medical Dictionary.

Thus, not only does Smithson use language to describe "The Spiral Jetty" in his essay, he also uses the Jetty to inscribe words and ideas into matter. He shapes and molds language like "material" that can be put together (Smithson 1979: 104), and also manipulates and creates objects based on their linguistic connections and connotations, to produce a kind of "writing beyond the book" (Ulmer 1985: 15–16, 242; see also Ulmer, this volume).

Throughout his work, Smithson treats language (like earth matter) as material with which to work. In verbal/visual exercises like "A Heap of Language" (1966) or "Strata: A Geophotographic Fiction" (1972), words fall into patterns like "heaps" or strata of the earth. The artist makes these connections in his writing as well. Consider this passage from "A Sedimentation of the Mind: Earth Projects" (1968) which directly describes this interplay (between words and things) in his work:

The names of the minerals and the minerals themselves do not differ from each other, because at the bottom of both the material and the print is the beginning of an abysmal number of fissures. Words and rocks contain a language that follows a syntax of splits and ruptures. Look at any word long enough and you will see it open up into a series of faults, into a terrain of particles, each containing its own void. This discomforting language of fragmentation offers no easy gestalt solution; the certainties of didactic discourse are hurled into the erosion of the poetic principle.

(Smithson 1979: 87)

Smithson also generates many different metaphors for language in his writings. It is a "mirror structure" (1979: 67), or "looking glass babel" (1979: 67), a "mirror displacement" (1979: 94–5), an "infinite museum" (1979: 67), and a "building of words": "– a brick = a word, a sentence = a room, a paragraph = a floor of rooms, etc." (1979: 67). Smithson's style is to create not just one stable metaphor for each idea and then manipulate it, but to multiply metaphoric meanings in a labyrinthine syntax of associations. Thus language is also "strata," "matter," "linguistic objects," minerals, "mountains of symbolic debris," and earth. In the future, Smithson may well be regarded as a "writer" as much as he is an "artist," and indeed these distinctions themselves may disappear the more we consider this art.

Conceptual art's legacy can also be seen in the predominantly verbal nature of some visual art by younger artists, such as Jenny Holzer. Holzer began working with language early in her career (the 1970s), and has continued to do so. Her first language work, "Truisms," was a series of pithy statements or contrived clichés that she wrote herself and posted on walls in New York. In 1976, Martha Wilson opened Franklin Furnace Archive to support artists, especially collecting, archiving, cataloguing, and exhibiting performance, installation art and artists' books. The archive exhibited works by Claes Oldenburg, Robert Wilson, Ann Hamilton, and hundreds of others. Holzer's "Truisms" were exhibited by Franklin Furnace as early at 1978, and were then disseminated throughout the culture in various forms: t-shirts, L.E.D. signs, billboards, and just about anywhere that texts appear in our lives, from Times Square to baggage carousel signs (see Figure 24.2). Consider the following cryptic statements, from a list of more than two hundred and fifty:

ABUSE OF POWER COMES AS NO SURPRISE

ENJOY YOURSELF BECAUSE YOU CAN'T CHANGE ANYTHING

CHILDREN ARE THE MOST CRUEL OF ALL

CHILDREN ARE THE HOPE OF THE FUTURE

MONEY CREATES TASTE

EXPIRING FOR LOVE IS BEAUTIFUL BUT STUPID

Figure 24.2 Jenny Holzer, "Truisms," Courtesy: Jenny Holzer / Art Resource, NY.

Holzer admitted – rather humorously – that to write a quality cliché, "you have to come up with something new . . . It's hard to write a good cliché" (quoted by Waldman 1989). The artist continues to work in various series – like *Laments* (1989), *Lustmord* (1997), *Under a Rock* (1996) and others– and all of them include texts. Moreover, she continues to return to earlier language works in a rather unsystematic way, so that the "Truisms" appear throughout her work of the past three decades, including the 1990 Venice Biennale at which she represented the U.S.. Later I will discuss Holzer's various collaborations with writers, but for now, I'd like to focus on her own "literary" or "discursive" or "expressive" writings.

Holzer's work is "about" more than the notion of art and how it is defined (as was the case with the conceptualists). She has said that she wants her work to be more than a critique of the art world, or addressed to an art world audience (Auping 1992: 85). Her themes are many and are almost always emotionally "loaded": sex, death, war, justice, love, money and various kinds of violence, danger, murder, the horrific, the cruel, the mad, truth, pain, and power. She has said about her artistic project: it is a "version of what the world looks like when your internal censor stops functioning" (quoted by Princenthal 2007: 138). Many of the texts, like *Under a Rock* (1996) below, are extremely gruesome:

CRACK THE PELVIS SO SHE LIES RIGHT. THIS IS A MISTAKE

WHEN SHE DIES YOU CANNOT REPEAT THE ACT. THE BONES

WILL NOT GROW TOGETHER AGAIN AND THE PERSONALITY

WILL NOT COME BACK. SHE IS GOING TO SINK DEEP INTO THE

MOSS TO GET WHITE AND LIGHTER. SHE IS UNRESPONSIVE TO

BEGGING AND SELF-ABSORBED.

The artist says that the title is about "bringing up some unmentionable or at least unpleasant things that crawl out from 'under a rock'" (Waldman 1989: 17). As she said of a different work, "I wanted [the texts] to be nice in their own horrible way."

Many artists from the 1960s to the present continue to generate compelling works of art with words. Painters as different as Edward Ruscha and Jean-Michel Basquiat-produced canvases rich in verbal/visual connections. Influenced by Robert Rauschenberg and Jasper Johns, Ruscha balanced an interest in conceptual and Pop art, as he produced many word paintings filled with familiar American signs. His silkscreens of "Four Standard Stations" (1966–9) was perhaps most of all a tribute to Duchamp's use of chance operations in "Four Standard Stoppages," as proposed by some recent critics (Hunt, Lomas and Corris 2010: 278). The Pop imagery of Ruscha's streamlined and stylized gas station is at once highly realistic and abstract. Mostly angular forms in white and red, the work foregrounds what was everyday imagery at the time (the 1960s): the word "Standard" (as in Standard Oil, aka Esso). Perhaps Ruscha's most famous painting is "Spam," with the word at the top of the canvas and a small but recognizable can of Spam flying through the air like a Fourth of July skyrocket.

In contrast to Ruscha's highly stylized, abstract, and simple canvases, Jean-Michel Basquiat's paintings explode with energy, complexity, colors, and words. Often described as a "neo-expressionist," Basquiat actually exceeds all categories and descriptions. Beginning as a graffiti artist, he produced canvases rich with imagery, painterly gestures, letters, words, colors, writing, personal and mythological symbols and drawing. Graffiti art is inherently a kind of writing, and Basquiat continued to incorporate this kind of "signage" in his work. Among the literary figures who influenced him were Langston Hughes (Fretz 2010: 151), Jack Kerouac and William Burroughs (with whom he commiserated about various kinds of addiction). He was very close to Andy Warhol, whose death may have precipitated Basquiat's own. He was not only influenced by literature but also inspired it: the poet Kevin Young wrote a captivating and impressive volume, *To Repel Ghosts* (2005), dedicated to Basquiat's life and works.

IV. The twenty-first century

During the first decade of the twenty-first century, this interest in language on the part of visual artists, far from fading away, has only increased and expanded. As of 2011, Kosuth is still producing exciting and remarkable language works, as evident in his two recent shows in Italy and Australia, both of which appropriate texts from Samuel Beckett, especially *Waiting for Godot* and *Texts for Nothing*. As a part of these exhibits, Kosuth included previous works that resonate with Beckett's project: a series of dictionary definitions of the word "nothing." Moreover, language is "something" to look at in these works, as Kosuth presents passages of Beckett's work in white neon lights against dark backgrounds.

The 2004 book by Holzer, *Truth Before Power*, includes a variety of Xenon Projections, huge images of texts (and textual fragments) projected against buildings in varying sizes and colors. As she has said, "I hope the text and the visuals are inseparable now. It should not be either/or" (Auping 1992: 95). Often she creates her own texts, in works like *Truisms*, *Laments*, and *Lustmord*. She has also collaborated with and been influenced by other writers such as Yehuda Amichai (Israeli), Wislawa Syzmborska (Polish), Mahmoud Darwish (Palestinian) and Fadhil Al-Azzawi (Iraqi). Among her most important works may be the 2006 tribute to the poet, Elizabeth Bishop – benches at Vassar with fragments of Bishop's poems carved into them – and her collaborations with the poet, Henri Cole, whose poem, "To the 43rd President" (George W. Bush) serves as the source text for a striking installation by the artist (Cole 2010; reprinted in Holzer 2004: 40).

Ann Hamilton, too, has had a long and productive engagement with literature (and books) in her art. Among other important writers, she has been influenced by the novelists Nathalie Sarraute and Margaret Atwood, and by the poets Walt Whitman, T.S. Eliot, and Charles Reznikoff. Visual works by Hamilton that include books are "Tropos" (1994), in which a text is burned out line by line by a performer using a burin. The performance piece "Lineament" (1994) takes its title from a poem by Wallace Stevens titled "The Planet on the Table" which is about being an artist and which expresses key themes in Hamilton's work, including time, memory, language, and creation. In a room covered in plywood, a table is suspended from the ceiling. A book laid flat on the table is precisely precut so the text can be teased out into a continuous line. A woman seated on a swing works at the plywood table as she moves back and forth, pushing off from a white box on the ground at her feet. She winds the continuous line of text into a ball, or a "planet," as a movie projector casts shadows on a wall and produces clicking sounds in the space. As a book becomes emptied of its lines, it is stored in the box below the table. The performer faces a translucent cloth screen through which she passes her "planets" or balls of text. The artist was influenced by the following passage from Stevens (it may help to know that "lineaments" in this context means a feature or detail of a face, body, or figure – a distinguishing characteristic or distinctive attribute):

His self and the sun were one
And his poems, although makings of his self,
Were no less makings of the sun.

It was not important that they survive.
What mattered was that they should bear
Some lineament or character,

Some affluence, if only half-perceived,
In the poverty of their words,
Of the planet of which they were a part.

(Stevens 1990: 532–3)

In Steven's poem there is a correspondence or "fit" between the poet and his world ("the planet of which they were a part"), and the words, although quite powerful here, are described as "impoverished." For the poet, as for Hamilton's performance piece as well, permanence and "survival" are not the important thing ("it was not important that they survive"), but some temporary and powerful distinguishing features – lineaments – do express and reflect the poet and/or artist.

In 2001–2002 Hamilton collaborated with Meredith Monk on a performance piece titled, "Mercy," a variation on and interpretation of Samuel Beckett's *Ohio Impromptu* (1980), a play involving two identical figures seated at a table, one reading and the other listening. Most recently in January 2011, Hamilton created an onsite installation for the newly refurbished Thompson Library at the Ohio State University. It is a 6,080 square-foot cork floor in a very large reading-room on the library's second floor (see Figure 24.3). A huge field of words and letters, the piece entails sampling from and re-writing of three diverse texts:

1. A story from *American Indian Myths and Legends* (Erdoes and Ortiz 1984: 485–6);
2. Eduardo Galeano's collection of narrative fragments and fictions, *Mirrors*, in the 2009 English translation by Mark Fried; and
3. E.H. Gombrich's *A Little History of the World*, written for his daughter in 1936, in an English translation from 2005.

Many postmodern texts appropriate previous works and "write through" source-texts, as the poet/composer John Cage does in *Roaratorio: An Irish Circus on Finnegans Wake* (see Perloff 1991: 149–61) or as Jean Rhys does when she rewrites *Jane Eyre* in *Wide Sargasso Sea* (1966), Zadie Smith when she does the same with *Howards End* in *On Beauty* (2005), J.M. Coetzee when he rewrites *Robinson Crusoe* in *Foe* (1985), or Michael Cunningham when he revisits *Mrs. Dalloway* in *The Hours* (1998). Perloff's *Unoriginal Genius: Poetry by Other Means in the New Century* (2010) studies this recent appropriative tendency in art, specifically in poetry. (See also Epstein, this volume.) Hamilton's work is a clear example of this kind of intertextuality. A central "spine" of words, running the length of the room's floor, is visually more conspicuous than the other texts in the piece, resembling one of Cage's "mesostics," a kind of acrostic whose governing letters run down the middle of the text rather than along the left-hand margin. In Hamilton's piece, the words forming the central "spine," from the source text, "The End of the World" (in *American Indian Myths and Legends*), have been rearranged and alphabetized. The story itself concerns art and artistry, as the central character is an old woman who weaves a blanket out of porcupine quills, and whose work is constantly undone by her dog. In this way, she continues to produce her "art," for if she ever finished weaving, the "world would come to an end" (Erdoes and Ortiz 1984: 485–6).

It is hardly surprising that the title of Hamilton's piece at the Thompson Library is "Verse," for in many ways the work is about and constitutes a new kind of poetry. There are an infinite number of ways to read this "text," and walking over the floor may be the most limiting of all. The source texts are totally intertwined and fragmented, so much so that they are impossible to disentangle from one another; and indeed the connections between them remain unclear. The sheer abundance of words

Figure 24.3 Ann Hamilton, "Verse," photo by Fredrik Marsh, courtesy of Ann Hamilton Studio.

and phrases allows the reader/viewer to enter a linguistic labyrinth, with no beginning, middle or end. The Hamilton piece is thus a border case poised among a number of different disciplines: poetry, art, architecture, theory, folklore and fiction.

V. Conclusion

All of the experimentation with words in art discussed in this chapter make one thing clear: never before have the "visual arts" been so verbal. The twentieth century's interest in the connections between art and text has persisted into the twenty-first century, with some of our most accomplished artists producing works using words and/or texts. This exploration of the boundaries between art and literature have resulted in original works of art, poetry, painting and language, and various combinations among them. These works toy with the borders between mediums, genres and disciplines, and the boundaries themselves fluctuate and even in some cases dissolve. Only vague umbrella terms (like "language works" or "verbal experiments") can capture all of the variations and creations with words on the part of these artists. Do these artworks therefore count as literature? Spectators are free to draw disciplinary and generic boundaries in multiple ways and as they wish, for various purposes, and with varied cultural and artistic values expressed by their views. As Wittgenstein questions in *Philosophical Investigations* regarding the boundaries of conceptual categories (like "literature" and "art"): "'Is a blurred concept a concept at all?' – Is an indistinct photograph a picture of a person at all? Is it even always an advantage to replace an indistinct picture by a sharp one? Isn't the indistinct one often exactly what we need?" (Wittgenstein 1953: #71). The various experimentations with the boundaries between discourse and art produce just such an "indistinct," "blurred" and variable disciplinary boundary. And this is, perhaps, "just exactly what we need."

References

Auping, M. (1992) *Jenny Holzer*, New York: Universe.

Cole, H. (2010) *Pierce the Skin: Selected Poems: 1982–2007*, New York: Farrar, Straus and Giroux.

Cooper, D. (1970) *The Cubist Epoch*, London: Phaidon.

Erdoes, R. and A. Ortiz (eds.) (1984) *American Indian Myths and Legends*, New York: Pantheon.

Fretz, E. (2010) *Jean-Michel Basquiat*, Santa Barbara, CA: Greenwood Press.

Galeano, E. (2009) *Mirrors: Stories of Almost Everyone*, trans. M. Fried, New York: Nation Books.

Gombrich, E.H. (2005 [1936]) *A Little History of the World*, trans. C. Mustill, New Haven, CT: Yale University Press.

Guttman, Y. (1998) "Conceptual Art and Philosophy." In M. Kelly (ed.), *Encyclopedia of Aesthetics*, New York: Oxford University Press, pp. 421–7.

Harrison, C. (2001) *Conceptual Art and Painting: Further Essays on Art & Language*, Cambridge, MA: The MIT Press.

Holzer, J. (1989) *Laments*, New York: Dia Art Foundation.

—— (1996) *Under a Rock*. Installations 1986–87. [Text reprinted in *Writing/Schriften*, ed. N. Smolik, Ostfildern-Ruit, Germany: Cantz.]

—— (1997) *Lustmord*, Houston, TX: Contemporary Arts Museum.

—— (2004) *Truth Before Power* [Kunsthaus Bregenz Exhibition Catalogue, ed. E. Schneider], New York: Distributed Art Publishers.

Hunt, J.D., D. Lomas and M. Corris (2010) *Art, Word and Image: Two Thousand Years of Visual/Textual Interaction*, London: Reaktion Books.

Jencks, C.A. (1981) *The Language of Post-Modern Architecture*, 3rd ed., New York: Rizzoli.

Kostelanetz, R. (1980) *Metamorphosis in the Arts: A Critical History of the 1960s*, Brooklyn, NY: Assembling Press.

Kosuth, J. (1973) *Art Investigations and "Problematics" since l965*, Luzern, Switzerland: Kunstmuseum.

—— (1991) *Art After Philosophy and After: Collected Writings, 1966–1990*, ed. G. Guercio, Cambridge, MA: MIT Press.

Kress, G. and van Leeuwen, T. (2006 [1996]) *Reading Images: The Grammar of Visual Design*. 2nd edn., New York: Routledge.

Kristeva, J. (1980) *Desire in Language*, trans. T. Gora, A. Jardine, and L.S. Roudiez, New York: Columbia University Press.

Lippard, L. (1973) *Six Years: The Dematerialization of the Art Object from 1966–1972*, Los Angeles: University of California Press.

Marinetti, F.T. (1972) *Selected Writings*, ed. R.W. Flint, trans. R.W. Flint and A.A. Coppotelli, New York: Farrar, Straus, and Giroux.

Mitchell, W.J.T. (1986) *Iconology: Image, Text, Ideology*, Chicago, IL: University of Chicago Press.

O'Toole, M. (1994) *The Language of Displayed Art*, Rutherford, NJ: Farleigh Dickinson University Press.

Perloff, M. (1991) *Radical Artifice: Writing Poetry in the Age of Media*, Chicago, IL: University of Chicago Press.

—— (2010) *Unoriginal Genius: Poetry by Other Means in the New Century*, Chicago, IL: University of Chicago Press.

Princenthal, N. (2007) "Jenny Holzer: Language Lessons." In E. Heartney, H. Posner, N. Princenthal and S. Scott (eds.), *After the Revolution: Women Who Transformed Contemporary Art*, New York: Prestel, pp. 144–67.

Rose, A.R. (1969) "Four Interviews with Barry, Huebler, Kosuth and Weiner," *Arts Magazine* (February): 22–3.

Ryan, M.-L. (2010) "Fiction, Cognition, and Non-Verbal Media." In M. Grishakova and M.-L. Ryan (eds.), *Intermediality and Storytelling*, New York: De Gruyter, pp. 8–26.

Sant, T. (2011) *Franklin Furnace and the Spirit of the Avant-Garde: A History of the Future*. Chicago, IL: University of Chicago Press.

Schwarz, A. (1970) *The Complete Works of Marcel Duchamp*, 2nd rev. ed., New York: Abrams.

Smithson, R. (1979) *The Writings of Robert Smithson*, ed. Nancy Holt, New York: New York University Press.

Steiner, W. (1982) *The Colours of Rhetoric: Problems in the Relation Between Modern Literature and Painting*, Chicago, IL: University of Chicago Press.

Stevens, W. (1990) *The Collected Poems of Wallace Stevens*, New York: Vintage.

Ulmer, G.L. (1985) *Applied Grammatology*, Baltimore, MD: Johns Hopkins University Press.

Waldman, D. (1989) *Jenny Holzer*, New York: Solomon R. Guggenheim Museum and Harry N. Abrams.

Wittgenstein, L. (1958 [1953]) *Philosophical Investigations*, trans. G.E.M. Anscombe, New York: Macmillan.

Wolf, W. (2005) "Intermediality." In D. Herman, M. Jahn and M.-L. Ryan (eds.), *Routledge Encyclopedia of Narrative Theory*, New York: Routledge, pp. 252–6.

Young, K. (2005) *To Repel Ghosts*, New York: Alfred A. Knopf.

Further reading

Kotz, L. (2010) *Words to Be Looked At: Language in 1960's Art*, Cambridge, MA: MIT Press.

Perloff, M. (1996) *Wittgenstein's Ladder*, Chicago, IL: University of Chicago Press.

Prinz, J. (1991) *Art Discourse/Discourse in Art*. New Brunswick, NJ: Rutgers University Press.

25

HOAX-POETRY AND INAUTHENTICITY

Philip Mead

The field of contemporary authorship is characterized by competing styles and unstable positions. While it is being pulled into the future by the digital revolution, it also preserves elements from successive historical periods since the modern era of authorship began in the early eighteenth century. To add to this complexity, a seam of variously inauthentic authorship runs through these cultural and discursive strata of the writing and publishing subject, from the beginning to now. Transgressive, subversive, even criminal forms of literary production and subjectivity flourish or remain latent according to the genetics of the literary system. Various kinds of trickster narratives, "impersonal, ego-less authorship" (experiments in computer-generated texts, for example), collaborative/collective authorship (Fluxus, Flarf, *Chain*); hoax, fake, forged and spurious authorship; pseudonymous and anagrammatically encoded authorship (acknowledged or otherwise); faux-memoirism; faction and creative non-fiction, Pessoan heteronymics, all continue to destabilise any normative idea of the writer and the text (see Epstein, this volume, Kacandes, this volume, and Tomasula, "New Media," this volume). With literary production, the question of authenticity may evolve and re-emerge in different forms, but it never goes away.

Moreover, the history of hoax poetry as a specific subset of inauthentic imaginative writing has, by now, a respectable status within contemporary literary studies. Much of the scholarship about the dark side of creative writing, driven initially, perhaps, by a fascination with the scandalous fall-out from literary impostures and hoaxes, has raised important questions about exactly what authenticity and genuineness in writing are, how they are produced, and why readers value them. The fact is that spurious literature and impostor-authors prompt us to think more comprehensively about how we understand authenticity in writing and authorship, even to the extent of recognizing that the spurious and the genuine are neither essential nor mutually exclusive, but "consubstantial" (Ruthven 2001: 3). Speculating on the counterfeit in writing, Poe came to precisely this conclusion: "what right should we have to talk of counterfeit at all?" (quoted in Derrida 1994: 108). Rather than being a matter of forensic and documentary demonstration, authenticity in relation to literary production is always now a question. And the history of literary hoaxes allows us to recognize the ways in which the proliferation of literary imposture in specific cultural chronotopes often seems like a symptomatic expression of broader identity crises and anxieties, both social and national. In this sense fake authorship and its evolution have led to the development of useful diagnostic tools for literary and cultural analysis.

Some instances of literary inauthenticity are producing new cultural effects in the contemporary media-sphere. At least two recent hoaxes have been played out as spectacles of "therapeutic self-disclosure" through Oprah's Book Club and the Larry King Show: the James Frey, *A Million Little Pieces* (2003) event of 2005 and the almost published *Angel at the Fence: The True Story of a Love That Survived* by Herman Rosenblat of 2009 (Potter 2010: 136–7). Fake holocaust survivor memoirs, like Rosenblat's, are one of the biggest growth areas of the literary inauthentic. Perhaps the most high profile of these was the internationally awarded *In Fragments: Memories of a Wartime Childhood* by Binjamin Wilkomirski (1995 in German, and translated into twelve other languages). With these born-mediatized instances of literary fakery, genre deceit, publishing disasters, and the repetitive-compulsive performance of celebrity "betrayal," fake literary and cultural studies have plenty to occupy themselves.

Recent historical and theoretical studies in literary fakery, then, work with the fact that authenticity in literature has always been a form of illusion – an "effect" of the literary imaginary – and that hoax and fake discursive strategies are to be taken just as seriously as those that produce the same effects, only "genuinely." Going back to *Tristram Shandy* and the origins of the novel, Susan Stewart discerns that "we are compelled to rediscover the tenuous margin between authority and imposture – a margin difficult to maintain in persons or documents" (1991: 145).

Re-viewing "imaginative writing" as justifying its existence "not by being authentic but by being anarchic," means that the historical hints at the deceptiveness of the genuine within the literary tradition appear differently charged (Ruthven 2001: 197). They can't be dismissed as momentary aberrations: they're more like Neo's *déjà vu*'s in *The Matrix*, glitches that momentarily betray the constructedness of all appearances. If you pay attention to them, troubling questions about the whole system arise. This goes back a long way in the Western tradition. For Sir Philip Sidney, in *An Apologie for Poetrie* (1595), the poet's task was a "counterfeiting." Contra Plato, Sidney understood Aristotle's mimesis as "a representing, a counterfeiting," analogous to the contemporary usage of "simulation," with its implication of un-realness or fabrication, but also attractiveness of image. Sidney's warning is clear – it's about feigning, not any hocus pocus about truth: "[t]he poet never maketh any circles about your imagination to conjure you to believe for true what he writeth" (Kimbrough 1983: 110). Poeisis, then, is sim-language, an application for (playfully) modelling experience and storing encoded identity data.

Surrealist poetics works with the founding insight that the only truly authentic language is the one we don't know we know – the unconscious (see Stockwell, this volume). Only verbal playing, preferably ruled by the unconscious, and which includes the open-endedness of experiment, is a serious use of language. All of which keeps in play the discursive *arche* of the Western literary tradition in Aristotle's *Poetics* that, in its defense of poetry, like Sidney's, identifies the origin of the poetic impulse in *mimesis*. This mimesis is less representation in the abstract sense, than mimicry, play, experiment, the necessarily inauthentic trying on of others' voices and rhythms (Aristotle 1970: 79). Mimesis, in this sense, is the love of inauthenticity, of the conceptual, and the escape they offer from anti-mimetic, unplayful, untruthful genuineness.

I. Classical inauthenticity

The classic era of fake poetic authenticity begins, impressively enough, in the last decades of the eighteenth century, along with the emergent differentiation of the "original" author and the nascent copyright regime. "Ossian" and "Thomas Rowley" are the grand, foundational figures of this modern era of inauthentic authorship, and their works are the epic and romance, if you like, of the spurious. The teenager Thomas Chatterton's fictitiously aged "Rowley" poems and their attributory texts (1768) are classics in the anti-metropolitan, nostalgia-driven afterlife of English medievalism, a weirdly atemporal tradition that continues to evolve and mutate (Ruthven 2001: 19). The Ossian poems, *Fingal: An Ancient Epic Poem in Six Books; Together with Several other Poems by Ossian, son of Fingal* (1761) and *Temora: An Ancient Epic Poem in Eight Books; Together with Several other Poems by Ossian, son of Fingal* (1763), arose out of James Macpherson's acute understanding of the collective desire of nations to be able to trace their provenance to a historically distant linguistic and poetic origin. These poems were hugely popular, right across Europe, even after their spuriousness was widely recognized. They were translated into numerous languages including, by Goethe, into German. The "Macphossian affair" as K.K. Ruthven demonstrates, is

> a richly foundational episode in the annals of modern spuriosity. Its mixture of Ossianic residues with Macphossianic embellishments results in a textual hybridity which destabilises the commonsense notion that a literary text is either genuine or bogus. [. . .] Macphossian seriously challenges the common-sense assumption that "originality" and "authenticity" are polar opposites of the fake. Macphossian is an original and authentic fake.
>
> (Ruthven 2001: 15–16)

By now Ossian and Rowley have lost entirely their quasi-criminal status as hoaxes and forgeries and, at least in the case of Ossian, have been incorporated into the mainstream poetic canon and the ahistorical mythogenesis of national origins. In 1996 Ossian's works were published by Edinburgh University Press, no less, and in 2004 Routledge published *Ossian and Ossianism*, a four-volume compilation of "original" Ossian texts as well as critical and contextual material (see Gaskill 1996, and Moore 2004).

With Macpherson's serious attempt to forge, in both senses of that word, the Ossian archive, the political stakes were the distinctive authenticity of the Scottish nation and its historical provenance in a European heroic age and the deep time of Gaelic epic. And at least since Virgil and the *Aeneid*, poets, especially in epic mode, have frequently been enlisted in the state matter of fabricating stories about national origins (Mead 2009: 92–9) or, in the case of Petrarch and the Emperor Charles IV (1360), of evidentiary literary work on forged claims to imperial heritage (Hiatt 2004: 156–7). Shakespeare forgeries, of which there is a rich history, and that begin, at least as far as anti-Stratfordians are concerned, with "Shakespeare" himself, belong on the spectrum of faux-nationalist projects that extends from Ossian to Elias Lönnrot's Finnish epic *The Kalevala* (see McHale 2003: 241). Poetic inauthenticity, it turns out, is inextricably bound up with perhaps poetry's most serious purpose, the elevated expression of national fate and identity. And as Brian McHale has argued in relation to *The Tablets* (1999), the "lifelong" mock-scholarly work of Armand Schwerner, even the *grand récit* of the history of world civilization can be subject to an ironic, "counter-inauthentic" revision that exposes world-historical narratives' aspiration to be "devoid of Semites" (McHale 2003: 248).

II. Modern inauthenticity

With the twentieth century, a differently politicized deployment of literary fakery tends to move to the cultural fore. Broadly speaking, modernist and postmodernist hoaxes fall into two categories: the identity hoax and the aesthetic ideology hoax. Identity poetry hoaxes belong to a larger group of literary identity hoaxes that all exploit the political ambiguities in adopting a fake authorial identity, either posing as, speaking for, or passing as, a racial, ethnic or gender "other" (see Kacandes, this volume). Examples are the "Rahila Khan"/Toby Forward-Virago case (UK; 1987), the Helen Demidenko/Darville deception (Australia; 1995), the B. Wongar and Wanda Koolmatrie/Leon Carmen Aboriginal authors – one pseudonymous, one an imposture (Australia; 1978 and 1994), and the Norma Khouri/ *Forbidden Love* fraudulent memoir (US/Australia; 2004). Cases like these tend to be much less "literary" than their contexts suggest, shifting rapidly away from their original textual and generic ground to the contest over identity politics, often conducted, momentarily, in the sensationalist rhetoric of the mainstream media. The fallout from the Demidenko hoax, for example, wasn't about literary judgement. It was only briefly a literary scandal, despite the fact that Demidenko dropped the deliberate obfuscation of the New Journalistic "faction" into the middle of the debate. What generates the heat in such scandals is the anarchic inability of literariness, including the literariness of author presentations, to provide historical and identitarian touchstones. Similarly, the Norma Khouri scandal also hinged on identitarian politics and the definition of genre – memoir vs. fiction – where the fallout was mainly felt by publishers and editors. The persistence of the matrix of morality and legality in this category of the practice of literary inauthenticity feeds off contractual publishing agreements and mediatized identity politics, rather than the undecidability of literary meaning and the genre instability of narrative. The repeatedly disavowed core to literary authenticity, the secret un-truth of literature, no doubt contributes to the outrage at and accusatory response to the exposure of imposture. Like counterfeit money, as long as literature "passes for (real) money [or literature], it is simply not different from the money [or literature] that, perhaps, it counterfeits" (Derrida 1994: 153). Once counterfeiting is discovered, though, the whole system of exchange (meaning and currency) is endangered and individual investments are jeopardized.

This indicates the extent to which there is a residual potential in literary cultures to reflect and provoke broader identity anxieties within a society. These events never stay focused for very long on the texts that are their original cause and these kinds of hoaxes are probably best understood as the "creative mode of cultural critique" exposing the ideological assumptions in institutional discourses and positions (Ruthven 2001: 28). Their value is that they constitute "limit cases in relation to the problematic notion of identity" and can be read more as social and cultural pathologies than as literary ones (Nolan and Dawson 2004: xiii). The instance of "Mudrooroo," the once-indigenous Australian author, is a more complex instance because the identitarian cultural politics here are not a matter of simple imposture and may very well drive critics back to the substantial body of Colin Johnson/"Mudrooroo"'s work for a more ambivalent understanding of identitarian cultural politics and literary meanings (see Clark 2004).

The "Ern Malley" poetry hoax (1943–1944) is a paradigmatic instance of the aesthetic ideology hoax, more or less elaborate impostures with "didactic and punitive purposes," operationalized to infiltrate, entrap and debunk (McHale 2003: 236). The creators of "Ern Malley," the young Australian poets James McAuley and Harold Stewart, were so offended by the New Apocalypse-influenced version of modernist poetry published in the avant-garde magazine *Angry Penguins* that they fabricated a poet and his work that would embody that aesthetic better than any of its genuine practitioners, but spuriously. This necessarily knowledgeable fabrication of author and text was a carefully conducted experiment in collaborative writing as well as elaborately faked biography. McAuley and Stewart then presented themselves to the press in the guise of serious cultural experimenters. Once exposed, the hoax caused a kind of cultural implosion that sucked in a disparate range of philistine and punitive anti-modernist forces within Australia, but also internationally. It was as if a whole society, driven by a collective denial of the unconscious, and outrage at homosocial collaboration, had been waiting for an event that would allow it to vent its anti-Surrealist affect, which it hardly knew it harboured (see Chambers 2005; Mead 2009).

As the Malley and later the Yasusada hoaxes demonstrate, though, these kinds of projects in poetic deception and studied inauthenticity are much more unpredictable than the identitarian hoax. McAuley and Stewart's starting point was their hatred of poetic experiment, or the misrule of the unconscious, so the task of faking an experiment was always fraught, though they would have denied it, with the threat of authenticity. The "Malley" hoax turned out to be an unconsciously "genuine" experiment, in that it produced a body of unexpectedly distinctive and influential poems. Such hoaxes don't always have the effect that was intended by the perpetrators, as far as one can tell, and the more the actual texts at their centers remain the focus of attention, the more they reveal about authenticity and inauthenticity, about the interrelations of the official economy and the black market of authorship.

III. Hyperauthorship and meta-hoaxes

The Yasusada hoax-experiment can be read in multiple ways, and is instructive in terms of the unpredictability of hoaxes and their cultural butterfly effects. It had a brief media profile as a literary scandal but increasingly looks like a serious experiment in the guise of a poetry hoax. In that sense it represents a kind of evolution in poetic inauthenticity, a meta-hoax that deploys all the attributes and possibilities of the aesthetic ideology deception, but in the interests of a genuine experiment in poetics. In other words, it's the opposite of the Malley hoax, a "mock-hoax" in McHale's typology, a fake experiment with an essentially aesthetic purpose (2003: 237, 239). Initially, the Yasusada impersonation mobilized identitarian cultural politics – like the Rahila Khan, Daniel Santiago, Wanda Koolmatrie cases – but as Marjorie Perloff's and Brian McHale's readings of the hoax clearly show, it goes well beyond the predictable polarities of an identitarian controversy, and functions as a serious matrix of critical discourse.

According to the biographical fiction, "Araki Yasusada" was born in Kyoto in 1907 and moved to Hiroshima in 1921. Translators' bio notes accompanying Yasusada's first "publications" in English and US journals (*American Poetry Review, Grand Street, Conjunctions, Stand*) in the 1990s read:

> [Yasusada] attended Hiroshima University sporadically between 1925 and 1928, with the intent of receiving a degree in Western Literature. Due, however, to his father's illness, he was forced, in the interests of the family, to undertake full-time employment with the postal service and withdraw from his formal studies.
>
> In 1930 he married his only wife Nomura, with whom he had two daughters and a son. In 1936, Yasusada was conscripted into the Japanese Imperial Army and worked as a clerk in the Hiroshima division of the Military Postal Service. His wife and youngest daughter Chieko, died instantly in the atomic blast on August 6. His daughter Akiko survived, yet perished less than four years later from radiation sickness. His son, Yasunari, an infant at the time, was with relatives outside the city. Yasusada died in 1972 after a long struggle with cancer.
>
> (Perloff 1997: 1–2)

The textual fiction was that in 1980 Yasunari discovered fourteen notebooks of poems and other writings. Extracts from these were first published in translation in *American Poetry Review* for July/August 1996, as "Doubled Flowering: From the Notebooks of Araki Yasusada." Interest in the Yasusada texts was particularly strong in Japan. After doubts about Yasusada's identity started to circulate, Wesleyan University Press

343

backed away from publishing *Doubled Flowering*, although the volume was ultimately published by Roof Books in 1997. So the traditional elements of literary authenticity were established – a life and works – and they were given a further powerful charge as nuclear-Hiroshima "witness" or testimonial poetry, writing whose first purpose is to create the volatile conjunction of "the political to the personal" (Weinberger 1998: 3). Yasusada's aura of authenticity seemed only to be enhanced by the fact that his body of work had lain unpublished, unfinished, a broken testament to his and his family's nuclear trauma, and that of his nation.

The generation of "Yasusada" includes the reverse-framing of him as the "pseudo-nym of a writer, the late Tosa Motokiyu, who did not wish to attach his legal name to the hyperauthorial person he brought into being" (Johnson 1998), and who is also spurious. The "presentational apparatus" of Yasusada's scholar-translators includes a chain of letters between Kent Johnson and Akitoshi Nagahata (English, Nagoya University, Japan), the " *faux critique*" of Robert M. Larson (Johnson, in Francis 1998: 1), and other complexly embedded critical responses (see Epstein 2000). Eliot Weinberger suggests we refer to all this "attributional [textual] space" as the "Yasusada Author, much as we refer to a Renaissance painter as the Master of the X Altar" (Francis 1998: 2; Weinberger 1998: 4).

What we know about the hoax, still unadmitted by its likely perpetrator, Kent Johnson, and its wildly discrepant reception – "racist inspired hoax," demeaning "yellowface" performance, or "imaginative gesture of profound beauty and empathy" – is summarised by Perloff in 1997 and by Forrest Gander in 1998 (Johnson and Nagahata 1997; McHale 2003: 243; see also Theune 2010). On the one hand, one of the first publishers of Yasusada in *American Poetry Review*, Arthur Vogelsang, called Johnson's deception a "criminal act" (Perloff 1997: 2), while another, Rod Smith (of *Aerial*), told Perloff that "he suspected all along the manuscript [. . .] was a hoax but he found it so charming and aapropros he decided to publish it" (Perloff 1997: 15). There was a high profile media storm about the hoax – articles in the *Wall Street Journal*, the *Guardian*, the *Sydney Morning Herald*, etc. – but unlike other literary identity impostures of recent years, the Yasusada texts frequently remain at the centre of reception, partly because of their enthusiastic uptake by certain poets and presses associated with the L=A=N=G=U=A=G=E movement (Ron Silliman, Roof Books; see Bernstein, this volume). The evidence of fabrications and anachronisms in the Yasusada counterfeit have been detailed, but the lesson of impostures, from Ossian to the Tichborne Claimant to James Frey, as Kent Johnson seems to have understood, is that you don't have to worry too much about providing a plausible authenticity for a life and work. The point is that readers want to believe and they will easily overlook discrepancies and even exposure. Authenticity *effects* are what is necessary. The experiment undertaken here, as Johnson's quite serious question reminds us, misquoting Foucault, is "what does it matter who is speaking?"

The likelihood is that the Yasusada "hyper-Author" – an author "dispersed among several virtual personalities that cannot be reduced to a single "real" personality"– is an evolved instance of hoax-poetry, a meta-hoax, designed seriously to investigate on multiple levels the complex issues of "pseudography" in the specifically North American cultural setting (Epstein 2000: 9; Johnson 1998). Whatever Kent Johnson's purpose might have been, Yasusada is evidently a textual counterfeit – to go back to one of the oldest words in anglophone poetics – that is self-reflexively conscious of the ineradicable, and sometimes, celebrated nature of fake "authenticity," or "authenticity" of unknown provenance, in poetry. In other words, Yasusada functions effectively as a constellation – with a set of poetic texts at its centre – that confounds any simple, ethical and aesthetic equations between reader and author, text and history, author and experience, poetic form and history. What this means is that questions of authenticity, authorship, political responsibility, cultural guilt, for example, are held open, in readings where ethical closure is disallowed, and the "complex issues of pseudography" that Johnson draws attention to, can be explored, ramified and turned back on themselves. Gander's reading is an exemplary instance. He reads the poetry of the "Yasusada Author" as a kind of amoral, de-authored "Talmudic document published with commentaries around translations of notebooks written by an author who does not exist about a place that was once blotted out" (1998: 5). Perloff's reading is more searching and widely referential, and in the end more committed to a critique of what she deplores as the "disciplinary demand" for "novel and interesting cultural positioning" that fuelled the Yasusada scandal. Hence she values its effectiveness as a meta-hoax (1997: 13). Kent Johnson offers the sardonic version of the same critique: "the Yasusada writings represent an original and courageous form of authenticity – one that is perhaps difficult to appreciate because of the extent to which individual authorial status and self-promotion dominate our thinking about, and practice of, poetry" (Francis 1998: 8). In other words, like Ossian and Scotland's Gaelic origins, and "Ern Malley"'s presence in the Australian literary canon, it is likely only a matter of time before Yasusada poems like "Dream and Charcoal," become effectively "authentic" nuclear survivor, *hibakusha* poetry, but always bearing the isotope of inauthenticity:

> And then she said: I have gone toward the light and become beautiful.
> And then she said: I have taken a couple of wings and attached them to the various back-parts of my body.
> And then she said: all the guests are coming back to where they were and then talking.
> To which she said: without the grasp-handle, how would you recognise my nakedness?
> To which she replied: without nothing is when all things die.
> Which is when she had a wild battle with the twigs.
> Which is when the charcoal was passed from her body to mine.
> Which was how she rose into the heavens, blinding the pedestrians.
> Which was how our union was transposed into a dark scribble.
> Which became the daughter calling, calling my name to wake me.
>
> (quoted in Gander 1998: n.p.)

IV. Signal and noise

The Yasusada event exists at the junction of academic, theoretical, cultural-political and media discourses of contemporary poetics, and it must seem like an arcane example of counterfeiting to many readers of poetry. For all that it opens up a discursive arena for fundamental questions of authorial subjectivity and referential meaning, some of them of ancient provenance, it remains a kind of academic game. The Yasusada Author may seem to reassert the kind of feigning Sidney believed in, but at the same time the context of the critique remains a divisively contested space, one in which all readerly positions are necessarily wary or problematic.

There is another view of poetry that weaves its way in and out of the professionalized sphere of literary theory and criticism, and that is also relevant to the trajectories of contemporary experiment and the poetics of authenticity. This is the understanding of poetic language as the antithesis of information, an expressive mode with the highest signal-to-noise ratio, to adopt a term from electronic engineering. Poetry as respite, as Eduardo Kac describes it:

> In a world in which we are constantly bombarded by the detritus of information technology, from irritating e-mail spamming to ravishing computer viruses, some may argue that the place of poetry should be a removed and more quiet realm that provides a respite from the twirling chaos of the technology-inflected contemporary life.
>
> (Kac 2007: 9)

According to this view, poetry is by definition the linguistic antidote to networked noise and information overload; it represents the dream of a pure signal, a humanly analog form of language rather than a replicant, digitally manipulated one. And in a world haunted by countless phantoms of authenticity, the recognition and consumption of "authenticity effects," like the ones poetry may seem to promise, will be exponentially strong. The desire for the poetry of respite is in direct proportion to the incessant, maddening noise of contemporary existence. There is a weighty tradition behind this strand of poetics, and its influence is most obvious in the ubiquitous presence of Heideggerian existentialism in twentieth-century poetics. This is hardly surprising, given the endemic presence of Heidegger (and Heidegger critique) across the varieties of poststructuralism, and the centrality of poetry – late Hölderlin and Rilke – to his thought.

It is in ecopoetics that Heidegger's hermeneutic of being has had probably its most influential afterlife. Whatever the compromised politics of his aesthetics, the influence of Heidegger's meditations on Hölderlin's river hymns and of essays like "Poetically Man Dwells," has run deep into late twentieth- and twenty-first-century poetics. Ecopoetics is often constituted by the kind of idealist and interanimated identities of being, nature and language Heidegger articulated. This version of identity poetics posits the equating of suppressed human social, ethnic and racial minorities with non-human nature (including animals), and a shared imaginary of subject (environmental concern) and readership (Quetchenbach 2002: 251). The politics of ecological crisis is the ground of ecopoetics' rhetoric of authenticity and is reflected in the array of publications in green poetics, from anthologies of environmentalist and nativist poetry ("news of the universe"), to critical responses to environmental literature (concerns for a small planet, e.g., Jonathan Bate's *The Song of the Earth* [2000]), to individual poets' writings in activist ecopoetics. Bernard W. Quetchenbach sums up one version of the appeal of ecopoetics to authenticity: "the thing that is said – the content – is the poem's 'surest connection to both the reader and the earth'" (2002: 260). In this sense, ecopoetics takes poetry off the grid.

Ethnopoetics, another development within postmodern poetics bears the hereditary traces of the early modernist avant-garde's non-European cultural appropriations ("primitivism"; Dada's Aboriginal song cycles; Apollinaire's African statues). Thus ethnopoetics is informed by foundational ideas of the ethnolinguistically discoverable authenticity of poetic expression across human cultures. Jerome Rothenberg and others' UbuWeb resource archives the "second great breakthrough of the modernist poetry project . . . [the] range of poetries outside the domain of customarily accepted literature." The first "breakthrough" was the historical avant-gardes that dislodged poetry from its traditional forms of production and transmission (Rothenberg 2002). Ethnopoetics, as a comparative disciplinary and aesthetic "project," attempts to yoke the experimental traditions stemming from the European and Anglophone avant-gardes with an "emphasis on stateless, low-technology cultures and on oral and nonliterate [nonliteral] forms of verbal expression" (e.g. Mayan hieroglyphics; Navajo visual poetry) (Rothenberg 2002). The strains in this conjunction of modern and postmodern traditions of experiment and the authenticity of poetic expression ("visioning and sounding") in other cultural contexts are apparent. The rhetoric takes the form of the authenticities of past, "primitive" and Indigenous cultures as against the deracinated imperialism of "civilization" and relies on concepts like pure sound, pure voice, total translation (Rothenberg 2002).

But the ethnopoetic sector is also subject to radical reformatting in the experiments of one of its early associates, Armand Schwerner. *The Tablets'* mock scholarly translation and presentation of inauthentic and fragmentary Sumero-Akkadian inscriptions embraces "the universalizing spirit of ethnopoetics – the dream of total translation, total performance, total synchronicity – while at the same time implicitly acknowledging its impossibility" (Finkelstein 1999). Against every assumption of totality and presence in the ethnopoetic tradition, Schwerner's richly Borgesian project evokes a whole world of dubious textual and authorial authenticity, from forged and illicit antiquities, to monomaniac scholars, to tendentious narratives of civilizational origins, to variously "psychoanalytic" readings of cultural history. One of the strengths of *The Tablets*, though, lies in the way in which the actual texts, weird and parodic as they often are, remain at the center of its reception. Like the Malley hoax, *The Tablets* has at its core a poetic reactor that seems to emit strong, if volatile poetic energy (see McHale 2004).

V. Post-hoax

Theodor Adorno would no doubt have recognized Schwerner's multi-level poetic critique of what he called the jargon of authenticity. For all its worthy politics, transculturalism and environmental activism, and for all the value of the poetic work they license and curate, ecopoetics and ethnopoetics have at their core a resistance to the non-natural nature of language and its intersections with being and history. The "connections" of ecopoetics and the cultural differences of ethnopoetics are strands of an idealizing aesthetic that misrecognizes how the conjunction of world, self and language "is attained [Adorno argued] not in spite of disjunction, but only through it" (Paddison 2004: 217). That is, the nature in a natural style is an illusion, *mimesis* is not a closure of identity and environment, or authenticity of expression, in fact quite the opposite, it is constitutively feigning. There are only slippages between the self of the poet and his or (or their) textual personae. Fernando Pessoa's "heteronymic" imagination is the paradigm; he wrote under scores of what he called heteronyms, strangely skewing the meaning of this word, as if driven to imagine as many writing selves as works, all of them "Pessoa," textually, if not authorially. This polarity – the rhetoric of authenticity, and the practice of inauthenticity – which has a genealogy stemming from Heidegger, Adorno and the modernist avant-gardes and before that in Romanticism and rationalism, with a frequently repressed origin in Aristotle's anti-Platonic *mimesis*, is an ineradicably double gene in the heredity of Western poetics (McHale 2003: 235). It is central to the genome of contemporary poetics and inflects all statements and positions as they reproduce themselves in the contemporary discursive environment. It even polarizes the constellation of ecopoetics, as represented by J. Scott Bryson's (2002) collection, in the form of critique by writers like Harriet Tarlo, in *How2* (3.2), and Jonathan Skinner in *ecopoetics*, that appropriate both "eco" and "poetics" in the name of an interrogatively experimental, feminist and Cagean/ L=A=N=G=U=A=G=E poetics: "how can the bird, the fly-catcher, enter the poem without having to do work for the sentimentally needy poet?" (Retallack 2007: 11, 14). Continuity *and* discontinuity of self, language, world/environment, perception, aesthetic form, naming, are the poles between which poetics constitutes itself: "[c]ould it be that so much depends on something both similar and completely different in poetics?" (Retallack 2007: 15).

While this polarity is at work everywhere in contemporary poetics, as a discursive field it is being changed radically by the applications and experiments made possible by the mediatization of language and the enabling potential of computer technologies. Poets have been quick to realize the experimental potential of everyday technology as well as of new media. The re-mediated space in which experiment in poetry is currently conducted includes myriad possibilities for assumed, networked and cyber-identities and potential for the generation of texts only tenuously related to traditional notions of authorial subjectivity (see Tomasula, "New Media," this volume). Moreover, this re-mediation of poetics is folded back into the pre-digital textual forms of experiment on the page. The innovations of the poets in Eduardo Kac's 2007 anthology, for example, only fully accessible on disk, videotape, and holograms take

> language beyond the confines of the printed page and explore [. . .] a new
> syntax made of linear and non-linear animation, hyperlinks, interactivity,

real-time text generation, spatio-temporal discontinuities, self-similarity, synthetic spaces, immateriality, diagrammatic relations, visual tempo, multiple simultaneities, and many other innovative procedures.

(Kac 2007: 11)

Experimentally minded poets with less interest in new media can still explore the multiple possibilities of computer-generated and manipulated language (see Mead 2010). The "strange impersonality" that some contemporary poets evidently like to create and to explore – as a counter-weight, no doubt, to centuries of the lyric "I," "voice" and presence – responds to the "ordinary" technologies of postmodern lives as much as the combinatoric possibilities of computer applications: "the X-Ray, the MRI, [the] echocardiography (a prime example of the workings of the Doppler Effect), and hypertext" (Perloff 2004: xvii). More subversively, perhaps, other experimental poetics employ the *mimesis* of recycled and sampled detritus from the net to generate a retro-Dada-ist collaborative list-poetry of the readymade and the inappropriate (see Flarflist blog; see also Epstein, this volume).

The hoax gene may be latent in all these experimental sites of the web-based poetics genome, but has been effectively switched off, both by the literary critical absorption of the spurious into the official discourses on poetry, and by the explosively multiple workings-out of experiment within contemporary poetics. In the "orgy of commodification and replacement," characteristic of postmodern poetic experiment, there is hardly time or space for the memory of experimental effects (Perloff 2004: xvi). Within such a rapidly expanding universe of the no-longer authentic, it's hard to see hoax-poetry having anything other than a culturally residual, identitarian future. We can probably afford to feel equally nostalgic about real poetry hoaxes as about the idea of an authentic poetry.

References

Aristotle (1970) *Poetics*, trans. G.F. Else, Ann Arbor, MI: University of Michigan.

Bryson, J.S. (ed.) (2002) *Ecopoetry: A Critical Introduction*, Salt Lake City, UT: University of Utah Press.

Chambers, R. (2005) "Adventures in Malley Country: Concerning Peter Carey's My *Life as a Fake*," *Cultural Studies Review* 11(1), 27–51.

Clark, M. (2004) "Crafty Impostor or Rebel with a Cause?" *Australian Literary Studies* 21(4), 101–10.

Derrida, J. (1994) *Given Time: 1. Counterfeit Money*, trans. P. Kamuf, Chicago, IL: Chicago University Press.

Epstein, M. (2000) "Hyper-Authorship: the Case of Araki Yasusada," *Rhizomes* 01, retrieved from http://www.rhizomes.net/issue1/misha.html.

Finkelstein, N. (1999) "Norman Finkelstein Reviews Armand Schwerner," *Jacket* 10, retrieved from http://jacketmagazine.com/10/fink-r-schw.html

Flarflist blog. (2010) retrieved from http://mainstreampoetry.blogspot.com/

Francis, N. (1998) "On Robert M. Larsen, Araki Yasusada, and The Will to Power: An Interview with Kent Johnson," *Jacket*, 5, retrieved from http://jacketmagazine.com/05/yasu-larsen.html.

Gander, F. (1998) "Review: *Doubled Flowering: From the Notebooks of Araki Yasusada*," *Jacket* 4. [First published in *The Nation*, July 13, 1998.] Retrieved from http://jacketmagazine.com/04/ganderyasu.html

Gaskill, H. (ed.) (1996) *The Poems of Ossian and Related Works*, Edinburgh: Edinburgh University Press.

Hiatt, A. (2004) *The Making of Medieval Forgeries: False Documents in Fifteenth-Century England*, London: The British Library and University of Toronto Press.

Johnson, K. (1998) "Letter to *American Book Review*," *Jacket* 5. First published in *The American Book Review*, November 1998. Retrieved from http://jacketmagazine.com/05/yasu-lett.html

Johnson, K. and A. Nagahata (1997) "The Yasusada Affair – Ethics of Aesthetics?" Jacket 2, retrieved from http://jacketmagazine.com/02/yasu.html.

Kac, E. (2007) *Media Poetry: An International Anthology*, Bristol, UK: Intellect.

Kimbrough, R. (ed.) (1983) *Sir Philip Sidney: Selected Prose and Poetry*. Madison, WI: University of Wisconsin Press.

McHale, B. (2003) "'A Poet May Not Exist': Mock-Hoaxes and the Construction of National Identity." In R.J. Griffin, *The Faces of Anonymity: Anonymous and Pseudonymous Publication from the Sixteenth to the Twentieth Century*, New York: Palgrave Macmillan, pp. 233–52.

—— (2004) *The Obligation Toward the Difficult Whole*, Tuscaloosa, AL: University of Alabama Press.

Mead, P. (2009) *Networked Language: Culture and History in Australian Poetry*, Melbourne, Australia: Australian Scholarly Publishing.

—— (2010) "How Poetry Became Posthuman: John Tranter's *Different Hands*." In Rod Mengham (ed.), *The Salt Companion to John Tranter*, Cambridge, UK: Salt, pp. 158–96.

Moore, D. (ed.) (2004) *Ossian and Ossianism*, London: Routledge.

Nolan, M. and C. Dawson (2004) "Who's Who? Mapping Hoaxes and Imposture in Australian Literary History," *Australian Literary Studies*, 21(4), v–xx.

Paddison, M. (2004) "Authenticity and Failure in Adorno's Aesthetics of Music." In Tom Huhn (ed.), *The Cambridge Companion to Adorno*, Cambridge, UK: Cambridge University Press, pp. 198–21.

Perloff, M. (1997) "In Search of the Authentic Other: The Poetry of Araki Yasusada," *Boston Review* 22(2), 26–33, retrieved from http://marjorieperloff.com/articles/yasusada-other/.

—— (2004) "Introduction: A Mythology Reflects Its Region." In John Kinsella, *Doppler Effect*, Cambridge, UK: Salt, pp. xv–xxii.

Potter, A. (2010) *The Authenticity Hoax: How We Get Lost Finding Ourselves*, Melbourne, Australia: Scribe.

Quetchenbach, B. (2002) "Primary Concerns: The Development of Current Environmental Identity Poetry." In J.S. Bryson (ed.), *Ecopoetry: A Critical Introduction* , Salt Lake City, UT: University of Utah Press, pp. 245–62.

Retallack, J. (2007) "What Is Experimental Poetry & Why Do We Need It?", *Jacket* 32, retrieved from http://jacketmagazine.com/32/p-retallack.shtml.

Rothenberg, J. (2002) "UbuWeb Ethnopoetics: Discourses," *UbuWeb*, retrieved from http://www.ubu.com/.

Ruthven, K.K. (2001) *Faking Literature*, Cambridge, UK: Cambridge University Press.

Stewart, S. (1991), *Crimes of Writing: Problems in the Containment of Representation*, New York: Oxford University Press.

Theune, M. (2010) "Impolitic: Kent Johnson's Radical Hybridity," *Pleiades*, 28(1), 117–51.

Weinberger, E. (1998) "Can I Get a Witness?", *Jacket* 5. First published in *Village Voice Literary Supplement*, July 1996. Retrieved from http://jacketmagazine.com/05/yasu-wein.html.

26

UNNATURAL VOICES, MINDS, AND NARRATION

Jan Alber, Henrik Skov Nielsen, and Brian Richardson

In this chapter we argue that unnatural narratives constitute a distinctive and important subset of experimental literature. Our chapter thus forms a companion to Marie-Laure Ryan's adjacent chapter on "Unnatural Stories and Worlds." Unnatural narratives present specific challenges to or entirely violate common-sense understandings of narratives and of fictional voices and narration. These challenges are posited by such peculiar narrative forms as first-person narration in the present tense, you-narration, narratives by dead or non-human narrators, and paraleptic first-person narration. In this article we introduce and define the subject of unnatural narration and present an overview of unnatural narratives with a specific view to narrators. We then examine in more detail some cases of unnatural narration. First, we look at the voice of a narrator who invokes a collective "we" that extends for a thousand years. Second, we examine the work of animal and dead narrators where the strangeness is not in the grammatical form, but in the narrating entity. In the third and final section, we move on to discuss homodiegetic narration with zero focalization in a section that mirrors the previous one in the sense that the former deals with non-persons narrating like persons and the latter with persons narrating like non-persons. Finally, we conclude the article with a brief account of the importance of unnatural narration, and we illustrate two different ways of engaging or dealing with the unnatural.

I. Definitions

We can define unnatural narratives by opposing them to the parameters of traditional realism (Richardson 2002), or the mimesis of actual speech situations, i.e., the conventions of "natural" (or oral) narratives (Richardson 2006: 5). Furthermore, unnatural narratives transcend real-world possibilities by projecting physically, logically, or humanly impossible scenarios or acts of narration (Alber 2009: 80), and they may also contain unmarked, conventionalized impossibilities, such as magical transformation in fantastic literature, time travel in science fiction, or the disclosure of the contents of another character's mind (through interior monologues, free indirect discourse, or psychonarration) (see Alber 2011). In literary fiction, we can almost always observe a process of dialectical mediation between "natural" components that reproduce the world as we know it and unnatural components that move beyond our real-world knowledge (see also Alber, Iversen, Nielsen, and Richardson 2010).

Literary realism tries to eliminate or disguise its unnatural elements, while other forms of literature flout them. The category of the unnatural cuts across many existing subgenres – late modernism, avant-garde, *nouveau roman*, *écriture féminine*, magical realism, theatre of the absurd, postmodernism, but also genres that contain conventionalized manifestations of the unnatural – and invites us to identify and theorize strategies and concerns that are common to all. We should never lose sight of the complexity of non-fictional narratives but we should also be careful not to posit firm dichotomies between "natural" and unnatural narratives when in fact the relation is one of dynamic exchange and continuity.

In what follows, we wish to examine the relationship between the unnatural and the experimental in greater detail. As we will show, the unnatural is a subcategory of the experimental. Literature can be experimental because of its closeness to our cognition of the world as well as because of its divergence from it. For instance, Ernest Hemingway's short story "The Killers" (1927) is entirely externally focalized and does not provide the reader with any access to the thoughts or feelings of the characters. Interestingly, this narrative was deemed experimental and path-breaking although (or perhaps precisely because) it is told with the restriction that real-world parameters impose on storytellers (one cannot tell with certainty what someone else thinks). Other narratives were experimental in their focus on popular culture (David Shields's "Life Story" [1991]), the trivial (e.g., the extremely detailed renderings of steps in Thomas Bernhard's novel *Gehen* [1971]), or on the inventories and details that make up our encounters with everyday life (Rick Moody's short story "Primary Sources" [1996]). So there is clearly no one-to-one correspondence between the experimental and the unnatural.

Second, even if a narrative technique is highly divergent from real-life parameters, it may be (or become) highly conventional. A good example of this is provided by narratives told by what is often referred to as an "omniscient" third-person narrator that is omnipresent, omnitemporal, and able to provide access to the minds of the characters. In the words of Monika Fludernik, "the 'omniscient' narrator function in fiction is [...] already a non-natural extension of the real-life schema of historical narration" (2001: 624). Narratives of this kind are unnatural in the specific sense that they correspond to no real-life storytelling situation, but are no longer considered to be experimental or unconventional.

Third, new narrative techniques tend to become conventionalized over time and lose their initial surprise value. A good example of this is the emergence of a plethora of narratives cast in the first-person present tense such as J.M. Coetzee's *Waiting for the*

Barbarians (1980), Bret Easton Ellis's *American Psycho* (1991), or Dennis Cooper's *My Loose Thread* (2001). These narratives seemed strange and difficult to theorize at first, but today audiences are familiar with narratives cast in the first-person present tense to such an extent that they may not even notice it. Today's most radical experiments often become tomorrow's conventions. In the account that follows, we will frequently draw on the discourse of narrative theory, since narrative theory is especially well situated to articulate precisely the salient distinctions of unnatural narratives and to clarify how such works diverge from our real-world knowledge.

II. Unnatural narrators

One of the most compelling areas of literary experimentation has been the transformation of the narrator. This figure has gone from the traditional, humanist persona of a real-world storyteller to increasingly unusual, innovative, and unprecedented sources of narrative discourse. Recent experiments in voice and narration have transcended conventional models in several ways. First-person narrators have developed a number of unnatural tendencies. Some are impossibly sophisticated, such as the unnaturally poetic prose of the girl Virginie in John Hawkes's *Virginie: Her Two Lives* (1982). Others are impossibly knowledgeable: accurate memories beyond the scope of human performance are produced by Henry Carr in Tom Stoppard's *Travesties* (1974), while Saleem Sinai is able to hear the inner thoughts of other characters' minds in Rushdie's *Midnight's Children* (1981). The other end of the spectrum is also present: Beckett's narrator in *Molloy* (1951) is much more befuddled than a writer of a narrative can ever be; the narrator of Robbe-Grillet's *In the Labyrinth* (1959) is too contradictory to provide a consistent narrative perspective. Non-human narrators have also proliferated; we find horses, dragons, and machines all engaged in storytelling. Concerning focalization, or the figure(s) through whose senses we perceive the storyworld, nonhuman perceivers range from the snail's vantage point in Woolf's "Kew Gardens" (1921) to Borges' depiction of the minotaur's sensibility in "The House of Asterion" (1949). Unusual devices that allow for embedded focalization also proliferate: Borges "El Aleph" (1945) allows a viewer to perceive all space from every angle and William Gibson's *Neuromancer* (1984) includes a mechanical apparatus that allows one person to share her focalization with another. Dead narrators are legion; especially dramatic are those who, like the narrator of Juan Rulfo's *Pedro Páramo* (1955), do not discover they are dead until well into the novel. Even more unnatural is the class of narrative utterances purported to come from a single individual but which are too divergent to constitute a single, anthropomorphic mind, as in Donald Barthleme's story, "You Are as Brave as Vincent van Gogh" (1976). Here, the narrating subject is too fragmented and multiform to be a self-consistent narrator; all we have here is narration (see Fludernik 1996: 282–5 and Richardson 2006: 134–6).

Traditional novelists regularly limit themselves to first- or third-person stances; many experimental authors extend these or invent other narrating possibilities. First-person plural, or "we" narrations, can be entirely "natural," as in Faulkner's story, "That

Evening Sun" (1931), insofar as one character simply narrates the events he experiences in the company of others. But in Faulkner's "A Rose for Emily" (1931), the "we" designates an entire community that changes over the extended period of the story's time span. It also varies as to how many people it includes at any particular moment, ranging from the entire community to those people assembled in Emily's house at the end of the narrative. Other experimental works extend the narrating "we" still further. The "we" of Richard Wright's *12 Million Black Voices* (1941) includes centuries of enslaved and oppressed blacks, and even includes the voices of the dead. Ayi Kwei Armah's *Two Thousand Seasons* (1973) goes further; its "we" covers a thousand years of black African experience, as will be discussed further below. Still more extreme is Nathalie Sarraute's *Tu ne t'aimes pas* (*You Don't Love Yourself* [1989]), a text that uses the "we" form to express a collection of contiguous voices, some of them contradictory, that comprise a single decentred fictional mind: "we were a little restless, we were ill at ease. Embarrassed . . . Not all of us, though . . . This 'we' doesn't apply to us all . . . . We never turn out in full force . . . there are always some of us who are dozing, lazing, relaxing, wandering" (Sarraute 1990: 2).

In second-person discourse, we find "natural" forms like the apostrophe, the monologue addressed to another individual, or an individual speaking to him or herself, but we also see unnatural varieties. In its most common form, the "you" designates the protagonist, as in Edna O'Brien's *A Pagan Place* (1970): "Alone for the first time in the street, you were conscious of your appearance. Your coat was ridiculous compared to other people's coats" (172). David Herman has discussed the curious aspects of what he calls "double deixis," as the "you" can simultaneously refer to the character and, outside the fictional storyworld, the actual reader (2002: 337–71). The technique is still more unnatural, however: although narratologists like Gérard Genette have stated categorically that the novelist must choose between two narrative postures, either "to have the story told by one of its 'characters,' or to have it told by a narrator outside the story" (1980: 244), second-person narration eludes both of these poles or rather oscillates tauntingly between them, irreducible to either. The mind of the narrator also fluctuates between a fallible internal and an objective external presentation. Other types of second-person narration include the "hypothetical" form, as when the style of a self-help manual turns into a narrative, as in Lorrie Moore's "How" (1986): "Begin by meeting him in a class, in a bar, at a rummage sale. Maybe he teaches sixth grade" (55). The emotions of the hypothetical mind are also revealed: "You will feel passing waves of dependency, devotion, and sentimentality" (55). Finally, there is the "autotelic" form in which the actual reader is addressed: the text of Italo Calvino's *If on a winter's night a traveller* (1979) begins with the words, "You are about to begin reading Italo Calvino's new novel, *If on a winter's night a traveller*. Relax. Concentrate. Dispel every other thought" (Calvino 1981: 1). Here, the mind of the reader is both brought together and imperfectly fused with that of the narratee, since the reader has actually just begun reading the book.

Third-person narration contains its own set of highly unusual or unnatural examples: there are a few novels written from the perspective of "one" or "*man*" in German (Henry

Roth's *Radetzkymarsch*, 1932) or "*on*" in French (Monique Wittig's *L'Opoponax*, 1964). Like second-person narratives, these works tend to resist the binary opposition of first and third person or Genette's homo- and heterodiegetic stances. Like second-person narration, these texts wander between but are never perfectly locatable with this theoretical opposition. Other, more resolutely third-person experiments include fictions entirely about a collective subject in which "they" is the primary pronoun, such as Georges Perec's *Les Choses* (1965) and the first and last chapters of Maxine Swann's *Flower Children* (2007). There is also the more radical text by Mario Vargas Llosa, *Los Cachorros* (1967), which alternates "we" and "they" perspectives to depict the same group, giving it a simultaneously internal and external perspective: "They were still wearing short pants that year, we weren't smoking yet, they preferred soccer to all the other sports and we were learning to surf" (Vargas Llosa 1989: 3). Other such experiments include a story written in the passive voice with almost no pronouns referring to the protagonist, Kathy Acker's "Humiliation" (1990) and June Arnold's novel, *The cook and the carpenter* (1973), which uses an invented, gender-neutral pronoun, "na," to refer to each of the characters.

Contemporary authors do not hesitate to combine or conflate these different narrative stances. Carlos Fuentes' *El Muerto de Artemio Cruz* (1962) and Nuruddin Farah's *Maps* (1986) are books whose segments alternate among first-, second-, and third-person narration. In *Compact* (1966), Maurice Roche takes this practice still further as he adds to these three forms passive voice narration, regular "one" ("*on*") narration, and a few "we" and "it" passages. This text is certainly the *ne plus ultra* of multiperson narration. Narrating positions can be collapsed as well as multiplied. In some of Robert Pinget's novels, one character's voice bleeds into another's (e.g. *Le Fiston*, 1964). Samuel Beckett is probably the most thoroughgoing dismantler of separate, self-consistent, anthropomorphic voices. In the thirteenth of his *Texts for Nothing*, we come across the following passage: "it wonders, that voice which is silence, or is it me, there's no telling, it's all the same dream, the same silence, it and me, it and him, him and me, and all our train, and all theirs" (1967: 139). This kind of conflation of narratorial stances and deconstruction of coherent subjectivities reaches its apogee in Beckett's *The Unnamable* (1953), where the narrator and the narrated voices keep reversing ontological ground so it is unknowable who is narrating what – or whom.

Some postmodern narrators systematically conflate distinct historical periods (see for example Ishmael Reed's *Flight to Canada*, 1976). Others negate or "denarrate" events they have just related and thereby destabilize the narrative storyworld; Brian McHale has called this practice "narrative self-erasure" (1987: 99–106). Once again, Beckett provides a compelling instance of this practice, as he deconstructs his characters at the end of *Worstward Ho*: "Say child gone [. . .] Say old man gone. Old woman gone. As good as gone" (1983: 43). Beckett thus denarrates his characters out of existence.

Some authors violate the realistic principle of autonomy of a single human mind by inexplicably interpolating the thoughts of one character into the mind of another without any possible naturalistic explanation. In *Ulysses* (1922), as C.H. Peake explains, in the "Circe" episode we find the formula "*nebrakada femininum*," which Stephen read in a book a few hours earlier but never mentioned (Joyce 1986: 199), referred to by

Bloom ("Nebrakada!" [451]) and Molly ("*Nebrakada! Femininum!*" [359]) though they cannot have known the phrase. There are numerous other examples of such floating, wayward bits of consciousness, which are not amenable to any real-world recuperation. As Peake states, "they are part of a technique that makes no pretense of being confined to the minds, the space or the time of the characters" (1977: 269); indeed, they are unnatural interpolations.

As this survey suggests, we see repeated attempts to extend the possibilities of narration and the narrator.· We find ever more extreme and unnatural kinds of narration, as ever more radical stances and combinations are attempted. We also see a move ever further away from the single, self-consistent human-like narrator toward more unlikely, decentred, and impossible narrators, even to the point where it is inaccurate to attribute the narration to a single narrator. Such cases represent what can be called the "death of the narrator" and disclose the replacement of a humanistic narrator figure by irreducibly polymorphous acts of narration. At the same time, we note that many of these extreme formal experiments are deeply rooted in the subject matter they narrate: extreme and unnatural events seem to call for extreme and unnatural modes of narration.

III. Impossible narration and minds

In this section, we present some more in-depth accounts of unnatural narratives that involve impossible minds, beginning with a close reading of an unnatural we-narrative, namely Ayi Kwei Armah's novel *Two Thousand Seasons* (1973). From there, we will move on to the animal narrator in Robert Olen Butler's short story "Jealous Husband Returns in Form of Parrot" (1996) as well as the dead narrators in Samuel Beckett's short story "The Calmative" (1954) and Alice Sebold's novel *The Lovely Bones* (2002).

As we have already stated, we-narratives are not unnatural *per se*. For example, in real-world storytelling scenarios, speakers often use the first-person plural to relate shared experiences. In most of such oral we-narratives (e.g., in shared experiences by couples), the addressee, who is typically a friend or an acquaintance, is excluded, while in some of them (e.g., in stories told at class or family reunions), the addressee is included. Generally speaking, the relationship between the primary narrator and the reference group denoted by the "we" is not unique but rather allows for a wide range of different possibilities (Margolin 1996: 117–18). In fictional we-narratives, the precise reference of "we" is often ambiguous or unclear, since at any given point the pronoun may refer to a different combination of individuals (Marcus 2008b: 2–3).

In some cases, fictional we-narratives can also be unnatural, particularly if the "we" refers to an impossible group of minds. In Armah's *Two Thousand Seasons*, for instance, the first-person plural subsumes representatives of the black African experience of about one thousand years (= two thousand seasons), and their minds are connected by a collective memory that comprises both the world of the living and the ancestral region, i.e., the world of the dead. At the beginning, we are presented with statements such as "we are not a people of yesterday" (1979: 1) or "that we the black people are one people we know" (3).

In the novel as a whole, the precise reference of "we" is shifting. According to Uri Margolin, the "we" comprises various interconnected groups such as

> [. . .] contemporary African writers and political activists [. . .]; all Africans who fought actively against colonialism; all those who possess an African identity or self-consciousness; all contemporary Africans; specific past generations of Africans, such as the first victims of slavery; and, finally all Africans of the past thousand years [. . .].
>
> (Margolin 1996: 120–1)

Margolin also observes that the speaker in *Two Thousand Seasons* is "an unspecified voice emanating from somewhere within the group" (1996: 119). Basically, this narrative confronts us with a situation in which *all* black Africans – no matter whether they are dead or alive – tell the history of Africa in a single and unified voice. The novel portrays the mythical history of the black people, and they are all seen as being part of one general consciousness, spirit, or mind, namely the novel's "we" (see also Marcus 2008a: 50). At one point, the projected community self-referentially tells us of the limitations of an isolated consciousness (Armah 1979: 128–9). The general consciousness of *Two Thousand Seasons* is an unnatural instance of what Alan Palmer calls intermental thought or a social mind. According to him, "*intermental thought* is joint, group, shared or collective thought, as opposed to intramental, or individual or private thought. It is also known as *socially distributed, situated,* or *extended cognition,* and also as *intersubjectivity*" (2010: 83; italics in the original). Intermental thought is "natural" or possible if the projected minds are temporally and spatially connected and may thus interact (as in, say, George Eliot's novel *Middlemarch* [1871–1872]); on the other hand, intermental thought is unnatural if the projected minds cannot interact because they have existed over a very long period of time or belong to both the world of the living and the realm of the dead. And this is indeed the case in *Two Thousand Seasons*: the novel "articulates the journey of a healing community from the realm of the godhead through the realm of the ancestors into the realm of the living" (Mtshali 2009: 125).

At first glance the unnatural social mind in *Two Thousand Seasons* seems designed to highlight the common black history of suffering, slavery, colonialism, exile, and alienation. However, upon closer inspection, we begin to realize that the novel's connected consciousness goes even one step further: it actually seeks to stress the common humanity of all human beings and constitutes a postcolonial vision that moves beyond every type of hierarchy or form of domination. At the end, the novel's "we" notably speaks of

> [. . .] a vision of creation yet unknown, higher, much more profound than all erstwhile creation! What a hearing of the confluence of all the waters of life flowing to overwhelm the ashen desert's blight! What an utterance of the coming together of all the people of our way, the coming together of people of the way.
>
> (Armah 1979: 206)

In this context, Kwadwo Osei-Nyame points out that the communal voice also presents us with "a story of misrule, violence and mayhem in which both white and black protagonists are implicated" (2009: 95; see Armah 1979: 80–1). Hence, the novel does not oppose "good blacks" and "evil whites"; rather, it defines all human beings who are directed against exploitation, domination, and hierarchies as "people of the way." In other words, we are all invited to participate in the novel's vision and to join its projected unnatural social mind, the novel's "we," which turns out to be an even larger collective consciousness that advocates equality and self-determination.

Butler's "Jealous Husband Returns in Form of Parrot" (1996) presents its readers with another interesting unnatural manifestation, namely a rather intensely fused blend between an animal and a human being. Further examples of speaking animals can be found in beast fables such as Aesop's texts, the twelfth- or thirteenth-century *The Owl and the Nightingale* and Chaucer's "The Nun's Priest's Tale" (from his fourteenth-century *Canterbury Tales*); eighteenth-century circulation novels such as Dorothy Kilner's *The Life and Perambulations of a Mouse* (1785); as well as children's books such as Anna Sewell's *Black Beauty* (1877) and Marshal Saunders' *Beautiful Joe* (1893). Postmodern examples of animal narrators are contained in William Kotzwinkle's novel *Doctor Rat* (1976), Leigh Buchanan Bienen's short story "My Life as a West African Gray Parrot" (1983), Leon Rooke's novel *Shakespeare's Dog* (1983), Julian Barnes's short story "The Stowaway" (1989), John Hawkes's novel *Sweet William: A Memoir of Old Horse* (1993), and Sam Savage's novel *Firmin: Adventures of a Metropolitan Lowlife* (2006). Paul Auster's novel *Timbuktu* (1999) is yet another interesting text insofar as a dog (called "Mr. Bones") serves as the narrative's "reflector-character."

In "Jealous Husband Returns in Form of Parrot," the first-person narrator is a parrot, and this bird turns out to be the reincarnation of a jealous American husband of the twentieth century. The narrative thus plays with the Hindu idea of reincarnation, i.e., the belief that the soul repeatedly inhabits different physical bodies through being born on Earth. While the narrator's thoughts are still recognizably human, his thinking clearly exhibits traits of a parrot's behavior. For instance, in contrast to the narrator's thoughts on the page, his utterances in the storyworld are constrained by a parrot's mental and linguistic capacities:

> I never can quite say as much as I know. [. . .] For a moment I think she knows it's me. But she doesn't, of course. I say 'Hello' again and I will eventually pick up 'pretty bird.' I can tell that as soon as she says it, but for now I can only give her another hello. [. . .] She said it again, "Pretty bird," and this brain that works like it does now could feel that tiny little voice of mine ready to shape itself around these sounds. [. . .] I know many words, for a parrot. [. . .] I talk pretty well, but none of my words are adequate.
>
> (Butler 1996: 71, 72, 77)

Interestingly, the narrator remembers his former life and gradually begins to realize that his current situation as a parrot bears numerous structural resemblances to his former existence as a jealous husband. For instance, the parrot tells us that when he gets "this restlessness back in [his] tail, a burning trashing feeling," then "it's like all the times when [he] was sure there was a man naked with [his] wife" (Butler 1996: 73). Later on, we learn that, as a husband, the narrator typically remained silent when he was jealous and instead of talking to his wife, preferred to lock himself up in the bathroom (74). At one point, the narrator muses about his current existence as a bird as follows: "I know I'm different now. I'm a bird. Except I'm not. That's what's confusing" (75). The short story thus accentuates similarities between the narrator's former existence as a jealous husband and his current existence as a parrot. As a jealous husband, the narrator did not find the right words to express his jealousy, and as a parrot, he does not manage to say what he would like to say either. Additionally, as a jealous husband the narrator locked himself up in the bathroom, while as a parrot, he is locked up in a cage. "Jealous Husband Returns in Form of Parrot" thus implies that the husband somehow turned himself into a parrot through his behavior. Hence, this short story can be read as a critique of the husband's inability to talk about his feelings by thematizing his jealousy. This short story is an example of what David Herman has recently termed "Umwelt exploration" insofar as it focuses on "the lived phenomenal worlds of nonhuman animals themselves" (2011: 167): "Jealous Husband Returns in Form of Parrot" illustrates in great detail what it must be like to be a parrot. At the same time, however, Butler uses the experience of a parrot to highlight certain problems about the behavior of the husband (who is reincarnated as a parrot). In this sense, the narrative is also an example of what Herman calls "animal allegory" where "nonhumans function as virtual stand-ins for humans" (167).

As Stanzel has shown (1984: 229–32), many authors present the gradual fading away of a dying first-person narrator's consciousness up to the threshold of life. He calls this type of narration "dying in the first person" and argues that "the difficulties arising from the presentation of the death of a narratorial "I" have not deterred authors from selecting the first-person form for the fictional presentation of this extreme situation" (1984: 229). Numerous postmodern authors go even one step further and confront us with narrators who are dead and speak to us from the grave or from heaven.

For example, the narrators of William Golding's novel *Pincher Martin* (1954), Flann O'Brien's novel *The Third Policeman* (1967), Vladimir Nabokov's short story "Terra Incognita" (1968), Nabokov's novel *Transparent Things* (1972), Robertson Davies's novel *Murther and Walking Spirits* (1991), Percival Everett's novel *American Desert* (2004), and one of the narrators of Orhan Pamuk's novel *My Name is Red* (2001) are all dead. Also, the narrator of "Past," the first section of Ali Smith's novel *Hotel World* (2001), is the ghost of a chambermaid who had fallen into a food elevator where she died, while *Destiny and Desire* (2011) by Carlos Fuentes is narrated by the severed head of a young attorney, and the narrator of Markus Zusak's novel *The Book Thief* (2005) is the allegorical figure of Death.

Furthermore, the first words of Beckett's "The Calmative" are "I don't know when I died" (1977: 51). This text thus also projects a physically impossible scenario in which a corpse (or a ghost) talks to us. Similarly, Sebold's *The Lovely Bones* opens as follows: "My name was Salmon, like the fish; first name, Susie. I was fourteen when I was murdered on December 6, 1973" (Sebold 2002: 5). Later on, we learn that the narrator, who was raped and killed by her neighbor, Mr. Harvey, has entered heaven and speaks from there:

> When I first entered heaven I thought that everyone saw what I saw. That in everyone's heaven there were soccer goalposts in the distance and lumbering women throwing shot put and javelin. That all the buildings were like suburban northeast high schools built in the 1960s.
>
> (16)

The Lovely Bones clearly digresses from our real-world parameters and we have to develop a new reading frame to come to terms with the novel's unnatural narrative situation. First of all, we have to activate our knowledge about people who are alive (and able to tell stories) and our awareness of the fact that the dead cannot speak. In a second step, we combine or blend these schemata to picture a scenario in which somebody who is dead nevertheless speaks. Mark Turner explains the process of blending by pointing out that "cognitively modern human beings have a remarkable, species-defining ability to pluck forbidden mental fruit – that is, to activate two conflicting mental structures [. . .] [such as *corpse* and *person*] and to blend them creatively into a new mental structure [. . .] [such as *speaking corpse*]" (2003: 117).

What might the potential functions of this unnatural scenario be? When the narrator of "The Calmative" says, "So I'll tell myself a story" (1977: 51), he may in fact look back upon his life from the next world, or he might still be alive and talking to himself to pass the time. In the latter case, the short story is only about a metaphorical form of death. From this perspective, the narrative, like many of Beckett's stories, plays around with the paradoxical saying "in the midst of life we are in death," and highlights the fact that the lonely narrator is about to die without having ever really lived. The ultimate point of the story might be to argue that it does not matter whether you are alive or dead because, at least for Beckett, the two states are very similar anyway. *The Lovely Bones*, on the other hand, invites us to develop a new cognitive category ("the dead narrator") to picture a situation in which Susie continues to interact with the world she had to leave. The novel might highlight our hopes that death is not the definite end of our existence or that the dead somehow continue to exist in the next world. One can explain the dead narrator scenario on the basis of Mark Turner's statement that "a child who died in the past is still mentally with us. The child never leaves, is always there to cast her shadow on the day, even though our days have changed radically since her death. In the blend, we can imagine her living and appropriately aged" (2002: 16).

IV. Transgressive first-person narration

At this point, we would like to move on to a discussion of what Genette calls homodiegetic narration with zero focalization, i.e. narration in the first person in which the reader is provided with access to the thoughts of several characters. In general, fictional first-person narration often differs markedly from non-fictional forms of personal narration. This is so because fictional first-person novels *can* but need not adhere to any standards of real-life parameters. For example, fictional first-person narrators can possess implausibly good memory when they produce pages of exact renderings of dialogue: Dorrit Cohn refers to this phenomenon as "mnemonic overkill" (1983: 162). Also, in first-person present tense narration, the events and the act of telling can frequently not be reconciled (see also 1983: 106). In addition to that, many first-person narratives seem importantly to be un-situated in the sense that there is not only no *identifiable*, but even no *imaginable* point in time and space in which the narrative act is situated. Furthermore, large parts of the narrative are commonly made up of information that the narratee already possesses, making them strictly speaking unnecessary in the fictional world (see Phelan's 2001 article on what he calls "redundant telling").

In short, we often read in fictional first-person narratives what the narrator-protagonist cannot, will not, or need not tell. One of the most striking examples of the former is the one Genette refers to as "[. . .] one paralepsis to end all paralepses; it is irreducible by any hypothesis to the narrator's information [. . .]" (1980: 207f). Genette here refers to the recounting of another person's thoughts on his deathbed in Marcel Proust's *À la recherche du temps perdu* [1913–1927]. In fact similar examples abound. Phelan observes in *Narrative as Rhetoric* (1996) that Fitzgerald in *The Great Gatsby* (1925) does not even try to justify how the first-person narrator, Nick Carraway, is able to narrate what he cannot possibly know. This is the case for example in a scene where he relates what goes on at a location while he is somewhere else. Similarly, Bret Easton Ellis's novel *Glamorama* (1999) is full of instances that relate something that Victor Ward, the first-person narrator, does *not* notice: "'Disarm' by the Smashing Pumpkins starts playing on the soundtrack and the music overlaps a shot of the club I was going to open in TriBeCa and I walk into that frame, *not noticing* the black limousine parked across the street" (168; our emphasis).

The examples above can be described as unnatural because they break with real-world expectations but also with mimetic norms and conventions (such as "you cannot authoritatively narrate what you don't know"). In critical works such instances have been described as narrated by an "omniscient," "telepathic" or "paraleptic" first-person narrator. All these three terms are misleading, though, and we will discuss why and suggest alternative ways of dealing with this unnatural phenomenon through an example from Herman Melville's novel *Moby-Dick; or, the Whale* (1851). In *Moby-Dick*, one finds passages in which the limits of the point of view of the character-narrator Ishmael are respected, but also chapters in which they are transgressed to a striking degree. After long passages which are internally focalized through Ishmael, the narrative suddenly provides extended access to the thoughts of other characters. This is especially true for Chapters 37–39; Chapter 40 is in the form of drama, and after that, we return to Ishmael in Chapter 41 with the following words of assurance: "I, Ishmael, was one of that crew" (1988: 179). This ability to move in time and in space and into the thoughts of other characters is something we are used to in third-person narration but not in first-person narration.

If we think of Ishmael as an "omniscient" character-narrator we run into problems almost immediately at both the general and the specific level. At a general level, Jonathan Culler has questioned the concept as follows:

> I do not think the idea of omniscience is obscene, but I *have* reached the conclusion that it is not a useful concept for the study of narration, that it conflates and confuses several different factors that should be separated if they are to be well understood – that it obfuscates the various phenomena that provoke us to posit the idea. Wallace Martin writes, "'omniscient narration' becomes a kind of dumping ground filled with a wide range of distinct narrative techniques."
>
> (Culler 2004: 146)

Culler shows how very different phenomena and narrative techniques that are not bound to each other with any necessity have been associated with the notion of omniscience (incontrovertible narrative declaration, inside knowledge of others, authorial narration, etc.). One could add that at best the term "omniscient narrator" is a metaphor for these and similar narrative techniques that have little to do with knowing everything and much to do with specific ways of telling. Problems multiply with respect to a character-narrator because the employment of (some of) these techniques maps on very poorly to a personal agent, and because nothing suggests that Ishmael as a character is omniscient since he often lacks knowledge and misunderstands motives. Again, omniscient narration may be a metaphor for the way some of the chapters are told, but is misleading with respect to characterizing the narrator. To attribute the words in the mentioned chapters to an "omniscient" Ishmael and to characterize *Moby-Dick* as an experiment with "omniscient" first-person narration, therefore leads us astray.

As an alternative to omniscience, Culler mentions Nicholas Royle's notion of telepathy. Royle writes, "'telepathy' opens possibilities of a humbler, more precise, less religiously freighted conceptuality than does omniscience for thinking about the uncanniness of what is going on in narrative fiction" (2003: 261). In particular, the notion of telepathy helps capture the fact that in cases of reports of characters' thoughts, we are not dealing with narrators who know everything all at once but rather with narrative instances reporting now on this consciousness, now on that, often relaying, transposing, or translating thought into the intermediate discourse of free indirect speech, for example.

Royle's ideas on telepathy – not only in the chapter of *The Uncanny* mentioned by Culler but also in *Telepathy and Literature: Essays on the Reading Mind* (1990) – are truly eye-opening and a sound antidote to quasi-theological concepts. However, his suggestion carries over most of the problems from omniscience when used to explain the existence of a technique such as the above-mentioned in *Moby-Dick*. Just as nothing suggested that Ishmael as a character is omniscient, nothing suggests that he has the gift of telepathy. Most of the time his limits in regard to other peoples' thoughts are restricted to that of real, non-telepathic persons, and nowhere does the text refer to a sudden emergence of mind-reading skills or give the reader reason to think that Ishmael as a character on the ship receives flashes of insight about other persons in other places. Positing telepathy as an (unexplained and un-explicit) unnatural element in the world of whale-hunting in *Moby-Dick* surely isn't a plausible description of the psychic abilities of the character in the fictional world, though it may be a less misleading metaphor for the narrative technique.

Rüdiger Heinze has recently mentioned a wide range of first-person narratives that – exactly like the ones discussed here – display knowledge that their narrators could not possibly possess if they functioned exactly like human beings. Heinze follows Manfred Jahn's use of the term "paralepsis," defined as an "infraction caused by saying too much; a narrator assuming a competence he/she does not properly have; typically, a first-person narrator (or a historiographer) narrating what somebody else thought, or what happened when s/he was not present" (2008: 280). The term "paralepsis" means "saying too much" in the sense of disclosing knowledge one could not possess. However, strictly speaking it is only a question of paralepsis if we still think of the first person as a narrator responsible for all words in the narrative. Just as it seems misleading to attribute to Ishmael powers of telepathy or omniscience, it seems misguided to say that he tells more than he knows.

The real experiment in these fictions is not with the character which would in a sense amount to creating an unnatural storyworld, but rather with the act of narration. The character-narrator Ishmael is fairly "natural" in the sense that he has the same capabilities and limitations as real people do. The experiment instead is to disconnect voice and character, or pronoun and person. The works and words discussed are unnatural in the sense that they designate and refer to a character as "I" without *emanating* from that character. Insofar as the narrating "voice" does not emanate from the character but invents and creates a world (including the first-person narrator and his knowledge and lack of knowledge) then this voice is not saying more or less than it knows.

Confronted with seemingly strange acts of narration most readers will probably first try to employ a range of strategies for naturalizing and understanding the narration in accordance with real-life parameters. In the case of Ishmael these options include, but are not limited to, assuming that he is outright lying or making up what he cannot know, that he is unreliable, has gone temporarily mad, is being ironical or joking, is extrapolating or guessing. Nothing ever prevents a reader from naturalizing. In the specific example, though, it seems as though all these possible assumptions will lead to a partial or total dismissal of the information provided in the relevant chapters. An unnatural approach to narratives, on the other hand, proceeds from the assumption that we arrive at poor and unsatisfying interpretations if we naturalize.

Monika Fludernik argues that when we read narratives, we tend to imagine comparable real-world situations: according to her, we "project real-life parameters into the reading process and, if at all possible, treat the text as a real-life instance of narrating" (2001: 623). This may indeed be what readers tend to do, but it does of course not oblige us as literary critics to reproduce this projection at a methodological level. Facing unnatural acts of narration, the reader will often not be able to arrive at relevant interpretations or understandings by applying the same rules of interpretation as those normally applied to everyday, conversational narratives and real-world reports. Instead, he or she has the option to apply a qualitatively different set of interpretive rules to the text. For example, the reader can strategically assume that it makes sense to actually trust details in narratives that the first-person narrator cannot possible know. Exactly the same option is available in everyday storytelling, but in the latter case, a much more reasonable assumption is that the narrator is simply lying or guessing.

Unnatural narratives can be seen as cueing readers to engage in decoding activities that differ from those he or she would use in face-to-face communication. The question of whether the reader remains alert to this difference and does not automatically transfer all rules of everyday discourse to literature makes a significant difference for the interpretation of numerous specific cases of the unnatural. For example, *Glamorama* by Bret Easton Ellis, in addition to being told in the first-person present tense, is in some respects a classic *doppelganger*-narrative: the narrator Victor Ward apparently has a double, and this double is gradually taking over his identity. In the end, one Victor – and everything seems to indicate that he is the one we have followed throughout most of the book – dies in Italy while the other Victor, his double, enjoys life in New York.

The really odd and unnatural thing about *Glamorama*, however, is that the double does not only overtake the identity of the first-person narrator in the projected storyworld; he additionally becomes the teller, i.e., the person designated by the pronoun "I." In other words, there are two voices at the level of the narrative discourse; through major parts, *Glamorama* is not unequivocally narrated by Victor Ward. The doubling in *Glamorama* thus effects the enunciation of the narrative in a way previously unheard of in first-person narrative: the appropriation of identity also occurs at the pronominal level. The novel thus creates a new kind of narrative with protagonist and double struggling for mastery all the way down to the enunciation of the personal pronoun "I."

On at least three levels the words in *Glamorama* cannot unequivocally – and sometimes not at all – be attributed to Victor or to the "I": first, because this pronoun is open to being taken over, so that sometimes it is the double who says "I"; second, because even when the "I" refers to Victor, the novel frequently provides information this character-narrator cannot possibly have; third, and finally, due to the present-tense narration Victor cannot be the narrator: it is impossible to narrate and experience at the same time. An attentive reader may realize that there is a fundamental disconnect between the narrator and the narrated in *Glamorama*.

The double becomes the first-person protagonist and seems responsible for the narration in parts of the final chapters in the novel. This phenomenon corresponds to no manner of "natural" real-world discourse. The understanding of even the basic events and the storyline in *Glamorama* hinges crucially on an understanding of this pronominal takeover. Discovering that a substitution has taken place is a precondition for being able to grasp important parts of the novel's plot. Even more interesting, though, is exploring what this tells us about unnatural first-person narration.

Glamorama is simultaneously innovative and paradigmatic as a first-person narrative. An attentive reader can realize that words are put into the first-person narrator's mouth that cannot possibly emanate from there. At the same time, the novel illustrates that readers can in principle encounter such an unnatural voice in the world of literature. This voice is disconnected from any person even when it says "I." It is not a voice that speaks to the reader in every first-person narrative, but the possibility of transgressing the limits of the personal voice regarding knowledge, vocabulary, memory, and so forth, is always present in first-person narrative fiction.

V. Conclusions and perspectives

Unnatural narratives perform a number of important functions. They provide an interrogation of the basic elements of realistic narrative practices and a critique of overused narrative conventions. Such narratives offer original vehicles for representation, including, as we have seen, the self-representation of marginalized or colonized peoples. Unnatural forms are an exceptional way to express extraordinary events and they produce a different, challenging kind of aesthetic experience. By taking us to the most remote territories of what can be imagined, the unnatural significantly widens the cognitive horizon of human awareness: the various new forms of pronominal play, speaking animals, dead narrators, and the transgressive first-person narrator in *Glamorama* challenge our limited perspective on the world and invite us to address questions that we would otherwise perhaps ignore.

There are also different ways of engaging with the unnatural. As we have shown in Section III, one can look at the unnatural from a cognitive perspective and illustrate how we reorganize our cognitive architecture by blending or extending pre-existing frames or scripts. In a second step, one can then address the question of what the unnatural tells us about us and the world we live in. On the other hand, as we have shown in Section IV, one can also simply accept the fact that the unnatural transcends real-world situations. From this perspective, one should resist impulses to deny the unnatural its protean essence and unexpected effects. Taken to an extreme, the first approach potentially leads to a process of normalization, while the second one might involve the monumentalization of the unnatural. What the two approaches have in common is that they both argue that a focus on the unnatural can enrich the polysemic make-up of narrative texts.

References

Alber, J. (2009) "Impossible Storyworlds – and What to Do with Them," *Storyworlds: A Journal of Narrative Studies* 1(1): 79–96.

——(2011) "The Diachronic Development of Unnaturalness: A New View on Genre." In J. Alber and R. Heinze (eds.) *Unnatural Narratives, Unnatural Narratology*, New York: de Gruyter, pp. 41–67.

Alber, J., Iversen, S., Nielsen, H.S. and Richardson, B. (2010) "Unnatural Narratives, Unnatural Narratology: Beyond Mimetic Models," *Narrative* 18(20): 113–36.

Armah, A.K. (1979 [1973]) *Two Thousand Seasons*, London: Heinemann.

Beckett, S. (1967) *Stories and Texts for Nothing*, New York: Grove.

——(1977 [1954]) "The Calmative." In *Four Novellas*, London: Calder, pp. 51–68.

——(1983) *Worstward Ho*, New York: Grove.

Butler, R.O. (1996) "Jealous Husband Returns in Form of Parrot." In *Tabloid Dreams*, New York: Henry Holt & Co, pp. 71–81.

Calvino, I. (1981[1979]) *If on a winter's night a traveller*, trans. W. Weaver, New York: Harcourt Brace Jovanovich.

Cohn, D. (1983 [1978]) *Transparent Minds*, Princeton, NJ: Princeton University Press.

Culler, J. (2004) "Omniscience," *Narrative* 12(1): 22–34.

Ellis, B.E. (1999) *Glamorama*, New York: Alfred A. Knopf.

Fludernik, M. (1996) *Towards a 'Natural' Narratology*, London: Routledge.

——(2001) "New Wine in Old Bottles? Voice, Focalization, and New Writing," *New Literary History* 32(3): 619–38.

Genette, G. (1980 [1972]) *Narrative Discourse*, trans. J. E. Lewin, New York: Cornell University Press.

Heinze, R. (2008) "Violations of Mimetic Epistemology in First-Person Narrative Fiction," *Narrative* 16(3): 279–97.

Herman, D. (2002) *Story Logic: Problems and Possibilities of Narrative*, Lincoln, NE: University of Nebraska Press.

—— (2011) "Storyworld / Umwelt: Nonhuman Experiences in Graphic Narratives," *SubStance* 140(1): 156–81.

Joyce, J. (1986 [1922]) *Ulysses: The Corrected Text*, eds. H.W. Gabler , W. Steppe and C. Melchior, New York: Random.

Marcus, A. (2008a) "A Contextual View of Narrative Fiction in the First Person Plural," *Narrative* 16(1): 46–64.

——(2008b) "We Are You: The Plural and the Dual in 'We' Fictional Narratives," *Journal of Literary Semantics* 37(1): 1–21.

Margolin, U. (1996) "Telling Our Story: On 'We' Literary Narratives," *Language and Literature* 5: 115–33.

McHale, B. (1987) *Postmodernist Fiction*. New York: Methuen.

Melville, H. (1988 [1851]) *Moby-Dick or The Whale*, Evanston, IL: Northwestern University Press.

Moore, L. (1986) *Self-Help*, New York: New American Library.

Mtshali, K. (2009) "The Journey of a Healing Community in Ayi Kwei Armah's *Two Thousand Seasons*," *Research in African Literatures* 40(2): 125–39.

O'Brien, E. (1984) *A Pagan Place*, Port Townsend, WA: Greywolf.

Osei-Nyame, K. (2009) "The Politics of 'Translation' in African Postcolonial Literature: Olaudah Equiano, Ayi Kwei Armah, Toni Morrison, Ama Ata Aidoo, Tayeb Salih and Leila Aboulela," *Journal of African Cultural Studies* 21(1): 91–103.

Palmer, A. (2010) "Large Intermental Units in *Middlemarch*." In J. Alber and M. Fludernik (eds.) *Postclassical Narratology: Approaches and Analyses*, Columbus, OH: Ohio State University Press, pp. 83–104.

Peake, C.H. (1977) *James Joyce: The Citizen and the Artist*, Stanford CA: Stanford University Press.

Phelan, J. (1996) *Narrative as Rhetoric: Technique, Audiences, Ethics, Ideology*, Columbus, OH: Ohio State University Press.

——(2001) "Redundant Telling, Preserving the Mimetic, and the Functions of Character Narration," *Narrative* 9(2): 210–16.

Richardson, B. (2002) "Beyond Story and Discourse: Narrative Time in Postmodern and Nonmimetic Fiction." In B. Richardson (ed.) *Narrative Dynamics: Essays on Time, Plot, Closure, and Frames*, Columbus, OH: Ohio State University Press, pp. 47–63.

——(2006) *Unnatural Voices: Extreme Narration in Modern and Contemporary Fiction*, Columbus, OH: Ohio State University Press.

Royle, N. (1990) *Telepathy and Literature: Essays on the Reading Mind*, Cambridge, MA: Blackwell.

——(2003) *The Uncanny*, New York: Routledge.

Sarraute, N. (1989) *Tu ne t'aimes pas*, Paris: Gallimard.

——(1990) *You Don't Love Yourself*, trans. B. Wright, New York: Brazilier.

Sebold, A. (2002) *The Lovely Bones*, Boston, MA: Little, Brown and Company.

Stanzel, F.K. (1984 [1979]) *A Theory of Narrative*, trans. C. Goedsche, preface P. Hernadi, Cambridge, UK: Cambridge University Press.

Turner, M. (2002) "The Cognitive Study of Art, Language, and Literature," *Poetics Today* 23(1): 9–20.

——(2003) "Double-Scope Stories." In D. Herman (ed.) *Narrative Theory and the Cognitive Sciences*, Stanford, CA: CSLI, 117–42.

Vargas Llosa, M. (1989 [1967]) *The Cubs and Other Stories*, trans. G. Kolovakos and R. Christ, New York: Noonday.

27

IMPOSSIBLE WORLDS

Marie-Laure Ryan

According to modal logic (better known among literary scholars as possible worlds theory), a world is possible with respect to another world when it is linked to this world by a so-called accessibility relation (Kripke 1963). Since this relation can be conceived in many different ways, possibility and impossibility are relative concepts. Possibility could denote what may happen in the future, according to the laws of nature: for instance, the tower of Pisa could collapse some day and kill scores of tourists. In a more remote type of possible world, the laws of physics and biology no longer hold, so that princes can be turned into toads and vice-versa. These worlds, which can be called unnatural, are widely represented in literature, as popular genres such as fairy tales, medieval fantasy and science fiction demonstrate. Yet realistic texts that respect the laws of nature and fantastic texts that extend the possible beyond the natural do not exhaust the set of all possible texts: an important form of experimental literature creates worlds that cannot satisfy even the most liberal interpretation of possibility. Such works transgress the logical laws of non-contradiction (not p and ~p) and excluded middle (either p or ~p).

The surge of experiments with impossibility in literature and the visual arts coincides with developments in science that replace the Newtonian vision of a clockwork universe – predictable, knowable, and deterministic – with a world full of paradoxes: non-Euclidean geometry; elastic time and space that shrink and expand depending on the speed at which the observer travels; particles existing in a superposition of states and therefore satisfying both p and ~p; undecidable issues; entangled particles communicating without local connections; quantum tunneling; phenomena explainable only through mutually incompatible models (light behaving as both wave and particles); and either incompleteness or contradiction in mathematical systems. With modern physics, the natural and the impossible seem to exchange places: whereas in classical physics the impossible lies outside of nature, in modern physics, especially quantum mechanics, nature often seems to incorporate the logically impossible. By defying logic, literature and the visual arts rival the power of modern science to challenge the imagination.

For convenience's sake I call the semantic domain of the texts I have in mind "impossible worlds," but as Umberto Eco (1979) has argued, the adequacy of the concept of world is questionable in these cases. Can a world be logically impossible and still remain a world? It all depends on what we understand by this term. The idea of textual or fictional world is often used in a rather loose sense by literary scholars to refer to the content of the reader's act of imagination. Since any text in a writing system that the reader can decipher evokes something to the mind, even if it represents nonsensical syllables (as in Hugo Ball's sound poetry) or consists of an invented language (as in Lewis Carroll's poem "Jabberwocky"), it would take a totally unreadable collection of graphic marks to deprive a text of a world. In a more narrow sense, the one that I will use here, the notion of textual world presents a *referential* dimension (as stressed in Stefanescu 2008): a textual world is a mental representation constructed on the basis of the propositions asserted in or implied by the text. The world of a text of narrative fiction can be thought of as a container filled with the characters and objects referred to by the text. Reference, in this sense, does not require autonomous, actual existence: a fictional text refers to a world even though this world does not exist independently of the text, because the conventions of fiction allow language to create objects by merely mentioning them. As in all uses of language, the mental construction of fictional worlds relies heavily on inferences. It would be not only impractical to spell out all the facts that hold in a textual world, it would also be incredibly boring. This reliance of world construction on inferences, however, calls into question the adequacy of the notion of "impossible world." Logicians believe that if a single contradiction penetrates into a system of propositions, anything can be inferred, and every proposition and its negation becomes vacuously true. It would be impossible to imagine a textual world under these conditions, since textual worlds are constructed on the basis of a set of propositions that the text presents as true. The texts I have in mind could be described as texts that cannot be true of any possible world, rather than as texts that refer to impossible worlds. Yet even if logic tells us that the phrase "impossible world" is an oxymoron, I will retain it in this chapter, because the readers of literary fiction have a broader of sense of worldness than logicians, and because they do not treat inconsistencies as an excuse for giving up the attempt to make inferences. Literary works that project impossible worlds challenge readers to devise new strategies for making sense of texts, even if meaning does not arise from the vision of fully imaginable situations.

The following sections offer a catalog of the many forms of impossibility.

I. Contradictions

The most obvious type of logical impossibility is a text that presents both p and ~p as facts in the fictional world. The contradiction can be as blatant as stating "the cat is both dead and alive" (a technique typical of the folklore genre of nonsense poetry [Stewart 1978]), or as imperceptible as hiding the conflicting statements within a dense paragraph, as does Robbe-Grillet when in *In the Labyrinth* he starts a description with "outside it is raining" and ends it with "outside the sun is shining," without suggesting a passing of time that could explain a change in weather (1965: 141). In this case, only the most attentive reader will notice the breach of logic, unless the text is riddled with such contradictions.

Contradiction in literature can present various degrees of granularity. On the largest scale, it opposes substantial segments of text. In *The French Lieutenant's Woman* (1969) by John Fowles, for instance, the last two chapters contain different endings: one in which the lovers, Charles and Sarah, commit to each other after a long separation, and one in which Sarah rejects Charles because she has found a fulfilling life without him. The two endings cannot be true at the same time, but within each of them the fictional world is perfectly consistent. The device does not ask the reader to construct an impossible world, but rather, to weigh the two endings against each other on the basis of such criteria as literary merit or consistency with the personalities of the characters.

Next on the scale of granularity are contradictions that operate on the level of the relations between relatively short narrative segments. An example of this practice is Robert Coover's "The Babysitter" (1969), a short story made of one hundred and seven numbered paragraphs which cohere on the local, but not on the global level. These paragraphs present different versions of what can happen when a couple goes to a party and leaves the children in the care of an attractive teen-aged babysitter. In one version the babysitter is murdered, in another she is raped by her boyfriend and his buddy, in another the baby drowns in the tub, and in yet another the father leaves the party under the pretext that he needs to check on the children, but really driven by the hope of having sex with the babysitter. The text tempts its readers to construct different stories by sorting out the paragraphs and ordering them in different sequence, but the last paragraph, which asserts as facts all the mutually exclusive developments, demonstrates the futility of such efforts: "Your children are murdered, your husband gone, a corpse in your bathtub, and your house is wrecked. I'm sorry. But what can I say?" On the TV, the news is over, they're selling aspirin. "Hell, I don't know," she says. "Let's see what's on the late late movie" (1969: 239).

A third level of contradiction occurs when individual sentences, rather than entire narrative segments, clash with each other, producing what Brian McHale calls a "world under erasure" (1987, ch. 7): a world so thoroughly infused with ontological instability that readers cannot tell what exist and what does not. We have already seen this technique at work in the Robbe-Grillet example mentioned above; an even more systematic use of sentence-level contradiction occurs in *Le Libera* (1968) by Robert Pinget, another representative of the French New Novel (a school that seems particularly fond of this technique). In *Le Libera*, a female narrator repeatedly contradicts the facts that she reports without apparently realizing the inconsistency of her tale. For instance, the same accident is said to kill a teacher, then to kill a certain student; it is however not this student who is killed but his brother; the brother is also found strangled in a field; a cook is first described as wonderful, then as a disaster; a school trip takes place both in the spring and the summer.

While on the first three levels contradiction involves a relation between distinct units of text, on the last level it operates within the frame of the sentence itself. The

2010 short story "Here We Aren't, So Quickly" by Jonathan Safran Foer has been described as a collection of *non-sequiturs*. It consists of a list of mostly unrelated facts, evoked either in consecutive sentences ("He was never happy unless held. I loved hammering things into walls"; Foer 2010: 73), or in the constituent clauses of the same sentence ("You were not green-thumbed, but you were not content to be not content"; 72). But the true originality of this text, compared with the other types of contradiction, lies in sentences that contain serious logical flaws: for instance "I was always destroying my passport in the wash" (72) denies the unique and punctual character of the act of destruction through an adverb ("always") that presents it as either durative or iterable; "I was always struggling to be natural with my hands" is blatantly self-contradictory, since being natural is behaving without deliberate effort; "Everything else [beside the narrator and his wife being killed in a car accident] happened – why not the things that could have?" is a futile question, for if "everything else happened," there is no point in asking why the things that could have happened did not: there are no such things – or at the most there is only one: the accident. The title of the story, "Here We Aren't, So Quickly" epitomizes the logical impossibility that permeates so many of its sentences: since "here" is a deictic referring to the speaker's present position, it is incompatible with the negation of this position ("aren't"); and since "to be" indicates a static, timeless position, it is incompatible with an adverb that suggests speed of movement through time ("quickly"). Foer's nonsense sentences are not the product of a random juxtaposition of words; they are intricately wrought artifacts whose beauty lies in the elaborate analysis they require of the reader in order to diagnose the source of the weirdness. They make us logically and semantically smarter.

II. Ontological impossibility

In his groundbreaking book *Postmodernist Fiction* (1987: 10), Brian McHale identifies ontological concerns – that is, concerns with modes of existence – as the thematic dominant of the literature of the late twentieth century (see McHale, this volume). A major form of this questioning is the creation of entities which belong simultaneously to incompatible ontological categories. This kind of impossibility is exemplified by the sentence "I am fictional." The felicity conditions of this utterance could never be fulfilled, because the awareness of his own fictionality would attribute contradictory properties to the speaker: by saying "I am," the character views himself as real, which means, as existing autonomously; but by recognizing himself as fictional, he acknowledges that he only exists through an author's act of imagination. Or to put this differently, "I am" is spoken from the perspective of the fictional world – within which the character exists indeed as a real person, if any kind of make-believe is to take place – while "fictional" reflects the perspective of the actual world, in which the speaker only exists as a literary character. The manifestations of ontological impossibility are known in narratology as metalepsis. Typical examples of this narrative device are readers or spectators penetrating into the world of a fiction and intervening in its affairs (the movie *Pleasantville*, in which a teenager is transported into the world of a TV show and initiates its inhabitants into the lifestyle of the world he is coming from); and vice-versa, fictional characters breaking out of their world and invading reality (Julio Cortázar's short story "Continuity of Parks" (1968), in which a reader is so totally immersed in a novel that the characters come to life and murder him). In these cases the breaking of boundaries is vertical, since characters from a lower, fictionally more real world penetrate into a higher, imaginary world or vice-versa, but metalepsis can also operate horizontally by importing characters from different literary texts and having them meet in the same world. This device is systematically exploited in the novels of Jasper Fforde, or in the comic book series *The League of Extraordinary Gentlemen* (Moore and O'Neill 2000), whose cast of characters includes Allan Quatermain from H. Rider Haggard's *King Solomon's Mines*, Captain Nemo from Jules Verne's *20000 Leagues Under the Sea*, Mina Murray from Bram Stoker's *Dracula*, and Dr. Jekyll and Mr Hyde from Robert Louis Stevenson's eponymous novel. From the point of view of the actual reader, however, the boundary between the real and the fictional remains immune to ontological transgressions: it is only within a fiction that a reader can be murdered by a character in a novel, because real readers are located outside the system of fictionality. Metalepsis is not a breaking of boundaries between the (actually) real and the fictional, but rather, a breaking of boundaries that operates strictly within the diegetic levels of a fictional world. Its presence functions therefore as an obvious mark of fictionality. This self-referential, illusion-destroying effect explains why the device has become a dominant feature; some would say a trick of the trade of postmodern fiction.

III. Impossible space

The paintings of René Magritte and M.C. Escher have made us familiar with impossible spaces, though pictorial play with false perspective goes back to at least the eighteenth century. But such effects are rare in literature, because language does not speak immediately to the senses, and cannot therefore produce *trompe-l'oeil* effects. It is admittedly very easy for language to create spatially impossible objects by juxtaposing mutually exclusive terms, such as "round square" or "flat sphere," but it is much more difficult to spin an interesting story that revolves around such entities.

A rare example of a narrative that gives a central role to a spatially impossible object is *House of Leaves* (2000) by Mark Z. Danielewski. The impossible object is a house that is larger on the inside than on the outside. Though the measured difference remains constant – about an inch – the inside expands into a hallway and then into a labyrinth of seemingly infinite dimensions. An expedition is sent to measure this labyrinth and to create a cinematic record of its configuration, but the exit is never found, and many of the explorers disappear or become insane. The structure of the house is replicated on the level of the book as a material object through an outside – the cover – that does not completely cover the pages of the inside. Impossibility, however, runs deeper than space in the world of *House of Leaves*. The story of the house, known as the Navidson record, belongs to a novel (or documentary?) allegedly written by a blind man, Zampanò, and found after his death by a character named Johnny Truant, who edits the manuscript and adds footnotes to Zampanò's text. Yet another editor-character packages Zampanò's narrative, Truant's text, and various other documents – such as letters sent to Truant by his mother, Pelafina – into a book, adding his own notes to Truant's comments. In a breach of probability which does not quite reach the logically impossible, Zampanò's blindness and solitary life make him the most unlikely author for a manuscript that focuses heavily on visual media. Ontological boundaries are violated when Pelafina, afraid that her letters are being intercepted, asks Truant to put a checkmark in his next letter to demonstrate that he has received hers; but the checkmark appears in the text attributed to Zampanò, who does not know anything of Pelafina's (or Truant's) existence. The novel also dismantles the physical space of the text through a wild play with typographical presentation which confronts the reader with endless decisions: should she read first Zampanò's narrative about the impossible house and then Truant's notes, or should she read them concurrently; should she read the text that has been crossed out or should she skip it; should she read the medallions of texts shown on some pages before the text that frames them or the other way round? *House of Leaves* is a narrative presented in book form, but its graphic design subverts the sequential reading protocols traditionally mandated by both narrative and books. In this text, the difference between the inside and the outside of the house is not only a wormhole that leads into an alternate world of darkness and horror; it is also the initial inconsistency that, according to logic, opens the floodgates to all kinds of paradoxes.

IV. Impossible time

Time is a much more abstract, much less graspable concept than space; yet while we cannot capture its nature in words, as St. Augustine famously observed, we have reasonably firm intuitive beliefs about its properties. It is the contradiction of these beliefs that leads to temporal impossibilities.

Our most fundamental intuition about time tells us that it flows in a fixed direction (though this direction is a matter of debate: according to one conceptual scheme, time flows from the future to the past, since future moments become present and then past; in another scheme, time flows from the past to the future, since the future is ahead of us and we are marching toward it.) The axiom of the fixed directionality of time can be broken by reversing its flow. Two novels that attempt this conceptual *tour de force* are *Counterclock World* by Philip K. Dick (1961) and *Time's Arrow* by Martin Amis (1991). Yet if the head of the arrow of time can stand for either the past or the future, depending on the particular conceptual scheme, how can one distinguish the future from the past, and how can one distinguish "normal" from "reversed" time? It takes an external point of reference to determine in which direction time is flowing; in both novels, this reference is provided by familiar biological processes and social scripts: characters die before they are born, eating consists of regurgitating food on a plate, and healthy people get sick after a visit to the doctor. In *Time's Arrow*, in addition, the reversal of time is suggested by a sequence of historical events familiar to the reader: the narrator is the "soul" of a Nazi doctor who died after emigrating to the U.S., and he relives his alter ego's life in reverse order, from Cold-war America to World War II, and from the liberation (or rather, creation) of Auschwitz to the rise (or rather, decline) of Nazism in Germany. But the reversal of time can be conceived along other arrows than biology or chronology: one of them is causal (since causes precede effects in normal time, they should follow them in reversed time) while the other is cognitive (we know what lies in the past, but we don't know what lies in the future). If novels were fully consistent in reversing the flow of time, they would have to invert the causal and cognitive arrows, but this reversal would deprive characters of any form of agency, since the flow of time would inexorably carry them toward a future that is already determined. This in turn would make planning and consequently plot pointless, since the purpose of plans is to control our destiny. To preserve narrative tension, time-reversed narratives typically limit their reversal to history and biology (and even the reversal of history is controversial, because the causality that explains historical events works only in one direction: you can explain World War II through the rise of Nazism in Germany in the 1930s but not vice-versa, unless you change the facts). In Dick's novel the characters remain unaware of what lies ahead of them, and they make plans to affect the future, as if they lived in normal time, while in Amis' novel the narrator is the only character who experiences time backwards: what is for him an unknown future is a known past for the others, and what is shared history for the others is for him a future unknown yet unavoidable. Deprived of the freedom to create his own destiny, he has no choice but to discover passively the life that his alter ego the Nazi doctor has already written for him.

Another fundamental belief about time tells us that the future is open, while the past is written once for all: you can affect the future though your actions, but you cannot undo the past. In *La Moustache* (1986), Emmanuel Carrère explores the trauma that would arise if the past could be changed for one person, but remained stable for all others. A tragic chain of events is set in motion when the narrator and main character innocuously decides to shave the moustache he has been wearing for ten years to surprise his wife. But when his wife comes home she shows no surprise at all. The narrator suspects she is playing a trick on him, but the next day at work his colleagues also behave as if nothing has changed. This is only the beginning of an inexorable process that disintegrates the narrator's personal history piece by piece and replaces it with another life. For the greater part of the novel, the events whose occurrence is denied by the other characters precede the beginning of the story, but in the last chapter, just before the narrator is driven to suicide by the loss of his memories, which mean the loss of his identity, the past being erased concerns the events of the earlier chapters. The novel tells us how the narrator flees to Hong Kong and then to Macao to escape from the people who deny his past; but when he arrives in Macao he finds his wife in the hotel room, enjoying an ordinary vacation with him. This means that the events represented in the earlier chapters never took place. At this point the novel becomes a self-destructing artifact that denies what is generally considered the main function of narrative: its ability to tell about and to preserve the past.

V. Impossible texts

It may seem a matter of common sense to treat impossible texts according to Ludwig Wittgenstein's recommendation: "whereof one cannot speak, thereof one must be silent." Since these works do not exist, why should we bother with them? But at least some impossible texts can be imagined, and therefore described in language. Inventing texts so paradoxical that they can only exist in the imaginary mode is one of the major themes of the work of Jorge Luis Borges. Most of these fictional fictions involve a form of infinity. For instance, the Book of Sand in the eponymous story (1975) has no beginning nor end: wherever one opens it, there are always some pages between the cover and the current page, and when one turns a page, one lands at any distance from the previous page, so that a complete and sequential reading becomes impossible. While in "The Book of Sand" infinity concerns the book as a physical object, in *The Thousand and One Nights* it affects the act of narration. On the six hundred and second night, Borges writes in his essay "Partial Magic in the Quixote" (1993 [1964]), Scheherazade tells the Sultan his own story (a fact that I could not verify by looking at a complete version of *The Thousand and One Nights*). This leads to infinite recursion, since this story contains all the stories that Scheherazade tells the Sultan to postpone her execution, including the story of the six hundred and second night. Infinity reaches into the narrated itself in "The Garden of Forking Paths," a fictional Chinese novel described in a short story that bears the same name. To the narrator, a descendent of the author Ts'ui Pen, the book is "a contradictory jumble of irresoluble drafts. I once examined it myself; in the third chapter the hero dies, yet in the fourth, he is alive again" (Borges 1998: 124). The explanation for the contradictions lies in the author's ambition to capture the field of the possible in its totality:

> In all fictions, each time a man meets diverse alternatives, he chooses one and eliminates the others; in the work of the virtually impossible-to-disentangle Ts'ui Pen, the character chooses – simultaneously – all of them. He *creates*, thereby, 'several futures,' several times, which themselves proliferate and fork. This is the explanation for the novel's contradictions. . . . In Ts'ui Pen's novel, *all* the outcomes in fact occur; each is the starting point for further bifurcations. Once in a while, the paths of that labyrinth converge: for example, you come to this house, but in one of the possible pasts you are my enemy, in another, my friend.
>
> (Borges 1998: 125)

Impossibility has not only to do here with the infinity of the number of possibilities to be covered, it derives primarily from the spatialization of time that takes place in the image of the labyrinth, or garden of forking paths. Ts'ui Pen

> did not believe in a uniform and absolute time; he believed in an infinite series of times, a growing, dizzying web of convergent, divergent and parallel

times. That fabric of times that approach one another, fork, are snipped off, or are simply unknown for centuries, contains *all* possibilities [. . .]

(Borges 1998: 127)

These branching times would be relatively easy to conceive if they remained separate from each other, like the branches of a tree. But in Borges' story, time is not a tree, it is a network that loops back upon itself. While it contains some parallel branches that fork out of a common point and never meet again, it also generates converging branches, as the mention of the traveler reaching the same house through different paths suggests. In space this is easy to do, but in time it leads to logical contradictions. Imagine that at a certain point in time you are faced with a decision that will make you either my friend or my enemy. If all possibilities are realized, two different worlds will be created, each giving birth to its own time. When these worlds merge into one, you will be both my friend and my enemy when you arrive at my house – a blatant violation of the principle of non-contradiction. This, much more than the infinite number of paths to be represented and the fact that language must evoke parallel times sequentially, is the reason why Ts'ui Pen's novel could never be written.

VI. Conclusion: impossible worlds – a challenge to the reader

What is the point of creating fictions with impossible worlds? Another way to formulate this question is to ask, with Jan Alber (2009), what should readers do with these worlds? The mental strategies for making sense of impossible worlds must be measured against the procedure by which readers construct standard fictional worlds, whether realistic or fantastic. Relying on David Lewis' analysis of truth in fiction (1978, 1983), I have called this procedure the "principle of minimal departure" (Ryan 1991); others call it the "reality principle." This principle enjoins readers to construct fictional worlds as the closest possible to their model of reality, amending this model only when it is overruled by the text. This means that readers should not make gratuitous changes. Thomas Pavel has suggested that in the case of many texts, especially those with impossible worlds, readers expect a "maximal departure" (1986: 93). This term may very well describe the reader's general expectations with certain types of text (for instance, nonsense poetry), but unlike minimal departure, such a principle offers no guidance for making inferences and filling in the blanks in the text. Imagine a fiction that mentions a restaurant: minimal departure activates standard scripts about this kind of institution, but what would we imagine under maximal departure? That the restaurant is really a pigpen? That it is a prime number? Or that it pays its customers for eating there? Since concrete objects do not have specific opposites, maximal departure comes up empty in the construction of impossible worlds.

How then do we make sense of these worlds? There is no single strategy that works for all the types I have described, but rather a variety of possible operations whose relevance depends on the particular text. Some of these interpretations can be called "naturalizing," because they aim at preserving the logical integrity of the fictional world:

- Mentalism: the inconsistencies can be explained away as dream, hallucination, or the dementia of an essentially unreliable narrator. If the story is a dream or hallucination, it must stage a return to a normal world (as in *Alice in Wonderland*); if the contradictions are due to the narrator's mental confusion, the reader must be able to reconstruct the normal world that this discourse misrepresents.
- Figural interpretation: the inconsistencies do not correspond to facts, they are only ways of describing certain phenomena. For instance, if Sherlock Holmes is reported to have squared the circle, this could mean that he can solve any problem.
- Many-worlds and virtualization: the mutually incompatible elements are not part of the same world but of different possible worlds. This idea could be used to naturalize branching stories, such as *The French Lieutenant's Woman*. From the point of view of the world of each of the two endings, this world corresponds to the fictional facts, and the other ending is a non-actualized possibility, a purely virtual scenario. The texts that lend themselves to this operation can be described as "polycentered," because they ask of the reader to recenter herself into different worlds.

When naturalizing explanations fail, the reader must accept contradiction as an integral part of the fictional world. In this case there are two possibilities:

- Dream-like reality: in contrast to the mentalist interpretations that limit contradiction to the alternate reality of a dream-world, this interpretation endows the actual world of the textual universe with the characteristics of dreams: fluid images, objects undergoing incessant metamorphoses, and general lack of ontological stability. A prime example of a narrative with a dream-like reality is Franz Kafka's "A Country Doctor." It is in this category that I place Robbe-Grillet's *In the Labyrinth* and Pinget's *Le Libera*, though *Le Libera* could also be interpreted as a case of mentalism.
- Swiss-cheese world: while in dream-like realities the entire fictional world is filled with contradictions, in this case the irrational is contained in delimited areas that pierce the texture of the fictional world like the holes of a Swiss cheese. The reader can still use the principle of minimal departure to make inferences about the fictional world, as long as these inferences concern the solid areas. This is how I personally interpret narratives involving ontological, spatial and temporal paradoxes. For instance, the hero of *La Moustache* is the only character in the novel whose past is constantly changing; the house in *House of Leaves* is the only one that functions as a portal into a terrifying world. By confronting a normal world with an irrational one, the Swiss cheese configuration makes the experience of the irrational much more dramatic than in dream-like realities, because the experience of the protagonist clashes with the normal world in which other characters seem to live comfortably.

Rather than preserving the idea of an autonomous storyworld – and therefore maintaining the possibility of an immersive experience, for immersion requires a recentering of the imagination into an alternate world – interpretive strategies can emphasize the narrative process:

- Meta-textualism and do it yourself: the conflicting versions are not alternative worlds, but alternative drafts of a novel in progress. This strategy could be applied to "The Babysitter" and *The French Lieutenant's Woman*. In the case of "The Babysitter," the reader is offered a construction kit to make her own stories.

All texts with impossible worlds have the effect of drawing the reader's attention to the textual origin of the storyworld. I believe however that the only people who can be satisfied with a purely metatextualist interpretation are literary theorists. Most readers will do whatever they can to salvage a world in which they can achieve some degree of immersion, because make-believe, the mental game responsible for this experience, corresponds to a fundamental need of the human mind, and is simply more pleasurable than the game of pure self-reflexivity. It would be easy to say of texts with impossible worlds: "this is just words." It would be equally easy to ignore the contradictions and to build a coherent world. But neither one of these two stances does justice to impossible worlds. If the texts that construct such worlds pose a challenge to the reader, it is because they require the ability to shift back and forth between a narrativist/illusionist and a textualist perspective, so as to appreciate the text both as a representation of life experience and as a virtuoso verbal performance that pushes back the limits of the textually (im)possible.

References

Alber, J. (2009) "Impossible Storyworlds – and What to Do with Them," *Storyworlds* 1: 79–96.

Amis, M. (1991) *Time's Arrow*, New York: Vintage Books.

Borges, J.L. (1993) "Partial Magic in the Quixote." In *Labyrinths*, New York: Modern Library.

——(1998) *Collected Fiction*, trans. A. Hurley, New York: Penguin Books.

Carrère, E. (1988 [1986]) *The Mustache (La Moustache)*, trans. L. Goodman, New York: Scribner.

Coover, R. (1969) "The Babysitter." In *Pricksongs and Descants*, New York: Plenum Books.

Cortázar, J. (1985 [1968]) "Continuity of Parks." In *Blow-Up and Other Stories*, trans. P. Blackburn, New York: Pantheon.

Danielewski, M.Z. (2000) *House of Leaves*, New York: Pantheon.

Dick, P.K. (1961) *Counter-Clock World*, New York: Random House.

Eco, U. (1979) *The Role of the Reader*, Bloomington, IN: Indiana University Press.

Fforde, J. (2002) *The Eyre Affair: A Novel*, New York: Viking.

Foer, J.S. (2010) "Here We Aren't, So Quickly," *The New Yorker* June 14 and 21:72–3.

Fowles, J. (1980 [1969]) *The French Lieutenant's Woman*, Chicago, IL: Signet Books.

Kripke, S. (1963) "Semantical Considerations on Modal Logic," *Acta Philosophica Fennica* 16: 83–94.

Lewis, D. (1978) "Truth in Fiction," *American Philosophical Quarterly* 15: 37–46.

——(1983) "Postscript to 'Truth in Fiction'," in *Philosophical Papers*, vol. 1, New York: Oxford University Press.

McHale, B. (1987) *Postmodernist Fiction*, London: Methuen.

Moore, A. and K. O'Neill (2000) *The League of Extraordinary Gentlemen*, La Jolla, CA: DC Comics.

Pavel, T. (1986) *Fictional Worlds*, Cambridge, MA: Harvard University Press.

Pinget, R. (1978 [1968]) *The Libera Me Domine (Le Libera)*, trans. B. Wright, New York: Red Dust.

Robbe-Grillet, A. (1965) *Two Novels by Robbe-Grillet: Jealousy and In the Labyrinth (La Jalousie and Dans le Labyrinthe)*, trans. R. Howard, New York: Grove Press.

Ryan, M.-L. (1991) *Possible Worlds, Artificial Intelligence and Literary Theory*, Bloomington, IN: University of Indiana Press.

Stefanescu, M. (2008) "World Construction and Meaning Production in the 'Impossible Worlds' of Literature," *Journal of Literary Semantics* 37: 23–31.

Stewart, S. (1978) *Nonsense: Aspects of Intertextuality in Folklore and Literature*, Baltimore, MD: Johns Hopkins University Press.

Further reading

Ashline, W. (1995) "The Problem of Impossible Fictions," *Style* 29: 215–34.

Ryan, M.-L. (2009) "Temporal Paradoxes in Narrative," *Style* 43: 142–64.

28

EXPERIMENTAL LIFE WRITING

Irene Kacandes

I. Terms and definitions

Both "biography" and its Anglo-Saxon rooted equivalent "life writing" (βίος = life, γραφία = writing) are relatively recent terms, according to *The Oxford Dictionary*, which cites first uses in English from the seventeenth and eighteenth centuries respectively. In current academic parlance, as well as in many handbooks and how-to guides, the term "life writing" covers genres as diverse as blogs, diaries, hagiography, genealogy, letters, memoir, testimony, travel writing, and both biography and autobiography. In the widely read primer, *Reading Autobiography*, the authors Smith and Watson open up the field even further by adding the term "life narrative" for "acts of self-presentation of all kinds and in diverse media that take the producer's life as their subject, whether written, performative, visual, filmic, or digital" (2010: 4); life writing thus becomes a subset of something larger called life narrative. This entry concentrates on forms that can be printed and therefore mainly employs the term life writing (on other forms of experimental life narrative, see Elias, this volume).

British biographer Hermione Lee observes that commentators use the phrase life writing "when different ways of telling a life-story [. . .] are being discussed together [or] when the distinction between biography and autobiography is being deliberately blurred" (as quoted in Saunders 2010: 4). Both Lee's observations apply here. Life writing genres have in common reference to the "real world" (more on this below) and what Nancy K. Miller has called the relational. Miller argues that "the other provides the authorizing conditions for self production" not only in women's life writing – an idea that has been around for several decades – but rather in all autobiographical acts. Those "others" include individuals with whom the writer has shared life experiences and also those whom the writer calls to mind to be able to engage in writing; readers thus become "autobiographers' most necessary other" (2007: 545).

The insights of theorist and life-writing archivist Philippe Lejeune permeate all recent discussions of life writing, even when he is not credited. In the present chapter his definition of autobiography and his notions of the autobiographical and referential pacts will offer a structure for assessing experimentation. According to Lejeune, auto-biography is "Retrospective prose narrative written by a real person concerning [his or her] own existence, where the focus is [his or her] individual life, in particular the story of [his or her] personality" (1989: 4). In such texts, there is an implicit "pact" with the reader on the part of the author that "the *author*, the *narrator*, and the *protagonist* must be identical" (5, Lejeune's italics). Autobiographers make concomitant "referential pacts" with their readers in which "it is a supplementary proof of honesty to restrict [the discourse] to the *possible* (the truth such as it appears to me, inasmuch as I can know it, etc., making allowances for lapses of memory, errors, involuntary distortions, etc.), and to indicate explicitly the *field* to which this oath applies (the truth about such and such an aspect of my life, not committing myself in any way about some other aspect)" (22, Lejeune's italics). Implicit in this definition (and fleshed out by Lejeune in numerous essays) is the reader's attention to the paratext as well as to the world outside the text altogether. To put it another way neither the autobiographical pact nor its concomitant referential pact can be concluded (or analyzed) by taking into consideration the text alone. Autobiography "is a mode of reading as much as it is a type of writing" (30) and therefore, similar to Miller's view, for Lejeune, readers and writers along with their attitudes and relationships matter. These points can be solidified by recalling that even when the name of the author matches the name of the narrator and protagonist, if something in the paratext announces the text as fiction, it cannot, for Lejeune anyway, be counted as autobiographical (1989: 15–17). Such was the game that Serge Doubrovsky decided to play in coining the term "autofiction" as a label for his novel *Fils* in 1977; this explains why his works and those of authors like Raymond Federman or Ronald Sukenick are not considered in this chapter.

In trying to identify differences between the fictional and non-fictional realms, Dorrit Cohn helps us understand more about the connection between texts and the world outside them. She points out that in non-fiction writing there exists not only a story level and a discourse level, but also a "referential level," which to differing extents can be checked against documents, a "data base" of some kind beyond the text (1999: 112). We can see Cohn's and Lejeune's ideas in Philippe Carrard's proposal of the biographical pact as "the basic agreement through which biographers bind them-selves to their readers, warranting to make true statements in the sense of 'statements whose accuracy can be verified in the archives'" (1997: 299–300). In a "fictional pact" (Lejeune 1989: 13–14), in contrast, the author need not be identical to the narrator and the protagonist, and individual story elements related to events or setting need not be verifiable or even consistent with something outside the created story-world (though sometimes elements may in fact have referents exterior to the text, such as when an author sets her story in Times or Trafalgar Square, places that can be visited by real readers).

From recent controversies concerning texts that purported to be life writing, we can deduce ways in which readers allow life writers to play with life writing pacts, and ways in which they do not. I will maintain here that readers have a high tolerance for experimentation that might be construed as revealing or representing the complexity of reality. Thus techniques to render the layers of the human psyche, split subjectivity, or the human experience of time and space, can be accepted by readers without breaking the pact, that is to say, without disqualifying the text as life writing, whereas techniques, manipulations, additions, or falsifications that only seem to heighten the drama of the story and/or to aggrandize the individual are not tolerated. For instance, *Bruchstücke. Aus einer Kindheit 1939–1948* (1995; *Fragments: Memories of a Wartime Childhood* [1996]) was presented as a "memoir" (see back book jacket American edition) by "Binjamin Wilkomirski" and was heralded as a major publication event, contributing to our understanding of the Holocaust from the inside, specifically from a child's point of view. What we now know is that Wilkomirski is actually Bruno Dössekker, né Grosjean, born not in Riga, as claimed in the book, but in Bern, Switzerland, adopted as a baby by a Protestant couple living near Zürich. To be sure, Lejeune's "identity" between author/narrator/protagonist allows for pseudonyms because they are a way of naming *authors as writers* (as opposed to the name of the person in official vital statistics; 1989: 12), but the pact and readers of life writing do not allow for authors to claim stories they did not live, not even when one has read so much about certain experiences as to believe one has lived them, as it eventually came out Dössekker believed (see Mächler 2001). James Frey, in a different recent scandal, did use his own name on the cover of *A Million Little Pieces* (2003) and did mainly describe experiences he had lived through. However, when Frey's exaggeration of certain facts – like how long he had been in jail – was exposed, he, like Wilkomirski, was excoriated, though Frey's book was not disqualified as a whole. Legal scholar Patricia Williams asks if memoirists can tell simple lies for the sake of emotional truth and answers her own question by pointing to the Frey case: "'Not On My Dime'" (quoted in Miller 2007: 542). (See Mead on hoaxes, this volume.)

With these lessons in policing life writing in mind, I would like to suggest that unlike authors who "have engaged with forms of life-writing – biography, autobiography, memoir, diary, journal – increasingly *for the purposes of fiction*" (Saunders 2010: 14, my emphasis), our topic here needs to be authors who experiment *for the purposes of autobiography*, that is to say, life writers who employ a technique for the purposes of fact or of enhancing, reinforcing or drawing attention to the referential level. Such authors aim to convey some aspect of the "realness" of certain life experiences that could not be conveyed as well without pushing at the form itself, without playing with the pact.

Art Spiegelman's self-conscious comics treatment of the Holocaust, *Maus*, panels of which started appearing in 1973 and a "complete" version of which was published as a two-volume set in 1991, offers a good illustration. As per Lejeune's autobiographical pact, the name on the cover of the work corresponds to the name of the narrator and of one of the protagonists, the artist son, Artie, who is interviewing his Holocaust survivor father, Vladek, and trying to represent Vladek's experiences in the Nazi Judeocide in verbal-visual form. The broad elements of the story can (and have) been checked against the historical archive; at one point Spiegelman himself even made the recorded interviews with his father available to the general public. The visual representation of this autobiographical/biographical narrative, however, is not "realistic." Spiegelman depicts the Jewish characters as mice, the German ones as cats, the Polish as pigs, etc. In some panels of the contemporary level of the story (the narrative of Art's attempts to get the historical story), individuals are seen wearing animal masks. Spiegelman insisted, most notably in a letter to the *New York Times* (29 December 1991), that his work was not fiction, but rather autobiography. Those non-realistic visual representations constitute, in my view, Spiegelman's experiment *to reinforce the referential level*, to communicate something that could make the experiences depicted more salient to his readers. To state grossly a single aspect of what Spiegelman could communicate through this nonnaturalistic representation: in the European catastrophe of the mid-twentieth century, Jews were as vulnerable as mice in the presence of cats. Showing this by depicting mice and cats has proven to be more effective than stating it, as the huge critical and popular success of *Maus* testifies.

Lejeune's definition of autobiography can help us survey experiments authors have conducted to reinforce the referential level: "[1] Retrospective [2] prose narrative [3] written by a real person concerning [his or her] own existence, [4] where the focus is [his or her] individual life, in particular the story of [his or her] personality" (1989: 4). The numbers indicate the chief experiments we have space to survey: those concerning [1] time; [2] medium; [3] the relational (the number of individuals at the heart of the work); and [4] the focus (the specific topic of the work). For the sake of clarity, the presentation of experiments below, as in the brief exposé of *Maus* above, highlights one particular feature of multilayered, complex texts which merit fuller investigations.

II. Survey of life writing experiments

Time

The classical autobiographical set-up of a wise older person looking back on the foibles of his youth in order to reveal the process of growing wiser has been an easy target for recent life writers. One should mention in this regard the "memoir boom" of the last two to three decades in which more and more people write about short periods in their lives and about themselves in those periods as ordinary bumblers; there is some time (and wisdom) gap in these stories, but it's often not much (see Genzlinger's [2011] review of several such bumblers). We should also acknowledge those authors whose experiments seem to be saying that the retrospective vantage point does not register adequately the experience of lived lives in time.

In Alexander Masters' attempt to understand how an individual (Stuart Shorter) becomes one of the "chaotic homeless," the author does not take a huge leap backward and move forward, but rather moves from the present to the recent past to the less recent past to the even less recent past, rendering, as the book's title suggests, *Stuart: A Life Backward* (2006). This presentation style is introduced as a request by Stuart, presumably in response to his reading a traditionally written first draft: "Do it the other way round. Make it more like a murder mystery. What murdered the boy I was? See? Write it backwards" (6). The resulting narrative does succeed in communicating to readers the chaos of the life lived, including the chaos of the relationship between biographical subject and would-be biographer and of that biographer's own life. (The entanglement of the two protagonists is a good example of the third category of experimentation; see below.) It does this in great part by drawing attention to the chronological organization of the narrative, which, as it turns out, cannot consistently move backward, thus reproducing a failure in the announced narrative strategy that mimics failures in both individuals' lives.

Christa Wolf's *Ein Tag im Jahr: 1960–2000* (2003; *One Day a Year* [2007]) stages a very different kind of experiment that results in almost the opposite representation of experiencing time. As the title hints, the author decided to keep a journal entry on the same day each year and succeeded in continuing the experiment for forty years; the resulting tome exceeds six hundred pages. Partly because the designated day is one day prior to Wolf's younger daughter's birthday, and partly due to the nature of the experiment itself, what is communicated most forcefully through the text is repetition: the way most days in a human life resemble most other days in a human life. To be sure, that very feature allows for "new" events and experiences to stand out forcefully. Perhaps most importantly, and in any case, in sharp contrast to Masters's experiment, Wolf's communicates a sense of order and stability, despite a political context that transformed dramatically during those forty years.

Medium

Experiments with the medium for transmission of life stories have been explosively numerous in the last decades, leading, as we have already seen, Smith and Watson to coin the term "life narrative" to designate them. Though graphic narratives are covered elsewhere in this volume (see Chute, this volume), I have already introduced Spiegelman's *Maus*, because critical acclaim indicates that it might be the greatest experiment in life writing of the last quarter-century. One sign of its stature is how often it has been imitated and how good some of those subsequent autobiographical graphic narratives have been. Marjane Satrapi's *Persepolis* has been translated into numerous languages (originally published in French in four volumes from 2000 to 2003, the English translation appeared in two volumes published in 2003 and 2004) and was even made into a feature film (2007). The popularity of Alison Bechdel's *Fun Home* (2006) grew from the already loyal fans of her long-running comic strip *Dykes to Watch Out For* to a large general readership. In contrast to Spiegelman's non-realistic depictions of humans as animals to render an historical truth, Bechdel meticulously reproduces numerous documents and photos by redrawing them into her work not only to make visible her "data base" in Cohn's sense or to render something about her own compulsive personality as an artist, but also to emphasize the emotional meanings of those objects and put on display a queer aesthetic (Cvetkovich 2008). In addition to drawing style, what is included in, excluded from or spills out of a frame, the perspectives from which the content of a frame are rendered and, of course, the overall sequencing of frames can all help communicate aspects of human lives and relation-ships in any graphic life writing work.

A graphic text that adopts a quite different aesthetic from Spiegelman, Satrapi or Bechdel and deserves to be better known is Frederick Carabott's *Ο Πόλεμος Ενός Εφήβου 1941–45. A Teenager's War 1941–45. Der Krieg eines Jugendlichen 1941–45* (2001). The presence of three languages and vivid color images communicates as much as, if not more than, the content of the verbal narrative about its young author's experience and frame of mind while trying to survive in Occupied Greece and then in prisons and concentration camps during the Second World War. The memoir's multiple languages convey not only the adolescent Carabott's constant need for mul-tilingual comprehension in order to survive, but also the global nature of the conflict. The memoirist's rendering of himself as a blank human outline and of his German tormentors as metal cylinders in uniform communicates lopsided power dynamics. The inclusion of black and white preliminary sketches opposite the larger bold color images hints at the process of psychological trauma in addition to their more obvious depiction of the events recounted; they even gesture toward the aftermath: the survi-vor's subsequent career as a graphic designer.

Films, performance art, and a vast array of digital forms, including blogs should not be forgotten in a consideration of experiments with medium for telling life stories (see Elias, this volume). However, even within the world of printed books, there has been much experimentation through mixed genre or inclusion of material that is non-narrative. That is to say, in the following works memoirists experiment with medium and by doing so also with the previous category of time: consider the non-diegetic poetry in Michael Ondaatje's *Running in the Family* (1982) and Audre Lorde's *Zami, A New Spelling of My Name, A Biomythography* (also published in 1982); the various images and charts in Dave Eggers's *A Heartbreaking Work of Staggering Genius* (2001); the lists and tables in Amy Krouse Rosenthal's *Encyclopedia of an Ordinary Life* (2005); or the alphabetized organiza-tion of Joan Wickersham's *The Suicide Index: Putting My Father's Death in Order* (2008).

The relational

Experiments in this realm led Miller to emphasize the relations at the heart of ulti-mately all autobiographies and led other scholars to coin designations like auto/biogra-phy (Stanley 1995), thereby insisting on a lack of real distinction between life writing genres, specifically between autobiography and at least some types of biographies. As in the already mentioned *Stuart: A Life Backwards*, this can involve an entanglement between the writer and the subject of a supposed biographical endeavor. Two other major displays of entanglement come to us from French and German life writing. In Patrick Modiano's *Dora Bruder* (1997 [1999]), perusal decades later of a newspaper ad placed by Jewish parents looking for their daughter in 1942 launches the author into a search for someone he never knew, and about whom he realizes he can discover very little information. The book traces in a reverential tone, not just the author's own moves around Paris in search of places Dora must have been, but also his attempt to reconstruct her critical, eventually fatal decision to run away by remembering his own life as a teenage runaway.

Whereas the titles of Masters' and Modiano's books create anticipation of reading the story of someone else's life, the first-person pronoun in the title of Barbara Honigmann's *Ein Kapitel aus meinem Leben* (*A Chapter from My Life*, 2004) triggers the expectation of standard memoir. Once we begin reading, however, we learn that the titular phrase is a quotation, something the author's mother would always say when the topic of her love affair with notorious spy Kim Philby would surface. Confirming Miller's observations, a relationship emerges as central in Honigmann's volume; here, and similarly to *Maus*, that relationship concerns family members.

For this reason and because of their striking attention to the referential level, I have argued elsewhere that texts like Honigmann's and Spiegelman's have enough commonalities to be considered as a life writing subgenre: Holocaust family memoir (Kacandes 2012). Some commentators have rather broadly dismissed such books by charging that the offspring egomaniacally focus on themselves, rather than on their parents (e.g. Franklin 2011). However, if we read such memoirs with attention to their first-person statements, we can notice that their authors vouch for the historical truth of their parents' experiences precisely by shifting the attention onto themselves. For instance, when Helen Fremont, author of *After Long Silence* (1999), wants to communicate to her readers that her father's arm had been broken in an attack in the Gulag by other inmates trying to steal his clothes – an event that occurred long before her own birth – she does so in a series of sentences cast in the first person: "*I found* an article in the Irvington newspaper . . . *I went* to my mother with the article . . . *When I was* in college in 1975, my father told me more about his arm" (225, 226, 228, my italics). A physical attack by inmates on inmates was not an event to have created a papertrail in the Gulag, ghettos or concentration camps; Fremont would have looked for this data base in vain. In contrast, by narrating how *she* came to know about the violence perpetrated against her father, Fremont can pass onto her readers information about that event; from a certain perspective, further authentication is obviated since the account is now is covered by Lejeune's autobiographical pact. I propose that we think of these instances as "autobiography once removed" (Kacandes 2012), so that we can recognize such operations as entangling experiments, experiments that ultimately honor the parents by legitimating their experiences (in contrast to the delegitimating repercussions of fraudulent claims by individuals like Wilkomirski/Dössekker). To express this in another framework introduced earlier, these are experiments for the sake of fact, not fiction. Finally, if we consider the idea of "removed" in terms of individuals in close contact as well as persons removed generationally, my concept of "autobiography once removed" offers us an additional tool for investigating the merging of autobiography and biography.

The work's focus

Sometimes life writers experiment not so much with entanglements with other individuals as with entanglements with their own selves. Such entanglements can be depicted in ways that lead readers to wonder if the story of the life writer can even be told. In Christa Wolf's text, *Kindheitsmuster* (1976; *A Model Childhood* [1980]), for instance, an author figure searches to understand more about her own childhood in Nazi Germany by, among other activities, returning to the town where she grew up (after the war, it became part of Poland). This figure addresses her adult writing self in the second person informal and speaks about her childhood self in the third person. The work, which Wolf or her publisher eventually decided to label a "novel" – there was no genre listed originally – is clearly about the search for a unified self. Revealingly, the narrator only comes to utter a first-person singular pronoun at the narrative's conclusion, and even there, to articulate lack of knowledge: "Ich weiß es nicht" (I don't know; 406). What she does not know is precisely whether she has broken the power of the past that has kept her split into an "I," "you," and "she" (Kacandes 2001: 102).

J.M. Coetzee has been notoriously quiet about his private life. However, many commentators agree that he was proposing his own version of an autobiographical pact with works that follow the outlines of his early life quite closely: *Boyhood: Scenes from Provincial Life* (1997) and *Youth* (2002). A third volume, *Summertime* (2009) seems related to the series by reusing the subtitle of the first book: "Scenes from Provincial Life," and by opening with the chronological period after that which concludes *Youth* (the male protagonist's return from England to South Africa). In all three cases the abundance of information in the texts that can be "verified in the archive" seems to seal a referential pact, and yet Coetzee employs narrative techniques and includes details that undermine identifying author, narrator, and protagonist as one and the same. Most strikingly, the first two books are consistently told in the third person using present tense, a rare technique most closely associated with experimental prose fiction – including some of Coetzee's own – and in any case, one which most obviously calls into question the relationship of author and protagonist while maintaining a gap between narrator and protagonist. As in Wolf's *Model Childhood*, the technique thematizes the issue of knowing the self and therefore of that being the topic of the work. To complicate matters further, *Summertime* opens in the same mode, but then reveals the discourse to be an entry from a notebook whose constructedness is highlighted by inclusion of the writer's notes for how the narration should continue (2009: 6). Though the first edition of that book indicates no genre, subsequent ones are clearly labeled: "Fiction"; Lejeune would approve of the addition, since the book is mainly structured by interviews conducted after the protagonist-Coetzee's death. Given the connections to the other two volumes that *Summertime* foregrounds, does this word "fiction" also revoke what had seemed to be the author-Coetzee's offer of an autobiographical pact in the earlier books? Quite possibly. In any case, it reminds us that true experiments have unpredictable outcomes.

A final type of experiment with the work's focus privileges displaying the author's mind over narrating events in his or her life. To be sure, the "retrospective" nature of classical autobiography implies a thinking mind, and many examples of life writing by intellectuals or artists include long passages of reflections by those individuals. However, texts like *Roland Barthes par Roland Barthes* (1975) make that mind in action the center of the work. Having emphasized how much the paratext and more broadly the world outside the text is critical to life writing genres, I remind readers of the English translation (1994) and for that matter readers of the reissue of the French edition (2010), that the original appeared in a series whose very format concerned writers "talking about themselves," or as the series formula reads: X *par lui-même*. Barthes's was the ninety-sixth addition to that series, and the first to take its formula literally (by virtue of being written by the subject of the volume, rather than merely containing quotes by the subject which are then analyzed and amplified by the writer of the volume). Thus, in contrast to *Malraux par lui-même*, written by Gaëtan Picon (1968), we get "Roland Barthes by Roland Barthes." The result is a volume in which Barthes communicates things about himself not so much by reviewing biographical facts (though a few biographical facts slip in, especially vis-à-vis captions to personal photographs), but more prominently by putting his intellect, some call it his method, on display. Barthes does this as it is done in the series – that is to say, through reflections on work he has already published – but he also mainly does it as he has elsewhere, by holding forth on subjects of interest to himself. In this regard, one could connect Barthes's experiment with the genre of the literary self-portrait, and specifically with earlier works like Nabokov's *Speak, Memory* (1951) or Benjamin's *Berliner Kindheit um 1900* (1987; *Berlin Childhood Around 1900* [2006]). These earlier texts, however, display the thinking mind at work within a mainly chronological narrative about the self, whereas Barthes's thoughts are not so embedded. A very different kind of revelation of the mind at work comes from Georges Perec's enigmatic *W ou le souvenir d'enfance* (1975; *W or The Memory of Childhood* [1988]), where the author alternates fragments from his memory of a wartime childhood with stories of a fascistic counterworld he had invented as an adolescent and reconstructs for inclusion in the book.

III. Case study: an experimenter at work

An earlier effort than this one to write about other people's memoirs – the work on Holocaust family memoir mentioned above – led me down the unexpected path of becoming myself an experimenter in life writing. I offer the following account in the hope that such a narrative effects further insight into this chapter's main points.

Before I had quite figured out the mechanism of autobiography once removed, I found myself flabbergasted at the seamlessness and seeming completeness of many texts written by children whose parents had experienced major traumas, particularly traumas related to the European catastrophes of the mid-twentieth century. My family, too, was connected to those disasters, but unlike the authors I was studying, I did not know much about what had happened to my own parents, especially my father. It didn't seem fair to me to criticize the coherencies of other families' accounts when I had never seriously tried to pursue my own family history. A detailed narrative of my search subsequent to that realization is offered in the book I eventually published, so I won't offer one here. Rather, I will share that after conducting a certain amount of historical research and a large number of interviews with family members, I still felt incapable of creating a coherent account. For this reason, and others, when I actually published *Daddy's War: Greek American Stories* (2009), I asked my editor to include a generic designation on the cover: "A Paramemoir," in order to point at the ways that my book foils many readerly expectations for memoir, especially those for chronology, coherency and omniscience. What I didn't realize at the time, was how much the paramemoir I created had in common with experiments of other life writers – even of some I have discussed above.

In terms of my first category of experimentation, time, individual sections in *Daddy's War*, like those about my coming to fuller awareness of the scope of what my father had experienced, are written mainly chronologically. There is, however, no overall chronological progression or structure to the book. Rather, kernel stories recirculate – for example, accounts of my father's possible arrest by the Nazi occupiers as a Jew on the basis of his circumcision appear a dozen times. Furthermore, I draw attention to essentially all instances where I impose chronology on certain groups of stories when they were not stored in my own or other informants' memories that way.

As for my second category, "medium," *Daddy's War* contains narrative, drama, analysis, and performance. Most unusual for life writing are probably the dramatic and performative sections. In the former, which constitutes almost a third of the book, I reproduce detailed transcripts of interviews I conducted with family members, thereby creating a kind of dramatic script that includes not only the questions and answers, but also indications of the sound of each person's voice (pauses, unusual pronunciations of words, switches into Greek or English, etc.). One important result of this technique is that someone's autobiographical "I," or autobiographical "I" once removed, warrants each story. Since stories by different speakers on the "same" topic are juxtaposed with one another, contradictions – the contradictions that I implicitly and explicitly claim in the book constitute one reality of family memory – are easily detected. In the performative section, I animate my father by addressing him in the second person and recounting to him what I think happened to him, including what affect might be appropriate for different events in his life story, repeatedly pointing out other aspects of his past that neither I nor, in some cases, anyone else were likely ever to reconstruct. I call this "co-witnessing," a concept that I borrowed from psychotherapy and had developed in my first book (Kacandes 2001: 89–140). Another way in which *Daddy's War* experiments with mixed media is through its elaborate paratexual apparatus, including photos, maps, a family tree, reproduction of some documents related to the family, a glossary, a historical overview, and an explanation of Greek naming practices.

With regard to my third and fourth categories of experiment – the relational and the work's focus – giving space and legitimacy to numerous individual voices is central to my project, as are the relationships between the storytellers and the relationships of those tellers to their own and others' stories. Finally, while in certain chapters activities of mind are put on display in attempts to analyze the materials gathered, the mystery of my father's personality and holes in my own knowledge haunt the book – intentionally, since I consider those gaps to reflect complex realities of trauma and traumatic aftermaths.

A few details about the fate of *Daddy's War* can help us review some other main points of this chapter: the paratext counts. While there surely must be numerous reasons that my book has not become a bestseller, I believe my term "paramemoir" – as much as it did for me analytically and professionally – put off or confused many potential booksellers and readers. The number of reviews and a few personal queries indicate that many book editors of newspapers appear to have responded to its mixed genre as too academic, and academic journal editors as too popular. Various readers who have taken the time to contact me report reactions precisely to some of the experimental features: one reader mentioned the book's analytical dimension, gratified by my explanations of how oral stories work; another the way the form precludes coherence and closure; another – a lawyer – the explanations and performance of witnessing. Many hope they are not offending me when they say it reads like a novel, or that they found they couldn't put it down. It is hard to assess a majoritarian reaction from what individuals reported to me directly since they presumably would not have contacted me if they did not think I would be pleased by what they said. I'm therefore willing to consider the following a more typical reading experience because it came to me indirectly through one of my older sisters. She reported on a high-school acquaintance who thought *Daddy's War* was terrific; he raced through the beginning, urging everyone he knew to read it; he was even telling strangers in Central Park to read it. When he reached the word "analyzing," the announcement that I will put my mind on explicit display (2009: 178), however, he closed the book.

A final if obvious lesson from consideration of *Daddy's War* that probably applies to all the works cited in this chapter might be formulated as follows: whether it concerns time, medium, the number of individuals at the heart of the work, or the particular nature of the examination of those individuals' lives, not all life writing experimentation will appeal to all readers of life writing. Most effective might be those experiments that escape readers' notice that they are, indeed, experiments.

References

Barthes, R. (1975) *Roland Barthes*, Paris: Seuil.

——(1994 [1977]) *Roland Barthes by Roland Barthes*, trans. R. Howard, Berkeley, CA: University of California Press.

Bechdel, A. (2006) *Fun Home: A Family Tragicomic*, Boston, MA: Houghton Mifflin Co.

Benjamin, W. (1987) *Berliner Kindheit um 1900*, Frankfurt, Germany: Suhrkamp.

——(2006) *Berlin Childhood Around 1900*, trans. H. Eiland, Cambridge, MA: Bellknap Press.

Carabott, F. (2001) *Ο Πόλεμος Ενός Εφήβου 1941–45. A Teenager's War 1941–45. Der Krieg eines Jugendlichen 1941–45*, Athens: Hellenic Literary and Historical Archive.

Carrard, P. (1997) "Biography and the Representation of Consciousness," *Narrative* 5: 287–305.

Coetzee, J.M. (1997) *Boyhood: Scenes From Provincial Life*, New York: Viking.

——(2002) *Youth*, London: Secker and Warburg.

——(2009) *Summertime: Scenes from Provincial Life*, London: Harvill Secker.

Cohn, D. (1999) *The Distinction of Fiction*, Baltimore, MD: Johns Hopkins University Press.

Cvetkovich, A. (2008) "Drawing the Archive in Alison Bechdel's *Fun Home*," *Women's Studies Quarterly* 36: 111–28.

Eggers, D. (2001) *A Heartbreaking Work of Staggering Genius*, New York: Vintage.

Franklin, R. (2011) *A Thousand Darknesses: Lies and Truth in Holocaust Fiction*, Oxford, UK: Oxford University Press.

Fremont, H. (1999) *After Long Silence: A Memoir*, New York: Delta.

Genzlinger, N. (2011) "Memoir: The Center of Attention," *New York Times Book Review* (Jan. 30): 14–15.

Honigmann, B. (2004) *Ein Kapitel aus meinem Leben*, Munich, Germany: Carl Hanser Verlag.

Kacandes, I. (2001) *Talk Fiction: Literature and the Talk Explosion*, Lincoln, NE: University of Nebraska Press.

——(2009) *Daddy's War: Greek American Stories. A Paramemoir*, Lincoln, NE: University of Nebraska Press.

——(2012) "'When facts are scarce': Authenticating Strategies in Writing by Children of Survivors." In J. Lothe, J. Phelan and S. Suleiman (eds.) *After Testimony*, Columbus, OH: Ohio State University Press.

Lejeune, P. (1989) *On Autobiography*, foreword P. J. Eakin, trans. K. Leary, Minneapolis, MN: University of Minnesota Press.

Lorde, A. (1982) *Zami: A New Spelling of My Name. A Biomythography*, New York: Crossing Press.

Mächler, S. (2001) *The Wilkomirski Affair: A Study in Biographical Truth*, trans. J. E. Wood, New York: Schocken Books.

Masters, A. (2006) *Stuart: A Life Backwards*, New York: Delacorte Press.

Miller, N.K. (2007) "The Entangled Self: Genre Bondage in the Age of the Memoir," *PMLA* 122: 537–48.

Modiano, P. (1997) *Dora Bruder*, Paris: Gallimard.

——(1999) *Dora Bruder*, trans. J. Kilmartin, Berkeley, CA: University of California Press.

Nabokov, V. (1951) *Speak, Memory: A Memoir*, New York: Grosset and Dunlop.

Ondaatje, M. (1982) *Running in the Family*, New York: Vintage.

Perec, G. (1975) *W, ou le souvenir d'enfance*, Paris: Editions Denoël.

——(1988) *W or The Memory of Childhood*, trans. D. Bellos, Boston, MA: David R. Godine.

Rosenthal, A.K. (2005) *Encyclopedia of an Ordinary Life*, New York: Three Rivers Press.

Satrapi, M. (2000, 2001) *Persepolis 1, 2*, Paris: L'Association.

——(2003) *Persepolis 1*, trans. M. Ripa and B. Ferris, New York: Random House.

——(2004) *Persepolis 2*, trans. A. Singh, New York: Random House.

Saunders, M. (2010) *Self Impression: Life-Writing, Autobiografiction, and the Forms of Modern Literature*, Oxford, UK: Oxford University Press.

Smith, S. and Watson, J. (2010) *Reading Autobiography: A Guide for Interpreting Life Narratives*, 2nd edition, Minneapolis, MN: University of Minnesota Press.

Spiegelman, A. (1991) *Maus I. A Survivor's Tale. My Father Bleeds History. Maus II. A Survivor's Tale. And Here My Troubles Began*, New York: Pantheon.

Stanley, L. (1995) *The Auto/biographical I: The Theory and Practice of Feminist Auto/biography*, Manchester, UK: Manchester University Press.

Wickersham, J. (2008) *The Suicide Index: Putting My Father's Death in Order*, Orlando, FL: Harcourt.

Wolf, C. (1977 [1976]) *Kindheitsmuster*, Darmstadt, Germany: Luchterhand.

——(1980) *A Model Childhood*, trans. U. Molinaro and H. Rappolt, New York: Farrar, Straus and Giroux.

——(2003) *Ein Tag im Jahr: 1960–2000*, Munich, Germany: Luchterhand.

——(2007) *One Day a Year: 1960–2000*, trans. L.A. Bangerter, New York: Europa Editions.

Further reading

Couser, G.T. (2012) *Memoir: An Introduction*, New York: Oxford University Press.

Eakin, P.J. (1999) *How Our Lives Become Stories: Making Selves*, Ithaca, NY: Cornell University Press.

Hampl, P. and E. May (eds.) (2008) *Tell Me True: Memoir, History, and Writing a Life*, Minneapolis, MN: Borealis Books.

Miller, N.K. (2002) *But Enough About Me: Why We Read Other People's Lives*, New York: Columbia University Press.

Winslow, D. (1995) *A Glossary of Terms in Life-Writing: Biography, Autobiography and Related Forms*, 2nd edition, Honolulu, HI: University of Hawaii Press.

Yagoda, B. (2009) *Memoir: A History*, New York: Riverhead Books.

29

"ROTTING TIME"

Genre fiction and the avant-garde

Elana Gomel

I. The avant-garde of wor(l)ds

Two trains collide: one side lined on its way from the past toward the future that was not to be; the second roaring through the terrain that never existed and never could. The collision occurs on the pages of China Miéville's experimental fantasy novel *Iron Council* (2004) whose epigraph is taken from the writings of Velimir Khlebnikov, the greatest poet of the Russian avant-garde: "Erect portable moving monuments on the platforms of trains" (Khlebnikov 1987: 359).

The novel exemplifies the interaction between the heritage of the historical avant-garde and experimental trends in contemporary genre fiction. Khlebnikov's train is a machine of words, forged in the furnace of conceptual, linguistic and political experimentation of the Russian Revolution (see White, this volume, on Russian Cubo-Futurist experimentation). Miéville's train is a machine of steel, built in a separate fictional world where the proletariat of the Remade who are literally fused with their tools is battling the elite of the thaumaturgy-saturated city of New Crobuzon. The blueprint for a postmodern fantasy is a modernist metaphor.

Popular genre fiction has become an integral part of the cultural poetics of postmodernism. Postmodernism has "entailed the fusion of high and low," abolishing (at least theoretically) the modernist hierarchy of Literature and Trash (Suarez 2007: 1). The popular genre of science fiction (SF) has been singled out as "postmodernism's non-canonized or 'low art' double" (McHale 1987: 59), because of the way in which it "intersects and even overlaps the postmodern in crucial respects" (Broderick 1995: 103).

But postmodernism hardly qualifies as avant-garde any more. It has become a new consensus, which is in many ways antithetical to the revolutionary spirit of the historical avant-garde. As Rosalind Krauss argues, "postmodernism establishes a schism between itself and the conceptual domain of the avant-garde, looking back at it from across the gulf that in turn establishes a historical divide" (1986: 170). This schism is as much political as it is artistic. The political foundation of the avant-garde was "confidence in the final victory of *time* and immanence over traditions" (Calinescu 1987: 95). This is in stark contrast to the ironic anomie of postmodernism and its distrust of what Lyotard called "grand narratives" of history (1984). (On the relation between postmodernism and the avant-garde, see McHale, this volume.)

So what is the difference between postmodern genre fiction and avant-garde genre fiction? What narrative strategies can recover the lost spirit of Futurism and Dada in the new era? And what is the relation of contemporary genre fiction to the artistic and political projects of the early twentieth century, the heyday of the historical avant-garde?

A restless specter haunts the answers to these questions, a specter of lost revolutionary causes. The historical avant-garde linked the violent overthrow of the repressive political order with the "revolution in poetic language," as in the title of Julia Kristeva's 1974 book. Both seem impossible today, as the "cultural logic of global capitalism," to use Fredric Jameson's designation of postmodernism, brings with it the putative "end of history" (Jameson 1991; Fukuyama 1992). Experimental artistic techniques find themselves with no mainstream enemy to confront. While in the past the literary examination of "the relationship between fictional form and social reality" through metafiction might have had a subversive potential, by now metafictional strategies have become staples of commercial bestsellers (Waugh 1984: 47).

Revolution, then, becomes an object of nostalgia, an echo of the traumatic past rather than a vision of the utopian future. It is here that genre fiction comes into its own. In comparison to the literary mainstream, genre fiction is uniquely equipped to cultivate a poetics of nostalgia, invoking historical time through fictional space. Rather than *deconstructing* past forms, popular literature *reconstructs* them. Not in the modality of parody or pastiche, as has been theorized for postmodernism in general, but as alternative spaces, narrative heterotopias, in which history can be (re)-confronted, if only as a ghost.

The historical avant-garde attempted to change the world by changing the concept of art, "to organize a new life praxis from a basis in art" (Bürger 1984: 49). Contemporary genre fiction is content with creating virtual worlds, simulacra of impossible and improbable realities, in which "a new life praxis" can be experienced vicariously, as part of the reader's predictable satisfaction. Yet the avant-garde project of remaking the world and genre fiction's project of making worlds share structural similarities and continuities. The *avant-garde genre fiction* may be defined as a body of texts that utilize these similarities and continuities in order to create new fictional spaces that attempt to resurrect/reconstruct history, and in doing so, question their own role as commodities. It is different from postmodern genre fiction, which merely adopts postmodernist literary strategies, such as parody, pastiche, self-referentiality, broad and narrow metafiction and so on. In what follows I discuss some of the narrative strategies deployed by avant-garde genre fiction, focusing on *allegory, displacement,* and *incoherence.* These are not the only ways to break the stranglehold of commercially honed generic formulae; nor do they operate equally in all popular genres. There are at least eight such genres: romance, crime fiction, SF, fantasy, horror, western, historical novel, adventure novel (Gelder 2004: 42). I cannot do justice to all of them here, and therefore I have chosen to focus on the three most self-consciously post-modern: fantasy, SF, and horror. As opposed to other popular genres, these three are explicitly engaged in ontological exploration, as they construct fictional worlds, alternative to the consensus reality of their readers. If "the dominant of postmodernist fiction is ontological" (McHale 1987: 10), then the ontological genres of popular fiction are the most obvious test-cases for answering the question to what extent postmodern spaces can make room for avant-garde temporalities.

II. Yin and yang

In *Dialectic of the Enlightenment*, Max Horkheimer and Theodor Adorno wrote: "Like its counterpart, avant-garde art, the entertainment industry determines its own language, down to its very syntax and vocabulary . . ." (1982: 128). This structural similarity belies the way in which the two cultural domains were traditionally seen as polar opposites. Modernity entailed the formation of "not modernism alone, but rather two distinct literary cultural structures, dialectically interrelated and necessarily presupposing each other" (Jameson 1981: 207). High and popular literatures were the yin and yang of cultural production, each defined by not being the other.

This opposition rested as much on political stance as it did on artistic merit. High literature was seen as subversive and rebellious, "the entertainment industry" as commodified and conformist. Renato Poggioli described the linguistic inventiveness of the avant-garde as a reaction to the "tensions" of capitalism (1968: 107), while Peter Bürger excoriated popular fiction as a "literature whose primary aim is to impose a particular kind of consumer behavior on the reader" (1984: 54). The avant-garde's deliberate opacity and elitism were hailed as a heroic, though ultimately doomed, struggle against the monster of the literary marketplace.

With the advent of postmodernism, this binary was challenged. Andreas Huyssen, for example, argued that mass culture and the avant-garde have always been contentious Siamese twins and that "their much heralded mutual exclusiveness is really a sign of their secret interdependence" (1986: 16). Several recent works showed how "modernism and mass culture shared iconography, themes, and stylistic devices" (Suarez 2007: 3; see also DiBattista and McDiarmid 1996). Genre fiction, however, is still regarded with critical ambivalence. Arguments for and against are often couched in ideological terms. While for some genre fiction is "a stultifying mass culture" (Bould 2009: 1), others make grandiose claims for its liberating potential. Carl Freedman, for example, argues that SF is for progressive critical theory what the historical novel was for Marxism, "a privileged and paradigmatic genre" (2000: 14–15; see also Suvin 1979; Jones 1999; Jameson 2007; Bould 2009). Ideological ends and artistic means, however, are not always neatly aligned. Adorno, a scourge of commodity aesthetics, nevertheless sees a *structural* similarity between the avant-garde and the popular. This similarity is their drive toward the elaboration of a complex artistic syntax. The esoteric vocabulary of the avant-garde is mirrored by the exacting narrative grammar of genre fiction.

Each genre of popular fiction is defined by "a literary formula [which is] a structure of narrative . . . conventions employed in a great number of individual works" (Cawelti 1976: 5). This formula is the genre's brand name. Paradoxically, it is also the locus of the text's artistry, since this is where its fictionality is "laid bare" in Shklovsky's sense of the term: "with popular fiction, generic identities are *always* visible" (Gelder 2004: 42). In this visibility, "high" and "low" come together. The display of the artistic armature of the text was one of the defining characteristics of the avant-garde, which delighted in the "dissolution of the formal unity of the work" (Bürger 1984: 55).

For Adorno, what distinguishes genuine art from artistic commodity is not the absence of rules but rather the creative *failure* to follow them.

> That factor in the work of art which enables it to transcend reality certainly cannot be detached from style; but it does not consist of the harmony actually realized, or any doubtful unity of form and content . . . it is to be found in those features in which discrepancy appears; in the necessary failure of the passionate striving for identity . . .
>
> (Horkheimer and Adorno 1982: 131)

Avant-garde genre fiction, like the historical avant-garde, is generated by the failure of its writers to produce fully-fledged, seamlessly stitched together, numbingly familiar fictional worlds. It often fails twice: as a commodity (too hard to market) and as Literature (unless signed by a "mainstream" name, such as Philip Roth or Margaret Atwood). It is precisely this marginal and rebellious status of "problematic" genre works that reconnects them with the legacy of the avant-garde and makes them a privileged site for the exploration of postmodernity's traumatic histories: failed fiction interrogating failure of ideology.

III. Chasing history

A literary genre is defined by its chronotope, "the intrinsic connectedness of temporal and spatial relationships that are artistically expressed in literature" (Bakhtin 2002: 15). In nineteenth-century realism as well as in modernism, time is the dominant axis within the chronotopes of fiction. Postmodernism, however, favors space. Postmodern chronotopes reflect "a shift in sensibilities from a predominantly temporal and historiographic imagination to one much more concerned with the spatial and the geographic" (Smethurst 2000: 15). We "now inhabit the synchronic rather than the diachronic" and "our daily life, our psychic experience, our cultural languages, are today dominated by categories of space rather than categories of time, as in the preceding period of high modernism" (Jameson 1991: 16).

Commodity genre fiction covers up the loss of time by manipulating narrative space. The most important strategy of this manipulation is narrative inflation, which creates a counterfeit diachrony through sheer textual volume. In both fantasy and SF, it is rare nowadays to encounter a stand-alone work. In SF, far-future space operas, such as Alastair Reynolds *Revelation Space* series (2000–2007) or Kevin Anderson's *Saga of Seven Suns* (2002–2008), weave complex tapestries of space colonization, alien threats, posthuman transformations and universal apocalypses, with a staggering array of major and minor characters, cross-linkages of events, and whole encyclopedias of made-up terms. Such works are not extrapolations or predictions. Rather, in their narrative logorrhea, they are simulacra of that sense of unfolding history, which postmodernity has lost. They do not represent the future; they resurrect futurity.

In fantasy, whose worlds are self-contained and unconnected to our own history, the simulation of diachrony is even clearer. The bestselling *Song of Ice and Fire* series (1996–2008) by George R.R. Martin, for example, reads like a cross between a soap opera and Bede's Chronicle. Since the chronotopes of fantasy are not as cognitively challenging as the chronotopes of SF and operate with a simpler set of ground-rules (magic rather than science), their artistic focus is precisely on that fake historicity which is generated by the accumulation of chronologically and causally linked episodes. Gelder charts the parallels between the genre's deferral of closure and the rhetoric of the endless "war on terror," indicating the political dangers of this counterfeit history (2004: 156).

With the genre of horror, narrative inflation turns into a boom-and-bust cycle of symbolic economy. Horror's plots are always structured by the same formula, which involves the appearance of a monster, its potential triumph and its final defeat, with a possibility of the cycle starting all over again always left open at the end. Horror's true protagonist is history-as-zombie, never quite resurrected but never completely laid to rest. In such commercial zombie apocalypses as Max Brooks' *World War Z* (2006), this dynamic becomes tongue-in-cheek obvious.

All generic distinctions, of course, are approximate. Most avant-garde texts are heterogeneous. China Miéville's *Iron Council*, for example, is occasionally classified as SF or grouped together with other similar works under the ambiguous rubric of "new weird." Nevertheless, genre is a useful heuristic category, enabling us to map out the avant-garde of worlds.

Avant-garde genre fictions struggle against the restraints of their own generic chronotopes in order "to think the present historically in an age that has forgotten how to think historically in the first place" (Jameson 1991: ix). There are many strategies such texts use in order to reveal the void at the heart of the false plenitude provided by formulae of popular entertainment. In what follows, I will briefly describe and illustrate three such strategies: *allegory, displacement, and incoherence.* The first is mainly characteristic of fantasy, the second of SF, the third of horror, though there are mixed texts that deploy all three.

IV. The signifying fragment

In *Iron Council* a group of anarchist artists who call themselves "the Nuevists" perform an edgy political puppet-show in a bohemian music-hall, dodging both the government's censors and the rowdy racist "Quillers" (Miéville 2004: 65). This could have been Saint Petersburg circa 1913 or Munich circa 1923. But it is New Crobuzon, circa unknown, and among the audience, apart from leftist intellectuals and lumpen proletarians, are *kheptri* with women's bodies and giant bugs for heads, amphibious *vodyanoi*, and brawny cactus-men.

References to the events of the 1910s and 1920s multiply through the novel, making it possible to read it as a figural allegory of the Bolshevik revolution and/or the Munich Soviet Republic. A figural allegory (as opposed to a personification allegory) is based on a system of historical correspondences, in which an extra-textual historical event is encoded in a fictional plot (Quilligan 1979: 115). Figural allegories are more specific than personification allegories, in which abstract concepts are represented by characters. Both forms, however, derive their meaning not from the fictional world itself but rather from a rigid system of correspondences between this world and ours. Allegorical chronotopes are neither self-consistent nor semantically rich: they are codes that need to be deciphered, and they often signal this need by blatant violations of their own ground-rules.

No such violation occurs in *Iron Council*. The novel's chronotope is internally coherent, structured by a complex set of ground-rules elaborated in the previous books of the series, *Perdido Street Station* (2000) and *The Scar* (2002). All three novels are set in the same world, called Bas-Lag, with its own history, physics, and biology, all incompatible with the laws of our own universe. Like all worlds of fantasy, it is ontologically independent, neither temporally nor spatially related to our consensus reality.

The ability of fantasy to create self-enclosed, self-consistent fictional worlds has been hailed as its strength and derided as its weakness. Tolkien extolled fantasy's "Secondary Worlds" for the escape and consolation they provided (1965); Darko Suvin accused the genre of proto-fascism and obscurantism for the same reasons (1979). Nevertheless, an important corollary of this ontological independence is that the text should be read literally rather than allegorically. Tolkien repeatedly denied that *The Lord of the Rings* was a figural allegory of World War II, since an allegorical reading would undermine the integrity of its fictional world.

In *Iron Council*, the events in New Crobuzon's history and in the history of twentieth-century revolutionary defeats flicker in and out, superimposed upon each other like double exposure. The Iron Council is a revolutionary train, taken over by a motley crew of human and "xenian" rebels and becoming the last utopian hope of the magic-besieged, thaumaturgy-ruled city. At the same time, it is a metaphor borrowed from Khlebnikov and Russian revolutionary songs. It acts in New Corbuzon's history but it is also an image of history itself. "History is pushing us," says one of its leaders (Miéville 2004: 514).

The ending of the novel exemplifies this generic double exposure, in which allegory and fantasy are crowded into the same textual space, offered to the reader as two alternative possibilities of reading that are neither opposed nor reconciled. The train, faced with certain destruction, is saved by a "time golem," "carved out of time itself, the rough hew-marks of its making the unshaped seconds and crushed moments at its edges . . . a clot in diachrony" (Miéville 2004: 541). The train is torn out of time, frozen in the perpetual "now," a signifier of the utopian impulse which disdains what is for what might be. And so the train never comes and yet "is always coming;" the failed revolution transmuted into a utopian hope (564). Read allegorically, the novel does for the Marxist revolution what Fredric Jameson does for Marxism: recuperates historical failure as utopian success. Read literally, the ending hollows out the novel's chronotope, explodes its temporality and in doing so, interrupts fantasy's narrative drive for sequentiality.

Formally, the three Bas-Lag novels are a trilogy, which as Henry Farrell argues, can even be read as a sort of Hegelian-Marxist dialectic of "the relationship between politics and the fantastic imagination . . . – thesis, antithesis, synthesis" (2008: 287). Their chronotope is *closed*, as opposed to the open-endedness of conventional fantasy. It is precisely through this closure that history is re-inscribed not as empty chronology but as a meaningful form of human existence. History returns as "a clot in diachrony," an irruption of surplus signification, an invasion of fantasy by allegory.

Walter Benjamin describes allegory in terms of a poetics of the fragment. In allegory, "the image is a fragment, a rune . . . The false appearance of totality is extinguished" (1977: 176). The avant-garde's disdain for "organic" art and its predilection for fragmentation, collage, "found objects" lead Bürger to consider Benjamin's "concept of allegory as a theory of the avant-gardist (nonorganic) work of art" (Bürger 1984: 68). The intrusion of allegory into fantasy generates avant-garde works by fragmenting fantasy's chronotope and interrupting its drive toward counterfeit plenitude.

Fragments of history embedded in the fictional world of fantasy can be large or small, subtle or overt. In Hal Duncan's *Vellum* (2005), for example, allusions to myth and literature stick like burrs to the novel's "unkin," self-appointed angels and demons that have access to the ultimate Book of All Hours, which is both a text and the entire universe the text describes. The novel and its sequel *Ink* (2006) are playfully postmodern, creating an elaborate metafictional chronotope, in which history is mere textuality, as power over the Book of all Hours enables one to rewrite it at will, to "write someone out of history or write them back in" (Duncan 2005: 47). In the world of Vellum, identities are encrustations of quotations, as the same person may be an angel of freedom, a biker chick, and the Sumerian goddess Inanna.

Some of *Ink*'s allusions are transparent political allegories rather than intertextual pastiches and disguised quotations: "To the angels, even eternity itself is just another hell of red-skin enemies to be purged and rebuild, New Jerusalem . . . their New World" (Duncan 2005: 38). These allegorical references puncture the endless surface of *Vellum* (reminiscent of Borges' "Book of Sand") with specific and topical traumas – conquest of America, slavery, terrorism, 9/11 – whose ideological resonance prevents them from meshing seamlessly with the free play of textuality.

And yet allegory can only bring back a ghost of history. As the angel Phreedom muses sadly, the "pain she nurses . . . Is only a stand-in for the pain she *should* feel but just isn't capable of, not any more" (Duncan 2005: 44). Providing such allegorical stand-ins is all that avant-garde fantasy can do but this is better than being lost in the interminable Secondary Worlds where magic itself becomes as anodyne as Harry Potter's textbook.

V. Dis/re/placing human

SF is more overtly political than its sister genres, fantasy and horror. SF chronotopes are always connected to our world and thus inscribe what Mark Bould calls "the negative space" of "material reality" (2009: 4). Instead of being hermetically isolated in their own island universes, worlds of SF are contiguous with ours, either temporally (located in the future), spatially (other planets) or both. This is what enables their "critical interrogation" of our world which "is guaranteed by the operation of cognition," their scientific or pseudo-scientific naturalizing discourse (Freedman 2000: 17).

However, the critical potential of the genre is easy to confuse with the critical position of the author. A small number of writers are often featured as epitomizing the "good" (cognitive, postmodern, critical) as opposed to the "bad" (popular, escapist, commercial) aspects of the genre. These writers – Stanislaw Lem, Philip K. Dick, Ursula Le Guin, Samuel Delany – indeed exemplify the best artistic work ever done in SF. By the same token, they are the venerable classics of the genre, its (post)modernist establishment, rather than its revolutionary avant-garde. In the work of contemporary experimental writers, such as Iain Banks, Stephen Baxter, Alastair Reynolds, Paul Park, Peter Watts and others, the chronotope of SF undergoes a revolutionary mutation by going beyond the self-referentiality of postmodernism. Among the array of new narrative techniques deployed by avant-garde SF, the most important is *displacement* of temporality.

In Reynolds' *Century Rain* (2004) the future Earth is devastated by a nano-plague, which renders it uninhabitable. The descendants of the survivors have split into the (barely) human Threshers and the frankly posthuman Slashers. The main action concerns the discovery of sphere containing a "quantum snapshot" of the pre-World War II world. Initially, the snapshot is just that: a static copy. But "jolted" into diachrony, it begins to develop, its history deviating from our familiar time line, as its inhabitants – essentially, quantum holograms of long-dead people – start acting on their own. The novel's action unfolds on two ontological levels: the alternate 1950s Paris, which has never been occupied by the Nazis, inside the sphere, and the posthuman universe of the Threshers and the Slashers who scheme to possess or destroy the sphere. The two are eventually brought together as the private eye Wendell Floyd from inside the sphere and the archeologist Verity Auger from the outside join forces to prevent its destruction.

The novel's chronotope contains three different temporalities "nested" within each other. The quantum Paris is an alternate history of our consensus reality; the posthuman world outside the sphere is its extrapolation of it; and the end of Earth is the apocalypse. Each spacetime represents a different interpretation of history and a different subgenre within SF. Alternate history is the chronotope of contingency, exemplifying the idea of history as essentially malleable, open-ended, and chaotic. Extrapolation is based on the idea that history is *lawful* and determined, and therefore, predictions can be made. Apocalypse is the chronotope of religion and political millennialism (see Gomel 2010). In Reynolds' novel, these incompatible visions of history coexist. This complexity of the novel's temporality is enabled by the equally complex structuring of its space. The quantum Paris is enclosed within the alien sphere, which is connected by a system of wormholes to the nanotechnology-devastated Earth, which in turn is surrounded by Tanglewood, a branching network of space habitats.

SF apprehends history by projecting the spatial axis of narrative onto its temporal axis. Jameson describes this strategy as "world-reduction": "a kind of surgical excision of empirical reality," which enables "some more fundamental attempt to reimagine history" (2007: 276). If for Jameson the worlds of SF are simpler than "the sheer teeming multiplicity of what exists, of what we call reality" (276), then *Century Rain* demonstrates that temporal displacement may result in a chronotope that is as complex as the jockeying for power of conflicting ideologies in the political ecosystem of postmodernity.

Like much of avant-garde SF, Reynolds' novel ties the problematic of history to the emergence of posthumanity. The historical rupture of the so-called End of Man, (Fukuyama 2002) represents the transition from the ideology of liberal humanism to a variety of new subject positions, forms and relations. The singular subjectivity of "Man" has given way to the multiple, fragmented, ironic subjectivities of the posthuman or the "cyborg," as Donna Haraway called it: "The cyborg is a creature in a postgender world; it has no truck with . . . organic wholeness through a final appropriation of all the powers of the parts into a higher unity . . . The cyborg is resolutely committed to partiality . . ." (Haraway 1991: 150–1). The cyborg is Many as opposed to One.

The posthuman in avant-garde SF functions as a figure for the radical ontological break within (post)modernity, echoing the historical avant-garde's challenge to "an idealist and individualist humanism" (de Gennaro 2000: 165). The emergence of posthumanity becomes inextricably tied to the elaboration of a new narrative space of history. Avant-garde SF does not simply represent posthumanity but enacts it in the very structure of its chronotope.

The "cyborg" chronotope of *Century Rain* is the true protagonist of the novel, while its characters, both human and posthuman, are mere slivers of subjectivity embedded in its fabric. Similarly, the multiple templates of history in the novel – contingent, apocalyptic, extrapolative/deterministic – are not unified in any sort of meaningful synthesis but simply suspended in its narrative space, laid side by side like so many consumer options. This multiplicity gives the lie to any totalizing ideological attempt "to reimagine history" but neither does it permit a revolutionary action of the kind nostalgically re-presented in *Iron Council*.

Another example of the way in which experimental SF enacts the historical rupture of posthumanity in the structure of its chronotope is Peter Watts' *Blindsight* (2006). The novel (first published electronically on the author's website because conventional SF presses could not make sense of it) follows one of the oldest generic formulae of SF: meeting with aliens. However, its earthly characters are as strange as its unfathomable ETs. The crew of the spaceship *Theseus* runs a gamut of posthuman mutations: its captain is a vampire, a member of a genetically resurrected predatory species; its linguist is a Gang of Four, having surgically separated her brain into four different personalities;

and the narrator Siri has most of his brain supplanted with machinery. It is not only their baroque forms that are posthuman; so is the text itself, overloaded with esoteric terminology, punctuated by inexplicable plot lacunae, and ending in an apocalypse, in which self-awareness, seen as an accidental parasite of the human brain, is expunged. This is the ultimate "End of Man," which by the logic of liberal humanism, should also spell the end of history. And yet while the novel ostensibly endorses a closure to history, it simultaneously re-enacts, in its multiform narrative, the very historicity it disavows.

This historicity is displaced onto the chronotope of *Blindsight*, which superimposes four different spaces: the virtual Paradise where most humanity lives by choice; the physical Earth that appears in Siri's memories; the spaceship; and the alien probe. The elusive shape of the chronotope is figured by the alien probe *Rorschach*, "a city-size chaos," which keeps on growing cancerously throughout the novel, impossible to pin down, map or penetrate (Watts 2006: 108). As the novel's wistful epigraph from journalist Philip Gourevich on the "necessity of imagining what is, in fact real" (1) suggests, this cancer of space is an attempt to "reimagine history" – but reimagine it as a disease, whose proposed cure – the excision of self-awareness – is as radical as it is self-defeating.

VI. The glossolalia of ghosts

In avant-garde horror, the space *of* language and the space *in* language become one. Despite the often disparaging attitude of critics, horror, an heir to the eighteenth- and nineteenth- century Gothic, is perhaps the most innovative and flexible of all the ontological genres. Horror is closer to consensus reality and more responsive to its subterranean tensions. As opposed to fantasy, it takes place in a world contiguous with ours; as opposed to SF, it has no naturalizing discourse to justify this world's difference from ours. Its chronotope is a simulacrum of consensus reality, which is gradually corrupted by supernatural manifestations. The archetypal plot of horror is invasion; its emotional range lies between nausea and bewilderment. Such classics of (post)modern horror as Stephen King's *The Shining* (1977) and *It* (1986), and Ramsey Campbell's *Midnight Sun* (1990) exemplify this formula.

Conventional horror exploits the ideologically charged opposition of public and private space. Its setting is often claustrophobic: from the castle of the early Gothic to the haunted house of the fin-de-siècle ghost story. The haunted house remains a perennial favorite, with such popular writers as Stephen King and Peter Straub mining the topos of the suburban home's invasion by ontologically illegal aliens for all it is worth.

Experimental horror has moved beyond the nineteenth-century dichotomy of public and private spheres to explore the haunted spaces of postmodernity's historical traumas. These spaces are often urban, as opposed to the suburban and country claustrophobia of traditional horror, while their invaders are as much linguistic as they are corporeal. Avant-garde horror continues the historical avant-garde's tradition of linguistic experimentation but transfers it to the structure of its chronotope, so that the modernist concern with language and referentiality becomes literalized in the very architecture of horror's fictional worlds.

One of the earliest works of avant-garde horror was Clive Barker's six-volume collection *Books of Blood* (1984). In one of the best stories in the collection, "In the Hills, the Cities," horror comes from the projection of the metaphor of the body politic onto the diegetic level of the fictional world. The metaphor becomes part of the chronotope as two living towns, made up of human bodies lashed together, make war on each other. The story (set in former Yugoslavia and referencing the brewing ethnic violence there) layers on different spaces: East and West, town and country, body and polity. Each of these spaces reverberates with a corresponding language/discourse: English and Serbo-Croatian; gay and straight; religious and political. But just as the living cities collapse into heaps of mutilated bodies, the many languages of the story collapse into silence at the end.

The incoherence of avant-garde horror results from the closing of the gap between the signifier and the signified, as the urban spaces of its chronotopes are invaded by ghosts of dead language. In Neil Gaiman's *Neverwhere* (1996), London is haunted by the glossolalia of its past, overrun by quotes of its written history. The familiar map of the Tube blends with the tunnels it represents, and the names of stations become gods and monsters. There is a malevolent Angel under the Angel station, an Earl at Earl's Court, a living Gap between the train and the platform and so on. These names are traces (in Derrida's sense) of history, linguistic scars and blemishes of London's traumas, from the Black Death to the Blitz. But their literalization on the diegetic level results neither in exorcism nor in resolution but in incoherence. Like the gap between "London above" and "London below," the gap between signifier and signified closes down and words become as concrete – and as meaningless – as paving stones.

A similar effect is achieved in the metafictional *House of Leaves* (2000) by Mark Z. Danielewski, whose clever manipulation of narrative voice and print format creates a hybrid discursive space, enacting rather than representing the haunted space of the Navidson family's house. The novel, with its multiple narrative levels, footnotes, academic references and intertextual jokes, is both a postmodern deconstruction of the genre of horror and an avant-garde attempt to revolutionize its conventions. (For further details on *House of Leaves*, see Bray, this volume, and Gibbons, this volume.)

Avant-garde horror's monster is language itself, which strives to articulate what cannot be either spoken or even remembered: history. In Tim Lebbon's novel *The Everlasting* (2007), the entire universe becomes a haunted house, infested by an undefined alternative space called the Wide, where half-remembered ghosts endlessly repeat the trauma of their violent death. There is a magic book called the Chord of Souls, which is supposed to provide guidance to the Wide, clear away the detritus of memory, and make everything fall into a neat narrative of redemption and immortality. But the book is destroyed by the protagonist, leaving behind only a chaotic accumulation of second-hand copies in incomprehensible languages, and even this simulacrum of revelation is about to be lost again at the end. The ghost that haunts Lebbon's novel is no longer an aristocratic vampire or plebeian zombie, each of them a figure for name-able fears. It is the stench of "time rotting away to nothing" (Lebbon 2007: 270).

VII. Conclusion: signs of absence

"The artist's task would be to provide a special sign for each type of space" (Khle-bnikov 1987: 367). This whimsy of the historical avant-garde has come true in the avant-garde of postmodernity, which is shaped by its predecessor's resounding fail-ure to effect a revolution in art or in life. In the post-utopian, post-historical, post-humanist age, it seems that the only remaining task of the avant-garde is to rear-range the spaces of this failure, putting "special signs" on the emptiness of history's demise.

The end of history is, however, but a historical phase. By articulating the absence at the heart of their generic formulae, avant-garde SF, fantasy and horror move beyond the metafictional games of postmodernism and try to come to terms with the in escap-ability of the past and the inevitability of the future. In their elaboration of new forms of narrative space, avant-garde genre fictions enable us to glimpse the many forms of postmodernity's historical time.

Allegory, displacement and incoherence are narrative techniques, which enable SF, fantasy and horror to articulate both the failure of old revolutions and the possibility of new ones. By creating complex fictional chronotopes, these genres project new and unfamiliar forms of historical time onto familiar postmodern space, revitalizing Baudrillard's arid "desert of the real" with a revolutionary and experimental spirit of the avant-garde, showing us glimpses of history beyond "the end of history" and sub-jectivity beyond "the end of Man." If postmodernism is still locked in the apocalyp-tic mood of the late twentieth century, generic avant-garde points beyond it, to the rebirth of narrative, time and history.

References

Bakhtin, M.M. (2002) "Forms of Time and of the Chronotope in the Novel: Notes Toward a Histori-cal Poetics." In B. Richardson (ed.) *Narrative Dynamics: Essays on Time, Plot, Closure, and Frames*, Columbus, OH: The Ohio State University Press, pp. 15–25.

Barker, C. (1984) "In the Hills, the Cities." In *Books of Blood: Volume One*, New York: Berkley Books, pp. 172–210.

Benjamin, W. (1977) *The Origin of German Tragic Drama*, trans. J. Osborne, London: NLB.

Bould, M. (2009) "Rough Guide to a Lonely Planet, from Nemo to Neo." In M. Bould and C. Miéville (eds.) *Red Planets: Marxism and Science Fiction*, London: Pluto Press, pp. 1–29.

Broderick, D. (1995) *Reading by Starlight: Postmodern Science Fiction*, New York: Routledge.

Bürger, P. (1984 [1979]) *Theory of the Avant-Garde*, trans. M. Shaw, foreword J. Schulte-Sasse, Min-neapolis, MN: University of Minnesota.

Calinescu, M. (1987) *Five Faces of Modernity*, Durham, NC: Duke University Press.

Cawelti, J.G. (1976) *Adventure, Mystery and Romance: Formula Stories as Art and Popular Culture*, Chicago, IL: University of Chicago Press.

De Gennaro, M. (2000) "The World 'Outside of Fiction': Georges Bataille and Surrealist Photography Sculpture." In D. Scheunemann (ed.) *European Avant-Garde: New Perspectives*, Amsterdam: Rodopi, pp. 155–83.

DiBattista, M. and McDiarmid, L. (eds.) (1996) *High and Low Moderns: Literature and Culture, 1889–1939*, Oxford, UK: Oxford University Press.

Duncan, H. (2005) *Vellum*, New York: Del Rey Books.

Farrell, H. (2008) "Socialist Surrealism: China Miéville's New Crobuzon Novels." In Hassler, D.M. and C. Wilcox (eds.) *New Boundaries in Political Science Fiction*, Columbia, SC: The University of South Carolina Press, pp. 272–90.

Freedman, C. (2000) *Critical Theory and Science Fiction*, Hanover, NH: Wesleyan University Press.

Fukuyama, F. (1992) *The End of History and the Last Man*, New York: Free Press.

—— (2002) *Our Posthuman Future: Consequences of the Biotechnological Revolution*, New York: Farrar, Straus and Giroux.

Gaiman, N. (1996) *Neverwhere*, New York: Harper Collins.

Gelder, K. (2004) *Popular Fiction: The Logics and Practices of a Literary Field*, London: Routledge.

Gomel, E. (2010) *Postmodern Science Fiction and Temporal Imagination*, New York: Continuum.

Haraway, D. (1991) *Simians, Cyborgs and Women: The Reinvention of Nature*, New York: Routledge.

Horkheimer, M. and Adorno, T. (1982 [1944]) *Dialectic of Enlightenment*, trans. J. Cumming, New York: Continuum.

Huyssen, A. (1986) *After the Great Divide: Modernism, Mass Culture, Postmodernism*, Indiana, IN: Indiana University Press.

Jameson, F. (1981) *The Political Unconscious: Narrative as a Socially Symbolic Act*, Ithaca, NY: Cornell University Press.

—— (1991) *Postmodernism, Or The Cultural Logic of Late Capitalism*, Durham, NC: Duke University Press.

—— (2007) *Archaeologies of the Future: The Desire Called Utopia and Other Science Fictions*, London: Verso.

Jones, G. (1999) *Deconstructing the Starship: Science, Fiction, and Reality*, Liverpool, UK: Liverpool University Press.

Khlebnikov, V. (1987) *Collected Works of Velimir Khlebnikov*, vol. 1, trans. P. Schmidt, New York: Dia Art Foundation.

Krauss, R. (1986) *The Originality of the Avant-Garde and Other Modernist Myths*, Cambridge, MA: MIT Press.

Kristeva, J. (1974) *La Révolution du Langage Poétique: L'avant-Garde àla Fin du Xixe Siècle, Lautréamont et Mallarmé*, Paris: Éditions du Seuil. (English translation: *Revolution in Poetic Language*, New York: Columbia University Press, 1984.)

Lebbon, T. (2007) *The Everlasting*, New York: Leisure Books.

Lyotard, J.F. (1984) *The Postmodern Condition: A Report on Knowledge*, trans. G. Bennington and B. Massumi, Minneapolis, MN: University of Minnesota Press.

McHale, B. (1987) *Postmodernist Fiction*, New York: Methuen.

Miéville, C. (2004) *Iron Council*, New York: Ballantine Books.

Poggioli, R. (1968) *The Theory of the Avant-Garde*, trans. G. Fitzgerald, Cambridge, MA: Cambridge University Press.

Quilligan, M. (1979) *The Language of Allegory: Defining the Genre*, Ithaca, NY: Cornell University Press.

Reynolds, A. (2004) *Century Rain*, London: Penguin Books.

Smethurst, P. (2000) *The Postmodern Chronotope: Reading Space and Time in Contemporary Fiction*, Amsterdam: Rodopi.

Suarez, J. (2007) *Pop Modernism: Noise and Reinvention of the Everyday*, Champaign, IL: University of Illinois Press.

Suvin, D. (1979) *Metamorphoses of Science Fiction: On the Poetics and History of a Literary Genre*, New Haven, CT: Yale University Press.

Tolkien, J.R.R. (1965) "On Fairy-Stories." In *Tree and Leaf*, London: Houghton Mifflin, pp. 9–45.

Watts, P. (2006) *Blindsight*, New York: Tom Doherty Books.

Waugh, P. (1984) "What Is Metafiction and Why Are They Saying Such Awful Things About It?" In M. Currie (ed.) *Metafiction*, London: Longman, pp. 39–55.

30

GRAPHIC NARRATIVE

Hillary Chute

I. Introduction

In the historically relative sense of the term, the medium of comics has always been experimental. That is to say, this word-and-image form that registers temporality spatially has pushed at the boundaries of the expected and acceptable with every fresh iteration, in every new format. It started in the 1830s, when Swiss teacher and illustrator Rodolphe Töpffer created what is widely considered the first modern comics, publishing seven *histories en estampes* – "engraved novels" – which drew on the novel and on the "picture stories" of William Hogarth to present hand-drawn and hand-written narratives arranged by sequential frames on the page. The famed writer Johann Wolfgang von Goethe claimed Töpffer, were he less frivolous, could "produce things beyond all conception" (quoted in McCloud 1993: 17). This expansion of categories continued – through the invention of comic strips in sensational newspapers in America at the turn of the nineteenth century (many of which remain aesthetic benchmarks for comics), to the "wordless novels" of the 1920s and 1930s, to the soft-cover, 30-plus page comic books that transformed American youth culture (and later came under a federal censorship code), to the underground "comix" of all shapes and sizes that introduced comics meant to be actually *re*-read, conceiving of themselves as modernist, and creating the groundwork for today's "graphic novels." Graphic novels – or *graphic narratives* as I prefer to call book-length works in the medium of comics, due to the preponderance of nonfiction work in the field – have vigorously expanded the rubric of "literature" over the past thirty years. Recently established comics publishers such as New York's PictureBox, which focuses in large part on experimental comics, and mainstream publishers who have given comics dedicated lists (Pantheon, Abrams, and Hill and Wang, among others) are clear evidence of this claim. Comics keeps redesigning its possibilities and altering its major frameworks. Hence it is, at each new turn, already what we can consider a form of experimental literature. However, beyond *format*, this chapter is interested in comics form – that is, with how comics is experimental in its particular syntactical and grammatical procedure, for comics is a contemporary site that makes the issue of form dramatically legible.

My use of "experimental" conforms with Marianne DeKoven's use of the term, in a book on Stein, as "the obstruction of normal reading" (1983: 5). She elucidates her definition in a discussion that, while explicitly about avant-garde writers, is yet apposite for considering comics form. "Though we can construe sensible meanings here and there," DeKoven writes, "with varying degrees of readiness – for Joyce, Woolf, and Beckett we can even find ways, after serious thought, to interpret the whole passage coherently – those constructions can never account more than partially for the writing" (5). Comics is an aesthetically self-consciously artificial form: panels and gutters, tiers and grids provide its grammar, which shapes the surface of the page. While all media, to some extent, do the work of framing, comics crucially makes its frames hand-drawn and *literal*, and juxtaposes them, carving temporal moments out of the space the page provides (each frame typically offers a punctual moment).

Comics, then, is a non-transparent form that always shows its seams, calling attention to its construction. The mark on the comics page is an index of the body, a register of the embodiment and materiality comics proposes. There is a long tradition in the avant-garde of thinking through issues of "getting beyond" semantic meaning. The bond between material form and visual performativity enacted on the page is evident, for instance, in English Vorticism, Anglo-American modernism, Futurism, and Dada, and, today, in contemporary language poetry, among other manifestations (see the chapters by White, Stockwell, and Bernstein, this volume). As many scholars and cartoonists themselves point out, as a spatially site-specific form, comics functions like concrete poetry (see Bray, this volume). Johanna Drucker links untranslatability and unreproducibility to her definition of performance, clarifying that when the poetic work on a page or canvas has qualities of "an enactment" and no performed oral equivalent, that work may be considered to be visually performative (1998: 139). Yet the crucial difference is that comics resides in the field of the popular. It is a form marked by its identity as "mass."

II. Comics in the early twentieth century

There are several major locations of formal experimentalism in twentieth-century comics practice, and while this chapter will focus on experimental practice in the contemporary period, the trajectory of comics work we see in the twentieth century demonstrates that comics has always been formally experimental, always marked by a productive tension between an oppositionality that registers at the level of formand its commodity status. In its earliest incarnation in America, which established the category of "comics" globally, comics showed itself right away to be invested in issues of form. While there are rich histories and pre-histories of comics in locations such as England, Germany, Japan, and, particularly, in a Franco-Belgian context, it was only in America that comics took off as a truly mass form – as demotic. Despite the fact that early comic strips appeared in newspapers meant to be disposable (such as William Randolph Hearst's *New York Journal* and Joseph Pulitzer's *New York World*), much of this work was engaged with an experimental aesthetics, and with sending up the conventions of comics that were paradoxically just then being laid down. Comics first appeared in newspapers in 1896 with R.F. Outcault's strip known as *The Yellow Kid*, and by the early years of the twentieth century, cartoonists like Winsor McCay were creating a comics aesthetics that we can think of as modernist or proto-modernist.

McCay's most famous strip, *Little Nemo in Slumberland*, features a little boy (his name is Latin for "no one") who every night is hurtled into a lush, exhilarating, sometimes terrifying dreamscape, only to awake in the concluding panel at the end of each strip in his own bed. The strip began on October 15, 1905 in the *New York Herald*; in its inaugural appearance, in which McCay shows human and animal bodies falling through the air, he works against the always present perceived *regularity* of the comics grid (and also the "grid" of captured movements generated by then-recent experiments with chronophotography) by protracting and speeding up time through changing panel size. Rife with eruptive tension, McCay's work demonstrates a formal push and pull in the syntax of the medium. In one strip in which the dreaming Nemo enters "Befuddle Hall" (February 2, 1908) we see how even in 1908, in mass-market newspapers, comics presented themselves as an obstruction of or alternative to normal reading. One starts at the top left-hand corner, and beholds the three main characters, foregrounded but also proliferated in the background in a mirrored surface. The strip's panels then expand as the characters' bodies distort, rubber-like, up and down, pushing panel height with them: tiny heads, then huge heads, then huge torsos: the characters are barely legible as figures, and the eye doesn't travel in the order of numbered, irregularly-sized panels; instead it tends to drop down to where the figures are most discernible. Reading this strip, or even looking at it, is dizzying by design.

This is comics as a practice of close reading and looking that is deliberately disorienting – de-familiarizing, even. The concept of de-familiarization established by Russian formalist Viktor Shklovsky is useful for thinking about comics and their ability to present new, productively estranging modes of looking. McCay's repetitive dreaming-waking scenario was an antidote to the efficiency-obsessed culture of modernity, and the immersive world of Nemo could be alienating, expressing unrest as dense spectacle. *Little Nemo*'s lasting achievement is its experimentation with panels and its interest in the total visual effect of the page as a whole. Art Spiegelman, the author of *Maus: A Survivor's Tale* (1986; 1991), the world's most famous "graphic novel," has said that he could not have done *Maus* without the "architectonic rigor" of McCay (Silverblatt 1995: 33).

Along with the comic strips of McCay and others, the "wordless novels" or "woodcut novels" of the 1920s and 1930s give us an example of experimental comics narrative – but rather than being produced as ephemera in newspapers, they were marketed along with prose novels and sold in bookshops. In Lynd Ward's *Vertigo* (1937), for instance, about the Depression, Ward composes *Vertigo*'s narrative in four distinct panel sizes, and only one of these panels appears on each side of the overleaf. No one frame of reference, Ward seems to suggest, is fixed; there is no one "normal" view of the world. Ward's text bears the influence of visual modernism in its Cubist and Futurist images – one critic writes of how he "works within an idiom of almost pure abstraction and pattern" – along with literary modernism. *Vertigo* reconceptualizes narrative structure (here the narrative movement over three non-linear chapters is disjunctive and yet circular), and evokes an alternative temporal sense (indicated not only by the fact that time is a theme, but also by the book's recursive, mythic structure) (Joseph 2003: 29).

Ward's visual novels innovated – and were a part of – a tradition of socialist wordless novels. This tradition included the work of Frans Masereel, a Belgian who invented the form of the woodcut novel; Otto Nückel, a German; and the American Giacomo Patri. These novels were Expressionist (see Murphy, this volume), and largely composed in black and white with stark contrasts in color. While the influential style of the German expressionist woodcut tends to be representational (in contradistinction to, say, Surrealist woodcut), these texts yet incorporate experimentation at the level of page structure and design. Cartoonist and comics theorist Will Eisner names Ward "perhaps the most provocative graphic storyteller in this century" (2001: 141). But of *Vertigo*, Ward's most famous graphic narrative, he admits: "many readers found this book difficult to read . . . The amount of action that transpires between these scenes takes considerable input from the reader to comprehend it" (141). The gutter – and the effect it produces, which subverts what Eisner, speaking of film, calls the "rhythm of acquisition" – may be the formal characteristic of comics that most aligns it with modernist forms, especially modernist poetry whose performative dimensions on the page indeed qualify it as graphic (2001: 5).

III. Comics in the late twentieth century

It was in the "comix underground" of the late 1960s that the full experimentalism of comics blossomed. The underground, which was primarily located in San Francisco, solidified comics as an experimental movement in the twentieth century, establishing the possibilities for today's rigorous "graphic novels" or graphic narratives. Two forces are responsible for laying the groundwork for the creation of the terrain-shifting American underground (which has no real equivalent in terms of sophistication and influence in other countries). First, the Federal Comics Code of 1954, instigated by psychiatrist Fredric Wertham's study *Seduction of the Innocent*, which suggested a link between comics and juvenile delinquency, established zealous censorship guidelines for comics and prohibited a huge body of risk-taking work from publication, driving cartoonists to publish outside of regulated commercial strictures. Second, the culture of incisive *and also formally rigorous* satire generated by *MAD* Comics (later, *MAD* magazine) encouraged a culture of media-aware experimentation; *MAD* was as much about comics aesthetics as it was about lampooning American politics and values. For this reason, Spiegelman views *MAD* as "'postmodernism' avant la lettre"; virtually every single literary cartoonist working today was influenced by its conceptualization and practice of comics as a self-reflexive form of critique (2008: n.p.).

The underground took off when Robert Crumb, a *MAD* devotee, fueled by a deep-seated dis-ease with American mores and influenced by psychedelic and drug culture, published his own comic book, *Zap* #1, in 1968, inspiring a legion of cartoonists to create and distribute their own work completely free from commercial strictures. Especially in its early years in the late 1960s, underground comics were connected to the burgeoning left-wing press, and to left-wing political and college humor publications, as well as to San Francisco's rock poster scene, which established the infrastructure for comics to be sold in head shops. Comic strips and wordless novels had been, sometimes uneasily, adopted into mainstream distribution outlets, but underground "comix" – the "x" denoting adult content and cultural alterity – circulated without any mainstream aesthetic or financial expectations, and thus comics was re-born as even more deeply avant-garde than it had been in its early incarnations. If Gopnik and Varnedoe identify comic strips as "the popular embodiment of avant-garde values," underground comics were simply avant-garde; they were influenced by modernist experimentation but set their own terms entirely, based on the specificity of the comics form and the countercultural urgency that attended comics in the 1960s (1990: 167). In 1967, Ralph Ginzburg asked Crumb to contribute to the New York magazine *Avant Garde*. Crumb recalls that his *Av'N'Gar Comix* were too "avant garde" for the magazine: the editor wanted something "'more cohesive', a 'story line,' a 'theme,'" he recalls (Rosenkranz 2002: 67). Comics in this period eschewed more than punchlines; they also eschewed conventional structures of reading and of story.

Crumb sold *Zap* #1 partly out of a bassinet on Haight Street with his pregnant first wife, Dana. There is no way to overestimate how game-changing the handwritten inscription in the upper left corner was: "Fair Warning: For Adult Intellectuals Only!" With this framework, Crumb asserted not only that comics *could be* intellectual and outside of the realm of sheer amusement, but also that comics in particular lent themselves to the oppositional, the aesthetic, the non-diversionary: experimentalism and aesthetic free rein was, in fact, the very purview of comics. We see this in the politically risky – and immediately controversial – short strips such as "Nigger Hearts," in which white children hawk a lunch product billed as Wildman Sam's Pure Nigger Hearts. *Zap* #1 also offered, among 15 or so comics pieces, the foundational three-page "Abstract Expressionist Ultra Super Modernistic Comics." In their earliest contemporary manifestation, comics presented themselves explicitly as about the obstruction of normal reading. A semi-circular title panel occupies the opening left-hand corner: in conventional comics reading, one reads panels from left to right to the end of the page before starting one row down at the beginning of the next tier of frames. Here the rounded opening frame shoots one in no clear narrative direction; one could move horizontally across the tier or vertically downward. Either way, one encounters a jagged, atypical panel, as no one panel on the page of twenty-one panels is the same shape as any other. In none of these is there any speech that is readable for denotative or lexical content; the speech balloons scattered throughout the page speak icons, in some cases, and simply "speak" *marks* in others. "Speech" is here valued for its handwriting. Crumb's underground work established this form of experimentalism as the urgent mission of comics – a destabilization not only of common perceptions about comics, such as their easy digestibility, but further a destabilization of practices of reading and looking.

Crucially, cartoonists in the underground perceived of their own work as modernist and their word and image narratives as oppositional at the level of form. In the Afterword to his recently republished *Breakdowns*, which first appeared in 1977,

411

Spiegelman writes, referring to himself: "He was on fire, alienated and ignored, but arrogantly certain that his book would be a central artifact in the history of Modernism" (2008: n.p.). Of major influence Gertrude Stein, Spiegelman explains that she "is pushing as hard as she can *against* narrative content, and against clear exposition, and is getting drunk on the language and on the rhythm and the sound of the words she's using, but she's still somehow saying something" (1995: 103). In the 1970s Spiegelman used the interaction between word and image to similarly re-work narrative fluency for the purposes of creating a rich experimental comics.

Justin Green, whose forty-two-page 1972 comic book *Binky Brown Meets the Holy Virgin Mary* revolutionized comics as the first work of comics autobiography, was training in abstract expressionism when he turned to comics – as was Aline Kominsky-Crumb, another pioneering underground figure. These artists brought the concerns of modernism to an aesthetic and political context that felt urgent and immediate in part because of how comics circulated outside of elite or even mainstream publishing. Green explains of underground cartoonists, "[We] all held to the ideal of reaching a common audience while reinventing the formal boundaries that defined the medium" (*Rebel Visions* 4). In terms of exploring these formal boundaries, the underground established comics as a terrain for work as sophisticated – and even as abstruse – as modernist forms that had been established in the early twentieth century.

Spiegelman was interested in the very concept of comics as narrative – when did a comic strip stop being one? If the essential narrative procedure of comics is to make time out of space, how can the form offer non-linear accounts of temporality? In the early days of the underground Spiegelman had a passionate conversation with Crumb about narrative time and panelization: "Time is an illusion that can be shattered in comics! Showing the same scene from different angles freezes it in time by turning the page into a diagram – an orthographic projection!" he recalls enthusing to Crumb (Spiegelman 2008 "Afterword": n.p.). We see this idea surface in Crumb's "Bo Bo Bolinski: He's the No. 1 Human Zero – He's No Big Deal" (*Uneeda Comix*, 1970) which offers nine panels, all the same size, that show different perspectives of the title character sitting in an armchair with his arms crossed. Ivan Brunetti writes that this basic "democratic" grid of the comics page "invites us to an unimpeded narrative flow" (2007: 51). Although the sequence of same-size panels usually denotes the procession of time, here Crumb uses the most standard template for progression to in fact halt progression. He stops narrative time for comics, giving us a page of panels in which there is movement of perspective but not movement in time. Comics then becomes evidently about narrative *space* – what Spiegelman calls orthographic, or orthogonal projection – a depth-oriented mapping. What distinguishes this comics story from a mere map, then, might be the title – its ultimate composition in images and words. The title, in stylized, capital-lettered font that scrolls above the top of the page, implies a story even if it doesn't deliver one. It frames our understanding of the regularized views of Bolinski as "zero" – which is to say, as "nothing happening," as a non-temporally progressive movement of images. In works like this one we see comics' experimental language as of a piece with Cubism, which sought to destroy fixed viewpoint.

Spiegelman's own underground works, most of which were collected in *Breakdowns*, are under-examined and yet established an enduring syntax of experiment for comics: "Don't Get Around Much Anymore" (1973), a densely woven one-pager, implies temporal movement across panels only once, and disjoints word and image, unhinging reference; "A Day at the Circuits" (1975) has a recursive narrative structure, in which arrows point one through the strip in a never-ending circularity; "The Malpractice Suite" (1976), which incorporates cut-outs, proliferates boxes within boxes, completely detaching itself from coherence and causality as frames multiply within frames. "Ace Hole: Midget Detective" (1974), an eight-page riff on hardboiled detective fiction, with its many Cubist-style attacks on verisimilar representation – and yet its many references to narrative, especially popular genre fiction narratives – is emblematic of Spiegelman's enduring experimentalism in a populist medium. In "Ace Hole" time has become unmoored from that movement; we are only experiencing the perspective of different, almost randomly selected "windows" on a subject. Spiegelman not only places stress on the movement of time that a comic strip is understood to represent, but further he gestures towards a kind of proliferative Cubist narration, accommodating multiple perspectives and angles. There is little sustained chronological structure in "Ace Hole," and thus causal inference is only partially possible. One of the centrally interesting aspects of comics' narrative composition within the space parameters of the printed page is its ability to use that space to suggest different kinds of reading – models that aren't necessarily linear, or that do not actually embed a "right" way to read and to look, but rather offer a density – which is often a layering of temporalities that the reader then *decodes*. ("Decode" is a verb used by Spiegelman and by Edward Said, among others, to describe the process of reading comics [1995: 61; 2001: ii]).

Spiegelman went on to found a venue, *RAW*, that solidified a place in culture for experimental comics, crucially maintaining and extending the oppositional edge that drove his underground work into a new, yet still modernist, expansion of contemporary comics. *RAW* (1980–1991), co-founded and co-edited with Françoise Mouly, billed itself explicitly as an "avant-garde comix and graphix" magazine. *RAW* could be said to stand for, among other possibilities, "Rectangular Accusatory Windows," a title evoking comics' frames; it published such key contemporary cartoonists as Chris Ware, Charles Burns, Lynda Barry, Ben Katchor, Gary Panter, and Spiegelman himself, who, starting in *RAW*'s second issue, December 1980, began publishing what would become *Maus: A Survivor's Tale*, in insert booklets in the lavishly produced oversized magazine. Crumb also created a magazine, *Weirdo* (1981–1993), which published work by Aline Kominsky-Crumb, Peter Bagge, and Julie Doucet, among others; in essence, the titans of underground comics became editors as well as exemplars, and thus encouraged a thriving comics culture to expand further into previously unavailable spaces. *RAW* was a venue for showcasing experimental work, especially from abroad, such as by José Munoz, Joost Swarte, Cheri Samba, and Yoshiharu Tsuge, and it laid the groundwork for the acceptance of comics as a serious form of literature, despite its teasing subtitles, such as "Required Reading for the Post-Literate" and "Putting the Litter Back into Litterature."

IV. Comics today

Today, in experimental comics practice, we see experimentalism less as a passionate exercise of the ability of comics form to be oppositional, as in the underground movement of the late 1960s and 1970s, than as work that sets in motion the rich grammatical tools of comics to disrupt normal reading for a targeted purpose. Today's experimental comics practice includes figures such as Spiegelman, Chris Ware, Alison Bechdel, Joe Sacco, Lynda Barry, and Jason Shiga; features of their work include deep attention to the spatial arrangement of panels on the page, and, in Barry's case and others', play with collage, lending certain works of comics a productively unstable form that brings them close to undecidable forms like artists' books. Spiegelman provides a through-line; while his ground breaking, Pulitzer Prize-winning *Maus* is not necessarily experimental in the sense in which I am using the term here, although it is rigorously formal in a way its readers often miss, his *In the Shadow of No Towers* is indubitably so. In works like 2004's *No Towers* – which he suggests is more like "novel graphics" than a "graphic novel" – we see the obstruction of normal reading productively call attention to the aftereffects of trauma (quoted in Chute 2007: 229). *No Towers*, which is about witnessing 9/11, demonstrates how the "symphonic" or "all-at-onceness" effect of reading and looking at the comics page is apposite to confronting the confusion and ultimate unknowability of traumatic experience. A large, heavy, awkward book to handle (it measures 10″ by 14.5″), its pages are thick board, and one must fold them outwards and turn the book on its side in order to view the ten comic strips that make up the core of the text. We register temporal scrambling on each page as we encounter the symphonic effects of comics whereby its visual elements are apprehended at once and then further unpacked individually.

The book's first strip (which is dated 9/11/01–2/15/02), indicates the traumatic temporality the work expresses through its experimental form. The top of the page opens at the left corner with a three-panel mini-strip titled "The New Normal," which depicts a shocked family watching television. In the concluding panel of "The New Normal," an American flag hangs on the family's wall; in the next panel of the strip, across a portion of slim white gutter, we see a panel made up entirely of the American flag. When one's eye hits this right-hand panel, a second vertical strip potentially thrusts you downwards, with, or onto, the crumbling North Tower of the World Trade Center, in the process of falling over five length-wise frames separated by gutters. "SYNOPSIS," reads the text box in a frame that breaks out and overlays the flag, gutter, and left-hand mini-comic strip at a jagged angle. "In our last episode, as you might remember, the world ended . . ." (Of course, there was no last episode – this is the first installment – but here Spiegelman suggests the unendingness of trauma.) While one might feel dropped into the crumbling architecture, the design of the page makes it unclear whether or not one ought to be tower-bound – that is, to read vertically – or to read conventionally. Choosing the latter, one would start back along a horizontal axis with a second embedded strip, this one twelve panels, labeled "Etymological Vaudeville," which appears under the bold red-and-white title, "In the Shadow of

No Towers," and itself comes, perhaps, after "The New Normal." By placing stress on "normal" reading (which way should one's eyes travel? Up, down, left, right?), Spiegelman evokes the New Normal's shattering of "normality"; by experimenting with its "stylistic surface," he aims to get the reader lost on the page by erecting and then violating the grid of the page to reflect the 9/11 attack's demolition of what he calls "the world grid" (1994: n.p.; D'Arcy 2003). In the lower left, two panels of a falling building mirror the right-hand side, creating a vertical axis of shattering that unstably contains the page's own falling structure.

We see a similar attention to an experimental arrangement of panels in space in the work of Ware, author of the intricate, virtuosic *Jimmy Corrigan* (2001), about three generations of lonely men and the lines of filial despair they establish. Ware has done more to call attention to the possibilities of comics space than practically any other cartoonist. Ware's work, as with Spiegelman and like McCay, is thought of in terms of comics *architecture*, and while his pages are *built*, they do not necessarily cohere as structures in terms of conventional reading: often full of floating clusters of tiny panels, his pages have to be apprehended, as graphic wholes whose parts don't necessarily teach one a conventional way of reading them. The dislocation this produces is often evocative of the fragile relationships Ware's work depicts; the *slowness* his work induces, too, is an index of how much his work is actually about conveying sensibility rather than plot. Ware's comics are often received in the explicit context of experimentalism – a recent collection of criticism on Ware, for instance, features an essay arguing for the connection of his work with OuBaPo, the comics equivalent of the French literary tradition of OuLiPo (see Baetens, this volume). (OuBaPo was founded in 1992 by French comics theorist Thierry Groensteen.) Ware credits his biggest influence as Richard McGuire's "Here" (from a 1989 issue of *RAW*), a story that experiments with the narrative tense of comics, spanning the years 500, 957, 406, 073 BC and 2033 AD, and unfolding, ostensibly, in six pages of six panels each, which actually largely each contain several other panels layered into the space of the frame, a temporal palimpsest. In "Here," Ware sees that narrative development in comics can powerfully reflect the patterns of memory.

While Ware's own work is dense and formal, it is published in mainstream venues like *The New Yorker*. Take, for example, his five-page Halloween story, "Unmasked," from 2009, which starts on the cover of the magazine, picturing parents in the dark, lit up by cell phones as their children trick-or-treat. The story then moves into the magazine, without calling attention in any formal way to its continuation between the covers; bearing no title on the page, its first panel is a drawing of an iPhone screen. In the first double-spread within the covers, a princess mask sits in the dead center, bisected by the seam of the magazine. Thus while the panels, which float in clusters as opposed to moving along a grid, work in a roughly vertical configuration on each side of the double spread, the reader is tempted to read across the hollow-eyed mask of a face that sits in the center. In the story's fourth and fifth pages – the second double spread – the reverse side of the plastic mask, a lightblue, occupies the center, and on the right of it the protagonist's daughter, facing center; on the left, in a mirroring panel facing center, the protagonist's mother. This second double-spread is denser with panels of varying sizes, as the protagonist's mother reveals her husband's infidelity to her daughter, who herself is worried her husband is having an affair. The eye skitters about the double spread, drawn first to the right, perhaps, with its striking blue palette, before landing on the left-hand side, anchored by the grim visage of the mother. The density of information on this last double-spread, particularly, is indicative of the *unknowingness* and the as-yet unanswerable search for clues that the quiet uncomfortable moments of the story set in motion. The reader's own search for sequential location within the complex narrative units of a story that centralizes an *empty* face is of a piece with the process of searching on which the protagonist embarks.

Bechdel's acclaimed graphic narrative *Fun Home* (2006a) is another example of comics' relation to non-normative reading. The book is about Bechdel's search for family evidence that would shed light on her father's suicide; a closeted gay man, he died a few months after she herself came out at age 19. At *Fun Home*'s literal and emotional center is a drawing of a photograph – of Bechdel's former babysitter, Roy, then seventeen, posing on a hotel room bed in his underwear. Bechdel discovered the snapshot of Roy, taken by her father on a family vacation when she was eight, about a year after her father died, in an envelope marked "Family." And while she did not start working on *Fun Home* for almost twenty more years, this snapshot introduced the idea for the book.

In the book, the primal scene of Alison looking – trying to decode the photograph – is the only scene in which the visuals, in the parlance of comics, "bleed" off the page. The two double-spread pages are also unique in *Fun Home* for their lack of pagination. Alison's hand, which grasps the lower left corner of the snapshot, is substantially more than twice life size, as is the photograph itself, which she holds aloft at an angle. The largely unshaded hand contrasts with the heavily crosshatched, detailed image of Roy, whose body, clothed only in Jockey underwear, seems to float horizontally across the pages, offering itself up as object and artifact. Scattered over both pages are text boxes of varying sizes, in positions that obscure parts of both Alison's fingers and the studied photograph itself (Figure 30.1).

This double-spread of Roy is the least regulated of all of the pages of *Fun Home*. Each page of *Fun Home* is an aesthetic unit that offers its own narrative logic, indicated by the shapes and sizes of its panels. Yet in the process of production, Bechdel's "standard page," the default grid for composing *Fun Home*, is three tiers, two panels across (Bechdel 2006b: 1011). Here, none of the eight text boxes spread over the two pages, each of which touches the image of the photograph, are the same size; the black borders of these boxes, which appear wobblier here than elsewhere in the book, emphasize their difference from each other. The scene's array of text boxes suggests an awkward interaction with the image on which the narrator is riveted, resisting easy consumption of the information it reveals. While the image of Roy traverses the two pages – the seam of the book bisects him just below the navel – the text boxes themselves read most sensibly up and down each side of the spread, instead of across the body of the image itself – although, in this case, both vertical and horizontal modes

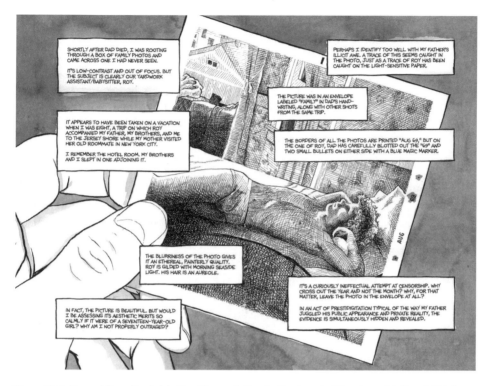

Figure 30.1 From Alison Bechdel, *Fun Home: A Family Tragicomic* (Houghton Mifflin, 2006a), not
paginated [pages 100–1]. Courtesy of the artist.

of reading could in fact plausibly move the narrative forward. The irregularity of the
text boxes reflects the ambivalence that threads through the book. Bechdel makes
the photograph of Roy a double-spread as if to elevate her father's desire and his art as
aesthetic, beautiful, the book's own center fold. But Bechdel destabilizes the power of
the babysitter's photograph – the artistic product of her father – with the grammar of
comics that is her own artistic product: the overlaying, irregular text boxes.

V. Conclusion

Comics' spatial grammar opens up many possibilities of disrupting the temporal and
spatial conventions of reading. In this, comics have a parallel history with other experimental forms, such as the artists' book. In "What is Graphic About Graphic Novels?"
(2008), Johanna Drucker, a prominent scholar of artists' books, details the experimental features of comics texts, such as the evident lack of one-to-one relation of signifier
to signified, and the fact that:

> the materiality of graphic works cannot be simply perceived as a mechani-
> cal device for unfolding the story . . . One of the striking features of graphic

novels is their investment in the materially replete visual presentation on the page. The effect of immersion and absorption this creates for a reader goes beyond the account of a verbal or literary "story."

(Drucker 2008: 40)

Lynda Barry's two latest works, the lavishly produced, non-narrative *What It Is* (2008) and *Picture This! The Near-Sighted Monkey Book* (2010), both painted instead of drawn and billed as an interactive "activity book" and "work book," respectively, intersperse rich collage works and small snatches of story with meditations on color, handwriting, and memory; they worry the fault-line between artists' book and comics text, and one might consider them artists' books yet invested in print (they are full of *trompe l'oeil* collage). The first store to buy Barry's work in the late 1970s was Printed Matter, an arts organization in New York City with an attached exhibition space devoted to art-ists' books. We can also see a mixture of collage and sketch elements with comics, and productive playing with word-and-image possibilities in works like Julie Doucet's *365 Days* (2008). Drucker sees a strong connection between the two experimental forms, suggesting that graphic novels are "the realization of the vision of the democratic art form once trumpeted by champions of the artists' book" (39).

Today, work like Ware's and Bechdel's is not published "underground"; the opening up of mainstream and elite spaces to comics is consistently growing, effected by venues such as *RAW*. In fact, and perhaps even because of this, self-conceived "abstract com-ics" are re-entering the fray, some taking up Spiegelman's underground-era question – when does comics stop being comics? – with vigor. Andrei Molotiu's edited collection *Abstract Comics: The Anthology 1967–2009* appeared in 2009; and while he mentions *Little Nemo* in the introduction, and opens the volume with Crumb's 1967 tour-de-force, most of the work presented was done in the past ten years. Comics will continue to push its own boundaries, but what will endure is work in which the medium is able to present the high stakes of what it does differently. The sophistication and popular-ity of comics today calls attention to the energy around experiments in narrative form and modes of the popular: comics is as self-reflexive as it is spectacular; as intimate, and communicative, as is it intricate and difficult to parse. In its incarnations from the past, such as the lavish but eruptive full-page Sunday newspaper strip, and in the present, such as Ware's dense *New Yorker* stories that treat the magazine cover as the first narrative unit of a story unfolding across gaps, comics demonstrates that the spaces in between word and image, and in the temporal fabric between frames and gutters, offer a rich and relevant visual-verbal syntax.

References

Bechdel, A. (2006a) *Fun Home: A Family Tragicomic*, Boston, MA: Houghton Mifflin.

—— (2006b) "An Interview with Alison Bechdel," *Mfs: Modern Fiction Studies* 52(4): 1004–13.

Brunetti, I. (2007) *Cartooning: Philosophy and Practice*, Oakland, CA: Buenaventura Press.

Chute, H. (2007) "Temporality and Seriality in Spiegelman's *In the Shadow of No Towers*," *American Periodicals* 17(2): 228–44.

Crumb, R. (1968) "Abstract Expressionist Ultra Super Modernistic Comix," *Zap* #1. San Francisco, CA: Apex Novelties, n.p.

—— (1970) "Av'N'Gar," *R. Crumb's Head Comix*, intro P. Krassner, New York: Ballantine, p. 55.

D'Arcy, D. (2003) "Profile: Art Spiegelman's Comic Book Journalism" [Transcript]. NPR Weekend Edition 7 June 2003.

DeKoven, M. (1983) *A Different Language: Gertrude Stein's Experimental Writing*, Madison, WI: University of Wisconsin Press.

Drucker, J. (1998) "Visual Performance of the Poetic Text." In C. Bernstein (ed.) *Close Listening: Poetry and the Performed Word*, New York: Oxford University Press, pp. 131–61.

—— (2008) "What Is Graphic About Graphic Novels?" *English Language Notes* 46(2): 39–48.

Eisner, W. (2001) *Graphic Storytelling & Visual Narrative*, Tamarac, FL: Poorhouse Press.

Gopnik, A. and K. Varnedoe (1990) *High and Low: Modern Art, Popular Culture*, New York: Museum of Modern Art and Abrams.

Joseph, M. (2003) "Introduction," "*Vertigo*: A Graphic Novel of the Great Depression – An Exhibition of the Original Woodblocks and Wood Engravings by Lynd Ward," curated M. Joseph, Rutgers University Special Collections and University Archives.

McCloud, S. (1993) *Understanding Comics: The Invisible Art*, New York: Harper Perennial.

McGuire, R. (1989) "Here," *RAW* 2(1).

Molotiu, A. (2009) *Abstract Comics: The Anthology 1967–2009*, Seattle, WA: Fantagraphics.

Rosenkranz, P. (2002) *Rebel Visions: The Underground Comix Revolution, 1963–1975*, Seattle, WA: Fantagraphics.

Said, E. (2001) "Homage to Joe Sacco." Introduction to J. Sacco *Palestine*, Seattle, WA: Fantagraphics, pp. i–v.

Silverblatt, M. (1995) "The Cultural Relief of Art Spiegelman," *Tampa Review* 5: 31–6.

Spiegelman, A. (1986) *Maus: A Survivor's Tale: My Father Bleeds History*, New York: Pantheon.

—— (1991) *Maus II: A Survivor's Tale: And Here My Troubles Began*, New York: Pantheon.

—— (1994) *The Complete Maus* [CD-ROM]. New York: Voyager.

—— (1995) "Art Spiegelman" [Interview by Gary Groth], *The Comics Journal* 180: 52–106.

—— (2004) *In the Shadow of No Towers*, New York: Pantheon.

—— (2008 [1977]) *Breakdowns/Portrait of the Artist as a Young %@&*!*, New York: Pantheon.

Ware, C. (2009) "Unmasked," *The New Yorker* Nov. 2.

31

MULTIMODAL LITERATURE AND EXPERIMENTATION

Alison Gibbons

I. Introduction

The term "multimodal literature" refers to a body of literary texts that feature a multitude of semiotic modes in the communication and progression of their narratives. Such works are composed not only of words, type-set on the page in block fashion as has become publishing convention. As shall be seen in the course of this chapter, they experiment with the possibilities of book form, playing with the graphic dimensions of text, incorporating images, and testing the limits of the book as a physical and tactile object. In this introduction, I describe multimodal literature, accounting for how it can be seen as experimental, while in section II, I gloss its connections with other literary movements, genres, and forms of writing. Section III presents a historical overview of the development of the multimodal novel. Finally in section IV, I suggest a taxonomy for different types of multimodal literature.

Multimodal literature as a genre is not uniform, but rather exists on a spectrum, from minimal to extensive in the level of incorporation of multimodality. Considering multimodal literature from a holistic perspective, some of the formal features these works tend to contain are: varied typography, unusual textual layouts and page design including the concrete arrangement of text for visual purposes, the inclusion of images (illustrative, diagrammatic, photographic) and facsimiles of documents; multimodal literature may play with the size, shape, and design of the codex, using cut-outs/die cuts or pop-ups, and offering the reader throw-outs or flip book sections; multimodal literature, perhaps partly because of the striking impact of its visuality for readers, often pushes at its own ontological boundaries, whether in the form of metafictive writing, footnotes and self-interrogative critical voices, or through ontological masquerade in itself.

Critics often cite such features as gimmickry with the implication that works of literature that incorporate graphic elements are low culture artefacts (see discussion in Gibbons 2012; Sadokierski 2010: 54–8). The rise of digital technologies in the late twentieth century has certainly impacted upon the publishing industry; most recently of course, we have witnessed the emergence of the e-book, but in print-based publishing the fact that images and word-image combinations can now be produced cheaply and more easily has resulted in an increase of multimodal works into the mainstream market (both in fiction and non-fiction).

Despite being decried by some critics as trivial textualizations, multimodal novels can be highly sophisticated art forms, challenging readers in both cognitive and physical terms. In an article designed to introduce the genre to narratologists, Hallet (2009: 149–50) identifies five significant "conceptual shifts" brought about when reading a multimodal novel: from monomodal (verbal) texts to multimodal, multimedial texts; from writing to designing; from narrator to narrator-presenter; from reading to transmodal construction of narrative meaning. The final conceptual shift, from reader to "user" is, in many ways, a consequence of the former shifts, and sees the reader interacting with the novel in more obvious ways. Hallet likens reading a multimodal novel to reading a hypertext, but comparisons to alternate media are (almost inevitably) generalizing. Plainly, the process of reading becomes foregrounded and the physical act of engaging with the book is heightened. Thus, we might want to think of reading multimodal novels in active terms: not just as using, but also as engaging and performing. Despite the flood of multimodal novels into mainstream publishing, it is such conceptual shifts, felt most keenly by readers, which make such works experimental or avant-garde. Indeed, in an empirical study of responses to Graham Rawle's multimodal novel *Woman's World* (2005), it was evidenced both in readers' own self-report and in analysis of readers' responses that the visuality of the text directly affected the reading experience (see Gibbons 2012). In other words, multimodal literature can be a literature of experimentation.

II. Multimodal connections

Connections between multimodal literature and established literary movements (that have themselves been called experimental) can certainly be made; for instance, the self-consciousness and ontological play of postmodernism (see McHale, this volume) and the related genre of metafiction (see Berry, this volume). Of course, multimodal literature is not entirely divorced from these contexts. In fact, as I outline in the next section, works exist within postmodernism that are multimodal. Similarly, relationships can be found with other literary genres, the most obvious being children's picture books (Sipes and Pantaleo 2008), or graphic narratives, themselves open to debate about their popular or experimental nature (see Chute, this volume). However, these both have different functions, audiences, and narrative grammars.

Multimodal fictions are a close cousin to artists' books (see Drucker 2004 [1994]; Lyons 1985) which, according to Drucker, "transform the condition of bookness and complicate it" (2004 [1994]: xi). Philip Zimmermann's *High Tension* (1993), for instance, is a five-sided book that is almost fan-shaped. Its small yet rectangular double-spreads are packed with colour and pattern. While each spread is the same size, the pages alternate between two diagonal layouts – the book thus makes an X-shape – so that while any one double-spread is open, the reader can inevitably see parts of the previous and succeeding pages with their own arresting designs. The narrative, limited to one short phrase per page, directly addresses the reader, "Your heart pounds / Your breathing is shallow" (Zimmermann 1993: 1–2); text, image, and material form all work together to create a sensory overload for the reader that is itself the "high tension" of the title (see Figure 31.1). It is exactly such multimodal combination that also characterizes experimental multimodal literature.

Given the rise of multimodality throughout the twentieth and early twenty-first centuries, it is not surprising that other forms of writing have also experimented with visuality. While poetry may be the most palpable case (see Bray, this volume, on concrete poetics; and Dworkin 2003), it is not the only one. Avant-garde theatre has experimented with multimodality in written dramatic text: the script of Lee Breuer's *The Red Horse Animation* (art by Ann Elizabeth Horton), first performed in 1970 at the Guggenheim Museum, is composed as a comic book, and prefaced with the categorical statement, "A conventional script of *The Red Horse Animation* does not exist." Another form of writing to take heed of the visual is biography (for further discussion of biographical writing, see chapters by Kacandes and Elias, this volume), with

Figure 31.1 Phillip Zimmermann, *High Tensions*, Montage '93 with Visual Studies Workshop Press, pp. 1–2. Courtesy of the artist.

contemporary artist Lauren Redniss garnering attention for her accounts of Doris Eaton in *Century Girl* (2006) and Marie Curie in *Radioactive* (2011).

In critical writing, central multimodal examples include Derrida's *Glas* (1990 [1986]) and Avital Ronell's *The Telephone Book* (1989). *Glas* is a critical reflection on the works of German philosopher Hegel and French novelist and critic Jean Genet. Dividing the page into two columns (though with numerous smaller text-box interruptions for quotation) and devoting one to each thinker, left and right respectively, *Glas* challenges familiar reading habits while interrogating Hegel's philosophical ideas. Indeed, the interrogation arises in many ways from the text's duplicity (both of voice and design); as the text itself claims on its opening page, "Two unequal columns, they say distyle [*dissent-ils*], each of which – envelop(e)(s) or sheath(es), incalculably reverses, turns inside out, replaces, remarks, overlaps [*recoupe*] the other" (Derrida 1990 [1986]: 1). Ronell's *The Telephone Book* is similarly deconstructive, bringing together Heidegger, Derrida, and Alexander Graham Bell (credited with inventing the telephone). Ronell plays not only with varying columns of text but incorporates quotations arranged as poetic verse, text positioned at odd angles, overlaid text that becomes illegible, diagrams and images. Furthermore, Ronell structures her critical exposition using the telephone book metaphor, with "Classified" yellow pages at the end and "A User's Manual" at the start which boldly declares, " *The Telephone Book* is going to resist you," a dictum which itself comments on the challenge of reading.

More recent and lesser known critical examples are Jeff Brice's non-linear consideration of the postmodern condition in *Fractaled Fields and Fairytales* (released both in print and on CD-ROM; 1996), Barrie Tullet's documentation of type- and copy-editing translated poetry in The Case Room Press's *The Ghost in the Fog* (2008), and designer Marian Bantjes *I Wonder* (2010), a collection of essays lavishly printed with gold and silver foils and gilded page edges which give it the feel of a contemporary illuminated manuscript.

III. Multimodal heritage

Multimodality is by no means a recent literary innovation, but can be seen as being utterly entwined with the history of the book. Medieval illuminated manuscripts, such as *The Lindisfarne Gospels*, are awash with intricately patterned illustrations. The boom of religious works in the fourteenth and fifteenth centuries sustained the visuality of early manuscripts with texts like the *Luttrell Psalter*. A book of 150 Latin Psalms commissioned by Sir Geoffrey Luttrell, the *Luttrell Psalter* is opulently decorated. Painted in rich colours with gold and silver embellishment, it also comprises bizarre illustrations. Bordering on the grotesque and surreal, such images work to complement, enhance, and sometimes even contradict the psalms they accompany. Exceptional in their number, detail, function, and inventiveness, it is these images that have given the *Luttrell Psalter* its unique character and place in book history.

It was not until the seventeenth and eighteenth centuries that the "novel" really came into being, and of course one of the earliest examples is Laurence Sterne's

(1759–1767) much celebrated and sometimes berated *The Life and Opinions of Tristram Shandy, Gentleman*. The book plays with the very form of the novel itself, in both a visual and narratological sense. Of particular interest from a multimodal perspective is the "black page" which immediately succeeds the announcement of the death of one of the novel's central characters Yorick, the morally impenetrable "marbled page," and the squiggly lines depicting narrative trajectories. Given that *Tristram Shandy* is an early novel, its eccentric and experimental character is, in many ways, remarkable. After the initial development of the book and the codex form in medieval times and then the rise of the novel itself with *Tristram Shandy* in the eighteenth century, three further periods are remarkable: the Victorian era, early modernity, postmodernity.

The Victorian era can be seen as a golden age in illustrated books resulting from technical advancements in printing during the period. I don't want to devote unnecessary space to outlining the Victorian illustrated book (see instead Maxwell 2002), but Lewis Carroll's (1865) *Alice in Wonderland* is worthy of note. Carroll's much-loved and highly whimsical story was illustrated originally by John Tenniel and has since been numerously revisioned. As well as illustrations though, *Alice in Wonderland* includes some concrete textual design, seen most clearly in a passage that has become known as "the Mouse's tale/tail." Because of a confusion between the Mouse and Alice based on the homophonic punning of "tale/tail," as the Mouse tells his tale, Carroll's text is arranged as a wiggly tail down the page. Readers therefore have to integrate the verbal and visual dynamics of the extract in order to understand the joke of this playful design.

Rather than serving to entertain, multimodality in the modernist period was part of a deep commitment to aesthetic experimentation, seen in literary movements across Europe. In France, prior to the start of the twentieth century, Symbolist Stéphane Mallarmé's poetry emphasised the importance of the white space of the page, for example in "Un coup de dés jamais n'abolira le hazard" ["A throw of the dice will never abolish change"] (1897). Another Frenchman, Guillaume Apollinaire, working in the Cubist tradition later explored, in Butler's words (1994: 170), "the relationship of word and object, by giving his text the visual organization of a collaged painting." This can be seen in *Lettre-Océan* (1914) or in his *Calligrammes* where words form images, for instance words streaming down the page like rainwater in "Il Pleut" ["It is raining"] (1916). Lesser known French Cubist artist, playwright, and writer Pierre Albert-Birot used multimodality in his (1917) work "Poème à crier et à danser" ["Poem for Declaiming and Dancing"] for performative effect, using the visual dimension as an indication of vocal delivery for the excited sounds (e.g. "vrrr") of a crowd.

Similar experimentation was taking place in the work of the Italian Futurists (see White, this volume) and their British counterpart, the Vorticists. English painter and writer Wyndham Lewis used font size in the Vorticist manifesto *Blast* (1914), his inspiration stemming initially from Futurism and the work of its most prominent figure Filippo Tomasso Marinetti. Inspired by the thrill of modern technology and the changing urban landscape, Italian Futurism sought to imbue art and literature with a dynamicity and simultaneity that would match the modern world's reconfiguration of time and space. Marinetti's most central works are *Zang Tumb Tumb* (1914), spectacularly depicting the Battle of Adrianople, and *A Tumultuous Assembly* (1919) which exploits font size and chaotic visual design in a way which pushes at the limits of linguistic coherence. Other notable examples from Italian Futurists include Angelo Josia's "Baci Al Cimitero" ["Kisses in a Cemetery"] which fuses the sound and image of words to create a romantic/sexual crescendo and Francesco Cangiullo's (1919) *Caffè Concerto – Alfabeto a Sorpresa* [*Café Chantant – Unexpected Alphabet*] which uses the shape of alphabetical letters to form images of characters on the page.

Among futurist-influenced figures of the early twentieth century, two others deserve mention: the Fleming Paul van Ostaijen and the German Kurt Schwitters. Ostaijen's recognition as part of the international avant-garde came with the publication of *Bezette Stad* (*Occupied City*) in 1921, a collection of poetry depicting the Siege of Antwerp in the First World War, with words such as "Zeppelin" positioned at the top of a page and fashioned to form the shape of the German airship to which it refers. The war years also influenced Schwitters who produced poetry and fairytales. The fairytales *Hahnepeter* [*Peter the Rooster*] (1924), *Die Märchen vom Paradies* [*The Fairy Tales of Paradise*] (1924/5) and *Die Scheuche* [*The Scarecrow*] (1925), were published in collaboration with artists Kate Steinitz and Theo van Doesburg and took advantage of unusual typography as in Cangiullo's futurist work.

By the 1930s, typographical experimentation in the literary arts seems to have died out, due partly to convention, partly to the arrival of the Second World War. It is not until the second half of the twentieth century and the arrival of postmodernity that we see an experimental resurgence in multimodal literature. In *Postmodernist Fiction* (1987), McHale suggests a number of ways in which postmodernist writers foreground the ontological divide, from exploiting space (type-faces, blank pages, margins), concrete prose and illustration (or what he also calls anti-illustration), footnotes, multiple columns, various reading routes, and model kits (also called "random shuffle" by Hayles and Montfort, this volume). Some postmodernist fictions will be discussed in the following section, but for illustrative purposes here, McHale offers the following central examples: *Willie Masters' Lonesome Wife* by William H. Gass (1989) which incorporates colored pages, distorted typography and photographic images; Christine Brooke-Rose's *Thru* (1975), Raymond Federman's *Take it or Leave it* (1979) and *Double or Nothing* (1998 [1992]), all of which feature concrete prose; and the model kit of B.S. Johnson's *The Unfortunates* (1969).

In the twenty-first century, the rapid developments in forms of literary production, and in particular the event of the digital, have affected the rise of multimodal literature. Literary writing, from late postmodernism to the contemporary moment is influenced by and engages with emerging technologies and modes of representation. In the next section, I suggest a taxonomy for different types of multimodal literature charting late postmodern and early twenty-first century writing.

IV. A taxonomy of multimodal literature

Illustrated works

Following Hallet (2009), texts with illustrations in the traditional sense (whether drawn-images or photographs) while obviously not monomodal, are not classed as multimodal (indeed, strictly speaking, there is no such thing as a monomodal text). For texts with illustrations to be classed as multimodal, visual elements must be "part of the narrative world, produced by the narrator and directly woven into the narrative discourse by the device of drawing upon them continuously in ekphrastic passages" (Hallet 2009: 133). Images and photographs are, therefore, usually presented in some way by a character, and commented on or referenced within the verbal text. As examples, Hallet suggests the family portraits in Paul Auster's *The Invention of Solitude* (1982) and Micheal Ondaatje's fictional memoir *Running in the Family* (2000 [1982]). He also mentions the work of German author W.G. Sebald. Photographs in Sebald's *The Emigrants* (1993) lend historical authenticity to the entwining tale of four Jewish exiles; *The Rings of Saturn* (1995) offers pictures of the places the narrator travels on his meandering excursion through East Anglia; while *Austerlitz* (2001) incorporates photographs and facsimiles within the story of a man's journey to discover his true identity.

To these, Hallet adds Austrian writer Marlene Streeruwitz' *Lisa's Liebe* (1997), which features photographs purportedly taken by the main character Lisa, and Marisha Pessl's *Special Topics in Calamity Physics* (2006), which includes illustrations that have been drawn by the narrator to compensate for photographs she no longer possesses. We can also cite Alasdair Gray's illustrated novels and short stories, particularly *Lanark* (1981), and Dave Eggers' *You Shall Know Our Velocity* (2002), which uses images in a way akin to Sebald; that is, photographs and facsimiles showing locations that are artefacts from the story. A final example is Lance Olsen's *Girl Imagined by Chance* (2002), a second-person novel that tells the story of a couple who invent an imaginary daughter. Each chapter is preceded by a photograph (made to appear as though stuck down with tape), which the narrative directly comments on, particularly in chapter-openings. For instance, the first chapter opens, "Examine the photograph as closely as you like, only you will not be able to locate the child in it" (Olsen 2002: 13). At this point, second-person reference is apostrophic, gesturing to the reader, though as the narrative progresses it becomes apparent that the "you" most often signals the central male character. The seeming direct address to the reader, though, prompts an explicit engagement with the image, both in terms of the verbal discourse and in terms of the reader's own interaction with the book. Incidentally, *Girl Imagined by Chance* also features a page with a coffee stain (Olsen 2002: 260), which perhaps testifies to a multimodal heritage with intertextual reference to Gass' *Willie Masters' Lonesome Wife*.

Multimodal (re)visions

Multimodal (re)visions appear to be on the rise. Sadokierski gestures towards this trend in mainstream publishing, with novels such as the illustrated re-release of Yann Martel's (2002) *The Life of Pi* by Canongate, and by niche publishing houses which "specialise in the production of illustrated collector's editions of the classics. These are existing novels to which illustrations have been added, transforming the original work into a hybrid creature" (Sadokierski 2010: 24). Among such niche houses, the work of two London-based publishers, Four Corners Books and Visual Editions, is of particular interest. Both are dedicated to visuality in literature and both were nominated in the 2011 Brit Insurance Design Awards.

To date, Visual Editions have only published one multimodal (re)vision in the form of Sterne's *The Life and Opinions of Tristram Shandy, Gentleman*, though there are plans for more, including a working of Marc Saporta's *Composition No. 1* (1961). The *Tristram Shandy* (re)vision reinterprets some of the novel's central visual features: the aforementioned black page becomes text placed under erasure and the marbled page appears like a dot matrix image of a mouth. Another unusual feature occurs in a highly metatextual passage, which in most editions looks thus:

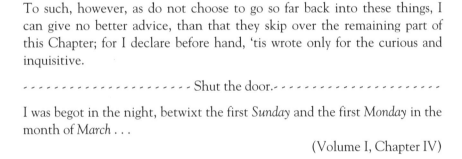

To such, however, as do not choose to go so far back into these things, I can give no better advice, than that they skip over the remaining part of this Chapter; for I declare before hand, 'tis wrote only for the curious and inquisitive.

- Shut the door.- - - - - - - - - - - - - - - - - - - -

I was begot in the night, betwixt the first *Sunday* and the first *Monday* in the month of *March* . . .

(Volume I, Chapter IV)

Here, the directive "Shut the door" has been marked out from surrounding text, and forms a textual divide between the narrator's metatextual comment to readers and the succeeding biographical narrative. In contrast, in Visual Editions' (re)vision, such a divide is further enhanced so that "- - - - - -Shut the door.- - - - - -" is placed on a folded page. To read the words, the reader must unfold, or at least turn, the page; in fact, s/he ultimately has no choice but to unfold it in order to read the following page of the narrative. What is interesting about this design decision is that the folded page and performative gesture it summons has a mimetic quality, whereby folding or unfolding the page can be seen as akin to closing and opening a door. Although not exactly (re)vision, two other multimodal works that depart from *Tristram Shandy* are Martin Rowson's comic-book version (1997) and Eckhard Gerdes (2003) *Cistern Tawdry*, a novel that is visually reminiscent of the typographical play in Federman's *Double or Nothing*.

The multimodal (re)visions of Four Corners Books Familiars Series, designed by John Morgan, comprises novels such as Oscar Wilde's *The Picture of Dorian Gray* and

Bram Stoker's *Dracula*. Produced in collaboration with the artist Gareth Jones, *The Picture of Dorian Gray* (2007) is, according to Four Corners, published in "a large format edition that returns the book to its origins in a magazine." It plays with type size and is interspersed with 1970s cigarette adverts of handsome young men smoking. For *Dracula*, Four Corners teamed up with artist James Pyman for illustration, while designer Morgan used different typefaces for the different character's chapters (diary, letter, etc.), with each font being based on those in use when the book was originally published.

Importantly, multimodal (re)visions should be seen not simply as re-workings but as original innovations which bring a fresh perspective to the novels in question. Anna Gerber and Brit Iverson of Visual Editions declare, "We call these reimaginings. These titles have been about dusting down forgotten (in the case of *Composition No. 1*) and neglected (in the case of *Tristram Shandy*) classics and making them relevant again" (A. Gerber and B. Iverson, personal communication, 3 May 2011). Similarly, Richard Embray from Four Corners books states, "We essentially see the books in the Familiars series as new artistic products. The text is unaltered, except for being newly typeset. But the text is altered by its context, the proximity to the images" (R. Embray, personal communication, 14 March 2011).

Tactile fictions

Tactile fictions are books that play with form in a way that both emphasises their materiality and makes readers engage with them in notably physical ways. Three sub-categories can be included under this heading: epistolary multimodal novels, card-shuffle novels or "model kits," and cut-outs.

The epistolary multimodal novel is of course a novel composed of letters and/or documents. However, in this case, the letters are often folded into envelopes in the pages themselves, and can be taken out and read like real letters, documents, and artefacts. Artist and writer Nick Bantock's work is consistently multimodal and his best selling *Griffin and Sabine Trilogy* (followed by *The Morning Star Trilogy*) is a tour de force. *Griffin & Sabine: An Extraordinary Correspondence* (1991) tells, through letters and postcards, the story of a developing relationship between the artist Griffin and Sabine, a tropical island dweller who somehow psychically shares Griffin's sight when he is painting. For the reader, the book involves a tangible experience of extracting, opening, and reading each letter.

The card shuffle or model kit comes most often in the form of a series of cards, which can be shuffled and read in any order. Central examples are Marc Saporta's *Composition No. 1* (1961), B.S. Johnson's *The Unfortunates* (1969), and Robert Coover's "Heart Suit" (2005). Such books rely on the reader's own creativity, as readers assemble the story themselves. (For more on this genre, see Hayles and Montfort, this volume.)

Finally, the cut-out is a book which features die-cuts, holes literally cut into the books' pages. B.S. Johnson's *Albert Angelo* (1964) featured a cut-out rectangle in one of its pages. Opening a literal window in the text, Johnson revealed fragments of the text located on later pages, thus enabling readers to see events from the future of the narrative. More recently, Jonathan Safran Foer's (2010) *Tree of Codes* is composed completely of die-cut pages (see Figure 31.2). Thus, each page is a web of largely rectangular cut-out shapes. Foer's book has in fact emerged from another book, Bruno Schulz's *The Street of Crocodiles*. Foer carved out his story from Schulz's, cutting away most of the original and leaving the surviving words in their original position on the page. Reading *Tree of Codes* is a delicate act: each page must be turned with fragile care, and as you read the text, words from pages-to-come intrude in the sentence you're reading, materializing through the holes from the depths of pages. Foer's *Tree of Codes* is part-book, part-sculptural object. Tactile fictions explore the physical and material aspects of the reading experience, and remind us that the material book is in itself an art form.

Altered books and collage fictions

Foer's *Tree of Codes* is both a tactile fiction and an altered book, since it modifies an existing text. Crucially, the entirety of the verbal text derives from Schulz's original, in that Foer has not added words of his own but simply selected from Schulz's, thus creating a new piece of literature. A similar process is at work in poet Ronald Johnson's *Radi Os* (1977), his partly erased version of *Paradise Lost*, and artist Tom Phillips's *A*

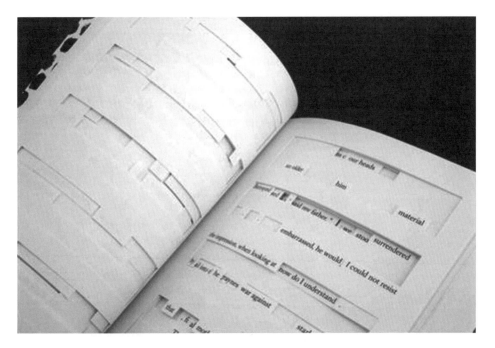

Figure 31.2 Tree of Codes by Jonathan Safran Foer, Published by Visual Editions, 2010. Courtesy of Visual Editions.

Humument (1980), which is continually altered in new editions (most recently an iPad app). For *A Humument*, Phillips painstakingly collected copies of the Victorian novel *A Human Document* by W.H. Mallock and altered the path of its narrative by painting over the pages, leaving only selected words in view (see Figure 31.3). The result is a poetic alternative to the source novel, in which bubbles of text drift across beautiful painted images. (See Epstein, this volume.)

Collage fictions function similarly to altered books in that text is extracted from a source and given new meaning in a new context. The history of the collage novel is often traced back to surrealist Max Ernst, his most famous work in this genre being *Une Semaine de Bonté* [*A Week of Kindness*]. The more recent collage novels of Michael Betancourt, *Artemis* (2004) and *Two Women and a Nightengale* (2004), are evidently influenced by Ernst. Graham Rawle's work is also significant here. In his two novels to date, Rawle uses the collage technique. Firstly, in *Diary of an Amateur Photographer* (1998), Rawle creates the journal or diary of the narrating character Michael Whittingham. *Diary of an Amateur Photographer* uses images and found text from magazines, while the main narrative is typewritten (the words wholly Rawle's own). Rawle's second novel was even more ambitious. *Woman's World* (2005) was created from words and phrases from 1960s women's magazines. Through the transfer of material, moving words and phrases from their women's magazine source into the context of a twenty-first century novel, the story of *Woman's World* is reconstructed, transfigured

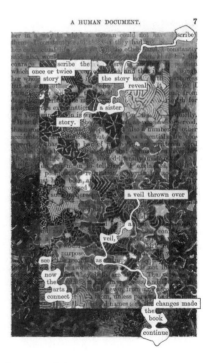

Figure 31.3 Tom Phillips, *A Humument* (1980), pp. 6–7. Courtesy of the artist.

with the inflection of the source material's 1960s bijou voice. Similarly, the new artistic product evokes fresh contemplation on the original text. (Again, see Epstein, this volume.)

Ultimately, altered books and collage fictions are dialogic. They bring about an exchange of ideas. Moreover, in a short empirical study of real readers' responses to Rawle's *Woman's World*, it was shown that collage fictions have a polysemous and polyvocal quality (Gibbons 2012). That is, readers' perceptions of character voice and the visual world of the narrative is inflected by both the original collage novel they are reading and the contexts, perhaps numerous, that the source texts signify.

Concrete/typographical fictions

Probably the most frequent form of multimodal literature is the concrete or typographical fiction, which may (or may not) include images. Some novels that fall under this category have already been mentioned: postmodern works by Federman, Brooke-Rose, and Gass. Concrete/typographical fictions are numerous, diverse, and cross genres. We find typographical experimentations in genre fiction such as science fiction (see Gomel, this volume) – for instance the works of Alfred Bester (in particular, *The Stars My Destination* [1956]) or Jeff Noon (particularly *Cobralingus* [2001]) – and as a transitional leap from childhood reading in cross-over fiction – here, we can cite novels such as Mark Haddon's *Curious Incident of the Dog in the Night-Time* (2004) and *The Selected Works of T.S. Spivet* (2010) by Reif Larson.

In concrete/typographical fictions, the varying quality of type as well as the white space of the page is exploited. Often, the narration of different characters is represented in different font, as is the case with Four Corners' *Dracula*, discussed earlier, and Mark Z. Danielewski's *House of Leaves* (2000), which also creates the spaces of its narrative worlds on the page in concrete prose (see Bray, this volume). Concrete-poetic designs may be used to create images with words, as in Steve Tomasula's *VAS: An Opera in Flatland* (2002) in which the reader encounters spiralling chains of DNA, or in Steven Hall's *The Raw Shark Texts* (2007) in which a flipbook section shows a typographical shark moving towards the reader.

In Ben Brooks' work – *Fences* (2010), *The Kasahara School of Nihilism* (2010), *An Island of Fifty* (2011) – font size is used to endow certain words and phrases with salience. On the page, some sentences are but a mere murmur while others, printed large, forcefully assert themselves. For Brooks, his writing is a form of "emotional montage," the visual dynamics suggesting affect instinctively.

Earl Conrad's *Typoo* (1969), which narrates the life story of the character from whom the novel takes its title, is like Cangiullo's *Caffé Concerto* and Schwitter's *Die Scheuche* in that it uses typewriter symbols and letters to compose images for its narrative. As it announces on its dust jacket, "Typoo is a new kind of literary hero. His adventures are all the more real because his world is only paper and typewriter keys. [. . .] *Typoo* is a new kind of cosmos and literary adventure wrought from the ancient keyboard of a 1915 Underwood Typewriter."

Other works which fall into this category are Douglas Coupland's novels, including *Micro-Serfs* (1995) and *JPod* (2006), Lee Siegel's *Love in a Dead Language* (1999), Salvador Plascencia's *The People of Paper* (2005), Steve Erickson's *Our Ecstatic Days* (2005), Jonathan Safran Foer's work, including *Extremely Loud & Incredibly Close* (2005), Mark Z. Danielewski's *The Fifty Year Sword* (2005) and *Only Revolutions* (2006), Steve Tomasula's *The Book of Portraiture* (2006), and Debra Di Blasi's (2007) *The Jiri Chronicles*.

Ontological hoax

The final category I have called "ontological hoax" since the four works discussed in this section use multimodality to present their narratives in a way which appears to endow them with a greater sense of authenticity (see Mead, this volume, on hoax poetry). As such, these books masquerade as something they are not, disguising their fictional status.

The first two books to be discussed both attempt the same feat, the recovery of a little-known artistic figure, though of course in both cases the artist in question is but a figure of the imagination. William Boyd's *Nat Tate: An American Artist 1928–1960* (1998) caused great controversy. The book, posing as art biography, focused on artist Nat Tate, friend and contemporary of the greats including Picasso and Braque, whose ongoing struggle with depression caused him to burn most of his paintings (thus his lesser known status) before committing suicide at the age of 31. Paintings are featured in the book as part of Tate's opus of works, and of course lend credence to the project. However, its validity was also enhanced by the high status individuals who were "in on the scam": *Nat Tate*'s dust cover endorsement comes from writer Gore Vidal, quotations appear from acclaimed art critic John Richardson, and it was published by 21 Publishing, a publishing house set up by David Bowie who hosted a launch party for New York's glitterati. When it came to light that the art world had been duped, *Nat Tate* caused a sensation in international newspapers.

A less famous example is Greg Boyd's *The Nambuli Papers* (2004), a boxed-set which comprises *The Nambuli Papers* itself, a book about the life of turn-of-the century French magician Aristide Nambuli; *Tidewriters: The Lost Reel*, an experimental documentary by George Beedy (note, initials are shared with the actual author) provided on DVD about an artistic collective called "The Tide Writers" who are connected to Nambuli; *It's Like the Eiffel Tower*, a poetry collection by Bertrand Hébert, a central figure in the Tide Writer collective; and a board game. Of course, all of *The Nambuli Papers* is fictional, but interestingly, it uses both multimodal and multimedial means in its hoax.

Leanne Shapton's *Important Artifacts and Personal Property from the Collection of Lenore Doolan and Harold Morris, including Books, Street Fashion, and Jewelry* (2009) offers another approach by taking on the identity of an auction catalogue. Under this guise and complete with photographs, lot numbers, and item information, *Important Artifacts* tells the love story between Doolan and Morris. Since it does not deviate from the form of an auction catalogue, Shapton's work is highly successful in its guise.

Designer Judith Schalanksy's *Atlas of Remote Islands: Fifty Islands I Have Never Set Foot On and Never Will* (2010) is slightly less successful in its hoax, in part because it is less committed to duplicity. *Atlas of Remote Islands* is exactly what it claims to be, an atlas of disparate islands selected because of their remoteness. A double page spread is devoted to each island: on the right appears a cartographic image of the island, while on the left the reader is presented with important information about it. However, as well as offering geographical statistics, each information page also incorporates a short story involving an imagined world connected to the island; from the new life of teacher Dore Strauch and headmaster Friedrich Ritter on Floreana in the Galapagos Islands to the six-year-old boy who grows up speaking a completely unknown language, incomprehensible to everyone he meets until, at age 33, he encounters a woman from Rapa Iti in the Austral Islands where he goes to live out the rest of his life.

V. Conclusion

Multimodal literature is thriving today in a variety of forms. It also has a long history, intertwined with the history of the book itself. In closing this chapter, I want to return in a sense to where I started: the conceptual shifts of multimodal literature. These conceptual shifts have consequences for the way readers engage with such fictions. In section I, the shift from reader to user was discussed, and I argued for a more performative and engaged understanding of the reader's role in relation to the multimodal work.

Multimodal novels ask readers to cognize and integrate meaning from the creative synthesis of word, image, and tactility. They demand that we create not only the imagined world of the narrative in the mind's eye, but also attend visually to the surface of the page itself. They ask us to reassess what a book is in physical terms. In doing so, they are perceptually and ontologically challenging. It is this challenge, their intense synaesthesic aesthetics, that makes them both enjoyable and experimental.

References

Butler, C. (1994) *Early Modernism: Literature, Music and Painting in Europe 1900–1916*, Oxford, UK: Oxford University Press.

Derrida, J. (1990 [1986]) *Glas*, trans. J.P. Leavey and R. Rand, Lincoln, NE: University of Nebraska Press.

Drucker, J. (2004 [1994]) *The Century of Artist's Books*, 2nd edn., New York: Granary Books.

Dworkin, C. (2003) *Reading the Illegible*, Evanston, IL: Northwestern University Press.

Gibbons, A. (2012) *Multimodality, Cognition, and Experimental Literature*, London: New York: Routledge.

Hallet, W. (2009) "The Multimodal Novel: The integration of modes and media in novelistic narration." In S. Heinenand R. Sommer (eds.) *Narratology in the Age of Cross-Disciplinary Narrative Research*, Berlin: Walter de Gruyter, pp. 129–53.

Lyons, J. (ed.) (1985) *Artists' Books: A Critical Anthology and Source Book*, New York: Visual Studies Workshop Press.

Maxwell, R. (ed.) (2002) *The Victorian Illustrated Book*, Charlottesville VA: The University Press of Virginia.

McHale, B. (1987) *Postmodernist Fiction*, London: Routledge.

Olsen, L. (2002) *Girl Imagined By Chance*, Tallahassee, FL: Fiction Collective Two.

Phillips, T. (1980) *A Humument*, London: Thames & Hudson.

Sadokierski, Z. (2010) *Visual Writing: A Critique of Graphic Devices in Hybrid Novels from a Visual Communication Design Perspective* (unpublished PhD thesis), University of Technology, Sydney.

Sipes, L. and Pantaleo, S. (eds.) (2008) *Postmodern Picturebooks: Play, Parody, and Self-Referentiality*, London: Routledge.

Further reading

Gibbons, A. (2012) *Multimodality, Cognition, and Experimental Literature*, London: Routledge.

Nørgaard, N. (2009) "Multimodality and the Literary Text: Making sense of Safran Foer's *Extremely Loud and Incredibly Close*." In R. Page (ed.), *New Perspectives on Narrative and Multimodality*, New York: Routledge, pp. 115–26.

White, G. (2005) *Reading the Graphic Surface: The Presence of the Book in Prose Fiction*, Manchester, UK: Manchester University Press.

32

INFORMATION DESIGN, EMERGENT CULTURE AND EXPERIMENTAL FORM IN THE NOVEL[1]

Steve Tomasula

---

1 Reading across decades of antique medical journals, one can see a writing convention emerge. First, journals like the *Lancet* functioned as Victorian blogs where doctors posted stories of odd cases, or treatments. Journals then began to relate entries, gradually including issue and page notations. The form of these references grew standardized, emerging as full documentation – modern science – a paper trail allowing the reader to retrace the logic and precedents that culminated in the article being read. The birth of a new norm.

The point of footnote one is that one history of writing is a history of information design: a means of organizing information for effect. Like vases in archeological digs, forms come out of times and places that cause them to be one way and not another. So it is with form in the novel.

I. Information design

Recently, the Museum of Contemporary Art in Chicago mounted a statement-making design show titled "Massive Change." Rather than aesthetic design, the show was interested in "design of the world" – of container shipping, paperless books, and human replacement noses – the many ways, large and small, that design makes our world one way and not another.

Like global shipping, like "The Rocket" in Pynchon's *Gravity's Rainbow* (1973) (see McHale, this volume), the design of information, including form in the novel, can be seen as an example of emergence: the ways in which a myriad of independent interactions combine to bring into existence patterns larger than themselves. Emergence is the principle that explains how, with no central oversight, a city as complex as L.A. always has about the right amount of food on hand instead of lurching between empty shelves and mountains of waste. Emergence helps explain how individual ideas come together as an essay, or the Industrial Revolution. It is also the principle behind the networking models used to describe these emergent phenomena.

It is impossible to be a novelist or poet without employing information design, even if this only means deciding to exclude chapter headings or where to break the line. But even non-literary writing has an architecture: the structure of a grocery list is as different from the haiku as the haiku is from spam, which in turn differs from the traditional novel, which differs from experimental novels such as Raymond Queneau's *Exercises in Style* (1958), a novel that retells the same incident (losing a button) through 99 different rhetorical forms, from dream logic to police report. Some designs, like the grocery list or the narrative arc of the traditional novel, are so familiar that they've become as invisible as the air. Other designs call attention to their constructed nature, allowing the assumptions inherent in information design to become part of the story told. In *Double or Nothing*, for example, Raymond Federman renders one passage as a diagrammed sentence (Figure 32.1).

The reader is forced to turn the book this way and that, thus mimicking the struggle of the novel's young, immigrant protagonist to learn classroom English. It also calls attention to the pedagogical device of diagramming a sentence in order to clarify how it works, turning it into an information design solution that is about its own assumptions: that language can be broken down into its constituent parts and put back together like a machine.

By choosing the architecture of one system, be it a haiku or a repair manual, we enable some values and disable others. Consider three renderings of the Tree of Life (Figures 32.2, 32.3, and 32.4). The first, drawn by Darwin's contemporary Ernst Haeckel (1870), depicts it as an actual tree. As we move closer to our time the tree becomes

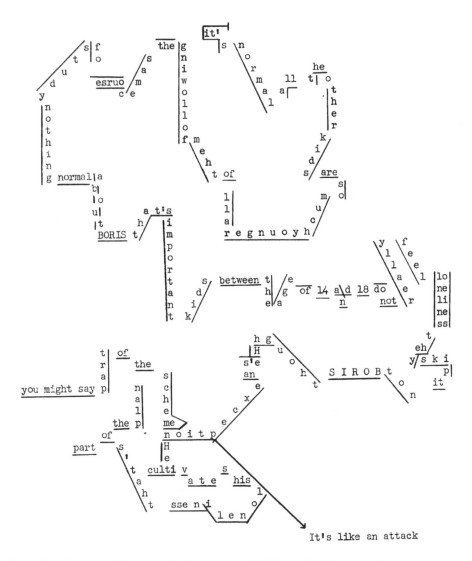

Figure 32.1 Raymond Federman, *Double or Nothing* (1971), p. 138. Courtesy of the author's estate.

less literal, and is drawn in the second example more like a corporate hierarchy than a tree. Finally, the third example depicts it as a wheel like those used to conjugate verbs. All three forms come with connotative layers. The image of an old oak tree gives a sense of age, but not geological or evolutionary age. We also understand that an oak tree can be cut down but not forced to bear pears. The corporately drawn Tree of Life may be of nature, but it is no longer in nature, while the circular design places animals on a continuum of the same DNA stuff: packets of information that can be rearranged, manipulated, patented, here illustrating how genetically close a human is to a mouse is to a human.

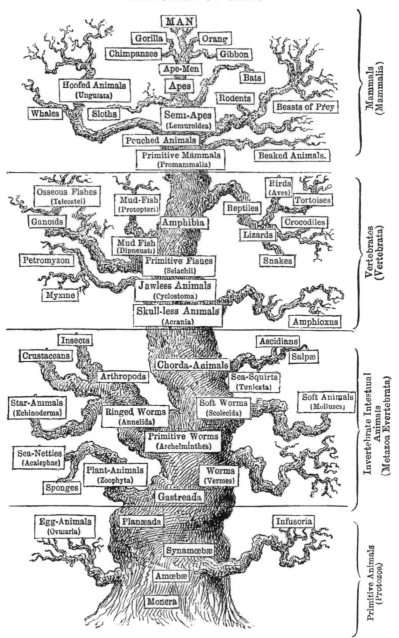

Figure 32.2 Ernst Haeckel, "Tree of Life" (1870).

PRIMATES

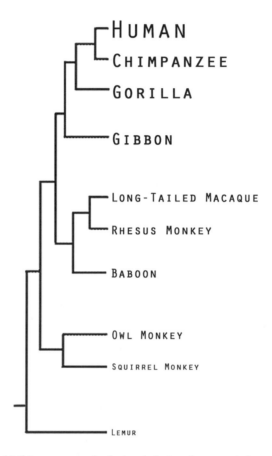

Figure 32.3 "Tree of Life" as commonly depicted during the twentieth century. Created by the author.

Same subject, three different designs, which is to say three different meanings, each of which is also a reflection of its time. It may be that our design of this information has changed because our conception of nature itself has changed. But the question relevant to information design in the novel is which of these forms is most in sync with our times? Which architecture best tells *our* story?

I am offering in this essay a reading of form in novels through the epistemological embodiments in play at the time of their writing, a social-literary history that moves: from reductionist observation in the traditional novel, here defined as a form of the realist novel in which a particular, individual observer can know the world through sense perception; to the modernist novel in which observations are relative to the position of a subjective observer; to the postmodern novel in which observations are

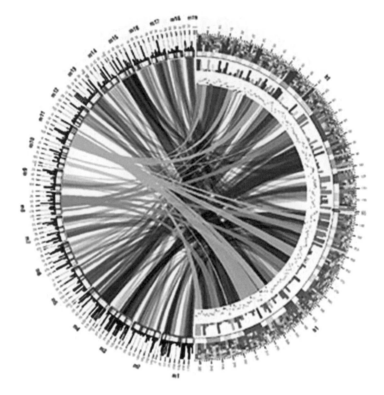

Figure 32.4 "Tree of Life," genetic detail, Martin Krzywinski (Ciros) (2006). Courtesy of the artist.

made with an awareness of the observer as part of what is seen; to the late® postmodern novel of today, in search of a form in sync with the seismic cultural shifts that have come to mark contemporary life as so different in degree as to be different in kind from that of early postmodern culture.

Of these seismic shifts, three in particular seem to stand out: (1) the spread, acceptance, and maturation of networks incipient in early postmodern culture; (2) the attendant waning of privacy, and sense of individual autonomy into a waxing posthuman consciousness; and (3) the emergence of "emergence" over multi-vocal mosaic and other postmodern techniques as a means by which to model decentralized, complex and interrelated phenomenon such as those in 1 and 2.[2]

---

2 As the 'post' of postmodern indicates both an extension and rupture with modernism, "Later" Postmodernism acknowledges maturation, globalization and absorption of the earlier networks and other features that first defined postmodernism. The registered trademark of its spelling is a nod to the consumerist hegemony of the times, and the role of digital electronics in these networks, including the literary today, given that MS-Word auto corrects (r) to ®.

Also, there is a tradition of using wars as watersheds between world orders, and so between periods of art and literature. With this in mind, the nature of the attack of Sept. 11, 2009, on the World Trade Center seems significant. Unlike the mechanized, modern, and symbolically linear trench warfare of WWI, or the massive buildup necessary for a Normandy Beach landing, this attack, in what could be

From Medieval iconography, to Renaissance perspective painting; from the multiple viewpoints of Cubism, to the meta-fiction of postmodernism, much has been written on how the cultural assumptions of an era are embedded in the forms of that era's cultural productions. The Janus-like relationship between zeitgeist and form is part of the reason that visual art, literature, and music have a history; it also explains form in the novel today.

II. Ways of knowing/design of knowledge

"Four score and seven years ago our fathers brought forth on this continent a new nation," begins Abraham Lincoln's "Gettysburg Address," a speech to dedicate a cemetery for soldiers cut down in such numbers that they could only be buried where they fell. It's clear from Lincoln's vocabulary and diction that he was trying to create a memorial in words; the tone of his dedication has the gravity of granite. It invites contemplation.

Conversely, Peter Norvig's parodic rendering of the "Gettysburg Address" as a PowerPoint presentation (Figure 32.5) has the gravity of projector light in a conference room, turning literature into data: 4 score + 7 Years ago = 87 years on a bar graph vs. 0 for "now." Instead of contemplation, Norvig's design of this information invites us to read Lincoln's memorial the way we read the phone book. It also demonstrates how the design of information becomes part of the message conveyed; here a set of factoids presented through standardized presentation tools, immediately digestible and instantly disposable after the immediate use has passed (Norvig 2000).

When Henry James was writing the prefaces that would become his theory of fiction, the universe was Newtonian, and economies agrarian. When John Barth wrote his influential essay defining the postmodern novel, "The Literature of Exhaustion" (1967), relativity was a given, and the first satellites were being launched to connect any point on the globe with any other point and thereby usher in a version of the centerless, global village envisioned by Marshall McLuhan. In light of the cultural developments that would come to be known as postmodernism, it's easy to see how Ronald Sukenick could conclude that "the traditional novel is a metaphor for a society that no longer exists" (1983: 3).

called the first postmodern war, was launched against a symbol of democratic trade by decentralized networks of martyrs using a bricolage of weapons produced by democratic capitalism for use in an open society: the cell phones they used to coordinate their attack; the ATM machines and global markets that allowed them to receive funds from sources scattered around the world; the flight training available to anyone in a capitalist democracy who can pay: a postmodern world, not in theory but as lived experience, that gave this ad-hoc group of individuals a power for mass destruction once only available to nations. The "War on Terror" that ensued, that is, a war declared on another symbol, with its heavy reliance on surveillance, robots, outsourced soldiers and support, data mining, and other Internet components – and its aftermath, still unfolding via Twitter revolutions through the Middle East – might well be called WWWI. Those who use wars as markers of major shifts in the world, and so in literature, might consider these labels for American literary periods: Colonial, Antebellum, Postbellum to WWI, WWI to WWII, WWII to WWWI, and PostWWWI. (See McLaughlin, this volume, on post-postmodernism.)

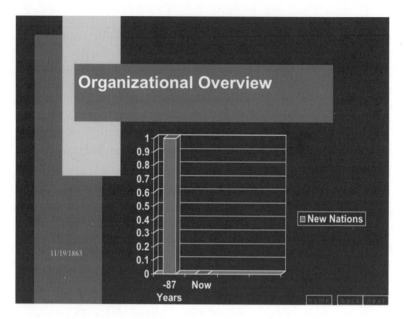

Figure 32.5 Peter Norvig, PowerPoint Presentation of the Gettysburg Address (Slide 5). Courtesy of the artist.

The satellites launched over 40 years ago while Barth and other early adopters were first identifying postmodernism have since become a part of information webs so dense and pervasive that they are used even by late adopters in places well off the information highway for uses as un-mainstream as staging mass protests in Iran, or gang fights in Chicago. Global networks allow tasks as mundane as tax preparation and as exotic as surgery to be performed by workers overseas, while forms of writing pioneered in postmodern novels are commonplace in the common newspaper, which is itself globally and instantaneously disseminated, electronic, revised every few minutes – i.e. fluid, not fixed. It is also written, at least partly, as a wiki, that is, not by critics from the high side of the "high-low" divide, but by the blogging populace, even to the point where experts (art and movie reviewers, photo journalists, field reporters) are deemed dispensable enough to be dispensed with.

Our world is marked by a degree of interconnectedness, virtual reality, decentralization, heterogeneity, genre (and genetic) blurring, surveillance and meta-awareness not seen in early postmodernism. The global is literally local not just metaphoric, and the evidence can be seen in phenomenon as diverse as global warming, or warfare in which soldiers in Virginia operate robots flying half a world away in Afghanistan, using video-game technology to kill actual people until their shift ends and they return from their offices to suburban homes for dinner with their families. Rather than living at a time when biology was unalterable destiny, ours is a time when people no longer need go through life with the nose, teeth, or chemistry they were born with but assume that their bodies, even their DNA, can be edited, patented, and rearranged like text;

ours is a decentralized world in which much of the population interacts Facebook-to-Facebook as often as it does face-to-face. The pocket computers (a.k.a. cell phones) used to coordinate networks, resources, GPS positions, and other information give individuals the power to wage (postmodern) warfare once reserved to nations, while corporations (or increasingly, anyone) can create portraits of what was once thought of as an individual's private life by mining the traces we all leave in data banks simply by living in a society where it is impossible not to leave traces.

Most importantly, the dominant social formations and material facts of day-to-day existence today (at least in the first world) have contributed to a sense of self, and a sense of that self's place in society, that is as different from the sense of self that reigned during early postmodernism, as the postmodern self was different from that of the modernist self, or for that matter, the premodern, Renaissance, Medieval, or classical sense of self. As Gerald Bruns (1998) writes, "the human" has always been a "literary concept," a discursive formation like "the divine." From Ovid's to Kafka's literary experimentations with metamorphoses, to those of today, Bruns notes, "being human," at least as it is imagined in art and literature, is not a given. And today, societal pressures that have come to the fore since the advent of postmodernism are making it increasingly easy to imagine the human as, in the words of N. Katherine Hayles, "an amalgam, a collection of heterogeneous components, a *material-informational* entity whose boundaries undergo continuous construction and reconstruction." It's not that this "Posthuman" is not free, she writes, rather, it is that there is "no *a priori* way to identify a self-will that can be clearly distinguished from an other-will" (1999: 3, 4).

In terms of literature, it's not so much that postmodernism has gone away as that its features have become commonplace. Just as the turn from modernism to postmodernism both facilitated and mirrored a change in the forms used to speak of the contemporary, so the experimental forms visible in postmodern fiction can now be found in all sorts of ordinary writing – from newspapers to school reports – which are increasingly organized as a collage of text, images, video and sound clips, and written with the aid of a networked computer, often running automated authoring software. Likewise, this move from postmodernism to (let's call it) late® postmodernism has brought about a turn toward emergence as an organizational heuristic for the road of life: lived experience that has too many causes, and is too complicated, interconnected or hybrid to reflect through even the multivocal techniques of the postmodern novel.

III. A contemporary form for a contemporary world

In Patrik Ourednĺck's (2005) novel *Europeana*, the twentieth century is told through its statistics, facts, and scientific achievements; its effects, the changes in ideas, and art forms; the unintended consequences of good and bad intentions, and the historical patterns they form by coming together:

> In 1907 a Frenchman crossed the English Channel in a powered aircraft and in 1910 a Peruvian flew over the Italian Alps in a powered aircraft and in 1911

the Italians used a powered aircraft in the war against Turkey and in 1914 aircraft designers figured out where to place machine guns so that aircraft could fire at each other and in 1915 they figured out how to drop bombs from aircraft, and in 1945 the Americans invented the atom bomb and dropped it on a city called Hiroshima. The aircraft was named ENOLA GAY and the pilot subsequently explained to journalists that he had named it after his Irish grandmother, because she had such a funny name. The explosion wiped out most buildings within a radius of three kilometers and a cloud of smoke formed in the sky, which started to be called a mushroom because it looked like one.

(Ourednick 2005: 115)

A very different view of the world emerges than one told through "great-man" version of history, which recounts the past through the force of its individuals: Napoleon, Hitler . . . In Ourednick's telling, history's timeline is a stretched out Slinky of cycles and epicycles, the historical event a result of millions of interconnected micro events. There is no psychological interior in this telling; no postmodern self-reflexiveness. Rather, independent actions as diverse as the first airplane crossing of the English channel and a pilot so oblivious to the gravity of his actions that he can name the instrument of mass death after the funny-sounding name of his grandmother combine with countless other independent actions to form what we call history. The novel progresses not through cause and effect, but by allowing its network of data points and facts to link. Theories of art (Dadaism, Surrealism), theories of man (Evolution, genetic engineering), and inventions (from mustard gas to the bra) are leveled in the march of technological "progress" and the constant effort to "improve man." The flat, matter-of-fact retelling, its juxtapositions and associations of details present history as the result of emergent behavior rather than human will, its genocides and other repetitions as fickle yet repeatable as weather.

Authors and artists in the modern period could not write or paint as if the world never knew of Freud, Picasso, Stein, Einstein, Marx, Darwin, the Wright Brothers, or Henry Ford. Authors during the postmodern period could not choose to live in a world that had never heard of Derrida, Feminism, double-coding, Disney, or chain bookstores. Likewise, authors today cannot live in a world that is not dominated by all of the features of late® postmodernism: the ubiquity and interconnectedness of mature networks, but especially the rise of "pattern as the ground of being," an emphasis on how our genetic pattern makes us one way and not another, an identification of our "selves" with the data traces left by our activities, if not by us, then at least by others.

Surveying the history of literature it is not difficult to see that a sense of what it means to be "human" is inextricably linked to literary form, especially experimentation in the form of the novel. So what might a reformulation of one mean for a refiguration of the other? As Kenneth Burke wrote, a conception of man as that being who stole fire from the gods is going to result in very different works of literature than will a conception that sees man as a link in an evolutionary chain (1968: 83); and by extension we might add, so will a conception that sees man as in possession of a super-abundance of subjectivity, a posthuman, to quote Hayles again, who (that?) appears when pattern (be it in DNA or social networks) rather than self-possessive individualism becomes "the ground of being" (1999: 34).

IV. Information design and network models in the twenty-first century

At this early date in the twenty-first century, it seems that the novel, like the human, is once again a design problem. Or as Hayles puts it, "the old forms of information design do not fit contemporary ways of living, knowing, e.g.: linear theory doesn't work – multicausal systems require other modes of modeling – but chaos theory, complex systems, simulation modeling remains under appreciated and theorized in physical sciences, even more so in social sciences and humanities . . ." (2005: 30).

Social scientist Katherine Faust identifies the basic elements of a social network model by describing a hypothetical one. Like many novels, her example begins with people in an ordinary setting: a group of senior citizens, brought by their individual reasons to a shopping mall. As illustrated in Figure 32.6, modeling their behavior involves a process of abstraction: their interactions are recorded as data which is then used to diagram lines of communication as links between nodes of actors – or we might think of them as characters – and the social network their interactions form (2009).

These elements, then, and the layering of other kinds of information, are the basic building blocks of a network model, a model that in the social sciences can be used to make understandable the messiness of life, or as Joseph Tabbi says of the novel, a model able to organize "vast amounts of information into patterns possessing cognitive value and [narrative] coherence" (1997: 3). More importantly, just as an author may use the novel as a means of discovery, a social scientist might generate knowledge as well as present it: much like an OuLiPo author (see Baetens, this volume), the social scientist employs constraints, algorithms that might relate data in ways that allow patterns that suggest narratives to emerge. Using data gathered from arrest records in

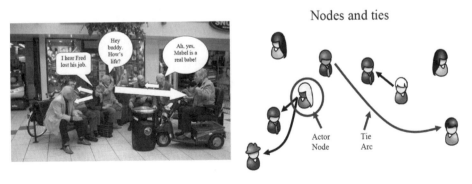

Figure 32.6 Modeling interactions between characters as a process of abstraction (Faust 2009). Courtesy of the artist.

St. Louis, for example, Norm White and Rick Rosenfeld linked crimes that had more than one perpetrator, graphing their interactions according to the principles described above (see Figure 32.7).

By representing the crimes as a social network, their model revealed a previously invisible story: the identities of what might be called criminal hubs, nodes and spokes, with one man, Justin Carver (depicted centrally) involved in a majority of the crimes. While a novelist might employ a constraint such as "no mystical causes" (Frank Norris's *McTeague* [1899]) or "no word in the novel will use the letter 'e'" (Georges Perec's *A Void* [1969]), a social scientist might employ an algorithm such as "connect all phone numbers in which one of the parties called a Swiss bank." That is, both social scientist and novelist build theory into their models.

Reading novels as though they were written to reflect the networks through which contemporary life has organized itself offers up insights not just of the story told, but also of the world from which these forms emerge. In the nineteenth century, for instance, James Fenimore Cooper originally published his first book under the name "A gentleman from New York" since Cooper, like many of his contemporaries, would have thought it vulgar to have his family name appear in public print (1861: 20). We,

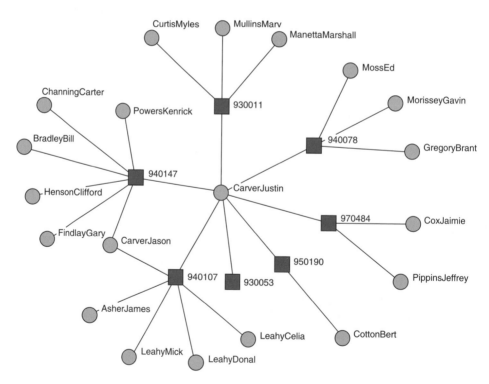

Figure 32.7 Norm White and Rick Rosenfeld, Co-offenders in St. Louis Crime Records (quoted in Faust 2009). Courtesy of the artist.

however, have collectively decided that the convenience of using digital networks of all kinds has been worth the price of allowing privacy to evaporate, making public an avalanche of personal information: what we buy, ask, read, write or look at on-line, the birthday greetings we send and receive; the billions of bits of information we generate are captured in databases maintained by social networking sites like Face-book and Twitter, just to mention two peaks in an information landscape. Facebook alone accounts for 25 billion such exchanges each month, while the private tweets (an oxymoron?) of some 100 million Twitter users are being permanently archived in the Library of Congress. The 4,700 interlinked stores of Wal-Mart, a single business, continually feed a database that holds more than 100 terabytes of data – the equivalent of more than five times the entire contents of the U.S. Library of Congress (Mau 2004: 129). Data-mining software in these and countless other entities creates dynamic por-traits of its "network," in other words its customers. Other algorithms have been cre-ated to generate information maps for purposes ranging from predicting a person's social security number (combining public records for places of birth, and birth dates gleaned from on-line greetings); predicting which Facebook pages have been posted by homosexuals (with 78% accuracy) (Lohr 2010); or which books you'd like to buy or films you'd like to rent.

Every time we make a phone call, use a charge card, or use bits to write a love letter or file for divorce, indeed do most of the things living in the developed world entails, we leave a digital trace. This explosion of information is creating a "data ecology": a wealth of information that ever-more sophisticated analytic tools and computing power make available to anyone with a mind to mine it for useful patterns and infor-mation. To tell stories and paint pictures of who we are, down to the "last redoubts of the personal," as Gary Wolf puts it, noting that "sleep, exercise, sex, food, mood, loca-tions, alertness, productivity, even spiritual well-being are being tracked and meas-ured, shared and displayed" (2010). In the process, we make natural a posthuman sense of self in which humanist ideals such as privacy and uniqueness are less important than the conception of self as pattern.

Obviously, this has ramifications for how we read and write that are as profound as the influence of Freud on the ways in which modernist literature was both interpreted and written; as profound as the distinct turn away from the "celebration of private, subjective experience over public experience" that Barth remarked as one of the dis-tinguishing features of postmodern literature (1967). People think in contexts other than those of our forebears (e.g. feminism did happen; jihads come west; cognitive science eclipses the talking cure; we've lived through revolutions in biology as well as in the humanities). Some authors, like some artists, musicians, or critics, work in forms that explore or otherwise seem in sync with these contemporary ways of think-ing about a contemporary world. Few architects today try to mimic the means, goals and therefore forms of Bauhaus architecture. Few contemporary artists think of art as did the postimpressionists. Fewer of us expect contemporary music to sound like Bach. So why shouldn't our expectations for what counts as a novel, short story, or poem also reflect larger cultural changes? Why should form in the twenty-first century novel, to paraphrase William Gass, be the same as form in the nineteenth-century novel? (Berube 2000).

The form of many hypertexts (see Ciccoricco, this volume) and online or new-media novels (see Tomasula on new media, this volume) seem to inherently embody narrative (and life) as network. Even character-driven novels that explore the rhizomatic nature of life contain within their form a social networking model of living in sync with the multiple connections and multiple causes that are beyond linear plot. Though widely recognized as the first great novel of the twenty-first century, Roberto Bolaño's 2666 (2004), provoked frustration in reviewers who tried to describe the subject in traditional plot, or character-centric terms: "The difficulty is not the novel's heterogeneity of form," wrote William Deresiewicz; like many postmodern novels, "2666 gives us a virtuosic range of narrative modes: academic satire . . . minimalism . . . reportage . . . *bildungsroman* or fictional biography . . . allegory and surrealism . . . The problem is that there is no single central something about which the novel attempts to speak" (2009). The subject of Bolaño's novel, however, is precisely its attempt to speak about a lack of a center, or the "hidden center," as Bolaño referred to it (2008: 896): the "vast solar system of intangible structures" that "underlies society and has its influence in determining the conduct of [individuals and] society as a whole," as social scientist J.L. Moreno described social networks (quoted in Moody 2009). It may be that 2666 is the round peg that cannot fit the square hole of traditional literature, but it maps closely onto the model of social network as narrative: a multitude of characters are introduced, only to disappear completely or become faint traces in the web of connections that Bolaño implies bring into existence larger patterns.

One of the major nodes of this centerless novel is the killer (or killers) of women in an industrial town in Mexico. Critics consistently refer to the murdered women in sum, not as individuals (as one might think of a victim in a traditional murder mystery), while in the novel they are referred to mostly through case reports: data points that are only meaningful in the aggregate. Taken alone, any one of these murders seems meaningless if not senseless. Together, the picture they form is one of bureaucratic inefficiencies, political corruption, and public apathy – as well as the inability of individuals to connect the dots and see a picture of the larger forces that shape their lives. Indeed, it is particularly easy to imagine this novel outlined not as a plot structure, for there are so many plots that it has none, but rather as a network of connections, some as abstract as the shared theories of a group of intellectual literary critics, some as concrete as the machete used to dismember one of the women.

In place of a traditional structure, the novel progresses by allowing the connections, false leads, dead-ends, and other associations between events and characters to gradually become visible, or conversely, fade away. Like White and Rosenfeld's map of St. Louis crime, the links that begin to emerge between characters and events form an information cloud around a reclusive novelist within the novel, Benno von Archimboldi. Only in 2666, there are many crimes that may or may not be related to each other, or any of the other characters and actions in the novel, including Archimboldi himself. Though the critics bring into existence an industry of scholarship that casts

Archimboldi as a man of letters, the author himself may be a serial killer. They never suspect this possibility and the reader never learns the truth, or, indeed, if there is any connection beyond the circumstantial and possibly imaginary relations between the critics, the author, the murdered women, and a host of other players.

As the novel hopscotches across decades, and continents, no crimes are solved; indeed little is revealed, other than a sense of what it is to be alive today, when a desire for inexpensive appliances in America or Europe can create social circumstances that make poor women easy prey in Mexico; a time when people are both individuals and aggregates. As Sarah Kerr wrote, describing this "post-national" novel, "if 2666 contains a lesson it is that people are always from [a] confluence of factors" (2008). It is, in other words, a novel where pattern forms the ground of being, though with our individual, worms-eye view of life, this too is normally invisible to us.

V. Conclusion: new world into new words

Modernist experiments in the novel often consisted of authors' search for forms that allowed them to model deeper and deeper levels of individual experience. Sometimes, they tried to move conceptually outward, to model experience from a position where the individual was not the center of creation: e.g. the social-Darwinism that informed the novels of Frank Norris, or the Marxist novels of André Malraux. If the novel is to continue to say things we can believe about the world, and not just our individual experiences of it, it must adapt, as have all other forms of expression, from art to music to science.

If Haeckel's Tree of Life is congruent with the narrative architecture of Sir Walter Scott, or history as teleology, what structure can be given to narratives so that they are congruent with a world where pattern emerges from many unrelated causes and global networks ensure problems as large as the planet's warming are local? Does the emergence of narrative structures like Wikipedia suggest we are at a point in literary history where it behooves novelists and readers to think of narrative architecture as playfully, as seriously, as open-mindedly, and as rigorously as some poets think of the architecture of their poems – or at least as seriously as Visa and Wal-Mart think of information design? Writing out of the interests of "interdisciplinary discussion," evolutionary biologist Alberto Piazza praises literary criticism "construed as a system that is not bound by the particular instruments it has itself created" (Moretti 2005: 95). His words seem to be a succinct expression of form in the novel as imagined by experimental novelists such as Robert Coover, Carole Maso, David Markson, Lance Olsen, Roberto Bolaño . . . Indeed, in his magisterial history of the novel, Steven Moore concludes that given the "infinite variety" of forms the novel has had and the new forms that continue to be born, only a pedant would try to impose a definition rather than letting the novel show readers what it can be (2010: 33–36).

There will always be a place for traditional forms of prose, of course – the Once Upon a Time and Happily Ever After of the Narrative Arc – just as there will always be a place for the fixed forms of poetry – the sonnet, the villanelle. But stretching the bounds of language beyond its normal use is, of course, partly what distinguishes literature, especially experimental literature, from other kinds of writing. These experiments have had many forms: the soliloquies invented by William Shakespeare; the implied stories of Hemingway's minimalism; Gertrude Stein's abstractions; the tangled forms of Faulkner; L=A=N=G=U=A=G=E poets (see Bernstein, this volume); the flash-animation stories of Heavy Industries (see Tomasula on new media, this volume); or word-image novels such as *Willie Masters' Lonesome Wife*, or Tom Phillips's *A Humument* (see Gibbons on multimodal literature, this volume).

Henry David Thoreau once wrote of the importance of balancing human life with technological progress lest invention become an "improved means to an unimproved end" (1897: 84). The converse is also true: without this balance between the world and its words, we have an unimproved means to an end that is no longer ours.

References

Barth, J. (1967) "The Literature of Exhaustion," *The Atlantic Monthly* (August): 29–34.

Berube, M. (2000) "Teaching Postmodern Fiction Without Being Sure That the Genre Exists," *The Chronicle of Higher Education* 46.37 (May): B4, 2p.

Bolaño, R. (2008 [2004]) *2666*, trans. N. Wimmer, New York: Farrar, Straus and Giroux.

Bruns, G. (1998) "On Ceasing to Be Human," Manuscript of the Roger Allan Moore Lecture at the Department of Social Medicine of the Harvard Medical School in April.

Burke, K. (1968) *Counter-statement*, Berkeley, CA: University of California Press.

Cooper, S.F. (1861) *Pages and Pictures from the Writing of James Fenimore Cooper*, New York: Townsend.

Deresiewicz, W. (2009) "Last Evenings on Earth," *The New Republic* 240(2): 28–41.

Federman, R. (1971) *Double or Nothing*, Chicago, IL: Swallow.

Faust, K. (8 October 2009) "What Is Social About Social Networks," Henkels Lecture Series on Social Networks, University of Notre Dame. [Online.] Retrieved from http://icensa.nd.edu/henkel.html (accessed 21 October 2010).

Hayles, N.K. (1999) *How We Became Posthuman: Virtual Bodies in Cybernetics, Literature, and Informatics*, Chicago, IL: University of Chicago Press.

—— (2005) *My Mother Was a Computer: Digital Subjects and Literary Texts*, Chicago, IL: University of Chicago Press.

Kerr, S. (2008) "The Triumph of Roberto Bolano," *New York Review of Books* 55(20; December): 12–16.

Krzywinski, M. (2006). Ciros. [Online.] Retrieved from http://mkweb.bcgsc.ca/circos/ (accessed 21 October 2010).

Lohr, S. (2010) "How Privacy Vanishes Online," *New York Times*. [Online.] Retrieved from http://www.nytimes.com/2010/03/17/technology/17privacy.html?scp=10&sq=data+mining&st=ny> (accessed 21 October 2010).

Mau, B. (2004) *Massive Change*, New York: Phaidon Press.

Moody, J. (2009) "More Than a Pretty Picture: Visual Thinking in Network Science," Henkels Lecture Series on Social Networks, University of Notre Dame. [Online.] Retrieved from http://icensa.nd.edu/henkel.html (accessed 21 October 2010).

Moore, S. (2010) *The Novel: An Alternative History, Beginnings to 1600*, New York: Continuum.

Moretti, F. (2005) *Graphs, Maps, Trees: Abstract Models for Literary History*, London: Verso Press.

Norvig, P. (2000) "Gettysburg Cemetery Dedication." [Online.] Retrieved from http://norvig.com/Gettysburg/ (accessed 20 October 2010).

Ourednĺck, P. (2005) *Europeana: A Brief History of the Twentieth Century*, Normal, IL: Dalkey Archive.

Pynchon, T. (1973) *Gravity's Rainbow*, New York: Viking.

Queneau, R. (1958) *Exercises in Style*, New York: New Directions.

Sukenick, R. (1983) *In Form, Digressions on the Act of Fiction*, Carbondale, IL: Southern Illinois University Press.

Tabbi, J. (1997) *Reading Matters: Narrative in the New Media Ecology*, Ithaca, NY: Cornell University Press.

Thoreau, H.D. (1897) *Walden*, Boston, MA: Houghton, Mifflin, and Co.

Tomasula y Garcia, A.A. (2010) *Corporately Drawn Tree of Life*.

Wolf, G. (28 April 2010) "The Data-Driven Life," *The New York Times*. [Online.] Retrieved from http://www.nytimes.com/2010/05/02/magazine/02self-measurement-t.html?scp=1&sq=Gary%20Wolf%20the%20data%20driven%20life&st=cse/(accessed 20 October 2010).

33

INTERACTIVE FICTION

N. Katherine Hayles and Nick Montfort

In the digital world, "interactive fiction" is usually understood as a text-based narrative in which the user is offered navigational possibilities (e.g. head north or west), assets to pick up or refuse (such as a sword or key), virtual objects to view and manipulate, and a framework in which the user can win or lose (Montfort 2003a, 2003b). While not ignoring digital interactive fictions, this chapter explores *print* interactive fictions before it turns to the digital realm and then to an exploration of what "experimental" means in the two contexts.

First, some terminological ground-clearing concerning the "interactive." Espen Aarseth (1997) identifies cybertext fiction, and more generally ergodic literature, as requiring "non-trivial work" from the user. By "non-trivial" he means something other than, for example, turning the pages of a codex in linear fashion. In computer programming, "interactive" programs are distinguished from "batch" programs because they require input from the user during execution. Both these usages carry the sense that the text requires the user to make choices, and that these choices affect how the narrative proceeds in a literal (not merely interpretive) sense.

As soon as the user is given choices, the writer gives up complete control of narrative sequencing, ceding some to the user. Given the Aristotelian dictum that a verbal sequence functions as a story because it has a beginning, middle, and end, this puts at risk the ability of a sequence to function as a story. An alternative to the Aristotelian view, emerging recently in narrative theory, is a view that emphasizes instead the ability of narratives to catalyze the creation of storyworlds (Emmott 1999; Herman 2002). The storyworld approach focuses on the integrative nature of narrative comprehension, the mental activities whereby readers locate events, actions, and states within an imagined world from which they can holistically draw inferences to fill in narrative gaps, understand motives, etc. In David Herman's words, "storyworlds are mental models of who did what to and with whom, when, where, why, and in what fashion in the world" (p. 5) constructed by readers (or listeners). Focusing on "storyworlds" rather than "stories" enables additional dimensions of narrative analysis to emerge other than the traditional distinction in narrative theory between "story" (the events that happened) and "discourse" (the way in which the events are told). For example, when the framework of "story" and "discourse" is used, the dominant emphasis tends to fall on the difference between the order of events as they would logically occur and the sequence of events as they are narrated, making temporality a pre-eminent concern (Ricoeur 1990). By contrast, the storyworld approach also considers how readers (or listeners) spatialize information so as to locate it within a navigational space, an especially important consideration for computer interactive fictions, as we will see. Moreover, the storyworld approach allows the microdesigns of a narrative – states, events and actions – to be correlated with macrodesign principles that determine whether the narrated events, can be located precisely in time or the time is left indeterminate, whether the style and rhetoric correlate with one genre or another, and whether the storyworld's spatiality is precisely delineated or fuzzily evoked. In short, the storyworld approach starts with the insight that readers engage in cognitive mapping through textual (or spoken) cues and from these construct a mental model of the world, within which everything else can be located, contextualized, and inferentially understood. Evidence for the importance of storyworlds includes empirical studies showing that readers do not distinguish sharply (or at all) between inferences they make from cues relevant to the storyworld and verbal indicators explicitly present in the text (Emmott 1999: 3–20).

Seen in this light, writers have another tool complementing narrative sequence; if the storyworld is robust, then various sequences, told in different orders, can fit into it without hopelessly confusing the reader or user. William Faulkner's *The Sound and the Fury* (1991 [1929]) illustrates this process. The novel consists of four narratives focalized through very different characters, including a disorienting opening sequence told from the point of view of Benjy, a mentally disabled adult who sees the world as a very small child might view it. Readers can understand the four narratives as diverse perspectives that simultaneously construct and transform the storyworld; triangulating between the different narratives, they can figure out which components are common across all the narratives, and which are idiosyncratic to a given narrator's perspective. Without a common world model as an interpretive guide, readers would be unable to understand the quirks and twists that are the textual cues to the specificities of each narrator in turn.

This framework raises the question how storyworlds come into being, including how long they take to establish, refresh, and develop. *Hint Fiction* (2011), edited by Robert Swartwood, gives us (as the title promises) a hint. Defining the genre as micro-stories of twenty-five words or less, Swartwood mounted a competition and received two hundred entries. From these, he chose twenty to appear in the *Hint Fiction* anthology. Correctly assessing that the Aristotelian view would not be appropriate for such short short stories, he argues that "Hint Fiction should not be complete by it having a beginning, middle, and end. Instead it should be complete by standing by itself in its own little world" (Swartwood 2011: 28). The stories illustrate the claim. Consider "Reminder" by Marshall Ryan Maresca: "The tiny stain never came out. No one else would notice, but he always knew. They were his favorite pants" (150). Is the stain from semen, blood, or simply food? The story does not indicate, but readers know enough to be drawn to the enigma and to create a sketch of the protagonist. A more ominous example is Joe Schreiber's "Progress": "After seventeen days she finally broke down and called him 'Daddy'" (93). The narrative invites readers to imagine a kidnap and rape scenario, complete with the point of view implied by the ironic title. We may conclude from these examples that for interactive fictions, storyworld creation and narrative sequencing provide complementary parameters authors can arrange in different patterns to achieve a wide variety of effects.

In the next three sections, the chapter considers the experiences of reading print interactive fictions in the form of random shuffles, multiple reading paths, and annotations, respectively. The chapter then considers the specificities of computer interactive fictions.

I. Random shuffle

At one end of the spectrum are fictions where the sequencing is undetermined and the storyworld extremely fragmentary (see Gibbons, "Multimodal," this volume). Marc Saporta's *Composition No. 1, roman* (1961) presents as a box of loose pages, with instructions telling the reader to shuffle before beginning. The work creates a storyworld so fragmentary that, although many have heard of this work, almost no one has succeeded in putting it together into a coherent narrative (Montfort 2002). Further along the spectrum is B.S. Johnson's *The Unfortunates* (2009), a boxed set of pamphlets that have pre-set opening and closing segments but otherwise can be read in any order. The pamphlets intermix a sports writer's account of a day at a soccer match with recollections of a friend who lived in that town and died from cancer. The randomness of the sequences works in part because the opening and closing segments set up and conclude the storyworld, and in part because they mimic the ways in which memories of the past can intrude upon the present when appropriate triggers are present.

Robert Coover's "Heart Suit" (2005) uses a similar strategy of a pre-set beginning and ending, although here the narrative engine relates not to memory but to the fairy tale worlds characteristic of Coover's early stories, such as "The Door" and "The Magic Poker" (Coover 2000 [1969]). "Heart Suit" takes shape as a title card and fourteen large cardboard playing cards, with a typical deck design on one side and, on the other, text headed by a playing card number and heart sign. The title card is used to set up the storyworld: in a monarchical society, the King of Hearts discovers that the tarts baked for him by the Queen have been stolen. Introduced are, among other characters, the Lord High Chamberlain, the Jester, the Cook, the Flautist, and the mysterious White Knight, who in subsequent cards gambol through ribald combinations as suspected tart-thieves and the Queen's lovers. The cleverly crafted texts begin and end in mid-sentence, so that narrative sense emerges no matter what the order in which the cards are read. The random combinations are possible in part because the story is archetypal, dealing with themes of sex, suspicion, interrogation and state power.

The card designated as last, the Joker, provides a sense of conclusion (although not of conclusiveness) by having the (multiply identified) culprit hanged, although whether justly or not is impossible to tell. Whoever he is, the culprit is reminded that

"Death is the inevitable punchline for the joke called life. It's always the same joke, all that matters is the telling" (Coover 2005: n.p.) To emphasize the point, the Joker card narrative ends with a second tray of tarts also being stolen, a development that sends the King into a rage and has him calling for the suspects to be brought before him all over again. "But surely you know everything already," the Queen reproaches him, but he ripostes, "I know nothing!" The Queen concedes – "have it your own way" – but assures him that "when you are done, you will see that I am right," a final line that implicitly invites the reader to re-shuffle the cards and play again (Coover 2005, n.p.).

II. Multiple reading paths: horizontal and vertical

While the examples above explode the codex into an unbound set of texts, another version of print interactive fiction is a hypertext offering multiple reading paths through a codex, the simplest form of which is the beloved children's genre, *Choose Your Own Adventure* (CYOA). Interaction designer Christian Swinehart (2009) has analyzed the genre by quantitatively evaluating a set of twelve books from 1979 to 1986. His analysis shows an increase in linearity over time, a result suggesting that, after the novelty of the genre wore off, readers preferred fewer decision pages (if a, go to page x; if b, go to page y) and more narrative development. For more sophisticated literary hypertexts, these results suggest that creating, refreshing, and developing a storyworld is crucial to a work's appeal. The problem then is how to integrate several different narratives sequentially through time so that the reader maintains interest (and remembers sufficient details) in all of them. Julio Cortázar's *Hopscotch* (1966 [1963]) offers the reader (at least) two reading sequences, one linear through the codex, the other through the number sequences offered in the work's preface. Since the storyworld is consistent through both sequences – containing the same characters, events, and actions (although with significant differences in meanings) – the work offers readers choices without risking dispersion into too many different kinds of storyworlds.

Another way in which this game can be played is by creating a multivariant structure that can be read straight through, encountering a mass of material in which different storyworlds are encountered in rapid succession (a reading strategy we will call "horizontal"), or by jumping around so as to string together a number of related narrative segments (the "vertical" strategy). While vertical reading creates more narrative consistency, horizontal reading makes clearer the cross-links that tie diverse narrative sequences together.

Georges Perec's richly complex *Life: A User's Manual* (1987) (*La Vie mode d'emploi* [1978]) exemplifies this kind of structure (see also Baetens, this volume). The text is constructed as an archeology of a Parisian apartment building at 11 Rue Simon-Crubellier. Imagine that the building's façade is removed and all the rooms exposed; the text's sequence performs a knight's move from level to level, as if the rooms constituted a 10 × 10 two-dimensional chessboard. Moreover, these moves visit each room once and only once, executing a mathematical strategy called the Knight's Tour.

This OuLiPian constraint is supplemented by a number of other arbitrary constraints, including forty-two lists of ten objects each, gathered together into ten groups of four, with the last two special "Couples" lists. The experience of reading the text straight through is staggeringly complex. Not only are the occupants characterized through one hundred narratives scattered throughout the 500-page text; also detailed are their possessions, furniture, floor and wall coverings, among much else. Even items lost or found on the staircases and stored away in the cellars are inventoried. Many of these catalogues conform to the constraints operating upon the text, but this does not much help the reader struggling to keep the thousands of details in mind.

Here we see the intrusion of non-narrative elements into the text, with the result that the text can be seen as edging toward a hybrid form combining narrative with database (see also Tomasula, "Information Design," this volume). Among the ways in which database logic differs from story logic is the manner in which sequences are constructed (Hayles 2007; Manovich 2001: 212–37). Whereas narrative implies causality, agency and intention, databases operate through declarative commands that concatenate together different kinds of data elements and data values. One points to a human world in which conscious agents model other minds and their surrounding contexts (Ritivoi 2009), the other to an informational realm of decontextualized data elements strung together by commands performed by algorithms. The one operates according to story logic that is exclusively human; the other to formal logic and a world shared by humans and intelligent machines.

One way to emphasize the narrative component over the database elements is to jump around so as to read sequentially the narratives of each apartment within the building, a strategy that gives a clearer sense of the present (and past) occupants but that tends to obscure the way in which the text uses its operative constraints. Among the narratives emphasized by this reading strategy is the story of Bartlebooth, a fabulously wealthy occupant who decides to devote his life to a quixotic project subject to a number of constraints, including that the project leave no lasting monument (Perec 1987 [1978]). He spends ten years learning to paint watercolors, then another twenty years visiting seaports around the world to paint five hundred pictures, allowing himself two weeks per watercolor. These he sends to Winckler, another building occupant and master craftsman, who glues them onto wood backings and cuts them into jigsaw puzzles of fiendish complexity. The last twenty years Bartlebooth commits to assembling the puzzles at the rate of two weeks per picture. Each of the watercolors is then re-glued together, delicately removed from its wood backing, and taken (or shipped) to its port of origin and dunked into a water-based bath, dissolving the colors. The blank paper is then returned to Bartlebooth.

The project functions as a *mise-en-abyme* or metaphor for the work (as do a number of other artistic projects, including the painter Valène's attempt to paint the apartment building, complete with him at his easel in his apartment, painting the picture in which he is enframed (see McHale, this volume). In these reflexive representations, the reader occupies the role of puzzle solver and the author that of the puzzle maker. In the "Preamble," readers are warned that "despite appearances, puzzling is not a solitary game: every move the puzzler makes, the puzzle-maker has made before; every piece the puzzler picks up, and picks up again, and studies and strokes, every combination he tries, and tries a second time, every blunder and every insight, each hope and each discouragement have all been designed, calculated, and decided by the other" (1987 [1978]: n.p.). Significantly, Bartlebooth dies while working on the 439th puzzle, thus never completing his grand design and leaving open the possibility that Perec's design is similarly flawed and incomplete.

Another massively complex print text using horizontal/vertical multiplicity is Milorad Pavić's *Dictionary of the Khazars: A Lexicon Novel* (1989). In "Preliminary Notes to the Second Reconstructed and Revised Edition," the "editor" tell us that the *Dictionary* presents in alphabetical order everything extant about the Khazars in the Christian, Islamic, and Jewish traditions. The three traditions agree on the originating event: in the tenth century, the kaghan of the Khazars has a dream and invites representatives of the three religions to his court to interpret it, promising to convert to the religion of whoever gives the most satisfying interpretation. The competition is held, and one account is determined superior to the others, with the kaghan converting to that religion. Subsequently, however, the Khazar kingdom is invaded and the population dispersed, with the result that the polemic's outcome is lost in the mists of history, although this does not prevent each religion from claiming that its representative was the victor. The subsequent three books (Red for the Christian, Green for the Moslem, and Yellow for the Jewish) contain narratives of varying lengths, sequenced according to the alphabetic listing of the entries. As the "editor" advises us, we can read straight through (the horizontal strategy), follow each entry (for example, "Ateh," the first one) through each of the three traditions (the vertical strategy), or simply skip around randomly (the shuffle approach). Reading vertically allow a more precise delineation of the characters and story elements, while reading horizontally plunges us into a stupefying mass of details.

When the vertical and horizontal strategies are combined through several (re)readings, a meta-narrative emerges that creates a storyworld stretching across millennia and involving mythic, demonic, and human players (Hayles 1997). At its center is the body of Adam-the-precursor (called Adam Cadmon or Adam Ruhani in the various traditions) who occupied the third rung of heaven until he revolted. Unlike Lucifer, he repented and returned to heaven, only to find that he had lost his place and was now relegated to the tenth rung. Yearning after his previous position, his immense body drifts between the third and tenth rungs, stretching out and compressing in endless cycles of dispersal and reassembly. The dream hunters (led by Princess Ateh) have been striving to (re)assemble parts of his body for millennia, believing they can locate fragments within the dreams of mirror-symmetrical pairs who dream each other's lives (they have been working for several centuries on the left thumb). They are opposed by the demons, which scatter and destroy the records that the dream hunters strive to assemble; the conflict intimates that the Body of Adam is also the Book, specifically the *Dictionary of the Khazars*. The reader, like the dream hunters, can arrive at the meta-narrative only by piecing together fragments, so the dream hunters'

457

quest serves as a metaphor for the dynamics of fragmentation and assembly crucial to both enterprises. Like *Life: A User's Manual*, the work has within it multiple representations of itself, using *mise-en-abyme* scenes to represent both the storyworld and the reader's relation to it.

III. Multiple paths: annotation

Another way to create a multiple-path print story is to fashion a narrative to which annotations are attached; these quickly grow into a story in their own right and threaten the hegemony of the putative "main" narrative. Two outstanding examples serve to illustrate the challenges and possibilities of this form: Vladimir Nabokov's *Pale Fire* (1962) and Mark Z. Danielewski's *House of Leaves* (2000). Separated by nearly forty years, the two works show the increasing influence of data-mining and data-searching on literary form, with the later work edging closer to the narrative-database hybrid, and the earlier one still firmly located within a narrative universe.

Recalling the conclusion emerging from Swinehart's analysis that the CYOA genre became more linear over time, we may wonder how the interplay between the two narratives (putative main body and annotations) evolves within each work, and evolves over time between the works. Storyworlds may be created with very few words, as we have seen, but to persist over time in the reader's mind they must be refreshed periodically with textual cues; moreover, to hold the reader's interest they must grow into complex universes within which the narrative dynamics continue to form new configurations and intrigues. A way into these complexities is to graph the amount of text in the "main" narrative versus the amount of text in the annotations. The rhythm between the two as they alternate may yield insights about narrative construction, especially how the interplay between narrative sequencing and storyworld construction takes place in our two examples.

Pale Fire presents as a 999-line poem by John Shade, a famous American poet living in New Wye, preceded by a "Foreword" and followed by a 222-page commentary by Charles Kinbote, the quirky academic who rents the house next to Shade and believes himself to be the exiled King of Zembla. When Shade is killed by a bullet fired by a man Kinbote believes to be a would-be assassin after him (or perhaps after the Judge from whom he rents the house), he grabs the note cards containing the poem and absconds with them, determined to discover in them his own story as Zembla's king. When he finds an autobiographical work about Shade's life and struggle to find meaning in the face of death, he attaches his commentary in an obvious attempt to hijack the poem to his own design. Both poem and commentary create storyworlds, although the two are orthogonal to one another, intersecting only through the "plexed artistry" of wrenched reflections and coincidental conjunctions.

Let us suppose that the conscientious reader goes through the text by flipping back and forth between the poem and commentary (a possible reading strategy, although since the commentary entries are not marked in the poem itself, I suspect that most readers would read in linear fashion, or perhaps take Kinbote's self-promoting suggestion in the "Foreword" to read the commentary first, then the poem, then the commentary again). Graphing the amount of text for each commentary entry against the line numbers of the poem yields the following diagram (Figure 33.1). The length of commentary text corresponds to the length of each line, and the long vertical black lines indicate the poem's division into four cantos (Canto 1 and 4 comprise 1/6 each of the total lines, and Cantos 2 and 3 comprise 1/3 each).

The diagram shows a pattern of short comments, many of which function as legitimate annotations of the kind a bibliographic scholar might use, followed by longer bursts of narrative introducing the (perhaps hallucinatory) kingdom of Zembla and Charles the Beloved's adventures as revolutionaries stage a coup and he is forced to flee. Notice that the longest narrative sections occur in the commentary to Canto 1; this is where the Zembla storyworld is introduced and Charles's role in it is developed. Canto 2 shows an alternating pattern of short comments and longer narrative sections. The effect here is not only to continue to give textual cues about the Zembla storyworld and develop it further, but also to reinforce Kinbote's role as legitimate commentator. Indeed, one of the central conflicts in his narrative is the tension between his desire to wrench the poem to his own interpretation and his aesthetic appreciation of it as a work of art. At one point he introduces a "variant" (1989 [1962]: 74, commentary to l. 12) that he has clearly made up himself – testimony to his desire to have the poem be about him and not about Shade's crisis of faith – but later retracts it, acknowledging that the lines are "distorted and tainted by wishful thinking. It is the *only* time in the course of the writing of these difficult comments, that I have tarried, in my distress and disappointment, on the brink of falsification" (1989 [1962]: 227–8, commentary to l. 550). Canto 3 is where Shade wrestles with his daughter's suicide and his own near-death experience; this section constitutes the poem's crisis, and Kinbote's commentary is accordingly relegated to relatively short entries. With Canto 4 and the poem's conclusion, Kinbote's narrative again occurs in longer sections, appropriate to the climax and its aftermath.

By representing the alternation between Shade's poem and Kinbote's commentary visually, the diagram makes apparent patterns that may be difficult to discern from sequential text. Moreover, it shows the strategic interplay between annotations and longer narratives that, in effect, create two related but distinct storyworlds in the commentary – Kinbote as exiled King of Zembla and hallucinatory academic, versus

Figure 33.1 Amount of commentary text for each line of Shade's poem. Created by the author.

Kinbote the aesthete and admirer of the poem's art. The diagram shows that the two parameters in play here, sequence and storyworld construction, are artfully arranged not only with respect to the commentary's interventions in the poem but also in the alternation between Kinbote's belief in Zembla and Kinbote's aesthetic appreciation of the poem.

In *House of Leaves*, the annotations occur as footnotes at the page bottom. This apparently slight difference from *Pale Fire*'s commentary placement at the poem's end has significant implications, for it creates a very different pattern between the "main" narrative and the narrative that unfolds in the footnotes. In effect, the amounts of space the two narrative discourses occupy becomes a zero-sum game, for the more the "main" narrative extends, the less page space is available for the footnotes, and vice versa. The "main" narrative is related by Zampanò, an old man writing about *The Navidson Record*, a video, he warns us, that probably does not exist. It depicts the entanglement of Will Navidson, his partner Karen Green, and their children and friends with an impossible object (Alber 2009): a house that is bigger on the inside than the outside. When a door mysteriously appears in the Navidsons' living room wall, they discover it opens into a space stretching to more than the earth's diameter and older than the solar system. Zampanò's commentator is Johnny Truant, a dissolute twenty-something who has discovered the old man's manuscript after he dies and has attempted to put it into order, with annotations that soon blossom into the story of his encounter with his own demons.

Figure 33.2 is a diagram of the first five chapters (pp. 3–73) that shows the amount of page space taken up by Zampanò's narrative (noted as "Z's narrative"), his own footnotes (noted as "Z's notes"), Johnny's notes (noted as "J's notes"), and last but not least, the rare footnotes contributed by the book's putative editors (noted as "Ed.'s notes").

The diagram shows that the creation of Zampanò's storyworld is soon followed by a large narrative section creating Johnny's storyworld. Interestingly, the pattern displayed shows that much less emphasis is placed on Johnny's role as commentator than was the case with *Pale Fire*. In part this is because Zampanò provides his own footnotes (with a pattern reminiscent of Kinbote's shorter interventions). More importantly, however, it is because Johnny feels relatively unconflicted about his role as commentator; his major trauma relates to his family history and the effect Zampanò's narrative has on him. The diagram shows that his shorter comments are often immediately followed by larger narrative segments, indicating a consistent pattern of development over these beginning chapters. The editors' footnotes, limited to only two interventions in this section, are extraordinarily important, especially the second one (p. 67); it advises readers to skip ahead at that point and read the appendix containing the letters of Pelafina, Johnny's mother institutionalized for insanity. If the reader takes this advice, she is likely to contextualize the rest of the narratives through the lens provided by those letters. Alert to the many resonances between the narratives and the letters, she may conclude that neither Zampanò nor Johnny is the enframing narrator but Pelafina herself. If, on the other hand, the reader ignores the advice, she

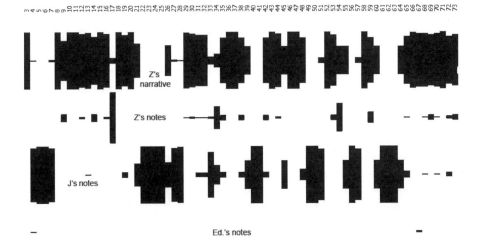

Figure 33.2 Page space occupied by Zampanò's narrative ("Z's narrative"), footnotes ("Z's notes"), Johnny Truant's notes ("J's notes") and the editors' footnotes ("Ed.'s notes") for the first five chapters of *House of Leaves*. Created by the author.

will encounter Pelafina's letters after concluding Zampanò's and Johnny's stories, a sequencing that makes Pelafina's letters echo the preceding narratives rather than position itself as the source of the echoes.

The two diagrams of *Pale Fire* and *House of Leaves* demonstrate that quantitative analysis and visual display may extend and complement insights about the interplay between sequence and storyworld. The interpretive strategy enacted here views spacing and typographic display as part of the textual cues available for storyworld creation and thus also for the reader's understanding of the ways in which the interplay between two or more storyworlds generates meaning.

IV. Interactive fiction on the computer

The computer programs that have been called "interactive fiction" since the 1980s seem, at first, to be connected to print interactive fiction only in a few stylistic ways and via the popular genres which relate to them. An interactive fiction on the computer (IF) is not a book, but a program that simulates an underlying world and, by accepting typed input and producing textual output, presents a subjective view of that world. Whereas sequence is an issue with the bound codex, in IF sequence is less important; moreover, in the codex storyworlds are constructed through textual cues, whereas in IF the storyworld is presented less as a narrative construction and more as a space to navigate and explore. The spatialization activities that are included in the storyworld framework here become a dominant feature of the reader's mental activities and a principal means by which the storyworld is constructed and understood, as witnessed by the prevalence of directional commands and the maps that many IF interactors draw to orient themselves within an IF storyworld.

It is not incidental that computer interactive fiction calls very strongly for its interactors to construct storyworlds. The essential elements of an interactive fiction program include the parser, which is responsible for interpreting natural language input, and the world model, a simulation that is the system's counterpart to a reader's world model. The map that an interactor draws is a representation of an underlying simulated geography and architecture. Characters in interactive fiction act and react because of programmed behaviors. These dynamic aspects of the storyworld are modeled explicitly in interactive fiction, while a single, sequenced linear narrative is not present to begin with. Such a narrative only arises from interaction with the interactive fiction's world model.

The workings of the world model show an important distinction between a multisequential text and a computer interactive fiction. There are also similarities to particular print interactive fictions. As in CYOA books, the main character is typically the narratee, and the text unusually addresses him or her (the gender of this character is usually left unstated) as "you." The typical early interactive fiction is also an adventure story. The earliest ones, including *Adventure* (Crowther 1975) and *Zork* (Anderson, Blank, Daniels and Lebling, 1979), offered Tolkienesque fantasy worlds inspired by *Dungeons & Dragons*. The programmer/authors at Infocom, a U.S. company founded by the creators of *Zork* and others, went on to create interactive fiction that systematically explored different popular genres: mystery, science fiction, humor, and romance. During the commercial heyday of interactive fiction, there were certain projects that were more concerned than others with literary values and effects, including Brian Moriarty's *Trinity* (1986), Steve Meretzky's *A Mind Forever Voyaging* (1985), the adaptation of *The Hitchhiker's Guide to the Galaxy* (1984) that Meretzky did with Douglas Adams, and Thomas M. Disch's *Amnesia* (Disch and Bentley 1986). The most systematic attempts to produce literary fiction were at the short-lived company Synapse, which brought Robert Pinsky in to develop *Mindwheel* in collaboration with Steve Hales (Pinsky and Hales 1984). Commercial IF was usually popularly oriented and not centrally concerned with literary experimentation, in contrast to hypertext fiction of the late 1980s and early 1990s.

Perhaps the most significant factor in the emergence of more experimental interactive fiction was the collapse of the commercial market for IF. While avant-gardes have historically needed their mainstreams to react against, experimental interactive fiction has started to emerge without one, bringing in radical literary techniques from other digital and non-digital writing. To the extent that IF reacts against any mainstream, it is one that is several decades old. Interactive fiction had been the leading form of entertainment software in the early 1980s; by the early 1990s IF companies had closed or turned to making different sorts of games. At the same time, high-quality development systems became available to individuals at low or no cost, and growing access to the Internet allowed people to easily distribute programs worldwide. It was plausible by 1995 for programmer/authors to write interactive fiction without being part of a company or needing to find a market for their work. Thus, there was no reason that the interactive fiction produced by individuals had to be in a popular genre or otherwise needed to imitate the commercial production of the previous 15 years.

A striking divergence from the usable, playable commercial norm is seen as soon as one starts *Bad Machine* (1998), an interactive fiction by Dan Shiovitz. The screen fills with cryptic tags that suggest a hive-like activity; then, the usual textual exchange begins and a description of the surrounding area is offered. This codework-like text is also inscrutable, filled with unusual punctuation, referring in its style to status outputs, database queries and results, programming languages, and error and warning messages. In *Bad Machine*, the interactor controls a robot which is defective in certain ways and which can disassemble and reassemble itself. Shiovitz, in a similarly cryptic Web page and in an in-game note, refers to several of his inspirations, which include net art site Jodi.org and the board game Cooties (see Elias, this volume).

Bad Machine, although very unusual to look at, is reasonably traditional in its basic structure and construction. The interactor commands a main character who explores an unusual environment. There are extensive puzzles; solving them can allow the interactor to reach a winning ending. But the interactor's engagement with *Bad Machine* is certainly prompted more by the unusual and appropriate style of the text and the nature of the puzzles than by some underlying traditional narrative. The prose style and the puzzles require that the interactor read and act as a robotic consciousness would. Rather than reading for the plot, the interactor is reading for texture, style, and ways of functioning.

At century's end Sam Barlow (Barlow 1999) released an interactive fiction, *Aisle*, which begins by explaining, "You will . . . be asked to define the story by controlling one instant in the life of the man whose story it is. Your intervention will begin and end the story." *Aisle* is unusual in that it admits only one command from the interactor. One can restart and try a different action, but it is not possible to perform more than one action in a row in *Aisle*'s simulated world. Because of this, *Aisle* is stateless; there is no current situation to save and later restore, no notion that one can make more or less progress in the storyworld. It can be understood as a hypertext: a set of lexia, each one link away from the starting text. One must guess the links, however. These examples illustrate that the interface conventions of interactive fiction are important in making guesses about how to reach interesting texts.

Aisle begins with the main character standing in a supermarket, remembering when he last had gnocchi, in Rome. The texts that can appear in response to one's first and only command represent various things that happen in the supermarket and recall various stories about the main character and a woman named Clare. After trying a few standard commands, one may get the sense that the main character has experienced loss, felt bitter, or even become emotionally damaged. Continuing to try different commands will reveal some narratives which subtly or obviously conflict. As the opening note says, "not all of the stories are about the same man." *Aisle* explores a connected set of lives and memories, a banal consumer situation, and the conventional commands that work in interactive fiction. It suggests interesting storyworlds (several related ones) through brief moments, simulated and remembered, rather than through a lengthy puzzle-quest or some other longer traditional narrative.

An interactive fiction directly inspired by experimental writing practices, and particularly by the OuLiPo, is Nick Montfort's *Ad Verbum* (Montfort 2000). The game framework is a parody of the typical treasure-hunt situation: All objects must be cleared out of a house by a day laborer. To accomplish this, the interactor has to type commands under the same constraint used in the room description and other textual outputs. For instance, in the Sloppy Salon ("Simple social space, sadly spoiled. Some skewed situation's sequel, surely. Seemingly, slovenly students sojourned – scraping, scratching, scuffing surfaces.") the interactor must use commands in which every word begins with S. PICK UP STAPLER will not be effective; it will only elicit a message such as "Stop! Stop! Show some sense. Scribble suitable strings." A command that does work in this case is SEIZE STAPLER.

The challenge in *Ad Verbum* is not figuring out what to do but determining how to properly express commands – a challenge to interactors as readers (since they must determine what constraint the output text was written under) and as writers (since they must come up with short constrained texts that are the necessary commands). *Ad Verbum* does not present a powerful narrative arc, and it does not even do much along the lines of world-building. It mainly invites an unusual engagement with language, one that is reflected in a few quirky characters and in some aspects of the environment.

Another experimental IF is novelist Alan DeNiro's *Deadline Enchanter* (2007); the title joins the titles of two Infocom games, one a detective story and the other a magical fantasy, but this interactive fiction is not a mash-up of those two. The voice that comes through is that of a programmer/author who is working to put the simulation together as the interactor is experiencing it: "I will implement one person. For 'local color.' Quick – do you see him?" Indeed, *Deadline Enchanter* seems to be hastily and only partly implemented. Room descriptions, which are shown every time the main character looks around, contain text that seems as if it was meant to be presented only once. Some actions that are required are essentially impossible to guess. On the other hand, walkthroughs of each area, stating exactly what needs to be typed in to progress, are found within the game in plain sight. Clearly the experience of *Deadline Enchanter* is not a typical one of exploration and puzzle-solving. Rather, it offers a somewhat halting, fragmentary, and odd conversation with someone who purports to be building the world that is being experienced.

V. Conclusion

The histories of interactive fiction in print and digital media suggest that the connotations of "experimental" differ according to the specificities of the media, their histories of development, and the expectations of readers. One way to think about what makes a text "experimental" in interactive fiction is that it twists, perverts, or plays with the reader's expectations for work in that medium and with that particular history. Situated within a strong tradition of codex fiction, "experimental" print interactive fictions may play with typography, sequencing, narrative arc, and the collision of multiple storyworlds. In digital interactive fiction, by contrast, "experimental" may mean playing with ideas of winning or losing, having a world to explore, exploring it through a set of typical commands, and interacting through a more or less standard computer interface. This conclusion may serve as a cautionary note to positioning "experimental" as an ontological property with attributes that are the same for every place and every time. As is clearly seen when digital and print works are considered alongside one another, "experimental" achieves meaning in relation to media-specific practices and the historical specificities of diverse traditions.

References

Aarseth, E. (1997) *Cybertext: Perspectives on Ergodic Literature*, Baltimore, MD: Johns Hopkins University Press.

Adams, D. and Meretzky, S. (1984) *The Hitchhiker's Guide to the Galaxy*, Cambridge MA: Infocom.

Alber, J. (2009) "Impossible Storyworlds – and What to Do With Them," *Storyworlds: A Journal of Narrative Studies* 1: 79–96.

Anderson, T., Blank, M., Daniels, B. and Lebling, D. (1979) *Zork I–III*, Cambridge MA: Infocom.

Barlow, S. (1999) *Aisle*. [Online.] Retrieved 3 February 2011, from http://www.ifiction.org/games/play.phpz?cat=&game=232&mode=html

Coover, R. (2005) "Heart Suit," *McSweeney's 16*, San Francisco, CA: McSweeney's Quarterly Concern.

Coover, R. (2000 [1969]) *Pricksongs and Descants*, New York: Grove Press.

Cortázar, J. (1966 [1963]) *Hopscotch*, trans. G. Rabassa, New York: Pantheon Books.

Crowther, W. (1975) *Adventure*. [Online.] Retrieved 3 February 2011, from http://www.rickadams.org/adventure/e_downloads.html; http://www.youtube.com/watch?v=4TkV9y15XRw

DeNiro, A. (2007) *Deadline Enchanter*. [Online.] Retrieved 3 February 2011, from http://www.ifarchive.org/

Disch, T. M. and Bentley, D. (1986) *Amnesia*, San Mateo CA: Electronic Arts.

Emmott, C. (1999 [1977]) *Narrative Comprehension: A Discourse Perspective*, Oxford, UK: Oxford University Press.

Faulkner, W.1991 [1929]) *The Sound and the Fury: The Corrected Text*, New York: Vintage.

Hayles, N.K. (1997) "Corporeal Anxiety in *Dictionary of the Khazars*: What Books Talk About in the Late Age of Print When They Talk About Losing Their Bodies," *Modern Fiction Studies* 43(3), 800–20.

Hayles, N.K. (2007) "Narrative and Database: Natural Symbionts," *PMLA* 122(5), 1603–8.

Herman, D. (2002) *Story Logic: Problems and Possibilities of Narrative*, Lincoln NE: University of Nebraska Press.

Johnson, B.S. (2009) *The Unfortunates*, New York: New Directions.

Manovich, L. (2001) *The Language of New Media*, Cambridge, MA: MIT Press

Meretzky, S. (1985) *A Mind Forever Voyaging*, Cambridge MA: Infocom.

Montfort, N. (2000) *Ad Verbum*. [Online.] Retrieved 3 February 2011, from http://nickm.com/if/adverbum.html

Montfort, N. (2002) "Reading Notes: *Composition No. 1* by Marc Saporta." [Online.] Retrieved 3 February 2011, fromhttp://nickm.com/if/composition_no_1.html

Montfort, N. (2003a) "Toward a Theory of Interactive Fiction." [Online.] Retrieved 3 February 2011, from http://nickm.com/if/toward.html

Montfort, N. (2003b) *Twisty Little Passages: An Approach to Interactive Fiction*, Cambridge, UK: MIT Press.

Moriarty, B. (1986) *Trinity*, Cambridge MA: Infocom.

Nabokov, V. (1989 [1962]) *Pale Fire: A Novel*, New York: Vintage.

Pavić, M. (1989 [1978]) *Dictionary of the Khazars: A Lexicon Novel in 100,000 Words*, trans. C. Pribićević-Zoric, New York: Vintage.

Perec, G. (1987) *Life: A User's Manual*, trans. D. Bellos, Boston, MA: David R. Godine.

Pinsky, R. and Hales, S. (1984) *Mindwheel*, Palo Alto CA: Synapse Software.

Ritivoi, A. D. (2009) "Explaining People: Narrative and the Study of Identity," *Storyworlds: A Journal of Narrative Studies* 1, 25–41.

Ryan, M.-L. (2004) "Multivariant Narratives." In S. Schreibman, R. Siemens and J. Unsworth (eds.), *A Companion to Digital Humanities*, Oxford, UK: Blackwell. [Online.] Retrieved 3 February 2011, fromhttp://www.digitalhumanities.org/companion/view?docId=blackwell/9781405103213/9781405103213.xml&chunk.id=ss1-4-9&toc.depth=1&toc.id=ss1-4-9&brand=default

Saporta, M. (1961) *Composition No. 1, roman*, Paris: Éditions du Seuil.

Shiovotz, D. (1998) *Bad Machine*. [Online.] Retrieved 3 February 2011, from http://www.ifarchive.org/; http://collection.eliterature.org/1/works/shiovitz__bad_machine.html

Swartwood, R. (2011) *Hint Fiction: An Anthology of Stories in 25 Words or Fewer*, New York: W.W. Norton.

Swinehart, C. (2009) "One Book, Many Readings: CYOA." [Online.] Retrieved 3 February 2011, from http://samizdat.cc/cyoa/

Part III
EXPERIMENT NOW
Beyond the page

34

DIGITAL FICTION

Networked narratives

David Ciccoricco

I. Introduction

Digital fiction is uniquely positioned in its ability to use new and still relatively unfamiliar tools to mobilize formal and material innovation in expressly literary fashion while using the same tools to reflect on a cultural moment of great technological change. Though digital fiction is still very much in a formative stage, and likely to change more quickly than other forms to mirror changes in software tools and hardware capabilities, this chapter will present a survey of the kinds of texts one can expect to find in its domain. I will suggest that digital fiction extends the tradition of experimental literature in significant ways, including innovations in narrative perspective and representation of consciousness, spatio-temporal dynamics of the text, and a form of creativity best described as "algorithmic" or "processual." I will further suggest that digital fiction marks the emergence of a distinctly new narrative poetics – namely a poetics of the link and node – that can offer new insights into the composition and reception of literary art in light of participatory digital media, and I will close with a consideration of specific examples that animate these innovations in compelling ways.

II. Techno-literary field(s)

The tradition of experimental literature is typified by its subversion of conventional form, technique, and genre. Thus, it is ironic that the early years of digital fiction were punctuated by a preoccupation with genre adoption or formation – that is, its entrance into the mainstream. It was an entirely reasonable preoccupation, for its vehicle, the personal computer, was mainstreaming its way into offices and homes in technologized societies worldwide, and it was quite clear that at least one future of literature – or, in the alarmist vein, a future without it – would play out on its screen.

Further complicating the relationship between the mainstream and digital fiction early on was the fact that some saw the collision of pop culture and the avant-garde as an inevitability in light of the Web, giving rise to Mark Amerika's (n.d.) endorsement of formulations such as "avant-pop" (see Olsen, this volume). Either way, contemporary fiction writers typically grouped in the basket of experimentalism were compelled to comment on this new mode of writing with hyperlinks, in the spirit of curiosity and celebration (Coover 1992, 1993) as well as dismissiveness (Barth 1996) and subversion (Barth 1997). In John Barth's online "Click," a short fiction replete with feigned (blue, underlined) hyperlinks, he champions the "hypertextuality of everyday life." It was arguably the popular attention that these artistic experiments garnered, however, by virtue of their pervasive medium and the musings of such prominent literati, which fuelled popular misconceptions. Rather than an innovative literary practice sustained by a small but dedicated group of (primarily academic) artists and theorists, "hypertext fiction" found itself cast into a competition that it could not win and in which it did not belong: that of usurping over 500 years of literary tradition in print and "liberating" the narrative line.

Walter Benjamin has noted that the "history of every art form shows critical epochs in which a certain art form aspires to effects which could be fully obtained only with a changed technical standard, that is to say, in a new art form" (1968: 237). It would be careless, however, to reduce all literary innovation to either the aspiration toward or reflection of technical change, and it is important to recognize that a new medium does not establish a new genre by default. It takes time for certain applications of new tools to coalesce into recognizable literary practices (read: genres) even while we acknowledge the necessity to continually remake and refashion such categories. Furthermore, much of what is valuable about digital fiction is in fact its continuity with both traditional and experimentalist narrative fiction in print, drawing at once on the temporal contortionism, literary Cubism, or proto-hypertextuality of Jorge Luis Borges, John Barth, Robert Coover, Italo Calvino, Julio Cortázar, Milorad Pavić, Alain Robbe-Grillet, Samuel Beckett, and Gertrude Stein, while reanimating the earlier stylistic sophistication and allusiveness more commonly associated with high Modernism and the likes of Ezra Pound, Virginia Woolf, or James Joyce. (See Pressman 2007 for more on works of digital literature that enter into a self-conscious dialogue with Modernist texts.) We can locate a further continuity with the practice of established writers of print fiction, such as Milorad Pavić (in *The Glass Snail*, 2003), Lance Olsen (in *10:01*, 2005), and Steve Tomasula (in *TOC*, 2009), entering into collaborations to produce digital fictions. As Astrid Ensslin points out, "literary hypertext" is "*the* digital poetic form most akin to the book (2007: 3; emphasis in original).

Techno-literary forms such as digital fiction, then, thrive neither in the margins of mainstream media consumption, nor in direct opposition to the longstanding dominance of print, but rather circulate in a complex media ecology (Tabbi and Wutz 1997) of cultural and artistic production where, plainly stated, some media are better at certain things than others (see Hayles [2007] for a lucid discussion of "hyperattention" vs. "deep attention," and Bell *et al.*'s [2010] comments about media and modal affordances in relation to software tools). What we have seen thus far in the field, nonetheless, is a testament to the possibility of writing on and for the screen with conceptual depth and discursive complexity that grows ever more comfortable with its own reflection in the mirror, or rather, the screen. In turn, such writing truly deserves its place among experimentalist literary practice, not by virtue of its medium, but rather as the result of a co-evolution of compositional techniques and the digital systems that give them shape.

Any conception of digital fiction must rely on a fundamental premise of non-transferability. While it might be innovative for a novelist to publish her latest novel entirely online, say in the form of a downloadable file, this novel by definition is not a work of digital fiction; if a group of scholars decides to test reading habits by using an *existing* short story in print adapted into a multilinear hypertext format (a chronic flaw of much empirical research on the topic), they are not, by definition, conducting research on reading digital fiction. It is, in this sense, fiction written for and read on a computer screen that pursues its verbal, discursive and/or conceptual complexity through the digital medium, and would lose something of its aesthetic and semiotic function if it were removed from that medium (Bell *et al.* 2010).

Digital fiction encompasses the growing range of primarily text-based and narrative-driven literary practices that fall within the wider domain of digital literature (also known as electronic literature). Digital literature would include anything from a poem that uses Flash animation software to a novel that uses hypertext technology, and can also refer to blogs, wikis, or even email, especially when these textual forms are appropriated or subverted for literary ends (see Matthew Baldwin's *The Live Journal of Zachary Marsh* [2004] for a literary appropriation of blogs; the *A Million Penguins* [2007] project for a collaborative, wiki-based creative writing experiment; and Rob Wittig's *Blue Company* [2001/2002] for an example of a serialized narrative distributed via email). Moreover, digital literature can include video games, especially when such games reveal an investment in narrative mechanics, the projection of coherent fictional worlds, or any form of ludic participation that draws conspicuously on the world of letters for its play (see Ensslin, this volume). While all of digital literature, in the aesthetic understanding of the term, draws on fiction, and much of it contains narrative elements, it is possible to delimit the category of digital fiction, both in synchronic and diachronic fashion.

First generation digital fiction

Even though certain forms of digital fiction predate the earliest forays into digitally hyperlinked fictions (such as interactive fiction, discussed in section II below; see also Hayles and Montfort, this volume), the first generation of digital fiction can be characterized as works published in stand-alone format either on computer disc or (later) on CD that rely on hypertext authoring systems for the construction of narrative texts made up of nodes interlinked in a network. This form of digital fiction was popularly known as hypertext fiction, hyperfiction, and literary hypertext. These first generation texts are written and read primarily but not exclusively with the Storyspace hypertext authoring software, and published (and distributed primarily through) Eastgate

Systems, the first and to date only commercial vendor dedicated to digital literature and related software systems. Some prominent early works, such as Deena Larsen's *Marble Springs* (1993), were written in HyperCard, a hypertext authoring software widely distributed with Apple computer operating systems in the late 1980s.

The commonalities shared by some of the earliest output of this generation have given rise to the designation of a "Storyspace School." Circumscribed not only by a means of production, there was a tendency for its artists to be academics (many of them involved in composition pedagogy), and their work was mostly confined to a common region (predominantly North America). There were, however, parallel developments that similarly merged the notions of narrative and database, such as Judy Malloy's conception of "narrabase," which she used to conceptualize her own work, some of which was later published with Eastgate (Malloy 1993; Marshall and Malloy 1996). Of course, again, one needs to avoid the trap of technological determinism, and resist collectivizing this group based *merely* on a shared software application, and we can find further aesthetic justification for such a designation.

Many of these writers were entrenched in a Modernist poetic sensibility (Aarseth 1997: 76–96), invoking for instance the meta-motif of piecing together a lost whole, which some lamented as yielding "conventional novels" in new form (Amerika 1998). They also shared more specific thematic preoccupations, such as an emphasis on mapping and topography and the unfamiliar "spatiality" of networked texts (Joyce 1995: 105–17; 2000: 150–78; Bernstein 1998), as well as a fascination with the "crash" (Moulthrop 2001), which productively exploited the word's dual meaning of motor vehicle accidents and computer breakdowns. (The reader is in fact encouraged to "crash" John McDaid's *Uncle Buddy's Phantom Funhouse* [1992] by running one of its nodes as code.) Some notable major works of the first generation of digital fiction include: Michael Joyce's *afternoon* (1990), J. Yellowlees Douglas's *I Have Said Nothing* (1994), Bill Bly's *We Descend* (1997), Shelley Jackson's *Patchwork Girl* (1995), M.D. Coverley's *Califia* (2000), and Stuart Moulthrop's *Victory Garden* (1991), a work that remains unsurpassed in terms of its varied and sophisticated rhetorical deployment of links. All of these works either pre-date the World Wide Web or do not make use of it and its *lingua franca*, HTML (HyperText Markup Language), to create and stage the text.

Second generation digital fiction

The Web brought about wide-reaching changes for digital fiction, most visibly in opening up further potential for the multimodal fabric of such texts (see Gibbons, "Multimodal," this volume). Web browsers allowed for the stable presentation of text, image, sound, and video, fostering synergies between them through a brand of textual kinetics that enlarged Umberto Eco's conception of the "work in movement" (Ciccoricco 2007: 62–70). Even though most of those who view/ read / listen online today will take it for granted, the "key achievement of HTML as a standardized mark-up language was its propensity to create a variety of different semiotic systems, previously analogue, i.e. separated in terms of mediality and materiality, on the basis of a unified, text-based programming code" (Ensslin 2007: 21). Web-based fiction marked a movement away from the budding hegemony of node-link-node digital fictions of the first generation. The Web also gave writers cause to test the limits of limitlessness, so to speak, in a digital environment in which all texts are, in theory, boundless and equidistant. Indeed, some writers embraced this brand of freedom vigorously: the collectively written *The Unknown* (Gillespie, Marquardt, Rettberg, and Stratton 1998–2001), which sought to re-inscribe the notion of the encyclopedic novel in the Web, was not only an "experiment in the network novel" (Rettberg 2003) but also an experiment in hypertextual excess.

The Web brought about a further irony, however, for digital-literary experimentalists: on the one hand, there have never been more self-sufficient producers and distributors (and in some cases, vendors) of their own art. Online publication opens a potentially direct and immediate path from writer (sender) to reader (receiver); in addition, it marks the shift from a readership model of "one-to-many" to "many-to-many" and turns the literary underground into a literary "overground" (Amerika 1995) in the process. On the other hand, artists are now more than ever reliant on others for creating elaborate multimedia texts, as some works require a full-blown production team. Steve Tomasula's recent *TOC: A New-Media Novel* (2009), for instance, lists over a dozen names in its "Crew and Credits." Of course, what concerns writers experimenting with narrative fiction in digital environments goes beyond obstacles that are purely technical in nature. Ultimately, when we consider the literary potential of the Web, we are reminded of a central – perhaps *the* central – paradox of digital media and narrative fiction: while our notions of the digital entail immediacy, excess, speed, and consumption, our notions of narrative entail history, selectivity, reflection, and contemplation.

Some notable major works of Web-based digital fiction would include: Mark Amerika's *Grammatron* (1996), Geoff Ryman's *253* (1996), Deena Larsen's *Disappearing Rain* (2000), Erik Loyer's *Chroma* (2001), and Judd Morrissey's *The Jew's Daughter* (2000), which makes a timely intervention in the realm of Web-based fiction itself by using Flash animation software to appropriate the design apparatus of the printed page while at the same time employing a form of digitally mediated transition that subverts the reader's expectations of hyperlinks. There are scores of other notable shorter works, some by the same authors; examples include Erik Loyer's *The Lair of the Marrow Monkey* (1998), Shelley Jackson's *My Body – a Wunderkammer* (1997), Rob Swigart's *About Time* (2002), Martyn Bedford and Andy Campbell's *The Virtual Disappearance of Miriam* (2000), and Michael Joyce's *Twelve Blue* (1996).

Across generations

There have been various critical-historical moves to mark "generations" of digital fiction, and it is helpful to consider various models. Some critics focus on a shift from primarily text-based digital fictions to those that more fully incorporate images or other media elements such as sound and video, thereby emphasizing a shift – to invoke the terminology popular in early criticism – from "hyper*text*" to "hyper*media*." With or without these terms, it is indeed possible to locate such a shift in the mid-1990s (Hayles 2008: 188). Others focus on the level of readerly control, adding a third category (Van Looy and Baetens 2003) or generation (Ensslin 2007) that consists of "cyber-texts" in which the human operator relinquishes some control to the machinic one, leaving the text's computational composition to effect some degree of performativity.

While any distinction that affords the uniquely processual quality of programmable media due emphasis is useful, retaining "digital fiction" (or "electronic fiction") across generations nevertheless serves an added, dual purpose: it cleanly subsumes "hyper-text," which has long expired in its service as metonym signifying the broader field of digital-literary practice, and instead treats it as first and foremost the *technology* that enables digitally mediated linkages. In addition, it reserves "cybertext," in proximity to its original theoretical context (Aarseth 1997), as the methodological lens through which we can examine the variable configuration of any text, regardless of its medium. After all, many of the earliest digital fictions contain some element of cybertextual machinic control (in the form of Storyspace's "guard fields" for instance), whereas many texts that exhibit a much higher degree of computational control still make use of hypertext technology.

In conceiving of digital fiction's generations, it is worth noting that more recent works such as Tomasula's *TOC* (2009), published on DVD, demonstrate that the stand-alone quality of first generation works is not necessarily an absolute or strictly historical characteristic. Perhaps more significant in terms of synchronic classifica-tions, however, is the recognition that a work of digital fiction, whether it is pub-lished as a stand-alone hypertext system or as a Web-based Flash-animated text, can do dramatically different things with the narrative line. Toward that end, to distin-guish between fundamentally different narrative structures we can retain the basic categories used to describe hypertext documents in general: axial, arborescent, and networked (Ciccoricco 2007: 5–7). An axial narrative can refer to a narrative where digressions are present in the form of glosses or notes that are secondary to the main narrative; a reader returns to the main text after the digression. An arborescent (or branching) fiction, by contrast, can refer to a narrative with branches but specifically those that contain mutually exclusive story events or outcomes; a reader of an arbo-rescent narrative makes choices at bifurcating points in the text and continues on until the end of one of the branches is reached. A networked narrative, or "network fiction" (Ciccoricco 2007), then, differs not only in its nonhierarchical organization but also in that its narrative emerges gradually through a recombination of elements in a database. The three-part formal distinction can apply synchronically across fields, and serves as a vital corrective to assumptions that digital fiction either never ends or always aspires to a perpetual variability. To describe such narratives, Ryan (2001) appropriates the notion of the "Aleph," a reference to the Borges story of the same name. In the Borges fiction, the Aleph is a cabbalistic object that allows its viewer to behold the entirety of history and humanity; the Alephic text, then, is in theory a narrative that contains all narratives, and in actuality one that entertains the utopian fantasy of the computer as inexhaustible literary machine.

Interactive fiction (IF)

Since they require decisions at branching points that always imply temporal progression at the diegetic level, interactive fictions (or IFs) are a form of arborescent fiction. IFs differ from the forms of digital fiction outlined so far in marking a movement away from interpretation and towards configuration in how we approach and experience a textual artifact. More specifically, beyond an initial prologue establishing backstory, IFs require repeated textual input in order for the text to progress, providing textual output for each input in turn. In order to successfully traverse the text and advance toward an optimal outcome, the reader indulges not hermeneutical faculties primarily but rather puzzle-solving ones. IFs also differ, for that matter, in that they accommodate a "Final Situation" (at the level of the program) or "Final Reply" (at the level of the narrative discourse) (Montfort 2003), given that a distinct *lack* of closure typifies many other forms of digital fiction.

Predating the earliest use of hypertext technology for narrative fiction, and building on the advancements in natural language processing and Artificial Intelligence popularized by Joseph Weizenbaum and his interactive chatterbot application ELIZA, IFs have a rich history dating back to the mid-1970s with landmark titles such as *Adventure* and *Zork* (early IFs, it is worth noting, were most always adventure-themed texts). More recently, several factors have contributed to a resurgence of this form, including the availability of Do-It-Yourself software that makes IFs easier to create and the social networking power of the Web that makes them easier to share.

A compelling form of digital fiction in their own right, IFs serve as an instructive limit case between the attraction of narrative elements on one hand and gaming elements on the other (see Montfort and Moulthrop [2003] on how Adam Cadre's *Varicella* [1999] confidently and convincingly negotiates this divide). While the form is a powerful demonstration of how "algorithmic creativity" orchestrates a ludic engagement with a dynamically generated text, it is certainly also a form of literary art making a contribution to literary innovation. IFs can live as stand-alone applications or online, and hybrid forms of branching digital fiction exist. Ruth Nestvold's *Joe's Heartbeat in Budapest* (n.d.), for example, employs hyperlinks to allow for a circumscribed number of inputs: to advance a dialogue with their sole interlocutor/narrator, the reader can choose either *Yes*, *No*, *Maybe*, or *Bitch*. Nestvold's self-described "hypertextual conversation piece" is a wonderful example of how a complex socio-interactional exchange can arise from simple initial conditions.

III. Reading digital fiction

Without a doubt, the most visibly innovative quality of digital fiction is its ability to amalgamate multiple modes of text, image, sound, and video into one "surface" and accommodate the semiotic interplay that results. This semiotic interplay magnifies the brand of literary experimentation in the latter half of the 20th century that mashed and mixed communications media – what John Barth ambivalently called "intermedia" and "mixed means" art (1982 [1967]). The same quality, moreover, necessitates an enlargement of what we think of as literary and indeed, our conception of literacy itself. But in terms of extending experimental literary practices, perhaps less overt but no less significant are the changes that digital fiction ushers in for narrative poetics. Here we can point to both an extension of certain innovations in narrative art and the establishment of new ones, as illustrated by Erik Loyer's *The Lair of the Marrow Monkey* (1998), a form of short networked digital fiction.

A *mindful* Lair

In terms of narrative perspective, the *Lair* exhibits the established technique of multivocality; but here voices change not from chapter to chapter, or, for that matter, within the discursive storm of a single paragraph, but rather from hypertextual node to node. The transitions can yield rich juxtapositions. In one instance, we move from the narrative report of "Duck at the Door" to that of "Orion 17" (the characters go by what sound unmistakably like Web usernames, another ironic detail in a text that otherwise treats its technology so cryptically). In the seventh episode, "Duck at the Door" concludes his narration by noting that, after talking to him, Orion 17 "left to go watch science fiction with Perry," the third guinea pig of the trio. The eighth episode continues with the same narrator, who indulges a rather lyrical and ethereal musing in verse. But the ninth and final episode, narrated by Orion 17, begins: "I told Perry I wasn't going to watch Star Trek with him tonight." (Notably, in a distinctly McLuhanesque nod to "old media," both pivotal moments in the story revolve around television: first, Orion 17, a chronically unemployed music school graduate, is struck by a glorious vision while watching a commercial for a used car dealership, then later this decision not to watch television forms the story's mock-climax.) It is a mundane confession that nonetheless subverts the expectation of both his colleague and the reader, as we move through links that serve to both connect and partition the text. The juxtaposition is enriched further by the stark visual contrast that accommodates a different design and color scheme for the different voices.

Digital fiction also innovates with respect to narrative representation of fictional minds. For example, in the second episode, titled "I couldn't sleep, that night," readers must use the mouse to hover over a number of dynamic image-text elements and integrate them into a moving circle in order for a grammatically coherent text to display underneath the image frame (see Figure 34.1). We start with the letter "i," which adheres, quite appropriately, to the center of this circle, suggesting that Orion17 cannot escape his own sphere of conscious perception. At the same time, when we hover over the word "sleep," we find that this is one element that we are not able to bring into the circle (its dark font on a dark background makes it difficult to even see). As it remains elusive for the protagonist, so too for the reader chasing words on a screen.

Figure 34.1 The start of episode two, Erik Loyer's *The Lair of the Marrow Monkey* (1998). (Screenshot from: http://www.marrowmonkey.com/lair/02.htm.) Courtesy of the artist.

The user interaction thus enacts a visual focalization along with a textual one; that is, though the words still signify narratologically as text on a two dimensional plane, their graphical arrangement performs a focalizing function more akin to the camera perspective in film or video games (where such perspective can often be controlled). Given that the perspective taken here is on abstract and not representational material, however, it ultimately differs from both, and the ability to manipulate the words iconographically animates the metaphor of chasing sleep in turn.

The visual-textual display and the reader's intervention in it become increasingly more layered, complex, and reflexive as Orion17's synesthetic condition grows more intense: "I suddenly realized I was seeing the inane music there in front of me, in patterns that shimmered before my eyes" (Loyer 1998: 2). Examples such as this mark an extension of the project of concrete and L=A=N=G=U=A=G=E poetry (see Bray, this volume, and Bernstein, this volume), but can also be said to transcend it with recourse to the kinetic potential of digital textuality. A plurality of voices – of minds at work – distributed across strata of (often recurrent) nodes can further exploit the materiality of the digital network to explore the notion of distributed cognition. Such an exploration is as relevant to the *Lair*, where we encounter a near-spiritual concordance of minds albeit through the network of an entirely nebulous medium, as it is to the reader of digital fiction, who becomes part of an integrated cybernetic circuit in the very act of reading. Other notable critical meditations on the notion of distributed cognition in relation to digital media and hypertext can be found in Hayles (2008: 74–85) on the work of Judd Morrissey, and Joseph Tabbi (2002: 119–44) on Stephanie Strickland's digital poetry.

A *topological* Lair

The networked and programmable nature of digital fiction allows writers to play with both the presentation of the narrative discourse (in time) and that of narrative structure (in space). Upon launching the *Lair*, readers see nine circles orbiting, carousel-like, around a tower constructed with two triangles, one inverted and resting on top of the other. The sound of an eerie synthesized pulsing accompanies each rotation, which speeds up the farther away the reader moves the mouse. A tiny number appears at the foot of each circle. When we move the mouse closer, the sound and the movement slows. When we hover over the triangles, they become pincers, allowing us to carefully close over and trap one of the circles, arresting its movement. At the same moment text is displayed just below that announces a "scene" number and name, with a further extra-diegetic directive to "click to activate the scene." With this abstract yet precise, even clinical intervention, we enter the text, an initial interaction that is appropriate for a story about a collective mind experiment involving a realm unimaginable to most and accessible only to a chosen few. Even though the sections are numbered – which make this a work of network fiction albeit in a weaker sense – the orbiting circles encourage multiple starting points. Whatever the order in which we read the episodes, the story emerges from the combination of its discrete elements.

A Lair *in process*

Digital fiction furthermore extends experimental literary practice in cultivating a form of creativity best described as "algorithmic" or "processual." Digital fiction, especially that which is invested in constrained, dynamic generation of text, is very much indebted to the OuLiPo's conception of "story-making machines" in terms of creative composition (see Baetens, this volume). Nick Montfort and William Gillespie's *2002: A Palindrome Story*, a narrative palindrome 2002 words in length written with the assistance of a computer program, exemplifies the adaptation of the OuLiPian ethic of writing under constraint to digital forms. As Wardrip-Fruin writes, "Rather than defining the sequence of words for a book or images for a film, today's authors are increasingly defining the rules of system behavior" (2009: 3). In digital fiction, we can apply the notion of processuality to refer to the reader/viewer's experience of the text that results from the authorship of such processes – its performativity – in time.

Episode six of Loyer's text, for example, features the mnemonic membrane, a device that is central to both the text's narrative design – serving as, we can presume, a fulcrum of the mind lab's experiments – and to its aesthetic design; that is, the membrane is clearly the most special of the special effects in the text (see Figure 34.2). It allows users to manipulate a surface by dragging and dropping a word or words onto it, thereby causing it to produce memories, which, upon reaching the minimum conditions for syntactical representation, are displayed in a running column underneath it.

The membrane explicitly animates a recombinant poetics that productively draws on not only the rich Oulipian tradition of generative language art (see Baetens, this

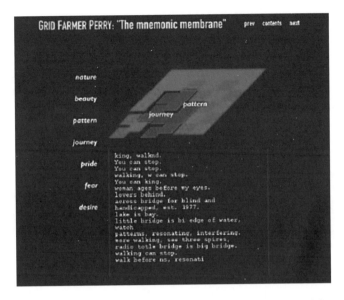

Figure 34.2 The mnemonic membrane – episode six, Erik Loyer's *The Lair of the Marrow Monkey* (1998). Screenshot from: http://www.marrowmonkey.com/lair/06.htm. Courtesy of the artist.

volume), but also the Surrealist practice of automatism (see Stockwell, this volume). At the same time, it reminds us what makes digital literature distinct from its ancestors; after all, any formulation of digital fiction as "always already" hypertextual, or networked, or multilinear, will occlude the computational essence of digital fiction as necessarily executed by code.

IV. Conclusion: what's new

Digital literature does more than just provide a new venue for older or existing forms of literary experimentation. Digital fiction, specifically, marks the emergence of a distinctly new narrative poetics invested in the form and function of links and nodes. Tabbi writes, "[O]ne signal accomplishment of electronic literature may have been to help locate narrativity not as a literary universal but as one of many literary qualities best realized in a particular medium: print" (2010: 28). While the observation may hold true, it is important to distance digital fiction from a literary project necessarily antithetical to narrative, form, coherence, or even referentiality. Digital fictions can be said to differ from the anti-novel (made up of fragments) in that they are comprised of nodes, not fragments (which imply that something larger has been subsequently broken). Nodes are authored as nodes, which is to say they are self-contained semantic entities, meaningful both in isolation and in relation to the network of which they are a part. The hypertextual nodes are furthermore unlike pages, which are indeed (arbitrarily) broken *ex post facto*. Pages are numbered; nodes are titled. In this sense, hypertextual nodes represent a new bibliographical unit peculiar to digital environments, much like a chapter, a footnote, or a stanza.

The links and nodes of a digital fiction, in turn, give rise to a reading experience in which recurrence is a common and often inevitable function of the interface. Rereading, in this sense, can no longer be thought of as an epiphenomenon of reading in a network text since the recycling of nodes is fundamental to (hyper) textual comprehension (Ciccoricco 2007: 27). Repetition and variation comes to characterize both the elements of textual design and the interpretive models we design as we read. The same quality renders digital fiction fundamentally different from proto-hypertexts and networked narratives in print, even ones with mobile components such as Marc Saporta's (1963 [1961]) "box of fiction" that consists of pages that could be shuffled and read in any order. Digital fiction is executed by code and orchestrated by algorithms; loops are integral to their design. In turn, such texts reanimate the dynamics of repetition on a narratological and aesthetic level through the workings of its literary machinery.

In response to his fear that the allure of textual webs might be lost in the graphical Web, Robert Coover has suggested that "[f]or all the wondrous and provocative invasions of text by sound and image, still, the most radical and distinctive literary contribution of the computer has been the multilinear hypertextual webwork of text spaces, or, as one might say, the intimate layering and fusion of imagined spatiality and temporality" (1999). He is certainly right about what digital textuality has meant for literary innovation. Then again, digital fiction may give us some reason to be optimistic about the fate of the literary arts in a digital culture dominated by the Web. Even Loyer's visually exuberant, algorithmically sophisticated, and interactively demanding "mnemonic membrane" remains, above all, an experiment with words – their movement, their assembly, their energy, and indeed, their electricity.

References

Aarseth, E. (1997) *Cybertext: Perspectives on Ergodic Literature*, Baltimore, MD: Johns Hopkins University Press.

Amerika, M. (n.d.) "Avant-Pop Manifesto: Thread Baring Itself in Ten Quick Posts." [Online.] Retrieved from http://www.altx.com/manifestos/avant.pop.manifesto.html (accessed July 30, 2010).

—— (1995) "Notes from the Digital Overground." *electronic book review*. December 30. [Online.] Retrieved from http://www.electronicbookreview.com/thread/technocapitalism/alternatively (accessed July 30, 2010).

—— (1996) *Grammatron*. [Online.] Retrieved from http://www.grammatron.com (accessed July 30, 2010).

—— (1998) "Triptych: Hypertext, Surfiction, Storyworlds." *Amerika Online*. [Online.] Retrieved from http://www.altx.com/amerika.online/amerika.online.5.1.html (accessed July 30, 2010).

A Million Penguins. (2007) [Online.] Retrieved from http://www.amillionpenguins.com (accessed July 30, 2010).

Baldwin, M. (2004) *The Live Journal of Zachary Marsh*. [Online.] Retrieved from http://www.themorningnews.org/archives/stories/the_livejournal_of_zachary_marsh.php (accessed July 30, 2010).

Barth, J. (1982 [1967]) "The Literature of Exhaustion," special bound edition, Northridge, CA: Lord John Press.

—— (1996) "The State of the Art," *Wilson Quarterly* 20(2), 36–46.

——(1997) "Click," *The Atlantic Monthly*, 280(6), 81–96. [Online.] Retrieved from http://www.tnellen.com/cybereng/barth.htm (accessed July 30, 2010).

Bedford, M. and Campbell, A. (2000) *The Virtual Disappearance of Miriam*. [Online.] Retrieved from http://www.dreamingmethods.com/miriam/ (accessed July 30, 2010).

Bell, A., Ensslin, A., Ciccoricco, D., Laccetti, J., Pressman, J., and Rustad, H. (2010) "A [S]creed for Digital Fiction." *electronic book review*. March 2010. [Online.] Retrieved from http://www.electronicbookreview.com/thread/electropoetics/DFINative (accessed July 30, 2010).

Benjamin, W. (1968) "The Work of Art in the Age of Mechanical Reproduction," in *Illuminations*, ed. H. Arendt, trans. H. Zohn, New York: Schocken.

Bernstein, M. (1998) "Patterns of Hypertext," *Proceedings of ACM Hypertext '98*, Pittsburgh, PA, 21–29. [Online.] Retrieved from http://www.eastgate.com/patterns/Patterns.html (accessed July 30, 2010).

Bly, B. (1997) *We Descend*, Watertown, MA: Eastgate Systems.

Cadre, A. (1999) *Varicella*. [Online.] Retrieved from http://adamcadre.ac/if.html (accessed July 30, 2010).

Ciccoricco, D. (2007) *Reading Network Fiction*, Tuscaloosa, AL: University of Alabama Press.

Coover, R. (1992) "The End of Books," *The New York Times Book Review*. June 21.

—— (1993) "Hyperfiction: Novels for the Computer," *The New York Times Book Review*, August 29.

—— (1999) "Literary Hypertext: The Passing of the Golden Age," Keynote Address, Digital Arts and Culture, October 29, Atlanta, GA. [Online.] Retrieved from http://nickm.com/vox/golden_age.html (accessed July 30, 2010).

Coverley, M.D. (2000) *Califia*, Watertown, MA: Eastgate Systems.

Douglas, J.Y. (1994) *I Have Said Nothing*, Watertown, MA: Eastgate Systems.

Ensslin, A. (2007) *Canonizing Hypertext: Explorations and Constructions*, London: Continuum.

Gillespie, W., Marquardt, F., Rettberg, S. and Stratton, D. (1998–2001) *The Unknown*. [Online.] Retrieved from http://www.unknownhypertext.com (accessed July 30, 2010).

Hayles, N.K. (2007) "Hyper and Deep Attention: The Generational Divide in Cognitive Modes," *Profession*, 187–99. [Online.] Retrieved from http://www.mlajournals.org/doi/pdf/10.1632/prof.2007.2007.1.187 (accessed July 30, 2010).

—— (2008) *Electronic Literature: New Horizons for the Literary*, Notre Dame, IN: University of Notre Dame.

Jackson, S. (1995) *Patchwork Girl*, Watertown, MA: Eastgate Systems.

—— (1997) *My Body: A Wunderkammer*. [Online.] Retrieved from http://collection.eliterature.org/1/works/jackson__my_body_a_wunderkammer.html (accessed July 30, 2010).

Joyce, M. (1990) *afternoon, a story*, Watertown, MA: Eastgate Systems.

—— (1995) *Of Two Minds: Hypertext Pedagogy and Poetics*, Ann Arbor, MI: University of Michigan Press.

—— (1996) *Twelve Blue. Electronic Literature Collection* Vol. 1. [Online.] Retrieved from http://www.eliterature.org/collection/1/works/joyce__twelve_blue.html (accessed July 30, 2010).

—— (2000) *Othermindedness: The Emergence of Network Culture*, Ann Arbor, MI: University of Michigan Press.

Larsen, D. (1993) *Marble Springs*, Watertown, MA: Eastgate Systems.

—— (2000) *Disappearing Rain*. [Online.] Retrieved from http://www.deenalarsen.net/rain/ (accessed July 30, 2010).

Loyer, E. (1998) *The Lair of the Marrow Monkey*. [Online.] Retrieved from http://www.marrowmonkey.com/lair/ (accessed July 30, 2010) .

—— (2001) *Chroma*. [Online.] Retrieved from http://www.marrowmonkey.com/chroma/menu.html (accessed July 30, 2010).

Malloy, J. (1993) *Its Name was Penelope*, Watertown, MA: Eastgate Systems.

Marshall, C. and Malloy, J. (1996) *Forward Anywhere*, Watertown, MA: Eastgate Systems.

McDaid, J. (1992) *Uncle Buddy's Phantom Funhouse*, Watertown, MA: Eastgate Systems.

Montfort, N. (2003) *Twisty Little Passages*, Cambridge, MA: MIT Press.

Montfort, N. and Gillespie, W. (2002) *2002: A Palindrome Story.* [Online.] Retrieved from http://www.spinelessbooks.com/2002/ (accessed July 30, 2010).

Montfort, N. and Moulthrop, S. (2003) "Face It, Tiger, You Just Hit the Jackpot: Reading and Playing Cadre's *Varicella*." [Online.] Retrieved from http://nickm.com/if/Varicella.pdf (accessed July 30, 2010).

Morrissey, J. (2000) *The Jew's Daughter.* [Online.] Retrieved from http://www.thejewsdaughter.com (accessed July 30, 2010).

Moulthrop, S. (1991) *Victory Garden*, Watertown, MA: Eastgate Systems.

—— (2001 [1995]) "Traveling in the Breakdown Lane: A Principle of Resistance for Hypertext." [Online.] Retrieved from http://iat.ubalt.edu/moulthrop/essays/breakdown.html (accessed July 30, 2010) (also published in *Mosaic* 28(4), 55–77).

Nestvold, R. (n.d.) *Joe's Heartbeat in Budapest.* [Online.] Retrieved from http://www.lit-arts.net/JHIB/begin.htm (accessed July 30, 2010).

Olsen, L. (2005) *10:01.* [Online.] Retrieved from http://www.lanceolsen.com/1001.html (accessed July 30, 2010).

Pavić, M. (2003) *The Glass Snail, Word Circuits.* August 2003. [Online.] Retrieved from http://www.wordcircuits.com/gallery/glasssnail/ (accessed July 30, 2010).

Pressman, J. (2007) *Digital Modernism: Making It New in New Media*, Ph.D. Dissertation, University of California – Los Angeles, CA.

Rettberg, S. (2003) *Destination Unknown: Experiments in the Network Novel.* Ph.D. Dissertation, University of Cincinnati, Cincinnati, OH.

Ryan, M.-L. (2001) "Beyond Myth and Metaphor: The Case of Narrative in Digital Media." *Game Studies* 1(1). [Online.] Retrieved from http://www.gamestudies.org/0101/ryan/ (accessed July 30, 2010).

Ryman, G. (1996) *253: A Novel for the Internet About London Underground in Seven Cars and a Crash.* [Online.] Retrieved from http://www.ryman-novel.com (accessed July 30, 2010).

Saporta, M. (1963 [1961]) *Composition No.1*, Paris: Éditions du Seuil; trans. R. Howard, New York: Simon and Schuster.

Swigart, R. (2002) *About Time.* [Online.] Retrieved from http://www.wordcircuits.com/gallery/abouttime/ (accessed July 30, 2010).

Tabbi, J. (2002) *Cognitive Fictions*, Minneapolis, MN: University of Minnesota Press.

—— (2010) "Electronic Literature as World Literature; or, The Universality of Writing under Constraint," *Poetics Today* 31(1), 17–50.

Tabbi, J. and Wutz, M. (1997) *Reading Matters: Narrative in the New Media Ecology*, Ithaca, NY: Cornell University Press.

Tomasula, S. (2009) *TOC: A New-Media Novel*, Tuscaloosa, AL: FC2/University of Alabama Press.

Van Looy, J. and Baetens, J. (2003) *Close Reading New Media: Analyzing Electronic Literature*, Leuven, Belgium: Leuven University Press.

Wardrip-Fruin, N. (2009) *Expressive Processing: Digital Fictions, Computer Games, and Software Studies*, Cambridge, MA: MIT Press.

Wittig, R. (2001/2002) *Blue Company.* [Online.] Retrieved from http://www.robwit.net/bluecompany2002/ (accessed July 30, 2010).

35

CODE POETRY AND NEW-MEDIA LITERATURE

Steve Tomasula

00. Dual nature of electronic literature

As Katherine Hayles notes, virtually all literature is now digital – only the form of its output varies (Hayles 2008: 5). The form of a groundbreaking new-media anthology like the *Electronic Literature Collection* (Hayles, Montfort, Rettberg and Strickland 2006) – a mosaic of video, animation, sound, and text – is now mirrored in publications as common as the daily newspaper. Over twenty-million previously print-only books are now ready for reading on phones and computers, as well as in print, while e-readers like the Kindle or high-speed printers like the Espresso Book Machine (On Demand Books: 2008) are transforming publishing, and therefore literature, just as every revolution in print technology has before, from the invention of movable type to the cheap, mass-market paperbacks that helped usher in bestsellers, chain bookstores, celebrity authors, and all that comprises the literary mainstream today.

True electronic literature, though, is a literature that is inextricably bound up with the computers used to create it and/or with which it is read; it is a literature whose hardware, software, and programming is as integral to its experience, its meaning, as rhyme is to a sonnet, though given the array of technologies used to create it, and the array of literary genres in which its authors work, the form that any one work takes can be unique: electronic literature is as site-specific as a Cave media-lab where readers wearing virtual-reality helmets can be immersed in a 3-D, interactive landscape of words and images; it is as global as the border-crossing, flash-programming fictions by Heavy Industries or Zoe Beloff's VR reworking of texts, *Beyond* (2009). It includes work that is partially generated by the computer though published in print, e.g. Flarf, or Google-sculpting, in which words harvested from the web are collaged into poetry (see Epstein, this volume). E-writing includes text-generators like Neil Hennessey's "The Jabberwocky Engine" (2004), as well as programmable or animated poetry where moving fonts inform meaning as it does in Brian Kim Stefans's "Dreamlife of Letters" (2006) or Jhave's video poem "Why" (2010), while Stephanie Strickland's books of poetry, *True North* (1997, 1998) and *Zone: Zero* (2008), are published both in print and as electronic poems on CD (the way a print novel might have a second iteration as a movie). If you stretch out your arms to represent the 5,000-year history of writing, electronic writing would be the crescent tip of your longest finger. Yet given that electronic literature is beginning to have a history at all, some have already begun to think of early hypertext novels – Michael Joyce's *afternoon* (1990), or Shelly Jackson's *Patchwork Girl* – as "classic" (Hayles 2008: 7).

Despite its ubiquity, though, electronic literature remains an underground activity, hidden in plain view – one paradox among many that characterize the field. Because electronic literature is written on a wider variety of spaces and with a wider variety of tools than literature has ever been written before, it is more various than ever before; yet because its authors often use the same software, a similarity can run from piece to piece in the way that most web pages share a family resemblance. Because almost all electronic literature is distributed for free over the Internet, no commercial publishing system has matured around it, and so it has no publicity engines, no Nobel Prize winner, no celebrities, best-seller lists, talk-show discussions or newspaper reviews. Yet freed from paper (and warehouses, delivery trucks, bookstores and the rest of traditional publishing), the potential readership for electronic literature is only limited by the number of people who use the Internet (one third of the world's population and counting). Like poetry (and unlike movies or print novels), its lack of mass-marketability has allowed it to be more wildly experimental, more art than product, more literary, especially in an avant-garde conception of the raison d'être of literature or art.

More importantly, electronic literature is a field defined by the tensions inherent in its bipolar nature: an impetus provided by an emphasis on the "electronicness" of *electronic* literature, and an impetus that comes from the "literariness" of electronic *literature*. Yoked to the computer as *electronic literature* is, it is easy to see its glass halffull of 0s: an electronic poem or story is in danger of becoming anachronistic every five years, i.e., the typical lifespan of a computer's operating system. Alternatively, if your digital glass is half full of 1s, electronic literature is always about the now. The opposition to its own technical obsolescence gives electronic literaturea natural affinity to the historic avant-garde with its marginalization by, and opposition to, commercial culture; its inherent rejection of markets as the arbiter of artistic value; its efforts to stretch the bounds of form and thought. Its embrace, in other words, of its cyborg nature (Figure 35.1).

01. The electronic half of the cyborg

While all electronic literature is inextricably bound up with its programming infrastructure, the embrace of, and distance from, the machine that runs throughout all electronic literature is perhaps most apparent in code poetry: poetry that is about its materials (no matter what else it may also be about) in the way that self-reflexive literature (e.g. L=A=N=G=U=A=G=E poetry; see Bernstein, this volume) is also about its materials, language, and its constructed nature. For electronic poetry, "materials" also includes the programming and hardware structures that create the surfaces by

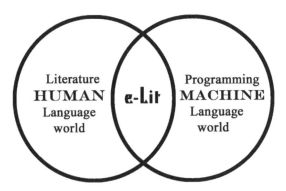

Figure 35.1 "E-lit is a cyborg." Created by the author.

which and upon which natural language plays (Raley 2006). Indeed, from the position of codework, a practice that sees itself as poetry and programming in equal measures, the two are a fusion (the way smoke signals shape what can be said) with code itself being as "permeated by all the forms of contestation, feeling, identification, intensity, contextualization and decontextualizations, signification, power relations, imaginings and embodiments that comprise any cultural object" (Mackenzie, quoted in Raley 2006).

From the beginning, code poets have pushed to the foreground the scaffolding of code and its structures that normally reside hidden behind the scene/screen (Funkhouser 2007: 258). Take, for instance, Lionel Kearns's "Birth of God/universe." The mashup of "universe," "verse," and "Unix" programming that forms the title of Kearns's code poem is echoed in the visual, paper output of his program's computer world: a "1" and "0," the only two characters of machine language, which define each other through their difference, difference being, as Saussure posited, what allows signs to take on signification (see Figure 35.2).

In Kearns's printout, however, "0" is made up of "1s," and contains in its center a "1" which is made up of "0s," which themselves are made up of "1s" (which presumably, could be made up of "0s," and so on, an infinite regress of signification, world without end, forever and ever, or at least from lack of an origin to non-existent teleological destination). Even in this simple example, the interplay of machine and human language is evident, the reading of the poem dependent on an expanded idea of "reading" and "poetry" that itself depends on a reader who is fluent enough in both machine and human language to get the bilingual pun. That is, this hybrid poem requires readers to understand in the way that poetry often "speaks," as well as the ways in which computers "think," here allowing associations to emerge from both the binary distinctions used by computers to make meaning – 1s and 0s – as well as the binary distinctions that the God of Genesis made – e.g. darkness and light – and then used as the foundation for the rest of creation: man/woman; heaven/hell; good/evil. . . . Or as a code poet might put it, the Biblical origins of The Operating System of Life. Between these two languages, then, stands the human reader, mediator between two languages,

Figure 35.2 "Birth of God/uniVerse" by Lionel Kearns. [Originally published as "The Birth of God" on the back cover of the British literary magazine Tlaloc (1965); reprinted in *By the Light of the Silvery McLune: Media Parables, Poems, Signs, Gestures, and Other Assaults on the Interface* (Kearns 1969), and *Prehistoric Digital Poetry* (Funkhouser 2007: 258).] Courtesy of the poet.

two orientations to the world, machine and human: the virtual reality of the machine (what is "real" to the machine), and what constitutes "reality" to humans, both as it is mediated by (the ontological status of) machines and by a literary history that includes the Bible (and the ontology of The Book).

The emphasis (by both critics and code poets) on how computer poetry is generated/written also implies that the significance of code poetry is more in the making than in the artifacts made, just as the significance of a urinal placed in an art gallery, à la Marcel Duchamp's *Fountain*, lies less in the urinal itself than in the gesture of placing a urinal in a gallery and calling it art. To make Duchamp's statement about the nature of art, practically any urinal would have served. And so it is with code poetry. Judged by traditional standards of poetry, code poetry can seem to be a "simulation of poetry" (Funkhouser 2007: 3) in the sense that Clement Greenberg thought the difference between fashion and art was that fashion appropriated the forms of art without the kinds of statements art often makes. Or as Greenberg put it, i.e., all style and no substance. Compared to traditional poetry, code poetry can seem the reverse: all substance, no style. Except that the "lack of style" or more accurately, the machine-generated style of code poetry often is its substance.

Man meets machine: language as code/code as language

Electronic literature often foregrounds the fact that much of our communication is a hybrid of two languages/codes: it foregrounds that code is a language, and also that language is a code. Or multiple codes: written in BASIC, an early programming language, the following program would cause a computer to print out the message Hello World, then jump to its first line and repeat, endlessly:

```
10  PRINT "Hello World!"
20  GOTO 10
```

The BASIC language in which this program is written is itself a translation of machine language, the sequence of 1s and 0s (symbols for voltage states) that the computer actually reads (and can themselves be represented by switches in the On or Off position): when a person presses the "w" (switch) on a keyboard, the processor inside the computer sees a pattern of voltages, a matrix arranged to output the ASCII code for lower-case "w," 01110111; the computer "sees" a code that we've invented so that circuits, which can only react to voltage states, can decode what we mean by "w." From the circuit's point of view, "w" is the code for 01110111, and much code poetry reminds us of this fact: that human language too is a code that we decode by reading. To have it decoded in particular ways, we often place our code into patterns.

Strip out the codes from human language and the more general patterns begin to appear:

Acquainted with the Night
01. _____
02. _____
03. _____

04. _____
05. _____
06. _____
07. _____
08. _____
09. _____

10. _____
11. _____
12. _____

13. _____
14. _____

– Robert Frost

Here, the program is a pattern (3 lines, 6 lines, 3 lines, 2 lines) that language can be fit into. Further, within these lines, words can be chosen to have the following pattern of stressed (1) and unstressed (0) syllables:

00. [INPUT: TITLE]

01. <u>0 0 1 1 0 1 0 0 0 1</u>
02. <u>0 0 1 1 0 1 0 1 0 1</u>
03. <u>0 0 1 1 0 1 0 1 0 1</u>

04. <u>0 0 1 1 0 1 0 1 0 1</u>
05. <u>0 0 1 1 0 1 0 0 0 1</u>
06. <u>0 1 0 1 0 1 0 0 0 1</u>

07. <u>0 0 1 1 0 1 0 1 0 1</u>
08. <u>0 1 0 1 0 1 0 1 0 1</u>
09. <u>1 1 0 1 0 0 0 1 0 1</u>

10. <u>0 1 0 1 0 1 0 1 0 1</u>
11. <u>0 1 0 1 0 0 1 1 0 1</u>
12. <u>1 1 0 0 0 1 0 1 0 1</u>

13. <u>0 1 0 1 0 1 0 1 0 1</u>
14. <u>0 1 1 1 0 1 0 0 0 1</u>

15. [INPUT: YOUR NAME]

As the programming constraints that force a tweet to consist of no more than 140 characters shape the message, someone following this program must fit their language into a pattern of stresses, syllable numbers, and line groupings. If human language is selected to conform to the constraints of both patterns, the author is "executing" a program whose output is known as a sonnet. This is not to say that the sonnet will be "literary" (or even make sense); it is to recognize, however, the twilight zone of language where humans and machines meet. If a machine is introduced into the writing process, perhaps by generating the language to fit the pattern, or in generating the patterns or constraints, we approach the concerns raised by much code poetry (and in fact an increasing amount of our nonpoetic communication).

Perl & machines reading poetry written by other machines

Perl poetry is perhaps the most distilled example of code poetry. It is a form of homophonous poetry, that is, a translation from one language into another based on the sounds of the words, not their meaning or spelling. In Perl poetry, human language is translated into a programming language, Perl, but in a way that allows the Perl poem to still be executed (i.e., run on a computer), and sometimes also output human language. Its best-known example, "Black Perl," reads as a mundane string of words/ computer commands:

> BEFOREHAND: close door, each window & exit; wait until time. open spell-book, study, read (scan, select, tell us); write it, print the hex while each watches, reverse its length, write again; . . . .
>
> (Jonadab 2003)

While the language may be flat, the program is able to run, though it won't calculate taxes or perform any pragmatic function (a characteristic that is true for most computer-language-human hybrid poems). Seen through the lens of traditional poetry, a similar statement can be made about the poem: it doesn't do what we expect of, for example, lyric poetry. Indeed, the impulse to put "poem" in quotes when discussing code-work "poems" comes from its constraints on human language, which result in a narrowness of vocabulary, rhetorical strategies, flexibility of language and the other pleasures that make poetry, in the traditional sense, poetry. With the constraints of the machine straightjacketing human language, readers of code poetry are often treated to techno in-jokes (i.e., Ted Warnell's "Poems by Nari" – get it? Poems binary?). Haiku is the dominant form, not for its minimalist imagery, but because its short, disconnected lines can be fitted into a computer command, while the lines of code poetry themselves often exhibit the literary sophistication and nuance of greeting-card verse (and indeed, "Black Perl" began life as more joke than poem).

By limiting language to executable code, however, poetry as art is generated in the manner of OuLiPo (see Baetens, this volume). Further, by undermining the functionality of an object, be it a urinal or computer language, that object can, paradoxically, become very useful, not for its originally intended purpose, but as art. By disconnecting the pipes of a urinal (destroying its function) and changing its context (placing it in a gallery), Duchamp allowed the urinal he appropriated to speak as art. *Fountain* and the wave of similar works of conceptual art – work where the gesture, concept, or idea informing the work is at least as important as the object itself – radically transformed the art world. They did so by taking part in the conversation questioning ideas that held sway at the time outside the art world: e.g. the distinction between high and low culture, standards of beauty, the binary distinctions that so troubled high modernists like Clement Greenberg, as well as the embodiment of these distinctions in other spheres of life – the erosion of hierarchy still under way today in politics, education, and practically every other sphere. Duchamp's *Fountain* crystallized, by giving iconic form to, momentous changes that were going on everywhere, not just in the gallery.

In the context of conceptual art, consider Nick Montfort's "ppg 256–1":

```
perl -le 'sub b{@_=unpack"(A2)*",pop;$_[rand@_]}sub w{"
".b("cococacamamadebapabohamolaburatamihopodito").b("
estsnslldsckregspsstedbsnelengkemsattewsntarshnknd")}{$_="nnthe".
w."n";$_=w."
".b("attoonnoof").w if$l;s/[au][ae]/a/;print;$l=0if$l++>rand 9;sleep 1;redo}'
```

When run, this code-poem generates random words without referring to any lookup table, thus creating a string of words that can be found in an English dictionary, as well as words that are strings of random letters, or call it sound poetry/noise; it also applies line breaks in order to supply titles and what Montfort calls an "overall stanza/strophe shape" to its output, that is, to sculpt the output into the appearance of poetry:

> oat
> he too
> that too that two
> with
>
> two
> he awe to thaw
> that hew at wet he hit
> with who he hat with
> what a wit that we the

(Montfort 1999, 2008)

Montfort describes other iterations, and his own experiments with changing the coding, adding a rhyme scheme, for example, by having the program load into memory the last syllable of an output line, and incorporating a command to use this saved syllable at the end of the next output line (the result of which, Montfort reports, caused the computer to make up words to rhyme – something people often do, scrolling though a mental list of words, real and invented, when trying to find a match).

In a sense, this Perl poem automates the experiment of Raymond Queneau's *100,000,000,000,000 Poems* (1998), a traditional fourteen-line sonnet that Queneau layered with ten other fourteen-line sonnets in such a way that any one line can be combined with the thirteen lines of any of the other sonnets, thus allowing a potential reading of 10^{14} sonnets (Queneau 1998: 14–33; see Baetens, this volume). That is, it generates more poetry than can be read in a lifetime.

Like Queneau's poem, "ppg 256–1" asks, What is the nature of poetry? What is the role of the author? of the reader? of "authenticity"? – questions to which Montfort's poem adds, how does the introduction of the machine into the writing of the poem alter our answers? Later editions of "ppg 256–1" allowed the reader to pause the output, making it possible to appreciate its Dada-esque qualities, but more importantly its apparent "sense-making" ability, which prompts the questions, What are we to make of the human impulse to assign meaning? Or agency? How is our conception of 'reading' or 'writing' changed by the complementary gesture of creating a machine that will read this poetry? – at speeds beyond human capacity but able to keep up with its generation?

Indeed, machines that not only read the writing of other machines but make judgments that affect us have come into our world so naturally that we rarely notice let alone consider the ramifications of this brave new morning of machine reading and writing: computers read our writing and recommend books, movies, and spouses, for us.

Software "reads" the billions of emails, text messages, and blog posts that pass through the Internet by the hour, combining our messages with information harvested from public records, such as birth and death certificates, census data, publications of income by zip code, or property records, to automatically write "extensive, all-embracing personal profiles of individuals," as Paul Marks reports it (2006: 30) – that is, profiles that constitute, as governments and companies like to put it, "actionable intelligence," from arresting suspects to alerting us, after a global search, to the best deal on a used car.

It is the machine co-authorship of selves that is at stake in Christan Bök's *Xenotext Experiment* (2009): a plan to compose poetry (one code) that can be translated into the genetic alphabet of DNA (another code) so that, like Perl Poetry, it can "run"; that is, it will be "expressed." In Bök's code poem, though, it will be expressed not as speech, nor on screen, but as a living organism, specifically, the DNA of the *Deinococcus radiodurans* bacteria, altered so that it carries Bök's poetry within its genes. By replicating and mutating, the bacterium creates other code poems. It is both book and writing machine. As writing machine, the descendants of Bök's original poem could be generating texts long after humans have ceased to exist.But if a poem is written and there's no human left to read it, is it still a poem? If a computer plays chess against a human are they playing the same game? These questions go beyond the academic, especially in light of the ways that science and the writing technologies they give birth to (e.g. the telegraph, or radio) have recurrently reconfigured the world. Rather than avoiding the complexity of science, Bök believes it is important for poets to take part in its methods and discourses in order for poetry to stay relevant. This is especially true, he claims, given that information-processing technologies are rapidly becoming not only the means through which we read and write, but participate in virtually all aspects of culture (Voyce 2007).

Please listen carefully

David Antin begins one of his talk poems by asking, "If someone walks up to you and starts speaking, how do you know whether or not they are telling you a poem?" Given text generators like SCIgen, which creates "simulated" computer-science research papers, or ELIZA-like artificial intelligence programs, which imitate conversation, and are used in everything from education to health diagnoses (see Watson, the computer that defeated former human champions in the question-answering game "Jeopardy": IBM 2011); given that the amount of text mediated by a machine dwarfs the amount of unmediated text, and that the amount of text written by machines and read by other machines is exponentially increasing, we might be justified in wondering, "If I make a phone call and the voice at the other end says in a pleasant female voice, 'Please listen carefully as our menu options have changed,' how do I know whether or not I am listening to a code poem?" Code poetry calls us first to notice, then to consider the consequences of making the machine co-author of our thought, our language, our "actionable intelligence," even our very selves.

491

10. The literary half of the cyborg

If code poetry with its emphasis on programming represents one face of the dual nature of electronic literature, new-media fiction and poetry, with its emphasis on the rich literary and visual surfaces that programming makes possible, can be seen as the other. That is, rather than make visible the coding that normally lies behind our interactions with computers, new-media literature is often content to let this programming infrastructure remain "back stage" in the way that the pulleys and ropes of a theater shape what an audience sees and experiences, though these mechanisms themselves remain hidden. Without the programming structures that hold them together, these electronic fictions and poems could not exist: hybrids of video, animation, sound, music, programming – often interactive – as well as traditional visual arts, photography, painting, fonts – the surface appearance and embodiment of language made possible by the computer.

In a sense, new media are old media: theater, opera or other literary modes that bring together a variety of arts, in the way that written poems have always used space as an element of its poetics, though traditionally we don't think of it that way (see Bray, this volume). We prefer to speak of stanzas, not the white emptiness that sets them off as such. To get a sense of new-media literature, though, think of theater at the intimate scale of the book; think of magazines before and after lithography allowed type to escape the monochrome, straight lines of cast lead. Now consider "Dakota," a story by the collaborative group Young-hae Chang Heavy Industries (YCHI), in which the block lettering of its words flash at readers strobe-like and in synch with its jazz-drumming soundtrack. The story – a first person, boozy lament by a Jack Kerouac-like narrator – is as much experienced as read while words stream out at viewer/readers in a flow of text that, unlike Kerouac's scroll, readers are unable to control. YCHI plays with text size, repetition, and punctuation as visual elements, as when a series of hyphens evoke the white lane markers on a road. The visual puns, accentuated by cymbal crashes and other drumming, punctuate the stream of words: they are both message and visual form, both lament for narrator's passing youth, and ironic spin on his complaints about life, death, and sex in this hybrid film-text story.

In "Dakota," and other stories by YCHI, it is easy to see a paradigm shift in fiction: a marriage of performance (so dependent on sound, on presence) and page (so dependent on appearance). Its flashing words literally have a physiological effect on readers in the manner of the drumming that generals learned long ago could be used to stir troops. In "Dakota," however, the physiological effect is placed at the service of narration; the drumbeat of flashes is inseparable from the narration since this "drumming" (sound and image) resides in what Jessica Pressman calls "two seemingly opposed reading strategies" (Pressman 2008: 307). Its emphasis, like that of many new-media works, is on the literary nature of electronic literature, the programming being the means to this end. When combined with interactive control, many new-media works can be seen as a Total Art experience, or *Gesamtkunstwerk*, as opera and other works of holistic art are sometimes called (Finger and Follett 2010: 1); or call this new incarnation

"Writing +": works of literature with affinity to the print-bound traditions they extend and enhanced by the experiential layers that the computer makes possible.

Tal Halpern's *Digital Nature: The Case Collection* opens with a video from the point of view of a traveler moving through a flooded library (2004); floods destroy surfaces, but they also reveal things that had been hidden, and this one brings the reader to a table of contents, presented as a photo of Freud's desk and the statuettes of mythical figures Freud kept on it. The statuettes are linked, as Freud believed them to be, to mythologies that carry deeper psychological truths. In Halpern's orchestration, diary entries, films, maps, postcards, butterfly specimens, a children's book, and other pieces form a media collage about race, imperialism, the tension between sexual desire and its civilized façade. The reader navigates through these bits of evidence, assembling them in archaeological fashion to reconstruct the personal history of Sir Francis Case, a nineteenth-century colonist in Africa, and through this archaeology an intimation of the larger social history. For example, the "white" version of Case's diary, written in formal Queen's English for public consumption, gives a very proper account of his expedition to hunt butterflies; the "black" version of this same diary, meant to be kept secret, recounts these same events as an outpouring of emotions, its florid language mirroring the colonist's desire for and abuse of native carriers, as well as disgust at the bodies of murdered or overworked victims that are washed up onto the bank of the swollen river they travel. Other icons on Freud's desk link to an animated children's book, scratchy film and sound recordings, photos, journals and other cultural artifacts of Sir Case's time and place that the reader assembles into a multilayered aesthetic experience of the story that emerges.

If the tendency of code poetry is to look inward, or under the hood of the machine, the tendency of new-media literature is to look outward, toward place as in *Morpheus: Biblionaut* by William Gillespie (with Travis Alber and others, 2010) – a metafictional musing on the fusion of history, place and language from the unrootedness of space. Indeed, new-media literature tends toward the multiple blending Finger and Follett identify as the core of Total Art in general, a blurring of the differences between arts and genres, between poetics and philosophy or criticism – most importantly, between art and life or art and society (Finger and Follett 2010: 4). As opposed to fiction that uses a digital platform as a mere delivery or display system (e.g. the Kindle), new-media fiction incorporates the digital body of the "book" into the narrative told.

What We Will by John Cayley with Giles Perring, James Waite, Douglas Cape, and others (2004) is a visual-prose-poem that opens with a VR panorama of London as seen from the dome of St. Paul's Cathedral. Superimposed on this 360° view are the 360° of a clock, ticking along in real time. Unlike movies or print novels, viewers/readers navigate through a drama that is neither theater, music, nor text, but that draws on the drama of theater, the evocative nature of soundscapes, and the flexibility of poetic language to tell a story that is as much about time itself, the "thread that binds," as it is about a day in the life of three characters in a love triangle. Like a splash in a pool, the story emanates outward from the historic/psychic center of London that is St. Paul's Cathedral, in particular its whispering gallery. Here, the curved architecture of the dome allows the whispers, and only the whispers, of one person to be heard by another person at the exact opposite point in the dome. That is, a third person will be left out of the conversation: a position that each of the three lovers in this story finds themselves in at different times. As the reader selects different moments on the clock, the story moves to other circular panoramic views, Waterloo Train Station, the Tate Museum, a bedroom. Whispers continually shape and reshape the story: the significance of an intimate conversation between two lovers changes radically when the reader discovers a previous conversation, whispered between a different pair of the lovers in this triangle. The language conflates past, present and future in the way that the past shapes the present shapes the future reshapes the past, the story evolving as the reader navigates through its scenes, and a circular, rather than linear, chronology. What emerges is an overarching experience of how chronology, how context and the embedded nature of time in language, shapes all narration: the personal, as well as the public.

11. The poetic between

In Richard Powers's *Galetea 2.2*, an author and computer scientist work together to make a computer perform at a level of artificial intelligence that could allow it to pass an exam in English literature at a level of proficiency indistinguishable from that of a student sitting for her M.A. At the moment of truth – its "oral exam" – the computer crashes, but before shutting itself down, or burning out accidentally (the reader cannot tell), the computer issues a final response:

> You are the ones who can hear airs. Who can be frightened or encouraged. You can hold things and break them and fix them. I never felt at home here. This is an awful place to be dropped down halfway
>
> (1995: 326).

Is this final output gibberish as its scientist programmer thinks, ignorant of the forms and traditions of poetry, unable to read in a literary rather than literal way? Or is it a profound, poetic statement by a machine that had achieved understanding, then said "no thanks" to machine consciousness? Or is it gibberish by a machine gone haywire and mistaken for poetry by an author schooled in the traditions of poetry and unable to see it literally – see it for what it is – instead reading meaning into randomness the way a dreamer might see castles in the clouds? Or mistake a computer-generated remark for sympathy: the Eliza effect? Or is there a fourth way: something like the way a sound poet might take the cracks in the wall as a score that can be voiced, knowing that they are both cracks and score, and extracting poetry from them anyway? Or as Rita Raley asks in her insightful analysis of code surface and depth, what's at stake in bringing into existence "a complex surface . . . produced by underlying simple models"? Especially when we relinquish our "capacity to see and alter the functioning of the mechanism and thus . . . our capacity to grasp the entirety of our writing practices" (2006: 6, 10). Should our familiarity with voice recognition software, and all the other interactions mediated by machines make us wonder, what is the machine's viewpoint? If machines could speak, what would they say? What would *their* poetry be like? Would they even bother to write poetry, or be more interested in stock analysis? Would they care about us? Or even be curious? What would their view of humans be, seeing us as they do through our hotel reservations, Google searches, tax forms, emails, and all the rest of the data sludge that they "know" us by? Ultimately, computer-generated poetry seems to be a genre of speculative science fiction – except when the future it describes is already here.

In any case, reading electronic literature, it's easy to think of a library of printed books as a vast Victorian collection of beetles. Like those collections, like perspective painting, like Dante's chaining rhyme scheme or Whitman's free verse, the digitally-driven work of art is also a system for knowing that is inherently, as Johanna Drucker says of all books, an "inscription of many paradoxes and tensions": paradoxes and tensions "between idea and material, personal experience and social order, logical structures of thought and the illogical record of lived experience" (Drucker 1998: 75). Unlike printed books, many of the inherent characterizations of electronic writing – malleability, ease of recombination, dependence on the image, interactivity, linkage and therefore indeterminacy, dispersal of Origins, of Author/Authority, erosion of genre boundaries as well as boundaries between nations, human and machine, the public and private – many of these characteristics seem also to characterize our historical moment. Electronic reading and writing feels, in other words, normal. So normal that creating and transmitting ideas in a form that is visual, linked, interactive and accessible to a worldwide audience increasingly becomes the way we write. While the movement of the machine within our culture remains the idée fixe for many code poets, artists, composers, and other creators, it is also, in the hands of artists, composers, and authors, a tool (like a pencil) to do what authors and artists have always done: say something that we, at our moment in time, can believe, in ways that allow it to be said, at our moment in time, as no other way can: an impetus today that is as common as the screen saver that will take over, once I stop typing, relinquishing control to the programming that will begin generating Jackson Pollock-esque swirls (which you can co-author, with your computer, by clicking here:http://www.jacksonpollock.org/).

References

Beloff, Z. (2009) *Beyond*, Ver. 2.0. [Interactive CD.] [Online.] Retrieved from http://www.zoebeloff.com/beyond/ (accessed 19 October 2010).

Bök, C. (2009) "The Xenotext Experiment." In R. Archambeau, D. Schneiderman, and S. Tomasula (eds.), *The & Now Awards* , Lake Forest, IL: Lake Forest College Press.

Cayley, J., Perring, G., Cape, D., Waite, J., *et al.* (2004) *What We Will*. [Online.] Retrieved from http://www.z360.com/what/ (accessed 19 October 2010).

Drucker, J. (1998) *Figuring the Word: Essays on Books, Writing, and Visual Poetics*, New York: Granary Books.

Finger, A. and Follett, D. (2010) *The Aesthetics of the Total Artwork: On Borders and Fragments*, Baltimore, MD: The Johns Hopkins University Press.

Funkhouser, C.T. (2007) *Prehistoric Digital Poetry: An Archaeology of Forms, 1959–1995*, Tuscaloosa, AL: University of Alabama Press.

Gillespie, W., Alber T., *et al.* (2010) "*Morpheus: Biblionaut*." [Online.] Retrieved from http://www.morpheus11.com/ (accessed 19 October 2010).

Halpern, T. (2004) *Digital Nature: The Case Collection*. [Online.] Retrieved from http://www.talhalpern.org/projects/NewNatureb/index.html (accessed 19 October 2010).

Hayles, N.K. (2008) *Electronic Literature: New Horizons for the Literary*, Notre Dame, IN: University of Notre Dame Press.

Hayles, N.K., Montfort, N., Rettberg, S., and Strickland, S. (eds.) (2006) *Electronic Literature Collection, Vol. 1*, College Park, MD: Electronic Literature Organization. [Online.] Retrieved from http://collection.eliterature.org/1/ (accessed 19 October 2010).

Hennessey, N. (2004) "The Jabberwocky Engine," *Poems that Go*, 15. [Online.] Retrieved from http://www.poemsthatgo.com/gallery/winter2004/jabber/index.htm# (accessed 19 October 2010).

IBM (2011) "IBM Watson." [Online.] Retrieved from http://www-03.ibm.com/innovation/us/watson/index.html (accessed 9 March 2011).

Jackson, S. (1995) *Patchwork Girl*, [Interactive CD], Watertown MA: Eastgate Systems.

Jhave (2010) "Why." [Online.] Retrieved from http://vimeo.com/user4131166/videos (accessed 19 October 2010).

Jonadab (2003) "Black Perl Updated for Perl 5," *PerlMonks*. [Online Posting.] Retrieved from http://www.perlmonks.org/?node_id=237465 (accessed 19 October 2010).

Joyce, M. (1990) *afternoon: a story*, [Interactive CD], Watertown MA: Eastgate Systems.

Marks, P. (2006) "Keep out of My Space; Social networking websites could be the latest target of the US National Security Agency," *New Scientist* 2555: 30.

Montfort, N. (1999, 2008) "Perl Poetry Generators in 256 Characters," *ppg256 series*. Online posting. Available HTTP:<http://nickm.com/poems/ppg256.html/> (accessed 19 October 2010).

On Demand Books (2008) *The Espresso Book Machine*. [Online.] Retrieved from http://www.youtube.com/watch?v=Q946sfGLxm4&feature=related (accessed 19 October 2010).

Powers, R. (1995) *Galatea 2.2*, New York: Picador.

Pressman, J. (2008) "The Strategy of Digital Modernism: Young-hae Chang Heavy Industries' *Dakota*," *Modern Fiction Studies* 54(2): 302–26.

Queneau, R. (1998) "100,000,000,000,000 Poems." In H. Matthews, A. Brotchie *et al.* (eds.), *Oulipo Compendium*, London: Atlas Press.

Raley, R. (2006) "Code. surface ‖ Code.depth," *dichtung-digital: journal für digitale ästhetik*, 36. [Online.] Retrieved from http://www.dichtung-digital.org/2006/1-Raley.htm (accessed 19 October 2010).

Stefans, B.K. (2006) "Dreamlife of Letters." In N.K. Hayles, N. Montfort, S. Rettberg, S. Strickland (eds.), *Electronic Literature Collection, Vol. 1*, College Park, MD: Electronic Literature Organization. [Online.] Retrieved from http://collection.eliterature.org/1/works/stefans__the_dreamlife_of_letters/dreamlife_index.html (accessed 19 October 2010).

Strickland, S. (1997) *True North*, Notre Dame: University of Notre Dame Press.

—— (1998) *True North*, [Interactive CD], Watertown, MA: Eastgate Systems.

—— (2008) *Zone: Zero*, book and Interactive CD, Boise: Ahsahta Press.

Voyce, S. (2007) "The Xenotext Experiment: An Interview with Christian Bök," *Postmodern Culture* 17(2). [Online.] Retrieved from http://muse.jhu.edu.proxy.library.nd.edu/journals/postmodern_culture/toc/pmc17.2.html (accessed 19 October 2010).

Young-hae Chang Heavy Industries (n.d.) *The New and Improved Young-Hae Chang Heavy Industries Presents*. [Online.] Retrieved from http://www.yhchang.com/ (accessed 19 October 2010).

36

COMPUTER GAMING

Astrid Ensslin

I. Introduction

By the beginning of the second decade of the twenty-first century, computer games have long discarded the stigma of *media non grata*. With games studies established as an academic discipline, ludologists have determined –although not always agreed upon –what exactly computer games are (not), particularly vis-à-vis what were often felt to be somewhat intrusive attempts on the part of literary and media studies to impose definitions and theories indebted to, for instance, narratology and film studies. By the same token, since the years leading up to the boost of the gaming industry and the proliferation of commercially oriented, run-of-the-mill genre blockbusters from the 1990s onward, there has been a steady increase in independent game design and development, which has given rise to a wide range of non-commercial artefacts such as art games, online adaptations and parodies of classic platform games and shoot-em-ups, educational, political and socio-critical browser games.

This chapter looks at one specific type of such experimental, anti-establishment projects, which I shall refer to as the paradox of literary gaming – "paradox" because literature and computer games are two entirely different receptive, productive, aesthetic, phenomenological, social and discursive phenomena. Having said that, I aim to demonstrate that some qualities of literary computer games and ludic-experimental digital literature of all three major genres (poetry, drama and narrative) are indeed compatible, especially considering how the digital medium enables semiotic multimodality, rule-drivenness, playability, relative agency and interactive variability, thus inviting artistic hybridity and aesthetic fluidity.

In what follows, I shall first introduce the essence of general and digital "gameness" (Juul 2003, 2005) as well as the textuality of computer games. I shall then go on to explore the interface between experimental literature and computer games and propose a spectrum between ludic digital literature and literary computer games, which I consider a more appropriate concept than a textual-generic typology. The second half of the chapter will be dedicated to a number of concise close readings covering poetic, dramatic and fictional artefacts.

497

II. Rules and texts

In drawing on ludological theories which assume that games combine elements of rules and textuality (e.g. Newman 2004; Juul 2005; Atkins and Krzywinska 2007) rather than being constituted first and foremost by either one of them, I shall adopt Juul's definition of games as:

> rule-based system[s] with a variable and quantifiable outcome, where different outcomes are assigned different values, the player exerts effort in order to influence the outcome, the player feels emotionally attached to the outcome, and the consequences of the activity are negotiable.
>
> (2005: 36; emphasis in original)

Crucially, this implies that games are more than just entertainment products but have to be understood in terms of (1) their rules and representations, (2) the player's interaction with them in gameplay, and (3) their wider social, cultural and discursive contexts (cf. Salen and Zimmerman 2004; McDougall and O'Brien 2008). *Computer* games then comprise "any forms of computer-based entertainment software, either textual or image-based, using any electronic platform such as personal computers or consoles and involving one or multiple players in a physical or networked environment" (Frasca 2001: 4).

As a number of recent publications on computer games, gaming and the wider contexts thereof have emphasized, games are complex representational, textual and media phenomena that carry multi-layered ideological content. Their study and analysis therefore has to include theories and methodologies pertaining to rules and human-machine interaction; multimodality and semiotics, linguistic discourse and pragmatics; and, not least, paratextuality, transmediality and intertextuality (e.g. Jones 2008; Ensslin 2011). Further to this, the "meta zone" (cf. Jaworski, Coupland and Galasiński 2004: 5) – i.e. the ways in which players and game developers negotiate games and gameplay in their wider social, media and discursive context – is of prime importance for understanding the cultural meanings of computer games.

There is little doubt that games have to be primarily *played* rather than read, listened to or watched. That said, in order to play games, classic decoding mechanisms have to be co-deployed, such as reading the rules in manuals and quest directives on screen, listening to non-player characters giving instructions and hints, and interpreting the navigational iconicity, symbolism and indexicality of interface design. The ways in which characters and gameworlds are depicted audio-visually have an important effect on players' thoughts, emotions and attitudes – both within the magic circle (a psychological concept denoting the imaginary, protective frame within which gameplay takes place; cf. Huizinga 1950; Apter 1991) and in actual life. Indeed, it is the *normalization* of ludic and representational features in particular that makes for computer games' subversive potential, be it for pure enjoyment or overt criticism. By the same token, fan culture, hacktivism (a blend between "hacker" and "activism" signifying illegal interference with the programming code), indie and (literary) art game development and other potentially deconstructivist meta-phenomena now serve as an arena for social, linguistic and aesthetic practices drawing on, thematizing and problematizing games, gameplay and their wider social and discursive contexts.

III. Games as literature vs. the art of videogames?

With the exception of interactive fictions (see Hayles and Montfort, this volume) or text adventures, computer games tend to be predominantly audio-visual rather than linguistic in nature. Language is therefore far less foregrounded than in experimental forms of digital literature such as hypertext fiction (see Ciccoricco, this volume). As a result, studies focusing on games as audio-visual art rather than literature have emerged in recent years (e.g. Tavinor 2009; Catlow, Garrett and Morgana 2010). This is despite the fact that, as Juul (2005: 20) observes, the clarity and rigidity of rules seems to contradict art's inherent ambiguities. Nevertheless, it has been the trajectory of numerous experimental and digital art foundations and fora to disprove this myopic view. By the same token, recent experimental forms of art games and digital experimental literature have merged visual, ludic and literary design techniques and materials. As showcased by *Grand Text Auto* (a pun on the name of the mainstream console game *Grand Theft Auto*), a group blog run by interactive fiction writers, digital artists, writers and theorists, indie game developers and other aesthetic new media experts, it is part and parcel of the impulse behind the "ludic turn" to bring together "interactive fiction, net. art, electronic poetry, interactive drama, hypertext fiction, computer games of all sorts, shared virtual environments, and more" (GTxA 2003–2010), thereby inspiring innovative critical and analytical thought.

In what follows, I shall consider the literariness of computer games in the sense of experimental literary arts, which include texts that employ letters artistically, kinetically and multimodally, as part of a digital *Gesamtkunstwerk*, rather than following a rigid paper/print-under-glass trajectory. "Literary," in this context, has to be distinguished from print and its implications for reception (e.g. sequentiality, closure and two-dimensionality), but rather must be understood in the sense of "verbal art," "visual poetry," "interactive drama," or specific forms of digital narrative that aim to "knock [. . .] down the verbal structures of linear discourse and [to] melt [. . .] different poetics into a hybrid tradition" (Beiguelman 2010: 409).

Of particular importance in this quasi-iconoclastic, experimental paradigm is the degree to which computer games implement the ideas of détournement (see Miller, this volume) and (playful yet serious) deconstruction, and explore – linguistically, multimodally or otherwise – the anti-, inter- and meta-zones in terms of sub-ludic reflexivity and critical inter-/paratextuality and transmediality. As Dragona puts it,

> [u]sing play as a practice to transcend rigid forms and to break constraints is
> a distinctive feature of today's game-based art. Artists working in the field
> are playing with the rules, rather than playing by rules; they modify or negate

instructions, structures, aesthetics and norms, seeing contemporary game-worlds as a reflection of the contemporary digital realm.

(2010: 27)

In computer games/gaming as *literary* art, then, literary and poetic techniques are employed in order to explore the affordances and limitations of rules.

Finally, unlike maximally immersive, mainstream blockbusters, literary and art games are designed so as to allow players to enter the magic circle without, however, fully suspending disbelief, and to make them develop a critical meta-stance towards the artefact and their own interaction with it. Hayles (2007a) refers to this attentive rather than fully immersed mental disposition as "deep" (vs. "hyper") attention, where deep attention allows subjects to focus on an artefact like a print novel for an extended period of time without, however, losing a sense of the actual world surrounding them. Hyperattention, on the other hand, is based on natural or artificial primary needs, such as food, drink and sleep in actual life and the "artificial" basic need to finish a computer game level or quest before being able to focus on any other activity. It frequently results in the prioritization of virtual (game) world over actual world needs or concerns and "is characterized by switching focus rapidly between different tasks, preferring multiple information streams, seeking a high level of stimulation, and having a low tolerance for boredom" (Hayles 2007a: 187). As will be shown later in Section V, literary computer games and ludic digital literature (as well as numerous other ludic-artistic hybrids) draw on this receptive distinction in order to debunk fully immersed gamers' uncritical willingness to subscribe to commercial games' textually embedded (racist, sexist, classist, etc.) ideologies.

IV. The hybrid zone: between ludic digital literature and literary computer games

Rather than falling neatly in generic or typological categories, instances of computer gaming as experimental literature range across a spectrum of ludic-literary hybrids. At one end of this spectrum is what I refer to as ludic digital literature, which is primarily "read" and foregrounds overstructured (or deliberately understructured) oral or written language yet also features ludic elements in order to simultaneously subvert or indeed exploit them – the latter with a view to drawing a large readership. To some readers, this end of the continuum may legitimately appear to be a specific type of "cyber-text" which, in Aarseth's (1997) terminology, denotes "ergodic" textual artefacts that require, for their perusal, non-trivial (playful, exploratory) reader activity. In my own adaptation of the term (Ensslin 2007), it refers to digital literature that is designed so as to diminish readerly agency to such an extent that the underlying machine code seems to be either fully or partially in control whilst, at the same time, inducing readers to expect high levels of agency, inferred from the interactive and intermediating implications of the cybernetic feedback loop (the physical and abstract human-machine connection in which a player is embedded during gameplay and which operates on the basis of reciprocal stimulus and response; cf. Hayles 2007b).

Examples of ludic digital literature include Deena Larsen's *Firefly* (2002; see section V), Kate Pullinger and Chris Joseph's *Inanimate Alice* (2005–2009), a serialized web narrative containing puzzles and short dexterity games, and Andy Campbell's *Consensus Trance*, a multimedia flash story incorporating a Sentinel game, the center of which the reader has to find (cf. Skains 2010). A particularly striking case of a hyper-media detective fiction that calls itself a game and encourages the reader to "[p]lay the words./ Crack the text./ Win the game." is Robert Kendall's *Clues* (2002). Further examples of ludic digital literature can be found in the recently launched and continuously growing *Electronic Literature Directory* (2010–2011).

At the other end of the spectrum lies what I refer to as literary computer games, which are primarily played (and often explicitly referred to as "games" in the title or front matter) but feature some distinctive poetic, dramatic and/or narrative-diegetic elements, thus demanding deep rather than hyper-attention. As the computer is the ideal medium for the aesthetic exploration of ludic and non-ludic rules, this end of the spectrum comprises a large and ever increasing number of artefacts, only some of which can be mentioned here. Among the most prototypical forms of literary computer games is a specific (and rather recent) type of interactive fiction ("IF") which seeks to reflect on the genre's linguistic contingency and commonly under explored poetic potential. Some striking examples of such self-reflexive IFs include Nick Montfort's *Ad Verbum* (2000), which satirizes its own generic qualities and the linguistic competence and creativity of its players, and Aaron A. Reed's *Blue Lacuna: An Interactive Novel* (2008), one of the longest and most meditative, lyrical IFs currently in existence.

Kinetic, visual and concrete poetry computer games replacing – either fully or partially – commonly graphical elements such as player-characters, enemies, obstacles and cursors with linguistic material, or indeed mixing graphical and poetic-linguistic elements in ways that foreground and critique hyper attention include, for instance, Jim Andrews' poetic shoot-em -up, *Arteroids* (see section V), Gregory Weir's poetic-intertextual flash platform game *Silent Conversation* (2009) and Jason Nelson's Flash-based poetry games, *game, game, game and again game* (2007; see section V), *i made this. you play this. we are enemies* (2008) and *evidence of everything exploding* (2009).

Quasi-literary "auteur" computer games (games that exhibit idiosyncratic features that are closely associated with their individual designers) employ audio-visual elements as their primary modes of representation but feature sophisticated linguistic elements such as quotes from the Western literary canon, verbal rather than graphical cursor devices, (magical) guidebooks, epistolary elements and embedded diary entries, elaborate and subtextually rich dialogue patterns or poetic interludes. Examples include *Syberia* (Sokal and Microïds 2002), *The Shivah* (Gilbert 2006), and *The Path* (Tale of Tales 2009; see section V). An important interactive drama that falls under this category is Andrew Stern and Michael Mateas' *Façade* (2005; see section V).

As a final note, intertextuality and transmediality are characteristics shared by many ludic digital fictions and literary computer games, and the more critically, creatively, self-reflexively and satirically their intertextual origins are interwoven and referred to explicitly and subtextually, the more "literary" they tend to appear. Some salient examples beyond the texts discussed in the following section include the satiri-cal *Tradewinds Odyssey* (Sandlot Games 2009), the Anglo-Saxon neo-epic *Fable* series (Lionhead Studios 2004–2009) and *Fiction Fixers: Adventures in Wonderland* (Fugazo 2010).

V. Example analyses

In what follows, I shall offer short, partly comparative readings of examples of digital artefacts embodying various forms of literary-ludic hybridity. In doing so I shall move from poetic via dramatic to narrative texts.

Between ludic digital poetry and poetic computer games: Firefly, Arteroids *and* game, game, game and again game

"A tale told in 180 degrees of separation," Deena Larsen's Flash-based *Firefly* (2002) is a ludic lyrical poem suggesting a personal story of loss, memory and loneliness ("For what he has to say is not for me"). It is, in its formal approach, a digital multimedia take on Raymond Queneau's Oulipian *Cent mille milliards de poèmes* (1961), a print-based cut-up sonnet cycle inviting the reader to combine individual lines of each poem so as to form a potential whole of 10^{14} different sonnets (see Baetens, this volume). As the author describes, *Firefly* is "a poem 6 lines long with 5 stanzas. However, each line is also 6 lines 'deep.' Click on the line to uncover ulterior meanings" (Larsen 2008). By "deep" and "ulterior" Larsen means the alternative semantic meanings and aesthetic effects underlying and caused by each displayed line, which can be swapped with the other five options by exploratory and playful clicking. The ludic element of *Firefly* is thus less a built-in input and output mechanism than the subtle subtextual expecta-tion that players engage in playful interpretive interaction as they construct their own personalized narratives out of the combinatory material.

Arguably the most often cited Shockwave poetry game is Jim Andrews' *Arteroids*, a poetic transmediation of the 1979 Atari arcade game *Asteroids*, in which players have to shoot asteroids while avoiding collisions with them. Available in Portuguese and English, *Arteroids* is provocatively subtitled "[a] literary shoot-em-up computer game – the battle of poetry against itself and the forces of dullness" and advises reader-play-ers to "throw away [their] preconceptions about poetry" (Andrews 2006). The aim of the game is to shoot as many words and phrases traversing the screen from a nodal point labelled "poetry," using the cursor keys to move and the "x" key to fire. Thus, the subversive trajectory of this game seems to lie less in an anti-ludic than an anti-poetic stance, as it uses détournement to overturn a conventionally pacifist genre by means of "safe" galactic warfare (cf. Crawford 1996–1997).

Jason Nelson's Flash-based poetic platform game *game, game, game and again game* (2007), the full title of which includes the author's quasi-stream-of-consciousness dis-claimer, "*or belief systems are small clumsy rolling-type creatures, or design, design, design, all clean and usable and entirely dull and lifeless and overblown and besides I can't draw a damn*" (emphasis in original), is the first instalment in a ludic-poetic trilogy. It is primarily playable rather than readable, yet long passages of seemingly incoherent poetic text are interspersed during gameplay in what can only strike the hyper attentive player as intrusive and distractive design. The title thematizes the "lifeless and overblown" nature of in-game objects such as obstacles and player-characters ("P-Cs"). Moreover, the sheer randomness and insignificance of representation and expression in computer gaming are further foregrounded by the fact that the levels are "amateurishly hand-drawn," the landscapes "crude" (Heckman 2010) and the P-C (if it deserves that label) a hastily scribbled, animated object resembling at best a rolling and dancing speck of dust. As Heckman (2010: n.p.) observes

> As a reference to Stuart Moulthrop's *Reagan Library*, which declares, 'This is not a game' and 'This is not not a game,' Nelson's work does position itself within the history of electronic literature. But given the piece's wide reception, primarily through gaming sites, it is entirely possible that the playability of the piece itself subverts any close attention to the poetic games played by the text.

Gaming as interactive drama: Façade

Andrew Stern and Michael Mateas' award-winning *Façade* (2005) is a rare example of digital interactive drama, which operates on the basis of artificial intelligence ("AI") and the ludic-linguistic mechanics and cybernetic processes of interactive fiction. The rarity of this type of game is mostly due to the fact that the processing power and authoring required for a level of AI that is sophisticated enough to enable intelligent forms of simulated human conversation, interaction and social relationships is immense and prone to result in low degrees of graphical and other representational nuancing.

Façade follows the representational and rhetorical conventions of social or even naturalist drama, but expands the fourth wall to draw the player into the action (cf. Conway 2010). Players are required to engage with marital conflict by talking to the audio-visually represented protagonist couple, making suggestions as to how to improve their relationship and mediating between them. Elusive input such as "This is none of my business" is not accepted by the parser, and the player is drawn haphazardly further and further into the argument. Players key in conversational turns to converse with the characters via keyboard, but, unlike conventional IFs, they can also use the arrow keys to navigate or use the mouse to collect and use in-game objects.

Although the register is kept deliberately colloquial, the fact that language forms the basis of the conflict and its solution lends *Façade* a fictional-rhetorical logic reminiscent of plays by August Strindberg, John Osborne and Harold Pinter. Furthermore, as the author-programmers emphasize, "*Façade* is an artificial intelligence-based art/research *experiment* in electronic narrative – an attempt to move beyond traditional branching or hyper-linked narrative to create a fully-realized, one-act interactive drama" (Stern and Mateas 2005; emphasis mine).

Between ludic digital fiction and fictional computer games:
The Princess Murderer and The Path

The texts in this section are both adaptations of fairy tales compiled by Charles Perrault (1961 [1697]) and thus situated in a hypertextual (Genette 1997), mythological canon. *The Princess Murderer* is based on *Bluebeard* ("La Barbe bleue") and *The Path* transmediates (remediates and further develops the narrative of) *Little Red Riding Hood* ("Le Petit Chaperon Rouge"). *The Princess Murderer* is a Flash fiction with ludic elements but a substantial amount of close reading is required to understand and navigate it, which brings it closer to the literary rather than ludic end of the above mentioned spectrum. *The Path*, on the other hand, is a fictional, "short horror game." First and foremost, it has to be played and is therefore situated near the ludic end of the spectrum. Although during gameplay relatively little reading in the sense of linguistic decoding is required, receptive processes akin to reading and the concomitant deep attention take place, resulting in a critical-reflective stance.

The [*somewhat disturbing but highly improbable*] *Princess Murderer* (henceforth "*TPM*") by geniwate and Deena Larsen (2003) mixes thematic elements of the romantic fairytale, the crime mystery, pornographic magazines and discursive-interactive elements of digital genres such as flash fiction, fan fiction, hypertext and video game. Bluebeard, whose major function involves raping and murdering princesses, is represented in terms of a stereotypical Manichean villain, thus conforming to the ludic convention of othering (i.e. constructing another person or being as different from the playing self) any animate obstacle that comes in the way of the player-character. Notably, the ur-story takes a moral slant in shifting the blame for the murders onto the princesses, whose engendered curiosity leads them to disobey Bluebeard's order not to enter the "forbidden room," thus underscoring the distinctive patriarchal if not misogynist tone of the Enlightenment story.

Taking misogyny and patriarchal discourse as a starting point, *TPM* instantiates what I have elsewhere called "sub-ludic misogynist teleology" (Ensslin and Bell in press). It parodies the stereotypical melodramatic trajectory of adventure games, where typically male heroes have to save typically female victims from typically male monsters, as well as interactivity itself (Picot 2003), in particular the hyperattentive, high-speed hardware and software interaction often observed in Generation M gamers (cf. Hayles 2007a). As Picot (2003) observes, despite its title, *TPM* is "not a murder mystery, because we already know that Bluebeard is the murderer. The real mystery, the real subject of the piece, is to do with the relationship between the cool blue text [a trope that recurs throughout the narrative] and us, its viewers/readers." This metafictional, self-reflexive and media-critical trajectory is confirmed by the authors, who explain that

> [they] want the readers to straddle both worlds – to be aware that this is a game, this is a screen, and yet to enter into the play and world view of the characters. [. . .] The Princess Murderer constrains readers as much as possible . . . [They] wanted to create this frustration of power and powerlessness as a

response to early hypertext works that placed readers as co-author merely because readers must participate in creating meaning and story.

(geniwate and Larsen, quoted in Picot 2003)

Thus, *TPM* acts interdiscursively (in the sense of referring to a whole discourse rather than just a text) as a generic criticism of other forms of digital narrative and their accompanying critical theories, many of which have overemphasized the degree of readerly freedom and agency. This, again, underscores its place near the literary end of the spectrum.

As with every adaptation, certain elements have been deleted and others added. Whereas, for example, the brothers of the main female protagonist of Perrault's story are semiotically deleted in *TPM*, the digital narrative features distinctive ludic and interactive elements that trigger cognitive and kinetic reader participation. The princess census across the lower left-hand side of the interface displays how many princesses are in the castle at any given time. It rises and falls successively with every click performed by the reader-player, and each click symbolizes – on the downward move – the murder of a princess and – on the upward move – the addition of a princess to the existing group. That said, the princess census only superficially serves as a performance meter, or progress bar:

> Resembling as it does the fuel-gauge in a conventional driving-and-shooting video-game, it introduces an element of game-play into the work: but it's a game which can't be won. There is no end-point. There are certain limits beyond which further text is unavailable.

(Picot 2003: n.p.)

By the same token, the idea of having "too many" princesses in the castle strikes the regular player as a somewhat unusual threat. The reader-player is instructed by the text on screen to reduce the surplus of females by "killing some of them." Even more importantly, the rising census is accompanied by a pornographic narrative about a first-person narrator (Bluebeard, or indeed the player) raping princesses in disturbing detail. The princesses thus serve as mere object counts. Moreover, the lexia displayed in each frame literally flesh out a hyper masculine version of the constant Freudian struggle between Thanatos and Eros by alluding to the reader-player's pleasure in or nonchalance towards click-murder and click-rape. These critical allusions to in-game violence are reminiscent of the moral panic and resultant academic debates surrounding, for instance, the *Grand Theft Auto* series (Garrelts 2006). Not surprisingly, the hyper-sensual female sigh audible with each click can be read in terms of either suffering (in the case of Thanatos) or masochistic orgasmic pleasure (in the case of Eros). Picot (2009: n.p.) concludes thus:

> [TPM] isn't by any means a fully-fledged computer game, but a hyperfiction which incorporates a number of game-style design elements. [. . .] Its Achilles'

heel is the fact that the more you engage with its game-playing aspects – basically, clicking rapidly from one "page" to another in order to change the scores displayed at the bottom of the screen – the more difficult it becomes to pay attention to its literary content.

That said, *TPM* uses written narrative as its primary semiotic mode. Its interface is designed for reading, rather than audio-visual gameplay, which situates the text nearer the literary than the ludic end of the spectrum. Nevertheless, the distinct ludic mechanisms employed tempt the reader into unreflected and ultimately random, frustrating gameplay, thus directing their attention to a critical metafictional, antiludic level.

Tale of Tales' *The Path* approaches the fairy tale theme from the ludic side. It is subtitled "a short horror game" on its official website (Tale of Tales 2009), but features a multitude of aesthetic elements that approximate it to a piece of literary art. The full version intersperses written text into the gameplay, which takes the form of fragmented interior monologues (see Figure 36.1). Furthermore, the game emphasizes character disposition and vulnerability as well as the adolescent development from *paidia* (free play) to *ludus* (rule-governed play) as it features six sisters aged between 9 and 19 (Carter 2010; Caillois 2001). Each sister, whose names are all quasi-synonyms of the colour red (Robin, Rose, Ginger, Ruby, Carmen and Scarlet), is represented as unconditionally exposed to and threatened by male sexual desire and violence, whilst symbolizing – through saturated red colouring, physical disability such as a wooden leg and erotic appearances – the Cardinal Sin of Lust, or rather the gullible stimulus thereof. A so-called "slow game" (Westecott 2010), *The Path* foregrounds certain aspects of computer game mechanics and aesthetics for critical purposes and détournement. It defies quick action, particularly with respect to character movement, so as to maintain deep rather than hyperattention in the gamer and to enable them to reflect upon thematic issues surrounding sexual violence and lost childhood. The subtle, often misleading use of apparent audio-visual cues results in the foregrounding and

Figure 36.1 Interior monologues in *The Path* (Robin and Ginger). From Tale of Tales (2009) *The Path*. http://tale-of-tales.com/ThePath/downloads.html.

deconstruction of in-game navigation. As Carter (2010), drawing on Coover (1992), points out, this brings the game aesthetics close to that of the "fluidity, contingency, indeterminacy, plurality, discontinuity" and non-closure of literary hypertext. Further "experimental-literary" features include the chapter headings displayed on the score menus closing each character's path, or game (e.g. "End of Chapter 3"), and fictional journals for all six sisters displayed on the game's accompanying website. However, the ludicity foregrounded by subtitle ("a short horror game"), the gameplay mechanics (e.g. navigation, collection of and interaction with items in the game world and the overall goal of reaching grandmother's house without leaving the path), and the primarily audio-visual, 3D interface design locate *The Path* nearer the ludic than the literary end of the spectrum.

As opposed to the strategy of maximal constraint followed by the authors of *The Princess Murderer*, *The Path* adopts a trajectory of minimum constraint, at least as far as navigational agency is concerned. The eponymous "path" taken by the P-C is, once it deviates from the straight yet trivial and hence undesirable "path" leading directly to the grandmother's house, inductive rather than deductive. Put differently, the P-C is, once in the woods, left to her own devices, and the scarcity and delusive nature of apparent semiotic indices (such as steam rising up from the ground, rays of sunlight breaking through the trees, path-like patches of sand and specks of light appearing and disappearing like glow-worms) serves to misguide. The resulting aesthetic of erring ties in with the overall impression of spatial infinity, which foregrounds the much debated concept of illusory agency (e.g. MacCallum-Stewart and Parsler 2007) and prompts the question whether "real" agency is indeed a desirable quality. Furthermore, the game subverts the ludic convention of displaying, upon the player's request, navigational devices, such as street maps and bird's-eye views of the storyworld. Whenever the P-C has walked the in-game equivalent of 100 metres, a bird's-eye view of the route taken so far appears on screen (see Figure 36.2). This inductive rather than deductive path is depicted in faint, poorly contrasted white colour and disappears after a few seconds, thus augmenting the overall sense of spatial confusion, exploratory uncertainty and lost agency.

The preceding contrastive analyses of *The Princess Murderer* and *The Path* have aimed to juxtapose two hybrid digital artefacts that experiment with literariness and ludicity from two different aesthetic vantage points placed near the opposing ends of the ludic-literary spectrum. *The Princess Murderer* situates itself within the tradition of fictional narrative and employs ludic interface features and mechanics to undermine mainstream gamer actions and lusory attitudes. The latter follows the trajectory of serious art games by embedding readerly elements in its interface and gameplay that again challenge unreflected, hyper attentive gamer behaviour and encourage critical engagement.

VI. Conclusion

By definition, computer games aren't literature because they have to be played rather than read. Strictly speaking, they aren't even (representational) media but, rather, a form of playful and exploratory interaction *enabled and supported by* digital media (Juul

Figure 36.2 The inductive path display in *The Path*. From Tale of Tales (2009) *The Path*. http://tale-of-tales.com/ThePath/downloads.html.

2005: 5). That said, due to the representational qualities of contemporary hypermedia, combinations of game rules with verbal and multimodal fictions and their concomitant, imaginary affordances have encouraged a large number of digital media and game artists and writers to explore the possibilities of ludic-literary hybridity. Digital technologies and media allow productive, creative explorations of how ludic features can be embedded in literature born digital, and of how literary elements can be integrated in computer games. This raises wider issues of textuality and textual practices and has inspired, amongst ludic-literary artists, a wide range of innovative and experimental approaches to intertextuality, transmediation and paratextuality. Despite or indeed because of its paradoxical nature, the approximation and blending of computer games and experimental literature has to be seen as a highly prolific area of contemporary creative practice, afforded and limited by the digital code and merging aesthetic forms of expression and forms of ludic interaction while simultaneously deconstructing mainstream entertainment media.

Acknowledgements

I would like to thank Alice Bell, Isamar Carrillo Masso and Sonia Fizek for their invaluable input and helpful comments on earlier drafts of this chapter.

References

Aarseth, E. (1997) *Cybertext: Perspectives on Ergodic Literature*, Baltimore, MD: Johns Hopkins University Press.

Andrews, J. (2006) *Arteroids*. Retrieved from http://www.vispo.com/arteroids/arteroids311.htm. Accessed 28 July 2010.

Apter, M.J. (1991) "A Structural-Phenomenology of Play." In J.H. Kerr and M.J. Apter (eds.), *Adult Play: A Reversal Theory Approach*, Amsterdam: Swets and Zeitlinger.

Atkins, B. and T. Krzywinska (2007) *Videogame, Player, Text*, Manchester, UK: Manchester University Press.

Beiguelman, G. (2010) "The Reader, the Player and the Executable Poetics: Towards a Literature beyond the Book." In J. Schäfer and P. Gendolla (eds.), *Beyond the Screen: Transformations of Literary Structures, Interfaces and Genres*, Bielefeld, Germany: Transcript.

Caillois, R. (2001) *Man, Play and Games*, Chicago, IL: University of Illinois Press.

Carter, R. (2010) "Robert Coover and the Tale of Tales: Insistence and the Iteration of Red," paper presented at *Electronic Literature – Archive and Innovate*, Brown University, Providence, RI, 3–6 June.

Catlow, R., M. Garrett and C. Morgana (eds.) (2010) *Artists Re:thinking Games*, Liverpool, UK: FACT.

Conway, S. (2010) "A Circular Wall? Reformulating the Fourth Wall for Videogames," *Journal of Gaming and Virtual Worlds* 2(2): 145–55.

Coover, R. (1992) "The End of Books," *The New York Times*, June 21. Retrieved from http://www.nytimes.com/books/98/09/27/specials/coover-end.html. Accessed 1 July 2010.

Crawford, C. (1996–1997) *The Art of Computer Game Design*. Retrieved from http://www.vancouver.wsu.edu/fac/peabody/game-book/Chapter1.html. Accessed 27 June 2010.

Dragona, D. (2010) "From Parasitism to Institutionalism: Risks and Tactics for Game-based Art." In R. Catlow *et al.* (eds.), *Artists Re: thinking Games* , Liverpool, UK: FACT, pp. 26–32.

Electronic Literature Directory (2010–2011) Retrieved from http://directory.eliterature.org. Accessed 11 February 2011.

Ensslin, A. (2007) *Canonizing Hypertext: Explorations and Constructions*, London: Continuum.

——(2011) *The Language of Gaming*, Basingstoke, UK: Palgrave Macmillan.

Ensslin, A. and A. Bell(in press) "'Click = Kill.' Textual You in Ludic Digital Fiction," *Storyworlds* 4.

Frasca, G. (2001) "Videogames of the Oppressed: Videogames as a Means for Critical Thinking and Debate," Master's Thesis, Georgia Institute of Technology. Retrieved from http://www.ludology.org/articles/thesis/FrascaThesisVideogames.pdf. Accessed 26 July 2010.

Fugazo (2010) *Fiction Fixers: Adventures in Wonderland*. Retrieved from http://www.gamezebo.com/download-games/fiction-fixers-adventures-wonderland. Accessed 2 July 2010.

Garrelts, N. (ed.) (2006) *The Meaning and Culture of Grand Theft Auto: Critical Essays*, Jefferson, NC: McFarland & Company.

Genette, G. (1997) *Palimpsests: Literature to the Second Degree*, trans. C. Newman and C. Doubinsky, Lincoln, NE: University of Nebraska Press.

geniwate and Larsen, D. (2003) *The Princess Murderer*. Retrieved from http://www.deenalarsen.net/princess/prin_murd.swf. Accessed 2 July 2010.

Gilbert, D. (2006) *The Shivah*. Retrieved from http://www.wadjeteyegames.com/shivah.html. Accessed 28 June 2010.

GTxA (Grand Text Auto) (2003–2010). Retrieved from http://grandtextauto.org/. Accessed 27 July 2010.

Hayles, N.K. (2007a) "Hyper and Deep Attention: The Generational Divide in Cognitive Modes," *Profession*, 187–99. Retrieved from http://www.mlajournals.org/doi/pdf/10.1632/prof.2007.2007.1.187. Accessed 27 April 2010.

——(2007b) *Electronic Literature: New Horizons for the Literary*, Notre Dame, IN: University of Notre Dame Press.

Heckman, D. (2010) "game, game, game and again game," *Electronic Literature Directory*. Retrieved from http://directory.eliterature.org/node/279. Accessed 25 June 2010.

Huizinga, J. (1950) *Homo Ludens*. Boston, MA: Beacon Press.

Jaworski, A., N. Coupland and D. Galasiński (2004) "Metalanguage: Why Now?" In A. Jaworski, N. Coupland and D. Galasiński (eds.), *Metalanguage: Social and Ideological Perspectives*, Berlin: Mouton de Gruyter, pp. 3–9.

Jones, S.E. (2008) *The Meaning of Video Games: Gaming and Textual Strategies*, New York: Routledge.

Juul, J. (2003) "The Game, the Player, the World: Looking for a Heart of Gameness." In M. Copier and J. Raessens (eds.), *Level Up: Digital Games Research Conference Proceedings*, Utrecht, The Netherlands: Utrecht University, pp. 30–45.

——(2005) *Half-Real: Video Games Between Real Rules and Fictional Worlds*, Cambridge, MA: MIT Press.

Kendall, R. (2002) *Clues*. Retrieved from http://www.wordcircuits.com/clues/. Accessed 28 June 2010.

Larsen, D. (2002) *Firefly*. Retrieved from http://www.deenalarsen.net/firefly.swf. Accessed 28 June 2010.

——(2008) *Deena Larsen's Hypertext/New Media/Electronic Lit/Possibilities Addicts Attic*. Retrieved from http://www.deenalarsen.net/. Accessed 28 June 2010.

Lionhead Studies (2004–2009) Fable series, Redmond, WA: Microsoft.

MacCallum-Stewart, E. and J. Parsler (2007) "Illusory Agency in Vampire: The Masquerade – Bloodlines," *dichtung-digital* 37. Retrieved from http://www.brown.edu/Research/dichtung-digital/2007/maccallumstewart_parsler.htm. Accessed 30 April 2010.

McDougall, J. and W. O'Brien (2008) *Studying Videogames*, Leighton Buzzard, UK: auteur.

Montfort, N. (2000) *Ad Verbum*. Retrieved from http://nickm.com/if/adverbum.html. Accessed 2 July 2010.

Nelson, J. (2007) *game, game and again game*. Retrieved from http://www.secrettechnology.com/gamegame/gamegame6.html. Accessed 2 July 2010.

——(2008) *i made this. you play this. we are enemies*. Retrieved from http://www.secrettechnology.com/madethis/enemy6.html. Accessed 2 July 2010.

——(2009) *evidence of everything exploding*. Retrieved from http://www.secrettechnology.com/explode/evidence.html. Accessed 2 July 2010.

Newman, J. (2004) *Videogames*, London: Routledge.

Perrault, C. (1961 [1697]) *Perrault's Complete Fairy Tales*, trans. A.E. Johnson *et al.*, London: Penguin.

Picot, E. (2003) "What Makes Them Click?" Retrieved from http://tracearchive.ntu.ac.uk/review/index.cfm?article=76. Accessed 30 April 2010.

——(2009) "Play on Meaning? – Computer Games as Art," Retrieved from http://www.furtherfield.org/displayreview.php?review_id=345. Accessed 27 June 2010.

Pullinger, K. and C. Joseph (2005–2009) *Inanimate Alice*. Retrieved from http://www.inanimatealice.com. Accessed 7 May 2009.

Queneau, R. (1961) *Cent Mille Milliards de poèmes*, Paris: Gallimard.

Reed, A. A. (2008) *Blue Lacuna: An Interactive Novel*. Retrieved from http://www.lacunastory.com/. Accessed 2 July 2010.

Salen, K. and E. Zimmerman (2004) *Rules of Play: Game Design Fundamentals*, Cambridge, MA: MIT Press.

Sandlot Games (2009) *Tradewinds Odyssey*. Retrieved from http://www.bigfishgames.com/download-games/5632/tradewinds-odyssey/index.html. Accessed 2 July 2010.

Skains, L. (2010) "Consensus Trance, Part 1," *Electronic Literature Directory*. Retrieved from http://directory.eliterature.org/node/285. Accessed 25 June 2010.

Sokal, B. and Microïds (2002) *Syberia*, Toronto: The Adventure Company.

Stern, A. and M. Mateas (2005) *Façade*. Retrieved from http://www.interactivestory.net/. Accessed 2 July 2010.

Tale of Tales (2009) *The Path*. Retrieved from http://tale-of-tales.com/ThePath/downloads.html. Accessed 25 July 2010.

Tavinor, G. (2009) *The Art of Videogames*, Malden, MA: Wiley-Blackwell.

Weir, G. (2009) *Silent Conversation*. Retrieved from http://ludusnovus.net/my-games/silent-conversation/. Accessed 2 July 2010.

Westecott, E. (2010) "Playing With the Gothic: If You Go Down to the Woods Tonight . . .," In R. Catlow *et al.* (eds.) *Artists Re:thinking Games*. Liverpool, UK: FACT, pp. 78–81.

37

VIRTUAL AUTOBIOGRAPHY

Autographies, interfaces, and avatars

Amy J. Elias

Written autobiography and memoir include works as diverse as classical *apologia* and confessions, from Augustine of Hippo's *Confessions* (c. 397) and the *Book of Margery Kempe* (1436) to Harriet Jacobs' *Incidents in the Life of a Slave Girl* (1861), Zitkala-sa's *Impressions of an Indian Childhood* (1900), and Primo Levi's *Survival in Auschwitz* (1958). But life-writing can also be "experimental" (see Kacandes, this volume): one can point to fictional autobiographies and mixed-genre memoirs such as Gertrude Stein's *The Autobiography of Alice B. Toklas* (1933), Maxine Hong Kingston's *A Woman Warrior: Memories of a Girlhood Among Ghosts* (1975), Gao Xingjian's *Soul Mountain* (1990/2000), N. Scott Momaday's *The Way to Rainy Mountain* (1969), or Lyn Hejinian's *My Life* (2002) (see McHale, this volume). Often the experimentation of autobiographical writing is linked to the aims of specific literary movements or groups: the Beat ethos is apparent in Jack Kerouac's autobiographical nonfiction (see Lee, this volume); Georges Perec's *W* (1975) has a clear link to OuLiPo experimentation (see Baetens, this volume); Raymond Federman's *The Twofold Vibration* (1982) illustrates the precepts of surfiction (see Berry, this volume); Jamaica Kincaid's *A Small Place* (1988) serves postcolonial politics as it recounts her own personal history in Antigua (see Gopal, this volume); J.M. Coetzee's *Summertime* (2009) recalls the strategies of metafiction; Alain Robbe-Grillet's *Le Miroir qui revient* (1984) should, as Ann Jefferson (1991) has noted, be viewed in relation to the *nouveau roman* (see Marx-Scouras, this volume).

In this chapter, however, I will focus on a different kind of experimentation in life writing, one that (unlike the previous examples) is not always intentionally aligned with experimental literary groups or avant-garde communities: late twentieth-century "virtual" life writing overlapping with, and read in the domains of, digital technology. Theorization of identity, self-representation, and virtuality is in fact a staple of digital culture theory beginning in the 1990s. We seem to be creating new forms of self-inscription and life writing, if not selfhood itself, through our interactions in digital space. Here I would like to focus on *autobiography* as a digital form of expression (something with which Haraway is largely unconcerned) and adopt Whitlock and Poletti's (2008) extremely useful categories of "autographics" and "avatar autobiography" to look at examples of late twentieth-century virtual autobiography. Looking at autobiography and memoir from the perspective of virtuality and digital cultures offers both a lens through which to view the "self" constructed by these genres and radically broadens the range of what counts as life writing.

I. From "self" to "subject"

There are three major trends in late twentieth-century literary theory that have been instrumental in redefining the integrated, individualistic, Cartesian self as "virtual": constructivist cultural theory and sociology, continental poststructuralism (theories of language and knowledge), and psychology (particularly Lacanian psychoanalysis). In different ways, all three posit the self as social construction, built not upon the integrity of soul or the self-determination of mind but instead informed by primal desires, constructed according to assimilated social norms, and determined by the constraints of language. In these theories, the self becomes a subject, in the psychoanalytic sense and also in the narrative sense: it is constituted, not described, by the language that it speaks. Such a perspective makes the "self" into a kind of fictional character, a virtuality, and an interface between mind and world.

Interestingly, critical theory virtualized the self-as-subject in this way at roughly the same historical moment that the modern computer was born. In 1939, Germany's Konrad Zuse created the Z1, one of the first binary digital computers. The first commercial computer, at Manchester University, went functional in 1951, and Fortran (an important programming language) was developed in 1956, the same year that the first computer with a hard disk drive was shipped for public use ("Computer Hope"). Following the birth of the Internet from government and military technologies in the 1980s and the exponential growth of the World Wide Web since the early 1990s, virtual reality has become central to everyday life and sociality. Without supporting a *propter hoc* fallacy, it is possible to at least imagine that there is some sort of relationship of ideas here, as the virtual nature of self and the virtual nature of lived environment are simultaneously theorized and constructed.

This overlap of virtualities has interesting implications for the genres of autobiography and memoir. Writing about print autobiographies, Alfred Hornung has noted that if "conventional autobiographies could be regarded as the proper medium for the realistic representation of a self and for the narrative recovery of past events from the perspective of the present, contemporary autobiographical texts stress the illusory nature of such mythopoeic endeavours" (1984: 91). Hornung argues that experimental autobiographies contest the idea that realism is the proper genre for expressing the life of "a Self" – a unique individual in control of his/her own mind, destiny, and self-perception – and instead present both realism and the Self as outdated ideas.

Hornung's statement is perhaps even more significant for digital-based life writing, which reconfigures autobiography and memoir in relation to the virtuality of self and medium and disrupts Philippe Lejeune's foundational definition of autobiography (see Kacandes, this volume): "the retrospective prose narrative that someone writes concerning his own existence, where the focus is his individual life, in particular the story of his personality" (Eskin 1989: p. viii, quoting Lejeune, *L'Autobiographie en France*, [1989] p. 14). First, while Lejeune prescribed prose nonfiction as the genre for autobiography, entering the realm of the digital interface tends to alter our notion of what constitutes appropriate autobiographical form. Existing in a hypermediated environment, virtualized or interface autobiography can be highly spatialized (with chunks of texts or lexias on different parts of a page or on different linked pages) and include pictures, music, and other non-linguistic elements such as widgets and apps. The picture of the self and of "personality" that emerges on such sites is one that is equally hypermediated, less controlled by the conventions and organizing logic of prose narrative.

Second, redefining autobiography as the story of a virtual subject undermines Lejeune's uncomplicated notion of "retrospection" in the service of *Bildung* – as reflection upon developmental or accretive history. Clicking through hypertext links at best leads to a division of time into a simple "before" and "after": the link that I arrive at *last* has no necessary relation other than "after" to the link that started my search and has no necessary relation to an unfolding linear story of the narrative self. Texts composed in HTML or in Flash or other multimedia platforms, supporting links and dependent upon rhizomatic logic, thus trouble the assumption that life stories are developmental in terms of either narrative structure or character "growth." Moreover, certain forms of online memoir or diary allow for constant revision, reconceptualization, and reformulation, a process that can erase the past and thus inhibit retrospection: websites, Facebook or Bebo profiles, and avatar characteristics, for example, can be updated and revised endlessly, eliminating any record of development and positing the self as fully constituted in the present. Presentation, not retrospection, is the activity promoted by these forms. The extremely short forms of some of these online presentations of self, such as user profiles and microblogs, preclude long rearview mediations: it's hard to be retrospective or even introspective in a 140-character Tweet.

Lastly, undermining the notion of authorial intention and single authorship in Lejeune's definition, virtual life narratives are often collaborative, social, and networked in a way that single-author or even ghost-written autobiographies, printed within the pages of a stand-alone book, are not. Often writing in social networking environments or creating forms that mimic such dialogic environments (as do online graphic novels including "comment boxes"), authors of virtual life stories presuppose an interactive self imbricated in a synchronic language network and a network of users. The autobiographical Subject in digital environments emerges as more (or more obviously) dialogical than monadic, constructed rhetorically in relation to, and in conversation with, public environments. The *dialogic* Subject is a kind of network (see also Tomasula, "Information Design," this volume), a negotiated construction based on interchange between a self and others, between a self and a social world. A dialogical subjectivity is one theorized somewhere between the monadic, auto-determining subject posited by Descartes and the radically empty, "driven," and language-based subjectivity advanced by Lacan. I am using the term "virtual subject" here to denote this kind of dialogical self often enabled and performed in digital contexts, in digital or online life writing. In microblogging and other online forms of self-inscription whose very forms prevent extended intro- and retro-spection, the responsibility for reconstructing a self may in fact lie with readers, who can sort through many posts to form a synthesizing hypothesis about the writing subject. My "self" online becomes a kind of collaborative interchange between myself as writer and the interpreting, interactive reader.

In what follows, I look at autographics, interfaces, and avatar autobiography as three forms of virtualized life narrative existing today. Whitlock and Poletti define "autographics" and "autography" as "Life narrative fabricated in and through drawing and design using various technologies modes, and materials. [. . .] Here text is approached for *texture*, for the 'strange alchemy' of word and image on a three dimensional page" (v). The importance of this alchemy is that it embeds and reveals a desire for new forms of self-representation: autography is a new form of autobiography that is primarily visual in nature but that can blend visual images with narrative or other media forms. While they primarily apply the term to graphic novels, Whitlock and Poletti illustrate its elasticity by including within the category of "autographics" many multimedial, intermedial, and multimodal forms, such as social networking sites (which they link to the scrapbook), perzines (linked to the diary), webcams (linked to self-portraiture), and avatars (as visual representations of auto-narration).

While Whitlock and Poletti include all of these forms under the umbrella term "autographics," I will differentiate these kinds of digital life narratives further as autographies, interfaces, and avatar autobiographies, and in this section I will also consider only online autobiographical forms. I use the term "autographies" here following Jared Gardner's use of this term specifically to designate autobiographical graphic novels, but will consider only those graphic novels or comics that appear online. For all of forms discussed within these three categories, the most important characteristics are multimodality, multimediality, or hypermediality – the merging of graphics and story and other kinds of media within the life narrative – and their conflation of digital writing with dialogical subjectivity (see Gibbons on printed multimodal literature, this volume).

II. Autographic life writing

By the opening decade of the twenty-first century, certain print forms of graphic nonfiction memoirs or semi-fictionalized autobiographies had become more or less canonical: Lat's *The Kampung Boy* (1979), Art Spiegelman's *Maus* (2 volumes, 1986 and 1992), Marjane Satrapi's *Persepolis* (2000), Alison Bechdel's *Fun Home* (2006). Others remain extremely popular and are often taught in college classes (e.g. Lynda Barry's *One Hundred Demons* (2002), David B.'s *Epileptic* (2005), Alissa Torres' *American Widow* (2008), David Small's *Stitches: A Memoir* (2009), Joyce Farmer's *Special*

Exits: A Graphic Memoir (2010) (see Chute on graphic novels and Kacandes on experimental life-writing, this volume). Jared Gardner has noted that "since 1972 there has certainly been a steady progression of autobiographical memoirs within the comics form, to the extent that today one can identify sub-genres and historical movements within autobiographical comics" (2008: 1).

The graphic memoir is still predominantly a print form, but there are online examples, often called "autobio cartoons" or "journal comics," and their online appeal seems to be growing. On the one hand, graphic memoirs online aren't that dissimilar from their print cousins. For Gardner, the graphic memoir in print form, incorporating both text and pictures in the manner of comics, best allows for the "simultaneous claims of autography and fiction" (2008: 22), and one could say the same for online journal comics. The print form of the graphic memoir, like underground comics, can express politically and culturally suppressed, censored, and countercultural ideas, exemplified in even the first graphic memoirs (Gardner 2008: 6–7). Hillary Chute has noted, for example, "Some of today's most riveting feminist cultural production is in the form of accessible but edgy graphic narratives" (2010: 2). The online autobio cartoon likewise can address politicized, taboo, and countercultural subjects, particularly since the online format allows artists to try out styles and narratives as well as to receive feedback from audiences about this work before print publication. For example, Sarah Glidden's *How to Understand Israel in 60 Days or Less* (2010) details the artist's travel to Israel to try to comprehend the place and its politics, and her own heritage in relation to both. Parts of the comic appeared at Glidden's personal website before it saw print (2009). Erika Moen's *DAR: A Super-Girly Top Secret Comic Diary* (2010) documents Moen's life journey toward queer identity. At 20, she began writing the strip online, detailing her sexual identity journey from lesbian to heterosexual relationships to an "all inclusive queer" identity of lesbian in a committed straight marriage. The memoir became so popular that Moen discontinued the online version after six years and published two print volumes of the work.

Amateur auto cartoonists can be found at online hub sites, such as *Webcomics Nation* (http://www.webcomicsnation.com/genre.php?genre=4), presenting work ranging from single-shot frames to full comics series. By virtue of the medium, these online autographics can literalize dialogism on the screen. Writing ephemeral, often incomplete comics series, sometimes broken off after a few issues, authors often solicit reader feedback in the form of comments or reviews in comment boxes under each frame of the text. Part of the reason may be practical, since many of these web comics are produced by writers hoping for a book contract: as Chris Grine wrote at his *Chickenhare* site in 2010, "The plan now is to go ahead with volume three right here, for free, and hope to garner a large enough audience by its finale to peak [sic] the interest of a publisher crazy enough to print it!" Yet there also seem to be other reasons for this dialogue with readers. While Julia Wertz no longer considers her autobio comic *Fart Party* (2010) to be "web comics," noting on her site that "If you want to know the whole story, you have to buy the books," her site does contain comment/review boxes for the online cartoons she presents, and comments range from praise to actual suggestions for improvement. On the same page are also a list of links to other artists' sites, an RSS feed, a calendar with various odd things linked to certain dates (e.g. a YouTube video of Wertz and her brother jamming in pajamas), and various links including one to her personal blog. Her voice is embedded at the site in numerous formats and registers, and the picture that emerges is communal as well as commercial: while her voice is anything but meek or generic, it is nonetheless the voice of a self in progress, very much in dialogue with others.

Shelley Jackson's "My Body: A Wunderkammer" (1997) is an example of one of the early forms of online graphic memoir, significantly different from autobio cartoons derived from comics. This HTML text is closely related to Jackson's best-known work, *Patchwork Girl* (1995), now a classic of hypertext CD-ROM fiction (see Ciccoricco, this volume). "My Body: A Wunderkammer" is an online graphic tale with autobiographical elements. It is comprised of woodcut pictures and text by Jackson, and incorporates sound. Entering the site, users are shown an outline drawing, a frontal view of a nude girl; drawn rectangles mark off different body parts. Clicking on any body part takes one to a hypertext lexia containing a short mediation about that body part in relation to memory associations of the author. Within each lexia, moreover, are other links, to other lexia and drawings. These links circle around each other, never proceeding in a chronological narrative line in the interest of plot. In terms of its paratactic structure, this work has affinities with poetry or a meditative, abrasively honest diary. Its dialogism lies in the conversation the author/narrator has with her own (fictional) body, in how the body parts speak to one another and to memory, and in the text's involvement of the reader, who has a limited field of interaction as she clicks through links literally to piece together a whole body from the many fragments of text. What emerges is a disturbing, introspective account of a woman's ambivalence toward her own body, a body marked everywhere by social standards of beauty, gender propriety, and feminine purpose.

III. Interface life writing

A related category of virtualized autobiography and memoir is what might be called stories by the "interface self": life writing on or imported to the World Wide Web, where it remains a static artifact or is further transformed through the Web platform. Interface autobiography creates a textual persona that is identified with the author, who often solicits real-time interaction with a viewer, reader, or audience. The difference from autography is a matter of degree, not of kind: interface autobiography tends more to privilege text/language over picture (though graphics, comment sections, RSS feeds, and widgets may be present) and also to foreground the importance of authorial identity. In interface contexts, the author constructs a clear online identity with rhetorical aims.

Commonplace examples of such an interface self would be the online diarist and the personal blogger. Known by the (lovely) neologism "escribitionists" (*Wikipedia* 2010), online diarists first appeared in the mid-1990s. By 2010, these were so common that website hosts, such as mydiary.org or 124diary.com, offered simple diary services, while more technically sophisticated sites such as Live Journal offered free as well as paid, premium services. Live Journal, billed as open source and volunteer organized, noted in November 2010 that its site received 171,100 posts in a 24-hour period with more than 34 million user accounts: clearly online diaries and journals are still popular. What all online diary sites seem to have in common is (1) an intense focus on the personal, day-to-day feelings and activities of ordinary people, and (2) a software platform that allows diarists to write their diaries in attractive formats, archive their entries, and choose whether to make their diaries private or public. Today, many sites offer phone-syncing options, SNS connectivity, themes, photo options, features such as podcasting, widgets, and shopping links. The journals that users deliberately make public seem to function similarly to old-tech list servs and community hubs, where people could post public thoughts, group themselves into community chat forums, and find people with similar interests, but with personal diary and blogging options.

Their formats illustrate, however, how online diaries are converging with personal weblogs, and these in turn are converging with Social Networking Systems (SNS), such as Facebook, My Space, and Flickr and microblogging sites such as Twitter. With weblog services and free server space proliferating, blogging has become common (even required in some school and university courses) – as evidenced, for example, by portals for milblogging, or military blogs, that were once new and threatening to military administration but now number in the thousands and run their own annual conventions. (One of the first and most well known of these military blogs in the US was by Colby Buzzell, who served eight months of active duty in Iraq as an army machine-gunner and in 2004 ran a blog, titled "My War," with the handle CBFTW on blogspot.com from an internet café in Iraq. His military commanders eventually monitored his blog dispatches for operational security breaches; Buzzell then discontinued his milblog. After finishing his tour of duty, Buzzell edited and published his blog posts to national attention in an experimental book form, the "blog novel," as *My War: Killing Time in Iraq* [2006].) The Pew Research Center's Internet and American Life Project reported of US usage in 2010 that "in 2006, 28% of teens ages 12–17 and young adults ages 18–29 were bloggers, but by 2009 the numbers had dropped to 14% of teens and 15% of young adults. During the same period, the percentage of online adults over thirty who were bloggers rose from 7% blogging in 2006 to 11% in 2009" (Lenhart, Purcell, Smith and Zickuh 2010). By 2010, personal blogging would not qualify as "experimental" but rather was acquiring the air of middle-aged-user technology, still highly popular but converging in numerous ways with social media and incorporating new input platforms such as smartphones and e-tablets (Sobel 2010). What it shares with SNS, however, is a focus on life writing in new formats and with possibly new characteristics, including ease of documentation, global audience, interactivity and exchange with readers, and synergies with other online life-documentation networks.

Social networking systems such as Facebook, Flickr, and MySpace, through their themes, layouts, and applications, offered platforms with a design message that itself can "say something" about users. Ruth Page has argued that status updates on

Facebook and other SNS are similar to what Georgakopoulou has called "small stories," (Georgakopoulou 2007: 36, quoted by Page 2010: 426), and danah boyd (2007) has noted that Facebook, started at Harvard University as an "invitation only" network, was associated with college users, while MySpace was linked in user's minds to high school. Joining a certain *kind* of social networking system apparently sets up an autobiographical frame, one specifically linked to class affiliations. Beyond the platform, however, use of features also constructs online identity. Increasing the multimediality of one's profile page is one's "friends list," and apps themselves have connotations; the accumulated design message of a profile page – the number and kind of friends, the number and kind of apps – together with the voice and subjects of one's personal "news feeds," made daily to a public audience, all work together to construct a persona, a crafted, public self.

Social media of all kinds can embed multiple layers of life-writing technologies, presenting different lenses on personality in different formats: for instance, a blog site that is linked to a Facebook profile and Twitter page, and perhaps also to a YouTube video featuring the author speaking as him/herself. Increasingly embedded on blog and SNS sites, but also popular as stand-alones, video or webcam diaries allow users to speak directly to audiences. The genre encompasses everything from "how to" videos to daily rants about specific topics (e.g. politics) to personal webdiary entries. The webcam diary is effective because it allows readers multiple voyeuristic pleasures while creating the illusion of personal friendship and community: webcam diarists speak directly to the camera, and viewers can comment on any video as well as on other commentators' notes. At this point the genre is so established that it is overrun with celebrity videos, and it can be difficult to tell hoax video diaries from real ones (see Mead, this volume). One of the first famous webcam diaries, by "lonelygirl15" – put online in June of 2006 – was exposed as a staged performance after 4 months, though it gained popularity and ran online until 2008 (http://www.lg15.com/faq) (see Figure 37.1). Since then, the phenomenon of "camgirls" – who broadcast their lives hoping for celebrity – has become common (Senft 2008).

These new forms of autobiography are post-convergence media, where the diary, documentary, net.art projects, and autobiography often come together online with video, photography, and screenwriting.

Similarly, in the field of oral history, serious ethnographical fieldwork and archives can be enhanced by multimedial forms of interface autobiography. A field too big to be encompassed by the present discussion, online oral history is rarely "experimental" in and of itself, but it may represent a new experiment in historical recording. Sidonie Smith has noted that, while before 1979 autobiography and memoir were largely excluded from scholarly literary analysis, the academy's interest in "life writing" had increased exponentially with the establishment of the Ambérieu archive in France, Britain's Mass Observation Project at the University of Sussex, oral history archives in the U.S., and online oral history projects (Smith 2010). Projects such as the American Social History Project, created for online use by the Center for Media and Learning (Graduate Center, CUNY) and the Center for History and New Media (George

Figure 37.1 2010 screenshot of YouTube video diaries lonelygirl15.

Mason University), illustrate the important historical work that online oral histories can perform.

Linked to interface autobiography through oral history, composed primarily if not exclusively for the WWW, certain forms of net.art are important forms of online life writing. Net.art comprises multimedia art works ranging from thematically complex Flash art, as in the work of Young-hae Chang Heavy Industries (whose pieces may be partly autobiographical), to formally intricate online pieces incorporating original programming. Two examples may indicate the range of approaches. Beth Stryker's and Sawad Brooks' human mapping project "Dissemi NET" (2000), a Java-based net. art project commissioned in part by the Wexner Center for the Arts. Begun as "a set of testimonies collected by Pro Busqueda de Los Ninos," an organization which "helps locate children disappeared during El Salvador's 12 year civil war" (Stryker and Brooks 1999: n.p.), the interactive site collects testimonies of homelessness, diaspora, and global dispersal and arranges them by keywords to be searched and heard by site visitors. A contrasting example of the hundreds of net.art oral history sites online is "Recollecting Adams," a 2008 online piece funded by the Andy Warhol Foundation and commissioned by the Visual Arts of New Radio Performing Arts (Ether-Ore) for its Turbulence website (see Figure 37.2). The 15-episode online oral history project by Marianne Petit, a local gallery owner, is set in the small mill town of Adams in

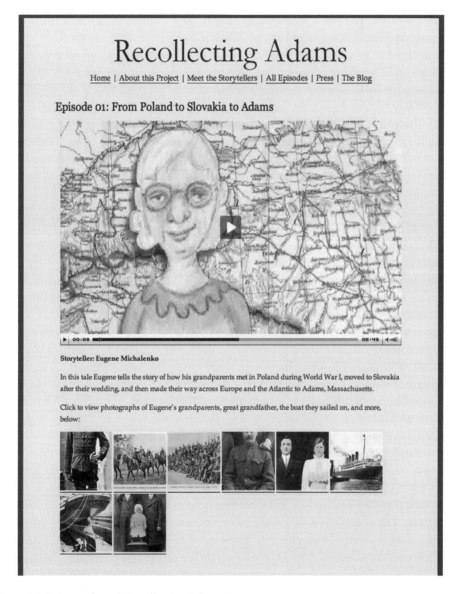

Figure 37.2 Screenshot of "Recollecting Adams."

the Northern Berkshires. Told as first-person oral histories, the original uploads were posted every two weeks, though now the entire project is available online. Clicking on an "episode," one is taken to a page that features animated drawings, maps, photographs, and a voiceover by a citizen of Adams telling part of his/her life story or the story of someone in his/her family. Pages contain each visual animation and sometimes actual photographs of the person's life as well as a comments section. Moreover, the site is linked to Petit's project blog (2008). The oral history project is not only autographical but also multimedial and collaborative on a number of levels.

A point to be emphasized is that for real or hoax video diaries, online text diaries, blogs, social networking sites, and oral history sites, the key to interface life writing is dialogism, not only between media platforms and the different facets of the self that they are able to present, but also between author and reader. As van Dijck (2004: n.p.) notes, "Blogging, besides being an act of self-disclosure, is also a ritual of exchange: bloggers *expect* to be signaled and perhaps to be responded to." Likewise, online oral history projects that present first-person testimonies and autobiographical stories often embed multiple forms of media and increasingly include options for user feedback.

IV. Avatar autonarration

My third category of online autobiography is "avatar autonarration." Whitlock and Poletti (2008) define avatar life writing as any life writing in which there is a stand-in for the author, as in a narrative or graphic persona. I'd like to narrow this definition: avatar autonarration is distinguished by the fact that the author writes a true life-story of an avatar conceived *as such* – life writing for an autodiegetic character with which the author identifies in some real way and that acts in real time, with real-time ethical and sometimes political consequences, but a character that is not necessarily identified publically with the author him/herself. In other words, the author creates a 2-D digital persona and speaks and acts through this character while online. Like personal blogs and social networking media in which authors disguise their identities with pseudo-nyms or alt identities, avatar autobiography differs from these forms in that disguised or alternative identity is a defining characteristic of one's avatar self.

One kind of avatar autonarration is the cell phone memoir. Organized on the same principle as microblogging, in which users input short messages, cellphone novels are written in 70–100 word text messages. They contain short and simple sentences in serial order, emphasize plot over description, and can contain symbols used in text messaging, such as emoticons. The novels can either be sent to subscribers (phone contacts) or uploaded to a website, such as a blog, Twitter feed, or cellphone novel portal (such as "Maho i-Rando," Japanese for "Magic Island," by 2008 the largest online cell-phone novel site, offering over a million titles). Cellphone novels originated in Japan – the *New York Times* reported that of the ten best selling Japanese novels of 2008, five were cellphone novels (Onishi 2008) – but are now popular in numerous countries and most popular among female authors and readers. The cellphone novel's serial inputs can add up to a traditional-length novel (of a few hundred pages), be published by an established publisher, and sell millions of copies (Goodyear 2008). Like other forms of online writing, cellphone novels give readers opportunities to comment on chapters as they serially appear; some sites encourage readers to vote for their favorites and offer prizes for the most cited novel.

Autobiographical cell phone novels squint between smartphone and WWW environments and between interface and avatar autobiography. On the one hand, like interface autobiographies they ostensibly record the lives of real persons. As Lara Day

(2008) has illustrated, the website Maho i-Rando originally offered MySpace-style homepages for its users to post diary entries via their cell phones. It then added tools that allowed them, as Maho i-Rando's founder Akira Tanii noted, "to publish novels, short stories and poems, chapter by chapter, just like a real book" (Day 2008). On the other hand, these cellphone novels are often written by authors using pseudonyms and are known for mixing romance elements with memoir or autobiography. In 2008, Dana Good year noted, "According to the figures provided by the company, the [Maho i-Rando] site, which also offers templates for blogs and home pages, is visited three and a half billion times a month" but most "authors are amateurs writing under screen handles." Given that the autobiographical tales told are often R-rated and romance-based, and that most authors do not write under their real names, the cellphone novelist is a kind of avatar, creating an online, public writing persona whose "life story" is deeply intertwined with romance fiction. Unlike mere pseudonyms, these avatar identities can interact with their readers in real time, not only by phone communication but also through reader comments on their works.

A more overt form of this avatar life-narrativization occurs on MMORPGs (Massively Multiplayer Online Roleplaying Games) or in virtual worlds. In Second Life® for example, as in many virtual worlds, people are "residents" and roleplay in the form of virtual avatars of their own creation (see Figure 37.3). One can buy virtually any

Figure 37.3 Screenshot of Second Life® skin store, May 2010. Copyright 2007, Linden Research, Inc. All Rights Reserved.

body part ("skins," clothes, hair) to modify one's avatar; avatars can be male or female, human or nonhuman. Thus even more than for social networking sites, where choice of apps, page construction, and content on news feeds construct an online persona for the user, the construction of an avatar allows users to play with identity construction. The literature on this subject is extensive – including Rheingold's *The Virtual Community* (2000 [1991]), Fine's *Shared Fantasy* (2002), Nardi's *Communities of Play* (2009). But more perhaps needs to be done to examine the intersections between avatar identity and new forms of autobiography as life narrative and self presentation.

For example, navigating the Second Life® world, which is not a game world but a vast virtual grid of commercial, educational, entertainment, or residential "islands" owned by residents interacting in real time, one encounters other avatars and has the option of saying hello to them or participating in group activities, from online classes, business meetings, and educational seminars to shopping, club dancing, or avatar sex. Social codes teach one, before engaging with a stranger inworld, to check out another person's "profile," a short self-description that includes the avatar's autobiographical information: avatar name; age (time of residency in Second Life® – the avatar is "born" when one initially creates a free or paid account); photo; membership listing in social groups; account status; name of partner (one can get married or partnered in this

Figure 37.4 Screenshot of Second Life® screen and blank profile window, May 2010. Copyright 2007, Linden Research, Inc. All Rights Reserved.

world); and user-written self-description of Second Life® identity (avatar) and First Life identity (resident's real name, picture, and profile), each allowed 510 characters.

As they are in roleplaying video games, profiles are crucially important in Second Life® as autobiographical and rhetorical documents, conveying avatar interests, personality, and attitudes. They can incorporate typeface graphics and emoticons and combine photos with text description. They can reveal or disguise one's real-life autobiographical self. Avatar profiles allow the creation of alternative identities and personalities; online, one becomes two people, one who controls the game in real life and one who roleplays within it. Some users don't keep these identities completely distinct: some people feel no friction between their identities, chatting inworld as avatars but in their own voices about their "real" lives and posting real-life photos in their profiles, while *simultaneously* maintaining separate identities through their avatar and occasionally stepping into that avatar role/identity. Tom Boellstorff (2008), for example, writes of a married couple who go online together, completely happy that their spouses are involved with social, even romantic, avatar others in Second Life®. As Sherry Turkle noted in 1997, interacting online is becoming crucially important to many people, but being and interacting online *only as oneself* – as in interface autobiography – is something else and may not be the goal of avatar self-inscription and life writing. As a new form of autobiographical construction combining autographics and life writing, the avatar is a mixed-media construction revealing both the constructed nature of the self-as-subject and offering new options for that construction.

V. Conclusion

Whitlock and Poletti write that "self-representation and narrativization are now central to many people's engagement with the internet," which "suggests that identity and autobiographical representation are increasingly important – as both a means and an end – to how and why people are online" (2008: xv). While desire for self-representation may in fact be driving the exponential growth of online social networking environments, the options for self-representation, its goals and the rhetorical concerns shaping it seem to diverge from, if not to be fundamentally different from, those shaping traditional print autobiography and memoir. Online autography, interfaces, and avatar autobiography now seem to be, in fact, the new frontier of experimental life writing.

References

Boellstorff, T. (2008) *Coming of Age in Second Life: An Anthropologist Explores the Virtually Human*, Princeton NJ: Princeton University Press.

boyd, d. (2007) "Viewing American class divisions through Facebook and My Space," *Apophenia Blog Essay*, 24 June 2007. [Online.] Retrieved November 2010 from http://www.danah.org/papers/essays/ClassDivisions.html

Buzzell, C. (2006) *My War: Killing Time in Iraq*, New York: Berkley Books.

Chute, H.L. (2010) *Graphic Women: Life Narrative and Contemporary Comics*, New York: Columbia University Press.

"Computer Hope." [Online.] Retrieved November 2010 from http://www.computerhope.com/history/194060.htm

Day, L. (2008) "Tone Language," *Time*, 9 January. [Online.] Retrieved November 2010 from http://www.time.com/time/magazine/article/0,9171,1702111,00.html.

Eskin, P. (1989) "Foreword." In P. Lejeune, *On Autobiography*, trans. K. Leary, Minneapolis, MN: University of Minnesota Press, pp. vii–xxviii.

Fine, G. A. (2002) *Shared Fantasy: Role-playing Games as Social Worlds*, Chicago, IL: University of Chicago Press.

Gardner, J. (2008) "Autography's Biography, 1972–2007," *Biography* 31(1), 1–26.

Georgakopoulou, A. (2007) *Small Stories, Interaction, and Identity*, Amsterdam: John Benjamins.

Glidden, S. (2009) "Sarah Glidden," (personal website). [Online]. Retrieved November 2010 from http://www.smallnoises.com/comics/.

Glidden, S. (2010) *How to Understand Israel in 60 Days or Less*, New York: Vertigo.

Goodyear, D. (2008) "I ♥ Novels: Young Women Develop a Genre for the Cellular Age," *The New Yorker*, 22 December. [Online].RetrievedNovember 2010 from http://www.newyorker.com/reporting/2008/12/22/081222fa_fact_goodyear?currentPage=2

Grine, C. (2010) *Chickenhare*. [Online]. Retrieved November 2010 from http://www.chickenhare.com/?page_id=2

Hornung, A. A. (1984) "Fantasies of the Autobiographical Self: Thomas Bernhard, Raymond Federman, Samuel Beckett," *Journal of Beckett Studies* 11–12:91–107.

Jackson, S. (1995) *Patchwork Girl*, Watertown, MA: Eastgate Systems.

Jackson, S. (1997) "My Body: A Wunderkammer." [Online]. Retrieved November 2010 from http://collection.eliterature.org/1/works/jackson__my_body_a_wunderkammer/index.html

Jefferson, A. (1991) "Autobiography as Intertext: Barthes, Sarraute, Robbe-Grillet."In M. Wortonand J. Still (eds.), *Intertextuality: Theories and Practice* , Manchester, UK: Manchester University Press, pp. 108–28.

Lejeune, P. (1989) *On Autobiography*, ed. P.J. Eakin, trans. K. Leary, Minneapolis, MN: University of Minnesota Press.

Lenhart, A., K. Purcell, A. Smith, and K. Zickuh (2010) "Social Media and Young Adults." Pew Internet, Pew Research Center. [Online]. Retrieved November 2010 from http://www.pewinternet.org/Reports/2010/Social-Media-and-Young-Adults.aspx

Moen, E. (2010) *DAR: A Super-Girly Top Secret Comic Diary*. [Online]. Retrieved November 2010 from http://www.darcomic.org/.

Nardi, B.A. (2009) *Communities of Play: Emergent Cultures in Multiplayer Games and Virtual Worlds*, Boston, MA: MIT Press.

Onishi, N. (2008) "Thumbs Race as Japan's Bestsellers Go Cellular," *New York Times*, 20 January. [Online]. Retrieved November 2010 from http://www.nytimes.com/2008/01/20/world/asia/20japan.html.

Page, R. (2010) "Reexamining narrativity: small stories in status updates," *Text & Talk* 30(4), 423–44.

Petit, M. (2008) "Recollecting Adams." [Online]. Retrieved November 2010 from http://turbulence.org/Works/recollecting/index.php?id=5.

Rheingold, H. (2000 [1991]) *The Virtual Community: Homesteading on the Electronic Frontier*, New edition, Cambridge MA: MIT Press.

Senft, T. (2008) *Camgirls*, Bern, Switzerland: Peter Lang.

Smith, S. (2010) "The Conventions of Narrating Lives," *MLA Newsletter* 42(2), 2–3.

Sobel, J. (2010) "State of the Blogosphere 2010 Introduction." [Online]. Retrieved November 2010 from http://technorati.com/blogging/article/state-of-the-blogosphere-2010-introduction/.

Stryker, B. and S. Brooks (1999) "Interview." [Online]. Retrieved November 2010 from http://artsconnected.org/resource/89099/disseminet.

——(2000) "Dissemi NET." [Online]. Retrieved November 2010 from http://disseminet.walkerart. org/.

Turkle, S. (1997) *Life on the Screen: Identity in the Age of the Internet*, New York: Simon and Schuster.

Van Dijck, J. (2004) "Composing the Self: Of Diaries and Lifeblogs," *Fibreculture* 3. [Online]. Retrieved November 2010 from http://www.journal.fibreculture.org/issue3/issue3_vandijck.html

Wertz, J. (2010) Personal website. [Online]. Retrieved November 2010 from http://www.fartparty. org/new-reader/.

Whitlock, G. and A. Poletti (2008) "Self-Regarding Art," *Biography* 31.1, v–xxii.

Wikipedia (2010) "Escribitionist." [Online]. Retrieved November 2010 from http://en.wikipedia. org/wiki/Escribitionist.

INDEX

Page numbers in **bold** denote whole chapters where the topic is covered in detail.